Postcard Jigsaw
(page 268)

Children can write a message to a friend and then mail it. The message will be a little "puzzling" to decode—and fun to create!

Each activity has also been rated with a difficulty level: easy, medium, or challenging. The number of symbols will guide you:

Activity is easy.

Activity is of medium difficulty.

Activity is challenging.

Fancy Flowerpot
(page 307)

This flowerpot is designed and painted by children. The flowerpot can then be used to hold those paints and paintbrush—or even a pretty plant.

These ratings are simply a guide, however. Again, you know your child best. The activities should be fun and enough of a challenge that they will be exciting for the child. On the other hand, you do not want to frustrate your child with activities that are beyond him or her.

Cut a Castle
(page 264)

Using a wide variety of tools, children can turn a cake box into a castle. Then they can pretend to be royalty or characters in a fairy tale.

1001 CREATIVE THINGS TO MAKE

pil

Publications
International, Ltd.

Contributors: Marilee Robin Burton; Jamie Gabriel; Kelly Milner Halls; Kersten Hamilton; Lise Hoffman; Rita Hoppert, Ed.D.; Lisa Lerner; Suzanne Lieurance; Susan Miller, Ed.D.; Donna Shryer

Illustrator: George Ulrich

Additional illustrators: Jim Connolly, Susan Detrich, Kate Flanagan, Yoshi Miyake

Covers: photography by Brian Warling; illustrations by Rémy Simard

Louis Weber, CEO
Publications International, Ltd.
7373 North Cicero Avenue
Lincolnwood, Illinois 60712

Permission is never granted for commercial purposes.

Manufactured in China.

8 7 6 5 4 3 2 1

ISBN: 0-7853-7209-1

CONTENTS

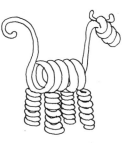

FOREWORD TO FUN

Dear Parents and Teachers—

Your child will be entertained for hours with *1001 Creative Things to Make.* Before letting your child create, be sure to note your child's abilities—craft knives are sharp, and stoves can be hot. And even if the child is able to handle all the tasks for each project, you should be present to prevent accidents or injuries! Occasionally instructions direct the child to ask for adult help. Be sure everyone understands the "Important Things to Know" section in this introduction.

We have given you some basic information about different topics, but this is a great opportunity for you and your child to learn more about the subjects in this book. If you have a computer, there are many Web sites you can explore together. Of course, the library is always a good place to find more information.

This should be an enjoyable, creative experience for children. Although we provide specific instructions, it's wonderful to see children create their own versions, using their own ideas. Encourage their creativity and interests!

Hey Kids—

With *1001 Creative Things to Make,* you have lots of fun ahead of you! This book is filled with exciting games to play, great gifts to make for family and friends, and terrific projects to decorate your room.

1001 Creative Things to Make was created with you in mind. Many of the projects are fun things you can make by yourself. With some projects, however, you will need to ask an adult for help. Not only can an adult help you with the projects, they can also admire your wonderful results!

It's a good idea to make a project following the instructions exactly. Then make another, using your imagination, changing colors, adding a bit of yourself to make it even more yours. Think of all the variations you can make and all the gifts you can give!

If you're curious about the topics mentioned in this book, do some exploring to find out more. Ask an adult to help you research—try the Internet (with adult permission, of course) and the library. Having some information makes you want more information—expand your world with knowledge!

The most important thing you need to remember is to have fun! Think how proud you'll be to say, "I made this myself!"

Key—

Each activity has been rated with a difficulty level: easy, medium, or challenging. The number of symbols will guide you:

 Activity is easy.

 Activity is of medium difficulty.

 Activity is challenging.

Important Things to Know—

Although we know you'll want to get started right away, please read these few basic steps before beginning any project.

1. For any project or activity you decide to do, gather all your materials, remembering to ask for permission first! If you need to purchase materials, take along your book or make a shopping list so you know exactly what you need.

2. Prepare your work area ahead of time. Clean up will be easier if you prepare first!

3. Be sure that an adult is nearby to offer help if you need it. An adult is needed if you will be using a glue gun, a craft knife, the oven, or anything else that may be dangerous!

4. Be careful not to put any materials near your mouth. Watch out for small items, such as beads, around little kids and pets. And keep careful watch of balloons and any broken balloon pieces. These are choking hazards—throw away any pieces immediately! Small children should not play with balloons unless an adult is present.

5. Use the glue gun on the low-temperature setting. Do not touch the nozzle or the freshly applied glue as the glue may still be hot. Use the glue gun with adult permission only!

6. Wear an apron when painting with acrylic paints; after the paint dries, it is permanent. If you do get paint on your clothes, wash them with soap and warm water immediately.

7. Cover your work surface with newspaper or an old, plastic tablecloth.

8. Clean up afterward, and put away all materials and tools. Leaving a mess one time may mean that your parents say "No" the next time you ask to make something!

9. Have fun, and be creative!

INSIDE FUN

Don't just pretend that being indoors is fun. Make it fun by playing and creating these great games and awesome activities. As unpredictable as the weather is, you won't question how to spend your time indoors when you have this chapter to shine light on your stay. No matter if you're alone or with friends, factor in fun as a force that will move you— from project to project to chapter's end.

All Mixed Up

Let's see how your story stacks up!

What You'll Need
• Sunday comics
• blunt scissors

Find your favorite comic strip, and cut apart the story frames. Mix up the pieces, and try to put them back in the correct order. Here's a goofy challenge: Lay them out in front of your friends in random order. Now have them try to make up a story that makes sense out of the scrambled pictures! Or show them the frames in the correct order, but leave off the last frame and see what kind of ending they come up with.

Early Animation

Cartoons have been around for longer than most people know. In 1928 Walt Disney created the first animated cartoon featuring Mickey Mouse, Steamboat Willie. Do you know what famous full-length animated cartoon was created just a few years later? If you guessed Snow White and the Seven Dwarfs, you're right!

Space Helmet

Practice "walking on the moon" with this cool space helmet, complete with its own make-believe oxygen tanks.

What You'll Need
- paper grocery bag
- markers or crayons
- scissors
- 2 oatmeal boxes with lids
- 2 paper towel tubes
- tape
- stapler and staples (optional)

Caution: This project requires adult help.

Put a paper grocery bag over your head. Using a marker, have a friend trace a circle on the bag where your face is. Take the bag off your head, and cut out the circle. You may also want to cut the bag around your shoulders so it is more comfortable to wear.

In the middle of each oatmeal box lid, trace the end of a paper towel tube.

Cut out the hole (have an adult help you, if necessary).

Tape or staple the oatmeal boxes side by side to the back of your helmet, lid side up. Stick an end of each paper towel tube through the top of each oatmeal box. If you like, tape the top of each tube to the helmet so the tubes look like oxygen tank hoses.

Decorate your helmet so it looks like one on a real space suit—or you can make your helmet look like one on an alien space suit. Use your imagination! Put on your new space helmet, and do your best moon walk.

Space Dust
Did you know that gravity on the Moon is only one-sixth as powerful as on Earth? The first Moon-walkers, astronauts Neil Armstrong and Buzz Aldrin, reported that when they kicked dust with their boots, every grain landed almost exactly the same distance away!

Story Characters

◆▶▶▶▶▶

Re-create your favorite hero or heroine from science fiction stories or fairy tales!
Use them for playtime or as decorations.

What You'll Need
- several colors of modeling dough
- toothpicks

Choose your favorite characters, and mold them out of modeling dough. Attach body parts by using toothpicks. Stick a toothpick or part of a toothpick into the top of the body. Then slide the head onto the other end of the toothpick. (Be careful to keep the toothpicks away from younger brothers and sisters. Let them have their own modeling dough to play with.) Two colors can be mashed together to form a neat, marbled color. Unfortunately, adding 1 shape on top of another without toothpicks won't work; the shapes will fall apart when dry. Let your characters dry for 2 or 3 days. Now use your desktop for a stage, and act out your favorite story!

Too Beautiful to Use
According to an article in Smithsonian Magazine, toothpicks were once valuable items, often made of gold, silver, or ivory, and sometimes they were encrusted with gems. When Princess Louise Marie Therese of Parma married a prince of Austria, her dowry included 12 such toothpicks.

Purple Cow Party

Say a big thanks to all the cows at this special party.

What You'll Need

- construction paper
- purple markers or crayons
- purple balloons and streamers
- purple nontoxic face paint
- vanilla ice cream
- ice cream scoop
- ripe bananas
- purple grape juice
- measuring cups
- blender
- glasses

Caution: This project requires adult help.

Make invitations for a purple cow party. Use a purple marker or crayon, and draw lots of purple pictures on the invitations. Ask your guests to wear only purple clothes! Decorate your party room with purple balloons and streamers. When each guest arrives, paint their face with purple face paint. For each purple cow shake, put one scoop of vanilla ice cream, ½ ripe banana, and ¼ cup purple grape juice into a blender. Blend until all the ingredients are mixed, and pour it into a glass. Say the purple cow rhyme as you serve each shake: "I never saw a purple cow, I never hope to see one. But I can tell you, anyhow, I'd rather see than be one!"

School Bus Game

This is one exciting bus ride!

Play this game at home or at school. To set up the game, put the chairs in rows, like on a bus. Write the names of all the players on the slips of paper, and put them on a table across the room from the chairs. One player is the school bus driver. She or he says: "The school bus is here. Let's all be on time. Pick up your tickets over there, so we can be in school by nine." After this is said, the other players run to the table to find the ticket with their name on it. If they find it, they run to the bus and get a seat. Whoever is left cannot ride the bus. Play the game over and over, and keep score for perfect school bus attendance. Whoever reaches a perfect score of 5 (for the 5 school days of the week) first gets to be the bus driver for the next round.

What You'll Need

- half as many chairs as there are players
- table
- a slip of paper for each player
- pencil

Silly Party

◆▶◆▶◆▶◆▶

Fool around at the silliest party of the year!

What You'll Need
- paper
- markers
- crackers
- cheese
- apple juice
- green food coloring
- old magazines
- blunt scissors
- construction paper
- glue
- pennies

Invite all your friends to act the fool at this silly party. You can make invitations by looking in a mirror and writing everything backward. (You might want to write a hint in regular writing that lets your guests know that they need a mirror to read their invitations!) Ask everyone to wear funny outfits, like a striped shirt with plaid or polka-dotted pants, mismatched socks, and a funny hat. When they ring the front doorbell, walk backward and greet them by saying "Goodbye" instead of "Hello." Ask everyone to do the same! Serve your guests inside-out sandwiches (a cracker between two pieces of cheese) and bug juice (apple juice with green food coloring). Have a box full of pictures of people and animals that you have cut out of magazines and have cut in half. Invite your guests to make wacky creatures from the pictures. They should glue the creatures onto construction paper. Later, you can use these wacky creatures as prizes for a silly stunt contest. To hold the contest, ask guests to do silly things, such as balancing pennies on their noses while walking across the room on their toes. Make up lots of silly stunts; it's a great day to be foolish!

The Fashion Set

◆▷◆▷◆▷◆▷◆

Doll up, dude up, and strut your stuff!

Borrow clothing from your parents, siblings, or any other people in your household. Be sure to ask for permission first! Now try dressing up as different people. See how many fashionable, funny, or downright strange outfits you can come up with. You'll have a roaring good time. Then plan a fashion show, dress up as your favorite celebrity, and see if your audience can guess who you are!

What You'll Need
- dress-up clothes (dresses, men's suits, shoes, hats, coats, purses, jewelry, gloves, etc.)

Puppet Paradise

◆▷◆▷◆▷◆▷◆

Perform with some fun puppets!

What You'll Need
- old, clean solid-color and patterned clothes (pantyhose, gloves, socks, etc.)
- old kitchen utensils
- old pantyhose
- cotton balls
- wiggly eyes
- poms
- yarn
- felt
- white glue
- glitter glue
- multicolored glue
- paint
- paintbrushes

These puppets are so much fun to make, you may be inspired to make a dozen of them. Take a good look at old clothes, such as pantyhose, gloves, and socks, and old kitchen utensils, and try to picture what creatures you could turn them into—let your imagination run wild! A striped sock might become a sleek jungle tiger. A mitten could turn into a hairy spider. A hand beater might be a mad beautician with a whirling hairdo. Once you have a personality idea, ask for permission and then use the craft materials to turn common household objects into fanciful puppets.

Hat Trick

◆▸◆▸◆▸◆

This one only sounds easy!

This is a game for 4 players. Divide the deck into the 4 different suits, and give a suit to each player. Set aside the jokers. Lay the hat on the floor, brim up. Stand back about 7 feet. Take turns tossing cards into the hat. When all the cards have been tossed, set aside the ones that missed the hat. Each player counts the number of cards in his or her suit that landed in the hat. If there is a tie, those players play another round to determine a winner. This is also a fun activity to play by yourself— you can practice your skills for the next time your friends come to visit!

Ring Toss

◆▸◆▸◆▸◆

This is a great game to play at birthday parties. And you can tell everyone you made it yourself.

To make the ring toss base, cut 2 paper towel tubes in half. Discard 1 half. Tape the remaining 3 to a 12-inch-square piece of foam core or cardboard as shown. Cut out 3 circles from a piece of construction paper. Cut a hole out of the center of each circle large enough to fit a paper towel tube through. Draw the point values on each circle. Place each circle over a tube, covering the masking tape. Cut out the centers of 3 coffee-can lids to make the rings. Decorate each rim with markers. To play, place the ring toss base flat on the floor, and throw the rings over the tubes.

One Peg at a Time

A pegboard solitaire game—or duel—is fast-paced fun.

What You'll Need
- thin poster board
- pencil
- ruler
- graph paper and glue stick (optional)
- pushpins
- thick stack of newspaper
- container to hold pushpins

Plan out any grid design you like (just make sure it has an odd number of dots or places where lines cross each other). If you're using graph paper, cut it to the desired shape and glue to the poster board. Lay the board on newspaper, and carefully stick a pushpin into every dot or line intersection. Leave one space open in the center. The object of the game is to "jump" pins over each other and remove them one at a time, as in checkers. The catch: You

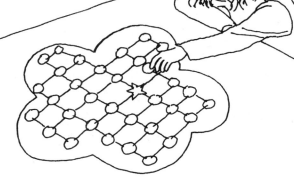

must end with the last pin in the center space. For a duel, have a friend make a board also. Then challenge each other to see who finishes first.

Grandma, What Big Teeth You Have

Who says theater has to be serious?

Fairy tales are great to perform because the audience recognizes the story. Pick a favorite fairy tale to make into a play. Have fun with the script, and spoof or exaggerate the story. Retell the ending the way you think it should have ended. Some of the funniest plays are written this way. Gather some hilarious costumes, and practice the play with a straight face, if you can! When you've achieved perfection, get ready to make your audience roar with laughter.

What You'll Need
- costumes

Felt Storyboards

Turn a pizza box into a storyboard, and bring the story to life with felt pictures.

What You'll Need

- unused medium-size pizza box
- felt in assorted colors
- blunt scissors
- craft glue
- markers
- trims (chenille stems, straw, yarn, etc.)

To make the storyboard background, cut 2 pieces of dark-colored felt to fit the inside of the top and bottom of the pizza box. Apply a layer of glue to the inside top and bottom of the box. Place both felt background pieces in the box over the glue. Let the glue dry completely.

Using assorted colors of felt, cut out felt pieces to make a picture. For example, if you were telling the story of *The Three Little Pigs,* you would need 3 pig cutouts, 1 wolf cutout, and 3 house cutouts. Draw features on the pieces with markers. Draw the eyes, noses, and mouths on the pigs. Glue on a small piece of curled chenille stem for the tail, and glue on cutout felt overalls. Draw in the eyes, nose, mouth, and teeth on the wolf. Decorate each house with markers, felt, and other trims. Glue or draw straw on one house, some twigs on another, and red felt bricks to the last house. Place your pieces on the felt background to tell your story.

What's Up My Sleeve?

And now, ladies and gents, it's time for some magic!

What You'll Need
- round, empty oatmeal carton
- blunt scissors
- paints and paintbrush
- stickers
- several old scarves
- a large jacket

This trick works because the audience's attention is distracted by the magic carton. Carefully remove the bottom of the carton. Decorate the carton with paint, and let dry. Then add stickers with a magic theme. Tie the corners of the scarves together so that you have a long chain of them. Take 1 scarf and thread it under your shirt and through a sleeve, with the tip of a scarf corner just inside your sleeve cuff. Stuff the rest of the scarves inside the side of your shirt, underneath your arm. Pop on your magician's jacket, and produce your magic carton with a flourish. Let a member of the audience examine it to prove it's not rigged. "Prove" it further by sticking the hand with the loaded sleeve into it. While you're using your free hand to pull the carton from your arm, pull loose the scarf corner from your cuff. Do not take the carton completely off your arm, but let it sit in the palm of your hand, with your fingers steadying it. It will cover the edge of your cuff. Then reach into the carton with your free hand, grasp a corner of a scarf, and quickly pull out a rainbow of scarves! Your friends will be amazed and swear that the jacket is rigged. But you can let them examine that, too. You can also use string, rope, or yarn for variations on this trick. (Hint: Be sure to practice this trick in front of a mirror until you can do it smoothly before you try it out on an audience.)

The Great Adventure

◆▶◆▶◆▶◆

Bring your favorite action hero or heroine to life.

What You'll Need

- action figure
- heavy poster board
- pencil
- thick black marker
- paints and paint-brushes, or colored markers
- clear adhesive vinyl
- thin poster board
- blunt scissors
- game pieces from other board games or colored glass pebbles
- die

Come up with an adventure for your favorite hero or heroine action figure. Give him or her a goal to reach and several funny obstacles along the way. Sketch in the starting point in a corner of the heavy poster board and the end in the opposite corner. Draw scattered obstacles in the middle. Draw a path, with marked spaces big enough for your game pieces, between the starting point and the end. Mark some spaces "hazard." Finish coloring in the board with paints or markers. Let dry. Cover with clear adhesive vinyl for lots of use. Use the thin poster board to make hazard cards to turn over when you land on one of these spaces. Name the hazard and the penalties, such as "Lose a turn," "Go back 2 spaces," "Start over," etc. Grab your game pieces, roll the die, and let your favorite action figure watch as you begin the adventure!

Stuffy Stack

Build an adorable mountain with stuffed animals you love.

What You'll Need
• stuffed animals
• tape measure
• paper
• pencil or pen

Is your room overflowing with stuffed animals? See how your plush pals really stack up in this silly game. Carefully stack your puffy pets, measuring the pile each time you successfully add another beast. Write down your totals as you go to find out how high a stack you can make before it all falls down. Compete against a friend or against your own best score. Put your bigger stuffed animals on the bottom of the pile, and save the smallest for your mountain peak.

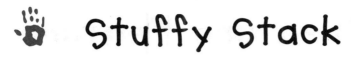

Play It Your Way

Who says you can't bring big Broadway musicals to your living room or school auditorium?

Choose a musical that most people in your audience would like. Then rewrite the story, and set the scene at your school. Narrow

What You'll Need
• costumes
• paper
• pencil or pen

the play down, and use just 2 or 3 musical numbers. You could also rewrite the song lyrics. Add costumes, singing (or lip-synching if you're not using new words), and dancing, and you may just bring the house down!

Creature Feature

◆▸◆▸◆▸◆

Make an appearance as your favorite animal!

What You'll Need
- paper bag or old mask
- blunt scissors
- glue
- 2 or 3 colors of felt
- yarn in colors to match felt
- black marker

Anything goes with this mask! Choose your favorite animal, or create a weird new one. (If you're making a new mask with a paper bag, remember to cut holes for the eyes and mouth.) Glue pieces of felt to the paper bag or old mask for the base color of the face. Let dry. Make more facial details out of felt, and glue them on. Let dry. Make eyebrows, short eyelashes, whiskers, and other details with the various colors of yarn. Add final details with the black marker.

Puppet Pageant

◆▸◆▸◆▸◆

Use puppets to perform a funny skit or silly song.

Choose a skit or song you already know, or make one up. If none of the puppets you made go with your skit or song, create some new ones to match! Practice holding your arm straight up in the air

What You'll Need
- handmade puppets

for long periods of time. Try to work up to 10 minutes; you'll need the stamina when you put on your show. To make sock-puppet characters look realistic when they talk, move only your thumb, not your fingers. After all, wouldn't we look funny if we moved the top of our heads when we talked?

Puppet Stage

▸▸▸▸▸▸

Even puppets need a stage to show off their talents!

What You'll Need
- brooms
- yardstick
- masking tape
- chairs
- old belts
- blankets or bedspreads

Here's how to make a stage for your puppet show. Ask an adult's permission to borrow 2 brooms. Lay them on the floor end to end, with the handles overlapping each other by 4 inches (try not to touch their ends since they might be dirty). Wrap the handles together with lots of masking tape. Next, arrange 2 chairs about 2 yards apart with their backs facing each other. Set the broom pole on the chairs, with the straw part of the brooms resting on the chair backs. Prop a third chair, facing the audience, under the part where the broom handles are taped together. Use a belt to wrap the broom pole to the top part of the chair back. Do this at both ends of the broom pole with the other belts. This makes your stage more stable. Throw blankets or bedspreads over the broom pole for curtains. Sit behind the stage, raise your puppets above the broom poles, and let the show begin!

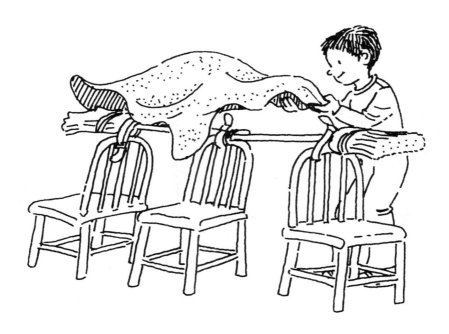

Coffee-Can Bug

◆▶◆▶◆▶◆

Make some plastic insects you can keep or catch.

What You'll Need
- coffee-can lid
- construction paper
- pencil
- blunt scissors
- craft glue
- markers
- chenille stems (optional)
- bowls or boxes (optional)

Grown-ups may use coffee as a morning eye-opener, and these fun, flying bugs are even better reasons for them to drink up!

Take the plastic lid from an empty coffee can (ask for permission before you take it). Decide what type of bug you'd like to make, and choose construction paper colors that correspond to that bug (if you were making a ladybug you would use red and black paper). Trace a circle on a piece of construction paper using the lid. Cut out the circle just inside the line so it is a little smaller than the lid. Glue the paper to the top of the plastic lid.

Decorate your bug, maybe adding a black head and black spots for a ladybug, green wings and black eyes for a fly, or a purple tail and pink legs for a bug from your imagination! If you'd like, add chenille stems for antennae.

Now it's time to toss your colorful insect through the air and see how it flies. For extra fun, set up bowls or boxes as targets and assign them points. Have a contest with a friend to see whose bug can accumulate the most points.

No-Bored Games

◆▶◆▶◆▶◆▶

Who said studying can't be fun? This dinosaur board game is not only fun—it may even help improve your grades!

What You'll Need
- poster board
- markers
- index cards
- 6 craft sticks
- small plastic cup

On the poster board, draw a snakelike road. Divide it into squares. Color each area with one of 6 colors. Draw dinosaurs, volcanoes, swamps, and tar pits alongside the road. Write "Jump ahead 1" or "Go back 1" on some squares. Draw question marks on 5 squares. On each index card, write a question about dinosaurs. If you land on a question mark, you must answer a question about dinosaurs to move. Make pick sticks to move. Color the bottom 1 inch of each craft stick with one of your 6 colors. Put the sticks, color side down, in a small plastic cup. Draw 1 pick stick to see what color you move to. Customize your game using the Game Pieces on page 69 or the Giant Dice on page 72.

Pictominoes

◆▶◆▶◆▶◆▶

Custom-make dominoes with pictures instead of dots.

Count out 28 index cards. On the blank side of each card, use a ruler to draw a straight line through the middle from one long side to the other. Take 1 of the ink stamps and make prints on 1 side of 4 of the index cards. Do the same with the rest of the ink stamps. This should leave you with 4 random spaces that are blank.

What You'll Need
- index cards in white or pastel shades
- marker
- ruler
- ink pad
- 6 small rubber stamps

That's OK; these are wild spaces. Play with your "pictominoes" as if they had dots, only match up the pictures instead!

Gotta Tap!

◄►►►►►►

Ever see Gene Kelly's dance routine in the old movie Singing in the Rain? Or Gregory Hines in the movie White Nights? That, my friends, is tap!

Make your feet sing, just like in the old-time Broadway and Hollywood musicals. Ask for permission to turn an old pair of shoes into tap shoes by attaching self-adhesive metal heel clips. (Don't use nails!) Attach the clips to the toes, balls of the foot, and heels. Tap dancers use these and other areas of the foot while doing their step combinations.

For beginning tap, first practice walking only on the balls of your feet, with your heels in the air. Like the sound? To place only the ball of 1 foot on the floor is called a "step." Transfer your weight to the ball of 1 foot, and let your heel down with a "click" sound. This is called a "heel." Try this beginning combination slowly: While standing in place, step right, heel right. Step left, heel left. Step right, heel right. Step left, heel left. Practice it until you feel a rhythm. When you feel comfortable, try picking up speed. Try walking that way with music. Very cool, huh? You might even want to try a beginning class just for fun.

What You'll Need
- comfortable, old pair of shoes
- self-adhesive metal heel clips from the shoe accessories department
- concrete floor, patio, or sidewalk
- your favorite music

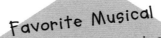

Favorite Musical

Gene Kelly's famous musical Singing in the Rain was named the tenth most popular movie ever made by the American Film Institute's 100 Years, 100 Movies Celebration.

# Balloon Badminton

Mom always said not to play ball in the house—until she learned this fun indoor game.

What You'll Need
- 2 craft sticks
- 2 plastic coffee-can lids
- craft glue
- markers
- newspaper
- blunt scissors
- string or yarn
- 2 chairs
- balloon

Glue a craft stick to each plastic coffee-can lid to make the badminton rackets. Use markers to decorate your rackets with opposing pictures. You might draw a sun on one and a moon on another, an elephant and a mouse, or a red and green light.

To make the net, fanfold a sheet of newspaper. Cut out V-sections as shown at right. Open the paper, and thread some string or yarn through the top row of the cutouts. Tie the net to 2 chairs. Blow up a balloon, and play a slow-motion, fun game of badminton inside the house. If you want, decorate the balloon to match your rackets (this is most easily done before the balloon is filled with air). You might draw a star, a peanut, or a yellow light.

Moon Rock Relay

◆▸◆▸◆▸◆

Step quickly on these moon rocks to race to the moon and back.

What You'll Need
- brown cardboard
- blunt scissors
- black marker

Cut 6 large rock shapes out of cardboard, and color them with a black marker to look like moon rocks. Divide players into 2 teams. Mark the start of the racecourse with a cardboard sign that says "Earth." Place another sign that says "Moon" about 20 feet away. The first player on each team has to toss out 3 moon rocks and step on them, each time picking up the back rock and moving it forward to the Moon. The players can only move forward by stepping on the moon rocks. When the player reaches the Moon, she or he picks up the moon rocks, tosses them out again, and repeats the process to get back to Earth. When the first player gets safely back to Earth, it's time for the next player to go to the Moon and back. When all the astronauts on a team have gone to the Moon and come back, they are the winners.

Cone Creatures

◆▸◆▸◆▸◆

***What kind of creatures do you like?
Martians? Purple People Eaters? Make them all!***

Cover the table and put on a smock or old shirt before beginning this project. Fill out your pinecone creatures with cotton balls. Paint them any color you like, and let dry. Adorn them with yarn for hair, chenille stems for limbs, and fabric scraps for clothes. Don't forget to glue on those wiggle eyes. Top off with touches of glitter glue, and let dry. Oh no—it's the attack of the cone creatures! Better go make some more!

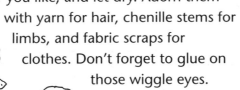

What You'll Need
- table covering
- smock or old shirt
- pinecones of various sizes
- cotton balls
- poster paint
- paintbrushes
- white glue
- yarn
- chenille stems
- fabric scraps
- wiggle eyes
- glitter glue

Feather Face-Off

Is soft still soft if you can't see what's touching you?

What You'll Need
- feathers
- cloth
- cotton balls
- anything extremely soft to the touch
- blindfold

Two players face each other, one blindfolded, one with a variety of soft objects in front of them. It's up to the blindfolded player to guess when the feather is being brushed across his or her cheek, rather than another very soft object. It's up to the sighted player to handle the objects so carefully that the blindfolded friend can't tell the difference. Remember, the gentler the pressure, the harder it is to tell what's touching you.

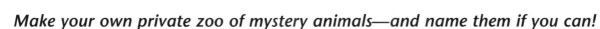 # Mixed-Up Menagerie

Make your own private zoo of mystery animals—and name them if you can!

With the chenille stems, make animals you are familiar with. Then make—and name—the mystery animals. Do a little mixing and matching, and create an animal with a giraffe's neck, a tiger's body, and a monkey's tail—or whatever you can come up with! Round shapes can be made by twisting the chenille stems around pencils and compressing the spirals. When the menagerie is complete, make name cards for each animal with index cards and markers. Invite visitors to admire your experimental zoo!

What You'll Need
- chenille stems in lots of colors and thicknesses
- pencil
- index cards
- markers

Rockin' and Rollin' Waves

◆▷▷▷▷▷◆

Rolling ocean waves always make a big splash—not to mention adding a really cool touch to your production.

What You'll Need

- heavy-duty scissors
- 3 big cardboard boxes of the same size
- pencil
- ruler
- duct tape
- 6 paper towel tubes
- newspapers
- old shirts
- poster paints
- paintbrushes

Caution: This project requires adult help.

These look fantastic when they're done. You may want an adult's help with this group project at first, but then you'll be able to make your own waves. Use the heavy-duty scissors to cut out the bottom of one box and cut down one corner of the box from top to bottom. Spread the box out, and cut off all the flaps. Do the same with the other boxes. Using one of the discarded flaps and a pencil, sketch a big curl of an ocean wave. Cut it out. This is your wave template, or pattern. Use the template to trace waves across each of the long cardboard strips you've made out of the boxes. Make sure there's at least 10 to 12 inches of space under each wave. Now cut out your rows of waves.

Next, wrap the duct tape from top to bottom around the curvy parts in each row of waves. This stabilizes the rows. To make a sturdy handle, cut down the length of a paper towel tube. Roll the cardboard into a tighter tube (until there's a double layer of cardboard all the way around), and wrap the tube in duct tape. Do the same with the other tubes. To attach the handles to a row of waves, lay 1 tube at the end of 1 row, on the back side. Half of it should be behind the wave and half below it. Tape the handle to the cardboard. The tape can be overlapped to the front, since you are going to paint it anyway. Do the same at the other end of the row.

Spread out the newspapers, and put on your old shirt. Paint a base color on your waves, and let dry. Then add details in several different colors. When your waves are finished, line up the lengths of waves, one in front of the other. One person will hold each handle. The middle row should be held a little higher than the front one and the back row a little higher than the middle one. Practice making the front and back rows sway in one direction while the middle row sways in the opposite direction. Talk about awesome wave action!

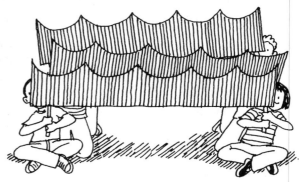

The "Shell" Game

Here's a twist—let the audience try to fool you.

What You'll Need
- 3 cups
- any object

You can do this with a table in front of an audience or around a dinner table. The "trick" is to pick a secret partner who won't tell the secret. Tell your friends you have developed amazing powers of X-ray vision. Arrange 3 cups in a row, and ask your secret partner to hide an object under a cup while your back is turned. Then have him or her mix up the cups several times. Whirl around and face the cups with a flourish. Glance at your partner out of the corner of your eye. If his or her hand is on his or her left hip, the object is hidden under the cup on the left. If the hand is on the right hip, the object is under the cup on the right. Both hands on the hips means the object is under the middle cup. Whip the cup up and away from the object, and declare, "Aha!" Then ask your amazed audience if someone would care to try to stump you. Repeat the trick several times. Your friends will be totally perplexed!

Stage Cycling

For a "wheely" good act, practice, practice, practice!

Caution: This project requires adult supervision.

What You'll Need
- bicycles and/or unicycles
- safety pads and helmets
- basketball and hoop
- juggling objects

With practice, cycling is a talent show crowd-pleaser. Gather a group of friends, and work up a routine for you and your bikes. For example, ride in formation and cross paths with each other (just like motorcycle police officers in parades). For those with access to and ability to ride a unicycle, try playing 1-on-1 basketball or juggling at the same time. Make sure you wear bicycle helmets and pads at all times and observe safety rules! Also for safety's sake, have an adult supervise your practices and performances. You've heard it before: Practice, practice, practice makes perfect!

Tip to Tip

❖❖❖❖❖

Try walking in a straight line as you've never done it before.

What You'll Need
• ruler

Have you ever seen an adult measure out the length or width of a room or space by walking very carefully, touching the heel of one shoe against the toe tip of the other? Try walking some of your favorite routes using that strange measuring method for steps. Does it take longer to accomplish the task? Is it harder to get from here to there? How many steps did you count to move from place to place? How did it make your legs feel? Measure a few of your favorite outdoor paths. Just for fun, measure your foot with a ruler to see exactly how long your favorite walks might be.

Shoestring Tie-Up

❖❖❖❖❖

You'll have your hands full with these shoes!

What You'll Need
• old sneakers with long shoelaces
• a stopwatch

Your shoe won't have to fit your foot for this fun race against the clock. The trick is in tying the shoe as you hold it in your hands. And did we mention, when you can't see it? How fast can you tie a shoe? How fast can you tie a shoe behind your back? This silly game will test your skills. Race against your own best time, or compete against a friend. Place untied shoes at one end of the room, players at the other. Say "go," and have the runners race to the shoes and tie them. Time each player with a stopwatch. Now untie the shoes and repeat the process, but this time tie the shoes while holding them behind your back. The player with the best scores wins.

Sneaker Fact
The first sneaker widely sold in North America was the Converse All Star basketball sneaker, and it debuted in 1917.

Beanbag Games

You can play lots of different games with beanbags. So get ready, aim, and toss!

Make one or all of the following games. Game 1: Draw a face on the bottom of a cardboard box with 2 big eyes and a big mouth. Cut out the mouth and eyes. To play, throw the beanbags through the holes. Game 2: Draw a tic-tac-toe board on poster board. Toss the beanbags on the board to get 3 in a row. Game 3: Draw a design on a sheet of construction paper. Tape the paper around a large coffee can. Standing at all different distances from the can, try to toss your beanbags in it. Game 4: Decorate 6 paper towel tubes. Stand them up, and try to knock each one down with a toss of a beanbag.

What You'll Need
- cardboard box
- markers
- blunt scissors
- beanbags
- poster board
- construction paper
- empty coffee can
- clear tape
- paper towel tubes

Boot Hill

Slip out of your shoes and into some fun!

What You'll Need
- players' shoes
- whistle

All players remove their shoes and put them in a pile at the center of the room. Mix the pile completely. The players form a circle around the pile, with everyone standing about 10 feet away from it. When the whistle sounds, the players head for the pile. The first player to find both of his or her own shoes—and to put them on!—wins.

Twirlies

◆▸◆▸◆▸◆▸

These bright umbrellas are fun to paint and add lots of eye appeal to your play or dance routine.

What You'll Need
• old umbrellas
• newspapers
• old shirt
• poster paints
• paintbrushes

Get your parents' permission to paint the umbrellas. Spread out lots of newspapers, and slip into your old shirt. Open up the umbrellas. You may give an umbrella a new base color if you wish or use the original color if it's a bright one. Wait a few hours for the paint to dry. Then paint a wild pattern in a contrasting color. Try spirals, dots, zigzags, and other shapes. If you want, you can also paint the inside of the umbrella a solid color. After they are dry, use the umbrellas in a show. You can have people crouch behind the decorated umbrellas and spin them for interesting backgrounds. Or have dancers dance around them, twirl them, and use them as props. (For eye safety, make sure each umbrella twirler is standing a good distance away from the next person!)

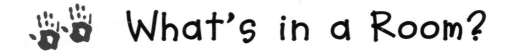

What's in a Room?

◆▸◆▸◆▸◆▸

Now you see it, now you don't. What do you remember?

This game is very simple and fun. Lead the group into a room with lots of things in it, both big and small. Give them 2 minutes to memorize what they see in the room. Then lead them back into the party room, and give them 2 more minutes to write down everything they remember seeing. Whoever remembers the most things correctly wins.

What You'll Need
• paper
• pencils

Dress-Up Relay

Can you change your clothes as fast as a superhero does?
If you can, you might be a dress-up champion.

What You'll Need
• old clothes, at least 10 pieces for each team

The object of this game is to dress and undress as quickly as possible, regardless of where on your body the clothes actually wind up. Divide into 2 teams. Pile 10 clothing items for each team or player—anything from scarves to pants to shirts to purses to hats—at the opposite end of the room. When someone says "go," the first player on each team runs to the pile and puts on all the clothes over his or her own, as quickly as possible. Anything goes, as long as nothing falls off your body as you run. The players run back to their starting point and take off the clothes. The next player on the team must put on the clothes, run back to the far side of the room, and take the clothes off. Then they sprint back to their team and touch the hand of the next player. The next player runs to the clothes and puts them on. The game goes on until the last player returns to the team. The first team to finish wins. You can even play this game on your own by racing against the clock. Keep trying to beat your best time!

Booting Up
Ever wonder why cowboys need boots? To keep their feet from slipping through their saddle stirrups, according to experts at the Cowboy Museum in Oklahoma.

Pencil Me In

◆▸◆▸◆▸◆

This game is tougher than you think.

Scatter the pencils on a tabletop, with several lying across each other. The object of the game is to remove 1 pencil at a time without making any of the other pencils move. It can be  done! The game ends when a pencil moves. Hint: You can use a pencil that's already been removed to try to push or flip out a pencil that's still in the pile. This is great fun to play alone, but it is also lots of fun with friends!

Milk Jug Catch

◆▸◆▸◆▸◆

This is a great game to play indoors or out, and it's especially fun since you made it yourself.

Caution: This project requires adult help.

With an adult's help, cut off the bottom of 2 clean plastic milk jugs as shown by the dotted line below. (For an easy game, use gallon 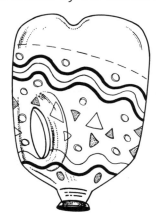 jugs. To make the game more challenging, use quart jugs.) Keep the caps on the jugs. Decorate the plastic jugs with permanent markers. To play the game, toss a ball to your partner. He or she catches it in the jug. Then your partner throws it to you. To make the game harder, throw the ball when it is still in the jug. You could use a soft foam ball to play the game inside, and use a plastic ball to play outside.

Double Dutch

Two ropes are twice as much fun as one!

What You'll Need
- 2 extra-long jump ropes

This talent is exciting to watch—but it takes lots of patience to perfect your skills! You may already know someone who can do this. Or you might be able to find someone at school or in your neighborhood who knows a little. Learning and practicing is easier and more fun together than alone! Rhythm plays a big part in this talent, too. That's why there are so many rope-skipping rhymes. Chanting the rhymes helps you keep the beat and tells you when to jump. Get 2 friends to swing the ropes for you. Practice first with 1 rope, doing simple tricks such as hopping in a circle. Then add a second rope. Just do the same trick at a faster tempo. Check out other people's moves, and adapt them to make up your own stunts. Then practice stunts with 2 or 3 jumpers. Add fast music, and you have a big crowd thriller!

I Feel Something Furry

Who knew so many animals could fit in this magic hat?

What You'll Need

- small cardboard box
- blunt scissors
- ruler
- one stuffed rabbit and other plush animals
- solid-color fabric remnant and felt the same color
- pencil
- glue
- black poster board
- black electrical tape

This trick uses the same principle as What's Up My Sleeve? (on page 15). The rabbit isn't actually in the hat. You're going to pull it from somewhere else. Cut a hole in the bottom of the cardboard box. It should be big enough for your hand and anything you want to pull out of the hat, but probably no wider than 5 inches across. Then cut off the flaps around the top (opposite the hole you cut). The box will serve as a platform for your hat, and it will hide the rabbit—and everything else you pull out of the hat. Put the box on a table (hole side up), and drape the fabric over it. With a pencil, trace the hole on the fabric. Cut out the hole. Cut a square of felt just large enough to cover the hole. Cover the hole with the felt, and glue 1 edge of the felt square to the fabric.

Make a top hat out of the black poster board. Cut a strip about 6 or 7 inches tall and long enough to fit around your head. Tape that piece together to form a cylinder, and place it standing up on the poster board. Trace around the circle, and cut it out; this will be the top of the hat. To make the hat brim, draw a circle around the one you've just cut out and then draw another one about 3 inches larger. Cut out the outer circle, and then cut out the inner circle, which will leave you with a large donut shape. Tape this brim to the hat with the black electrical tape. Tape the top of the hat on only halfway around. When you perform, use a tiny strip of tape on the open end to make the hat appear closed.

For your magic trick, hide all your plush animals or other objects under the box. Then drape the fabric over it, centering the felt-covered hole over the hole in the box. Bow and tip your hat to your audience, showing them that there is absolutely nothing in it. Set your magic hat on top of the box. Reach into the hat, breaking open the small piece of tape, and reach through the felt into the box. Stick your arm in up to your elbow and "root around" in the hat for that silly rabbit. Start pulling out everything else but the rabbit. Say, "No, I didn't want a tiger (or whatever animal you pull out). Where is that rabbit?" The suspense builds until...out pops the rabbit!

Flyers, Posters, Invitations, Tickets, and Programs

Now that you've gone to all the trouble to put on a show, let the world know about it!

What You'll Need
- typewriter or computer
- white and colored paper
- copy machine
- poster board
- paint and paintbrushes, or markers
- gift wrap
- blunt scissors
- glue
- envelopes
- postage stamps
- heavy card stock

Flyers and Posters: Type up your announcement on the typewriter or computer. Add graphic art, if you want. Next, print it on white paper, take it to a copy store, and copy the flyers in bright colors (if you want, just print the top flyers on colored paper). Post them wherever your audience will be. Paint or draw some special posters to go in high-traffic areas where lots of people will see them. Ask for permission before posting the flyers and posters.

Invitations: Follow the basic instructions for the flyers and posters. If you don't have access to computer graphic art, cut out colorful pictures from gift wrap that fit the theme of your show, and glue them on the invitations. Decorate the outside of the envelopes, too, if you like. Then address, stamp, and mail the invitations to all your friends and family members.

Tickets: Use little information on the ticket, and make it easy to read. Include the name of the show, location, time, day of the week, date, and "presented by" information. Print or make one original of the ticket on heavy card stock. Check it carefully! Make more copies of the ticket on the same page. Copy or print your page on colored paper. Cut the tickets apart, and hand them out.

Programs: Make enough programs for everyone in the audience. If you have a computer, explore type styles to find a fun one for the show title. Place the show title at the top of the page. Below it, list the acts in the show and names of the actors in each. Then list everyone who helped with the presentation. Make sure you thank any sponsors who helped you put on your show and mention what they donated. Let the show begin!

# Crafty Animals

These soft and cuddly animals will never run away from home.

What You'll Need
- cardboard
- blunt scissors
- ruler
- craft glue
- yarn
- paper scraps

It's hard to believe you can turn cardboard and scrap yarn into fun animals, but it's true!

Cut 3 strips of scrap cardboard; make 2 the same length and the other about 2 inches longer. The longest strip will be the body, neck, and head of the animal. The other strips will be the animal's legs. Make a bend in the longer piece of cardboard, about ¼ of the way down from an end; make another bend another ¼ of the way down from the first bend. This is the head and neck of the animal. Your animal should look a bit like a backward Z.

Bend the shorter 2 pieces in half. Fold 1 over the "shoulders" of the animal, just behind the neck, and the other at the opposite end or "bottom" of the animal. (You'll need to rebend the legs so they lay flat on top of the animal's body.) Glue the legs in place.

Wrap your animal's body with yarn. Work your way down the body, circling it again and again with soft, fluffy yarn, passing over the legs at first. Once the body is covered, slowly work your way back to the legs and start wrapping those pieces of cardboard until they are covered and plump. Work your way back up to the belly of the animal, and tie off the loose end of yarn. Glue on scraps of yarn for ears, a mane, and a tail. Use bits of paper to add animal eyes and other features.

Make a zoo full of animals!

 # Giant Maze

◆◇◆◇◆◇◆

Create a maze, and challenge your friends to get through it!

Use a pencil to draw a maze on a large piece of bristol board or light- to medium-weight cardboard. Draw the correct route through the maze (all the way to the exit) first. You might want to get ideas for drawing your maze from other mazes you find in coloring books or activity books. Start drawing other routes through the maze that look like they lead to the exit but only lead to dead ends.

Why not pick a theme for your maze, with traps and decorated dead ends. Use the markers to illustrate your theme. Is Roger running from the vampire? Is Sara searching for her cookie? After you've finished drawing and decorating the maze, go back over all the pencil lines you want to keep with the small-tipped marker and erase the other ones.

Cover the board with clear vinyl adhesive paper so your friends can try escaping from your maze again and again. (Have them use their fingers or a wax crayon, which can be wiped off.)

What You'll Need
- bristol board or light- to medium-weight cardboard
- pencil
- markers
- small-tipped black marker
- clear vinyl adhesive paper
- wax crayon (optional)

Make a Tangram

◄►◄►◄►◄►

A tangram is like a recyclable puzzle, because you can make so many shapes and patterns with it.

What You'll Need
- 8×8-inch sheet light cardboard
- ruler
- pencil
- blunt scissors

The Chinese call this puzzle *ch'i ch'iao t'u,* which means "ingenious puzzle with seven pieces." Seven geometric shapes make up the puzzle. Rearranged in different ways, these 7 pieces can make as many as 1,600 different designs!

Look closely at the pattern in the accompanying picture. Use your ruler and pencil to draw an 8×8-inch square on the cardboard. The heavy black lines are the cutting lines. If you'd like, you can decorate your tangram—color each piece a different color, create different patterns on each one, or whatever you like. (NOTE: It is easier to color or decorate your tangram puzzle before you cut it apart.)

Try to re-create the design shown here. Then invent new shapes of your own. Trace the outside shape of your new designs, and challenge friends and family members to arrange the tangram pieces to match your designs.

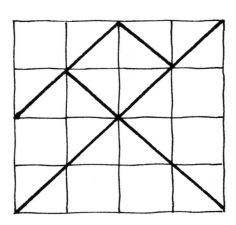
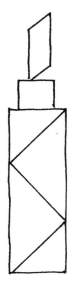

Shadow Puppets

*Even with all the lights on, these funny shadow shapes
stay around to play some more.*

Pick out a room with a light-colored wall. Turn on a lamp. Practice making shadows on the wall with your hands. Cross your thumbs over one another and spread your fingers apart to make a bird. Or hold one hand sideways with your thumb sticking straight up on top and your pinky separated from your other fingers at the bottom to make a dog.

What You'll Need
- drawing paper
- masking tape
- pencil
- colored pencils, crayons, or markers
- blunt scissors
- craft glue
- poster board or cardboard
- craft sticks

When you're done practicing, tape a piece of paper on the wall. (Don't press the tape too hard or leave it on too long—you don't want to remove any paint or wallpaper.) Make a shadow puppet on the paper, and have a friend draw an outline around the shape. Use household items, such as gloves, strainers, and staplers to make more shadow puppets. Take turns with your friend making shapes and drawing outlines until you have a whole zoo. Color in your animal shapes.

To make your shapes into stick puppets, cut out an animal shape, and glue it on a piece of poster board or cardboard. Cut around the shape, and glue a craft stick to the back.

Cat Walking

This purrrfectly wonderful activity will keep you on your toes.

Scientists say cats actually walk on their toes at least 80 percent of the time. Could you manage that? Practice walking on your toes to your favorite song, counting 1, 2, 3, 4, 5, 6, 7, 8 as you go. When you get to 9 and 10, walk as you normally do. Start your cat walk again, counting 1, 2, 3, 4, 5, 6, 7, 8, then walking flat-footed again for steps 9 and 10. How do your legs feel? Want to test a new catlike rhythm? Do the same cat walk to the beats of your name.

Traffic Signs

◆▶◆▶◆▶◆▶

These signs are fun to make for toy cars. They're also a great way to learn all your road signs.

What You'll Need
- 5 boards, 1×2 inches each
- 5 wood dowels, ¼ inch each
- saw
- power drill and ¼-inch drill bit
- sandpaper
- tape measure
- wood glue
- cardboard
- blunt scissors
- markers
- clear tape

Caution: This project requires adult help.

Have an adult saw and drill all the wood pieces. Make sure you sand the wood smooth. Saw the 1×2-inch boards into 2-inch pieces for the base of the signs. Drill a ¼-inch hole in the center of each wood base. Saw the dowels into 4-inch pieces for the sign posts. Glue each dowel in a base.

To make a sign, cut a 4×1½-inch piece from the cardboard. Fold it in half, and draw a traffic sign on both sides. Tape the sides closed to make a pocket. Slip it over a dowel sign post. Repeat to make 4 more signs. For instance, you could make a stop sign, yield sign, traffic signal, railroad crossing, or a walk/don't walk sign.

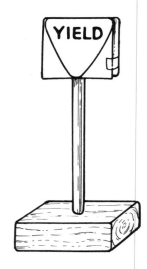

 # Mystery

◆▶◆▶◆▶◆▶

Everyone loves a mystery, especially trying to guess whodunit before the play is over!

Rewrite a short classic mystery story as a play with modern characters and situations. Hunt for costumes in thrift stores and at garage sales. This will keep you busy for at least a month! Practice by yourselves, then perform it before an audience.

What You'll Need
- short classic mystery story
- paper
- pen or pencil
- costumes

# Shape It Up

Teach your favorite young child about different shapes.

What You'll Need
- foam food trays (from fruits or vegetables only)
- pencil
- ruler
- permanent markers
- colored shoelaces or yarn with taped ends

You can be a real teacher when you help some young friends learn about circles, squares, triangles, and other shapes. First make sure the foam trays are clean. You may want to have an adult help you do this because the trays must be really clean. Let them dry if you had to wash them. Use a pencil to poke out the outline of a shape (triangle, circle, square, etc.) on one of the foam trays. Leave ¼ to ½ inch between each hole, depending on the size of the shape you want. Use a marker to write the name of the shape underneath the shape. Repeat these steps with each of the other trays, using a different shape on each one. To teach younger children the names of the shapes, help them lace up the outline with a piece of yarn or a shoelace. Show them the name of the shape that you have written. Make sure you tell your young students what a great job they did! (Be sure that young children do not play with yarn or shoelaces without supervision!)

Marble Menagerie

Round out your animal collection with this marble magic.

What You'll Need
- 4×6-inch piece stiff cardboard
- markers
- colored marbles
- craft glue
- colored paper

If you love marbles and animals, this is the activity for you.

Decorate cardboard so it looks like an animal habitat or a cuddly pet bed. Now, follow the patterns below—or try some creatures of your own—to make a marble mate. Make a turtle (glue a circle of marbles for the shell, 1 marble each for the turtle's head, feet, and stubby tail), snake (6 marbles laid end to end), or a cat (a pyramid of marbles with paper ears and tail added).

Cut out small pieces of paper for eyes, ears, and other body parts to finish your creatures; add the details to the paper with markers. When the glue is dry, put your animal in its habitat!

snake

cat

Presidential Marbles

If you enjoy playing marbles, then you have something in common with several past presidents of the United States. It's said that George Washington and Thomas Jefferson both enjoyed the game of marbles and Abraham Lincoln was an expert at a marble game called "old bowler."

Mighty Masks

◆▸◆▸◆▸◆

These easy-to-make masks look hilarious!

Leaf through old magazines (ask for permission first!), and cut out individual facial features from pictures of faces. Divide them into piles of ears, noses, eyebrows, chins, hair, heads, etc. Don't forget animal faces! Cut eye and mouth holes out of a paper plate. Pick out a goofy arrangement of facial features, and glue them onto the plate to make a mask. Let the glue dry. Next, punch holes in the sides of the mask with a pencil. Tie a piece of yarn to the hole on each side to hold the mask on your head. Admire the crazy results.

What You'll Need
- several old maga-zines to cut up
- blunt scissors
- thin paper plates
- glue
- pencil
- yarn

Toothpick Towers

◆▸◆▸◆▸◆

Stacking toothpicks is harder than you think.

What You'll Need
- clean large bottle
- toothpicks

Sliding 1 toothpick across the mouth of a bottle is easy. But stacking 10 or 20 toothpicks across the same small space is a fun challenge, with or without a play partner.

Clean the bottle well with soap and water. Take 10 toothpicks in your hand. Start stacking them across the mouth of the bottle, then stack them across the first layer you set down. See how many toothpicks you can safely stack without knocking the whole experiment down. Store your toothpick game pieces inside your bottle after you're done playing.

Story Scroll

▶▶▶▶▶▶▶

Make one of these and you'll really be on a roll!

Choose a folktale or a play you've seen, or make up your own story. Find a TV-size box, and cut out a screen-size hole in the front. Cut round holes in the top and bottom of the left-hand and right-hand corners, so you can thread 2 gift wrap tubes through the holes. Next, pick 10 key scenes in the story. Draw or paint the scenes from the story in panels on the white butcher paper. Make sure the panels fit the size of the TV "screen." Don't forget to make a title page and a closing page. The pictures can be done by several people, if you wish, and then taped together later in the cor-

rect order. Thread the gift wrap tubes through the holes above and below the "screen." Once the artwork is finished and taped together, tape the ends of the scroll onto the tubes. Roll the scroll around the tubes. Choose a narrator to tell the story while someone rolls the panels forward.

Ancient Scrolls

Probably the most famous scrolls in the world are the Dead Sea Scrolls. They were found by a young Bedouin shepherd in the Judean Desert when he was searching for a lost goat. He entered a cave and found ancient clay jars filled with some of the scrolls.

Flying Machines

People have dreamed of flying ever since...well, ever since there have been people. Now it's your turn to make a flying machine!

What You'll Need
- 2-liter soda bottle with black base and a cap
- craft knife
- small stuffed animal
- tape
- paints
- paintbrush
- plastic coffee-can lid
- straight pin with a ball head
- cool-temp glue gun

Caution: This project requires adult help.

Why not invent your own incredible machines? They won't really fly, but they will be fun! Here's one that's easy to make: Pull the black bottom off a 2-liter soda bottle. Have an adult cut the bottle in half with the craft knife. Set a stuffed animal "pilot" in the top of the bottle. Push the top of the soda bottle into the base to make the body of your flying machine (with the pilot inside). Wrap tape around the seam between the top and the base. Paint the machine, leaving the front half clear for the windshield. Cut 4 sections out of the coffee-can lid, but don't cut the rim! (Have an adult help you with the craft knife and glue gun!) Push the pin through the center of the coffee-can lid and into the center of the soda pop lid. Paint and then glue the plastic cutouts on as wings for your airplane. Happy flying!

Butcher, Baker, Candlestick Maker

◄►◄►◄►◄►

Have fun acting out different careers. Try them all!

What You'll Need
- secondhand clothes
- newspaper or construction paper
- blunt scissors
- markers
- stapler and staples
- clear tape
- glue
- cardboard

Make your own costumes for various jobs, such as a doctor, nurse, firefighter, lawyer, schoolteacher, and so on. You could use secondhand clothes (wash them first!) or cut the costume pieces out of newspaper or construction paper. If you're making your own clothes, decorate the paper pieces with markers. Fasten them with staples, clear tape, and glue. Use the cardboard to cut out props, such as stethoscopes, swords, shields, computers, and so on. Don't forget to create really fun hats to go along with your costumes! Do this just for fun or put on a show for your friends.

 # Box Maze

Make 2 box mazes, and have races with a friend. If you can finish without losing your marbles, you win.

What You'll Need
- drawing paper
- pencil
- shoe box with lid
- blunt scissors
- markers
- ruler
- craft glue
- small marble

Practice drawing a maze design on a piece of paper. Think of a theme for your maze. For example, it might be a swamp game, such as "Watch out for the Alligator Ponds." Draw lines for the maze walls, and mark places along the maze to cut holes (the ponds) for the marble to fall through. Mark the starting and finishing points of the maze. Once you've created a design you like, draw the maze lines and hole marks on the inside of the shoe box lid. Cut the pond holes where indicated. Make sure the holes are slightly larger than the marble. Decorate the maze with markers. To make the maze walls, cut ½-inch-wide strips of cardboard from the rest of the shoe box. The strips should be the length of each maze line. Apply glue along the lines in the lid, and stand a cardboard strip in the glue to make each wall. Let the glue dry. To play, place a marble at the starting point. Then tilt and turn the lid to move the marble along the maze to the finishing point. Be sure to watch out for the alligator ponds!

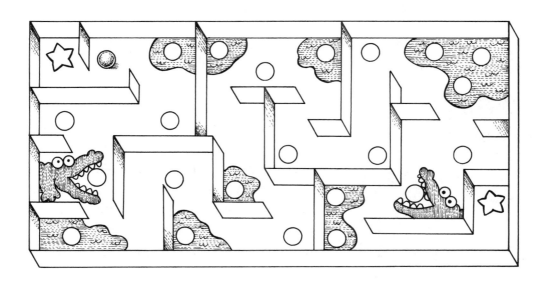

What Is That?

◆▶◆▶◆▶◆▶

This guessing game makes everyone use more than their sense of sight!

What You'll Need
- hat or stocking cap
- 3 differently textured objects that are hard, rough, and silky
- pencil
- paper
- bowls (optional)
- cardboard box (optional)
- black cloth (optional)
- grapes, noodles, and gelatin (optional)

Put all 3 objects into the hat or stocking cap. In a separate room, have each player reach into the hat (without looking) and try to guess what each object is. After everyone has had a try, meet together in a room and have everyone write down the mystery objects. The winners are those who guess correctly. For a more gross-out version of this game, put 3 bowls in a cardboard box covered with black cloth. Place peeled grapes; cold, cooked noodles; and cut-up gelatin in the bowls. Now have your friends guess what they are touching! Yucky!

Domino Duplex

◆▶◆▶◆▶◆▶

Patience, not speed, wins this game.

The object is to build a house, 1 player and 1 domino at a time. The first player lays a domino down on its side. The next player adds another domino in such a way as to start building a house. Keep in mind

What You'll Need
- standard set of dominoes

that you will have to lay dominoes on their long or short sides so that they stick up to make walls. Players take turns adding dominoes to build up the building—it gets tricky pretty quickly! The game is over when the first domino falls down. An alternative is to play this game by yourself, each time trying to add more dominoes. Keep track of how many you add. You can also time yourself; see how many you can place before the timer goes off!

Art Flash Cards

◆◆◆◆◆◆◆

Teach yourself to see basic shapes in your art with a fun flash card game.

What You'll Need
• 10 blank index cards, 3×5 inches each
• markers

Divide the index cards between you and a friend. Draw crazy shapes on the cards. Start with simple shapes without too many intersecting lines, then make each shape a little more complicated. Don't draw letters or specific objects. The idea is to draw unfamiliar shapes. Color in

the shapes. Now flash 1 card at a time to each other. See if you and your friend can redraw the shape you were shown. Hold the picture at different angles and distances. Can you see any objects in your art?

Ballet Brainstorm

◆◆◆◆◆◆◆

Looking graceful and flowing with the music can be hard work, but the results are worth it.

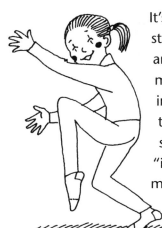

It's very important to begin slowly by stretching out your arms, torso, back, legs, ankles, and feet. Don't bounce. Listen to the music as you warm up your muscles. Imagine what you might do with each part of the music. When you're done warming up, start the music again and use your body to "interpret" what you hear. How would you move to soft parts? How would you move to fast, dramatic parts?

What You'll Need
• soft, flexible shoes or socks
• music from your favorite ballet
• smooth floor
• mirror (optional)

 # Hidden Coin

◆▶◆▶◆▶◆

You should be making a million dollars, because you can find money anywhere!

What You'll Need
• 2 quarters

This trick takes a little practice. Ask someone to come forward and stand up in front with you. While the audience's attention is on the person coming forward, slip a quarter far enough into one sleeve so that it doesn't slide out. Be careful never to let this hand drop to your side. Move fast!

Both you and the participant should face the group, and you should be slightly facing one another. Make sure no one can see your back. Now, hold out both palms for everyone to see. Put a quarter on one palm. Then put your hands behind your back, and count "1, 2, 3" while pretending to switch the quarter from hand to hand behind your back. Actually, you slip the quarter down your waistband. (Hint: Your shirt must be tucked in to do this.) Bring your closed fists forward for the participant to choose. Have the participant tap one fist: "Darn, it's empty." You open the other fist—surprise, it's empty, too! Say, "Now where is that quarter? Hmm." Keep talking while you finally drop the hand where the quarter is hidden. Wiggle the hand behind your back until you feel the quarter slide into your palm. With the quarter in your loosely closed fist, reach up behind your participant's ear and exclaim, "Hey, how did that get there?" Then show the quarter.

Fast Clap

◆◇◆◇◆◇◆▶

How fast can you clap your hands? It's not as easy as you think.

What You'll Need
- paper
- pen or pencil
- stopwatch or clock

We often clap our hands together to express our approval—to say we loved a musical show, to praise our favorite football players, to say we agree with something we've just heard. But how fast can you clap your hands? And how do those numbers change with the position of your arms? Write down your numbers to find out. Clap your hands in the usual position, right in front of your body, for 30 seconds. How many claps did you manage to make? Now do the same with your hands over your head. Now do the same with your hands behind your back. What muscles did you use when you clapped over your head that you didn't use clapping in front of you or clapping behind your back?

Ten-Penny Pickup

◆◇◆◇◆◇◆▶

Once you toss these pennies, the race is on!

What You'll Need
- 10 pennies
- small box or bowl
- stopwatch or clock
- paper
- pencil or pen

Hold 10 pennies in your hand, and softly scatter them just a few feet in front of you. See how fast you can gather the pennies and drop them in the box or bowl. Write down your time. Now repeat the process. But this time, gather them with your toes before dropping them in the bowl or box. How long did that take? Want a few more choices? Try picking up the pennies with only your right hand. Now, only your left hand. For extra fun, invite a friend to play with you, and see who's the penny pickup champion. Don't forget to wash your hands after you have finished playing. Coins are valuable, but they are not very clean!

Fox and Hounds

Who will outfox whom? Play the game to find out!

What You'll Need
- a group of people, the more the better
- deck of cards

Everyone sits in a circle. Remove all the face cards from a deck of cards except for 1 joker. Choose a person to be the game leader. Count out as many cards as there are people playing, except for the game leader, making sure to include the joker. The game leader deals out the cards face down to the other players. Whoever gets the joker is the fox. After the cards have been passed out, they are collected again. Now the game leader instructs the group, or "hounds," to "fall asleep" by bowing their heads and closing their eyes. Only the fox stays "awake" so the game leader can identify him or her. The game leader calls for the hounds to "awaken." The group plays the game in rounds, eliminating 1 person from the game at a time.

When the hounds "awaken," the players stare closely at each others' eyes and suggest one or more people they believe to be the fox. When they decide on a person to question, he or she must tell the group why he or she couldn't be the fox. If the group believes that person, they choose another until they find a person they decide to eliminate. While everyone is staring at each other, the fox carefully winks at someone (without being seen by the others) and eliminates them. That person waits a few seconds, and then announces, "I've just been outfoxed."

The game leader calls for the hounds to "fall asleep" again, and everyone except the fox and the eliminated players bow their heads and close their eyes. Once someone is eliminated,

they can remain and watch the rest of the game, but they may not speak at any time or give clues about the fox's identity. Play continues until 1 person is left—either the fox or a hound. The hounds win the game if they manage to find the fox in this manner before he or she outfoxes them.

Dinosaur Finger Puppets

Make a little thunder with a dinosaur on your hand!

What You'll Need
- green paper
- blunt scissors
- ruler
- markers
- glue
- tape

This unusual puppet's body is formed by your own hand. Paper cutouts make the long neck, the head, and the feet!

Cut out 2 identical head pieces. Cut out a neck piece that is 2 inches high and 2 inches wide. Decorate the head to look like your favorite dinosaur. Glue the tops of the 2 heads together. Roll the neck piece around your middle finger, and tape it. Slide the roll off your finger, and glue the bottom of the heads to the roll. For fun dino feet, cut 4 strips of paper that are 1 inch high and wide enough to wrap around your fingers.

Now it's time to dress the dinosaur! When the glue is dry on the head, slide your middle finger inside the neck piece. Tape the strips of paper around the tips of your other fingers.

Now you have a miniature dinosaur in, or should we say ON, your hands.

# Beanbags

These soft bags can be used for target practice or a fun game of catch.

Cut three 4×8-inch pieces of fabric. Fold them in half vertically to form a square. Sew 2 sides closed on each square of fabric. At the open end, fill the squares with stuffing materials. Make them heavy or light, depending on how you will use the beanbags. To make heavy bags, use aquarium rocks; to make light bags, use packing peanuts; and to make medium-weight bags, use dried beans. Sew the last side closed. Use the bags to play the Beanbag Games on page 29.

What You'll Need
- ⅔ yard of fabric
- blunt scissors
- tape measure
- needle and thread
- dried beans, aquarium rocks, or small packing peanuts

Marble Toss

◄►◄►◄►◄►

Playing this game is easy. Scoring high is not so easy!

What You'll Need
- clean, dry egg carton
- black crayon
- large beach towel (optional)
- five marbles

With the black crayon, write "15" in the bottom of 1 egg section, "10" in 2 sections, "5" in 3 sections, and "1" in the remaining 6 sections. Either play this game on a rug or carpet or spread out a beach towel on the floor. Lay the carton on the rug or beach towel, and stand about 5 feet away. Toss your marbles, 1 at a time, into the egg carton, and add up your score. When you think you're getting pretty good, challenge your friend to a game! The highest score wins.

Triangulation

◄►◄►◄►◄►

In a race of triangles, who will make the most?

This is a game for 2 or 3 players. With the ruler and a pencil, the first player makes a small triangle. The player's score for that turn is 1, since 1 triangle was formed. The second player is allowed to draw 3 lines. They may make the lines anywhere they like. If they make them around the first triangle,

What You'll Need
- sheet of white, unlined paper
- ruler
- pencils

with 2 sides overlapping 2 sides of the first triangle, their score is 2; 1 for the triangle they made and 1 for the triangle within the triangle they just made. By overlapping lines, they also set up an opportunity for multiple scores in the future. Play continues with each player making 3 moves and scoring according to the number of triangles contained in the triangle just formed. The game ends when players run out of room on the paper.

Balancing Act

◆▶◆▶◆▶◆▶

Can you improve your balance? This game will help you find out.

What You'll Need
- book
- stuffed animal
- ball
- paper cup

You may have seen people from other countries carrying jugs of water from village wells on their heads. How hard can it be? Find out by using different objects around the house. Set a book on your  head, and keep track of how many steps you can take before the book topples. Do the same with a stuffed animal, a ball, and a paper cup. Compare your results. See if you can improve your balance by taking longer or shorter steps. Try moving your arms in different ways. Can you keep the objects on your head as you run or skip?

Silly Sandwiches

◆▶◆▶◆▶◆▶

You can't eat these "sandwiches," but you'll have fun coming up with all sorts of silly ingredients!

Cut out 4 light brown or white pieces of construction paper in the shapes of pieces of bread. Glue 3 edges of 2 bread-shaped pieces together, leaving an edge unglued. When the glue is dry, stuff small scraps of paper between the 2 layers. Glue the open end closed. Repeat for the other 2 pieces of bread-shaped paper. Then cut out other ingredients to fill your sandwich. Lettuce could be made from green paper, crumpled up, then glued to a bread slice. Tomato slices could be "stuffed" to look more realistic (just as you did with the bread slices). Use markers, the hole punch (to make Swiss cheese), and any other craft supplies you'd like to make your sandwich. When you're done making all your ingredients, glue the layers together to make delicious-looking artwork!

What You'll Need
- construction paper
- blunt scissors
- glue
- markers
- hole punch
- other craft supplies

Pretend Store

◄►►►►►►

Invite your friends over, and have each of you design your own store. Together you can make a mini-mall.

Make several different types of stores for your mini-mall. All you need is some play money and a cash register to get started. To make play money, cut several 2½×6-inch pieces from green construction paper. Decorate them to make your own dollar bills. Add the amounts—$1, $5, $10, and even $100. Cut several circles from foam food trays to make the coins. Decorate them with markers.

Make a cash register from a shoe box. Cut the lid in half. Use one half as the cash drawer. Place the lid half back on the box, and turn the box upside down. Pull out one half of the lid, and place your play money inside. To make the cash register buttons, cut small circles from different colors of construction paper. Write numbers and words such as "Total" and "Void" on the buttons. Glue them to the box.

Now you're ready to play store. For a grocery store, gather food cartons and boxes. Collect junk mail for a post office. Use stuffed animals for a pet store. Gather old shopping bags for your purchases. Draw your store's sign on a piece of construction paper.

What You'll Need
- ruler
- blunt scissors
- assorted colors of construction paper
- markers
- foam food trays (from fruits or vegetables only)
- shoe box with lid
- craft glue

# Step by Step

◄►►►►►►

Count on this step-by-step activity to be fun!

How many steps does it take to get from your room to your front door? How many steps to walk to school? How many steps to explore your local mall? You've never thought about it, right? Well, slip on your thinking cap, and take it step by step. You might be amazed at how busy your feet actually are. Want an extra mind-bender? Get an adult in your house to count his or her steps on the same routes you selected, then compare the numbers. Why are they different?

3-D Tic-Tac-Toe

Here's an old favorite made into a brain-bender.

This is a game for 2 players. Draw 3 tic-tac-toe grids side by side. Label them "top," "middle," and "bottom." The goal is still to make 3 of your own marks in a row. However, you can now score a win by placing a mark in the upper left of the top level, 1 in the

What You'll Need
• sheet of white paper
• pencil

center of the middle level, and 1 in the lower right of the bottom level. The same goes for vertical or horizontal lines. Try playing fast— it's trickier than it looks. Once you've mastered 3 levels, try 4, 5, 6, or more levels. Remember, there must be as many rows across and down in each grid as there are levels played on. For instance, if you play on 5 levels, each grid must have 5 rows across and down.

Flip Ball Paddle

Challenge your hand-eye coordination with this easy-to-make paddle game.

What You'll Need
• paper plate
• markers
• blunt scissors
• small rubber ball
• paint stirring stick
• craft glue
• hole punch
• netted fruit bag
• string

Draw a fun character's face on a paper plate. Cut out the eyes and mouth. Make sure the holes are slightly bigger than the ball. Glue the paint stirring stick to the back of the plate. Punch a small hole in the plate just below the mouth. Cut a piece of netting from a fruit bag large enough to cover the ball. Wrap the ball in the netting, and tie it closed with one end of the string. Tie the other end of the string through the small hole in the plate. Try to flip the ball through the holes.

Puppets with Legs

◇▸◇▸◇▸◇▸

With the help of your fingers, these puppets come alive and dance across the stage.

What You'll Need
- poster board
- markers
- blunt scissors
- feathers, yarn, or felt scraps
- craft glue

On a piece of poster board, draw an animal or person from the thighs up. For example, draw a bird's head, body, wings, and tail for the puppet shape. Use markers to color in the details. Cut out the puppet shape. Cut 2 holes at the bottom of the shape. Make sure they are large enough for your middle and index fingers since your fingers will be the bird's legs. Glue on trims, such as feathers, to decorate your bird. Put your fingers through the holes, and make your bird puppet dance. Make more puppets to put on a show with your friends and family.

Le Jazz Hot

◇▸◇▸◇▸◇▸

Move to your own groove!

Explore some types of jazz music (if you want, ask an adult for help finding radio stations that play jazz). Find the kind of music you feel like dancing to. Listen to the rhythm, and then try to follow it with your feet and other parts of your body. Be creative! If you want, practice in front of a mirror to refine your moves. You "interpret" the music with your steps and with your movements.

What You'll Need
- comfortable shoes
- fast or slow jazz music
- smooth floor
- mirror (optional)

Wonderful Wizard or Crowned Royalty

◁◆▷◆▷◆▷

You can be a wizard or the king or queen of your castle.

What You'll Need
- colored poster board
- tape
- clean, round, empty ice cream tub
- pencil
- yarn
- gold star stickers
- markers
- poster paints
- paintbrush
- glitter glue
- sheer or sparkly fabric
- blunt scissors
- glue

Use the colored poster board to shape a cone for the wizard's hat; tape the cone in place. The ice cream tub is a perfect base for building a crown, or make a base out of poster board. Don't worry if the base shapes of your hats are a little too small for your head; you can always make holes at the sides and tie the hats on with yarn. The decorations can be as plain or fancy as you wish. For the wizard's hat, use the gold star stickers, markers, poster paints, and glitter glue. When the decorations are dry, use glue or tape to fasten a corner of the sheer or sparkly fabric just inside the top of the

hat. If you're making the king's or queen's crown, cut the poster board to make a saw-toothed strip. Glue the strip around the base of the ice cream tub to make the points, then bejewel and bedazzle your crown.

Costume Origins
People have been dressing up for thousands of years. Men and women would dance while wearing animal skins and masks that resembled animal faces. They danced to celebrate good hunting, plentiful crops, the birth of a child, and other milestones in their lives. Some cultures still maintain that tradition today.

Star Search

◆▶◆▶◆▶◆

The next big star could be you!

What You'll Need
• costume (optional)
• mirror (optional)

If you want to put on a talent show, you'll need all different kinds of acts. Learn a song or two, or come up with a really funny comedy routine. You'll want to place these solo acts between the group numbers. If you're a singer, try performing your number in the character of the person the song is about and in costume. If you're a comedian, practice your timing and try to use topics that everyone can relate to; you'll "hook" your audience early on. Have your friends audition with their special solo acts. (Hint: You may want to practice in front of a mirror. It will give you more confidence later.)

Waiting Kit

◆▶◆▶◆▶◆

No more boring waiting rooms with nothing interesting to do. This project creates activities for you to do anytime, anywhere.

Hem the 2 short ends of muslin. Fold the muslin in half, bringing the 2 hemmed ends together with the hems facing out. Cut a few small holes in the hemmed ends for the drawstring. Thread a piece of yarn or string through the holes, and tie it in a knot. Sew the 2 side seams closed. Turn the bag inside out. Place a piece of cardboard inside the bag. Decorate the bag with permanent markers or fabric paint. Let the paint dry. Remove the cardboard. Fill the bag with a notepad, colored pencils, crayons, scissors, a glue stick, a travel game, or a good book.

THE WAITING KIT

What You'll Need
• 10×24-inch piece of muslin
• needle and thread
• blunt scissors
• yarn or string
• cardboard
• permanent markers or fabric paint

Feather Float

Can you keep your fluffy feather afloat?

What You'll Need
• small feather

As light as a feather—we've all heard it said. But how light are feathers? And how easy to keep afloat? Lightly toss your small feather in the air. Now try to position yourself exactly beneath the feather. Use your own personal air power to blow upward and keep the feather in the air. Note how long you can keep it from touching the ground. For extra fun, play the game with a friend.

Juggle This!

It takes patience to learn this skill, but your friends' amazement will make it all worthwhile!

What You'll Need
• 3 small beanbags or soft balls

There are many different skills and talents; this one dates back to medieval times. Start with 1 beanbag or ball. Throw it from 1 hand to the other by making scooping loops in the air. Scoop it underhanded, then throw it in a "loop" over the opposite hand, about 2 inches over your head. Let it drop into the opposite palm. This "hang time" in the air is what gives you time to throw more balls or beanbags later. Make sure you throw the ball in loops directly over your body. If the loop veers forward, you may end up chasing balls! Now throw the ball in the same kind of loop from the opposite hand back to the first hand. Practice throwing it back and forth without stopping. Keep going until you feel an easy rhythm, almost like you could do this and talk at the same time. Now you're ready to add a second ball. Follow the same pattern as with 1 ball. When you're comfortable again, add a third ball. See, you're doing it!

Car Race Game

◆▶◆▶◆▶◆

Draw your own grand prix track, and race a friend to the finish line.

What You'll Need
- graph paper
- ruler
- markers
- die

Draw a curvy track at least 1 inch wide on a piece of graph paper. Draw a tiny grandstand, start/finish line, pit stop area, and walls. To make your "race cars," cut 2 squares from another piece of graph paper the same size as the squares on the graph paper track. Mark one with an X and one with an O. Or instead, you can draw 1 type of car on a square and a different car on the other square.

To play the game: Place your cars at the start line. Roll the die to determine how many squares to move. You may move your car in only 1 direction—either across or down. You may not move diagonally. If your move sends your car off the track, you lose a turn. When it's your turn again, you come back to the last spot you were on inside the track. If you land on the same spot as the other car, go back to the last spot you were on and skip a turn. Take turns with your friend moving your race cars. The first one to cross the finish line wins.

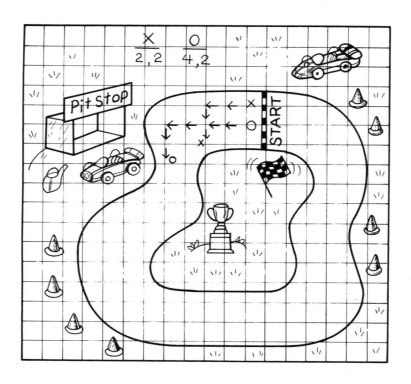

Turkey in the Straws

◆►◆►◆►◆►

This game is tricky because straws don't have flat sides!

What You'll Need
• large, empty margarine tub
• drinking straws
• plastic cup

Lay several drinking straws crosswise on a clean margarine tub. Now balance a cup, turned upside down, on the straws. Each player takes a turn removing 1 straw at a time. Whoever pulls the straw that makes the cup fall down is the "turkey." He or she must gobble out loud! Practice this game by yourself—you won't be the turkey next time you play with friends!

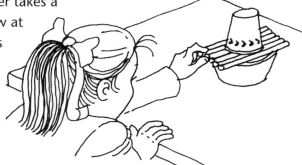

 # Roadblock!

◆►◆►◆►◆►

This is HUGE fun and a great way to get to know people.

One person stands in the middle of the group and tells one thing about himself or herself, such as "My name begins with A." Then everyone for whom that statement is true—in this case, anyone else whose name begins with A—jumps up and dashes for a different empty seat (including the person in the middle). It can't be right next to the seat you just had. If only 1 other person jumps up, they are next to stand in the middle. If no one jumps up, the same person must tell something new about himself or herself. Here's the tricky part—no item can ever be repeated. If

What You'll Need
• group of people, the more the better
• living room furniture
• 1 less chair or seat on the couch than the number of people playing

you can't think of something new, yell "Roadblock!" Then everyone must jump up, grab another seat, and avoid being the person left standing.

Flying Disk Game

◆◆◆◆◆◆◆

Don't let the rainy weather stop you from having fun. Play an exciting indoor game of flying disk golf.

Decorate the foam with markers. To make the golf targets, stuff 3 paper grocery bags with newspaper. Tape or tie the bags closed. Decorate the bags with funny faces or a bull's-eye design. To play the game, place a target bag in a room and stand a distance away from it. Throw the foam disk until you hit the target. Count how many throws it takes to hit the target, and write down your score. Place the next bag in another room, and throw the disk. Finish the game with the third bag. Whoever has the lowest score wins.

What You'll Need
- 8-inch circle of ure- thane foam, 1 inch thick (available at fabric stores)
- markers
- 3 paper grocery bags
- newspaper
- clear tape or string
- paper
- pencil

Twist-Tie Pickups

◆◆◆◆◆◆◆

Get hooked on this fun game. But be careful—one wrong move and your chain falls apart.

What You'll Need
- large piece of tag- board or thin poster board
- pencil
- blunt scissors
- markers
- twist ties (about 40)
- craft glue

On the tagboard, draw a figure with a head and body. Cut it out, and trace it 19 times on the remaining tagboard. Cut out all the figures, and decorate them. Glue 2 figures back to back with twist ties between the pieces for legs and arms. Make 9 more 2-sided figures the same way. Let the glue set. Bend the arms and legs in different directions to make hooks. To play the game, hold 1 figure and try to pick up another by hooking it to the first.

Holding only the first figure, hook another figure to the second figure. See how many figures you can pick up before the chain breaks.

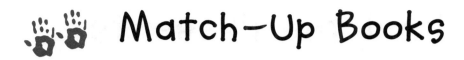# Match-Up Books

◁▷▷▷▷▷▷

Create your own collection of kooky characters.

Cut each sheet of paper into 3 equal-size rectangles. (Cut across the short side of the paper.) This will give you 6 rectangles. Cut a piece of light cardboard the same size as the rectangles. Stack the 6 paper rectangles on top of each other. Fold them down twice, dividing the papers into 3 sections.

Unfold the rectangles, and draw a different person, family member, animal, or monster on each page. Draw the head in the top square, the body in the middle square, and the legs at the bottom. (NOTE: The drawings should all be about the same size, and the heads, bodies, and legs should all line up in the same place. This way the head of one figure will line up with the body on every other drawing.)

After you finish drawing, put the piece of cardboard on the bottom of the stack. Then staple the left side of your drawings together to make a book. Carefully cut across the papers along the folds, stopping before you get to the left side. (Don't cut the cardboard!) Your book is done. Flip through your book, turning different flaps at a time, to see what silly characters you can create!

Find the Presents

◆▶◆▶◆▶◆

In this game of strategy, race your opponent to locate the hidden presents.

What You'll Need
- drawing paper
- ruler
- markers
- construction paper
- blunt scissors

To make the game board, draw an 8×8-inch square on a piece of drawing paper. Divide the square into 64 squares, 1 inch each, by drawing lines 1 inch apart down and across. There should be 8 squares down each side. Label the rows across A through H, and label the columns down 1 through 8 as shown. Have an adult take your original game board to a copy center, and make 4 copies— you'll need 4 copies to play 1 game. (Be sure to save your original game board to make more copies later.)

On a piece of construction paper, draw 10 presents. Make four 1×2-inch presents and six 1×1-inch presents. Decorate your presents, and cut them out. Each player gets 2 large presents, 3 small ones, and 2 game boards.

To play the game, arrange your presents on 1 game board. Then take turns guessing the location of your opponent's presents by calling out the name of the square. For example, you might ask if the present is in E-3. If the answer is no, mark the E-3 spot on your blank game board with an X; if the answer is yes, mark it with a star. Then your friend takes a turn. The first person to find all the presents wins.

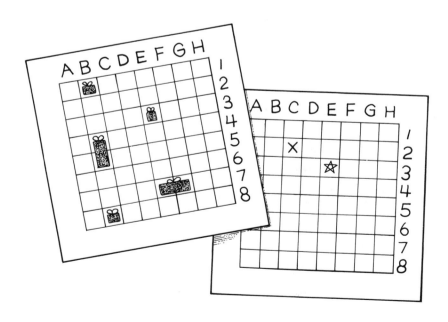

Motor Mat

◀◆▶◆▶◆▶

With your motor mat, you can drive yourself to the movies, mall, or any other place you want to go.

Cut a 40-inch square of vinyl fabric. Cut holes in the fabric, and string cord in and out of each hole as shown in the illustration. Use permanent markers to draw roads, rivers, and railroads on 1 side of the vinyl fabric. Start in the middle and work out. Let the markers dry before you play. Make roads just like the ones in your neighborhood. Add parking places, a pond, and squares where wooden buildings might be placed. Use a green marker to draw trees and bushes. Let the markers dry. Use the Traffic Signs on page 40 and the Block Buildings on page 304 with your mat. When you're done playing, pull the cord to close the mat into a bag.

What You'll Need
- 1¼ yards of vinyl fabric
- blunt scissors
- tape measure
- cord
- permanent markers

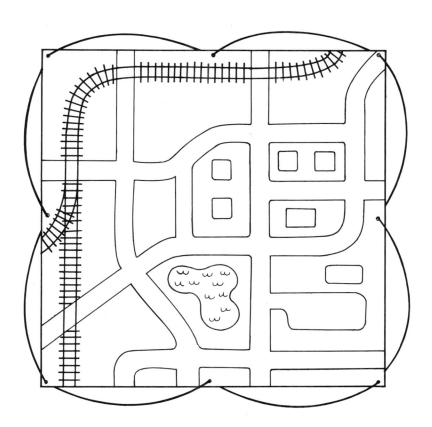

Losing Your Marbles

◆▶◆▶◆▶◆▶

Can you shoot your marbles straight enough to win this game?

What You'll Need
- carpeted room
- about 10 marbles
- clock
- paper
- pen

Shooting marbles—using one marble's motion to slam another marble into action—is a game almost as old as time. Now see if you can master this fun, new marble twist. Move all the furniture aside so you have a nice straight line across your carpeted room. Set 1 marble in the middle of the room, 1 near one end, and 1 near the other end. Keep the rest of the marbles with you. The object of the game is to move from one end of the room to the other. But you can go only as far as your marbles go. Start at one end of the room. Shoot your marbles at the marble you placed close to the end of the room where you are. Go up to the marble that came closest to your target, and start over. When you hit the first target marble, pick it up and start shooting toward the marble in the center of the room. Keep track of how long it takes you to make the journey to the far end of the room, or keep track of how many shots it takes to get there. This will work only on smooth, thick carpet. Textured carpeting will make the journey tough. And tile or wood floors will send your marbles rolling out of control.

Game Pieces

Design custom game pieces for your family and friends, or replace missing pieces from your favorite board game.

What You'll Need
- craft foam (available at craft stores)
- blunt scissors
- permanent markers
- craft glue

Cut out 2 identical shapes from the foam. Cut out geometric shapes, such as a square, circle, or hexagon, to replace missing pieces from a board game. You could also customize the pieces for your family or friends by drawing their features on both pieces— same color eyes, hair, and so on. Add earrings, a hat, or any other feature that represents that person.

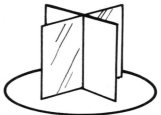

In the top of 1 shape and the bottom of the other, cut a slit about ½ of the length of the shape. Fit the shapes together. Cut a circle about the same size as the shapes from the foam. Glue the circular base to the game piece. Let the glue dry.

Ball Gown Dress-Ups

Turn mom's old skirt into a long dress just for you to dress up in.

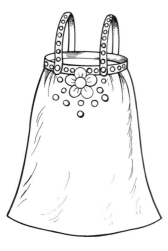

Ask your mom for an old skirt. Hold it up to you at your chest. The skirt should fall to the floor from under your arms. Cut the elastic in half. Sew a piece of elastic at the skirt's waistband to make a shoulder strap. Repeat with the second piece of elastic. Sew on sequins, old jewelry, and lace at the skirt top, the waistband, and the straps to decorate your dress.

What You'll Need
- old skirt
- blunt scissors
- 14 inches of elastic
- needle and thread
- sequins, old jewelry, and lace

Floppy Horseshoes

◆◆◆◆◆◆◆

Unlike most other games, in horseshoes you get points when you hit the mark and even when you're close!

What You'll Need

- 8½×11-inch piece of cardboard
- markers
- ruler
- blunt scissors
- 1 yard of foam sheet, 1 inch thick (available at fabric stores)
- drinking straw or unsharpened pencil
- tape (optional)
- paper
- pen

On a piece of cardboard, draw a horseshoe 8 inches long, 7 inches wide, and 2 inches thick. Cut out the horseshoe pattern. Following the arrangement shown, trace six horseshoes on the foam sheet. Draw two 12-inch circles on the foam. Cut out the circles and horseshoes. Cut a tiny slit in the middle of each circle. Insert a thick drinking straw or an unsharpened pencil for the post. (You may need a little tape to help the post stand up straight.) If you want, decorate the circles and horseshoes with markers.

To play a game of horseshoes, you and a friend each get 3 horseshoes. Place the posts about 6 feet apart. Standing next to 1 post, throw your horseshoes at the opposite post. Take turns with your opponent throwing horseshoes at opposite posts. Give yourself 3 points for a ringer (around the post) and 2 points for a leaner (touching the post). If no horseshoes touch the post, the person with the closest horseshoe gets 1 point. To make the game more challenging, move the posts 1 foot farther apart after each round. Keep track of your points—the first person to reach 50 points wins!

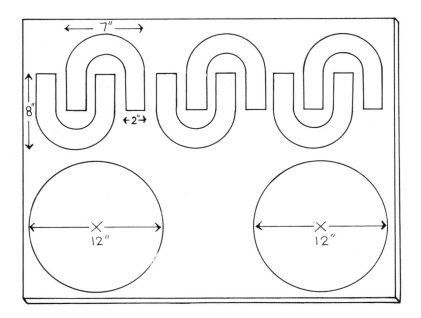

Face Charades

Can you let everyone know how you feel—without saying anything?

What You'll Need
• pens or pencils
• paper
• cup or hat

This game is a lot like regular charades, but instead of acting out a word or phrase, you act out a feeling or emotion and have the other players guess what it is.

Before you begin, have each person write 3 or 4 emotions on different pieces of paper. Fold them up, and put them into a cup or hat. Each player takes a turn drawing an emotion out of the cup and then acting it out for the other players. This must be done without making any sound and without moving any part of the body except for the face and head. That's right—no hand, arm, leg, or other motions.

The following are some feelings and emotions to start out with. How many more can you think of?

HAPPINESS	SADNESS	SHYNESS	SURPRISE
HUNGER	ANGER	LOVE	CONFUSION
FRIGHT	SLEEPINESS	DISGUST	BOREDOM

Lots and Lots of Words

When you use words to communicate, you have a lot to choose from. The average American's vocabulary is around 10,000 words—15,000 if you are really smart! The famous writer William Shakespeare had a vocabulary of over 29,000 words.

Giant Dice

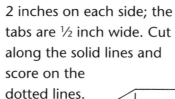

No more lost dice. These oversize cubes are fun to use and hard to lose!

What You'll Need
- pencil
- poster board
- ruler
- blunt scissors
- markers
- craft glue

Draw the pattern shown on the poster board (at least 8½×6½ inches). (Make a bigger pattern for larger dice or a gift box.) Be sure to follow the dimensions exactly. Each square is 2 inches on each side; the tabs are ½ inch wide. Cut along the solid lines and score on the dotted lines.

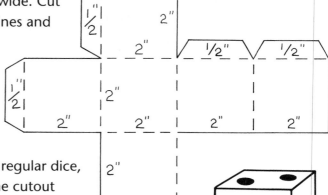

Scoring makes it easier to fold the poster board. To score, use a ruler to guide the point of your scissors as you "draw a line" along the dotted lines.

Decorate the 6 squares. Make dots as on regular dice, or draw numbers, letters, or shapes. Make the cutout into a box by folding along the scored lines. Place glue on the tabs, and tuck them inside the box to hold it together.

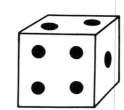

Foam Core Puzzle

To make your puzzle more challenging, use a picture with only a few colors.

Caution: This project requires adult help.

Ask an adult to help you with this project. Select a picture from a magazine, a large photograph, or your own artwork. Glue the picture to the foam core board or picnic plate. Cut out the picture in a square or circle with a small border for edge pieces. Have an adult help you cut your picture into curvy and zigzag pieces with a craft knife. Now mix the pieces up, and try to put the picture back together.

What You'll Need
- magazine picture, photograph, or artwork
- foam core board or plastic foam picnic plates
- craft glue
- craft knife

Wherefore Art Thou Romeo?

◆◇◆◇◆◇◆

Ah, the romance of a dramatic balcony scene!

What You'll Need
- heavy-duty scissors
- cardboard refrigerator box
- duct tape
- pencil
- tape measure
- newspapers
- bricks or concrete blocks
- old shirt
- poster paints
- paintbrushes
- scrap fabric (optional)
- aerobic step bench or small step stool

Caution: This project requires adult help.

Many dramatic plays have a balcony scene. Here's how you can carry off yours. You may want an adult to help you with some parts. Using the heavy-duty scissors, cut out all the way down one corner of the box. You will have 3 vertical "bends" in your box where the corners used to be. Lay the box on the floor, and bend up the left and right bends, leaving the middle one flat. At the left and right bends, tape the upper flaps together to form corners. (Don't do anything with the lower flaps yet.) Stand the box up, and reinforce the corners, from top to bottom, with tape. Then tape together the middle flaps at the top, but do not bend them.

About 6 inches from the very top of the box, draw your balcony window. Make it 2×2 feet. Have an adult help you poke the scissors into a corner of the window, and cut it out. Spread the newspapers out under the box. Bend the bottom flaps to the inside. These are the "feet" for your balcony. The corner flaps will overlap the middle flaps. Tape these together, then put bricks or concrete blocks on the flaps to stabilize the balcony. Now for the messy part. Put on your old shirt, get out the paint, and go! Paint a base color, and let dry. If you want bushes or flowers at the foot of the balcony, paint those in next. Finally, with a color darker than the base color, brush in the outlines of bricks or stones. Then add curtains if you wish. Inside the balcony, put an aerobic step or small step stool beneath the window. Step up to the window, and make your speech to thundering applause!

The House that Cards Built

◆▸◆▸◆▸◆

Sure you can build a house, but you have to get cards from your own suit first!

What You'll Need
• standard deck of cards

Before play starts, each of 4 players must pick a suit to call his or her own: hearts, diamonds, clubs, or spades. Pull the jokers from the deck, and deal out all the cards to the players. The game is played in rounds. If any of the players have 3 cards of their own suit right after they are dealt, they may put the 3 cards together to begin to build their house. Try holding 2 cards upright and placing a card flat on top of them. In the next round, each player passes 1 card to their right. If a player already has another suit card or just gained 1, they may add it to their house. If they don't have another suit card, they wait until the next round. The rounds continue until someone's house falls down. Then that player's cards are dealt out to the remaining players. This is repeated until only 1 house is standing—the house belonging to the winner of the game!

State Capitals Matching Game

◆▷◆▷◆▷◆

This game, made with craft sticks, comes in handy when you want to know your states and capitals.

What You'll Need
- reference books
- 100 large craft sticks
- markers

Print the names of all the states on craft sticks. Next, print the name of each state capital on a separate stick. Decide which you prefer for each state: the state bird or the state flower. Draw whichever one you like more on the back of each of the corresponding state stick and capital stick. Then when you play the game, you'll know that if the backs match, you've correctly matched the state with its capital. Now it's time to play the game! Lay all the sticks on a big table or on the floor. See if you can match the states to their capitals.

Pantomime

◆▷◆▷◆▷◆

Try acting out a story without words!

What You'll Need
- pencil and paper, or instrumental music
- white mime makeup (optional)
- makeup
- clothing in all one color
- background music (optional)

Write a very simple story, or choose a piece of instrumental music. Then use your imagination to show the story you hear in it. If you can get some, put on the classic white mime makeup. If not, ask permission to use some makeup to highlight your eyes and mouth. Also, make sure to pull your hair away from your face. This helps the audience see your expressions better. Choose a color, and wear it from head to toe so the emphasis will be on the story you are miming, not the costume. Now act out your story using exaggerated facial expressions and body movements. If you are acting out a simple story, you may want to use background music.

Go Outside

Some of this chapter's activities are for when the ground is dry; some can be played when the grass is covered with snow. But before taking the fun out the front door, be sure to get your parents' permission and to dress properly. A little caution can make the outdoors more enjoyable. So go and have fun!

 # Animal Tracking

◆◆◆◆◆◆◆

Find an animal track outside, and make a record of it.

What You'll Need
• 4 cardboard strips
• paper clips
• coffee can
• plaster of paris
• water
• measuring cup
• mixing stick
• newspaper

Search outdoors for a paw print or animal track left imprinted in the dirt. Using 4 strips of cardboard, make a square collar around the track by inserting the cardboard into the dirt surrounding it. Fold and clip the edges of the strips together to secure the collar, if needed. Mix the plaster of paris with water in a coffee can according to the directions, and pour the plaster into the collar. Let the plaster set for ½ hour. Then lift the plaster out, and set it on newspaper with the track side facing up. Dry overnight. Now you have a permanent record of the animal track. (When you are done, throw out the coffee can; do not pour the remaining plaster of paris into the sink!)

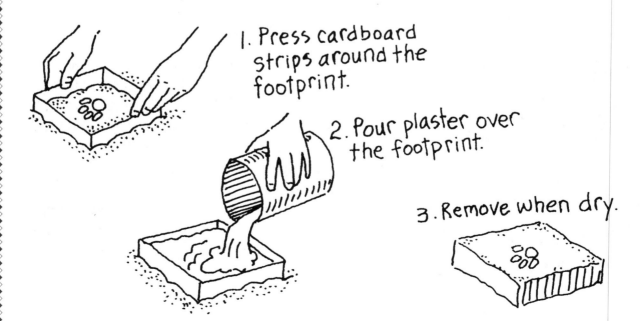

1. Press cardboard strips around the footprint.

2. Pour plaster over the footprint.

3. Remove when dry.

Icy Animal Wagon

❖❖❖❖❖❖➤

Hurry up and eat this wagon before it melts in all that sunshine!

A wagon made of ice cream? Why not? This is a cool treat for a long, hot summer day. On a square of Neapolitan ice cream, add 4 round mints for the wheels and put 2 animal-cracker elephants or horses at the front to pull the wagon. You can add other small plastic animals to ride on top of the ice cream wagon (but be sure people know these are not to be eaten!). This makes a cheerful centerpiece, but don't wait too long to eat it!

What You'll Need
- square of Neapolitan ice cream
- round chocolate mints
- animal crackers
- small plastic figures of animals

 # Sailboats

❖❖❖❖❖❖➤

Sailboat racing is a time-honored sport. Make your own swimming pool competition with these tiny floating boats.

What You'll Need
- foam food trays (from fruits and vegetables only)
- ballpoint pen
- blunt scissors
- permanent markers
- fabric glue
- straight pin

Draw a boat hull and a triangular sail on foam food trays. Cut out the pieces. Decorate the pieces with permanent markers. Draw a sail emblem and your boat's name. Put a line of fabric glue (it's waterproof) on the boat hull, and stand up the sail in the glue. Use a straight pin to keep the sail straight until the glue dries. Make a fleet for swimming pool races. If there is no wind, blow your boats from the start to the finish line!

Toss and Catch Game

◆▸◆▸◆▸◆▸

Invite a friend—or a group of friends—to play this special game of catch.

What You'll Need
- 2 disposable wooden paint paddles
- paints
- paintbrushes
- 2 paper cups
- blunt scissors
- glue
- tissue paper or table tennis ball

For each player, paint a disposable wooden paint paddle with bright colors and designs. You can write a special friendship message on one side, such as "I'll always be there to catch you when you fall!" Cut 2 paper cups in half, then glue the bottom of each cup to the end of each paddle. Let this dry for at least an hour. Crumple tissue paper into a ball, or use a table tennis ball. Take your toss-and-catch game outside or where there's room. Put the ball into one of the paper cups, and fling it

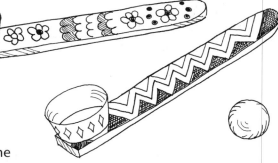

lightly so your friend can catch it in her or his paper cup. Take a step back each time the ball is caught. Get a group of friends together, and play in a circle. Or 4 players can form a cross and play 2 games at once, trying not to let the 2 balls hit each other.

Holding Hands Games

◆▸◆▸◆▸◆▸

Holding hands has never been so much fun!

Divide the players into 2 equal teams. Have each team line up and clasp hands by weaving their fingers together. Put a dish with 10 peanuts at one end of each line and an empty dish at the other.

What You'll Need
- 4 dishes
- 20 peanuts

The first player in each line picks up a peanut with her or his free hand and then passes it to her other hand (the one that is clasped with the hand of the next player). The next player must use his clasped hand to pass the peanut to his other hand, and so on until the peanut gets to the last person, who drops it in the empty dish with her free hand. As soon as the first player has passed the first peanut, she picks up another peanut and begins again. The team that passes all 10 peanuts into the empty dish first, without unclasping their hands at any time during the game, wins. Hold on tight!

Paper Plane Liftoff

◆▷◆▷◆▷◆▷

How your plane flies depends a lot on you!

Fold your favorite airplane out of a crisp, clean piece of paper. Decorate it with crayons or markers. Now launch your flying machine at your favorite playground, and mark where it lands with a piece of chalk. Try tossing it with your other hand, and mark where it lands. Toss it twice as hard, and mark where it lands. Try it

with half the force you originally used. Has the wind picked up? Has it gone still? See how that affects your flights. Will your paper plane fly straight up? Will it crash if you launch it toward the ground? Who knows? But give it a try, and be sure to mark where the flights land. Then compare your marks on the ground, and try to figure out just what it would take to launch the perfect flight.

Spin and Touch

◆▷◆▷◆▷◆▷

How does balance affect the simple things you do?

Our balance depends on the workings of our inner ear. And spinning around in circles certainly affects our sense of balance. But how does being dizzy affect the little things we do? To find out, spin around in place 10 times or so. (Be sure you are somewhere that you won't hurt yourself if you fall!) Now see if you can touch your nose on the first try. See if you can easily walk a straight line. See if you can stand on 1 foot without a sway or tilt.

Hike and Hunt

◆▶◆▶◆▶◆

Keep your eye on the great outdoors!

What You'll Need
- plastic magnifying glass
- paper
- pencil

The next time you take a hike in the woods or a nature area in your neighborhood, keep your eyes open for signs of wildlife. Are there bird feathers on the trail? Have local animals left tracks in the mud or sand? Are there bits of fur trapped in the bushes? What signs of nature can you find? What clues do those signs offer to the animals' ways of life? Use the magnifying glass for close-up looks at items that catch your eye. Make notes of your observations. Then, hike the same path a week later and make more observations. What has changed? What hasn't? You can hike and observe regularly over a longer period and keep a nature journal. So learn something while you are exercising those legs!

Snow Snakes

◆▶◆▶◆▶◆

Create wondrous winter snakes that won't hibernate!

Everyone's heard of a snowman. But making a slithering snow snake is ssssserious fun. Instead of making a snowman of 3 large balls, try a snow snake made of as many basketball-size snow sections as you can make. Once you've lined your snow-snake balls up, carve

What You'll Need
- snowy field
- warm clothes and gloves
- bits of food

out a pointed head and rattling tail at either end of the snake. Decorate your snake with bits of food, such as raisins. These will be good treats for hungry birds and squirrels.

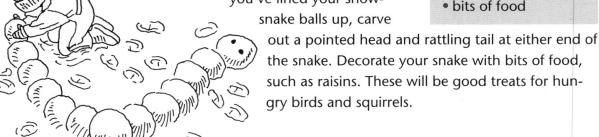

Workout Stations

Have fun exercising at your own workout stations. Add posters that have directions for what to do at each one.

What You'll Need

- sticks or pieces of rope
- bath mat or nonslip rug
- poster board
- markers
- jump rope
- canned goods (or plastic water bottles with lids)
- blank cards
- clear tape

Make 4 workout stations, each with a poster explaining what to do there. Mark off each station with sticks or pieces of rope. At the first station, place a bath mat or nonslip rug for sit-ups. The poster here should explain or show what a sit-up is. It should also say, "Do 10 sit-ups before moving to the next workout station."

At the second station, make a poster that explains or shows what a push-up is, and the poster should say, "Do 10 push-ups before moving to the next workout station." The third workout station should include a jump rope. The poster at this station should say, "Jump rope 10 times before moving to the next workout station."

At the fourth station, place some canned goods to use as lightweight dumbbells (or make your own by putting some water into water bottles and closing the lids). Make a poster that says, "Do 10 curls for each arm with the dumbbells to complete your workout."

Before you begin working out, make sure you stretch out all your muscles: Do some side bends, toe touches (no bouncing), and arm stretches. When you are done stretching, start your workout routine.

After you have mastered your circuit of exercises, add 2 more reps (repetitions of the exercise) to each workout station. Tape a blank card over the number on each poster, and write in the new number. After mastering each new number, add another 2 reps. You will be the most fit kid on your block, and your muscles will be active and healthy!

Butterfly Net

Make your own net to capture butterflies and other small creatures for examination and study. This net won't hurt them; they can be safely released.

What You'll Need
- plastic mesh bag (such as the bag onions come in)
- blunt scissors
- chenille stems
- tape
- long cardboard tube
- drawing paper (optional)
- markers or crayons (optional)
- butterfly reference books from the library (optional)

Cut the clamp off one end of a plastic mesh bag (leave one end clamped). Next, make a circular rim for the net, using 2 chenille stems. Twist 2 ends together, and thread the stems in and out along the top edge of the mesh bag. When you're finished, secure the ends of the rim with a piece of tape.

For a handle, use a very stiff cardboard tube (like the kind found in a roll of wrapping paper). On one end of the tube, cut 2 slits opposite each other. Insert the rim of the net into the slits, and tape it in place.

Now it's time to go out and explore the natural world. When you find and capture a butterfly, examine it quickly and then draw it. After you let the butterfly fly to freedom, you can look up the butterfly in a book to determine what type it is and to read more about it. Collect several pages of drawings, and make your own butterfly book.

You'll be a butterfly expert in no time!

# Parachute

◆▶◆▶◆▶◆▶

***When the spring winds blow, get out your parachutes and let
Mother Nature help you play a game.***

Here's an easy way to make a hexagon: Draw and cut out a triangle with 14-inch sides from a piece of heavyweight paper. Trace it on the cloth, then set the heavyweight paper triangle on top of the original tracing so that a hexagon is formed. Trace it, and cut it out. Use markers to write the name of your skydiving company with an insignia on the parachute. Cut a tiny hole in each corner. Tie 2 ends of each string in a knot through each hole. Hold all the strings together, and make a slipknot 7 inches from the cloth parachute. Tie an action figure on the ends of the string. Bunch up the fabric, and throw it up in the air. Watch the parachute float back to you.

What You'll Need
- blunt scissors
- ruler
- heavyweight paper
- pencil
- thin cotton or nylon cloth
- markers
- 6 lengths of cotton string, 12 inches each
- action figure

Squirt Bottle Art

◆▶◆▶◆▶◆▶

***Since the summer heat quickly dries your artwork, race your friends to see
who can finish their picture the fastest.***

What You'll Need
- clean plastic dish detergent bottles with a squirt lid
- water
- safe sidewalk or concrete driveway

Here's a project that's a lot of fun on a sunny day. Fill a plastic dish detergent bottle with water. Squirt the water to "draw" a picture on the sidewalk or driveway. Shade and color in your picture with the bottle's water. You must work very quickly before the sun "erases" your design. That's the fun part of this project. You get to start all over again.

Hop (and Pop) Scotch

◆▶◆▶◆▶◆

Hop up for a surprising new twist on an old game.

What You'll Need
- chalk
- small balloons

Hopscotch just got explosive, thanks to this new idea. Rather than hopping on 1 foot, hold a small air-filled balloon between your feet as you hop. How long will your balloon last? Only time will tell. No matter how long you keep your balloon from bursting, no matter how good you get, there's always room to compete with yourself. For an extra challenge, hopscotch backward. Set up your hopscotch course on grass using thick, oversize color chalk to make the game a little safer if your balloon bursts. (Always remember to pick up balloon pieces, which are dangerous for small children and animals!)

No-Sting Bubbles

◄►◄►◄►◄►

These bubbles won't sting your eyes if you get
some of the mixture near your face.

What You'll Need
- ¼ cup baby shampoo (no-sting type)
- ¾ cup water
- 3 tablespoons light corn syrup
- mixing bowl
- mixing spoon
- thin wire
- pie plate

This is a great project to do outside on a summer day!

Mix the baby shampoo, water, and light corn syrup in a bowl. Stir the ingredients gently so you don't create lots of bubbles; if any bubbles are created, let them settle. Bend an end of a piece of thin wire into a circle; this is your bubble blower. Pour some of the bubble mixture into a pie plate, dip the circle into the bubble mixture, then blow to create some bubbles!

For more bubble experimentation, make a triangle, square, hexagon, or other shape out of the thin wire. See if the bubble shapes are any different depending on the shape of the blower. You can also blow bubbles through a plastic berry basket.

Can you find any other things that would make good bubble blowers? Explore and experiment, using No-Sting Bubbles!

Walk the Line

◆▶◆▶◆▶◆

See if you can walk the walk the same way twice.

What You'll Need
- 2 colors of chalk
- colored yarn
- old clothes

Can you walk a straight line with your eyes open? Can you walk a straight line with your eyes closed? How about while you're holding your breath or singing a song? This will help you find out. Cover the bottom of your feet or shoes with dark-colored chalk.

Now walk along a line of colorful yarn stretched across a safe sidewalk. Be sure you've used enough chalk on your shoes to leave a trail behind. Repeat the experiment with your eyes closed, using a different color of chalk. Compare the 2 trails. Remember that chalk can stain clothing, so wear old clothes when you experiment with this activity. And be sure to scrub your shoes or feet before you go into the house!

Bike Spectacle

◆▶◆▶◆▶◆

Get together with the kids on your block and decorate your bikes for a neighborhood parade.

Decorate your bike with pom-poms, paper fringe, and flowers. To make pom-poms, fanfold 2 pages of newspaper together. Make a long cut through each crease to about 3 inches from the end. Wrap tape around the uncut end. Repeat to make another pom-pom. Tape the pom-pom to your handlebars. To make paper fringe, cut a 9-inch-wide strip of colored tissue paper. Fold it in half lengthwise. Cut slits along the open edge about ½ inch apart up to about 2 inches from the folded edge. Tape the fringe around the

What You'll Need
- newspaper
- blunt scissors
- ruler
- masking tape
- colored tissue paper
- twist tie

bars on your bike. To make flowers, cut 3 large circles from colored tissue paper. Place the circles on top of each other and gather them into the middle so that they look like a bow. Secure the centers with a twist tie. Separate the paper layers, and fluff them into a flower. Tape the flower to the front of your handlebars.

Mud Pies

◆▶◆▶◆▶◆▶

They're not too tasty, but they're a whole lot of fun to make—and the only ingredients you need to get started are dirt and water!

Put on some old clothes. Mix some dirt and water in a throwaway container to make mud. Mix in some grass to add texture to the mud. Line a disposable pie pan with leaves. Pour some mud into the pan over the leaves. Sprinkle your mud pie with seeds, and add flowers and twigs to decorate it. Let the mud set until it dries. Make more pies with your friends, and pretend you have an outdoor bakery. "Sell" the mud pies to your friends and family members.

What You'll Need
• old clothes
• throwaway containers
• plastic spoon
• dirt and water
• grass
• disposable pie pans
• leaves
• seeds, flowers, and twigs

Exploding Glider

◆▶◆▶◆▶◆▶

Here's a project you can throw together quickly. Just be careful to toss your glider away from other people.

What You'll Need
• 6 craft sticks
• markers
• cardboard (optional)
• paper
• pen

Decorate the sticks with markers. Arrange the sticks in the window pane pattern shown in the illustration. The cross pieces go over and under the outer pieces to provide the tension that holds the sticks together. Now go outside and throw your glider. When you throw it, it explodes! You can make glider games. Draw a big bull's-eye pattern on a piece of cardboard, assigning the different rings point values. Place it on the floor. When you throw the glider, add up the points you score as it lands on different sections.

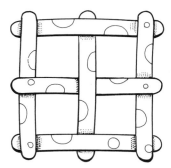

String Rocket Races

Invite some friends over for rocket races.

What You'll Need
- small milk carton
- blunt scissors
- glue
- aluminum foil
- markers
- soda straw
- ruler
- masking tape
- kite string
- long balloons

Cut the bottom (the square end) off a small milk carton and discard. Spread glue on the outside of the remaining milk carton, and cover it with aluminum foil. Smooth the foil with your fingers to make sure it's all stuck down. Use markers to draw windows on your rocket, with an astronaut looking out. Cut a 1-inch piece of soda straw. Tape it on top of the milk carton. Thread the string through the straw. Tie one end of the string to a tree limb 10 to 20 feet away. Tie the other end of the string to a chair or limb. Put a balloon in the rocket, with the nozzle facing back. Blow up the balloon as big as you can. Release, and watch your rocket go! For rocket races, set up 2 string rockets. (Balloons are choking hazards—keep them away from small children!)

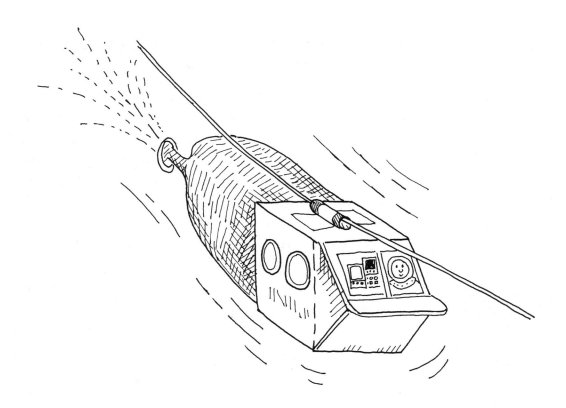

Leave It to Me

◆◆◆◆◆◆

When autumn leaves are falling, drop in on this sneaky game.

What You'll Need
- fall leaves
- cardboard boxes

The object of this fast-paced game is to see how many leaves each player can collect without having them stolen by other players. Set boxes (one per player) about 15 feet apart in a leaf-covered park, yard, or play-

ground. One player says "go," and the game begins. Grab handfuls of leaves, and put them into your box. But watch carefully. You can steal leaves from other boxes to fill your own, so you'll want to guard your box as you go. Remember, your box can be robbed while you're out searching or stealing!

Basketball Buddies

◆◆◆◆◆◆

You could sink this one with a smile!

Love shooting hoops? Why not add a few extra "grins" to the game? Each time you sink a basket, draw a facial feature on your ball. It could be an eye, a mouth, ears, even long, lush lashes. You're the winner—it's up to you to decide! Want to turn this activ-

What You'll Need
- basketball
- chalk

ity into a competition? Decide on 5 facial features in advance. Each of you label a side of the basketball for your face. The first person to sink 5 baskets (and complete the facial expression) wins the game!

 # Sidewalk Art

◆▶◆▶◆▶◆▶

Create a sidewalk gallery for your neighbors. They'll be able to enjoy your artwork while they walk.

What You'll Need
- safe sidewalk or concrete driveway
- colored chalk
- paper towel

Find a safe sidewalk area away from traffic. (Be sure to ask permission to draw on the sidewalk.) Use colored chalk to draw your art on the sidewalk. Try chalking a sunset. Start at the top with blues, then add purples, reds, and oranges.

Work in some fluffy pink-tinted clouds. Finish up with some snow-capped mountains. Rub a paper towel across the edges of your colors to blend them. Instead of a square picture, be creative with your concrete space. Chalk a long skinny dragon down the sidewalk or a school of fish on a concrete walkway. Another idea is to trace the shadow of an object, such as a tree, on the concrete. Then, color in the outline.

 # Apple Walk Game

◆▶◆▶◆▶◆▶

Apples are not just for eating!

What You'll Need
- apples
- 2 large empty buckets

This is a relay race for 2 teams. For each team, set an empty bucket 20 feet away from the players. The first player on each team puts an apple between his or her knees, runs or walks to the bucket, and drops it in. The first player then picks up the apple and runs back to hand it to the next player. That player must do the same thing the first player did, and so on until everyone has had a turn. The first team to finish wins the game. Make sure you have plenty of apples to snack on—after all that hard labor, you're bound to be hungry!

Milk Carton Waterwheel

◄▶◄▶◄▶◄▶

Newton's third law states, "Every action has an equal and opposite reaction." Have fun proving that law by making a waterwheel—but do this project outside because it is quite wet!

What You'll Need
- paper ½-gallon milk carton (washed and clean)
- pencil
- blunt scissors
- string
- water

Caution: This project requires adult help.

This is a fun way to play with water on a hot, sunny day. Put on your thinking caps and your bathing suits! Use a pencil to poke a hole in the bottom left-hand corner of each of the 4 sides of a paper ½-gallon milk carton. With scissors, poke a hole in the top flap of the milk carton (you may need adult help with this). Tie a string through this hole, and tie the carton to a branch or something from which it can suspend. While covering the holes in the milk carton with your fingers, have a helper pour water into the carton.

When the carton is filled, take your fingers off the holes and see what happens to the milk carton as the water flows out. You've created a waterwheel!

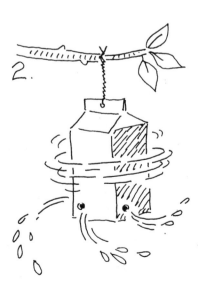

The Great Bug Search

◄►◄►◄►◄►

Go on a Great Bug Search in your own backyard, and find out where bugs and worms like to make their homes. See how much information you can gather!

What You'll Need
• white fabric
• stick
• notepad
• pencil
• magnifying glass

Discover secret places where insects make their homes.

Spread a piece of white fabric on the ground beneath a low-hanging branch. With a stick, give the branch a short, sharp rap. In your notepad, write down the number and kinds of insects that come tumbling down onto the fabric. Use the magnifying glass to examine the bugs closely. If you don't know the bug, draw a picture of it in your notepad and go to the library for a bit of bug sleuthing! After you've written down all the bugs, let them go without harming them.

Now roll over a rotting log, and see what you find (probably slow-moving pill bugs, sow bugs, slugs, snails, and earthworms, among others). Do you see any tiny seedlings, mosses, lichens, or mushrooms? Again, use your magnifying glass to examine the objects closely. Write down whatever you see, then roll the log back in place. (You wouldn't want someone coming along and moving your house, would you?)

How much did you learn about bugs?

Rolling Riot

"The more the merrier" applies when it comes to this rolling riot.

What You'll Need
• as many soft, rolling balls (of all sizes) as you and your friends can find

To get this game started, gather up your friends and all the rolling balls you have. Sit in a circle with your legs spread extra wide, the tips of your toes touching. Put the balls in the middle. Once the circle is formed, sit cross-legged, with gaps in the circle on

either side of you. Count "1, 2, 3" with your friends, and then go! Start those balls rolling all at once. The object of the game is to keep the balls moving as fast as you can while you try to stop them from leaving the circle. Keep the rolls low to the ground so no one gets a ball in the face. And have fun. Remember, there are no losers in this game—you're all winners because you're all having a good time, no matter how long the crazy game lasts.

Ball for All

Have a ball finding out how different "different" can be.

Playing ball is pretty easy. But how simple is it really? Does one ball kick like another? Can you throw one ball as far as the next? Select 4 different balls (of 4 different shapes and sizes). Toss each ball as hard as you can. How far does the first ball go? How far does the second ball go? Now try to bounce each ball. How hard (or how easy) is that task? This fun experiment will help you find out how complicated playing ball can be.

What You'll Need
• variety of balls (kick ball, football, baseball, basketball, table tennis ball, golf ball, tennis ball, etc.)

Cricket Kit

◆◆◆◆◆◆

This chirping chum is a good-luck friend everyone can enjoy.

What You'll Need
- clear plastic jar
- nail
- cotton ball
- cat food
- cricket

Caution: This project requires adult help.

Most kids love keeping pets. But some apartment landlords won't allow the privilege. If you have a friend who really wants to care for a critter, this cricket kit could be the perfect gift. Keeping crickets is fun and easy. Search your yard or a neighborhood park (take an adult along!) for a cricket. If it's winter or extremely cold outside, you might have to turn to your local pet store to buy a cricket (for about a dime). Wash the plastic jar (you could use an empty peanut butter jar) thoroughly. Have an adult help you poke a few air holes in the upper edge of the clean plastic jar with the nail. Slip your cricket into the jar along with a cotton ball soaked with water and a little cat food crushed to a fine powder. Give the jar to your friend, and watch him or her grin. Remind your friend to feed and water the cricket every other day. Give your friend a few extra cotton balls for water and a plastic bag full of crushed cat chow, just to get them started. And tell them the cricket should live at least 3 months (sometimes longer).

Treasure Map

◆▶◆▶◆▶◆▶

It's fun to have your friends hunt for buried "treasure" using a treasure map!

What You'll Need
- object to hide (for the treasure)
- brown paper
- markers or crayons
- twine or string

First you'll need some treasure to bury (just something you can hide—maybe some small toys). Hide the treasure in your yard someplace; you can bury it, put it in some bushes, or place it under a rock, etc. (If you are digging in your backyard, be sure to ask permission first!)

Use a piece of brown paper (part of a paper grocery bag will work) to create a map of your yard. The map will show where the treasure is hidden. Put a large X on the map where you hid the treasure. Include the number of paces (footsteps) from place to place (oak tree to large rock to gate to treasure), so you'll have to be good at both counting and writing directions.

Roll the map up, and tie it with twine or string so it looks like a real treasure map. Then give the map to a friend, and see if he or she can find the hidden treasure.

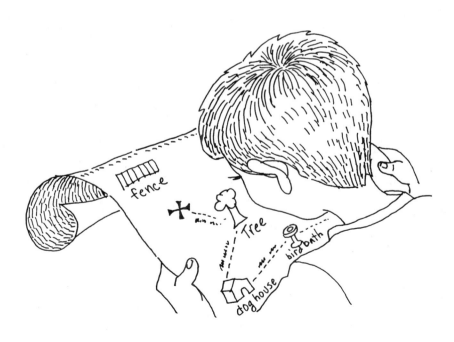

Snow Boot Two-Step

❖❖❖❖❖❖

Track down this snowy game for frosty winter fun.

When snowfall threatens your outdoor adventures, try this game on for size. This tough-to-master version of follow the leader requires 2 or more players. The leader makes a path in freshly fallen snow. His or her teammates must try to step in exactly the same spots. The object of the game is to make it seem as if only one person has taken a walk through the snow. Can you pull it off? It takes balance and agility! Be sure to bundle up to stay warm and dry.

Drop and Splat Painting

❖❖❖❖❖❖

Put on a bathing suit or shorts, and experiment outside on a warm summer day with drop painting.

Food coloring stains, so wear clothes your parents have approved! Fill several plastic cups with water. Take the cups and the rest of your materials outside. Add a few drops of food coloring to each cup to make different colors. Place a sheet of newspaper or a large piece of paper on the ground. You can put rocks on the corners to keep the paper in place. Put a straw in a cup of colored water, and place a thumb or finger over the top end of the straw. This will keep water inside the straw when you remove it from the cup. Lift the straw out of the cup and over the paper. Release your finger from the straw end so the colored water drops onto the paper. Experiment by raising straws full of water to different heights and observing how the height of the drop changes the splat.

 # Pinwheels

When your pinwheel catches the wind, the colors come alive as they spin and swirl in the breeze.

What You'll Need
- 2 squares of different-color lightweight paper, 8 inches each
- blunt scissors
- ruler
- small nail
- hammer
- 12-inch wood dowel with ¼-inch diameter

Caution: This project requires adult help.

Place the squares on top of each other. Cut a line 4 inches long from each corner toward the center. With an adult's help, use a nail to poke a hole in each corner and in the center of the combined squares. Fold the corners into the center of the square, lining up the holes on top of each other. Place the pinwheel over one end of the wood dowel. Have an adult help you use a hammer to tap the nail through the holes into the dowel. Take your pinwheel outside, and watch it spin in the wind!

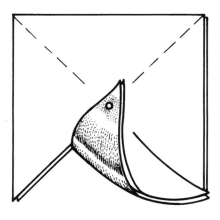

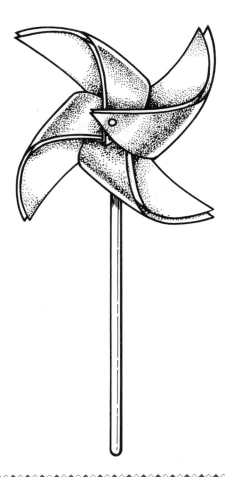

Sundial

◆◇◆◇◆◇◆◇

As the sun moves throughout the day, so does the shadow it casts.
A sun clock tells the time by the position of the shadow.

What You'll Need
- newspaper
- colored poster board
- blunt scissors
- plaster of paris
- large plastic coffee-can lid
- markers

Cover your work surface with newspaper. Cut a triangle from colored poster board. Have an adult help you mix the plaster of paris according to package directions. Carefully pour the plaster into the plastic coffee-can lid. Stand the triangle up in the plaster. Let the plaster dry.

Use your sundial to tell the time. Take the sundial outside early on a sunny day. Place it where the sun will hit it all day. Every hour on the hour, make a mark at the shadow of the triangle. Write the hour on the plaster. Once you've marked off the hours, keep your sundial in the same spot so you can tell the time on sunny days.

String Me Along

◆◇◆◇◆◇◆◇

String your friends along for follow-the-leader fun!

Playing follow the leader may seem easy, but this tied-up version adds a new challenge to the mix. Each player holds one end of a string that leads to the next player. The leader must come up with silly activities that can be accomplished without letting go of the string. For an extra-tough game, string all players together in a circle, and alternate leaders. Caution: Never wind a string around your neck or anyone else's, and play this on soft grass or carpeting!

What You'll Need
- 2-foot lengths of string or yarn (one for each player)

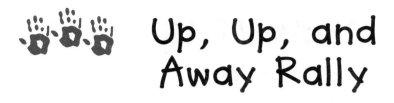

Up, Up, and
Away Rally

◆▶◆▶◆▶◆▶

Invite your friends over for an Up, Up, and Away Rally. Make paper planes or fancy flyers; the only rule is they must really fly!

What You'll Need
- construction paper
- ruler
- blunt scissors
- tape
- drinking straw
- large trash bag
- hula hoop
- marker
- duct tape

Here are a few fancy flying machines to make:

Baby UFO: Cut 2 strips of construction paper, one ¾×6½ inches and the other ½×5½ inches. Make both into a loop. When you make the loops, overlap the ends ¾ inch. Tape the ends of the strip on the inside and on the outside. Insert the ends of a drinking straw into the space between the overlapping ends. Fasten the straw to the loops with tape. Hold the UFO horizontally, with the small loop in front, and toss.

Mama UFO: Cut along one side of the trash bag, and open it up. Lay the hula hoop on it. Trace around the outside of the hoop with a marker. Cut out the circle. Tape it to the hula hoop with duct tape. Fly it like a giant flying disk!

How many fancy planes or flying machines can you invent?

Chalk It Up

◆▸◆▸◆▸◆▸

Blending swirls has never been more fun!

What You'll Need
- colorful chalk
- ruler
- sidewalk (if the weather is warm and dry) or plain paper
- paper towels
- old clothes

Everyone knows how much fun chalk can be when it comes to games of hopscotch or tic-tac-toe. But have you ever experimented with the swirling strokes of a piece of chalk and discovered what blending can do to those same strokes?

Put 5 thick lines of colored chalk, about 3 inches long, on a sidewalk surface (be sure to ask for permission first!) or paper. Make your colorful lines bold and dark, with less than 1 inch between each line. Once your lines are clearly in place, set your chalk down, and get ready to use your fingers.

Start rubbing the first chalk line, blending it toward the thick line of color next to it. Wipe your finger on a paper towel, and repeat the same experiment with the second line of color, letting the lines overlap. Wipe your fingers, and do the same with each line.

What happens as the colors mix? Do the shapes and textures of your lines change? Do shadows and highlights appear? This chalky fun will help teach you how to use color blending to make artistic magic.

Make sure you wear old clothes when you play with chalk. And be sure all the chalk dust is off your clothes, shoes, and hands before you go back into the house.

# Time Capsule

◂▸◂▸◂▸◂▸

Time capsules help people in the future understand past cultures.
Help future generations learn about your life!

Caution: This project requires adult help.

Gather objects that represent the current year. These can be baseball cards, newspapers, magazines, fashion items, or anything else you can imagine. You might write a letter that tells about you, your family, or your community. Put these items into a plastic container, and seal it securely. Put the plastic container into a plastic bag, and tie the bag closed.

What You'll Need
• various objects
• paper
• pen
• resealable plastic container
• plastic bag
• shovel

Find someplace to bury the time capsule; make sure you have permission to do so. Dig a 3-foot hole in the ground (you might want to ask an adult for help), put your time capsule in, and cover it with dirt. Make a sign and put it on the ground above the capsule, or make a map to the capsule. On your map or sign, indicate what year the time capsule should be opened. When it is opened, people will find artifacts that will give them some information about how you lived.

Balloon Toss

Test your aim in this cool point-scoring game.

Caution: This project requires adult help.

Very carefully (and with permission, so you get to do this again!), slip a regular balloon inside a metallic balloon. Blow into the balloons to straighten the inside balloon. Next, stretch the neck of the double balloon over the narrow end of the funnel, and fill the inside balloon almost full with flour. Have an adult help you securely tie off the end. Make 4 balloons for each player—with each player having different colors. Find a piece of heavy poster board big enough to fit over a big cardboard box. Lay the poster board on the floor, and trace around a coffee mug near the top center. This is the top of a "pyramid." Trace 2 more circles centered underneath the first circle. Leave about 4 inches between rows. Trace 3 more circles centered under the 2 circles. Cut out the circles. Over the top circle, mark "10" points. Over each of the 2 circles in the middle, mark "5" points. Over the remaining circles, mark "1" point. Lay the poster board over the box, and tape the edges down with masking tape. Stand back from the box about 5 to 7 feet. Play by yourself, or have friends over for a challenge match. Players take turns throwing the balloons into the holes to score points. Start tossing balloons!

What You'll Need
- bag of regular party balloons
- metallic balloons, 4 of each color per player
- plastic or paper funnel
- flour
- heavy poster board
- big cardboard box
- coffee mug
- pencil
- blunt scissors
- jumbo marker
- masking tape

Squirt Bottle Tag

◂▸▸▸▸▸▸▸

Here's a wet wonder to heat up (and cool down) your summer.

What You'll Need
- tissues
- masking tape
- clean, empty dishwashing liquid bottles
- water

This fun tissue tag is a great way to beat the summer heat. Slip into your favorite swimming suit. Then tape an ordinary tissue to each player's back. The object of the game is to flood your fellow players' tissues with enough

water to cause them to tear from the masking tape and fall to the ground. The last player with a tissue still in place wins the game.

Frantic Flying Disk

◂▸▸▸▸▸▸▸

Free your flying disk to sail to new heights!

Tossing a flying disk with a friend or a dog is a great way to keep fit—and it's fun to do all by yourself also! And you can add a new challenge to the popular game. See how easy (or how hard) it is to send your flying disk sailing through a hula hoop from 5 paces

What You'll Need
- flying disk
- hula hoop

away. Too easy? Move back 10 paces from the hoop. Still not tough enough? Try it from 16 paces away. This game makes a great competition between friends or whole teams.

 # Ice Patrol

◆▶◆▶◆▶◆

Sidewalk ice can be a serious danger for the elderly.
You can help keep them safe.

What You'll Need
- cat litter
- sand
- rock salt
- bucket

Winter snowfall means fun to most kids—sledding, snowball fights, and frosty activities galore. But to senior citizens, winter weather means icy sidewalks and all the danger that goes with them. If you have elderly people in your neighborhood, do a weekly ice patrol to help keep them safe. If you find a patch of stubborn ice on the sidewalk that just won't go away, ask your neighbor if you can sprinkle it with a mix of sand, rock salt, and cat litter. The rock salt will help melt the ice. The cat litter will soak up the frosty water. And the sand will help keep the ice from being slippery until the whole process kicks into action. But don't forget to ask permission first!

Long Lives
The average American now lives to be 75 years old—or older.

Square-a-Round

Square up with this ball-tossing fun!

First, using fabric paints you can buy at a craft or hobby store, decorate your square of fabric or bandanna to reflect your own personal style. If you love astronomy, you might decorate it with stars and planets. If you love dinosaurs, draw a Tyrannosaurus rex on your cloth. Once the paint dries, use the cloth to toss and catch tennis balls. How many tosses can you catch in a row without dropping your ball? How high can you make your toss? How many balls can you toss and catch in 1 minute? The possibilities are endless. For an extra challenge, play this game with a partner, tossing a single ball from cloth to cloth or making 2 balls cross in midair.

What You'll Need
• 15×15-inch cloth squares or bandannas
• fabric paint
• paintbrush
• tennis balls

Alphabet Jump Rope

Have some alphabet fun without skipping a beat.

What You'll Need
• jump ropes (one for each player)

Pick a subject, such as animals, flowers, girls' names, or food. Then as you jump rope, name members of that group alphabetically (for the topic animals: ape, bear, cat, dog, elephant, fish, etc.) every other hop. If you miss while jumping or can't come up with the next animal or item in the alphabetical list, start over at the beginning. This game is great alone, but it's also fun to do with a friend.

Snowscape Stomp

◆▶◆▶◆▶◆▶

Splashes of color make winter white a little warmer!

What You'll Need
- food coloring
- paper cups
- measuring spoon
- water
- snow boots
- paintbrush

Does it look like winter weather has put a freeze on creative fun? Think again! Grab your gloves and your paintbrush. That snowy hillside has just become an artist's canvas. Mix 2 tablespoons water with 10 drops food coloring in a paper cup (make as many colors as you desire). Go outside, and march out a playful pattern of footprints in the snow. Splatter splashes of color in each frosty track, and watch the magic begin. Be sure to check for chilly changes later as the snow begins to melt and the colors soften.

Remember that food coloring stains if it gets on clothing or light-colored boots, so be sure to wear old clothes your parents won't mind getting splattered. And don't forget to bundle up.

What a Flake!

While it's true that no two are exactly alike, snowflakes can be broken down into six different six-sided crystal categories: needles, columns, plates, columns capped with plates, dendrites, and stars.

Coded Message Kite

◆▸◆▸◆▸◆▸

Make an easy kite to send a coded message to a friend.

What You'll Need
- permanent markers
- plastic shopping bag
- ball of string
- blunt scissors
- ribbon
- tape measure
- stapler and staples

With the markers, draw some pictures on the plastic bag to make a coded message for a friend to read when the kite is in the air. Tie the handles of the plastic shopping bag together with the end of a ball of string. Staple a few 2-foot lengths of ribbon to the bottom of the bag for kite tails.

Find a windy spot outdoors (away from any overhead wires), and start running. As the bag fills with air, slowly let out the string. The kite should begin to soar and dive. See if your friend can figure out the message you drew on the kite.

Don't forget to take your kite in the house or put it in a trash can when you've finished playing with it—plastic bags are dangerous for small children and animals.

Yards of Helpfulness

◆▸◆▸◆▸◆

Help good feelings grow by cleaning up a neighbor's yard.

What You'll Need
- lawn mower
- rake
- weed trimmer
- work gloves
- trash bags
- ice water

Is your neighbor disabled? Overworked? Sick? Ask if you can help by taking care of some of the yard work. Once they say it's okay, why not mow the lawn? Rake the leaves? Pull those ugly weeds? Not good with yard tools? Volunteer to baby-sit your neighbor's children as they do the difficult work. Offer to wash their dishes to free up a little extra time. Do what you can to grow some neigh-

borly smiles and prove you care. Don't forget to bring a big bottle of ice water with you when you volunteer; yard clean-up can be hot and thirsty work. Remember to ask your parents for permission before you volunteer.

Butterfly's Delight Muffin

◆▸◆▸◆▸◆

Butterflies love these flowery treats.

Choose a nice sunny day to whip up a batch of these sweet "mud muffins," and watch to see who flies by! You won't want to place these muffins too close to the house, since there might be bugs in addition to butterflies also dropping by for a snack. Mix the soil and water together to make a nice, firm mud. Collect some wildflower petals, and stir these in. Add the honey or corn syrup, and stir well. Then spoon the mix into individual muffin cups, and top each with a pretty flower top. Set them in a place where you have seen butterflies before. These muffins look good enough to eat, but unless you're a butterfly, don't try them!

What You'll Need
- soil
- water
- plastic spoon
- disposable bowl
- wildflower petals
- ½ cup honey or corn syrup
- muffin cups
- flowers

Happening Joints

❖❖❖❖❖❖❖

Celebrate the bends and bounces of your body!

Every joint in your body is a kind of engineering wonder, designed to make your body move in amazing ways. So why not celebrate every single bend? Move from the tips of your fingers to the tips of your toes, flexing each joint. Count how many joints you can move independently. Imagine what it would be like if that particular joint didn't exist.

Straw Glider

❖❖❖❖❖❖❖

With a little help from the wind, your straw glider will take to the air and soar across the sky.

Tape 3 straws together at 4 points. Draw the wing and 2 tail sections on a piece of craft foam or foam food tray. Cut out the pieces, and decorate them with markers. Draw a design of your own airline company. Insert the foam pieces in between the 3 straws. Add a dab of glue to hold them in place. Let the glue set. Hold the glider in 1 hand, then throw it in the air and watch it fly.

What You'll Need
- 3 plastic drinking straws
- masking tape
- pencil
- craft foam or foam food tray (from fruits or vegetables only)
- blunt scissors
- permanent markers
- glue

WORDPLAY

What do words mean to you? Do you play with their meanings? Do you string them together to express how you feel? These activities let you play with words whimsically. This chapter is your recipe for great new literary kicks!

 # Word Chain

◄▷◄▷◄▷◄▷

Explore and express how you feel, one word at a time.

What You'll Need
• paper
• crayons, markers, or colored pencils

Sometimes the reasons for our moods hide at the back of our minds. We might be really happy or a little sad and not quite understand why we feel what we feel. If you ever wonder what you're feeling and why, try this word game to help you find out.

Pick a word that seems to describe what you are feeling. It might be "excited" or "blue"; it might be "confused" or "angry." Pick whatever word best describes how you think you feel. Write it out in a color that matches the mood.

Now, ask yourself why you feel that way: Is it because of your parents, your dog, your best friend, or the weather? Write the first word that comes to your mind in a color that helps describe it. But here's the trick: Try to build that word on the word you already wrote, like a crossword puzzle. Keep up with the game until the page is full or you run out of words.

Doing this game may help you understand yourself a little better!

Good Sport

Complete this play to find out if sliding into home can have a whole new meaning.

What You'll Need
- paper
- pen
- dictionary

Do you love baseball? Live for football? Shoot for record-breaking hoops? Write out the special terms used in your favorite sport (words such as *base, plate,* and *mound* for baseball; *dunk, court,* and *foul* for basketball, etc.). Now ask yourself: *Do these words have other meanings?* Look the words up in a dictionary to see if they have other meanings. How would those meanings change your favorite sport? What would happen if Sammy Sosa slid into a home plate made of good china? Could Kurt Warner score if all the receivers were telephone receivers? Explore the magic of words and meanings—these would also make great pictures!

Favorite Sports
The top five sports in America are football, baseball, basketball, golf, and hockey (not necessarily in that order).

Word Wonder Magnets

Make headlines of your own that inspire and delight!

What You'll Need
- old magazines or newspapers
- blunt scissors
- cardboard
- glue
- magnet strips (available at craft stores)

Ever seen a word or a headline that inspired you? Hold on to that spirit with these terrific Word Wonder Magnets. Go through a stack of old magazines or newspapers (be sure to ask for permission first!) until you see a word or headline that reminds you to do your best work, try a new sport, be a friend to someone who needs one, or do some other worthy activity. Cut out the word or words, and glue them to the cardboard. After the glue dries, cut away the excess cardboard and attach a small piece of magnet strip to the back. Hang up your headlines where they will remind you to always do your best!

Animalriffic

Is your favorite animal hiding in your favorite words?

What You'll Need
- pen
- paper

Have you ever thought about how often your favorite animal is mentioned in another, often unrelated word? Take the ant, for instance. You find it in *anticipation, antiperspirant, tyrant,* and thousands of other words. Now pick your favorite animal (simple animal names such as "dog," "cat," "bug," etc., work best), and see what you can come up with. Illustrate your animalriffic words for an extra dose of fun.

Word Pictures

Paint a picture with powerful words!

Some words seem more powerful than their quiet cousins. "Big" seems small when compared to "enormous." "Wet" seems a little dry when held up next to "drenched."

What You'll Need
• blank paper
• markers, crayons, or colored pencils

Pick your favorite powerful word, and carefully draw it in large block letters on a blank piece of paper. Then decorate the block letters with pictures and designs that help illustrate just what this blockbuster word means.

Book Page Bingo

Search the pages of your favorite books to win!

What You'll Need
• books
• bingo game
• blank paper
• pen or pencil

Try something new with an old favorite. Pass out 1 bingo card and 5 books to each player. As the caller announces each letter/number combination (for example, B 12), players check to see if they have that square on their card. If they do, they must search through their books for the page number (page 12) and find a word that begins with that letter (B). The first person to raise their hand and show that combination claims that bingo square and covers it on their card. The first person to cover a row—vertical, horizontal, or diagonal—on their card wins the game. For even more fun, keep track of the words you find by writing them down on a piece of paper. When the game's over, everyone can compare their words.

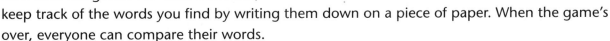

Journal Jam

Writing in a journal is great fun now, and the journal will be even more fun to read in a few years!

What You'll Need
- spiral notebook (plain colored front is best)
- pen
- family pictures, or magazines and newspapers
- craft glue

For ages, people have explored their feelings and their ancestry by writing and reading personal journals. Young people, such as World War II's famous heroine Anne Frank, have left behind important messages for future generations.

You can join in this proud tradition by writing in your own journal. Once a week, or once a day if you're really anxious to speak your mind, sit down and write out what you've done, what you've seen, and how you feel. Date each page with the month, day, and year. Be sure to mention how much things cost; popular trends; and troubling, interesting, and exciting things you hear about in the news. Ask for permission to glue in family pictures or images from magazines and newspapers to verify what you say.

Five, ten, even a hundred years from now, people could be using your journal to better understand the times in which you lived.

Mother Moose Illustrated

◆◆◆◆◆◆◆

Change the key words of old nursery rhymes or your favorite story to make a silly poem. Then draw pictures to match your new story.

What You'll Need
- drawing paper
- blunt scissors
- colored pencils or markers
- construction paper
- hole punch
- yarn

Cut several sheets of drawing paper in half, depending on how many pages you want your book to be. Write a silly story on a page, and draw matching illustrations. For example, instead of Mary having a little lamb, she can have a giant ham. Make yourself, your family, or your friends the characters in the story. Rewrite and illustrate several stories for your Mother Moose storybook. If you want, add a table of contents and a dedication page.

After you've finished the inside pages, bind your new book. To make the front and back covers, fold a sheet of construction paper in half and punch 4 holes near the fold. Decorate the front page. Then punch 4 holes in each page, making sure they line up with the holes on the covers. Place the pages inside the covers. Cut a piece of yarn, thread it through the holes, and tie it in a bow.

Blankity Blank

◆◆◆◆◆◆◆

Even ordinary words can take on zany new meanings when you use them.

Pick out a page from a story you've just read, or choose a poem you know. Write down a few of the key words from the story or poem. Now ask your friend or family member to replace those words on the page with words of their own, without reading the story first. Then insert their words in the real story or poem—the results will be rib-tickling surprises that really change the meaning of the story, 1 random word at a time!

What You'll Need
- paper
- pencils

Paper Promises

◄►►►►►►

Cut out some favors the people you love can really use.

What You'll Need
- old magazines
- blunt scissors
- paper
- glue

Can't think of what to give Mom for her birthday? Dad for his special day? Grandma for Christmas? How about a promise on paper? Pledge to clean up your room, wash the dishes, or walk the dog—then put it in writing. Cut the letters you need to spell out the task from old magazines. Glue them on a piece of paper. Then watch their eyes light up when they discover their "gift."

Headline Hunt

◄►►►►►►

Craft a crazy idea, using five words or fewer!

Newspaper editors spend hours writing the perfect headlines. Now you can get a laugh out of their hard work. Clip all the headlines from an old newspaper, cut the words apart, and drop them in a box. Mix them up. Now try to make goofy headlines of the bits and pieces you've collected, and glue

What You'll Need
- newspapers
- blunt scissors
- box
- paper
- glue

your favorite combinations on a page. Headline a crazy story only you could imagine—with a little help from the real news!

# To the Letter

Stick with one letter for storytelling fun.

Just for fun, see if you can write a simple story using words that start with the same letter of the alphabet. Writing an "A" story? Start with, "An ant ate apples at Aunt Alma's." See how long you can continue without breaking the letter chain. Don't get discouraged—this is sometimes difficult but always a blast! For extra fun, illustrate your story.

What You'll Need
• paper
• pens or pencils
• colored markers or crayons

# Picture Inspiration

Have fun putting pictures into words!

What You'll Need
• old magazines
• paper
• pens or pencils

Here's your chance to prove just how many words 1 picture can inspire. Go through a stack of old magazines (be sure to ask for permission first!), and pull out pictures that appeal to you. The picture could be a dog running through a field. It could be a baby crying with a fever. It could be a grandmother opening gifts. Now see how many single words you can come up with to describe the picture. Take your time. This is a game you can play alone or with a friend. If you play with a friend, talk about the words you picked and why.

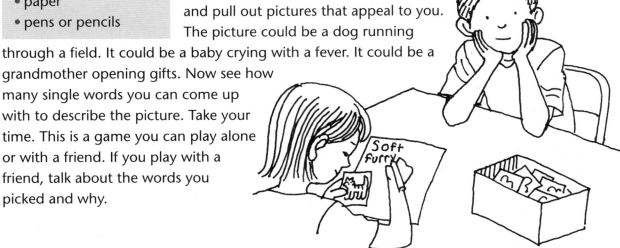

Family Newsletter

◆▸▸▸▸▸▸◆

Stop the presses! Report on your family's latest news!

What You'll Need
- typing paper
- typewriter and copy machine or computer and printer
- postage stamps
- envelopes

You can bring the whole family together by writing and distributing this fun family newsletter. First, ask your parents for the addresses, birthdays, and anniversaries of all your relatives. Then drop your relatives notes asking them what's been happening in their lives. Once you get your answers, write short reports on each family group and add a reminder box of their special dates. Print out copies for each family, and drop them in the mail. (You can e-mail those who have computers.) Before you know it, you'll be getting announcements from your long-lost Uncle Harold (not to mention thank-you notes from Aunt Lucy).

Doggie Diary

◆▸▸▸▸▸▸◆

Can you talk to the animals? Can they talk back?

What You'll Need
- notebook
- pen

Some experts say our pets have their own distinctive languages, even if we don't know how to interpret what they say. This fun experiment might help you get a clue to doggy dialogue. The next time you have a free day at home with your dog, pay close attention to how he "talks." Does he whimper when he wants to go outside? Write it down. Does he give a loud, short bark when he's hungry? Make a note of it. Now see if you can duplicate the sounds to communicate with your dog.

Senior Interview

◄►►►►►►

We can shape the future if we learn about the past.

What You'll Need
- tape recorder
- notepad
- pen

Do you think all the good stories will spring out of the future? Think again. Interview a friendly senior citizen about what it was like growing up in the "old days." First, call to arrange a time for the interview. Prepare some questions in advance. You can ask, "How were things different when you were a kid?" "How much did gum cost?" "What did you do for fun?" "What was the scariest thing about life in your early years?" "What really made you laugh?" Record your interview with a tape recorder, and take written notes. You can write a story about your interview, and then share your discovery with teachers, parents, and friends.

Long Life

No one knows for sure which individual has lived the longest. But the Guinness Book of Records says Frenchwoman Jeanne Calment must have been among the top contenders. She passed away in August 1997, at the ripe old age of 122.

Rebus Romp

❖❖❖❖❖❖

Turn your favorite story into a rebus!

What You'll Need

• favorite book
• old magazines
• blunt scissors
• crayons or markers
• pencil or pen
• paper
• glue

What is a rebus? It's a fun story in which key words, such as favorite characters or important settings, are replaced by illustrations. Maybe you wonder what your favorite classic story would look like as a rebus. Make a rebus version of a favorite story, and find out. Cut key images in the story from old magazines (ask for permission first!) or draw them yourself. Then write out the story, leaving spaces to glue the illustrations to your paper in the correct places. Glue on the illustrations, and share your finished rebus with a younger reader, your parents, or your friends.

Newspaper Caper

❖❖❖❖❖❖

Check out the who, what, when, where, why, and how of reporting the news!

Ever wondered what a real reporter does for a living? Why not do an interview of your own to find out? Thumb through a newspaper until you find an article that's interesting to you. Did the writer answer all your questions? Would you like to know more? Write down your questions and a short note of introduction. Send both to the reporter whose name is on the article, in care of the newspaper office. Don't forget to include a self-addressed stamped envelope and your e-mail address if you have one.

What You'll Need

• newspapers
• paper
• pencil
• envelopes
• postage stamps

Poetry in Motion

◆▶◆▶◆▶◆▶

Poetry is like painting pictures with words.

Think of sights you've seen that interested you or made you feel something. Maybe it was a bird flying, a dog chasing its tail, or a horse galloping across a field. Why not take a stab at writing a poem about it? Try to use powerful words—words that say

What You'll Need
• paper
• pens

more than you might think. For example, why use "big" to describe that Clydesdale horse when you could say "monumental"? Why say the dog was brown when you could say he was the color of chocolate? And remember, poetry doesn't have to rhyme to be good.

Internet Bingo

◆▶◆▶◆▶◆▶

Surfing the Internet can really spell F-U-N!

What You'll Need
• notebook paper
• pen or pencil
• computer with Inter-
net connection and
Web browser

You'll need adult permission for this activity. Internet bingo is like an electronic scavenger hunt. Spell out the word *INTERNET* on a sheet of notebook paper. Go to your favorite search engine (www.yahoo.com or www.excite.com are good possibilities), and type in what-

ever word comes to mind. It could be dog, kite, or cantaloupe. Spend the next hour searching for subject links that start with each letter in the word *INTERNET*. E-mail a friend with the great new cyber stops you find along the way. (Remember, never give out your name, age, address, or e-mail address to any strangers you meet on the Net without your parents' permission.)

Play Day

◆▶◆▶◆▶◆

The play is the thing—and you can be the star.

If you've been bitten by the drama bug, you might want to put on your own performance. You can write, direct, and star in your own creative play. Make up 4 important or interesting characters. They could be rock stars or scien-

What You'll Need
• spiral notebook
• pen or pencil

tists, police detectives or circus clowns. What do they look like? Where are they from? Write it down. Now imagine what might happen to your characters. How did they meet? What do they do when they get into trouble? How do they get out of the fix? Write down everything you imagine they would say. Then get 3 of your friends to help you read the finished script.

Pass It On!

◆▶◆▶◆▶◆

Say what's on your mind, then pass it on!

What You'll Need
• paper
• pen

With parents working and kids participating in after-school activities, one thing is for certain: Today's families are busy! Keep track of what's going on in your world—and in the worlds of your other family members—with this fun, "pass it on" weekly communication. Write a sentence about what you're doing or feeling, then pass it on to another family member. That member comments on your sentence and adds another. The note is again passed on to another family member, who comments on each of the previous comments and adds another of their own. Before you know it, the original letter comes back to you—and you have a quick idea of what everyone is doing and what each of your family members has to say.

Reach for the Stars

Reach for the stars through the mail!

What You'll Need
- notebook paper
- pen
- envelope
- postage stamp

Ever wished you could write to your favorite TV celebrity? What's stopping you? With a little research, you can tell the stars exactly what's on your mind. Write a short letter to the glamour queen or king of your choice (be careful with spelling, and write neatly). Now comes the research. Grab your local newspaper television listings. What network makes your star's show? Match it up to the address below, and you'll know where to mail your message. In 4 to 6 weeks, you may even get a reply.

ABC: ABC, Inc., 77 W. 66th St., New York, NY 10023
CBS: CBS Television Network, 51 W. 52nd St., New York, NY 10019
FOX: Fox Family Channel, P.O. Box 900, Beverly Hills, CA 90213
NBC: National Broadcasting Company, Inc., 30 Rockefeller Plaza, New York, NY 10112
UPN: United Paramount Network, 11800 Wilshire Blvd., Los Angeles, CA 90025
WB: The Warner Brothers Television Network, 4000 Warner Blvd., Burbank, CA 91522

Puzzle Poems

Puzzling over poetry? Try this activity on for size.

What You'll Need
- paper
- markers
- cardboard
- glue
- blunt scissors
- resealable plastic bag

Craving a puzzle with personal appeal? Write your favorite poem, classic or original, on a blank sheet of paper. Illustrate the poem with bright colors and drawings. Glue the paper to a piece of cardboard, and let it dry completely. Once it's dry, cut the stiff page into small pieces. You'll have your own personal puzzle poem to

put back together and enjoy. Hint: Keep the pieces in a resealable plastic bag when you're not putting your puzzle together.

Color of Color

◆▶◆▶◆

Why use red to describe your favorite flower when scarlet waits in the wings?

Professional writers know words have the power to paint pictures. Find out how great that power is with this colorful exercise. When you describe a red rose, is red really just red? Or is that vivid rose really scarlet? Is your blue sky just blue? Or is it a robin's-egg-blue

horizon? Is the sun shining yellow, or is it bathing your world in gold? It's up to you. How many words can you come up with for the colors of the rainbow? Make a list to find out.

 # Picture Perfect

◆▶◆▶◆▶◆

Capture your life and loves in pictures, then share them with the world.

What You'll Need
• disposable camera
• poster board
• glue
• markers or pen
• index cards
  (optional)
• photo album
  (optional)

Work around the house and neighborhood doing chores until you earn enough money to buy a disposable camera and to have the pictures developed. Then see if you can tell the story of who you are, using pictures alone. Are you messy? Take a picture of your room. Do you love animals? Take a picture of your favorite kitty. Take your time and really make every picture count. Mount them on poster board with glue, and write a few words

under each picture describing why it means a lot to you. Or write your captions on index cards, and arrange the cards and photos in a photo album.

Step In, Step Out

◆▷◆▷◆▷◆▷

When you write the sequel, you can become your favorite hero!

What You'll Need
• favorite novel
• paper
• pen

Do you have an all-time-favorite book? An all-time-favorite book character? If you do, and you've ever wondered what happened after the story's final page, this is your chance to take control.

Become your favorite hero or heroine when you write the sequel. Ask yourself a few important questions: How did the events in your favorite story affect and change the character? How did it affect the characters around him or her? And most important, what might have happened next in your favorite character's life? Write it out in a short story follow-up. For more fun, invite a few friends over to act out your new story. Write speaking parts for everyone, rehearse, and then put on a show!

# Quick Draw

◆▷◆▷◆▷◆▷

Can you use words to describe an object without using the word that names the object?

Play this game with a partner. Find photos of simple objects such as dogs, cats, cereal boxes, and baseballs in old magazines (be sure to ask for permission first!). Cut them out, and glue them on 3″×5″ cards. Put the cards in a box, and mix them up. Take a card from the box, and say words that describe the object without saying what the object is. See how long it takes your friend to guess what object you're describing. Then it's your turn to guess!

What You'll Need
• old magazines
• blunt scissors
• glue
• 3″×5″ index cards
• box

"Touching" Mail

◆◆▶▶▶◆◆

Express how you feel, feel what you express.

Caution: This project requires adult supervision.

Feel the need to say "hello"? "I love you"? "Goodbye"? The next time you want to write what you feel, why not give your friends and family the chance to feel what you write?

Create your note using Braille. First, pick a simple message—1 to 3 words, tops. On a piece of scrap paper, translate the letters into the dot-patterned letters used by the visually impaired. (See the Braille chart below for guidance.)

When you've translated your message, carefully copy it onto a clean piece of white card stock, leaving lots of space between letters and words. Drip small blobs of nail polish over the alphabet dots. This works best if the nail polish is old and slightly thickened. If you need to, go back over the dots with a second coat so the letters dry slightly raised. (Work in a well-ventilated room and away from any flames when you use nail polish.) On the back of the card, translate your message in ordinary letters.

Decorate the card once it dries, and pass it on. This note will be remembered for a long time!

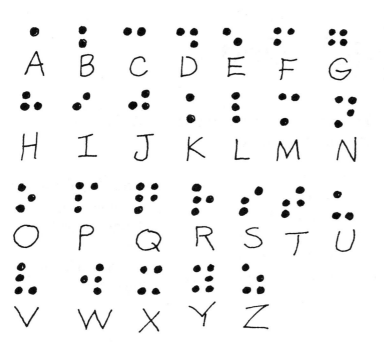

Opposite Ads

Make 2 or 3 ads for the same pretend product. Then show them to your friends to see which one "sells" your product the best.

GROSS   Now 10 years old

yucKy CooKies made with 100% REAL SLIME

BAT FREE

How would you sell the worst video game, the yuckiest cookies, or the dullest school? How could you eat, much less sell, computer-chip or slimy cookies? Advertisements always have a picture or a photo, writing called *copy,* and a headline. Invent your own yucky product. Draw a picture and headline for the worst ad, and give your product an awful name. If you don't want to sell something bad, sell something that isn't usually for sale. For instance, you could try to sell a field trip, honesty, or a dentist appointment.

What You'll Need
• drawing paper
• colored pencils, markers, or crayons

Wild & Crazy Monsters

In this project, you begin with a good story and make it even better. It's a test for your imagination.

What You'll Need
• drawing paper
• pencil
• markers

Read a book about imaginary monsters, like *Where the Wild Things Are,* and create your own make-believe creatures. Sketch a fun or scary monster on a piece of paper, and color it in. Or use the drawing technique in The Art of Tracing on page 257 to create an outline of a shape, such as a bear. Turn it into a monster by adding horns, sharp teeth, and a tail. Then color it in. Make all kinds of monsters—a giant one, a ghostlike creature, or a dragonlike animal—to create your own picture book.

Spool-a-Word

◆▷◆▷◆▷◆

Spin the spools to make real or pretend words. Even better, spin letters with your friends and invent new word games.

What You'll Need
- empty wood or plastic spools
- unsharpened pencils
- permanent markers

Find 3 empty spools and 1 unsharpened pencil. Using a blue marker, write the letters *s, r, l, g,* and *f* around the first spool. Around the second spool, write the letters *a, e, i, o,* and *u* in red. Around the third spool, write the letters *n, t, d, p,* and *b* in blue. Put the spools on a pencil (in order), and turn them to form a word. Make other spools with more letters, and pick spools with your friends. Put them on a pencil and see who can come up with the most words in 1 minute.

Alphabet Art

◆▷◆▷◆▷◆

Spell out the objects in your picture with pasta letters. This art form is called word graphs and it's F-U-N.

Word graphs use words to draw an outline of an object. For example, the words *sun* and *shine* form a sun's shape. The word *sun* is used to outline the round part of the sun, and the word *shine* is used to outline the sun's rays. Gather letters from alphabet pasta to

What You'll Need
- alphabet pasta
- drawing or construction paper
- markers
- craft glue

make your picture with words. If you don't have any alphabet pasta, you can still make a word graph—just draw the letters. Glue the alphabet pasta to a piece of paper to make your picture. Fill in any missing letters or add more details with markers.

TV Word Tag

❖❖❖❖❖

This fast-paced channel-surfing game will keep your mind hopping!

What You'll Need
- coin
- TV and remote control
- timer
- paper
- pencils

Flip a coin to see who goes first in this fast-paced game. The first player holds the remote. Set the timer for 1 minute, and the first player has that amount of time to select a word heard on TV, shout it out, and write it on a piece of paper. Once that word is selected, the remote control is passed to the next player, who has 1 minute to flip through channels until he or she finds a word that rhymes with the first word. Once that word is discovered and called out, the remote goes to the next player, who must do the same.

TV tag continues until a player can't find a rhyming word. The player who can't find a rhyme gets a point. The player with the least points at the end of 20 minutes is the winner.

You can also play this game by trying to find synonyms rather than rhymes. A synonym is a word that means the same or almost the same as another. For example, "garbage," "trash," and "rubbish" are synonyms.

Back Talk

❖❖❖❖❖

Can you talk backward? Nac uoy klat drawkcab?

Ever imagined what it would be like to say all your words backward? Why not give it a try? Write out a few sentences, carefully spelling each word backward. Practice reading the words aloud that way. Once you feel confident, record the backward phrases. Play them for your friends or parents to see if they can figure out the trick!

What You'll Need
- paper
- pens or pencils
- tape recorder

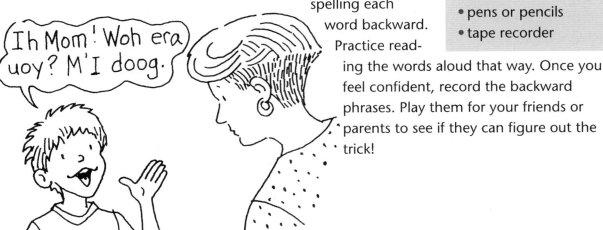

Ih Mom! Woh era uoy? M'I doog.

Name Game

◆▸◆▸◆▸◆

Who's who in the land of make believe?

What You'll Need
- old newspapers or magazines
- blunt scissors
- blank paper
- glue
- markers
- pencils or pens

Flip through an old newspaper or magazine, and look for the names of famous or infamous people, such as Madonna, Butch Cassidy and the Sundance Kid, Elvis Presley, Michael Jordan, and Savage Garden. Cut out the names (ask for permission first!). Make a new name out of pieces of existing names—Savage Madonna, Elvis Jordan. Glue that name at the top of your blank piece of paper. Now make up a personality, a personal history, a whole new person to go with that made-up name. Maybe Elvis Jordan sings "Love Me Tender" as he makes jump shots!

Splitting Ends (and Beginnings and Middles)

◆▸◆▸◆▸◆

What if "Once upon a time" could change with the turn of a page?

What You'll Need
- ruler
- paper
- pens or pencils
- blunt scissors

Are you a natural-born storyteller? Would you like to be? This crazy cut-up of a project can make it easy. Using a ruler, take 10 pieces of paper and divide each into 6 even sections. Write a very simple story, using 6 sentences, with a sentence in each section. Make the first sentence a "Once upon a time" character introduction, such as "Once upon a time, there was a green tree frog." The second describes where your character lived: "He lived in the wilds of a South American rain forest." The third sentence tells your character's special talent: "He was able to hop better than any animal in the realm." The fourth sentence explains the character's feelings: "But he was sad." The fifth says why the character felt that way: "He was a very lonely frog." The last line describes how the character solved the problem: "So he found a friend in the pond." Write a story for each of the pieces of paper. Now cut the sections of each page so you can mix and match the lines of the stories. See what wacky combinations you can come up with.

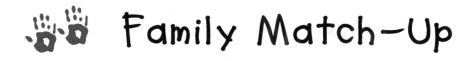

Family Match-Up

◆▸▸▸▸▸◆

What's another word for sister*? That depends on the sister.*

What You'll Need
- scrap paper
- pencil
- card stock (cut in 3″×3″ pieces)
- markers
- resealable plastic lunch bag

If you've ever played memory match-up games—those face-down card games that dare you to find the 2 zebras for a match—this game gives a new twist to the age-old challenge. On a piece of scrap paper, make a list of the names of 10 family members and friends: Mom, Dad, Sis, Cousin Bob, best friend Karen, etc. Then write down the 1 or 2 words that best describe each person. Funny? Computer wizard? Tall? Skier? Those descriptive words will represent the perfect match in this memory card game.

Write each name and each word on its own 3″×3″ piece of card stock. For each pair, mark a color-coded X so you'll know you've made the right match (for example, the card with "Dad" and the card that matches him, "Tall," will each have a purple X on them; the set for "Mom" and her match will each have a red X on them).

When you are finished making the game, mix up the cards and spread them all out, face down, on a flat surface. It's time to try your luck. Put all the pieces in a resealable plastic bag after you've finished playing your game. Lost pieces will make it hard to win (or play) the game!

Finger Plays, Fingers Play

Let your fingers do the talking.

What You'll Need

- children's storybook
- paper
- pen
- copy machine (optional)
- highlighters (optional)
- cardboard box
- blunt scissors
- paint and paintbrush (optional)
- washable markers
- fabric scraps (optional)
- washable glue (optional)
- video recorder (optional)

Is there a picture book you can't get enough of? A short children's story you never get tired of hearing? Why not put on a finger play based on that children's classic? Go through the story, and write out the main parts. For example, in *The Three Little Pigs,* the narrator, each pig, and the big bad wolf are the main characters. You could also photocopy the pages of your favorite picture book and highlight each part in a different color: for instance, blue for the narrator; red, green, and yellow for the pigs; and purple for the big bad wolf.

Cut a stage out of a cardboard box, and decorate it if you'd like. Now it's time to get the actors ready! Use washable markers to decorate your fingers to look like the main characters. Draw pig faces on your middle, ring, and baby fingers. Add wolf ears to your index finger. Draw a big smile and bow tie for the narrator thumb. You can also make clothes out of fabric scraps. Act out the play for younger relatives or friends. You might want to ask a few teachers if you could perform this play in their classroom for the children. Have an adult videotape your play for an extra measure of fun. You'll giggle every time you watch it!

"Who Am I" Word Collage

◆▶◆▶◆▶◆

Even words can be art when self-expression is the goal.

What You'll Need
- plain white paper or card stock
- colorful markers
- scrap paper (optional)

When you think of the things you love, what words come to mind? Cooking? Dogs? Helping others? Painting? Now imagine: How can you bring those important words to life, using color? Choose a few of your favorite words, and write them on a large, sturdy piece of paper. (You may want to practice on scrap paper first, if you want to be extra neat.) Use lovely, unique lettering on your final collage, and decorate the letters with stripes and shapes. Use bold or pale colors to create the lettering, and you can surround the letters with tiny drawings and other descriptive words. It's your choice. Just experiment with colors and designs to make a single word or phrase paint a bigger picture. Share your artistically worded art with a friend or family member.

What's in a Word?

◆▶◆▶◆▶◆

Pull words out of words with this fun puzzler.

Find a long and complicated word in your favorite dictionary. Write it out at the top of a blank sheet of paper. Now try to find words made up of the letters in the word you've selected—you can use the letters only as many times as they appear in the word. Give yourself 1 point for each word built from rearranging letters. Give yourself 2 points for words you find in the original word without switching the letters around. To add more of a challenge, put a 2-minute time limit on each round of your game.

What You'll Need
- dictionary
- paper
- pens or pencils
- timer

Pick-a-Day Brightener

◆▶◆▶◆▶◆

Pick a flower of encouragement that will bloom all year long.

What You'll Need
- pencil
- paper
- colored markers
- blunt scissors
- ruler
- book of good quotes
- paper plate
- tape

Everyone could use an encouraging word from time to time. This basket of flowers will make it easy to pick a positive message when you need it most. Draw and cut out colorful paper blossoms about 3 inches wide. Write an inspirational quote or saying on the back of each flower. Ask your school librarian to suggest a book of good quotes to help you get started. But be sure to write some of your

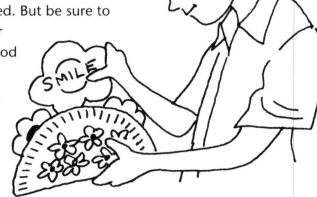

own quotes—you can come up with lots of good ideas. Fold a paper plate in half, and tape the sides together, leaving 4 or 5 inches at the top untaped. Decorate the folded plate to resemble a basket or flower pot. Slip your flowers into the paper basket, and pull one of them whenever you need a lift.

Rosy News
Though thousands of kinds of roses have been grown for centuries, these five are among the current American favorites: Angel Face, Fragrant Cloud, Heritage, New Dawn, and Peace.

 # Picture Puns

◆▶◆▶◆▶◆

Draw pictures that stand for a word. Have your friends and family guess the words!

What You'll Need
- 8 to 11 sheets of drawing paper
- markers
- stapler and staples

Draw 2 pictures that stand for a word on a sheet of drawing paper. You might choose the word *snowman* and draw snowflakes and a man or *starfish* and draw a star and a fish. Write the word on the back of the paper. Make 8 to 10 picture puns. Make a book out of your drawings. Decorate a sheet of drawing paper for the cover. Set all the pages together and staple the top of the pages to bind your book. Show your book to family members and see if they can guess your words.

Try other picture puns with homonyms. These are words that sound alike but have different spellings and meanings. An example is *aunt* and *ant*. Draw as many as you can and add them to your book.

Fantasy Creature

◆▸◆▸◆▸◆▸

Build a body with scissors and glue!

What You'll Need
- old magazines
- blunt scissors
- glue
- paper
- pen or pencil

Find out what it's like to be a mad scientist with this goofy cut-and-paste activity. Thumb through magazines until you find an interesting head, 2 unusual hands, a couple of dazzling eyes, some

really amazing teeth, and a wildly dressed body. Cut them out. Mix and match these body parts to create a fantasy creature sure to make you laugh. Glue your creature to a piece of paper to show it off. Write a funny story or poem about your crazy creature!

Matter of Opinion

◆▸◆▸◆▸◆▸

What you think matters. It's time to speak your mind!

Has a news event ever made you mad? Has crime ever made you afraid? Has a sports hero ever made you proud? Why not tell your community how you feel? Write a letter to your local newspaper. Explain which current event made you think, and just what those thoughts were. End your opinion letter with your name, your age, and your phone number. Mail it to the editor of your local paper. Watch the editorial page to see if your words make it into print.

What You'll Need
- notebook paper
- pen
- envelope
- postage stamp
- newspaper

Creative Crosswords

◆▷◆▷◆▷◆▷

Make up your own crossword puzzles, then share them with a friend!

Add a new twist to an old favorite by making up crossword puzzles based on your favorite hobbies, books, animals, or celebrities. Arrange your "down" and "across" words on the graph paper, writing 1 letter in each square. After you arrange the puzzle words, write your clues to match. Don't forget to number the words and clues. (Hint: Don't make your word clues too difficult.) Then copy the puzzle on a clean sheet of paper, and see how long it takes a friend to complete.

What You'll Need
• pens
• ruler
• graph paper
• pencil

Magazine Match-Up

◆▷◆▷◆▷◆▷

One person's trash is another person's great read!

What You'll Need
• old magazines
• wagon
• paper bags

Once you've read a magazine cover to cover, is it time to throw it away? Not necessarily. Why not match old magazines with new readers? Gather up your old magazines (be sure to ask for permission first!). Ask your friendliest neighbors to do the same. Take an adult along, and go door to door with your wagon collecting magazines. Mix and match the pile into paper bags. Now make a few telephone calls. See if neighbors, senior citizen homes, or local hospital wards would like to participate in the drop-off. Even people in homeless shelters might like to catch up with the latest in magazines, and you can help!

Boxing Match

How do you see things? Chances are, a lot differently than your friends might.

Playing with enormous boxes is always fun so this activity is sure to be a knockout. Two teams each get a slip of paper with the same phrase written on it. The phrases will be instructions such as "Make your box a watery wonder" or "Make your box really fly." Without looking at the other team, you and your creative friends have exactly 15 minutes to decorate half the box to reflect that phrase. Do the decorations match? How did you interpret the phrase differently? Try another phrase on the other side of the box.

What You'll Need
- large cardboard boxes
- paper
- markers
- timer
- blunt scissors
- glue
- crayons
- paints
- paintbrushes

Word Picture Book

One picture is worth a thousand words—or is it the other way around?

What You'll Need
- dictionary
- blank paper
- crayons or markers

Thousands of new words are waiting for you to discover them in your favorite dictionary. So why not get started learning every single one? Open your dictionary to a page at random. Find a word you've never seen before. Read the definition carefully. Once you understand what the new word means, illustrate it on a piece of blank paper. Add a new page to your Word Picture Book each week.

Personal Headlines

◆▶◆▶◆▶◆

Make a collage for friends and family to let them catch up on your life.

What You'll Need
- old newspapers
- blunt scissors
- card stock (cut in 4"×6" pieces)
- glue
- markers
- postage stamps

Who are you? Where have you been? What are your hobbies? This fun fact-finding activity will help you express yourself—and share those expressions with the people who love you.

Go through a pile of old newspapers, cutting out and gathering words that express who you are, what you've done, and how you feel. Creatively position and glue those headlines on a side of a 4"×6" piece of card stock. Make sure you glue all the edges down securely so they can't be ripped off. Decorate those words with colorful markers, if you like. Once the glue and ink are dry (plan for overnight drying time in most climates), add a stamp, an address, a quick "hello" to the back of the card, and drop it in a mailbox.

Your personal headlines will update your friends and family on your life. The headlines might even inspire them to create their own.

Wacky Word Search

❖▸❖▸❖▸❖▸❖

Can you find yourself in the mix?

Have you ever done a word-search puzzle? Found the names of
your favorite animals, rock bands, or cartoon characters mixed in a
sea of random letters? This is your chance to make a word search
of your own, starring—who else—YOU! First make a list of words
that sum up who you are and what you like. Include your first, last,
and middle name, of course. Then think about what things make you unique. Do you speak
Spanish? Put "Spanish" on the list. Do you collect glass horses? Include the word "horses" in
your search. Do you jump rope for fun? Don't forget to include "jump rope." Now mix those
words, up and down, side to side, backward, and diagonally, in an ocean of unrelated letters.
Make a few copies of your puzzle. Then see how long it takes your mom, dad, and best friend
to find all the words. Or wait a few days, and test yourself!

What You'll Need
- paper
- pens
- copy machine

Chalk Talk Hop

◂▸◂▸◂▸◂▸◂

Chalk it up to your winning ability to rhyme!

What You'll Need
- sidewalk chalk
- knee pads (optional)

Take action with words in this colorful rhyming/jumping game.
Draw five 2-foot squares in different colors on a cement or black-
top surface (such as a driveway, a side-
walk, or a playground—be sure to ask
for permission first!). The squares should touch each other. Now
hop from one square to the next. If you hop on the pink square,
stop and write a word that rhymes with pink (such as "ink")
in the box before you move on. Hopping on blue?
Write a word such as "true." Get the picture? Can't
think of a word that rhymes? You'll have to skip
that box and leap to the next one. Any direction,
forward, backward, or sideways is fair. A round is complete
as soon as you rhyme every square. Be careful of your knees when
jumping across pavement. Knee pads will come in handy for this game.

Tell a Story

❖▸❖▸❖▸❖

Writing a story is a team event when you pass it on!

Most writers work alone. But thanks to this activity, storytelling can be friendly fun. Go through a stack of old magazines, and find a picture that really makes you think twice. Write a paragraph about the person, animal, place, or thing in the picture. Then pass the picture and your paragraph on to a friend. Ask them to add to the paragraph and pass it on to another friend. The next person adds a few sentences and passes it along, and so on, and so on, until you've built a whole story around the photo. Gather together, and read the story aloud.

You could also play this game on the Internet via e-mail. Just find a picture on a Web site. Pass the Web address to your friends, along with your story. (Don't give out your name, address, or age to anyone you meet on the Web without your parents' permission!)

What You'll Need
- old magazines
- notebook paper
- pens or pencils
- computer with Internet access and Web browser (optional)

Word Scramble

❖▸❖▸❖▸❖

What will you say when you have to say it fast?

What You'll Need
- card stock
- markers
- dictionary (optional)
- blunt scissors
- box
- timer

If you think you're good with words, this is the game for you. Write 20 of your favorite nouns (person, place, or thing words), 20 of your favorite verbs (action words), 20 of your favorite adverbs (words that modify verbs), 20 of your favorite adjectives (words that modify nouns), and a dozen each of "the," "a," "but," "or," "when," "why," "how," and "with." (You can use a dictionary if you want.) Cut each into 1-word strips, and toss them all into a box. Shake them up, dump them out, and see how many crazy sentences you can come up with in 2 minutes.

Code Wheel

◆▶◆▶◆▶◆▶

You and a friend can pretend you're secret agents and send each other important messages in code.

What You'll Need
- poster board or 2 small paper plates
- blunt scissors
- ruler or compass
- pencil
- brass paper fastener
- ballpoint pen

Cut out 2 circles, 6 inches each, from poster board. (You can also use 2 small paper plates.) Cut a ½-inch-wide V-shape and a ½-inch-round window in 1 circle wheel as shown. Use the pencil to poke a small hole in the center of both wheels. Attach the wheels with a brass paper fastener. Write the letter *A* in the V, then turn the wheel ½ inch and write the letter *B*. Continue with the rest of the alphabet around the wheel. (Hint: You can measure ½ inch without a ruler. Make a small pencil mark on the right side of the V, then turn the wheel so the left side lines up with the mark.)

Now fill in the window. Turn the wheel. Write the letter *A* in the window. (Make sure the V is not pointing to the letter *A!*) Turn the wheel several inches, and write a *B* in the window. Place the rest of the alphabet in the window, always making sure the window letter is different than the V letter. Make a second wheel for your friend that matches yours exactly so you can write and decode secret messages.

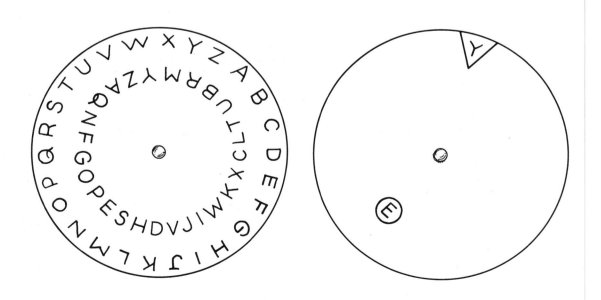

Frankenstein's Animals

Bits and pieces come together to make a new beast!

What You'll Need
- blank paper
- markers
- old magazines
- glue
- blunt scissors

Do you love animals? Here's your chance to create a whole new species...or 2...or 3. Using animal body parts you find in magazine pictures, mix and match to make a whole new beast. Think a flying sea horse would be fun?

How about a dog with 4 eyes? Or a turtle with fur! Anything is possible with a little imagination. Once your animal is captured on the page, write a short story about what makes it unique.

# Mysterious Secrets

Can you solve the mystery of the mystery? Check this activity to find out.

What You'll Need
- classic mysteries (such as *Sherlock Holmes, The Hardy Boys,* or *Nancy Drew*)
- notebook
- pens

Mysteries are some of the most popular books sold in the United States and around the world. But what's the secret to a good mystery? The hidden treasure? The butler? The mysterious house guest? As you read your favorite mystery, take a few notes. Keep track of the secrets your fictional sleuth uncovers as he or she goes about solving the mystery. Then rewrite key scenes, changing those secrets. How would your changes affect the outcome of the story? Only you can decide!

Movie-Time Scrapbook

You become the film critic!

Are you a film buff? Does going to the latest movie totally rev your jets? Then this fun project is custom made for you. Keep a movie scrapbook!

Decorate the cover of a spiral notebook any way you'd like—be creative. Dedicate each page of the notebook to a movie you want to see. Headed for the latest superhero flick? Check magazines and newspapers for print advertisements or reviews of that film. Cut them out, and glue them to the page. Once you actually see the film, date the page, glue on your ticket stub, and take a minute to jot down whether or not the movie was all you'd hoped it would be. Years from now you'll look back on the scrapbook as a sign of the times. When you're older, you can see how your taste in movies has changed or stayed the same.

Galloping into the Movies

Would you believe that movies got their start because of a horse? A row of cameras was lined up to take pictures of a moving horse. When the horse galloped by, each camera got a slightly different picture. Showing the still pictures quickly created a film by tricking the viewer's eyes into seeing motion!

Calligraphy

◇▸◇▸◇▸◇▸◇▸◇▸◇▸

Thanks to calligraphy, now you write can be as expressive as what you write.

What You'll Need
- an assortment of pens and papers

Have you tried exploring the fonts (type styles) on your home computer? Maybe you've seen an unusual letter style in your favorite book. Or maybe you've noticed surprising or interesting letter styles on book covers or in magazines. Each of these are examples of calligraphy, the art of lettering. Now's your chance to come up with a lettering style all your own. Try to develop letters A to Z that reflect your personal style. Ask your librarian to help you find books on calligraphy if you need inspiration.

Author! Author!

◇▸◇▸◇▸◇▸◇▸◇▸◇▸

Tell your favorite author just what his or her words mean to you.

Is there an author who writes books that you can't put down? Why not drop your favorite author a line to tell them exactly what their books have meant to you? You can write to the company that published the books—the address will be inside your book. Keep your letter neat and brief, but don't hesitate to tell the writer exactly how you feel. Did the book make you happy? Sad? Thoughtful? Mad? Tell the author. And if you decided to try writing a sequel to one of their books (as in Step In, Step Out on page 125), send that along with your note. If you have a computer, you can try looking up the author's name on an Internet search engine.

What You'll Need
- stationery or lined paper
- pen
- envelope
- postage stamp
- computer with Internet access and Web browser (optional)

Your favorite author will be pleased and flattered and might even write you back!

Crossword Puzzle

◄▶◄▶◄▶◄▶

This crossword puzzle has a surprising twist because your clues are pictures instead of words.

What You'll Need
- graph paper
- pencil
- tracing paper (optional)
- black felt-tip pen
- markers

Think of nouns to go in your crossword puzzle, making sure 1 word can connect with another word. Make your answer key using the graph paper. Draw a square for each letter of each word in your puzzle, connecting the words with a shared letter. Write each letter in. Then number each word going across and each word going down.

Cover the crossword puzzle with tracing paper to copy the squares without the letters in them, or redraw the puzzle without the letters on a new sheet of graph paper. Draw a clue for each word, and number the clues to match the word. If the word for 1 across is dog, then draw a dog for clue 1 across. Draw a decorative border around the puzzle. Make photocopies of the crossword puzzle to give to your friends and family.

Pet Cam

◆◆◆◆◆◆◆

How does Rover see the world?

If you're old enough to use a video camera, this is a great way to understand your pets a little better. Get down on your hands and knees, grab your camcorder, and follow your dog or cat around the house. What do they

What You'll Need
• video camera or pen and paper

see? What do they do? How do you think they might feel? Videotape "A Day With My Pet." (Be sure you get your parents' approval before using the video camera!) If you don't have a video camera, make 4 or 5 illustrations of your own based on what you saw during your animal observations. Add captions; the results can be hilarious!

Channel Changers' Word Search

◆◆◆◆◆◆◆

Channel surfing takes on alphabetical appeal!

What You'll Need
• notebook paper
• pencil
• TV
• remote control
• timer

On a blank piece of notebook paper, make a column listing each letter in the alphabet. Using the remote control, move from channel to channel, searching for words that begin with each letter. Play once, keeping track of how long it takes to complete your alphabetical search. Then play again to beat your own time. To make this a 2-player game, you and a friend can each go after words beginning with every other letter in the alphabet.

SCIENTIFIC SLEUTHS

Scientists probe the questions of how things work and why things act the way they do. But science is not just for scientists. Everyone is interested in the world around them and what makes things tick. You can learn a great deal about the world by observing and performing experiments. Here are some activities to get you started investigating!

Blowing in the Wind

How does a weather vane work? Find out by making your own.

What You'll Need
- heavy cardboard
- 2 pencils
- ruler
- blunt scissors
- aluminum foil
- hole punch
- string
- nut, bolt, or other weight

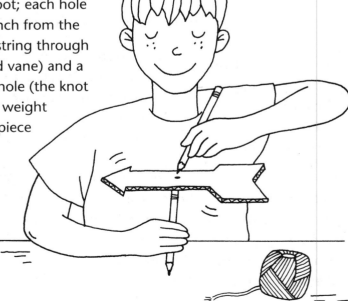

Draw a wind vane, in the shape of an arrow, on a sheet of heavy cardboard. Your vane should be about 14 inches long and 5 inches wide, and the tail should be wider than the point. Cut the wind vane from the cardboard with scissors. Cover the arrow with aluminum foil.

Balance the cardboard wind vane on the eraser of a pencil, and mark the top of the wind vane above where the pencil balances the wind vane. Punch 2 holes side by side in the wind vane by this balance spot; each hole should be ½ inch from the edge of the vane. Tie an 18-inch piece of string through 1 hole (the knot should be below the wind vane) and a 12-inch piece of string through the other hole (the knot should be above). Tie a nut, bolt, or other weight to the bottom piece of string. Tie the top piece of string to a tree branch where the vane can swing easily without hitting anything.

When the wind blows, your wind vane will point directly into the wind. The larger surface of the tail provides more resistance to the wind and causes the point to face into the wind.

Kaleidoscopic View

Make your own kaleidoscope, and view fantastic symmetrical patterns.

To make the kaleidoscope, tape 3 mirrors together, with the reflective sides facing in, to create a triangular shape. Set one of the open ends of the triangle on a piece of cardboard, and trace it. Cut out the cardboard triangle, and tape it over one open end of the mirror triangle. Set the mirror triangle on its cardboard bottom

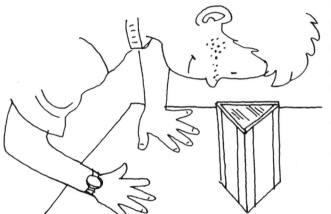

What You'll Need
- 3 rectangular mirrors
- masking tape
- cardboard
- pencil
- blunt scissors
- small pieces of colored paper, glitter, buttons, or other small, colorful objects

end. Drop small pieces of colored paper, glitter, buttons, and other objects inside. Then peek inside to see the colored patterns created and reflected in the mirrors. Gently shake the kaleidoscope to make new patterns!

Magnet Making

Magnetize an ordinary nail by rubbing it with a magnet.

What You'll Need
- iron or steel nail
- paper clip
- metal magnet

Try picking up a paper clip with an iron or steel nail. What happens? Now rub the nail with a magnet 50 to 100 times, always rubbing in the same direction. Try picking up the paper clip again. The atoms in the nail lined up in the same direction when you rubbed it with the magnet. This causes the nail to become magnetized, which means it will act like a magnet. Test your new magnet, and see what small objects it attracts. If you rub it more, does it become stronger? You can also magnetize a paper clip and test the comparative strength of the 2 magnets you have made.

Electro-Detecto

Make a device that detects electrical charges.

What You'll Need
- bottle
- cork
- nail
- ruler
- electrical wire
- aluminum foil
- blunt scissors

Find a bottle and a cork that will seal it. With a nail, make a small hole through the center of the cork from top to bottom. Remove the nail, and push a 6-inch piece of heavy electrical wire through the hole. Leave about 1 inch of wire above the top of the cork.

Bend the wire coming out from the bottom of the cork into a flat hook, shaped like the bottom of a coat hanger. Use the scissors to cut a piece of aluminum foil into a strip 1 inch long and ¼ inch wide. Fold the strip in half, and hang it on the flat hook. Put the hook and foil into the bottle, and seal the opening with the cork. Make sure the foil and the hook do not touch the sides or bottom of the jar. Roll up another piece of aluminum foil into a tight ball, about 1 inch in diameter, around the wire sticking out of the top of the cork. Make sure that the ball is smooth and tightly packed.

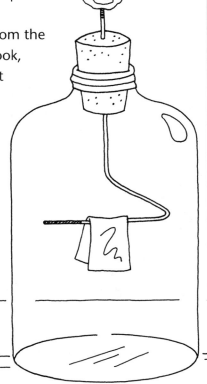

You have just built a functional electroscope that will tell you if an object carries a charge. If you hold an object with a charge near the foil ball, the object will draw the opposite charge through the wire from the foil strip. The 2 sides of the aluminum strip will then have the same charge and repel each other.

Rocking Candy!

◆▶◆▶◆▶◆

When liquids evaporate into gases, they can leave material behind.

What You'll Need

- pan
- water
- pot holder
- hot pad
- sugar
- measuring spoon
- mixing spoon
- string
- pencil
- glass
- blunt scissors
- button

Caution: This project requires adult help.

Have an adult help you bring a small pan of water to a boil on the stove. Turn off the heat, and move the pan to the table using a pot holder (have an adult do this for you). Place the pan on a hot pad. Add 1 tablespoon of sugar, and stir until it dissolves. Continue adding sugar, 1 tablespoon at a time, letting each tablespoonful dissolve completely before adding the next. When no more sugar will dissolve in the water, allow the saturated solution to cool (be sure it is in a safe place so it can't be bumped or spilled).

Tie a string to the middle of a pencil, and set the pencil across the rim of a glass. Cut the string so that it just touches the bottom of the glass. Tie a button onto the bottom of the string. Pour the cooled sugar water into the glass. Leave the pencil across the rim of the glass so that the string and button are in the solution. Allow it to sit in a warm place without being disturbed for several days so that the water evaporates. As the water evaporates, it will leave sugar crystals on the string. You can eat these crystals like rock candy.

Twig Collecting

Make a collection of twigs gathered from trees in winter.

What You'll Need
- tree identification book
- plant shears
- index cards
- tape
- pencil
- magnifying glass
- hole punch
- string or ribbon

Caution: This project requires adult help.

The twigs of each kind of tree have unique shapes and characteristics. You can collect an assortment of winter tree twigs, note the variety of characteristics, and compare and sort them. If you have a good twig or tree identification book, you can even identify the trees they came from using the pictures in the book. The best time for collecting twigs is in February or March, long after trees have lost their leaves but before they have begun to bud. (Get permission to do the following! You may need adult help!)

Carefully cut twigs from a variety of trees (1 twig from each tree), and tape them to index cards. Write down the color and texture of the twig (these may change as the twig dries; you can record differences later on, if you want). Also, write down the name of the tree if you know it. Study the different characteristics of the twig parts using the magnifying glass, and compare them. Twig parts include the terminal bud (called the "bud" on our diagram) that will become new growth; bud scales to protect new leaves or flowers; leaf scars that show where stems of old leaves were attached; bud scale scars that show where last year's buds were and how much the twig grew over the year; bundle scars that show where sap flowed to leaves; lenticels, the tiny holes or openings through which bark "breathes"; and the pith, the twig center. Make your own tree booklet: Use a hole punch to make 2 holes in the left side of each index card, and tie the cards together with string or ribbon.

Capturing Leaf Vapor

◆▸◆▸◆▸◆▸

Do leaves actually "breathe"? Check it out!

What You'll Need
- plastic sandwich bag
- small pebble
- twist tie
- measuring spoon

Capture and measure how much water vapor a leaf releases into the air in a week's time. Trees drink water through their roots and send it up to all parts of the tree. Leaves use the water they need and "breathe" out the excess in the form of water vapor. You can catch and measure the vapor using a plastic bag.

On a warm, sunny summer day, put a pebble in a plastic bag and place the plastic bag over a tree leaf that gets a lot of sun. Secure the bag over the leaf with a twist tie. After a few hours, return to observe the leaf. You will begin to see moisture collecting inside the bag. Leave the bag on the leaf for 1 week. After a week, take it off and carefully measure the water collected with a measuring spoon. This will tell you how much water vapor your leaf has produced in a week's time. (A small leaf will produce approximately ¼ teaspoon of water in a sunny week.)

Rain Gauge

◆▸◆▸◆▸◆▸

Measure, record, and chart daily, weekly, or monthly rainfall.

What You'll Need
- cylinder-shaped jar or square container with straight sides
- ruler
- permanent marker
- chart paper
- pencil

Compare your measurements to those recorded in the newspaper! Use a cylinder-shaped jar or a square container with straight sides for your gauge. (You can also use several containers of different sizes to test if the results will be the same in different places in your yard.) Measure and mark inch and half-inch marks on the side of the jar or container, measuring from the bottom up. Place the gauge outside in an open area. Check the rainfall in each 24-hour period. You can use separate gauges for daily, weekly, and monthly recordings. Empty the daily gauge after each recording, and set it back outside to measure the next day's rainfall. Chart your results.

Look-Alike Testing

Salt and sugar look alike, but how, besides taste, are they different?

What You'll Need
- waterproof table covering
- smock
- salt
- sugar
- measuring spoons
- frying pan
- spoon
- timer
- clear plastic cups
- water
- measuring cups
- food coloring
- ice cube tray

Caution: This project requires adult help.

You can perform several tests to find out how the molecules in these 2 look-alike substances act differently under different conditions. With adult supervision, you can perform a melting test. On your own you can do a dissolving test and a freezing test. Be sure to cover yourself and the work surface when doing these experiments.

Melting Test (ask an adult to help you): Place ½ teaspoon of salt on one side of a frying pan and ½ teaspoon of sugar on the other side. Tap down each pile with a spoon so it is flattened. Heat the pan slowly for 3 minutes. Then remove the pan from the heat. Watch and see what happens to the different piles.

Dissolving Test: Fill 2 plastic cups with ½ cup of water each. Add 2 teaspoons of salt to one cup and 2 teaspoons of sugar to the other cup. Add a different color of food coloring (1 drop) to each cup to distinguish the solutions from each other. Let the solutions stand for an hour, and then check for crystal formations. Crystals will form differently in each solution.

Freezing Test: Fill 2 plastic cups with ½ cup of water each. Add 2 teaspoons of salt to the first and 2 teaspoons of sugar to the other. Color each solution a different color with a drop of food coloring. Pour 1 solution into the cups at one end of an ice cube tray and the other solution into the cups at the other end. Place the tray in the freezer for 2 hours. Then check to see if there is a difference between how the substances reacted to the cold.

Waterwheel in Motion

◆▶◆▶◆▶◆▶

Make a miniature waterwheel, and put it to work under a water faucet.

What You'll Need
- empty plastic yogurt container
- blunt scissors
- modeling clay
- ruler
- pencil
- toothpick

Wash an empty plastic yogurt container. Make spokes for your waterwheel by cutting the sides of the yogurt container into 8 spokes. Then roll a lump of modeling clay into a ball about 2 inches across. Insert the spokes parallel to each other in a row around the ball of clay. Use the pencil to make a hole through the ball at a right angle to the row of spokes. Insert the toothpick through the hole. Turn on a water faucet in a sink, make sure the water is cold, and hold the waterwheel by the ends of the toothpick under the slow-moving running water. The stream of water will turn the wheel.

plastic spokes

clay ball

toothpick

Clean Living?

In Idaho Springs, Colorado, Charlie Tayler built a waterwheel in 1893 for gold mining. Mr. Tayler lived a long, healthy life, and he said it was because he never kissed women or took a bath!

Personal Shadow Clock

▷▷▷▷▷▷

Create a personal shadow clock, and tell time with your own shadow!

What You'll Need
• chalk, rocks, or sticks
• watch
• permanent marker

Find a sunny spot outside to make the clock. Choose a place for the center of your clock. If you are making your clock on a patio or concrete area, mark the center with chalk. If your clock will be on a lawn or dirt area, use a rock or insert a stick in the ground to mark the center. To make the hour markings, go outside every hour, on the hour, and stand on the center of your clock. Then make a mark on the ground where the tip of your shadow hits. (Have a friend or family member help you!) You can make the hour markings in the same way you marked the center, using a rock, chalk, or a stick inserted in the ground. But this time, you'll need to label the time, too! Write the hour number on concrete with chalk or use a permanent marker to write the hour on a rock or stick. After the clock is made, you can return to it at any time on another day, stand in the center, and determine the time of day by noting where the tip of your shadow lands.

The U.S. Timekeeper
The U.S. Naval Observatory, in Washington, D.C., is the official source of time for the Department of Defense and is the official timekeeper for the United States.

Balloon Rockets

◆>◆>◆>◆>◆

Your balloon engine takes your homemade rocket to new and exciting places.
Just hold the end, aim, let it go, and watch it fly.

What You'll Need
- markers
- lightweight paper
- clear tape
- long, thin pencil balloons
- blunt scissors
- ruler

Draw a design for your rocket on a piece of paper. With the design side facing out, bring the ends of the paper together to form a tube. Overlap the ends until the diameter of the tube is slightly larger than the diameter of a blown-up pencil balloon. Tape the ends to secure them.

Cut a piece of paper in half, horizontally. Using one half, bring the top ends together and overlap them to form a cone. Tape the ends to secure it. Trim the excess paper at the bottom of the cone. Tape the cone to the top of the rocket. Use the other half of the paper to make the rocket fins. Cut the paper in half, vertically. Cut a triangle from each half. Fold in the long side of 1 triangle about ¼ inch. Tape it to one side of the rocket. Repeat with the other triangle.

Blow up a pencil balloon. Do not tie the end in a knot. Hold the end closed, and place it inside the rocket tube. Let go of the end, and send your rocket to the moon. (Note: Be sure to throw away any discarded balloons when you're finished (they are a choking hazard), and please don't shoot your rocket into anyone's face.)

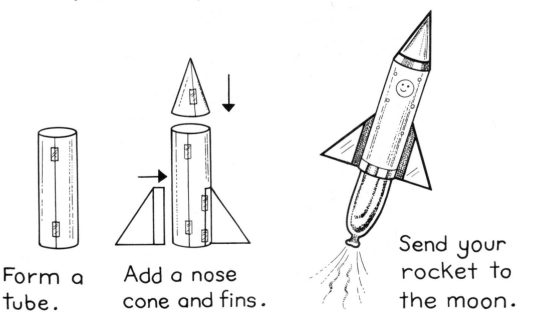

Form a tube.

Add a nose cone and fins.

Send your rocket to the moon.

 # Worm Condo

◄►◄►◄►◄►◄►

Worms are fascinating creatures. Watch them tunnel through the dirt, then return them to their natural environment after a few days!

What You'll Need
- 2 clear plastic containers (one slightly smaller than the other)
- soil
- worms
- screen or stocking
- rubber band

First, you'll need a clear plastic container. Place another container, an inch or so smaller in diameter, inside the larger container. You are creating a narrow enough space between the containers so you'll be able to see the worms tunnel.

Fill the space between the 2 containers with a good supply of fresh soil (not potting soil), and keep it moist (but not soaked). Put in some worms, then cover the container with a piece of screen or stocking for good airflow. Secure this cover with a rubber band.

Now watch the worms as they tunnel through the soil! (Be sure to keep this out of the hot sun and free the worms after a few days of observation.)

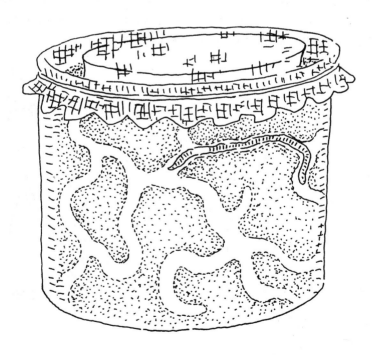

 # Helicopters

◆▷◆▷◆▷◆

This helicopter can help you figure out how propellers work.

What You'll Need
- 6-inch wood or plastic propellers (from hobby store)
- unsharpened pencil
- drill
- glue

Caution: This project requires adult help.

Buy a wood or plastic propeller at the hobby store. Have an adult help you drill out a hole in the center of the propeller until a pencil will just fit inside. It must be a tight fit. Push the pencil into the propeller. Make a little mark on the top of the propeller so you will know which end was up when you took your test flight. Now you're ready for the test. When the blades of the propeller turn they will either push down on the air, making the helicopter go up, or they will push up on the air, making the helicopter go down. Hold the pencil between your hands, and slide the palm of one hand quickly across the palm of the other to make the pencil and propeller turn. Let go. Did the helicopter go up or down? If it went down, pull the propeller off the pencil and turn it over. Try again. When you have the propeller on the correct way, glue it in place.

 # Expanding Hot Air

◆▷◆▷◆▷◆▷◆

Perform a balloon experiment to see hot air expand.

Stretch the end of a balloon over the top of a bottle. Carefully set the bottle in a pan of hot water. After a few minutes the heat will cause the air in the balloon to expand, making the balloon begin to blow up. This happens because the hot water heats up the air inside the bottle. This causes the air to expand, filling up more space inside the balloon. You can also cause a balloon to inflate slightly by making carbon dioxide gas. Put a cupful of water into an empty bottle. Add a spoonful of baking soda. Pour in a little bit of vinegar, and quickly put a balloon over the bottle top. You can tell carbon dioxide has been created when you see the balloon expand slightly. Make sure you do this experiment in a well-ventilated place!

What You'll Need
- balloon
- bottle
- pan
- hot water
- baking soda
- spoon
- vinegar

Testing Balance and Gravity

◄►◄►◄►◄►

Turn an experiment into a magic trick!

What You'll Need
- large index card
- pencil with an eraser
- blunt scissors
- markers
- paper clips
- string

Cut out a symmetrical (both sides the same) clown, and watch how symmetry can work with gravity to create balance.

To make a symmetrical clown, fold an index card in half and draw half of a clown on one side. The fold line in the middle of the card is the middle of the clown. Cut out the clown, and unfold the paper. Decorate. Attach a paper clip to each arm for weight. Try balancing the clown on the eraser tip of a pencil. Then try balancing the clown with just 1 paper clip on 1 arm, and see if there is a different effect. Can you figure out the reason for the different results? To balance your clown on a tightrope, tie a string between 2 chairs or 2 legs of a table. Cut a notch in the clown's hat, and set the notch on the taut string.

1.

2.

 # Anemometer

◆◆◆◆◆◆

Measure the wind's strength, and make a pretty outdoor decoration, too.

What You'll Need
- hole punch
- 39-ounce-size plastic coffee-can lid
- $\frac{3}{8}$-inch wood dowel
- blunt scissors
- plastic foam egg carton
- stapler and staples
- 12 strips of yarn, 6 inches each
- 2 pieces of electrical tape, 4 inches each
- 1-inch circle from foam food tray (from fruits and vegetables only)

Punch a hole in the center of the coffee-can lid. The hole should be large enough to fit the wood dowel. Cut out 4 cups from an empty egg carton. Staple the cups to the lid as shown in the illustration. Staple 3 pieces of yarn between each cup. Roll a piece of tape around the dowel about 3 inches from the end.

To make the washer, cut a hole in the center of the foam circle large enough to fit the dowel. Place the dowel through the center hole on the plastic lid. The lid should be just below the tape. Place the washer on the dowel under the plastic lid. Wrap another piece of tape around the dowel under the washer. Stick the dowel in the ground outside your house in a windy place and watch the anemometer turn.

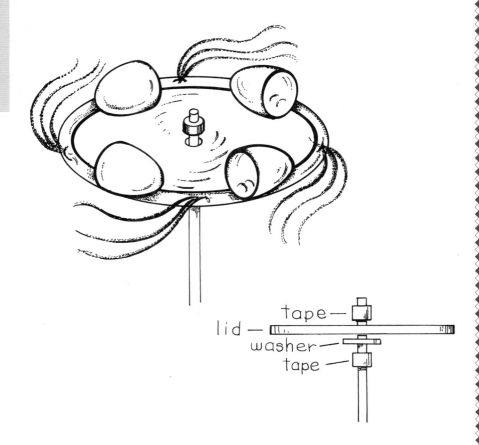

lid —
tape —
washer —
tape —

Full to the Rim

Discover how many pennies you can add to a full glass of water!

What You'll Need
- waterproof table covering
- glass
- water
- pennies
- sugar
- teaspoon
- straw

In this experiment, the surface tension of water will keep the water from overflowing, creating surprising results.

Cover the table. Fill the glass with water all the way to the rim. Make a guess of how many pennies you can add to the full glass. Then test by carefully inserting a penny slightly into the water and then letting it go so it gently drops into the glass. Observe the top of the glass from the side so you can see the water level rising above the glass! Keep adding pennies until the water begins to overflow. The experiment can also be performed using sugar instead of pennies. Fill the glass to the top with water, and then add a teaspoon of sugar. Gently stir the water with a straw to dissolve the sugar. After the sugar is dissolved, add a second spoonful of sugar and stir, then a third, and a fourth! Perform the sugar experiment twice, first with cold water and then with hot, and compare the results.

Water Strider

The water strider is an insect that uses the surface tension of water to its advantage. When it hunts for prey, it runs along the water's surface.

Periscope

Turn an empty waxed paper box into a spy tool for looking around corners, over walls, and out of windows.

What You'll Need
- empty waxed paper box
- blunt scissors
- masking tape
- 2 small mirrors (about 2×3 inches)

Caution: This project requires adult help.

Ask an adult to cut off the cutting edge of the box. Tape the box closed with masking tape. Cut out a small square on the top end of one side of the box. Cut another small square out at the bottom end of the opposite side of the box. On a third side (a side between the 2 sides with the cutout holes) cut a diagonal slit at each end of the box. Cut each slit so that the bottom of the slit is level with the bottom edge of one of the cutout squares, and the top of the slit is level with the top edge of the cutout square. The bottom slit's bottom should be close to the cutout hole and slant away from the hole. The top slit should slant in the same direction as the bottom one. Cut identical slits on the opposite side of the box. Each slit should be a little bit wider than the mirror width so the mirrors will fit in the slits. Slide a mirror into each slit. If the mirrors are 1-sided, slide them in so the reflective sides face the holes. Secure the mirrors in place with tape. Hold the periscope upright, and look into the hole at the bottom. You'll see what's caught in the reflection from the top hole!

Up Periscope!

A submarine has two periscopes: an attack periscope and a search periscope. The search periscope is used to look for targets and also for guidance as the sub navigates through the water. The attack periscope is smaller than the search periscope and is used if a sub is ready to attack—hence its name.

# Sound Wave Model

Use this model to find out how sounds move through the air.

What You'll Need
- thread
- blunt scissors
- ruler
- 6 metal ball bearings
- tape
- clothes hanger
- shower-curtain rod

Cut 6 pieces of thread, each 10 inches long, and attach an end of each thread to a ball bearing using tape. Tie the other end of each thread to the horizontal piece of a clothes hanger, leaving about 1 inch between each thread that you tie.

Hang the hook of the clothes hanger from a shower-curtain rod. Pull back one of the end bearings. Let the bearing go so that it strikes the next one. Watch what happens. It hits the second, which swings and hits the third, and so on.

Sound travels through the air in the same way. A vibration causes 1 molecule of air to move and bump into another molecule, which then moves at the same rate and bumps into a third molecule, and so on.

Choose a Compass

◆◆◆◆◆◆

Make a compass, and you'll always know in what direction you're headed. You can make either a floating compass or a Chinese hanging compass—or both!

What You'll Need
- 1 or 2 needles
- magnet
- pin
- cork
- blunt scissors
- 2 clear plastic cups
- water
- thread
- pencil

Rub the pointed end of the needle along a side of the magnet, always rubbing in the same direction. Do this about 30 times to magnetize the needle. You can test it by picking up a pin with it. If you will be making both compasses, repeat the process with the other needle.

Floating Compass: Cut a small piece of cork, and push the magnetized needle through it. Fill a plastic cup with water. Carefully place the cork with the magnetized needle into the cup so it floats in the center. The magnetized end will face north.

Chinese Hanging Compass: Tie an end of a short piece of thread to the center of the magnetized needle, and tie the other end of the thread to a pencil. Place the pencil over the rim of the plastic cup. Again, the magnetized end of the needle will point north.

floating compass

chinese hanging compass

Fossil Imprints

◆▶◆▶◆▶

Learn about fossils by making a few of your own.

What You'll Need

- 2 cups flour
- ½ cup salt
- ¾ cup water
- mixing bowl
- mixing spoon
- measuring cups
- objects for fossil making (leaves, shells, twigs, or boiled and washed chicken leg bones)
- rack

Measure and mix together the flour, salt, and water to make a salt dough. Knead the dough for 5 minutes, and form it into small balls. Flatten the balls to prepare them for a fossil print. Make impressions in the dough with different objects. Make 1 print in each flattened ball. Place the fossils on a rack, and let them dry for several days.

 # Balancing Act Mobile

◆▶◆▶◆▶

Notice that one heavy and one light object can still balance, depending on where you position the items.

Cut the following pieces of yarn: one 15-inch, one 9-inch, five 5-inch, and one 4-inch. Tie one end of the 15-inch piece of yarn to the center of the 12-inch dowel to hang the mobile. Tie one end of the 9-inch yarn piece to the center of a 6-inch dowel. Tie the other end of the yarn piece to one end of the 12-inch dowel. Tie one end of a 5-inch yarn piece to the center of the remaining 6-inch dowel. Tie the other end of the yarn to the other end of the 12-inch dowel. Tie the 4-inch yarn piece to the center of the 12-inch dowel. Tie the remaining 5-inch yarn pieces to the 6-inch dowels. Tie natural items, such as shells, bark, and rocks on the yarn ends to balance the mobile.

What You'll Need

- 1½ yards of yarn
- blunt scissors
- ruler
- wood dowel, 12 inches long, ¼ inch diameter
- 2 wood dowels, 6 inches long, ¼ inch diameter
- shells, bark, and rocks

Indoor Rain

***

Perform an experiment to observe how rain is produced when warm, moist air rises up and hits the colder air above it.

What You'll Need
- jar with lid
- hot water
- ice cubes

Put a small amount of hot tap water in the jar. Place the lid upside down on top of the jar. Put several ice cubes on top of the lid. You will be able to observe moisture forming on the lid top inside the jar, and you'll see the moisture drip down like rain. Warm air can hold more moisture than cold air. When warm air in the sky hits cold air higher up, it condenses, turns into water vapor, and rains!

Clay Boats

***

Mold and model clay to find what shape floats best.

Fill a bucket (or even a large bowl) with water. Cover the table with a plastic table covering. Then take a lump of modeling clay, and experiment! Try shaping the clay into different kinds of boats until you find shapes that will float successfully. Once you have figured out what kind of clay shape will float in water, experiment further by testing how many pennies, paper clips, or marbles your boats can carry without sinking. Make an estimate before testing. Then keep adding a penny or paper clip until you've sunk your boats!

What You'll Need
- bucket or large bowl
- water
- plastic table covering
- modeling clay
- paper clips, pennies, or marbles

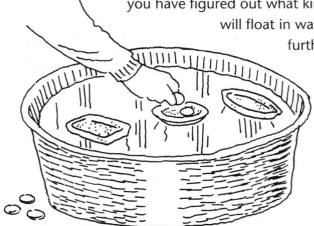

Water on the Move

Explore the capillary action of water.

What You'll Need
- celery
- glasses
- water
- food coloring
- white carnation
- blunt scissors
- string
- small bowls
- paper towel

To watch water move through plant material, stand a stalk of celery in a glass of water that has been colored with food coloring (see illustration 1). You will be able to see the water traveling up the celery as the celery stalk changes color.

If you can get a white carnation, you can create a more dramatic demonstration (see illustration 2). Snip the stem of the white carnation to divide it in 2. Set each stem section in a separate glass of water that has been colored with a different color of food coloring. The colored water will travel up the halves of the carnation stem and mix at the top in the flower.

To watch water make its way through a piece of string (see illustration 3), fill 4 bowls with water and add a different color of food coloring to each bowl. Cut a piece of string, and dip the end of the string into 1 bowl. Then drape the string over the edge of the bowl and over the next bowl so that it dips slightly into the water in that bowl. Continue until the string touches the water in each bowl. Soon you will observe the colored water creeping along the string out of the bowls.

For another experiment to give you more experience with capillary action (see illustration 4), fill a glass with water and set it beside an empty bowl. Twist a paper towel around and around to form a wick. Set one end in the full glass of water and the other end in the empty bowl. The water will travel up the towel wick and then drip into the bowl.

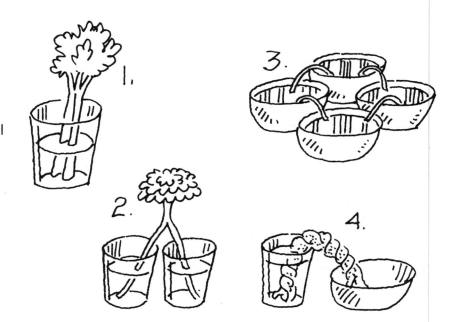

Ocean in a Bottle

◆▸▸▸▸▸▸▸

Try a test on oil and water, then turn your experiment into a decorative display.

What You'll Need
- funnel
- clear soda bottle with a lid
- water
- cooking oil
- measuring cup
- blue food coloring
- glitter

Using a funnel, pour ½ cup of water and ½ cup of oil into a soda bottle. Put the lid on tightly, and shake the bottle vigorously to mix the substances. After shaking, put the bottle down and let it sit for a few minutes. What happens to the oil and water after you mix them? To turn your experiment into an ocean display, remove the top and add enough

water to fill the bottle ⅔ full. Add a few drops of food coloring and some glitter, and shake the bottle gently to mix in the color. Then fill the rest of the bottle almost to the top with oil. Put the top back on tightly, and gently tilt the bottle back and forth to create an ocean wave effect.

Frozen Bubbles

◆▸▸▸▸▸▸▸

Blow a soap bubble, then turn it into a delicate, frozen orb.

This is an activity for a cold, cold (below-freezing) day when there is no wind in the air. Start by making a strong bubble solution. Mix the soap powder, sugar, and hot water. (This mixture will help the bubbles last longer.) Take the bubble solution and a bubble wand outside. Blow a bubble, and catch it on the wand. Let the bubble sit resting on the wand in the cold air. In the below-freezing chill, the bubble will soon freeze into a fragile crystal ball.

What You'll Need
- ½ cup soap powder
- ½ cup sugar
- 3 cups hot water
- mixing bowl
- mixing spoon or whisk
- bubble wand

 # Discover Hidden Leaf Colors

◆▷◆▷◆▷◆

Preview fall colors in a spring or summer leaf.

What You'll Need
- green leaves
- plastic bowl
- sand
- measuring spoon
- rubbing alcohol
- rock
- glass jar
- paper
- paper clip

Caution: This project requires adult supervision.

The reds, yellows, and oranges seen in fall leaves are always there, but they are hidden during the year by the greater amounts of green pigment in the leaf. You can perform an experiment to separate the colors in a leaf so you can see some of the hidden colors. Gather some green leaves. Put a few tablespoons of sand in a plastic bowl, and add the leaves. With adult supervision, add enough rubbing alcohol to cover the leaves. Crush them into little pieces using a rock. (Be sure to wash your hands after touching the rubbing alcohol, and keep alcohol away from younger children in the house.) Crushing the leaves in the rubbing alcohol will pull the pigment out of them and turn the alcohol green. Carefully pour the green alcohol out of the bowl and into a glass jar. (Discard the sand.) Now roll a piece of paper into a cylinder, and clip the ends together with a paper clip. Place the paper cylinder in the jar of alcohol, and leave it overnight (keep it away from any flame). The leaf pigments will creep up the paper. The pigments climb at different speeds, causing the different colors to separate from each other. In the morning, when you check the paper, you will be able to see the colors that were hidden in the leaf on the paper cylinder.

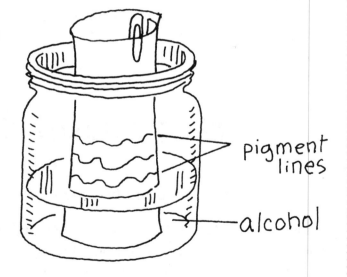

pigment lines

alcohol

Comparative Parachuting

◆◆◆◆◆◆◆

Make parachutes from different materials, and observe how air pressure helps them float!

What You'll Need
• paper grocery bag
• blunt scissors
• string
• tape
• washer

Paper-Bag Parachute: Cut a large square out of one side of a paper grocery bag. Cut the corners off the square to make it into an 8-sided shape. Cut 4 long pieces of string, and fold them in half. Tape the ends of each piece to one of the 4 original square sides to form a loop. Tie the loop ends of the 4 strings together, and then tie them to a washer.

Fabric Parachute: Cut 4 pieces of string, and tie 1 to each corner of a handkerchief. Tie the ends of the strings to a washer or weight.

You can also experiment with making parachutes out of other materials and comparing the results. Make parachutes from plastic garbage bags, paper towels, or burlap fabric. Experiment using different weights, such as nuts, bolts, clothespins, and pieces of wood. Drop your parachutes from different heights, and watch them float. Try dropping a parachute from the top of a staircase to see what happens. Try folding up a cloth parachute and throwing it up in the air to see if it floats down. Compare your results with different materials, weights, and heights.

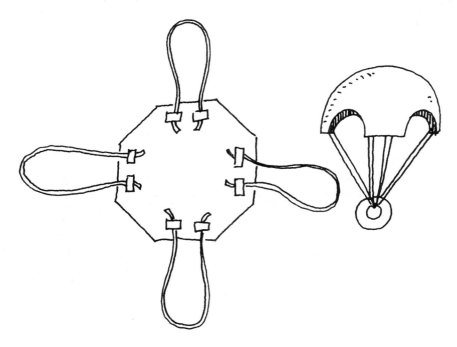

Flower Press

◄►◄►◄►◄►

With your flower press you can preserve the beauty of the season and its lovely flowers.

What You'll Need

- 2 squares of thin plywood, 12 inches each
- C-clamp
- power drill
- ¼-inch drill bit
- sandpaper
- blunt scissors
- 4 squares of cardboard, 10 inches each
- 6 squares of construction paper, 10 inches each
- assorted flowers
- 4 bolts, 2×¼ inches each
- 4 wing nuts

Caution: This project requires adult help.

Clamp the pieces of plywood together. Have an adult drill a ¼-inch hole in each corner all the way through both boards. Unclamp the plywood pieces, and sand the edges. Cut the corners off each square of cardboard and construction paper. Place a cardboard square on top of a plywood piece and a square of construction paper on top of the cardboard. Arrange your flowers on top of the construction paper. Place a second square of construction paper on top of the flowers, then add another cardboard square. Continue with additional layers of materials following the same order.

After all the layers are arranged, place the second piece of plywood on top of everything. Insert the bolts in each hole, and tighten down the wing nuts. Put your flower press in a warm, dry place for at least 6 months. The longer the flowers are allowed to dry, the less likely their color is to fade when you use them in a design.

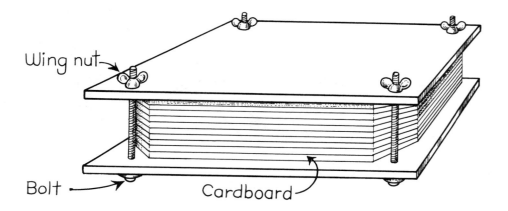

Wing nut

Bolt

Cardboard

# Wind Whirl

◆►◆►◆►◆►

*This simple wind whirl, when placed over a hot lamp,
shows how heat affects the air.*

Caution: This project requires adult help.

Draw a large spiral, like the one shown here, on a sheet of stiff
paper. Following the line on the spiral, cut along it with scissors.
Punch a hole through the center of the spiral. Thread a piece of
string through the hole in the center of the spiral, and tie the string
to the spiral's end.

You will need an adult's help with this part of the project—do
not attempt this without supervision! Holding the string with one
hand, hang the spiral over a hot lamp. Keep the end of the paper at least 2 to 3 inches away
from the lamp.

What happens to the spiral, and why? The heat from the lamp warms the air, and the
heated air moves upward. This rising air causes the spiral to move.

Water Scale

◆▸◆▸◆▸◆

Measure an object's volume using water.

What You'll Need
- large bowl
- baking pan
- water
- assorted items (apple, rock, etc.)
- clear measuring cup

Place a large bowl in a baking pan, and fill the bowl to the rim with water. Gently drop an apple, a rock, or another item inside the bowl. The water will overflow into the baking pan to make room for the object dropped into it. Now, care-  fully remove the bowl from the pan and pour the displaced water into a clear measuring cup. The amount of water tells you the volume of the object. Use the information to compare the volume of different objects.

Spin a Color Wheel White

◆▸◆▸◆▸◆

Spin a color wheel, and watch it turn white!

What You'll Need
- white poster board or paper plate
- blunt scissors
- protractor
- pencil
- paint
- paintbrush

Cut a circle out of white poster board (or use a white paper plate). Using the protractor, measure and mark 7 even, pie-shaped sections on the circle. Paint each section with one of the 7 colors of the rainbow. The colors must be in the order in which they appear in the rainbow (violet, indigo, blue, green, yellow, orange, red). When the wheel is dry, punch a pencil through the middle to make a spinner. Spin the wheel, and watch what happens. If you spin the wheel fast enough, the 7 colors blend and appear as white.

 # Pinhole Camera

◆━◆━◆━◆━◆

Unfortunately, this camera can't really take pictures. But you will learn something about how the human eye works.

What You'll Need
- clean, empty coffee can with plastic lid
- nail
- hammer
- scissors
- waxed paper
- ruler
- towel

Caution: This project requires adult help.

Make a pinhole camera, and view an image inside the camera reversed in the same way an image appears reversed on the retina of the eye.

To make the camera, have an adult help you hammer the nail through the middle of the coffee can's bottom. Remove the nail. Cut the center out of the plastic coffee-can lid. Cut a piece of waxed paper, approximately 8×8 inches, and place it over the open end of the can. Secure the waxed paper in place by putting the lid back on top of the can. Cover your head and the bottom (with the nail hole) of the camera with a towel, and look through the waxed paper end of the camera at an object. The object will appear upside down.

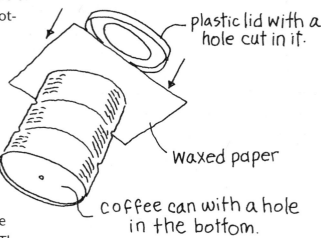

plastic lid with a hole cut in it.

Waxed paper

coffee can with a hole in the bottom.

A Young Photographer

Ansel Adams, one of America's most famous photographers, knew at age 14 that he wanted to be a photographer. He convinced his parents to take him to Yosemite National Park in the summer of 1916, and he began taking pictures. For the rest of his life, he returned to the park at least once a year to take pictures.

Find Earth's Poles

Make your own compass, and observe the magnetic pull of the poles.

What You'll Need
- modeling clay
- pencil
- horseshoe magnet
- needle
- waxed paper
- blunt scissors
- bowl
- water

Roll out a lump of modeling clay to form a firm base for a compass stand. Set the eraser end of a pencil in the base so the pencil is standing upright with the point up. Balance a horseshoe magnet on the tip of the pencil. Once balanced, the magnet will align itself on a north-south line. This happens because the earth itself acts as a huge magnet with lines of force running between the north and south poles. The compass automatically aligns itself with these invisible magnetic lines. You can also make a compass using a needle, a magnet, and a piece of waxed paper. Rub one end of the needle on the positive side of the magnet and one end on the negative side (run the needle in 1 direction only—not back and forth). Then cut a small piece of waxed paper, and stick the needle through the paper. Gently place the waxed paper in a bowl of water so it floats, and give it a spin. When the paper stops spinning, the needle will be lined up on a north-south line.

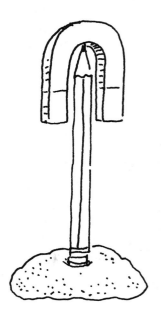

waxed paper

needle

 Blubber Bag

<>━━━━━<>

Find out how seals and whales stay warm, even in very cold water!

What You'll Need
- bucket
- ice
- water
- 2 large plastic bags
- vegetable shortening
- paper towels

Do this experiment with a friend for extra fun. Fill a bucket with ice and water. Let the water get very cold.

Be sure there are no holes in the plastic bags. Fill 1 bag about half full with vegetable shortening. Have your friend slip the second bag over his or her hand, like a glove, and put the gloved hand into the shortening-filled bag. Your friend should mush the shortening around until it surrounds the hand. Now plunge your bare hand into the bucket of ice water, and hold it there for 20 to 30 seconds. Is it cold? Your friend should plunge his or her blubber glove into the ice water. How long can your friend keep his or her gloved hand in the water without getting cold? Why do you think the gloved hand stayed as warm and comfortable as a seal in the winter?

Now take your turn with the blubber bag, and see for yourself what a difference the "blubber" makes. (Be sure to wipe all of the shortening from your hands onto paper towels when you have finished the experiment.)

Create Crystal Creatures

Dip decorations and paper sculptures in a crystal solution, and watch your work crystallize overnight!

What You'll Need
- waterproof table covering
- water
- measuring cup
- saucepan
- sugar
- plastic cups
- chenille stems
- string
- blunt scissors
- pencils
- paper towels
- food coloring (optional)
- Epsom salts
- alum
- spoon
- index cards
- permanent markers
- pie pan

Caution: This project requires adult help.

Have an adult help you throughout this activity. Cover your work surface. Heat a cup of water until it begins to steam. Remove it from the heat, and stir in 2 cups of sugar. Then pour the solution into plastic cups. Mold chenille stems into decorative shapes (star, heart, cat, initials). Tie one end of a piece of string to a chenille-stem shape and the other end around a pencil. Let the shape sit in the solution by balancing the pencil on the rim of the cup. Leave it overnight, and then remove it from the solution and let it dry on a paper towel. When dry, the decorations will be covered with shiny crystals. They can be hung in a window, from a shelf, or anywhere! For larger crystals, allow the chenille stem to soak for a longer time in the solution. For colorful crystals, add food coloring to the crystal solution.

Create crystals of a different texture by using different materials. Follow the same recipe, replacing the sugar with Epsom salts (wash your hands after touching Epsom salts). Or try adding alum (available at the drugstore) to hot water for a different crystal solution: Ask an adult to heat a cup of water until it steams, pour it into a cup, and stir in alum spoonful by spoonful until no more will dissolve. Then suspend the chenille-stem shape in the solution. To make a crystal sculpture, fold an index card in half. Draw an animal, person, creature, or shape on the card using the edges of the card as the bottom. Cut out the shape. Pour one of the crystal solutions into a pie pan. Stand the paper shape in the solution, leave it for several days, and watch the crystals grow to cover it!

pencil

sugar water

pipe cleaner

# Fingerprint Fun

Have fun uncovering fingerprints with this easy-to-make fingerprint kit!

Collect all your family members to play this fingerprint game. Have everyone gather in another room where you can't see them. Before they go, give them a jar of cold cream and 1 white envelope. Tell them that only 1 person should rub cold cream into his or her hands and then hold the envelope. They shouldn't tell you who does it, but you'll be able to tell by matching the fingerprints.

To Solve the Mystery: Before starting the game, you need to create a fingerprint file for each member of the family. First, write each person's name on a separate index card, and draw two 1-inch squares for the fingerprints. Rub the point of a No. 2 pencil on a separate piece of paper until you have a solid 1-inch square. Roll each person's left thumb on the square to coat it with graphite, then press it down on the sticky side of a piece of tape. Gently lift off the tape, and press it onto one of the squares on the file card. Repeat this procedure for the right-hand thumb. Be sure everyone washes their hands after being fingerprinted.

What You'll Need
- cold cream
- white envelope
- no. 2 pencils
- index cards
- ruler
- paper
- clear tape
- emery board
- small dish
- soft bristle paint-brush
- dictionary
- magnifying glass (optional)

To Dust for Prints: In a small dish, make some graphite powder by rubbing a pencil point against an emery board. Dip your paint-brush into the powder, and gently brush the entire surface of the envelope to expose the hidden prints. They will appear like magic.

To Match the Prints: Examine the prints on the envelope for arches, loops, and whorls (look in the dictionary under "fingerprint" for more information). Are there any broken lines in the ridges? Compare the dusted prints (which are backward) with the fingerprint file cards. Use a magnifying glass if you need to. This should tell you who touched the envelope.

Secret Message Making

◆▷▷▷▷◁◁◁◆

Write an invisible message, and then amaze your friends by making it appear.

Caution: This project requires adult help.

Invisible messages can be written using several different kinds of substances. You can experiment with different "secret inks." Try writing messages with lemon juice, grapefruit juice, milk, or baking powder.

Write your message on a piece of paper using a paintbrush or a cotton swab. Write carefully because you won't be able to see the message while you're writing it! To make the message appear, have an adult help you place the message paper between 2 sheets of scrap paper on an ironing board, and then iron the papers with a warm iron. Your message will appear as if by magic—but it is really a chemical reaction that happens quickly because of the heat of the iron.

What You'll Need
- lemon juice, grapefruit juice, milk, or baking powder
- paper
- paintbrush or cotton swab
- scrap paper
- iron and ironing board

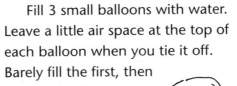

The Big Freeze

◆▷▷▷▷◁◁◁◆

Chill out to find what's what when it comes to things that freeze.

What You'll Need
- small balloons
- water
- freezer
- ruler or tape measure
- paper
- pen or pencil

Have you ever slipped a full plastic drink bottle in the freezer at bedtime, only to find it cracked at the crack of dawn? It's a fact of physics—frozen things expand. To find out how much, try this chilly challenge.

Fill 3 small balloons with water. Leave a little air space at the top of each balloon when you tie it off. Barely fill the first, then

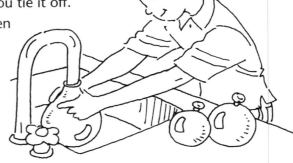

tie it. Double the water in the second balloon, and tie it. Triple the water of the first in the third balloon, and tie it. Measure the water balloons, and record the measurements on paper. Put all 3 in the freezer overnight. Measure the balloons again after they are frozen. Compare the results.

Jiggly Gelatin Lenses

Make these Jiggly Gelatin Lenses, and find out how eyeglass lenses work.

What You'll Need
- water
- saucepan
- pot holder
- hot pad
- small mixing bowl
- package of lemon, pineapple, or other light-colored gelatin
- measuring cup
- mixing spoon
- variety of rounded containers (ladles, ice-cream scoops, wine glasses, round-bottomed bowls, round-bowl measuring spoons)
- tray
- clear plastic wrap
- knife (optional)
- newspaper

Caution: This project requires adult help.

Have an adult heat the water in a saucepan until it boils and then, using the pot holder, measure out 1 cup. Pour the gelatin into a mixing bowl, and carefully add the cup of boiling water. Stir until all the gelatin dissolves. Choose a variety of containers to pour the gelatin into; use containers with round, smooth bottoms to give the lenses smooth, curved surfaces. Set the containers on a tray, and fill them with the gelatin mixture. Put the tray into the refrigerator, and chill the gelatin for at least 4 hours or until fully set.

When the gelatin is set, run hot tap water over the outside of the containers, and if necessary, coax the gelatin out with the tip of a warm, wet knife.

Place the plastic wrap over a sheet of newspaper. Moisten the top side of the plastic wrap (to avoid sticking), and place the lenses on the wrap. Be sure the flat side is down. Slide the plastic wrap slowly over the paper while looking through a lens. Try all the lenses on the same word, then look at some pictures. Which lenses make the words look bigger? Which

make them look wiggly? Why do different lenses make the same thing look different?

If you'd like to do some more exploring about lenses, check out some books from your school or local library.

# So Much Pressure!

Make a water barometer that will show you changes in air pressure.

What You'll Need

- 2 rulers
- modeling clay
- bowl
- water
- narrow, clear plastic bottle
- string
- blunt scissors
- paper
- permanent marker
- tape

Stick a ruler into a lump of modeling clay, and put the clay and ruler in the bottom of a bowl. (The ruler should be upright.) Pour about 3 inches of water into the bowl.

Get a narrow, clear plastic bottle. Fill it about ¾ full of water. Cover the top of the bottle with your hand, turn it upside down, and put it into the bowl next to the ruler. Once the bottle top is underwater and close to touching the bowl's bottom, you can take your hand away. With the bottle upside down, tie the ruler to the bottle with string.

Cut a strip of paper 4 inches long. Make a scale on it by making a mark every ¼ inch. Halfway down the strip (at 2 inches), make a longer line to show the halfway mark. Tape this strip of paper to the bottle with the halfway mark at the same level as the water in the bottle. The water level in the bowl should be below the paper.

You have made a water barometer. As the air pressure in the room increases, it will push down on the water in the bowl, forcing water into the bottle. You can see that the air pressure is high. If the air pressure is low, the bowl's water will rise, the bottle's water will sink, and you'll get a low pressure reading.

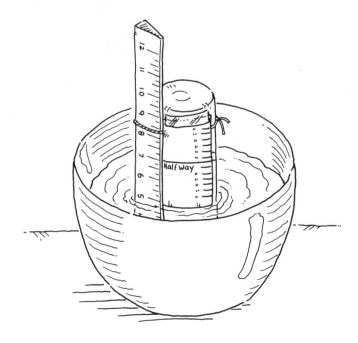

Scientific Sifter

Archaeologists and other scientists often sift through sand, dirt, and other materials to find small artifacts and treasures. Make your own scientific sifter to find treasures.

What You'll Need
- mesh onion or potato bag
- blunt scissors
- cardboard
- ruler
- stapler and staples
- packing tape
- magnifying glass (optional)
- notebook (optional)
- pencil (optional)
- reference books (optional)

Cut the metal clips off an onion or a potato bag, then cut the bag so you have a flat piece of mesh. Cut 2 rectangles the size of the mesh out of cardboard. Cut a matching hole in each piece of cardboard that is at least 2 inches smaller than the size of the mesh. Using one piece of cardboard, stretch the mesh over the hole and staple it in place. Take the second piece of cardboard and lay it on top (over the staples). (If you'd like to make an extra-fine sifter, use 2 or 3 pieces of mesh.) Tape the cardboard pieces together at the outside edges with packing tape.

Now it's time to go outside to explore! Sift through some dirt in your backyard, some sand at the beach, or some soil in the garden. (Of course, you need to ask permission before digging or sifting!) How many treasures can you come up with? Did you find living creatures (be sure to put them back after examining them), interesting rocks, shells?

If you want, examine your findings with a magnifying glass, and draw them in your notebook. Then you can sort, classify, and identify your treasures by comparing your drawings with pictures from reference books.

Remember: Mom will appreciate that you bring only pictures of your treasures into the house!

Gyrocopter

This paper gyrocopter is just the thing to enjoy outside on a warm spring day—or anytime it's not too windy or cold.

What You'll Need
- paper
- ruler
- blunt scissors or pinking shears
- paper clip

A "gyre" is a circular motion, so that means a gyrocopter spins when it flys. To explore gyre motion, make your own gyrocopter.

Cut out a 6½×1½-inch strip of paper. (Note: Using pinking shears will make the gyrocopter fly better, but ordinary scissors will work well too.) Starting at the top, cut a 3-inch slit down the middle of the strip to create a pair of wings. Fold the wings in opposite directions (see the diagram below). Attach a paper clip to the bottom of the strip for additional weight.

Drop the finished gyrocopter from an elevated spot, and watch it spin to the ground.

Now try experimenting. Make larger and smaller gyrocopters to see if size makes a difference when they fly. Think up other experiments you can try (for instance, make the wings longer or add 2 paper clips to the bottom).

Have gyrocopter races with friends who have made their own 'copters!

Dirt Discovery

◆◆◆◆◆

There's more to dirt than you think! Find out what it's made of.

What You'll Need
- waterproof table covering
- jar with lid
- dirt
- pitcher of water
- plastic spoon
- paper towels
- magnifying glass
- markers
- paper

Cover your work surface. Fill a jar halfway with dirt. Add water nearly to the top of the jar. Put the lid on, and tighten it securely. Shake the jar vigorously for a half a minute, and then set it down. Let the jar stand until the dirt and water settle. The soil will settle into layers. Observe the layers in the jar, and see what you can tell about them. How many layers are there? Which layer is made of the biggest particles? Which is made of the smallest? Can you guess why? To further examine the different layers and what they are made of, you can sort out the soil materials and examine them. Use a spoon to skim off the objects floating in the water. Place them on a paper towel. Then carefully pour off the water on the

top and scoop out the grains of the next level onto another paper towel. Do the same if there is another level. After each layer has been placed onto towels, they can be examined with the magnifying glass. What else can you tell about the different layers after further examination? You can also do this experiment with dirt you have collected from different areas and compare your findings. Draw pictures of each jar full of soil after you have shaken it and the dirt has settled to make picture comparisons.

Magazine Page Envelopes

◆◆◆◆◆

How can you help save trees? Reuse and recycle the paper you already have!

A good way to recycle is to make your own envelopes out of magazine pages. Pick a page with a pretty picture on it. Fold ⅓ of the page over, and tape up the sides. Fold the last part of the page down to make the flap. When you put your letter inside, seal the flap with a piece of tape. Use an address label on the front so the postal carrier can read the address!

What You'll Need
- magazine pages
- tape
- address labels

Reflective Experimenting

Mirrors and light are fascinating—reflect on them and experiment!

What You'll Need
- cardboard
- blunt scissors
- ruler
- comb
- tape
- flashlight
- mirror
- paper
- pencil
- 2 small rectangular mirrors
- small object

Perform several experiments to explore mirrors and the reflections they can produce.

Experiment 1: Cut a 1-inch hole in a piece of cardboard. Tape a comb over the hole. In a darkened room, hold the cardboard upright and set the flashlight behind it so it shines through the hole. Hold a mirror in front of the hole to capture the reflection. Turn the mirror to investigate how it reflects light at exactly the same angle it hits the mirror.

Experiment 2: Write something backward on a piece of paper. Hold the paper in front of a mirror; your backward message will read forward in the mirror!

Experiment 3: Tape 2 small mirrors together on one side to form a right angle. Set the mirrors on their sides, and place a small object between them. You will be able to see many sides of the object in the mirrors. Move the mirrors closer together and farther apart, and observe what happens to the images. You can also try placing the mirrors (untaped) facing each other with the object between them in order to see an endless reflection.

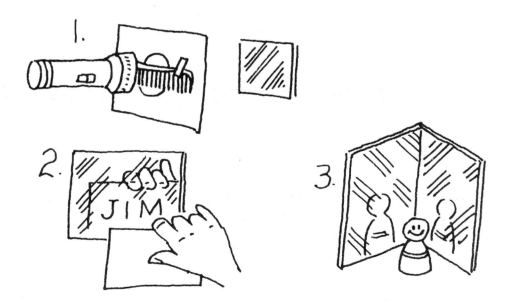

 # Astrolabe

Learn how to measure the position of stars with this simple instrument.

When scientists describe the position of a star in the sky, they measure its position relative to the horizon. An instrument called an astrolabe measures how high above the horizon the star is in degrees. Here's how to make your own astrolabe.

Tie a 12-inch piece of string to the hole in the middle of the crossbar on a protractor. Tie a weight to the other end of the string. Hold the protractor so that the curved part is down and the zero degree mark is closest to you. Sit on the ground, and look along the flat edge of the protractor with your eye at the zero mark. Point the flat edge at the star whose position you want to measure. Once you have the star at the end of your sight, hold the string against the side of the protractor.

Note the degree mark the string touches. Write this down in your notebook. This number tells you how many degrees above the horizon your star is.

Take readings for several stars. Return every 30 minutes, and take new readings. Notice the pattern of the stars as they appear to move across the sky as the earth turns.

What You'll Need
- string
- ruler
- plastic protractor
- weight (washer, rock, or fishing weight)
- pen
- notebook
- flashlight (to see what you're writing)

Liquid Density Test

◀▶▶▶▶▶▶

Do all objects of the same size have the same density? Find out!

What You'll Need
- clear plastic cup or glass jar
- corn syrup
- salad oil
- water
- small objects (paper clips, buttons, macaroni, etc.)

Use the density of liquids to test the density of small objects. Fill a clear cup or jar a third full with corn syrup. Fill the next third of the jar with salad oil. Then add water to fill the top third. Drop small objects into the jar, and observe on what level they stop and float. Objects will float at different levels depending upon their density in relation to the density of the different liquids. If the density of an object is greater than a liquid's density, it will sink

through that liquid. If an object's density is less than a liquid's density, it will float on that liquid. After experimenting a little, choose some new objects to test and try predicting the level on which they will float or sink before dropping them into the jar!

Pipe Cleaner Backbone

◀▶▶▶▶▶▶

Use sculpture to learn that some animals have backbones that run through the center of their bodies, just like humans!

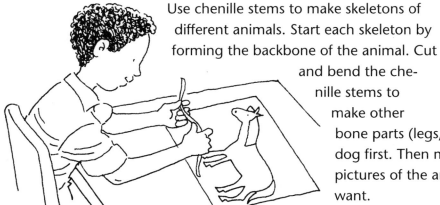

Use chenille stems to make skeletons of different animals. Start each skeleton by forming the backbone of the animal. Cut and bend the chenille stems to make other bone parts (legs, heads, tails). Try to make a

What You'll Need
- chenille stems
- blunt scissors
- pictures of various animals (optional)

dog first. Then make other creatures. Use pictures of the animals as a guide if you want.

Bark Casting

Record and compare the bark patterns of different trees.

What You'll Need
- modeling clay
- rolling pin
- self-hardening clay

To make a tree bark impression, roll out a piece of modeling clay into a flat sheet. Press the clay onto a tree trunk hard enough for the bark to create an impression in the clay. Then carefully peel the clay off the tree, keeping the molded texture intact. To make a permanent cast of the tree bark, roll out a piece of self-hardening clay. Flatten it into a sheet the same size as the modeling clay impression you made. Place it on top of the modeling clay, and gently press it onto the ridges so that it captures all the textures but does not erase them. Gently lift off the clay, and let dry for 2 or 3 days. Do this for several types of trees, and compare the different textures.

Spore Prints

Discover the tiny mushroom spores that can grow into new mushrooms.

Caution: This project requires adult help.

What You'll Need
- mushrooms or toadstools
- knife
- white paper
- black paper
- magnifying glass
- bread
- jar with lid
- water

Mature, ripe mushrooms can produce as many as 1,000,000 spores per minute for a period of several days! Find 2 mature mushrooms or toadstools whose gills are exposed (have an adult help you choose them). Cut the stems off the mushrooms. Place 1 mushroom on white paper and 1 on black paper. After 24 hours, lift the mushrooms off the paper and check for spore prints. Use a magnifying glass to look at the tiny mushroom-producing spores. Algae, lichen, moss, and mold are some other plants that grow from tiny spores. The spores grow into plants when the conditions for growth are right. To explore spores further, put half a piece of bread in a jar. Sprinkle the bread with water, and cover the jar. Leave the jar in a warm, dark place. You will be creating a warm, moist food source that will encourage growth of any spores in the air. After a few days, look at the bread in the jar. What is happening? (Note: Wash your hands well after handling your experiment, and don't eat the results of either experiment!)

Animal Litter Bags

◆▷▶▶▶▶▷◆

These handy litter bags are decorated to look like animals, so you "feed the animals" each time you throw away trash.

Caution: This project requires adult help.

On the plain side of a large grocery bag, cut out a big opening that will be the mouth of your animal. Be sure the mouth is high enough on the bag so it will hold trash. Then, staple the top of the grocery bag closed.

Color eyes, ears, nose, and feet on the bag to look like any animal you choose. If you'd like, use construction paper and cut out shapes for the body parts. Tape or glue them onto the bag in the proper places. You can also cut strips of paper for fur or a mane and attach them to the bag. Use your imagination—your creation doesn't have to be an animal you've ever seen before!

When your animal is completed, put on your work gloves and walk around your yard or neighborhood. Pick up litter, and put it in the bag through the animal's mouth. Don't pick up any broken glass, needles, or other dangerous materials. Have an adult come along on your garbage hunt to help out with those things!

Felt Weather Channel

◆▷◆▷◆▷

Use colorful felt weather symbols to predict tomorrow's weather.

What You'll Need
- cardboard
- blunt scissors (optional)
- colored felt
- glue
- pencil
- ruler
- clear cellophane
- colored tape
- puffy fabric paint

If you've ever dreamed of becoming a weather person, here's your chance. Make your own weather channel, and treat the family to a morning and evening forecast.

Find or cut 2 same-size pieces of cardboard. Glue a piece of dark felt onto one so the felt covers the cardboard completely. On the other piece of cardboard, draw a large square opening with a 1-inch border all around. Cut out the opening so you have a frame. Cut a piece of clear cellophane to match the frame's size. Glue the cellophane to the wrong side of the frame. This is the TV screen. Attach the screen to the dark-felt background by taping a piece of colored tape along the length of the top borders to make a hinge. Tape it loosely so that the screen can be lifted easily enough for you to place your weather symbols inside. Cut different weather symbols out of colored felt. Cut a sun, puffy white clouds, dark storm clouds, umbrellas, snow people, snowflakes, raindrops, and lightning bolts. Decorate them with puffy fabric paint. You are ready to forecast. Use your best weather person announcer voice to let folks know that a storm is coming their way.

Compost Sculptures

◄◄◄►►►►

These decorative bags make interesting lawn sculptures, and you'll end up with some handy compost in the spring!

What You'll Need
- paper yard-waste bags
- crayons or permanent markers
- leaves
- string
- twigs (optional)
- smaller brown paper bags (optional)
- tape (optional)

You've probably seen those orange plastic bags that look like pumpkin faces and are filled with leaves. The ones you make will be even better for the environment. If you place them where they'll be protected during the winter, in a few months you'll have some compost in the bottom of the bags—just in time for your spring garden!

Before filling the yard-waste bags with leaves, decorate the bags with the crayons or markers. Animal faces, funny faces, or designs of any kind make interesting sculptures.

When finished, fill the bags with leaves. Tie the tops shut. You can add twigs for arms, use a smaller paper bag to make a hat— who knows where your imagination will take you!

Come spring, you'll have compost to fertilize your garden!

Pop-Can Cut-Ups

Save an animal's life with scissors and glue.

Caution: This project requires adult help.

Every year, thousands of birds, sea creatures, and forest animals lose their lives after becoming entangled in plastic pop-can caddies, those plastic binders that keep aluminum six-packs together until shoppers get them safely home. You can help save animals' lives by spreading the word.

Make simple flyers that ask your neighbors to snip those dangerous bits of plastic into harmless strips. Pass your flyers out to your neighbors. Be sure to ask for permission before you post them in public places, such as malls or schools. And always take a trusted adult with you.

A Green "Valentine"

This is a heart-shaped valentine you can give all year-round.

What You'll Need
- table covering
- ivy plant
- small- or medium-size pot
- potting soil
- spoon or small trowel
- a roll of florist wire
- tape measure
- blunt scissors
- red ribbon

Cover the table you will be working on. Pot the ivy according to the plant directions. Measure and carefully cut three 40-inch-long pieces of florist wire. Match up the ends, and twist the 3 pieces together into 1 strand. Bend the twisted strand of florist wire into a heart shape, with the loose ends forming the V at the bottom of the heart. At the bottom of the V, twist the ends together, leaving about a 5-inch "stem" to stick into the potting soil. Stick the heart into the pot near the base of the plant. Tie a red bow at the top of the heart. Loosely wrap strands of the ivy around the heart.

Be an Eager Beaver

Beavers build their dens with mud and sticks. Build a miniature beaver den from common items.

What You'll Need
- toothpicks or twigs
- modeling clay
- lid from a shoe box or other shallow box
- rocks
- leaves
- twigs
- shallow saucer or container
- small plastic cup
- blunt scissors

Use your hands to mix the toothpicks or twigs into the clay. (Be careful not to poke yourself!) Shape the clay into a den (like a small cave) with an opening.

To make a beaver habitat, get the lid from a large shoe box or other shallow box. At one end of the lid, pile up some more clay, and place the beaver den on it. Place more clay, small rocks, leaves, and twigs over the bottom of the lid.

Beavers build tunnels from their dens into nearby ponds. Put a small, shallow container in the bottom of the lid as a pond. (A small saucer that goes under a flower pot makes a good pond.) Use a small plastic cup as your tunnel. Cut the bottom out of the cup. Put the bottom piece into the den opening for support and the top of the cup by the pond. Use clay to attach the cup to the den and to cover the top of the cup so it looks like a tunnel.

This model shows the ingenious home design of beavers. They scurry down to the pond to get water and plants for dinner, then go back home without ever venturing outside where predators might see them.

Now the challenge is yours: What other kinds of animal homes can you make? Do some research in the library, collect your craft supplies, and build!

Reverse Garden

Plant a garden in reverse, and investigate what "biodegradable" means.

What You'll Need

- deep pan
- soil
- old spoon
- variety of garbage (apple core, dried leaves, newspaper, plastic foam, old sock)
- watering can
- paper
- pen or pencil
- water
- disposable gloves

Instead of planting seeds and bulbs and watching plants and flowers sprout blossoms, bury different kinds of garbage and observe them as they decompose.

Fill a deep pan with soil, and bury several kinds of garbage under the soil (an apple core, some dried leaves, a crumpled piece of newspaper, a piece of plastic foam, and an old sock). Water your garden every couple of days. Dig up the garden after a week, and see what is happening to the items. Rebury your plantings, and continue to water every couple days. Dig up the garden again, and observe it after 2 or 3 more weeks. Then replant it one more time, and check it in several more weeks. Note which objects change and how. You may want to keep a journal and make sketches each time you unearth your garden for observation. (Be sure to wash your hands or wear disposable gloves when you work in your reverse garden.)

Secret Garden

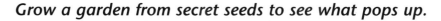

Grow a garden from secret seeds to see what pops up.

Collect spoonfuls of dirt from 3 different places. Keep the samples of soil separate. Divide the inside of a shoe-box lid into 3 sections with a marker. Label each section with the name of the place where you collected the soil sample. Line the lid with a plastic bag that has been cut open or a piece of plastic wrap (make sure there are no holes in the plastic). Put each sample in the section with its place name. Sprinkle water over the soil. Cover the lid with a piece of plastic wrap or another plastic bag. Seal the cover with tape to create a greenhouse. Set it in a sunny window, and check every day or two.

What You'll Need

- 3 scoops of dirt from 3 different locations
- plastic spoon
- shoe-box lid
- marker
- plastic bags or plastic wrap
- blunt scissors
- water
- tape

Button Park

◆▷◆▷◆▷◆▷

Don't have room in your yard for a tree? Even tiny plants become towering trees in a button park!

What You'll Need
- large button
- baby food jar with lid
- cool-temp glue gun
- tiny pebbles
- tiny air plants
- dry moss
- small ceramic animal
- eyedropper or mister
- water
- small buttons

Caution: This project requires adult help.

Get the biggest button you can find. Have an adult help you glue the button to the top of the lid of a baby food jar with the cool-temp glue gun. Collect tiny pebbles for boulders. Ask your florist to help you select tiny air plants. Some possibilities are silver beads, toy cypress, *Sedum Moranenci, Sedum dasyphyllum,* cobweb houseleak, and *Echeveria microcalyx.* These tiny plants need no soil or sand. You can attach them to your button with a drop of cool-temp glue. Fill the spaces between your plants with little bits of moss, pebbles, and a tiny ceramic

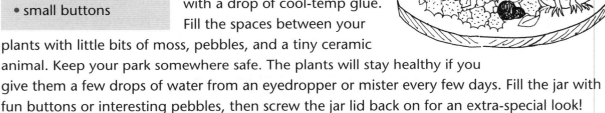

animal. Keep your park somewhere safe. The plants will stay healthy if you give them a few drops of water from an eyedropper or mister every few days. Fill the jar with fun buttons or interesting pebbles, then screw the jar lid back on for an extra-special look!

Save It!

◆▷◆▷◆▷◆▷

Is the wilderness around you vanishing? You can help stop the destruction!

Is there a wetland in your hometown? An old-growth forest? A rare bird nesting site? Is it safe, or is it in danger of being destroyed? The Center for Children's Environmental Literature can help. Write for special suggestions on how to save wilderness areas in your own hometown. Then get busy putting the suggestions into action. Write to: Center for Children's Environmental Literature, P.O. Box 5995, Washington, D.C. 20016.

What You'll Need
- notebook paper
- envelope
- pencil
- postage stamp

Nature Bookmark

Make a bookmark to remember your garden.

Caution: This project requires adult help.

Put fabric flat on your work surface with the right side up. Arrange some pressed flowers on the fabric, and glue in place. Add more decoration with markers. Let dry. Slowly peel the backing of the flexible vinyl about 2 to 3 inches down from the vinyl. Put the sticky side of the vinyl at one end of the bookmark. Continue peeling the backing from the vinyl as you press the vinyl in place on the bookmark. Be sure to keep the edges even. Turn the fabric over to continue pressing the vinyl in place. Once the vinyl is in place, put the paper backing, shiny side down, over it. With an adult's help, press with an iron for 3 to 4 seconds. Remove the paper, and let cool. Trim the edges.

What You'll Need
- 2×6-inch piece of fabric
- pressed flowers (see Flower Press on page 172)
- craft glue
- fabric markers
- 2×12-inch piece of iron-on flexible vinyl
- ruler
- iron and ironing board
- blunt scissors

Garden Markers

Now you'll never forget where you planted the carrots! You can even make notes about watering needs and harvest time.

What You'll Need
- plastic milk jugs
- permanent markers
- scissors or craft knife
- garden seeds

Caution: This project requires adult help.

Refer to the illustration and draw the cut lines of a square with a spike on a clean plastic milk jug. With an adult's help, cut out the garden marker shape. Draw the plant's picture shown on your package of garden seeds. Write the name of the plant as well. Add the plastic markers to your garden. You can also make a set of garden markers for your houseplants. Learn all the names and how to care for them, and write the instructions on the plastic markers.

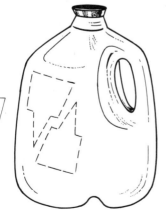

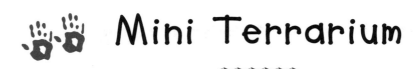 # Mini Terrarium

◄►►►►►►

Make your own little terrarium in a plastic cup, and watch tiny greenery grow.

What You'll Need
- waterproof table covering
- 2 clear plastic cups
- pebbles or gravel
- potting soil
- pitcher of water
- seedlings
- florist's moss
- water-resistant tape

Cover the table. Cover the bottom of a clear plastic cup with a layer of pebbles or gravel. Add a little more than an inch of potting soil above that. Sprinkle the soil with water to dampen it, and gently tamp it down. Make holes in the soil with your fingers for the seedlings, and place them in the holes. Carefully pack the soil around the seedlings. Cover the soil with moss, and water again to wet the soil. Place the second cup upside down on top of the first to create a greenhouse cover. Tape the second cup to the first. Set your mini greenhouse in a sunny spot, and watch your seedlings flourish.

clear tape

seedling

moss

soil

gravel

Recycle, Recycle, Recycle

When you check to see if that plastic cup is recyclable, do you know what the number means? It refers to the type of plastic resin that is used to make the product. If you see the number 1, then this product can be recycled into bottles for cleaning products and nonfood items, egg cartons, and even for polyester fibers that are used in T-shirts, carpets, and fleece. Products with the number 2 on them can be recycled into flowerpots, toys, traffic cones, bottle carriers, and trash cans! Numbers 3 through 7 are not usually recyclable.

Backyard Bingo

Become a bingo winner, and recycle at the same time.

Caution: This project requires adult supervision.

Gather a team of friends and neighbors together for a clean-up day. Grab some trash bags, and put on your work gloves, then search your yard or neighborhood park for bits of trash with the letters "b," "i," "n," "g," and "o" printed on them. The first person to collect all 5 letters—and securely dispose of the garbage—wins the game. But in the long run everyone wins because a cleaner park is a safer park. Be extra careful of broken glass. Ask for adult assistance to clean up dangerous shattered glass or any other items you're unsure of.

 # Bonsai

Small is beautiful—even when it comes to trees!

Select a shallow clay pot with a hole in the bottom for drainage. Put a 12-inch piece of copper wire in the pot with 1 inch sticking out the bottom hole. Spread a layer of gravel in the bottom. Set the tree in the pot. Wrap the wire around the root ball; keep 1 inch sticking out of the bottom hole. Bend the end flat to hold the tree in place. Fill the rest of the pot with a mixture of ¾ potting soil and ¼ sand, and water it well. After a few weeks, wrap pieces of copper wire around the tree's branches, and carefully twist them. Clip the tips of the branches so they do not grow too long. Water your bonsai well once the soil has dried out completely.

Recycling Round-Up

◆▶◆▶◆▶◆

Don't wait for recycling to come to your neighborhood—start some yourself!

What You'll Need
- large cardboard boxes
- markers
- magazine pictures
- glue
- blunt scissors
- large plastic trash bags

Decorate large cardboard boxes, such as fruit or moving boxes, with words or phrases about recycling or pictures of pop cans and other recyclables. Give the boxes to trusted friends and neighbors, and ask them to keep their empty soda cans in their boxes. Collect the cans in large plastic garbage bags each week. Check your Yellow Pages to find your local recycling center. Turn in the bags of soda cans each week—you may even make a small profit!

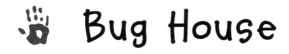 # Bug House

◆▶◆▶◆▶◆

Make a simple bug home, and capture an insect to observe for a day or two.

Scoop a few spoonfuls of dirt into a plastic cup. Add some leaves, twigs, and a rock. Moisten the soil and leaves with a few drops of water. Set the cup inside the end of the nylon stocking. Now find an interesting bug. Place the bug inside the cup. Seal the top of the stocking with a twist tie. Observe your insect guest for a day or two, and then set it free outside again.

What You'll Need
- clear plastic cup
- plastic spoon
- dirt
- leaves
- twigs
- rock
- water
- bottom of a leg of a nylon stocking
- twist tie

 # Growing Up

◄►◄►◄►►

No matter how you try to fool them, seeds know which way is up!

What You'll Need
- glass or plastic jar
- potting soil
- lima bean seeds
- water
- black paper
- tape
- plastic wrap
- rubber band

Fill a glass or a plastic jar with potting soil, and push a seed right next to the side of the jar where it can be easily seen. Place 3 more seeds around the jar where they can also be seen. Moisten the soil with water, and check daily to see if the seeds have begun to sprout. Once the seeds have sprouted, cover the outside of the jar with the black paper. Make a lid for the jar with plastic wrap and a rubber band. For the next 12 days you will be changing the position of the jar. During those 12 days, check the moisture level of the soil each day or two and add a little water whenever needed to keep the soil moist. To begin the position-changing experiment, lay the jar on its side for 3 days. After 3 days, turn the jar upside down and keep it that way for the next 3 days. Then lay the jar on its side again for 3 days. And finally, set the jar right side up for 3 days. After the 12 days of position changing, remove the black paper. You will discover that the beans kept changing their growth pattern in order to keep growing upward even though there was no light to show them which way was up.

Awesome Art

Look to the ideas presented in this chapter for eye-catching art. Inspire and awe others with the works you make from these activities. Motivate yourself to use these projects as taking-off points to create new crafts. You might end up living inside a gallery when you find these decorative creations plastered all over your home's walls.

 # Double Drawing

You may think you're seeing double, but you're not. You're seeing a cool design drawn with two crayons at once.

What You'll Need
- crayons, colored pencils, or markers
- masking tape
- drawing or construction paper
- watercolor paints and paintbrush (optional)

Hold 2 crayons, colored pencils, or markers side by side, and tape them together. You can tape together two of the same color or two different colors. Draw a picture on a piece of drawing paper. Your picture will have double lines. Write your name a few times or make the same design, such as a heart, over and over in different colors and sizes. Change color combinations often. After you've finished drawing your picture, color the space in between the lines to create a bold design. If you use crayons to draw your picture, color it in using watercolor paint to create a resist effect.

Animal Combos

❖◆❖◆❖◆❖

Mix and match animal features and colors to draw the most unusual zoo in the world.

Find pictures that are about the same size of 2 different animals. Place a piece of tracing paper over one animal, such as a giraffe, and use a black felt-tip pen to trace the head and neck. Then place the tracing paper over the other animal—perhaps a fox—and trace the body and legs. You've just created a giraffox!

Place a sheet of drawing paper over your tracing paper, and trace the giraffox. Using colored pencils, give your giraffox a wild coat. Add feathers, fur, horns, or tails of other creatures to make your animal look even more different. Use this drawing technique to create all kinds of original animals. Think of combinations to make the most ferocious, the fastest, or the most colorful creature.

What You'll Need
- old magazines or books
- tracing paper
- black felt-tip pen
- drawing paper
- colored pencils

Mosaic Art

❖◆❖◆❖◆❖

A mosaic is a realistic picture or an abstract design made up of small colored pieces placed side by side.

What You'll Need
- assorted colors of construction paper
- blunt scissors
- ruler
- pencil
- drawing paper
- craft glue

Make a picture from cut-up pieces of paper. Cut assorted colors of construction paper into ½-inch squares. The easiest way to do this is to gather a stack of the same-color papers, measure and mark ½-inch increments on the top sheet, then cut the ½-inch-wide strips. Gather the strips, and snip them into squares. Continue with the other colors, keeping the colors separate.

Draw an outline of a simple picture on a piece of drawing paper. Start by covering the outline of your picture with the paper squares. Glue the squares down one by one, leaving a little space between each piece. Then fill in the design and the background with squares of other colors, following the shape of your outline.

# Leaf Stencils

Leaves make lovely artwork—and unique greeting cards and stationery.

What You'll Need
- tempera paints
- water
- spray bottles
- leaves
- newspaper
- white paper
- crayons (optional)

Caution: This project requires adult help.

Make easy and safe spray paint by adding water to tempera paint to thin it. Put the different colors of paint in different spray bottles.

Collect a variety of leaves with interesting shapes. Cover your work surface with newspaper. (The newspaper should be bigger than the paper you will be using so it will catch the "over spray" when you paint.) Put a few leaves on a piece of paper.

Spray-paint the leaves. (Be sure to spray around the leaves, too.) Let the paint dry, then remove the leaves. The image that remains on the paper is called a stencil. You can also rub crayons around the edges of the leaves instead of using paint to create your stencil.

Make your leaf stencils into greeting cards, or make stationery by painting with light-colored paints. Overlap several leaves for an intricate design.

Dot Art

Here's a whole new angle on dot-to-dot pictures!

Want a new art project? Try dot art. Draw a picture on a plain sheet of white paper. Punch tiny round dots from sheets of colored paper, using a hole punch. When you punch, hold the colored paper over a different sheet of white paper to catch the dots as they fall. Glue the colorful dots in place on your drawing, leaving as little white as possible without letting the dots overlap. Your finished work will have a bright, unusual look.

What You'll Need
- white paper
- markers
- colored paper
- hole punch
- glue

 # Flying Fish

Fish seem to fly through the air with this attractive mobile.

What You'll Need

- reference books
- 6 sheets of paper
- pencil
- ruler
- blunt scissors
- paper clips
- stapler and staples
- newspaper
- paints
- paintbrush
- hole punch
- string
- coat hanger

Find reference books about fish in your local library. There are many differently colored and shaped fish in the world. Find your favorite in the books, and make a fish mobile that will be sure to catch everyone's attention!

Draw the outline of the fish you have chosen, making sure the outline is about 7 inches long and at least 5 inches high. If you'd really like to go all out, choose 3 different fish and make a large outline shape for each. Trace your initial outline on 5 more sheets of paper, making a total of 6 fish, and cut them out. (If you are making 3 different fish, copy each outline once more, making a total of 2 outlines for each fish, and cut them out.) Use paper clips to hold 2 fish shapes together (if you made more than 1 fish, hold 2 of the matching fish shapes together), then staple them together at the edges. Staple all around the body except the back of the tail. Make a total of 3 fish this way.

Paint the fish anyway you like. You can paint them so they are realistic, or you can be fanciful with your painting! Let them dry. Tear sheets of newspaper into thin strips. Scrunch up the strips, and stuff them into the fish. When each fish is full, staple across the tail to keep the stuffing inside.

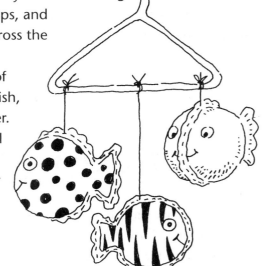

Punch a hole in the top of each fish. Cut 3 lengths of string. Tie an end of a piece of string to the top of the fish, and then tie the other end of the string to a coat hanger. Repeat for the other 2 fish. Hang your fish mobile for all to see!

If you don't like fish, why not try a bird, dog, cat, or bear mobile. Your local library has all the books you need to do research on any of these animals!

Patterned Butterflies

◆▷◆▷◆▷◆▷◆

These beautiful butterflies look like they're made from stained glass! Study the patterns on real butterflies, and see if you can re-create some of those patterns.

What You'll Need
• butterfly reference books (optional)
• large sheet of paper
• marker
• tissue paper in many colors
• ruler
• waxed paper
• liquid starch
• paintbrushes
• blunt scissors
• tape

Study some reference books about butterflies to decide which butterfly you want to create. Draw a butterfly outline on a large sheet of paper. Tear the colored tissue into 3-inch shapes. Place a sheet of waxed paper over the butterfly outline. Use the liquid starch to paint tissue pieces onto the waxed paper, filling in the outline of the butterfly with a mosaic of different colors. Add 1 or 2 more layers of tissue, and allow your butterfly to dry overnight. Cut out the butterfly, following the outline on the underlying paper. Slowly peel the tissue-paper butterfly off the waxed paper. Tape your butterfly to the window, and let the sun shine through!

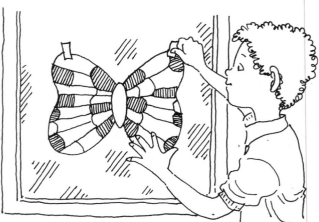

 # Blot Painting

◆▷◆▷◆▷◆▷◆

It's like looking in the mirror. Whatever goes on the left side of the paper is reflected on the right.

Cover your work surface with newspaper. Fold a piece of construction paper in half, then unfold it. Use a paintbrush to dribble small amounts of poster paint on one half of the paper. Refold the paper, and rub it gently. Unfold it, and let it dry. Your picture will have blots of color. To create rainbow-colored blots, mix dots of colors when you dab the paint on the paper. Use markers to draw a design around the blots of color. For example, your blot painting might look like 2 seals balancing 2 balls, so draw in flippers on the seals and stripes on the balls.

What You'll Need
• newspaper
• construction paper
• poster paint
• paintbrush
• markers

Resist Painting

Here's an idea no one can resist. Use masking paint to block out watercolors and create crisp edges and white spaces.

What You'll Need
- newspaper
- white art paper
- masking paint (available at art supply stores)
- watercolor paint
- paintbrushes

Cover your work surface with newspaper. Draw a picture, such as a candy cane, on a piece of white art paper. To paint in the white part of the candy cane, fill it in using the masking paint. The masking paint covers the areas of your painting that you don't want to fill in with color. Let the paint dry. Then paint in the rest of your picture using watercolor paints. Let it dry. Now rub off the masking paint with your fingers. If your picture needs layers of colors, repeat the masking and painting process.

Another idea is to paint a soccer player against the blurry background of a stadium. Paint in the player using masking paint; then use watercolor paints to color in the bleachers, the fans, and the grass. When the paint is dry, rub off the masking paint and color in the detail of the player.

Art for Seniors

Brighten a senior's world with your art!

Many senior citizens find themselves in rest homes far from their own kids and grandkids. You can help brighten their days with a splash of color: bright and lively artwork only you can give. Draw and color your favorite scene—anything from animals to airplanes. Add your first name and your age.

What You'll Need
- paper
- crayons
- cardboard
- large envelope
- stamps

Glue your artwork to cardboard, and mail it off to a nearby home for the elderly. If you can share art once a month, your gift will keep on giving. Try to enlist your entire class to join in the fun and inspire dozens of smiles and warm feelings.

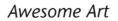

Grease Casting

◆▷◆▷◆▷◆▷

Try a different technique to make plaster casts. This one is so much fun since you can easily "erase" your design and start over.

Caution: This project requires adult help.

Cover your work surface with newspaper. Fold up the sides of your aluminum foil square or circle about 1 inch. Use a butter knife to spread a ⅛-inch thick, even layer of shortening in the foil shape. Press the ballpoint pen into the grease to draw your design. Don't worry if you make a mistake or want to change your design. Just use the knife to smear the grease, and start your design over again.

With an adult's help, mix the plaster of paris according to package directions. Carefully spoon it over the grease. If you'd like to hang your plaster casting, press a paper clip into the top edge. When the plaster is set, pop it out of the foil. Let it dry completely. Clean the plaster casting with warm, soapy water.

What You'll Need
- newspaper
- 4×6-inch square or 6-inch circle of heavy-duty aluminum foil
- shortening
- butter knife
- ballpoint pen
- plaster of paris
- spoon
- paper clip (optional)

Tessellations

◆▷◆▷◆▷◆▷

A tessellation is like a mosaic, using small squares to make a repetitive picture. Try one on your own. It's fun!

What You'll Need
- drawing paper
- pencil
- ruler
- colored pencils

Draw a grid of 9 squares on a piece of drawing paper. On the left side of 1 square, draw a curvy line. Repeat that same line on the left side of each square. Now draw a different curvy line at the top of the first square. Then draw the curvy line at the top of each remaining square. Take a look at the squares to see what the shape is starting to look like. Fill in more lines to create a shape, repeating the same line in each square. Each line creates part of the next square's design. When you are done, you should have the same shape in each square. Color in your design using colored pencils.

Paper Weaving

◆◆◆◆◆◆◆

Go ahead! Make waves as well as zigzags and curves—all with one fun and colorful paper-weaving technique.

Cut out several 1-inch strips from different-colored sheets of construction paper, lengthwise. Fold another piece of construction paper in half. Starting at the fold, cut straight, zigzag, or curvy lines about 1 inch apart, ending 1 inch from the edge of the paper. Open the paper, and weave paper strips over and under each cut. Alternate colors of strips as you weave. Continue weaving until the paper is full. Trim the strips. If you want, glue your paper weaving on a larger piece of paper and hang it on the wall.

 # Toe Painting

◆◆◆◆◆◆◆

Create a work of art with your feet. Play some tunes, dip your feet in paint, and tap your toes to the music's beat.

Cover your work surface (the floor works best) with newspaper. Place a chair on top of the newspaper. Pour finger paints on paper plates. Arrange them within close reach of the chair. Fill a bucket with warm water, and place it next to the chair. Tape drawing paper to the newspaper in front of the chair, then sit on the chair. Dip your big toe in the paint, and make a design on the paper. Paint heel prints and dots with your toes. When you are done with each color, dip your feet in the water to rinse the paint off your foot. Dry your foot with an old, clean towel.

Painting in Opposites

◆▶◆▶◆▶◆▶

Every color has a complementary, or opposite, color. Use the opposite color than what's expected, and create a surprising world.

What You'll Need
- pencil
- drawing paper
- ruler
- newspaper
- watercolor or poster paints
- paintbrush

Do you know which colors are the primary colors? They are red, blue, and yellow. Which colors are the secondary colors? (Here's a hint: Mixing the primary colors creates the secondary colors.) They are green, orange, and purple. Now that you know which colors are which, draw a color wheel. To create a color wheel, draw a circle on a piece of drawing paper. Use a

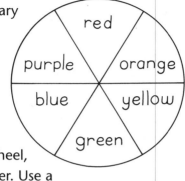

ruler to divide it into 6 equal "pie" pieces. Label or color in every other "pie" piece as a primary color. Then fill in the opposite secondary colors. Label the "pie" piece opposite of red as the secondary color green. Finish labeling the remaining colors.

Cover your work surface with newspaper. Draw a summer scene of a field with flowers and trees. Paint it in opposite colors. Use your color wheel to pick the opposites. For example, your grass will be red, and the sky will be orange with a purple sun. Let the paint dry.

 # Thummies

◆▶◆▶◆▶◆▶

With your thumbprint as a starting point, you can come up with all sorts of art creations.

Press your thumb on an ink pad, then press it on a piece of paper. With a fine-point felt-tip pen, add details to your thumbprint to create an animal, a person, or a silly character. Draw ears, whiskers, and a tail to make a cat, or add spots, legs, and antennae to make

What You'll Need
- waterbase ink stamp pad
- drawing paper
- fine-point felt-tip pen

a ladybug. There are so many fun creations you can make with Thummies. Try using your pinky or index finger for prints in different sizes and shapes. Or press 4 or 5 Thummies in a row to make a caterpillar. Use Thummies to decorate greeting cards and stationery or to illustrate a story.

Salt & Watercolor Picture

Salt is great on popcorn, but did you know it's also fun to sprinkle it over a wet painting?

What You'll Need
- newspaper
- pencil
- drawing paper
- watercolor paints
- paintbrush
- salt

Cover your work surface with newspaper. Sketch a picture, such as a panda bear in a forest, on a piece of drawing paper. Paint the drawing using watercolor paint. While the paint is still wet, sprinkle it with salt. Let it dry. The painting will take on a textured look, and the paper may even crinkle and pucker. You can use this painting technique to make textured backgrounds for holiday cards, stationery, and more.

 # Foil Printmaking

This printing technique allows you to transfer a picture piece by piece.

Cover your work surface with newspaper. Use a ballpoint pen to draw a square on a sheet of foil. Make the square slightly smaller than the sheet of paper you will print on. Then draw a picture in the foil square. Select 1 color of paint, and paint in the parts of the picture using that color. Then place a sheet of paper over the foil print, and press. Carefully peel off the paper, and let the paint dry. Use a damp paper towel to wipe off the old color from the foil. Now select a different color, and paint in another area of the picture. Reprint it on the same paper as before. Continue reprinting the paper until you use all your colors and your picture is complete.

What You'll Need
- newspaper
- heavy-duty aluminum foil
- ballpoint pen
- ruler
- poster paints
- paintbrush
- drawing paper
- paper towels

Ironed Collage

This project re-creates a stained-glass effect when you hang it in a window.

What You'll Need
- resealable plastic sandwich bag
- colored tissue paper, doilies, glitter, and tinsel
- iron and ironing board
- aluminum foil
- clean, old towel
- needle and thread

Caution: This project requires adult help.

Working on a flat surface, carefully arrange colored tissue paper, doilies, glitter, tinsel, and any other thin, flat items in a design or pattern inside a plastic sandwich bag. Overlap different colors of tissue paper to create new color combinations, sprinkle glitter to add

sparkle, and create flowers with doilies. Keeping the bag on the flat surface, gently seal it shut. Then place the bag between 2 pieces of aluminum foil. Cover with an old towel. With an adult's help, iron the "sandwiched" bag for about 15 seconds. The bag will melt and hold your collage in place. After the collage has cooled, poke a hole in the top center of the bag with a needle. String it with thread to hang it in a window.

2-Day Paintings

This art project uses both your painting and drawing skills!

Cover your work surface with newspaper. Use watercolor paints to paint the background of a scene, such as a sunset beach or desert dunes, on watercolor paper. For the sunset beach, paint brown sand, blue water, and an orange-yellow sun setting on the horizon. Blend your colors, and let the paint dry. The next day, draw over the dry painting with markers to create sharp edges and lines. Add the silhouettes of palm trees on the beach or yucca, cactus, and roadrunners to your desert.

What You'll Need
- newspaper
- watercolor paints
- paintbrush
- watercolor paper
- markers

You can also create a still life painting using this technique. Try painting a bowl of fruit in washes of color without adding any detail—just use splashes of purple for grapes, red for apples, and yellow for bananas. Wash in a background, too. The next day, draw in the shapes of the fruit and the bowl.

Paper Cutouts #1

◆▶◆▶◆▶◆

Begin with a flat shape, add a few simple cutouts, and make a three-dimensional picture.

What You'll Need
- poster board
- pencil or black felt-tip pen
- blunt scissors
- construction paper
- craft glue

Draw an animal shape on a piece of poster board. Cut out the animal shape. Now make its "coat" using paper cutouts. To make fish scales, cut out small semicircles from construction paper. Glue the straight edge of the semicircles to the poster board animal shape, and bend the other ends of the semicircle up to create a three-dimensional look. To make bird feathers, cut out small triangles, glue them to the poster board, and bend them up. For alligator teeth, cut a zigzag line and score each side. Then glue the teeth to the poster board, and bend them up. To make a curly animal coat, cut out small rectangular strips. Wrap each strip around a pencil to curl it. Glue the curled strips to the poster board.

Brayer Scraper

◆▶◆▶◆▶◆

This artwork is all your own since you choose the colors, you select the designs, and you even make the painting tools.

To make painting tools, draw a comb on cardboard. Cut it out. Make different combs to create different paint patterns. Make a comb with lots of tiny teeth or a few spaced-out teeth.

What You'll Need
- pencil
- cardboard
- blunt scissors
- newspaper
- finger paints
- palette
- brayer
- finger-paint paper

Cover your work surface with newspaper. Put some finger paint on a flat palette. Roll the brayer in the paint, then roll the inked brayer in stripes on the finger-paint paper. Run the cardboard combs over the wet paint to create a design.

Scrape each comb in a square section of paint to make patchwork designs. Let your painting dry flat on the newspaper. Use this painting technique to decorate gift boxes, book covers, and notecards.

Half & Half Picture

Picture this—half the design is a photograph and half the design is original artwork. What a surprise!

Look through old magazines for a picture of a person's face. Make sure it is somewhat symmetrical (a picture with similar halves). Cut the picture out, then cut it in half down the middle of the face. Glue one half of the picture on a piece of drawing paper; discard the other half. Use a pencil to sketch in the other half of the face. Try to match the facial features. Then color it in with charcoal or colored pencils.

Once you've practiced this drawing technique, try sketching some other symmetrical pictures, such as a person's body, a penguin, or a house. Then instead of gluing the magazine picture to the paper, use removable tape to set the cutout half in place. Sketch in the other half of the picture, then remove the original half and sketch in the rest of the picture.

What You'll Need
- old magazines
- blunt scissors
- craft glue
- drawing paper
- pencil
- charcoal or colored pencils
- removable tape (optional)

Still Life Photography

Use light and texture to tell something about what you like.

What You'll Need
- interesting objects (for the still life arrangement)
- camera
- black-and-white or color film

Instead of photographing people or scenes, experiment with making a still life. A still life is an arrangement of objects that have interesting shapes and textures. Artists often use strong light to make interesting shadows. Many artists arrange fruits and vases as subjects; you can try a basketball, shoes, hoop, and net or whatever else interests you. Look for some interesting objects and arrange them on a table. Take a picture of your still life arrangement. Try using different kinds of light, such as natural light, spotlight, or colored light when taking your photos. Take pictures from different angles as well.

Sculpting Clay Statues

◆▷◆▷◆▷◆▶

The only difference between a great sculptor and a really great sculptor is imagination. So let yourself go wild.

Caution: This project requires adult help.

Make a wire shape base for your clay statue. (See the Wire Santa project on page 417 for the bending technique.) Create any shape you want—a person, an animal, or even common objects. Artist Claes Oldenburg copied common household objects, such as a can opener, for his statues.

Cover your work surface with waxed paper. Roll clay into a thin pancake. Place pieces of clay over the wire shape, covering it completely. Use your fingers to smooth over any gaps. Add dimension to your statue by pinching patches of clay over one another or cutting away small areas of clay.

Place your sculpture on a foil-covered baking sheet. To support the shape, crumple some foil pieces and place where needed. With an adult's help, bake the clay statue. (If you are using the Sculpting Clay Dough on page 240, do not bake; let air dry.) After the sculpture has cooled, paint it with acrylic paints.

What You'll Need
- uncoated wire
- waxed paper
- rolling pin
- white polymer clay (or Sculpting Clay Dough on page 240)
- aluminum foil
- baking sheet
- acrylic paints
- paintbrush

Self-Portrait

◆▷◆▷◆▷◆▶

Mail a self-portrait to a friend.

What You'll Need
- blunt scissors
- grocery bags or brown mailing paper
- masking tape
- pencil
- markers
- glue (optional)
- yarn and fabric scraps (optional)
- mailing tube

Cut off the bottom and 2 shortest sides of 2 or 3 grocery bags, and tape the bags together end to end; or unroll a long sheet of mailing paper. Place the large sheet on the floor, and use masking tape to hold it down. Lie down on the paper, and have a friend or family member trace around your body. Decorate your outline with markers. If you want, glue on yarn for your hair and fabric scraps for your clothes. Make yourself into anything you want. You can be yourself, an astronaut, or a ballerina. Roll up the paper when the glue is completely dry, place it in a mailing tube, and send it to someone special.

Shades of Color

One color can be quite interesting. Just add a little white or black to create different tones.

Cover your work surface with newspaper. Sketch a picture on a piece of paper. In the empty, clean egg carton or on the small dishes, put a small amount of 1 watercolor or poster paint in 7 different sections. Mix in 1, 2, and 3 drops of white paint with 3 of the sections. Then mix in 1, 2, and 3 drops of black paint with 3 other sections. Do not mix any other colors in the 7th section.

Now paint your picture using the 1 color and the various tones of that color. For example, if your picture is a baseball game and the color you choose is green, then you can paint it in shades of green: dark green stands, light green uniforms, and medium green grass. Think about the direction the sun will shine on the field. Place lighter shades facing the light and darker shades away from the light to make shadows.

What You'll Need
- newspaper
- pencil
- drawing paper
- plastic egg carton or small dishes
- watercolor or poster paints
- paintbrush

Yarn Collage

The yarn gives your picture a furry, three-dimensional appearance. Stringing beads on the yarn adds even greater depth.

What You'll Need
- pencil
- drawing or construction paper
- craft glue
- assorted colors of yarn
- blunt scissors
- beads (optional)

Draw a picture, such as a plane in the sky, on a piece of drawing or construction paper. Apply a line of glue along the outline of the picture. Then place yarn along the glue. To "color in" a space, coil the yarn around itself until the space is filled in. Keep outlining and filling all the spaces in your picture with yarn. Trim off any excess yarn. To add more dimension to the picture, string a few beads on the yarn as you go along.

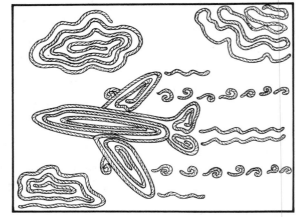

Crayon Sun Catcher

Melted crayons swirl around to become a kaleidoscope of colors, and the bumpy surface makes a wonderful texture.

Caution: This project requires adult help.

Twist old crayons in a small handheld pencil sharpener to make shavings. Spread them on a sheet of waxed paper, and place another sheet on top. Cover your "sandwich" with a towel. With an adult's help, iron over the towel until the crayons are melted. Remove the towel, and use a pot holder or oven mitt to smooth over the waxed paper. This will spread the crayons, mixing the colors together. After the crayons have cooled, cut the waxed paper into a flower, a star, or any shape you want. To make a hanger, poke a hole through the top of the sun catcher with a needle. String with thread to hang it in your window.

What You'll Need
- crayons
- handheld pencil sharpener
- waxed paper
- clean, old towel
- iron and ironing board
- pot holder or oven mitt
- blunt scissors
- needle and thread

Pencil Painting

Draw a picture and then turn it into a painting with these "magic" pencils.

What You'll Need
- water-soluble colored pencils (available at art supply stores)
- drawing paper
- water
- small bowl
- paintbrush

Draw a lion on a sheet of drawing paper using yellow and brown water-soluble colored pencils. (They feel and look just like colored pencils.) Use a wet paintbrush to blend the colors of the lion's mane. Clean your paintbrush. Let the painting dry. Add other details, such as big green eyes, one at a time; blend with the damp paintbrush; clean the paintbrush; and let the painting dry. Repeat as often as you like. Then experiment with other scenes and colors.

Decorate a Door

◆◇◆◇◆◇◆

Turn your bedroom into a magical wonderland. Decorate the door as the entrance to your favorite place.

Measure the outside of your bedroom door. Cut a rectangle the same dimensions as your door from paper. Cut a hole for the doorknob. Use markers or poster paints to decorate the paper. You can create an underwater scene, a skiing scene, or a giant "do not disturb" sign. Tape it to your door.

If you don't want to draw or paint a scene, make a giant collage for your door decoration. Cut out pictures from old magazines (ask for permission first!). Glue them to the paper, covering the whole sheet. After the glue has dried, tape the collage to your door.

What You'll Need
- tape measure
- blunt scissors
- butcher, wrapping, or mailing paper
- markers or poster paints and paintbrush
- removable tape
- old magazines
- craft glue

 # Catching Rays

◆◇◆◇◆◇◆

Recycle old yogurt lids to make dazzling stained-glass sun-catchers.

What You'll Need
- white paper
- permanent markers in several colors including black
- yogurt lid with clear plastic "window"
- tape
- gold thread

Practice drawing a simple geometric design on white paper. Make thick, black lines around large, simple areas. Fill the areas with color. When you create a design you like, copy the black lines onto a clean, see-through yogurt lid. Then fill in the blank areas with colored markers. Tape a loop of gold thread to the lip of the lid. Hang your sun-catcher!

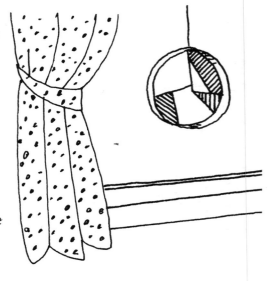

Point of View Photo

With photography, you can make objects bigger than a building or smaller than a stone. It all depends on the angle.

What You'll Need
• camera
• color film

Take pictures from a different angle than usual. For example, photograph your dog from a ladder, your brother from down by his feet, a nature scene from between 2 branches, or a group of friends from one end of the group. It's an easy thing to do, and it will give your photos a new twist. Make a study of a series of items by examining them from different angles and from close and far away.

 # Pointillism Picture

Many famous painters have used this technique: They paint a picture using lots of dots to create solid shapes. It's amazing but true!

What You'll Need
• newspaper
• old magazines
• blunt scissors
• craft glue
• drawing or construction paper
• cotton swabs
• watercolor or poster paints

Cover your work surface with newspaper. Find a colorful picture in a magazine. Cut it out (ask for permission first!), and glue it to a piece of paper. Use a cotton swab to paint over your picture with dots. Cover each color in the picture with the same color of paint. To change the shading of the picture, paint white dots to add highlights and black dots to add shadows.

As you dot in the colors, you can mix them together to create new colors. Mix red and yellow dots together for orange areas; mix blue and yellow dots together for green areas. Use dots to add shading and highlights to your picture. You can darken green areas with blue dots or lighten red areas with pink dots. Use your imagination and experiment with different color combinations.

Crayon & Paint

◆▸◆▸◆▸◆▸

It's fascinating to see how crayon and paint mix together to make a most unusual texture.

What You'll Need
- newspaper
- drawing paper
- crayons
- watercolor paints
- paintbrush

Cover your work surface with newspaper. Draw a beach scene on a piece of paper using crayons. Lightly color in the blue sky, the light brown sand, and the bright beach towels and umbrellas. Now recolor the picture using watercolor paints. Use blue paint over the blue crayon, light brown paint over the light brown crayon, and the same paint colors over the bright beach towels and umbrellas. Let the paint dry.

Now try creating an abstract design. Draw geometric shapes and patterns using crayons. This time, paint over the crayons using different colors. Try to create a mood with your color combinations. (See Emotional Painting on page 241 for mood colors.)

Quilt Picture

◆▸◆▸◆▸◆▸

This looks like an old-fashioned quilt, but there's no sewing and it takes less time than the real thing.

Practice drawing a quilt design on a piece of graph paper. Use a ruler to help you draw the triangles and squares of the quilt pattern. Then measure the exact size of the triangles and squares in the design, and cut them from cardboard to make the pattern

What You'll Need
- pencil
- graph paper
- ruler
- blunt scissors
- lightweight cardboard
- fabric scraps
- craft glue
- old paintbrush

pieces. Place each pattern piece on the fabric scraps, and trace around them. Cut out the fabric pieces. Use an old paintbrush to coat the back of each piece with glue. Following the quilt design you drew on graph paper, glue the fabric on the cardboard. After the glue has dried, trim the cardboard and frame your quilt picture.

Sponge Sculpture

◆◆◆◆◆◆◆

Build fun soft sculptures that you can even use in the tub!
Watch them grow as they absorb water.

Cut up sponges to make a sponge boat. To make the base of the boat, cut off the corners of one end of a sponge so it comes to a point. Cut an oval shape from another sponge in a different color. Use a third color to cut 2 small squares for the top of the boat. Glue the oval shape on top of the boat base.

What You'll Need
• assorted colors of
  unused sponges
• blunt scissors
• fabric glue

Glue the 2 small squares on top of the oval shape. The fabric glue allows you to use the sponges in the tub without having them fall apart. Make more sponge sculptures for the tub. Cut out fish shapes—even little hamburgers and hot dogs!

Positive–Negative Cutouts

◆◆◆◆◆◆◆

Yes, you'll have lots of fun. No, you'll never run out of ideas.
You'll want to do this project again and again.

What You'll Need
• construction paper
• ruler
• blunt scissors
• craft glue

Cut a shape into each side of a 4×4-inch square of construction paper square, saving the cutout pieces. Place the cut square and the cutouts on another piece of construction paper. Arrange the cutouts in a mirror image of the square's side shapes. After you've positioned the pieces, glue them to the background.

Experiment with all kinds of shapes. You can even glue small cutouts in the center of bigger ones. Or you can tear out the pieces instead of using scissors to cut them. After you've created several cutouts, make them into a collage or frame the finished pieces.

Weave a Plate

◆▸◆▸◆▸◆▸

Jazz up this wall hanging with all sorts of trim—some rough, some smooth, some shiny, and even some unexpected, such as wire.

What You'll Need
• markers
• paper plate
• pencil
• ruler
• blunt scissors
• yarn
• pony beads or feathers (optional)

Use markers to draw a small design in the center of a paper plate. With a pencil, lightly mark 3-inch increments around the plate edge to indicate spacing. Starting about ½ inch from the plate's outer edge at one of the pencil marks, cut a 2½-inch slit toward the plate's center. Make sure you don't cut into your center design. Repeat around the whole plate.

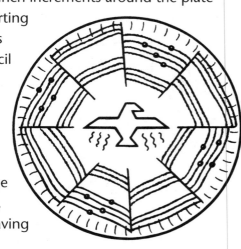

Weave pieces of colorful yarn through the slits. Change colors by tying 1 color to another. As you weave the yarn, thread on beads or tie in feathers. When you're done weaving the yarn, knot it in back and cut off excess yarn.

Coffee Filter Art

◆▸◆▸◆▸◆▸◆

With a coffee filter as your canvas, the paint seems to come alive, moving and blending with other colors.

Cover your work surface with newspaper. Use your hands to flatten out a coffee filter. Tape it flat if necessary. Paint a picture on the coffee filter using watercolor paints. Since coffee filters are made of porous paper, the paint spreads and blends with the colors next to it. Experiment with different abstract designs, then try to make a specific scene. Paint a sun with rainbow rays. Or, since you are working on a round shape, think of painting round pictures like a sleeping puppy or a baseball mitt. Try painting on other porous papers, too. You can use light-colored tissue, paper towels, and cotton fabric to create more "blended" pictures.

What You'll Need
• newspaper
• coffee filters
• removable tape
• watercolor paints
• paintbrush

Picture Perfect Progress

◆▶◆▶◆▶◆▶

Who are you? How have you changed?

What You'll Need
- old photos
- copy machine (optional)
- white glue
- blank paper
- pen

What will you look like when you grow up, grow older, and even grow old?

Ask your parents for a box or scrapbook of old photographs of yourself. Then ask if there are a few copies you can keep for yourself. (You can make photocopies of the pictures—this works just as well.) Select photos that show how you've changed . . . and how you've stayed the same. Want some examples? How about the picture taken at the hospital on the day you headed home after being born? How about a photo showing your first tooth? A picture that shows how you got that cute little scar on your left cheek?

Arrange those telling photographs on a blank page of paper, and write a caption under each shot. Ask your parents for help if you're not totally clear on the details. Now study those photos. Close your eyes, and look to the future. You might get a better idea of what's to come.

Now draw a picture of what you think you'll look like in the coming years. Keep this portrait someplace safe so you can look at it later to see how accurate you were!

A Grandparent's Story

◆▶◆▶◆▶◆▶

Combine your drawing with a grandparent's story.

Make a book about your grandparents. Think of at least 10 questions, and write each on an index card. You can ask, "What was your favorite toy?" or "Where did you live when you were 10 years old?" Have them write their answers on the cards. If your grandparents live far away, mail the cards to them and have them mail them back.

Once you have all the answers, glue each one to the bottom half of a sheet of construction paper. Draw a picture above the card to illustrate the answer. Use markers or colored pencils to decorate a separate sheet of construction paper for the front cover of your book. To bind your book, set all the pages together and punch 4 holes along the left edge. Cut a piece of yarn, thread it through the holes, and tie it in a bow.

What You'll Need
- 3×5-inch index cards
- pen
- envelopes and postage stamps (optional)
- construction paper
- craft glue
- markers or colored pencils
- hole punch
- blunt scissors
- yarn

Toothpick Sculpture

◆▸◆▸◆▸◆

You need patience and a steady hand to create these toothpick designs, but the effort is well worth it.

What You'll Need
- waxed paper
- flat, round, or colored toothpicks
- craft glue
- blunt scissors
- blue construction paper
- crayons or markers

Cover your work surface with a sheet of waxed paper. Glue toothpicks together to make a skeleton shape of a shark. Dip the toothpick ends in glue; then glue each toothpick together piece by piece. After you've created the base of the shark, fill in the body with long and broken toothpicks until the shape is rounded. Then add fins and a tail. Let the glue dry. Now make a display stand for your sculpture. Fold a piece of

blue construction paper in half lengthwise. Draw on some waves. Glue the shark to the paper.

Corn Syrup Paint

◆▸◆▸◆▸◆

Corn syrup paint dries with a shiny gloss. It almost looks as if the colors are still wet.

Cover your work surface with newspaper. To make the paint, mix 1 tablespoon of corn syrup with 5 or 6 drops of food coloring in one section of an empty egg carton. Repeat with the other colors of food coloring, keeping each paint mixture in a separate egg carton section.

Using a black crayon, draw a design with thick outlines on a piece of heavyweight white paper. If you draw a baseball player, outline his pants, shirt, arms, and head with thick black lines. Color in each section with the corn syrup paint; don't let the colors touch one another across the black lines. This homemade paint is also great for drawing a jack-o'-lantern or Christmas tree. Since the paint is so shiny, it will seem like your pictures are all lit up!

What You'll Need
- newspaper
- corn syrup
- measuring spoon
- food coloring
- clean plastic foam egg carton
- heavyweight white paper
- black crayon
- paintbrush

All that Glitters

◆▷◆▷◆▷◆

Reflections of light turn your glitter art into sparkling masterpieces.

What You'll Need
- newspaper
- stiff paper or card stock
- blunt scissors
- hole punch
- white glue
- glitter
- waxed paper
- string

Cover your work surface with newspaper. Cut your favorite shapes out of stiff paper or card stock. Punch a hole in the top of each shape, and cover one side of the shapes with a fine layer of glue. Sprinkle your favorite color of glitter over the shapes. Place the glittered shapes on waxed paper.

As soon as the glue dries, shake the loose glitter onto a sheet of paper. Put the excess glitter back into the bottle to recycle it. Flip the shapes over, and repeat the process for the other sides of the shapes.

Once the glue is dry, thread string through the holes to hang your glittering objects in the sunniest window. You'll soon discover all that glitters is not gold—but it can be pretty stunning. (Be careful not to get bits of glitter in your eyes. Be sure to wash your hands as soon as you have finished this activity.)

 # Foot Drawing

◆▷◆▷◆▷◆

It's hard to say which is more fun: trying to master foot drawing yourself or watching someone else try it.

What You'll Need
- large pieces of paper
- markers
- bare feet

Foot drawing makes a great party project. Have everyone sit in a chair, and place a large piece of paper by the foot of each chair. Give everyone a marker to draw with. Don't let them hold the markers in their hands—instead they have to hold the markers between their toes! Now everyone can start drawing. Have them start by trying to write their name, then have them draw a picture. When everyone's done, compare their foot drawings. Save the drawings as souvenirs from your party.

# String Art

This project has a three-dimensional feeling. It looks as if the objects you form are actually leaping off the background.

What You'll Need

- 8×8-inch square of wood
- 29 small nails
- hammer
- pencil
- yarn
- blunt scissors
- markers

Caution: This project requires adult help.

Have an adult hammer the nails into the wood base following the illustrations on this page. Using the illustrations, pencil in a number next to each nail. The numbers will serve as your guide when you start to string the design.

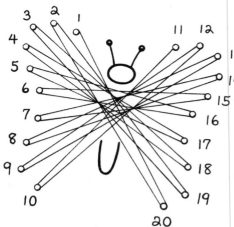

To string the butterfly, tie one end of the yarn to nail 1. String the yarn from nail 1 to nail 20, then bring the yarn back up to nail 2 and down to nail 19. Continue stringing the yarn using the illustration as your guide. Once you're finished, tie the yarn to nail 11. Trim off excess yarn.

To make the flower, tie one end of the yarn to nail 1. Then string the yarn from nail 1 to nail 5, nail 5 to nail 9, and nail 9 to nail 4. Continue stringing, using the illustration as your guide. When you come back to nail 1, tie yarn to the nail. Trim off excess yarn.

After you've finished stringing, use markers to draw on a head, body, and antennae for the butterfly and a stem and leaves for the flower.

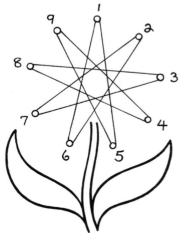

Magical Mosaic Puzzle Picture

◆▷◆▷◆▷◆▷◆

Recycle an old puzzle by painting a picture on it. Play with it or frame it!

What You'll Need
- newspaper
- old shirt
- discarded puzzle, either 8×10 or 10×17 inches in size
- opaque white and other colors of poster paint
- paintbrush
- pencil
- frame for framing or box for storing puzzle

Spread out the newspaper, and put on an old shirt. Assemble the puzzle on the newspaper. Paint the entire surface of the puzzle with the white paint. Let dry. If you can see any of the original picture underneath, paint on another coat of white and let dry. If necessary, add a third coat and let dry. Lightly sketch an original picture or copy one of your favorite drawings on the puzzle with the pencil. Get out the other colors of paint, and paint away. Let the paint dry overnight. Your puzzle picture is ready for playing or framing!

Flower Explosion

◆▷◆▷◆▷◆▷◆

If you thought sponges were only for cleaning up messes, you're in for a surprise with this colorful project.

Fold a piece of construction paper in half. Draw half of a vase shape at the fold. Cut along the lines of the shape, and unfold the paper. Glue the vase shape on a piece of heavyweight paper.

Cover your work surface with newspaper. Place poster paints on paper plates. Dip a damp sponge in the paint, and then sponge paint "flowers" on the paper above the vase. Twist the sponge to create swirled flowers, or press the sponge on the paper for stamped flowers. You can use this technique to make a bowl of sponged fruit, a tree with sponged leaves, or a cornucopia with sponged vegetables.

What You'll Need
- construction paper
- pencil
- blunt scissors
- craft glue
- heavyweight paper
- newspaper
- poster paints
- paper plates
- sponge

 # Poster Redesign

◆─◆─◆─◆─◆─◆

Take an old poster, and make it brand-new. All you have to do is let your imagination run wild.

What You'll Need
- newspaper
- large poster
- poster paints and paintbrush or markers
- blunt scissors
- pencil
- construction paper
- removable tape

Tired of the same old poster hanging in your room? Ask your parents if you can make your old poster into a new one. For example, you could make Michael Jordan play football.

First cover your work surface with newspaper. Now paint a football helmet and uniform on Michael Jordan. Let the paint dry and hang your new poster on the wall. Or make a poster of puppies into a poster of the latest space aliens. Use markers to draw in antennas on the puppies, spaceships in space, and stars in the sky.

You could also use these new posters as a game for your next party. Play pin the helmet on Michael or pin the antenna on the space alien puppies. Just draw helmet or antenna shapes on construction paper. Cut them out, put a piece of removable tape on the back of each, and use them as the game pieces to "pin" on the poster.

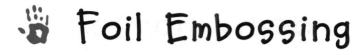 Foil Embossing

*Whether you emboss one pretty flower or a wild abstract design,
these wall hangings will shine in any room.*

What You'll Need
- poster board or cardboard
- blunt scissors
- craft glue
- pencil (optional)
- aluminum foil
- markers

Cut 2 backing pieces of poster board or cardboard into the size of the picture you want to make. It's best to start with a small piece, about 8×10 inches. Cut out some geometric shapes from poster board or cardboard. Glue them in a design on one of the backing pieces. For example, arrange triangle shapes into a pinwheel or square shapes into a checkerboard. Or ask a friend to trace your profile from a shadow, cut it out, and glue it on the backing.

After the glue has dried, place a piece of foil over the top of the shapes and rub until the design is raised onto the foil. Leave the foil in place and color the raised design with permanent markers. Then carefully remove the foil, and glue it on the other backing piece.

 No-Drawing Design

*How can you make a design without drawing? It's easy—
just use the sun to "draw" a picture.*

Gather several small household objects, such as a wrench, key, or small bowl. Place a piece of dark-color construction paper in a sunny spot outside or near a window. Arrange your objects on the paper. Leave the paper in the sunny spot for a week. After a week, remove the objects and you'll notice that the areas where the objects were are darker than the other areas. Now you have a no-drawing design. If you want, add some drawing to your picture to make the objects into something specific such as a person from the wrench or an alligator from the key.

What You'll Need
- household objects
- dark-color construction paper
- crayons or markers (optional)

Tracing Horses

*This project shows all the ways you can "see" a horse—
realistic, imaginary, colorful, or fuzzy.*

Look through a book or a magazine to find a picture of a horse. Using tracing paper and a pencil, trace the horse shape several times. Now use different coloring tools to decorate the horses. Color one in with crayons, and use chalk to fill in another. You can even cut and glue felt to cover one of the horses. Use as many different mediums to color your pictures as you can. Be creative with your colors, too. Your horses can be red and orange, or they can have purple and green stripes. Cut all your new horses out, and glue them into a poster picture on a piece of poster board.

What You'll Need
- book or magazine with pictures of horses
- tracing paper
- pencil
- crayons, pastel chalks, markers, or colored pencils
- felt
- blunt scissors
- craft glue
- poster board

Markers & Lines

*Draw shapes within shapes to create an optical illusion.
The picture is still there, but it becomes harder to see.*

What You'll Need
- drawing paper
- pencil
- markers

Sketch an outline of a house, yard, tree, and sun. Instead of coloring in the drawing with solid colors, use the markers to "color" it in with lines. Outline each element with marker, and fill in the shape with a continuous line. Or draw concentric shapes within each element until the area is filled in. You can also fill an area with a swirl of lines. If you want to "color in" a sky, draw several smaller areas of shapes and lines to divide it up. Another idea is to write your name and keep outlining it with markers. Use different colors for each outline to create a rainbow progression of colors.

Picture This

◆▶◆▶◆▶◆

Turn discarded frames into jeweled masterpieces.

What You'll Need

- newspaper
- plastic gloves
- old shirt
- small, old picture frame with wide, flat borders
- paper towels
- margarine tub
- plaster of paris
- old butter knife
- "glass pebbles" in gemstone colors

Caution: This project requires adult help.

Spread out the newspaper, and put on your gloves and an old shirt. Ask an adult to remove any glass from the frame and set it in a safe place. Wipe the frame with a damp paper towel, then dry it.

In the clean margarine tub, mix a small amount of plaster of paris according to package directions. (Have an adult help you with this part.) Use an old knife to spread plaster on the picture frame. Place a row of "glass pebbles" around the inner edge

of the frame. Make sure the pebbles are evenly spaced and in a variety of colors! Finish covering the frame surface in rows of "jewels." Let dry for a day. Use the leftover plaster to bejewel a flowerpot or throw it away in the trash, but don't pour it down the sink—it could cause a nasty clog! Enjoy your "jewel" of a frame!

Straw–Blown Painting

◆▶◆▶◆▶◆

*Here's a great way to make a splashy picture in wild colors—
without even touching the paper!*

Cover your work surface with newspaper. Tape a piece of drawing paper in the center of your work area. Dilute the poster paint with a little bit of water. Place 1 color of diluted poster paint on the paper. Now use your straw to blow the paint around on the paper. Before the paint dries, add another color and blow it around. Let the paint overlap and blend. Try blowing your paint from one corner or out from the center. When you're finished painting, let the paint dry.

What You'll Need

- newspaper
- removable tape
- drawing paper
- poster paints
- water
- plastic drinking straw

Toothpick Architecture

◆▸◆▸◆▸◆▸

***Create a tiny city, geometric shapes, or a circus tent with clowns.
You can build whatever your imagination dreams up.***

What You'll Need
- waxed paper
- plastic-based clay
- ruler
- toothpicks
- poster board

Place a sheet of waxed paper over your work surface. Roll the plastic-based clay into several ¼- to ½-inch balls. The number of balls you need to make will depend on what you're making, since the clay balls are the anchor joints of your toothpick creation. To make a person, you will need 7 balls of clay; to make a pyramid shape, you will need 4 balls of clay.

Insert a toothpick into a ball of clay. Connect the toothpicks with the clay balls until you have completed your structure. Place your finished projects on a piece of poster board to display your handiwork.

 # Snow Mobile

◆▸◆▸◆▸◆▸

Bring a little winter inside the house with a sparkling, snowy mobile.

What You'll Need
- silver or white glitter
- clear adhesive vinyl paper
- blunt scissors
- hole punch
- fishing line or white string
- white plastic-coated hanger
- tape
- flashlight (optional)

Spread silver or white glitter onto the sticky side of a piece of clear adhesive vinyl paper. Smooth another piece of vinyl paper over the top, and press out the air bubbles. Cut the glittered adhesive paper into snowballs, snow people, and snowflakes. Punch a hole near the top of each shape, and thread different lengths of fishing line or white string through each. (If you use fishing line, your shapes will look like they are floating mysteriously in the air.) Tie the other end of the fishing line or string to the hanger. Make sure some shapes hang lower than others to make your snow mobile more interesting. To hold the shapes firmly in place, tape the tied ends of the string to the hanger. Hang your mobile in a dark room, and shine a flashlight for some sparkling fun.

Advanced Paper Folding

Learn how to use "scoring" to create fancy paper-folding projects. This technique turns a flat piece of paper into three-dimensional art.

What You'll Need
- heavyweight paper or index cards
- ruler, compass, or French curve ruler
- blunt scissors
- clear tape

Scoring creates an impression on paper to use as a folding guide. This makes it easier to fold the paper into straight, curved, or wavy lines. To score a piece of paper, use a ruler to guide the point of your scissors as you "draw a line" on the paper. To make curvy or wavy lines, use a compass or French curve ruler. Here are some paper-folding ideas to get you started.

Cut out a big circle from a piece of paper. Use a compass to score 2 circles inside it. Cut a slit from the outer edge into the center. Fold 1 inside circle, pinching it along the score line. Turn the paper circle over, and fold the other inside circle. Overlap the cut ends, and tape them together to secure.

Cut out a curved shape from a piece of paper. Use a compass to score 4 curved lines on the shape. Fold each line, turning the paper over after each fold to alternate the fold direction.

Score some straight lines on a piece of paper. Fanfold the paper along the score lines, then fold in the corners. Open the fanfold, and pinch the top and bottom triangle folds in the opposite direction of each fanfold crease.

Storybook Quilt

▶◀▶◀▶◀▶◀

Stitch together squares of family pictures, sayings, stories, and more to make a quilt that tells the story of your family.

What You'll Need

- poster paper
- ruler
- blunt scissors
- family pictures
- markers
- glue
- clear vinyl adhesive paper
- hole punch
- large plastic needle
- yarn

Cut the poster paper into 6×6-inch squares. Make as many as you'd like, but make enough so that there are the same number down as across when placed as a grid pattern (for example, 4 down and 4 across).

Glue a picture of each family member on a separate square (don't forget your pets, and don't forget to ask for permission first!). Then write anecdotes (interesting stories), family sayings, or anything else that explains who your family really is. When all the squares are completed, cover each one with clear vinyl adhesive paper.

Punch holes around the outer edges of the squares, making certain they are evenly spaced by using a ruler. Be sure the holes of each square line up with the holes of the squares next to it. Thread a large plastic needle with yarn, and sew the squares together for a Storybook Quilt.

Hang your quilt with pride!

Crazy Putty Dough

With this putty dough, you can make all sorts of silly shapes or magically lift pictures off the funny pages.

What You'll Need
- ⅓ cup liquid starch
- baking sheet
- 1 cup craft glue
- craft stick or mixing spoon
- Sunday comics
- drawing paper

Pour liquid starch on a baking sheet. Using a craft stick or mixing spoon, slowly stir in craft glue. After it starts to clump, let the mixture set for 5 minutes. Dab a small amount of starch on your fingers, and knead the mixture. Now you can pull it, roll it, and stretch it—just like putty!

As you experiment with your homemade putty, use the baking sheet as your work surface. (Be careful not to get it on the carpet or furniture.) Use the putty to make prints of your favorite comics.

Press it on the comic strip, peel it back, and then press the putty on a piece of paper. When you're finished playing with the putty, store it in a small airtight plastic container.

Salt Clay Dough

Do something unexpected. Sculpt sports equipment, such as a bat and ball, or even food like pizza and hot dogs.

Caution: This project requires adult help.

Mix salt and flour in a bowl. Slowly add water until the mixture forms a doughlike consistency. Place a sheet of waxed paper on your work surface, and sprinkle it with some flour. Knead the clay dough until smooth. Sculpt clay into any shape you want, and then bake your sculpture on the aluminum foil. Have an adult help you bake thin objects for about 30 minutes at 350 degrees. Larger or thicker objects will require more baking time. After your clay creations have cooled, add some color with acrylic paints. Let the paint dry. Store unused clay in a resealable plastic bag or airtight container.

What You'll Need
- 1 cup salt
- 4 cups flour
- mixing bowl and spoon
- 1½ cups warm water
- waxed paper
- aluminum foil
- acrylic paints and paintbrush (optional)
- resealable plastic bag or airtight container

Feather Painting

Feathers are good for the inside of pillows, to tickle your friend's nose, and to make beautiful paintings!

What You'll Need
- newspaper
- India ink
- foam food trays (from fruits or vegetables only)
- poster paints
- 3 feathers (available at craft stores)
- drawing paper
- scissors or craft knife

Caution: This project requires adult help.

Cover your work surface with newspaper. Pour a bit of India ink on a clean foam food tray, and pour some poster paints in another tray. Paint a picture on a piece of drawing paper with one part of each feather: the quill end, the feather tip, and the feather web (edge). Dip the quill end in ink to create sharp lines, dots, and points. Dip the feather tip and the feather web in poster paint to create soft, sweeping lines.

To make a quill pen, ask an adult to cut off the end of the quill at an angle so that it tapers to a point. Then have the adult make a small slit in the middle of the tip. Dip the quill pen in some India ink, and write a letter or draw a picture. When the tip wears down, ask the adult to snip a bit off again for a fresh, sharp tip.

Hardware Sculpture

Nail down a fun metal sculpture.

Caution: This project requires adult help.

What You'll Need
- hardware (washers, nails, nuts, screws, bolts, etc.)
- household cement

Ask your parents to go through their spare hardware, or head for a hardware store to get started. Pick out a good-size washer, some tiny nails, drapery hooks, and anything else that captures your imagination. Have an adult help you glue the hardware together using household cement. (Be sure the room is well ventilated, and keep the glue out of your eyes.)

Want to make a ladybug? Try a washer with 6 tiny nail legs and miniature nut eyes. You are only limited by your supplies and your imagination!

3-D Picture

Outline a simple picture with colorful paper to make it a three-dimensional work of art.

What You'll Need
- pencil
- black and assorted colors of construction paper
- blunt scissors
- ruler
- craft glue
- pastel chalks

Draw a car on a piece of black construction paper. Then cut ¾-inch-wide strips from bright-color construction paper to outline the wheels, doors, and hood of the car. If your car is winding down a country road, outline a tree and a fence. Put a line of glue around the wheels, and stand the paper up in the glue. Bend the paper to match each part of the outline. Outline the whole car in stand-up paper. Use pastel chalks when you are finished to add more color to your picture.

You can also make great ornaments using this technique. After you've outlined your ornament shape, cut it out. Then outline the same design on the other side.

Fuzzy Photos

You can make special effects just like in the movies by putting something over the camera lens.

Stretch a piece of strong plastic wrap over the lens of your camera. Try to make the plastic wrap as smooth as possible without any wrinkles. Lightly rub a very thin coating of petroleum jelly over the plastic wrap. This technique creates a special effect with your photos. Take some pictures of different objects and people. Once the photos are developed, you'll notice they have a soft, fuzzy look.

What You'll Need
- heavy-duty plastic wrap
- camera
- color or black-and-white film
- petroleum jelly

Stencil Tiles

◆▸◆▸◆▸◆▸◆

You can make cheerful ceramic tiles.

What You'll Need
- tile
- stencil
- glass and tile paint
- clear gloss
- paintbrush

Caution: This project requires adult help.

Making lovely tile works of art is an easy way to make a great decoration! Buy craft tiles (about $1 each) at your local hobby or craft store. Decorate them with cheerful designs using a stencil and tile paint. (Have an adult read the paint label for precautions—are paints nontoxic, and do they need good air circulation for fumes? Always have an adult help you follow the label instructions!) Allow tiles to dry, then apply a thin layer of clear gloss to protect your hard work. Give the finished artwork as a gift to someone you love.

Brainteaser Art

◆▸◆▸◆▸◆▸◆

Be sure to count your shapes as you draw the picture or you could end up teasing yourself.

Use a stencil to create pictures out of geometric designs. Try a butterfly with lots of circles within circles or a house with squares for windows, shutters, chimneys, and even bricks. Keep track of the number of shapes you draw. If you want, use markers to make your brainteaser a kaleidoscope of color. When you're finished, challenge a friend or family member to count the shapes.

What You'll Need
- paper
- stencil shapes (available at office supply, craft, or art stores)
- pencil
- markers (optional)

Finger Paints #1

*Find tools that imitate nature's own textures. A sponge makes a great tree trunk.
A comb makes super ocean waves.*

What You'll Need
- newspaper
- 1 cup soap flakes
- mixing bowl and spoon
- warm water
- small dishes
- food coloring
- tape
- finger-paint paper
- comb, cotton swab, craft stick, and sponge

Cover your work surface with newspaper. Place soap flakes in a mixing bowl. Slowly stir in small amounts of warm water until the mixture is thick like pudding. Spoon mixture into separate dishes. Stir in a few drops of food coloring in each dish.

Tape a piece of finger-paint paper down on your work surface. Spoon some finger paint onto the paper, and use your fingers and hands to swirl it all over. Blend the colors—especially red, yellow, and blue—to make new ones. Use the painting

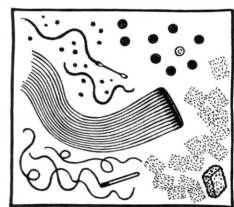

tools to scratch designs in the paint. Experiment with other types of paper, too. Try finger painting on foil, cardboard, and even plastic wrap.

 # Quilt-Patterned Collage

*Use quilt shapes, such as squares, triangles, and hexagons,
to piece together a patterned collage.*

Make a quilt-patterned collage using magazine pictures instead of fabric. Look for a magazine picture in colors that you like. Once you have selected a picture, cut it into several 2×2-inch squares (be sure to ask for permission first!). Then cut some of the squares in half, diagonally, to form triangles. Now piece your quilt collage together on a piece of construction paper. Once you have arranged the pieces in a pattern you like, glue them in place.

What You'll Need
- old magazines
- blunt scissors
- ruler
- construction paper
- craft glue

Sculpting Clay Dough

◆◆◆◆◆◆

Ever wondered what a yellow elephant looks like? Or a purple spaceship?
Find out when you sculpt and paint your wildest fantasy.

What You'll Need
- saucepan
- 1 cup cornstarch
- 2 cups baking soda
- 1¼ cups water
- mixing spoon
- waxed paper
- poster paints
- paintbrush
- resealable plastic bag or airtight container (optional)

Caution: This project requires adult help.

In a saucepan, mix cornstarch, baking soda, and water. With an adult's help, heat it on a medium setting. Stir the mixture continuously until it thickens. Let it cool.

Place a sheet of waxed paper over your work surface. Knead the clay dough for a few minutes. Roll the clay into a ball, and shape it into small sculptures. Pinch ears and legs to make bears, bugs, and bunnies. Let the figures air dry, then paint them using poster paints.

You can also use this homemade clay for the Sculpting Clay Statues project on page 215—just let it air dry instead of baking it. If you want to play with the clay another day, store it in a resealable plastic bag or an airtight container, and keep it in the refrigerator.

Big Brush Art

◆◆◆◆◆◆

All the best artists know that sometimes an unusual paintbrush creates
the most remarkable picture.

Caution: This project requires adult help.

With an adult's help, cut out a large panel of cardboard. Cover your work area with newspaper. Paint a painting on your cardboard "canvas" using a 1-inch paintbrush and poster paint.

What You'll Need
- large cardboard box
- blunt scissors
- newspaper
- 1-inch paintbrush or foam brush
- poster paints

Illustrate something big like a skyscraper, the Grand Canyon, or even a Ferris wheel. You can also paint something that is small on a large scale. Try filling the whole space with one autumn leaf or a bouquet of sunflowers.

Acrylic on Acrylic

If you color outside the lines, it really doesn't matter. They're your guide for coloring in a design, and then you erase the lines anyway.

What You'll Need
- scrap paper
- ⅛-inch-thick sheet of clear acrylic (available at hobby stores or home centers; cut to fit your desk top)
- grease pencil
- acrylic paints
- paintbrush
- paper towels

Cover your work surface with scrap paper. Use a grease pencil to draw a design on a sheet of acrylic. Create a theme to match your room, hobbies, or interests. Turn the acrylic sheet over on the paper with the drawing side down. Using the grease pencil outlines as your guide, fill in the design with acrylic paints. Start painting in the middle of the sheet first, then work toward the edges. Let the paint dry. Turn the sheet over and wipe off the grease pencil using a paper towel. Place the acrylic sheet on your desk, paint side down.

Emotional Painting

Are you feeling blue, green with envy, or pretty in pink? Color a self-portrait to match your mood.

Cover your work surface with newspaper. Draw a picture on a piece of drawing paper. Draw the same picture on another piece of paper, or make a photocopy of your first drawing. Now think of warm and cool colors. Warm colors are the colors of fire: red, orange, and yellow. Cool colors are the colors of ice: blue, green, and purple. Think of what the colors would be for opposite emotions, such as love/hate, happiness/sadness, and anger/peace. Once you've assigned colors to the different emotions, paint your

What You'll Need
- newspaper
- drawing paper
- pencil
- watercolor or poster paints
- paintbrush

pictures. Paint 1 picture in the colors of 1 emotion, then paint the other picture in the colors of the opposite emotion. Let the paint dry, and compare your paintings.

Foam Tray Casting

◆▶◆▶◆▶◆

Look for small, flat objects, and reproduce their shapes.

What You'll Need
- newspaper
- foam food tray (from fruits or vegetables only)
- craft knife, cookie cutters, keys, or screws (to press in foam tray)
- plaster of paris
- paper clip (optional)
- acrylic paints
- paintbrush

Caution: This project requires adult help.

Cover your work surface with newspaper. Use a craft knife (adult use only!), cookie cutters, keys, and other objects to carve and press shapes in the foam food tray. Press objects in a design or a picture. To create more detail, press hard into the foam, but don't cut all the way through the foam!

Have an adult help you mix the plaster of paris according to package directions. Carefully pour the plaster in the foam tray. (Be sure to throw unused plaster away. Do not pour it down the sink; it will clog the pipes.) If you'd like to hang your plaster casting, press a paper clip into the top edge. Let the plaster set. When it's dry, pop it out of the tray. Add color to your plaster casting with acrylic paints.

Spin Art

◆▶◆▶◆▶◆

This art project will have your head spinning.

Caution: This project requires adult help.

With an adult's help, carefully push a nail down through the middle of the bottom of a cardboard box so the nail pokes through to the outside of the box. Your box should have high sides to prevent paint from splattering. Push a cork onto the nail, or use a hammer to gently tap a wood block onto the nail.

Cover your work area with newspaper. Cut a piece of paper to fit inside the box. Tape the paper to the sides of the box to hold it in place. Put dabs of slightly watered-down poster paint on the paper. Hold the cork (or wood block), and spin the box. The paint will fly toward the sides of the box. Untape the paper from the box. Place your artwork on newspaper to dry.

What You'll Need
- cardboard box
- nail
- cork, or small wood block and hammer
- newspaper
- drawing paper or construction paper
- blunt scissors
- removable tape
- poster paints
- water

Seed Collage

◆▸◆▸◆▸◆▸

When you recycle seeds from fruits and vegetables, it's as if you're growing a beautiful piece of artwork.

What You'll Need
- dry seeds (from fruits, vegetables, or plants)
- paper plates
- construction paper
- craft glue
- markers (optional)

Gather seeds from melons, squash, pumpkins, and other plants. Look for different colors. Wash the seeds. Spread the seeds out on a paper plate, and place it in a sunny window. They should be dry in a few days. Once the seeds are dry, use them to create a collage. Apply lines of glue to a piece of construction paper. Sprinkle the seeds over the glue. Let the glue dry. Shake off the excess seeds. Continue gluing and adding seeds to your collage. Try sprinkling white pumpkin seeds with black watermelon seeds to create a contrasting design. You can also use markers to make part of the picture, and then add the seeds to fill it in.

Marble Painting

◆▸◆▸◆▸◆▸

You're never boxed in with this unpredictable painting technique. No two designs are ever alike.

What You'll Need
- drawing paper
- blunt scissors
- cardboard box
- removable tape
- rubber gloves
- poster paints
- marbles

Cut a piece of drawing paper to fit the bottom of your box. Tape the paper to the bottom of the box. Wearing rubber gloves, dip a marble in poster paint. Place the marble on the paper. Now tilt, wiggle, and twirl the box around to make designs—the marble is your paintbrush! Let the paint dry. Use more marbles dipped in other colors to add to your design. Experiment with different colors of paper and paint. Start with red paper and make only white marble tracks. Or try black paper with fluorescent-colored paints. Once all the colors are dry, remove the paper from the box and display your artwork on the wall.

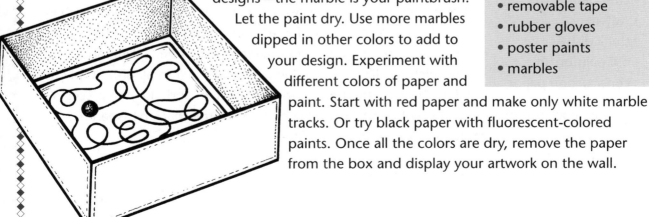

Paint with Texture

◆▶◆▶◆▶◆▶

Painting with bumpy paint creates a three-dimensional effect that will make everyone say, "Wow!"

What You'll Need
- newspaper
- sawdust, dry coffee grounds, sand, dried herbs, or washed and crushed eggshells
- plastic egg carton or small dishes
- poster paints
- pencil
- drawing paper
- paintbrushes

Cover your work surface with newspaper. Place small amounts of textured materials, such as sawdust, in sections of the empty egg carton or on small dishes. Add poster paint in each section, and mix the textured materials and the paint together.

Draw a picture on a piece of drawing paper. Paint it in with the textured paint. Whether you draw a porcupine or a fire truck, your painting will have a 3-D effect. Use plain poster paint to create smooth areas of paint on your picture.

 # Tear-It-Up Mosaic

◆▶◆▶◆▶◆▶

Take apart a picture to find the basic shapes that make it up, and create an interesting final picture.

What You'll Need
- old magazine
- craft glue
- water
- small dish
- old paintbrush
- construction paper

Find a picture you like in an old magazine, and tear it out (be sure to ask for permission first!). "Take apart" the picture by tearing it up into separate pieces. Look at the major shapes or colors in the picture and tear these pieces out. For example, if your picture has a large area of a color, tear that area into tiny pieces and the rest of the picture into bigger pieces. After you're done "taking apart" your picture, dilute some glue with water in a small dish. Apply the diluted glue to the back of the torn pieces, and glue the pieces of the picture back together on a piece of construction paper. Leave some space between the pieces. This makes your picture look like a mosaic. Let the glue dry.

Pyramid Pictures

◆▷◆▷◆▷◆

*By overlapping several pieces of construction paper, you're building
a picture to create depth.*

What You'll Need
- assorted colors of construction paper
- blunt scissors
- markers
- craft glue

Cut a small rectangle from a piece of construction paper. Draw an object or design on it. Cut a slightly larger rectangle from another piece of construction paper using a different color. Glue the small rectangle on top of the larger one. Add more detail to your picture. Then cut an even larger rectangle from another piece of construction paper using a different color. Glue the previous rectangles on top of the bigger rectangle. Draw more designs around your picture. Repeat the process as often as you like to make a pyramid of pictures.

As a variation, you can draw parts of a picture on each piece to create one complete scene. Or instead of rectangles, cut out octagon shapes. Glue them on top of one another, turning them a bit each time to make your picture into a star.

Crewel Burlap

Artwork can be drawn with pen, pencil, or paint, but it can also be drawn with yarn.

What You'll Need
- craft burlap (available at craft or fabric stores)
- markers
- assorted colors of yarn
- needlepoint needle

Draw a picture on burlap with markers. You could make a picture of a garden with a scarecrow and a split-rail fence with a line of crows. Following the outline, sew yarn around your picture in long and short stitches. Go in and out with a needlepoint needle using different colors of yarn to match what you are outlining. You can even fill in areas by going back and forth with the yarn. Pick small areas to fill in that need emphasizing in your picture, such as the black crows and the scarecrow's face.

Continuous Picture

Here's a drawing challenge. Create a picture using only one line—a long, continuous line.

Draw a picture on a piece of paper, but don't lift up your pencil or pen as you draw. Make a picture with 1 long, continuous line. Start drawing a person, then make him or her into a vampire. Start with the mouth, add pointy teeth, and then draw the nose and eyes. Next, fill in the head and body with a bat cape. Just don't pick up your pencil or pen! Try drawing a continuous picture using colored pencils or crayons. Start your drawing in 1 color, then when you change colors, continue the drawing at the ending point of the last color.

What You'll Need
- drawing paper
- pencil or pen
- colored pencils or crayons

Art in Pieces

◆▷◆▷◆▷◆

One picture is worth 1,000 giggles when you try drawing
a picture in nine separate sections.

What You'll Need

- old magazines
- ruler
- pencil
- blunt scissors
- drawing paper
- craft glue
- colored pencils
- crayons, chalk, or acrylic or watercolor paints and paintbrushes (optional)

Find a picture you like in a magazine. Draw a large square around it, then divide it into 9 equal squares. Cut out the small squares (be sure to ask for permission first!). On a piece of drawing paper, draw the picture in 1 cut square; you can even turn the square upside down to concentrate on the lines. As you draw, concentrate on the spacing of the lines rather than the outline. Repeat this drawing technique for each square.

After you're done drawing, cut out the squares, reassemble your picture on a piece of paper, and glue in place. Color in your picture. Another idea is to fill in your square pieces before you put them together using different coloring tools. Color some in with crayon, chalk, and even acrylic or watercolor paints.

Ghost Pictures

◆▶◆▶◆▶◆▶

With a little trickery, you can make the camera see things that aren't really there, such as a ghost.

What You'll Need
- white sheet
- flashlight
- camera with adjustable shutter speed
- black-and-white film
- markers
- construction paper
- tape or glue

Have a friend or family member wear a white sheet. Shine a flashlight on the "ghost." Set the camera on the table. Look through the lens, and adjust the position of the camera so that the ghost is toward the left in the viewfinder. Set the shutter speed for 1 second. Now turn off all the lights in the room. Push the camera button to take a picture, then move the camera slightly. Take more ghost pictures. This time instead of moving the camera, tell the "ghost" to move very slowly. Draw a picture of a haunted house, then add the ghostly photos to your picture.

Rice Picture

◆▶◆▶◆▶◆▶

Colored rice gives your picture a grainy texture. Experiment with different dyes, such as chalk or even spices.

Caution: This project requires adult help.

With an adult's help, grate one color of chalk onto a paper plate using a cheese grater. Repeat with other colors, keeping them separate. Or place different colors of spices on paper plates. Mix white rice in with each color. Dilute craft glue with water in a small dish. Use an old paintbrush to paint a picture with the diluted glue on a piece of construction paper. Choosing one color of rice, hold the paper plate like a funnel and pour the colored rice over the glue. Let it set, then pour off the excess rice. Repeat the process with another area of the picture using a different color.

What You'll Need
- pastel chalk or spices like ground mustard, cinnamon, and paprika
- paper plates
- cheese grater
- uncooked white rice
- craft glue
- water
- small dish
- old paintbrush
- construction paper

Finger Paints #2

This is two projects in one. First you finger paint a design, then you transfer it to another piece of paper.

What You'll Need
- newspaper
- mixing bowl and spoon
- 1½ cups liquid starch
- ½ cup water
- 1 cup flour
- small bowls
- food coloring
- baking sheet or plastic tablecloth
- finger-paint paper
- airtight containers
- plastic wrap

Cover your work surface with newspaper. To make the finger paint, mix the liquid starch, water, and flour together. Stir until it reaches a smooth consistency. Divide the mixture into several small bowls, and add a few drops of food coloring to each bowl. Dip your fingers in the paint, and draw your design right on a baking sheet or plastic tablecloth. (Cleanup is easy since this finger paint washes off easily.)

To make a print of your picture, place a piece of finger-paint paper over your artwork and press. Lift the paper off, and let it dry flat. Store any extra paint in airtight containers. Place plastic wrap over the surface of the paint to keep the air out.

Bed Banner

Every night before bed, admire your banner to ensure good dreams throughout the night.

Fold the shorter ends of the felt over about 2 inches, and glue them in place to form pockets. Insert a dowel through each pocket, then glue the beads on each end. Cut pieces of fabric and felt to make a picture. Do you dream of being an astronaut, a ballet dancer, or a basketball player? Cut out shapes to match your dreams. Apply a thin film of glue on the back of each cutout shape. Assemble the pieces on the felt banner to make your picture. Tie a piece of yarn or string to the ends of the top dowel. Hang the banner above your bed.

What You'll Need
- 36×48-inch piece of felt
- ruler
- fabric glue
- 2 wood dowels, 36 inches long, ½ inch diameter
- 4 large wood beads
- fabric and felt scraps
- blunt scissors
- yarn or string

Kitchen Collection Art

◆►◆►◆►◆►

It's hard to believe that such a beautiful picture started out as odds and ends headed for the garbage can.

What You'll Need
- plastic cup
- markers
- collection of throw-away items, such as bottle caps, string, or rubber bands
- craft glue
- construction paper or cardboard

Place a plastic cup in the kitchen to collect all kinds of throwaway items. Label your cup "Kitchen Collection" so that everyone knows to put the items in the cup. Once the cup is full, take a look at what you have collected. Arrange and glue the objects into an interesting collage on a piece of construction paper or cardboard. You'll have so much fun collecting the items that you may want to put a cup in the laundry room and your bedroom for other kinds of objects.

 # Sand Jars

◆►◆►◆►◆►

If you think sand belongs only at the beach, think again. This project lets you turn ordinary sand into artwork.

Cover your work surface with newspaper. Mix small amounts of sand with different colors of powdered poster paints in small dishes. Carefully pour one color at a time into a glass jar. Tilt the jar, and add about ½ inch of one color

of sand. Tilt the glass the other way, and add another ½ inch of sand using a different color. Keep tilting the glass and alternating colors until the jar is full. Decorate the lid of the jar with acrylic paints. When the paint is dry, place the lid on the jar. Be careful not to shake your sand picture.

What You'll Need
- newspaper
- sand
- small dishes
- powdered poster paints
- spoon
- clean glass jars with lids
- ruler
- acrylic paints and paintbrush

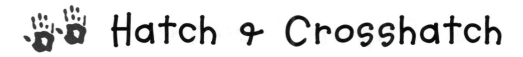

Hatch & Crosshatch

◆▸◆▸◆▸◆▸

***This art technique uses lines to create highlights
and shadows in your drawing.***

What You'll Need
- drawing paper
- pencil, ballpoint pen, or felt-tip pen

The hatch-crosshatch technique uses small lines to create dark areas (shadows) and light areas (highlights) in a drawing. Hatch marks are lines drawn in the same direction, and crosshatch marks are lines crossed over each other in 2 or 3 directions. Fewer lines create light areas and more lines create dark areas. Practice this technique to add shadows and highlights to your drawings.

Sketch an outline of a picture, such as an apple, on a piece of drawing paper. Make hatch and crosshatch marks to "color" in the apple. Create shadows along the side and bottom of the apple with crosshatch marks. Highlight the center and the top of the apple with hatch marks.

Sand Casting

◆▸◆▸◆▸◆▸

***If you take your time and have a little patience, you can create beautiful
sculptures to enjoy forever.***

Caution: This project requires adult help.

Cover your work surface with newspaper. Fill the pie pan about half full with sand. Add oil until the sand sticks together. Pat the sand base down to about 1 inch thick in the pie pan. Build up a ½- to ¾-inch rim around the edges. Use a small spoon or knife to press in a design, dig holes, or build ridges in the sand. Use a toothpick to create finer lines or letters. If you are making projections like legs or stems, place straightened paper clips in the sand to strengthen your plaster casting.

What You'll Need
- newspaper
- pie pan
- brown or white sand
- vegetable oil
- ruler
- small spoon or knife
- toothpicks
- paper clips
- plaster of paris
- mixing spoon

Have an adult help you mix the plaster of paris following package directions. Carefully spoon the plaster into the sand mold. If you'd like to hang your plaster casting, press a paper clip into the top edge. Let the plaster set overnight. When it's dry, remove your cast from the sand and brush off excess sand.

 # Paper Mosaic

◆▶◆▶◆▶◆

Original mosaics were made with small pieces of tiles. You'll use small pieces of paper to make this mosaic. Awesome!

What You'll Need
- scratch paper
- pencil
- white drawing paper
- blunt scissors
- ruler
- construction paper (or colored foil or wallpaper sample pages)
- paper cutter (optional)
- glue stick

Caution: This project requires adult help.

Make a sketch of a scene on a piece of scratch paper. Fill the entire piece of paper with the scene (flowers, birds, tropical fish, and fruit are things that work well for this). When you are happy with your sketch, draw it again on the drawing paper.

With scissors, make ½-inch strips of the construction paper (or foil or wallpaper samples). If you have a paper cutter, have an adult make the strips. Cut the strips into small squares. Again, an adult can do this on the paper cutter, or you can do it with scissors.

Glue the paper onto the objects in your picture, and use the colors you have creatively. An apple, for example, can have many colors: light red, dark red, and red-brown that could be used to show shading. Place the squares as close together as possible, leaving white paper showing through to look as though the mosaics are embedded in plaster.

When you are done with your picture, mount the finished work on a larger sheet of construction paper for display.

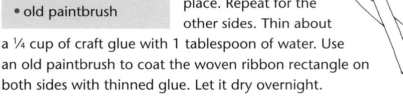

Ribbon Art

Use this weaving technique to create textured artwork you can hang on the wall.

What You'll Need
- assorted colors of 1-inch-wide satin ribbon (about 3 yards)
- blunt scissors
- ruler
- aluminum foil
- removable tape
- craft glue
- water
- measuring cups and spoons
- small dish
- old paintbrush

Cut ribbon into five 9-inch strips. Use remaining ribbon to cut seven 7-inch strips. Cover your work surface with a sheet of aluminum foil. Place the five 9-inch strips on the foil side by side, vertically. Tape the edges of them down. Starting 1 inch from the top of the strips, weave a 7-inch strip over and under each ribbon horizontally. Position the 7-inch strip so that 1 inch of each end is left unwoven, and tape it securely down. Repeat the weaving technique with the remaining 7-inch strips. When you are finished, you should have a 1-inch unwoven border around the edges of the ribbon rectangle. Remove the tape from one side, and weave each end of the ribbon back into a square. Glue in place. Repeat for the other sides. Thin about

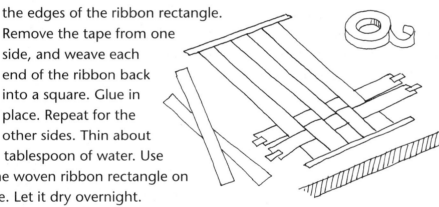

a ¼ cup of craft glue with 1 tablespoon of water. Use an old paintbrush to coat the woven ribbon rectangle on both sides with thinned glue. Let it dry overnight.

Rubbings

It seems like all you're doing is moving a crayon back and forth. Then almost like magic, an object appears.

Place a piece of paper over some leaves. Rub a crayon back and forth over the paper to show the texture of the leaves. Use this technique to experiment with other textures. Use paper and crayons to rub over textured surfaces around the house, such as wood floors, tile, bulletin boards, or greeting cards with raised designs. Mix and match textures on one piece of paper to create a textural collage.

What You'll Need
- drawing paper
- leaves
- crayons

 # Snowstorm Art

◆▷◆▷◆▷◆

*You don't need snow to create a snowstorm. Starch or glue and
a little rice will make a dazzling storm!*

What You'll Need
- construction paper
- markers or crayons
- liquid starch or glue
- paintbrush or cotton swabs
- uncooked rice

Do you love the winter weather, even when it's too cold outside to play? Well, make a winter project in your warm house that expresses how much you love the snow!

Draw a winter scene on the construction paper. Do you like sledding or building snow creatures? Then draw that! A pretty cabin in the woods with smoke curling out of the chimney would also make a pretty picture. Create whatever scene you'd like.

When you are done drawing and coloring your picture, brush a generous amount of starch or glue over your picture on the construction paper. Sprinkle the rice over the glue on the paper. Shake off the excess rice, and discard. (Don't put the rice back in the package—you won't want to be eating starched or glued rice for dinner!)

Now watch out for the blizzard!

 # Scratch Board

◆◆◆◆◆◆

Etch a design on scratch board, and you'll see the contrast between dramatic black and bold brights.

What You'll Need
- newspaper
- card stock or poster board
- crayons
- black poster paint
- dish soap
- spoon
- bowl
- paintbrush
- metal nail file, toothpick, or pointed craft stick

Cover your work surface with newspaper. Color a piece of card stock or poster board with crayons in assorted colors, covering the paper completely with a thick layer—color very hard. Mix black poster paint and 2 drops of dish soap together. Paint the mixture over the layer of crayon coloring. Let the paint mixture dry completely. Use a nail file, toothpick, or craft stick to scratch off the paint in a design or a picture, just as if you were drawing a picture on a piece of paper. Now your picture practically jumps off the paper!

 # Chalk It

◆◆◆◆◆◆

It's incredible how one piece of pastel chalk creates two different colors when you draw on wet paper and then on dry paper.

Caution: This project requires adult help.

Fold a piece of construction paper in half. Dampen one half of the sheet by dabbing it with a moist sponge. Draw a design on both the wet and dry halves of the paper with pastel chalks. Make a squiggle picture by drawing a continuous curvy line all around the paper. Add more squiggles, and color in the spaces. Now compare the colors on the wet and dry surfaces of the paper. When the paper dries, you can have an adult seal the picture with a fine mist of hairspray.

What You'll Need
- construction paper
- moist sponge
- pastel chalk
- hairspray (optional)

# Net Scape

◆▸◆▸◆▸◆▸

Use the Internet to express your artful side.

Are you in full command of the World Wide Web and eager to make that connection clear? Why not surf the Net for a few cyber sensations, and turn those discoveries into art?

Go to your favorite Internet search engine. Type in a fun topic (a name, a band you like, a country in Asia, a flavor of ice cream), and see what comes into view. If you find a picture, statement, or logo that really makes you smile, print it out and set it aside. Once you get 4 or 5 great printouts, turn them into an expressive cyber collage. Be sure to date the back of the page and put it in a safe place. Pull it out in weeks or years to enjoy it all over again.

What You'll Need
- computer with Internet access and Web browser
- printer
- blank paper
- white glue
- pen

Photo Collage

◆▸◆▸◆▸◆▸

You can describe a particular object with a series of photographs and never even say or write a word.

What You'll Need
- camera
- color film
- craft glue
- long matboard (available at art supply stores)

Take a series of different photos of the same thing, such as several types of dogs or closeups of a variety of flowers. Glue the photographs in a row on a colorful piece of matboard. Choose a color that picks up something in your pictures. You can also take a series of pictures of parts of an object. For instance, take photos of car tires, the trunk of the car, and the car grille. Put them together on the matboard. Make several photo collages and have a showing of your photography.

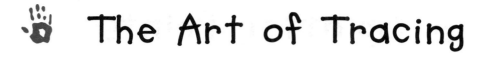

The Art of Tracing

◆◆◆◆◆◆◆

Tracing an object is just the beginning. The fun comes when you color it in, using imagination and wild designs.

You can trace any picture without tracing paper. Pick a picture from a magazine that you want to trace, and cut it out (ask for permission first!). Tape the picture with a piece of paper over it on a window. You can see the outline of the picture through the paper. Use a black felt-tip pen to trace the outline of the picture. Take the picture and paper off the window. Now add your own details to the outline, and color them in. For example, if you traced a picture of a dog, then draw and color in the eyes, a nose, the fur—or whatever else you want to add. Another idea is to use the shape to make it into something else. Use the outline of a dog to make a monster or space alien instead.

What You'll Need
• old magazines
• blunt scissors
• lightweight white paper
• masking tape
• black felt-tip pen
• colored pencils or markers

Assemblage

◆◆◆◆◆◆◆

Collect objects with interesting shapes and textures, and assemble them to make a unique sculpture.

What You'll Need
• household objects
• shoe-box lid
• craft glue
• poster paint and paintbrush (optional)

Look around your house for a variety of objects, such as empty spools, buttons, and paper clips. Try to find items in different sizes, shapes, and textures. You might look for all round items, all long items, or all rough and smooth items. Once you have gathered the objects, assemble them in a design on the inside of a shoe-box lid. Try for balance in shapes, textures, or size throughout the arrangement. After your design is in place, glue the objects to the lid. If you want, paint everything in one color before you glue them to the lid to add emphasis to your design.

# Splatter Prints

◆▶◆▶◆▶◆▶

You're in good shape when you use this terrific painting technique to outline favorite objects.

What You'll Need
- newspaper
- old paint shirt
- drawing paper
- large cardboard box
- pressed flower, leaf, or key
- old toothbrush
- watercolor or poster paints

Cover your work surface with newspaper. Put on an old paint shirt. Place a piece of drawing paper in a large cardboard box. Place a pressed flower or other item on the paper. Dip the bristles of an old toothbrush in watercolor or poster paint. Point the toothbrush down at the paper. Now rub your finger over the bristles toward yourself to splatter the paint around the flower. Remove the flower. The splattered paint looks like confetti outlining your picture. Let the paint dry. To create rainbow splatters, use different colors of paints.

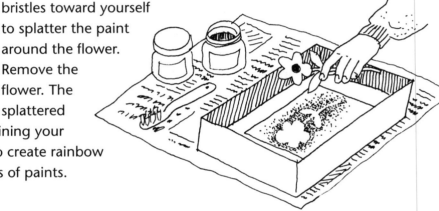

Palette Painting

◆▶◆▶◆▶◆▶

This technique uses dabs and dots of paint instead of straight lines, adding dimension to your artwork.

In a small dish, mix a small amount of cornstarch with poster paint until the mixture becomes thick like pudding. Repeat with other colors of paint. Now "paint" a picture on a piece of cardboard. Use a craft stick or butter knife to apply the thick paint to the cardboard. The paint will "stick up" from your paper. Try an abstract design first. Create "heavy" areas of color by building up the thick paint; to make "light" areas of color, spread the paint out. Then try to "paint" a portrait of someone. Since you are painting with a craft stick, you won't be able to add a lot of detail.

What You'll Need
- cornstarch
- poster paints
- small dishes
- cardboard
- craft stick or butter knife

Brayer Printing

◆▸▸▸▸◆

A brayer applies paint evenly to larger areas without brush lines.
These are important goals for fine printmaking.

What You'll Need
- brayer
- palette (sheet of acrylic or glass)
- duct tape
- newspaper
- masking tape
- finger-paint paper
- poster paints

Caution: This project requires adult help.

A brayer, or ink roller, rolls paint evenly and is great for printmaking. To "ink" a brayer, you'll need something smooth and flat to roll the paint on, such as a sheet of acrylic or glass. With an adult's help, place duct tape around the edges of the palette to cover any rough ends. Cover your work surface with newspaper.

Place pieces of masking tape across a piece of finger-paint paper to create a stripe design. Put 3 dots of paint on the palette in a row. Roll the brayer 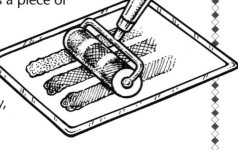 in one direction until it is coated with 3 stripes. Roll the inked brayer over the paper to make a stripe design. When the paint is dry, peel off the tape.

Cutout Collage

◆▸▸▸▸◆

This cutout collage will look like ones made by Henri Matisse,
a famous French painter who created similar designs when arthritis made it
impossible for him to paint in his later years.

Matisse used geometric (squares, rectangles, triangles, circles, etc.) and organic (those found in nature) shapes in his compositions. Geometric shapes are symmetrical; if you were to fold them in half, they would touch equally on all sides. Organic shapes, on the other hand, are not symmetrical; they include squiggles and blobs.

Begin cutting out shapes in many different sizes and colors from the colored paper. Once you have a collection of shapes, arrange them on a sheet of white or black paper. Glue the cutouts in place. If you made your collage on white paper, mount the work onto black construction paper to create a striking contrast.

What You'll Need
- colored construction paper or tissue paper
- blunt scissors
- white or black construction paper
- glue

Glitter Globe

◆◆◆◆◆◆◆

Snow globes are fun to watch, and these miniature glitter globes are fascinating.

What You'll Need

- small baby food jar
- acrylic paint and paintbrush (optional)
- clay
- any small metal or plastic trinket
- iridescent confetti flakes
- teaspoon
- water

Remove labels from the baby food jar. Wash and dry the jar thoroughly. If you wish, you may paint the outside of the lid with acrylic paints. Let the paint dry. Then put a dime-size amount of clay on the inside of the jar lid, and stick the bottom of the trinket into the clay. Place 1 teaspoon of confetti in the jar; use more or less confetti depending on the size of the jar. Slowly let water trickle into the jar until it's full. Screw the lid on tightly, and turn over the jar. Watch the sparkling glitter rain down!

Bathtub Art

◆◆◆◆◆◆◆

When you're done with one foamy picture, lightly wipe your hand over the surface and you have a new canvas.

Here's a fun project to do while you are in the bathtub. Cover a side wall of the tub with a big handful of shaving cream. Use your fingers, a comb, a washcloth, or a sponge to draw a picture in the shaving cream. If you want to make a different picture, wipe your hand over the surface of the shaving cream and start all over again. When you are done creating your bathtub art, make sure you rinse off the shaving cream from the bathtub wall.

If you are not in a bathtub, use a baking sheet as your canvas. Place a handful of shaving cream or nondairy whipped cream on the sheet. Add a drop of food coloring to the cream, and blend together. Now you're ready to create some fun art.

What You'll Need

- shaving cream or nondairy whipped cream
- bathtub wall or baking sheet
- comb, washcloth, or sponge
- food coloring

 # Things on Springs

◆▶◆▶◆▶◆

Anybody can make a mobile, but can they make one as springy as yours?

What You'll Need

- coat hanger
- brightly colored electrical tape
- 4 to 6 little trinkets or game pieces
- construction paper
- blunt scissors
- ruler
- black darning thread
- needle

Wrap the coat hanger in brightly colored electrical tape. Choose 4 to 6 trinkets or game pieces to hang from the mobile. Now make large and small "springs." Start by cutting a 3-inch square out of construction paper. Starting at the outside edge, cut the square, turning at the corners and spiraling inward to the center. Leave a "knob" the size of a penny in the center.

Thread the needle, make a knot, and poke through the underside of the "knob." Cut the thread about 5 inches from the knot, and tie the end around the bottom part of the coat hanger. Knot another piece of thread, and going from the top of the spring to the bottom, poke the needle through the outside edge of the square. Next, knot the thread around a hanging trinket. Notice how the square looks like a spring? Make springs unique by starting with triangular or other shapes and cutting toward the center. To make a longer spring, start with a bigger shape. Use a smaller shape for a shorter spring. Finish making springs and hang your trinkets. Display your springy mobile!

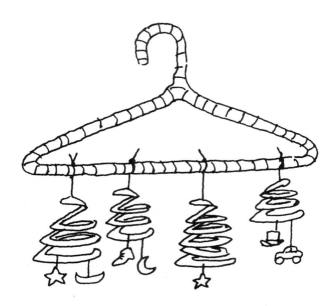

CREATIVE CRAFTS

These crafts are fun to make and fun to use. Create these functional projects once, then alter them to make them unique—you can even combine one idea with another for something really original. After you work on these activities, these activities will work for you!

 ## "Record" Achievement

◆▶◆▶◆▶◆▶

When you want to recognize someone for a major achievement, surprise them with this!

What You'll Need
- newspaper
- inexpensive 8×10-inch picture frame and cardboard liner
- discarded music CD
- acrylic gold paint
- paintbrush
- small game pieces or metal charms
- clear gel glue
- white paper
- pencil
- blunt scissors
- low-plush velvet fabric remnant
- rubber cement
- gold glitter marker

Spread out the newspaper, and lay the CD and the picture frame on it (use the glass of the frame for some other project). Set the cardboard liner from the picture frame aside. Paint one side of the CD and the frame gold. When the frame is dry, use clear gel glue to attach the game pieces or metal charms to the outside of the frame. While they dry, trace around the cardboard liner on white paper. Cut this out, and use it as a pattern to cut out the velvet.

Practice writing on velvet scraps with the gold glitter marker. Plan what to write. Be brief! You will write the name of the person receiving the award first, then the kind of award. Brush the back of the velvet and the front of the cardboard liner with rubber cement. Then put them together, and let dry.

Next, use the rubber cement to glue the CD to the top center of the velvet (be sure there is enough room around the edges to put

this piece into the frame). Write the award information on the velvet with the marker. Let the words dry, and put it into the frame. Surprise your super-achieving friend!

 # Breakfast for the Birds

This breakfast is strictly for the birds—don't you taste it!

What You'll Need

- 2 cups biscuit baking mix
- water
- tablespoon
- mixing bowl
- mixing spoon
- rolling pin
- cookie cutters
- spatula
- baking sheet
- straw
- 2 tablespoons margarine
- small saucepan
- pastry brush
- 2 tablespoons sesame seeds
- 2 tablespoons sunflower seeds
- fork
- cooling rack
- ribbon

Caution: This project requires adult help.

Ask an adult to preheat the oven to 425 degrees. Add enough water (just a few tablespoons) to the baking mix to form a soft dough. Roll out the dough to ¾-inch thickness, and cut it into shapes with the cookie cutters.

Using a spatula, put the shapes on a baking sheet. Use the straw to punch a hole in the top of each cookie.

Ask an adult to melt the margarine. Brush the melted margarine over the dough. Sprinkle the seeds onto the dough, and press them in firmly with a fork.

Bake for 15 to 20 minutes or until light brown. Remove cookies with a spatula, and place them on a cooling rack.

When the cookies are cool, thread brightly colored ribbon through the holes. Hang the bird snacks in a tree. Now wait for the birds to enjoy their breakfast! (Note: If birds don't eat the biscuits right away, check after a few days to be sure the biscuits aren't moldy. If they are, remove them from the tree and make fresh ones.)

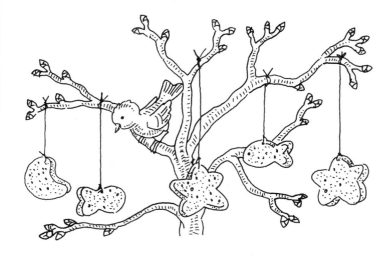

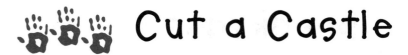

Cut a Castle

◄▶◄▶◄▶

You'll be the ruler of the land in your very own castle.

What You'll Need
- white cake box
- blunt scissors
- 4 paper towel tubes
- white paper
- clear tape
- markers or poster paints and paintbrush
- construction paper scraps
- craft glue
- toothpick

Cut a drawbridge in the side of the clean cake box. Cut out a square from the top of the box. The hole is the opening for the courtyard, and the rim is the base for the battlement. Make 4 towers from the paper towel tubes. Wrap white paper around the tubes, and secure with tape. Make a cone for the roof of 1 tower. Tape it to the top of a tube. Tape a tower to each corner of the box. To make the wall

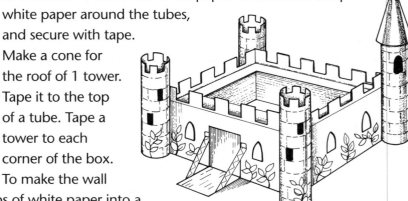

around the battlement, cut 4 strips of white paper into a comb shape. Make them long enough for each side of the box. Tape them around the castle's top edge. Use markers or paint to decorate the castle with windows, vines, and bricks. To make a flag for the castle tower, cut a scrap piece of construction paper in a triangle. Glue it to a toothpick. Insert the toothpick in the top of the cone on the tower, and glue it in place.

Post Office

◄▶◄▶◄▶

Say you care, even if you don't know the person you're saying it to.

Everyone loves getting mail—especially soldiers far from home or senior citizens without families of their own. You can help cheer up these sometimes forgotten citizens by writing short, encouraging notes all your own. Remind the folks you write to that people care about them. Tell them to have a great day. Fold the letter into a

What You'll Need
- paper
- pens or markers
- tape

rectangle, and seal it with a piece of tape. Address it to "You" from "Me," but don't include your real name or address. Ask your parents to take your letters to your local senior citizens home or Red Cross office. The home or office will do the rest.

 # Tees, Please

◆▷◆▷◆▷◆

You don't have to be a great artist to make a terrific T-shirt.

What You'll Need
- cotton T-shirt in any color
- pictures cut out from printed fabric (the bigger, the better) of cars, aircraft, horses, stuffed animals, flowers, etc.
- scissors
- dual-sided fusible interfacing
- iron and ironing board
- sewing machine (optional)
- wide piece of cardboard
- fabric paint in tubes

Caution: This project requires adult help.

Wash and dry the T-shirt first; don't use fabric softener. (Fabric softener keeps the interfacing and paint from bonding completely.) Cut out pictures and other shapes from the fabric. Plan your original design. Then cut out interfacing to match the fabric pieces. Iron the interfacing onto the fabric pieces following package instructions. (Have an adult help you use the iron.) Then iron the fabric pieces onto the T-shirt. (To make the shirt even more durable, an adult could use a sewing machine to make small stitches around each picture.) Slip the wide piece of cardboard into the T-shirt to make the fabric taut before painting. Using fabric paint in a tube, outline all edges of the pictures. This helps anchor them to the T-shirt. Let the paint dry, and then outline the edges again. Let dry for 24 hours. Try to avoid using fabric softener in the wash later because it could loosen the fabric pictures.

Mount a Leaf Collection

◆▷◆▷◆▷◆

Gather a colorful collection of leaves, and mount them for display.

Collect leaves in a wide array of colors in the fall, or gather leaves of different shapes and sizes at any time during the year. After you have assembled the leaves, gently dry each with a paper towel to remove any moisture. Then set the leaves between layers of newspaper. Place heavy books on top, and weigh them down for 2 weeks. Then take the leaves out, and glue them to stiff paper. Paint the leaves with decoupage glue to strengthen them and give them a shiny surface. On each page, note the name of the tree the leaf came from as well as when and where the leaf was collected. Using the hole punch and yarn, tie the pages into a book.

What You'll Need
- leaves
- paper towel
- newspaper
- heavy books
- glue
- stiff paper
- decoupage glue
- marker
- hole punch
- yarn

Clean Hands Dish

This pretty soap dish will help everyone remember to wash their hands!

What You'll Need
- air-drying clay
- rolling pin
- ruler
- pencil
- butter knife
- toothpick
- acrylic paint
- paintbrushes
- sealer

Roll the clay to about ¼ inch thick. Lay your hand on top of the clay with your fingers together. Use a pencil to trace the outline of your hand onto the clay. Use a butter knife to cut the clay hand out. Smooth the edges with your fingers. Using a pencil, draw a design, maybe a heart or star, in the palm of the hand. Poke 6 small drainage holes through the center of the palm with a toothpick. Make sure the holes go all the way through. Bend the edges of the hand and fingers up into the shape of a dish. Prop up the edges so that they won't sag as it dries. Paint the dish with 2 coats of acrylic paint. Let dry between coats. Waterproof the dish with a sealer.

Fan-Tastic

On the next hot summer day, create your own gentle, cooling breeze with a pretty paper fan.

What You'll Need
- 6×12-inch piece of construction paper
- pastel chalks or markers
- ruler
- clear tape or stapler and staples

Draw a picture on the piece of construction paper using pastel chalks or markers. Draw pretty butterflies, yummy birthday cakes, or stars in a deep blue sky. Now fold the paper back and forth in a fanfold. To start the fanfold, fold one end over about 1 inch. Turn the paper over and fold the end up. Continue folding the paper in accordionlike pleats. Once you've finished folding, tape or staple the folds together at one end to hold it in place. Make bigger fans to decorate your room.

Bulletin Board Display

With your very own bulletin board, you always have a place to keep important notes, party invitations, or special photographs.

What You'll Need
- newspaper
- corkboard or bulletin board with a flat wood frame
- masking tape
- acrylic paint
- paintbrush
- paper towels
- blunt scissors
- plastic coffee-can lid
- pencil or pen
- sponge

Cover your work surface with newspaper. Place masking tape around the edges of the board, inside the frame. Paint the frame in a color to match your room. If any paint gets on the board, wipe it off with a damp paper towel. Let the paint dry.

Cut a small circle from the plastic coffee-can lid. To make your stencil, sketch a shape on the plastic circle; make sure it is not wider than the board frame. Cut the shape out. Dip a damp sponge in paint, and dab off the excess. Place your stencil on the frame, and fill in the stencil by dabbing the sponge straight up and down. Repeat your pattern all around the frame. Let the paint dry.

 # Bookmarks the Spot

Make someone's leisure reading even more fun.

People who can't get around much, such as the elderly or sick, often find reading to be a cheerful escape. You can add an extra spark of warmth to their reading by making colorful bookmarks. Cut 2×5-inch strips of card stock. Decorate the strips with colorful designs or inspirational sayings cut out from magazines or greeting cards (ask for permission first!) and lots of bright bits and pieces you find around the house. Ask your local senior center or home for the elderly to pass them out to folks who might need a little lift—or ask permission to go to the center and hand them out yourself. You may really touch some seniors' lives!

What You'll Need
- card stock
- blunt scissors
- ruler
- markers
- glue
- magazines, greeting cards, sequins, ribbon, stickers, buttons, etc.

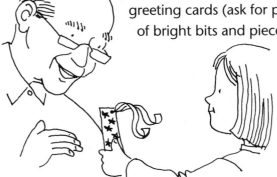

Postcard Jigsaw

Make this "puzzling" message, and send it to a friend.

What You'll Need
- postcards (larger ones work best)
- pencil
- blunt scissors
- envelope
- postage stamp

Write a note to your friend on the back of a postcard. Use the whole back if you want, even the part where you're supposed to put the address. Next, draw a jigsaw pattern on the back of the postcard. Make sure that the pieces are different shapes and sizes, but don't make the pieces too small because it might be too tough to cut them out. Now carefully cut out your pattern to make a mini-puzzle out of your postcard.

Put the pieces of the puzzle into an envelope, and mail them to a friend to figure out. He or she will have to put the puzzle together to read your message! For more of a challange, make jigsaw puzzles out of several postcards that are the same size and mix them together before mailing them.

Sewing Cards

Who says you need needle and thread to sew? Use yarn to decorate these special shapes that you cut out.

Make several outline drawings—animals, people, whatever you want—on a piece of cardboard. Cut out the shapes. Punch holes around the edges every ½ inch or so. Next, tie a knot in one end of a piece of yarn, then wrap a small piece of tape around the other end (just like on the end of a shoelace) so that you can easily push the yarn through the holes in the cardboard. After you're done, sew the card by threading the holes with different pieces of colored yarn.

What You'll Need
- 6×6-inch sturdy cardboard
- blunt scissors
- hole punch
- ruler
- 2 feet of yarn
- clear tape

You can try sewing pieces together to make three-dimensional shapes. For example, sew 6 squares together to make a cube. Sew 8 triangles to make a diamond, or 4 triangles and 1 square to make a pyramid. What other shapes can you make?

Gift-Wrapping Paper

◆▶◆▶◆▶◆

Make the gift wrapping as special as the gift!

What You'll Need
- food coloring or tempera paint
- liquid starch
- bowl
- cardboard
- ruler
- blunt scissors
- newspaper
- spoon
- paper
- sea sponge

For patterned gift wrap, mix food coloring or tempera paint with liquid starch in a bowl to make a thick paint. Make design combs by cutting cardboard into small rectangles 1 to 3 inches wide. Cut notches on one side of each rectangle, making variations in the rectangles so that each comb can be used to create a different effect. The notches can be cut closer or farther apart, the teeth can be wider or narrower, or you can even vary the width of the notches and teeth on a rectangle! Spread newspaper to cover the working surface. Lay your paper on the newspaper, and using the spoon, cover it with the finger

paint. Use the notched edge of the cardboard squares to create designs in the paint by combing over the surface of the paper. For a textured wrapping paper, use the sea sponge to dab paint onto a piece of unpainted paper. Let the paper dry overnight.

Mailing Tube

◆▶◆▶◆▶◆

Imagine the expressions on your friends' faces when they receive mail in a tube!

To make a mailing tube, decorate a cardboard tube from a roll of wrapping paper. Use markers to color it in a wild and colorful pattern. Stick a white mailing label on the tube for the sender's address. Add another label for your return address. To make the end caps, trace the end of the roll on the cardboard twice. Cut out both circles. Securely tape 1 circle to one end of the mailing tube. Roll up a letter or artwork you want to send, and insert it into the tube. See Self-Portrait on page 215 to send a picture of yourself. Tape the other end cap to the open end of the tube.

What You'll Need
- wrapping paper tube
- markers
- white mailing labels
- pencil
- cardboard
- blunt scissors
- packing tape

Embossing Paper

This is a double treat since collecting your supplies is as much fun as making the embossed paper itself.

What You'll Need
- flat household objects (paper clips, keys, buttons, etc.)
- lightweight paper
- poster board (optional)
- blunt scissors (optional)

Look around your house for flat objects, such as paper clips and keys. Place a piece of lightweight paper over one of the objects, and rub over the paper with your finger. Lift the paper, and notice the textured shape on the paper. You've created Embossing Paper.

To make embossed designs, rub over an object and move it around under the paper. Use a key to make the petals of a flower. Or cut a wavy edge on a strip of poster board, and use it to make an embossed line at the top and bottom of your paper. It's a pretty decoration for stationery.

Clay Pencil Holder

This unique holder keeps all your pens and pencils close at hand and neatly organized.

Caution: This project requires adult help.

What You'll Need
- assorted colors of polymer clay
- waxed paper
- rolling pin
- butter knife
- ruler
- pen cap
- pencil or pen
- aluminum foil

Roll pancakes of red, orange, yellow, green, blue, and purple clay on waxed paper. Stack them on top of each other in the colors of the rainbow, then cut them into a 1½×7-inch rectangle. Bend the rainbow clay into a big arch with your hands. Using a pen cap, poke a hole in the clay about ¾ inch from one end. Make sure it is deep enough to hold a pencil or pen. Make 7 more holes, each about ¾ inch apart.

Wad up some foil, and place it under the arch for support. With an adult's help, bake the clay arch according to package directions. Once the clay has baked, let it cool and then put your pencils in the holder.

Scrapbook Binding

Save memories from a vacation, jot down your thoughts, or sketch drawings in your own special book.

What You'll Need
- 2 pieces of cardboard (for the panels), 11×2 inches each
- 2 pieces of cardboard (for the covers), 11×12 inches each
- 2 pieces of cloth, 17×20 inches each
- ruler
- blunt scissors
- craft glue
- old paintbrush
- typing or construction paper
- hole punch
- yarn

1. Using the illustration below as your guide, place 1 cardboard panel piece and 1 cardboard cover piece on 1 piece of cloth. Leave a ¼-inch space between the cardboard pieces. Cut out the corners from the cloth.

2. Remove the cover board from its position, and apply an even coat of glue with an old paintbrush on one side of the board. Place it back onto the cloth to glue it in place. Repeat with the panel board. Fold the cloth over the boards, and glue in place. Let the glue set.

3. Cut a 7×7-inch square from a piece of paper. Glue the square of paper over the cloth edges on the cover board.

4. Repeat steps 1 through 3 to make the other cover.

5. Punch 2 holes in the panel of the front and back covers, making sure they line up. To make the inside pages, punch 2 holes in several sheets of typing or construction paper in the same position as the cover holes. Tie the scrapbook together using yarn.

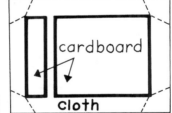

1 Place cardboard on cloth.

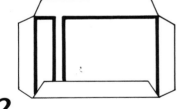

2 Fold cloth over cardboard.

3 Glue a square of paper over cloth edges.

5 Tie pieces together.

Letter Designs

Use your imagination to make your own personalized nameplate for your bedroom door or to create a fun alphabet game.

What You'll Need
- colored pencils or markers
- drawing paper
- ruler
- cardboard
- blunt scissors
- craft glue
- hole punch
- yarn

On a piece of drawing paper, draw an object in the shape of its first letter. For example, the word *snake* starts with an *s*. Draw a snake in an s shape, and then write out the rest of the letters. Color in your letter design. Try making a poster of all the letters in the alphabet with letter designs.

To make a nameplate, cut a 3×8-inch rectangle from a piece of paper and one from cardboard. Draw an object in the shape of each letter in your name on the paper. Then color in each letter design. Glue the paper on the cardboard, then punch a hole in the top 2 corners of the nameplate. String it with a piece of yarn to hang it up on your door.

Coiled Bowl

This is truly a bowl of a different color, and it becomes extra special when you make it yourself!

Caution: This project requires adult help.

What You'll Need
- assorted colors of polymer clay
- waxed paper
- ruler
- blunt scissors
- aluminum foil
- ovenproof bowl (about the size of a salad bowl)
- craft knife

Using the palms of your hands, make 9 to 10 rolls of clay about 10 inches long on waxed paper. Then roll each clay piece into a circular coil. Cut a circular piece of foil slightly larger than the ovenproof bowl. Put coiled clay pieces on the foil close together like puzzle pieces. Use your fingers to smooth the surface until the clay blends together. (Water helps to smooth the clay.) Make sure no gaps exist between the pieces. Ask an adult to use a craft knife to trim edges if necessary. Turn the bowl upside down, and press the clay sheet over onto the bowl. With an adult's help, bake the bowl according to package directions. After the clay has cooled, remove foil and bowl from clay.

Paper Making

◆▶◆▶◆▶◆▶

Learn the basics of paper making to create pretty, textural paper for art projects or stationery.

What You'll Need
- junk-mail envelopes, old letters, or news-paper
- dishpan
- warm water
- wire whisk or blender
- 8×8-inch piece of small-hole screening
- towel
- smooth board (to press the paper)
- cotton cloth

Caution: This project requires adult help.

Tear up junk-mail envelopes (without the windows), old letters, or newspaper into small pieces. Soak pieces overnight in a dishpan with warm water. The next day, add more warm water to the paper, and hand-beat the mixture until the pulp is broken apart. Or use a blender to mix it by placing the soaked paper in the blender and filling it half full with water. With an adult's help, blend it in short bursts to break up the pulp.

Spread some pulp evenly on the screen. The screen should be covered with the paper pulp. Place the screen on a towel. Press a board down hard on the paper to squeeze out any excess water. Remove the board. Place a piece of cotton cloth on a flat surface. Turn the screen over onto the cloth to remove the paper. Let the paper dry.

Craft Stick Stick-Ins

◆▶◆▶◆▶◆▶

Dress up hospital plant life with colorful craft-stick fun.

Many hospital patients and senior citizens get plants as gifts. These adorable stick-ins can spruce up those plants to make a cheer-up treat. On colored paper, draw and cut out a butterfly, a ladybug, a bird, or any other design you like. Decorate your designs so they are really special. Glue your paper design to the end of a craft stick (or a clean ice cream stick). Use the other end of the stick to anchor the paper design in the potting soil. Share these cheerful stick-ins with people who might not be able to get out and enjoy the great outdoors.

What You'll Need
- colored paper
- blunt scissors
- markers or crayons
- glue
- craft stick (or clean ice cream stick)

Kitty's Favorite Mouse

Your cat may like this mouse so much that you'll have to keep more than one mouse in the house!

What You'll Need
- scrap paper
- ruler
- pencil
- felt scraps
- blunt scissors
- yarn
- yarn needle
- catnip
- black marker

On the paper, draw a small hill shape about 2 inches high and 2 inches wide, with a straight line at the bottom. Cut it out, and use it as a pattern to cut out 2 pieces of felt. Match up the 2 pieces of felt, and stitch them together around the outside top curve. Stuff the mouse with catnip until it's plump. Stitch the bottom edge closed. Draw in the eyes, one on either side of the seam. Cut out 2 circles of felt that are 1 inch wide. These are the ears. Sew them on, just above and slightly to the side of each eye. Use a few tight stitches on the part of the ear that is nearest the eye. Draw on a nose and whiskers with the marker. Sew a yarn tail on the other end.

Pattern

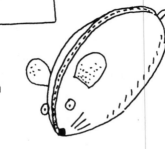

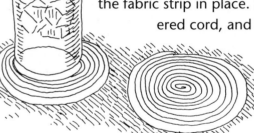

Coiled Coasters

These soft coasters are remarkably sturdy, making them not only pretty to look at but useful, too.

What You'll Need
- clothesline cord
- blunt scissors
- tape measure
- 1¾ yards of fabric
- fabric glue

Cut four 54-inch pieces of clothesline cord. Cut four 1×54-inch strips of fabric. Wrap a fabric strip around a 54-inch piece of clothesline. Dot some glue along the cord to hold it. Once you reach the end of the cord, glue the end of the fabric strip in place. Start a small coil of the covered cord, and use fabric glue to hold it together. Continue coiling the cord around itself. Put glue on the cord as you coil it. When you get to the end, tuck it in between the last coil. Add a dab of glue to secure it. Let dry overnight. Repeat to make 3 more coasters.

 # Book Pillow

After you get home from the library, curl up with your reading pillow and dive into your books.

What You'll Need
- 1⅓ yards of fabric
- blunt scissors
- tape measure
- newspaper
- fabric paint
- fabric glue
- cotton batting
- bias tape
- black fabric marker

1. Cut a 12×19-inch piece and a 3×28-inch piece of fabric. Cover your work surface with newspaper. Place the 12×19-inch piece of fabric on your work surface right side up. Divide the fabric as shown in the illustration for the front cover, spine, and back cover, and decorate it with fabric paint to look like your favorite book. Paint on the title and illustrations. Let the paint dry.

2. Use fabric glue to put together the seams to make the pillow. Apply a line of glue along the edges of the 3×28-inch piece of fabric. Attach one end of the 3×28-inch piece of fabric to the bottom of the spine. Continue gluing and attaching the long strip around the edges of the book fabric until you get to the top edge. Leave it open. Stuff the book with batting, then glue the last edge closed.

3. Place bias tape over the edges with more fabric glue. Draw some lines on the long strip to create the pages of the book.

1

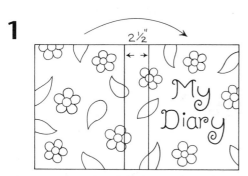

2½"

Decorate the fabric to look like your favorite book.

2

glue

Glue the long strip of fabric to the book edges.

3

Draw lines on the long strip to make pages.

You're a Star

Show someone they're appreciated or reward them for a special deed.

What You'll Need

- 2 cups flour
- ½ cup salt
- 2 tablespoons cream of tartar
- measuring cups and spoons
- saucepan
- mixing spoon
- 1 cup water
- 2 tablespoons cooking oil
- waxed paper
- rolling pin
- cookie cutters
- pencil or straw
- wire cooling rack
- poster paints
- paintbrush
- glitter markers
- ribbons

Caution: This project requires adult help.

Have an adult help you make the clay. To mix up a small batch of play clay, stir together the flour, salt, and cream of tartar in a saucepan. Then add the water and cooking oil. Put the pan over medium heat, and cook for 3 to 5 minutes. Stir the mixture constantly until it looks like mashed potatoes. Dump the clay out on a sheet of waxed paper, but wait until the clay is cool enough to touch. Roll out the play clay to a layer about ¼ inch thick. Cut out stars (or other appropriate shapes) with cookie cutters. With a pencil or straw, make a hole in the top, but not too close to the edge. The size of the hole depends on the thickness of the ribbon you're using. Let the cutouts air-dry for 24 hours on a wire rack. Paint them with poster paints, and let dry. With the glitter markers, write on the names of the people who are receiving your awards and add any other messages. Thread ribbons through the holes, and present your awards!

Arctic Light

This arctic light gives off a warm, welcoming glow.

Caution: This project requires adult help.

Pour a few inches of water into a mixing bowl. Center a clean yogurt container with stones or coins in the bowl. Slowly pour more water into the bowl so that it nearly reaches the rim of the smaller container. Freeze.

When frozen, remove the ice from the mold. Dump out the stones or coins. Pour in warm water to loosen the container. Remove the container, and put the candleholder on a large tray. Put a votive candle in the opening, and have an adult light it.

What You'll Need

- water
- large metal mixing bowl
- plastic yogurt container
- small stones or coins
- large tray with sides
- votive candle
- matches (adult use only!)

No, No, Fido!

◆▶◆▶◆▶◆▶

Dogs don't like the noise a shaker can makes. Shake the can whenever you catch them misbehaving.

Put the pennies in the can. Cover the top of the can with clear packing tape. Cut a 9×4½-inch label out of white paper. Decorate the label with markers. Tape one end of the label to the can. Make small rolls of tape, and stick them between the label and the can. Over-lap the other end of the label over the first end, and tape it down.

What You'll Need
- clean, empty diet shake can
- 5 pennies
- clear packing tape
- white paper
- ruler
- blunt scissors
- markers
- clear tape

Cinnamon "Scent"-sations

◆▶◆▶◆▶◆▶

These beads not only look good, they smell good, too!

What You'll Need
- ¼ cup (really!) cinnamon
- ¼ cup applesauce
- mixing bowl
- mixing spoon
- aluminum foil
- rolling pin
- butter knife
- toothpick
- wire rack
- tiny cookie cutters (optional)
- string or embroidery floss

Mix the cinnamon and the applesauce. Lay a sheet of foil on the counter. Put the cinnamon clay on the foil, and cover the clay with another sheet of foil. (This keeps your hands from getting stained.) Roll the clay out into a "snake" about a ½ inch thick. Cut the beads to the desired length. Shape them in rounds, squares, cylinders, etc. Use the toothpick to put a hole through each bead. Make sure the hole is wide enough at both ends for the string you will use. Let the beads dry for a day or so on a wire rack. For a variation, you can roll the cinnamon clay out in a sheet and use tiny cookie cutters to carve out flat, shaped beads. Very carefully stick a toothpick through the flat beads to make the holes. String the beads into a "scent"-sational necklace, bracelet, or whatever you'd like.

 # Flapping Bird

◇▷◇▷◇▷◆

Time flies when you're making these unique birds. It's so much fun, why not make a whole flock!

Caution: This project requires adult help.

Draw a bird body and 2 wings on foam core board. Have an adult help you cut out the pieces with a craft knife. Color the foam pieces with markers to make a dove, flamingo, eagle, or parrot. Poke 2 holes in the side of the bird body. Poke 2 holes at the end of each wing, the same width apart as the 2 holes on the bird body. Poke 2 more holes about ⅓ of the way down each wing.

To connect the wings to the body, thread a piece of fishing line through one end hole of 1 wing. Continue threading the fishing line through one hole on the bird body and

on through to an end hole on the other wing. Bring the ends of the fishing line together, and tie a knot. Repeat for the other end hole on the wings. Thread a piece of fishing line through each wing hole, and knot the end. Tie the other ends of each fishing line to the dowel. To hang the bird, tie a line from one end of the dowel to the other.

To make the pull string, poke a small hole at the bottom of the bird body. Cut a 10-inch piece of fishing line. Thread it through the bottom hole. Thread a small bead on the end of the line. Tie a knot under the bead to secure it. Pull the line to flap the wings.

 # Fabric Tubes

◆▶◆▶◆▶◆▶

These tube projects are just the beginning. When your creative juices are flowing, see how many more ideas you can come up with.

What You'll Need
- 1 yard of fabric
- blunt scissors
- tape measure
- needle and thread
- cotton batting
- felt
- 2 buttons
- markers
- ribbon

1. To make a snake, cut a 5×30-inch piece of fabric. Fold the fabric in half lengthwise with the wrong side of the fabric facing out. Sew a seam along the long end, then turn it inside out. Sew one end of the tube closed.

2. Stuff the fabric tube with batting at the open end. Sew the open end closed.

3. Cut a piece of felt for the tongue. Sew it to the snake. Sew on 2 buttons for the eyes. Use markers to decorate the snake.

4. To create a wreath, make 3 tubes just like the snake but use 3 different colors of fabric. Braid the tubes together, then sew the ends together forming a circle. Use ribbon to tie a bow around the ends. Make a bed bolster using an 18×54-inch piece of fabric. Repeat steps 1 and 2 to make the tube.

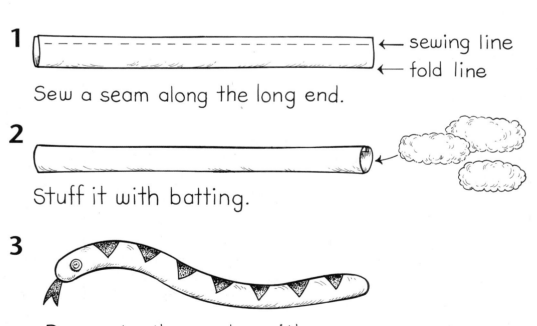

1 ← sewing line
← fold line
Sew a seam along the long end.

2 Stuff it with batting.

3 Decorate the snake with a felt tongue and button eyes.

# Childhood Home

You'll always remember the place you grew up when you look at this homey model.

What You'll Need
- construction paper the color of your house
- clear tape (optional)
- glue
- blunt scissors
- old home-decorating magazines and catalogs
- markers

Homes are the places that families create together. In the home, a family eats, sleeps, laughs, cries, and plays together. Memories are created there every day.

To form a house, fold in the 2 sides of a large sheet of construction paper to meet at the middle, so that each side opens and closes. You might need to tape a few sheets together to get a piece that is large enough. Cut a triangle-shaped roof for your house, and glue it to the top of the flaps of the closed house. (If you live in an apartment building, you might not have a roof like this.) Then cut up from the bottom of the triangle to the point so that the roof will open and close with the flaps. Cut out and glue on a chimney as well. Use colors that match your actual house.

Find pictures of doors, windows, outside shrubbery and flowers, front steps, and other details in old home-decorating magazines. Cut these out (ask for permission first!), and glue them to the outside of your house. Then open your house, and divide it into the number of rooms that are in your house. You might want to leave space for a staircase if you have more than one floor. Cut out furnishings from the home-decorating magazines, and glue them in the rooms where they belong. Find rugs, beds, tables, chairs, curtains, and plants that look similar to things you have in your house. You can change the color of objects with markers. If you want, write the names of the people who live in your house in the different rooms. Or you might want to write a sentence or two telling what the people in the house are likely to do in each room. As you get older, you will always want to remember this special place where you shared so much with your loved ones.

Edible Necklaces

◆▶▶▶▶▶

Jewelry you can eat makes a super gift for yourself or others.

Special snacks are hard to afford when you live in a homeless shelter. So give a needy kid a treat by making and sharing these delicious edible necklaces.

Wash your hands carefully. Spoon the cereal and other snacks into a plastic sandwich bag. Use the curling ribbon to tie off the bag. Leave the ends of the ribbon long so you can curl them so they look pretty. Make a long necklace out of more curling ribbon, and tie it to the bag so the bag looks like a large charm—be sure the necklace is long enough to slip over someone's head. Call your local YMCA or social services hotline for suggestions on where to donate your snacks.

Show Them You Care
Sadly, children are one of the fastest growing groups of poor people in America. Helping homeless children will let them know that someone really cares.

Custom Pillowcase

◆►◆►◆►◆►

Stencil on your own custom border to turn a plain pillowcase into something special for your room.

Draw a flower shape on 1 plastic coffee-can lid. Draw leaf shapes on another coffee-can lid. Cut out the shapes to create a flower stencil and a leaf stencil. Put a plain pillowcase flat on your work surface, and place a plastic garbage bag inside the pillowcase. Place the flower stencil on the edge of the pillowcase, and secure it with a binder clip. Pour some acrylic paint on a paper plate. Dip a stencil brush in the paint, and dab off the excess paint on a piece of paper. Dab the brush inside the stencil shape until it is filled in. Continue stenciling the flower design along the edge of the pillowcase to make a border. Once the paint has dried, repeat the stenciling process using the leaf stencil and a different color paint. Let the paint dry. If you want and after you get permission, stencil the same border on your bed's dust ruffle or curtains to match your bedroom.

What You'll Need
- pencil
- plastic coffee-can lids
- blunt scissors
- plain pillowcase
- plastic garbage bag
- binder clips
- acrylic paints
- paper plates
- stencil brush

Neighborhood Birdbath

◆►◆►◆►◆►

Birds love taking a bath. Make a bathtub just for them, and have the cleanest birds in the neighborhood!

What You'll Need
- plastic gallon milk jug
- heavy-duty scissors
- sand or a brick
- shallow plastic bowl
- water
- small rocks

Caution: This project requires adult help.

First make the pedestal base for the birdbath out of a gallon milk jug. Have an adult slice off and cut curves into the top of the plastic milk jug. The curves should allow the shallow plastic bowl to sit securely on the milk jug. Put enough sand or a brick in the bottom of the milk jug to keep it from toppling over. Place the bowl on the jug-pedestal, and fill the bowl with water and a layer of small rocks. Then wait for the birds to come take a dip in their new tub. Don't be surprised if neighborhood cats, squirrels, rabbits, or other wildlife also love this backyard addition!

 # Polymer Clay Beads

◆▶▶▶▶▶

Use these 4 clay beads—rolled stripe, sculpted, impressed, and marbleized—
to make beautiful necklaces and bracelets.

Caution: This project requires adult help.

Place a sheet of waxed paper on your work surface. Choose the beads you want to make, and follow the instructions below.

Rolled Stripe: Use your hands to roll out 2 thin pancakes, each a different color. Cut a rectangle from each. Place 1 rectangle on top of the other, then roll up tightly. Slice the roll into beads.

Sculpted: Cut a small circle from clay. Cut tiny pieces of different colors, and press them onto the circle to create a design.

Impressed: Cut a small circle from clay. Press a coin into the circle to create an impression.

Marbleized: Roll out 2 colors of clay. Twist them together, and roll into a ball.

After forming your beads, carefully insert a toothpick through the clay to create a hole. Then have an adult help you bake the beads following package directions. After the beads have cooled, string them on thread, and tie on the end clasps to complete your necklace.

> ## What You'll Need
> • waxed paper
> • assorted colors of polymer clay
> • single-edged razor blade (use with an adult's help)
> • toothpick
> • jewelry thread
> • necklace end clasps

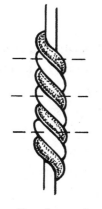

rolled stripe

sculpted

impressed

marbleized

Stick Wreath

◆▷◆▷◆▷◆▷

Hang your natural wreath on the front door. It will be a welcome symbol to all who visit your home.

What You'll Need
- 10 long, thin branches
- large tub or bucket (to soak sticks)
- warm water
- silver cord
- dried flowers (see Flower Press on page 172)

Find about 10 long, thin branches in your yard. Soak them in warm water overnight. The branches will become soft so that you can bend them. The next day, twist and braid the branches together in a circle. Overlap several branches around the circle of sticks to secure it. Bring the branch ends together, and overlap them. Tie a piece of silver cord around the ends to hold the wreath in place. Tie more silver cord in a few spots around the wreath. Tuck dried flowers into the branches.

Fun Foam Stampers

◆▷◆▷◆▷◆▷

These stamps are ideal for making holiday greeting cards or invitations to your birthday party.

Cut out shapes from craft foam. Glue each shape on a block of wood. You can make 1 large stamp to decorate the front of a birthday card or small stamps to create repeating shapes on wrapping paper or gift bags. Combine 2 or 3 small shapes on a single block of wood to make interesting repeating patterns. Try hearts, circles, squares, or stars. You can also make letter or word stamps. Cut out letters or words that you want to print, and glue them to a block in a mirror image. Use poster paints or stamp pads to ink your stampers. Wash stamps after each use.

What You'll Need
- craft foam (available at craft stores)
- blunt scissors
- fabric glue
- blocks of wood
- poster paints or stamp pads

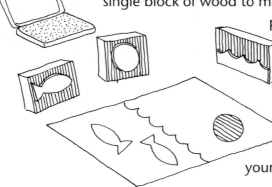

Precious Belongings Pouch

◆▶▶▶▶◀◆

Make this pouch to carry all the precious belongings you'll collect as you go exploring on field trips or nature walks.

What You'll Need
- different-colored sheets of felt
- blunt scissors
- ruler
- stapler and staples or glue

Cut a 5×12-inch rectangle out of a piece of felt. Fold up the long end of the strip about ⅔ of the way. Staple or glue the edges together to form a pocket. If you'd like, you can make 2 parallel slits in the back of the pouch so you can thread your belt through the slits. Decorate the pocket by cutting out shapes from the felt (maybe nature shapes, such as leaves, animals, flowers, etc.) and gluing them to the pocket. Now it's time for that nature walk!

Pencil Pals

◆▶▶▶▶◀◆

Coil up with a new friend!

Kids with learning disabilities sometimes need a special friend to help them stay focused and eager to learn. These cute pencil pals might be just what the teacher ordered.

Roll the clay into 3-inch "snakes" that are ¼ inch wide. Glue 2 wiggle eyes to the head end of the snake, and draw on a silly smile. Coil the snake around the eraser end of a number two pencil.

What You'll Need
- self-hardening (air-drying) clay
- ruler
- white glue
- wiggle eyes
- markers
- pencils
- wire rack

Use markers to decorate the snake's skin with fun patterns and colors. Make a few different snakes. Lay the pencils on the wire rack, and allow 2 days for the clay to harden. Add a little white glue around the snake to guarantee that it will stay put. Donate these pencil pals to your school's special education or resource room teachers.

 # Fancy Envelopes

Make your own special envelopes to send letters or artwork to your friends and family.

Draw the envelope pattern shown here on a piece of cardboard. Cut out the pattern. Trace the pattern on a piece of medium-weight paper. Cut out the envelope pattern, and fold it along the lines indicated on the illustration. Glue all edges except for the top flap. Place your letter or picture in the envelope, and seal the top flap. Now you're ready to send your letter.

You can make fancy envelopes using a magazine picture (ask for permission first!) or your own artwork—just make sure it's at least 9×12 inches. Trace the envelope pattern on the back side of the magazine picture or your artwork. Fold and glue your fancy envelope as described above. Stick on 2 white mailing labels for the return and the sender addresses, and it's ready to go. Once you get the hang of this, you can design your own pattern for specialty envelopes of a different size.

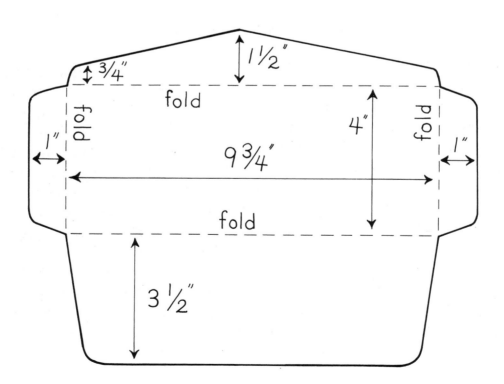

Fancy Fabric Frame

◆▸◆▸◆▸◆▸

Photos help us preserve precious moments. What better way to display them than in their own customized frame?

What You'll Need

- wooden picture frame
- paper towels and glass cleaner
- printed fabric
- blunt scissors
- craft glue

Caution: This project requires adult help.

With an adult's help, carefully remove the glass and backing from a wooden picture frame. Wipe off any dust or smudges from the glass using a paper towel and glass cleaner. Cut strips of printed fabric. Apply glue to the frame, and wrap the strips of fabric around it. Cover the whole frame with fabric strips, smoothing them in place as you wrap it. Trim off any excess fabric, then glue the ends to the back. Let the glue set. Put the frame back together to display your favorite photo.

India Ink Smoke

◆▸◆▸◆▸◆▸

Your finished artwork will look like swirled marble. Use the paper to make notecards, book covers, or smoky backgrounds for pictures.

What You'll Need

- newspaper
- warm water
- craft stick or paint-brush
- India ink
- construction paper
- blunt scissors
- drawing paper

Cover your work surface with newspaper. Fill a sink or basin with ½ to 1 inch of warm water. Use a craft stick or paintbrush to swirl the water around, and add 2 drops of ink to the water while it's still swirling. Place a sheet of construction paper on top of the water for about 3 seconds. Slowly lift the paper out of the water. The wet paper will curl a bit. Turn it over, ink side up, and lay it flat on newspaper to dry.

If you want to make more smoky ink designs, drain and clean the sink and repeat the previous process. For instance, to make a notecard, cut a sheet of drawing paper smaller than the inked paper. Glue drawing paper on the blank side of the inked paper, and fold the notecard in half.

No matter what artwork you create, make sure to clean the sink when you're done.

 # Clay Printer

◆▶◆▶◆▶◆▶

Print a special message or a unique design with your very own printing blocks to make wrapping paper, notecards, or a wall picture.

Caution: This project requires adult help.

Roll out an even pancake of clay about ¼-inch-thick on waxed paper. Have an adult help you cut it into a 3×5-inch rectangle with a craft knife. Sketch a design on the clay using a toothpick. If you are using letters in your design, write them in backward. (The design will be the raised part of the clay that will print.) Use the knife (have the adult help you) and paper clip to scrape away clay from the design so it is raised.

Place some poster paint in a pie pan, and roll a brayer in the paint. Using the brayer, cover the clay printer piece with paint. If you don't have a brayer, paint the raised part of the clay with a paintbrush. Lay the painted clay over a piece of drawing paper. Press gently to imprint your design on the paper. If you want to use a different color, carefully rinse the paint off the clay printer and repaint it with the brayer to make another print.

What You'll Need

- plastic-base clay
- waxed paper
- rolling pin
- craft knife
- toothpick
- paper clip
- poster paint
- pie pan
- brayer or paintbrush
- drawing paper

 # Note-Keeper Keepsake

◆▶◆▶◆▶◆▶

Create a special place to keep special things.

What You'll Need

- old photographs, magazines, and newspapers
- blunt scissors
- small wooden or paper box (a shoe box is okay)
- craft glue
- paintbrush

Go through boxes of old family photos, magazines, and newspapers, and cut out pictures and words that are special to you. (Be sure to get permission before cutting anything!) With the paintbrush, paint a thin coat of glue over the lid. (Be sure the glue you use will be clear when it dries.) Attach the pictures on the lid of your keepsake box.

Your box has become more than just a box—it's a reflection of who you are. And it's the perfect place to keep your most private possessions.

Star Power

Create a little sparkle power for your youngest friends.

Cut out 8 poster-board stars of different sizes. Cover both sides of the stars with aluminum foil. Use the glitter glue to decorate them if

you'd like. Carefully poke a hole with scissors in a tip of each star. Slip a piece of string through each hole. Using string, tie 2 of the drinking straws to the ends of the other. Dangle the sparkling stars from drinking straws, and sus-

What You'll Need
- poster board
- blunt scissors
- aluminum foil
- glitter glue (optional)
- string
- 3 drinking straws

pend the finished mobile (out of reach) from a toddler's ceiling or door frame. It's sure to cheer up even a cranky little friend.

Big Box Bonanza

Turn an ordinary box into something special. With a little imagination, you can make it into a pretty house or a favorite store.

What You'll Need
- big appliance box
- scissors or craft knife
- newspaper
- poster paints
- paintbrush

Caution: This project requires adult help.

Have an adult help you cut out windows, shutters, and a door. Then cover your work area with newspaper. Paint flowers, bricks, shingles, or a store sign on the box. Add any trims you want to decorate your house or store. Allow the paint to dry completely.

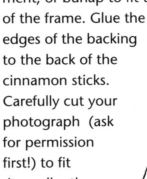

Stick Picture Frames

In the early days of the United States, picture frames might have looked like these. But these probably smell better!

What You'll Need

- 4 cinnamon sticks
- raffia or twine
- craft paper, parchment, or burlap
- blunt scissors
- craft glue
- photograph
- picture hanger or soda-can pop top

Tie the cinnamon sticks together at the corners with raffia or twine. To make the background, cut out craft paper, parchment, or burlap to fit the size of the frame. Glue the edges of the backing to the back of the cinnamon sticks. Carefully cut your photograph (ask for permission first!) to fit

inside the frame; you can make it smaller than the inside of the frame. Center and glue the picture inside the frame. Glue a picture hanger or metal soda-can pop top to the back of the frame for hanging.

A Spicy Tree

Do you know how cinnamon is made? It comes from the dried bark of a tree. The waste and other parts of the bark are called oil of cinnamon, which is used as a flavoring and has also been used in medicines. Cinnamon was a favorite spice in biblical times when it was used for perfume and incense.

Forever Friends

◆▷◆▷◆▷◆▷◆

Is anybody else at your school wearing a velvety friendship bracelet?
All it takes is five minutes to start a trend!

What You'll Need
• 3 different colors of thick, chunky-weight chenille yarn
• blunt scissors
• ruler
• masking tape
• 2 large wooden or plastic beads

Make bright friendship bracelets using 3 strands of yarn that are 9 inches long each. Line up the strands, and knot them; leave 1 inch free at the end. Tape the knotted end to a table edge, then thread a large bead next to the knot. Braid the yarn down to 1 inch from the end. Thread on the other large bead. Tie an end knot after the bead. Wrap your cool bracelet around your wrist, and push the beads through the braids on the opposite sides, or simply tie the ends off. Make plenty of bracelets for your friends, too.

 # Bookworm Book Buddy

◆▷◆▷◆▷◆▷◆

Use this friendly stretch of a worm to keep track of how many books you've read!

Cut out a 3-foot-long strip of construction paper; you may need to tape shorter pieces of paper together. On another piece of paper, draw and cut out a fun, wormy head. Tape the head to the top of the body, and add worm markings along the body. Tape the worm to your wall (after getting your parents' permission!). Each time you finish reading a book, make a miniature book report. Write the title and the date you finished the book on the report, and tape it to your bookworm. Before you know it, your bookworm buddy will have a library on its back.

What You'll Need
• blunt scissors
• construction paper
• tape measure
• tape (optional)
• markers

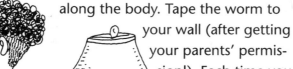

Stationery Set

Use these cards to write thank-you letters or to just say "hi" to faraway friends.

What You'll Need
- envelopes
- blunt scissors
- construction paper
- ruled writing paper
- craft glue
- markers

Use plain envelopes or make your own (see Fancy Envelopes on page 286). To make the notecards, cut and fold over a piece of construction paper, making sure it will fit inside the envelope. Unfold the construction-paper notecard. Cut a piece of writing paper to fit on the card, and glue in place. Repeat to make a set of notecards. Use markers to decorate each card. Draw a simple design like a series of stripes, curvy lines, or polka dots. Or cut a rippled edge at the bottom of each notecard so a bit of the writing paper shows. This gives the card a lacelike look. Draw a matching design on the envelopes, leaving room for the postage stamp, mailing address, and your return address.

Personal Postcards

Why not send a personal "hello" to your friends and relatives with handmade postcards?

What You'll Need
- cardstock or 4×6-inch blank index cards
- ruler
- black felt-tip pen
- colored pencils or markers

On one side of the cardstock or index card, create the back of a postcard. With the ruler, draw a straight line down the center of the card to divide one half for the address and the other half for the greeting. On the half for the address, use a ruler to draw 3 straight horizontal lines from the middle to the bottom of the card. On the other side of the card, create the front of a postcard. Draw yourself at the beach, on a roller coaster, or hiking up a mountain to illustrate your vacation. Your postcard doesn't have to show a real vacation: You could draw yourself piloting the space shuttle. Color the picture with colored pencils or markers, and write a greeting on the other side.

Fabric Fruit

◆▷◆▷◆▷◆▷◆▷

Fabric fruit makes a pretty table decoration, especially when you put it in a handmade bowl.

What You'll Need
- red, yellow, orange, purple, and green felt or cotton cloth
- ruler
- blunt scissors
- fabric glue
- yarn
- cotton batting
- green construction paper
- markers

1. To make round fruit, cut an 8×11-inch piece of felt or cotton cloth. Bring the short ends together to make a tube, and glue them in place. To make a banana, bring the long ends together to make a tube.

2. Twist one end, and tie it closed with yarn.

3. Turn the fabric inside out. Stuff it with cotton batting. Twist the other end, and tie it with yarn to close it.

4. Cut a leaf shape from a piece of green construction paper. Tuck one end of the leaf into the yarn. If you want, draw decorations on your fruit with markers. Make more round fruit with different colors of fabric, and arrange them in a pretty bowl. (See the Coiled Bowl on page 272.)

1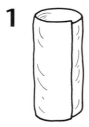

Make a tube.

2

Tie one end with yarn.

3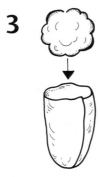

Turn fabric inside out, and stuff with cotton.

4

Tuck a paper leaf into the yarn.

 # Tote It

◆▷◆▷◆▷◆▷

This tote is the most usable piece of art you'll ever create. You can even personalize it for yourself or a friend.

What You'll Need
- 1 yard of bright-colored denim fabric
- blunt scissors
- tape measure
- sewing machine and thread
- iron-on fabric adhesive
- iron and ironing board
- fabric scraps
- fabric paint

Caution: This project requires adult help.

1. Cut a 14×9-inch piece of denim fabric for the bag and a 3×15-inch piece for the handle. (To make a book bag, cut a 22×12-inch piece for the bag and a 24×3-inch piece for an over-the-shoulder handle.) (Have an adult help you with the sewing in this project.) Hem one 14-inch side on the larger piece of fabric. Fold the fabric in half with the seam of the hemmed edge facing out. Sew the 2 sides of the fabric together, running a stitch along the bottom and up the side of the folded fabric. Turn the bag inside out.

2. To make the tote bag handle, fold the 3×15-inch piece of fabric in thirds. Sew along the length of the fabric to stitch it together. Sew each end of the handle to the inside of the bag. Sew several stitches to secure the handle.

3. Decorate your bag with fabric. Have an adult help you iron the fabric adhesive to the back of some fabric scraps. Cut out shapes or a design from the fabric. Remove the paper backing from the adhesive. Place a fabric shape on the tote bag, and iron it in place with an adult's help. Continue decorating the tote bag with the remaining fabric shapes. Use fabric paint to outline the shapes or to add more shapes. Let the paint dry.

1

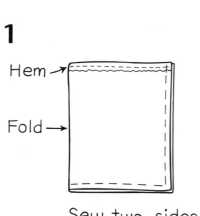

Hem →

Fold →

Sew two sides of fabric together.

2

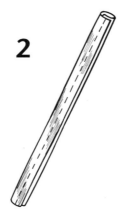

Fold 3×15-inch piece of fabric in thirds and stitch together.

3

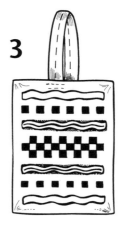

Decorate your tote bag.

Berry Basket Weaving

◆▶◆▶◆▶◆▶

This is a great basket to hold your treasures. Fill it with dried flowers or candy treats, or give it as a gift.

What You'll Need
- plastic berry basket
- fabric or ribbon
- blunt scissors
- 1-inch-wide strip of construction paper
- stapler and staples
- tissue paper
- goodies

Cut several strips of fabric or ribbon as wide as the openings in your basket. Weave the strips in and out of the slots around the basket. Tie each strip in a knot and trim the excess. To make the handle, secure one end of the construction paper strip to each side of the basket with a stapler. If you want, use a strip of fabric or ribbon to tie a bow around the handle. Line your basket with tissue paper, and fill it with goodies.

Dried Flowers

◆▶◆▶◆▶◆▶

Big bouquets can be used as door decorations or table centerpieces. Tiny bouquets can decorate hats or jewelry.

With an adult's permission, gather some flowers from outside. Collect ones that are not quite in full bloom. Gather the stems together, and bind them with a rubber band. Thread a piece of string through the rubber band, and tie it in a loop. Place the loop over a hanger, and hang the bouquet of flowers in the sun upside down. Bring them in at night so dew doesn't collect on them in the morning. Put them back in the sun the next day. They should be dry in about a week. If the sun has bleached out some of the colors, touch up the flowers with watercolor paints. Add a few drops of dish detergent to the paint water to help the paint stick to the flowers. Arrange your bouquet in a vase, or tie a ribbon around it and hang it on the door.

What You'll Need
- flowers
- rubber band
- string
- hanger
- watercolor paints and paintbrush
- dish detergent
- vase or ribbon

No-Stitch Pillows

◆▷◆▷◆▷◆

Create fluffy pillows all by yourself!

Cut a 20×24-inch piece of fabric. Roll a 12-inch strip of cotton batting. Place the batting on the wrong side of the fabric. Roll the fabric around the batting. Glue the end seam in place to close the roll. Cut the grosgrain ribbon in half. Tie each piece in a bow around each end of the fabric roll. Fringe the edges of the fabric. Use permanent markers to draw on your favorite candy flavor label to make the pillow look like taffy.

What You'll Need
- ⅔ yard of fabric
- blunt scissors
- tape measure
- cotton batting
- fabric glue
- 1 yard of grosgrain ribbon
- permanent markers

Zipper Chic

◆▷◆▷◆▷◆

These are easy, believe it or knot! Make your own unique zipper pulls.

What You'll Need
- colored leather cords, wild colored shoelaces, lanyard lacings, or satin cords
- ruler
- jacket, backpack, or purse zipper
- big beads
- metal spring clip or key ring (optional)

Choose the color, pattern, and type of cords or laces according to how you plan to use the zipper pulls. Mixing colors creates cool effects and makes learning this process easier. Start with 2 laces, one of each color, about 12 inches long. Thread the 2 laces through the zipper's pull, and fold the laces in half so the bottoms are even. You now have 4 laces to work with. Arrange the light-colored laces in the middle and the dark ones on the outside. The lighter laces will always hang straight down the middle. With the 2 dark laces, make a simple knot in front of the lighter laces. Pull tightly. Now use the dark laces to tie a simple knot behind the lighter laces.

Pull tightly, and continue knotting above and behind the light-colored laces until the zipper pull is as long as you want it. Thread a large bead on the end of the laces, and tie them off.

Make an easy variation by using a metal spring clip or a key ring. Use the same instructions for Zipper Chic, only thread the laces through the swivel base of the metal clip instead. Now slip your metal key ring onto the swivel base of the spring clip. Clip your keys onto your belt loop and voilà! Funky, cool keys to go.

Military Dog Tags

◀▶◀▶◀▶◀▶

These dog tags aren't for dogs! They're ID tags like the metal ones American soldiers wear. Cool!

What You'll Need
- pencil or pen
- aluminum pie pan
- ruler
- work gloves
- heavy-duty scissors
- needle-nose pliers
- stack of newspapers
- paper clip
- hole punch
- 18-inch ball chain

Caution: This project requires adult help.

You must have an adult help you with this project. Use a pencil or pen point to mark two $1\frac{1}{2} \times 2\frac{1}{4}$-inch rectangles on the flat portion of the pie tin. Wearing work gloves, cut out the tags with scissors. Trim the corners of the tags diagonally to make a pair of octagons.

Have an adult use the pliers to bend back the edges of the tags about $\frac{1}{8}$ inch. Fold corners first, then tops and bottoms, and then the sides. Again wearing your work gloves, place each tag right-side up on a hard surface and use the ruler to gently smooth the edges of the tags by rubbing the ruler along all the folded-down edges. (Have the adult check to make sure there are no sharp edges remaining.)

Now it's time to emboss your initials on the tags with the end of a paper clip. Place the tags on a soft surface, such as a stack of newspaper, and use just enough pressure to raise the letters without poking through the aluminum. Punch a hole in each tag $\frac{1}{4}$ inch from the top.

String your tags, back sides together, onto the ball chain. Wear your tags with pride!

Reusable Calendar

◆◇◆◇◆◇◆

***This calendar can be used again and again, since you simply turn
the spools over to the correct month and day.***

What You'll Need
- 3 large spools
- paint
- paintbrush
- paper
- blunt scissors
- markers
- craft glue
- clear tape
- 2 pieces wood
- 1 wooden dowel

Paint the spools, and let them dry. Cut out 3 paper strips, one to fit around the middle of each spool. Use a marker to print the months on the first strip; the numbers 0, 1, 2, 3 on the second strip; and the numbers from 0 to 9 on the third strip. Glue a strip to each spool.

Cut out 3 more strips that are slightly longer than the first 3. Cut out a window in each; the windows should be large enough to show the month and date on the first strips made. Place each strip over a spool, and tape the ends of each strip together. Be sure the sleeves move freely around the spools.

For the base, use 2 pieces of wood that are the same size. Paint them however you want. Glue the dowel to the center of one piece of wood. When the paint and glue have dried completely, place the spools on the dowel. Place the month spool first, the spool with the numbers 0 through 3 next, and the spool with the numbers 0 through 9 last. Glue the dowel to the middle of the other piece of wood. Let the glue dry completely.

Turn your spools to the correct month and day. Keeping track of the date was never so much fun!

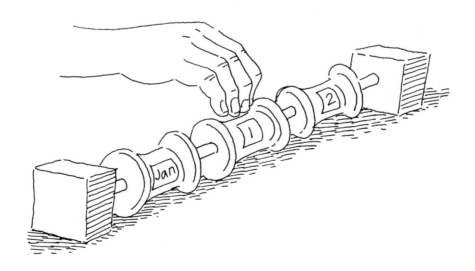

Decoupage Art Box

Decorate a plain box using fun cutouts. Find pictures of your favorite things, or choose a theme, such as dinosaurs, angels, or flowers.

What You'll Need
- newspaper
- blunt scissors
- wrapping paper or old magazines (for cutouts)
- wooden box (available at craft stores)
- craft glue
- water
- bowl
- old paintbrush
- water-based polyurethane

Cover your work surface with newspaper. Carefully cut out the pictures that you want to paste on your box. Once you have gathered all the pictures you will need to decorate your box, position them on the box to create a scene. Dilute some glue with water. Remove the pictures from the box, and coat the back of the pictures with the diluted glue completely and evenly. Press them back onto the box. Smooth out any bubbles. Let it dry. Apply a coat of polyurethane to the box. Let it dry completely, then apply a second coat.

Pom-Poms

Make a pom-pom in your school colors. Bring it along to the next game, and cheer on your team.

Collect 2 different colors of plastic bags. Cut along each side of the bags. Then cut the bags into 24-inch strips, about 1 inch wide. (The more strips you cut, the fluffier your pom-pom will be.) Hold several strips together, and tie them to a long piece of cord. Repeat until you have used all the strips. Slide the knotted strips together on the cord so that they are bunched up next to each other. To make the pom-pom handle, tie the ends of the cord together. Wrap the cord handle with masking tape.

What You'll Need
- white kitchen bags, clear dry-cleaning bags, black trash bags, or colored shopping bags
- tape measure
- blunt scissors
- heavyweight cotton cord
- masking tape

Terrific Tassels

Look around the house for objects that need a splash of color.
Then decorate them with tassels.

What You'll Need
- 2½-inch square of cardboard
- yarn
- blunt scissors

1. Wrap yarn around a cardboard square 10 to 15 times. To make the tassel hanger, thread a piece of yarn under the wrapped yarn at the top edge of the cardboard. Bring the hanger ends together to form a loop, and tie a knot to secure it. Carefully slip the wrapped yarn loops off the cardboard.

2. Tie another piece of yarn around the top third of the yarn loops. Cut the loops at the bottom to make the tassel.

3. Repeat steps 1 and 2 to make more tassels. Use the tassels to decorate shoes, barrettes, bicycle handlebars, place mats, hats, and more. Make 2-color tassels in your school's team colors, and tie them on your gym shoes.

1

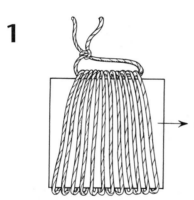

Slip the yarn loops off the cardboard.

2

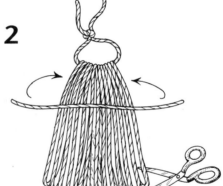

Cut the loops at the bottom.

3

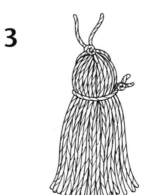

Use tassels to decorate
shoes, barrettes, and more.

Seashell Frame

◆▸◆▸◆▸◆▸

Collect shells along the shore to decorate a picture frame. Put a photo of yourself or your pet playing at the beach inside the frame.

What You'll Need
- seashells
- plain wooden picture frame or wooden box (available at craft stores)
- craft glue or epoxy

Find a variety of small seashells. Glue them on the picture frame. Start in the corners, and make the same arrangement in each one. Then glue small shells between the corner decorations. Let the glue set, then put your picture in the frame. You can also decorate a wooden box with seashells. Just glue the shells on the lid. Give your seashell frame or box as a gift to a friend or family member.

 # Family Flag

◆▸◆▸◆▸◆▸

A family is a team, and every team needs a flag. Make a team flag for your family, and hang it high.

Cut out a V-shape at one 8-inch end of the felt. Make a pocket for the dowel at the other short end of the felt. Apply a line of glue along the end of the felt, and fold over 1 inch. Let the glue dry. To make a coat of arms for your family flag, cut a shield shape from felt. Glue the felt shield to the center of the flag. Cut up other shapes of felt to glue on the shield shape. Think of things your family likes to do. If you like to go camping, cut a tent shape. Glue these other shapes to the shield shape. Let the glue dry, and then insert the dowel in the pocket. If you want, add a tassel to the top of the dowel. See Terrific Tassels on the previous page to make a tassel.

What You'll Need
- 8×12-inch piece of felt
- blunt scissors
- craft glue
- ruler
- assorted colors of felt scraps
- 18-inch wood dowel with ¼-inch diameter

"Pin"–demonium

Make one for each of your friends! Have fun collecting each other's artwork.

What You'll Need
- diaper pins with animal faces or large safety pins
- brightly colored nail polish (optional)
- newspaper (optional)
- clear nail polish (optional)
- small beads that fit the open shaft of the safety pin
- clear gel glue
- colored ribbons

If you don't have diaper pins with animal faces, spread out newspaper and paint large safety pins a bright color of nail polish. (Make sure you have good ventilation.) Let dry, then paint the other side. It will take 3 or 4 coats, depending on the thickness of the polish. Give the pins 2 coats of clear polish, and let dry. Thread the beads onto the lower, open pin shafts. Make sure to leave enough room to close the safety pins. Now spread clear gel glue over the beads with your fingers, making sure

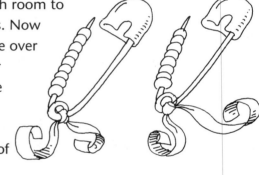

some glue gets between all the beads. Let pins dry for a few hours. Add a second coat of glue, and let dry again. Tie coordinating ribbon through the hole at the bottom of the pin.

Recycled Jewels

Take apart several pieces of old jewelry, and combine them to re-create your own jewelry for special occasions.

Caution: This project requires adult help.

Ask your mother or grandmother for some old costume jewelry. With an adult's help, take apart the rhinestones, beads, and pearls. Cut a circle or a different shape from a plastic coffee-can lid. Arrange your "jewels" in a new jewelry design.

Glue them to the plastic base, covering the whole piece. Glue a metal barrette or brooch pin to the back of the jewelry base. Let the glue set.

What You'll Need
- old costume jewelry (or buy rhinestones and other faux gems at a craft store)
- scissors
- plastic coffee-can lids
- jewelry glue (for plastic and metal)
- metal barrettes or brooch pins

Gift of Giving

◆▶▶▶▶▶▶

Give the ability to give (the greatest gift of all).

Nothing feels better than the chance to give a heartfelt gift. So why not give a less-fortunate person that opportunity? Gather together materials, such as beads, ribbons, key chains, colorful paper, glue, and fabric paints. Bag or box them up as a craft kit, and ask your local YMCA, Salvation Army, or social services offices to help you give them to people who will appreciate them most. Write instructions for specific crafts, or leave it up to the gift-giver's imagination.

What You'll Need
- beads, key chains, ribbons, and other gift goodies
- bag or box
- paper and pencil (optional)

 # Papier–Mâché Mash

◆▶▶▶▶▶▶

This pulpy mash is great for adding dimension to papier-mâché projects.

What You'll Need
- newspaper
- bucket
- water
- saucepan
- strainer
- mixing bowl and spoon
- 2 tablespoons of craft glue
- 2 tablespoons of dry wall-paper paste
- aluminum foil
- paper towel tube
- sandpaper
- acrylic paints
- paintbrush

Caution: This project requires adult help.

Tear up 4 sheets of newspaper into postage-stamp-size pieces. Place the newspaper pieces in a bucket, and soak them in water overnight. After the paper has soaked, have an adult boil the paper and water in a saucepan for 15 minutes. Stir the paper mixture until it is pulpy. Once the mixture has cooled, use a strainer to press out the excess water. Place the paper mixture in a bowl, and add glue and dry wallpaper paste. Stir well until it thickens. Set the mash aside.

To make a puppet head, create a base form with crushed foil. Wrinkle and crush the foil into the head shape you want. Position the shape over the top of a paper towel tube. Cover the shape with the papier-mâché mash, and sculpt out features. Let it dry overnight. Once it's completely dry, smooth any rough edges with sandpaper, and paint the puppet head with acrylic paints.

Doorknob Hangers

◆▷◆▷◆▷◆▷

These doorknob hangers have a notepad so you can leave notes for your family all year round.

What You'll Need
- poster board
- pencil
- blunt scissors
- markers
- self-stick removable notes
- construction paper
- craft glue

Make a doorknob hanger for each season. Refer to the illustration to draw a 4×8-inch doorknob hanger pattern on a piece of poster board. Cut out the pattern, and trace it 3 times on poster board. Cut out each piece. You should have 4 doorknob hangers. Decorate each one to match a season. A summer hanger might have a sprig of flowers with summer bugs crawling up it or children diving into a pool. Leave a space toward the bottom for the notepad. For the notepad, place the self-stick removable notes on the doorknob hanger. Cut a strip of construction paper to make a pencil holder loop. Glue it to the side of the notepad.

Block Buildings

◆▷◆▷◆▷◆▷

Create your own miniature city with buildings that look just like the ones in your town.

What You'll Need
- 2×2-inch and 2×3-inch wood boards
- saw
- tape measure
- sandpaper
- markers
- cardboard
- scissors
- wood glue
- paper towel tubes

Caution: This project requires adult help.

Have an adult saw all the wood pieces. Make sure you sand the wood smooth. To make a house or store, saw a 2-inch piece from a 2×2-inch board. Draw windows, doors, and shingles on the wood. Cut a roof piece from cardboard, and glue it to the wood. To make a tall building, saw a 6-inch piece from a 2×2-inch board and an 8-inch piece from a 2×3-inch board. Stand them up, and draw on the windows of a bank or the balconies of an apartment. To make a barn, cut a 5-inch piece from a 2×3-inch board. Decorate it with markers. Place the wood piece on its side, and add a cardboard roof and a paper towel tube silo.

Batik T-Shirt

❖▶▶▶▶▶❖

The great thing about batik T-shirts is that no matter how many you make, each one will be different.

What You'll Need
- large plastic bag
- white T-shirt
- pencil
- old crayons
- paper cupcake liners
- disposable paint-brushes
- fabric dye
- rubber gloves
- paper towels
- iron and ironing board

Caution: This project requires adult help.

Cover your work area with a large plastic bag. Lightly draw a design on your T-shirt. Remove the paper wrapping from the crayons. Have an adult melt the crayons in paper (not metallic!) cupcake liners in the microwave. Paint the melted crayons on your design. Let dry. Then crumple up the T-shirt. This is what creates the cracked look of batik. With an adult's help, mix the fabric dye according to package directions. Be sure to wear rubber gloves. Soak the T-shirt in the dye for about 10 to 15 minutes. Cover an area of your work surface with paper towels. Place the T-shirt flat on the paper towels to dry. With an adult's help, iron the T-shirt between 4 layers of paper towels. The paper will soak up the excess wax.

Airplane Flyer

❖▶▶▶▶▶❖

Hang your airplane from the ceiling. If you use fishing line, it looks as if the plane is really flying.

What You'll Need
- pencil or black felt-tip pen
- foam food trays (from fruits or veg-etables only)
- craft knife
- permanent markers
- craft glue
- masking tape

Caution: This project requires adult help.

Refer to the illustration and draw the body, wings, and tail pieces of an airplane on a clean foam food tray. With an adult's help, cut out the pieces with a craft knife. Decorate the pieces with perma-nent markers. Cut 2 slots in the body of the plane for the wings and the tail. Insert the wings and tail, adding a dot of glue to hold them in place. Now you're ready to test-fly your plane. If you need a weight adjustment in the nose or tail, use some masking tape to add weight.

# Pencil Cup Possibilities

*Jazzing up your room will take the boredom out of homework.
Try making other items for a desk set.*

What You'll Need

- newspaper
- tin can or old coffee mug
- poster paints (optional)
- colorful pictures cut from old magazines, calendars, greeting cards, gift wrap, etc.
- blunt scissors
- old margarine tub
- clear gel glue
- water
- tablespoon
- paintbrush
- clear, nontoxic acrylic gloss
- yarn, ribbon, rubber stamps and ink pads, glitter glue, or glitter marker

Caution: This project requires adult help.

Spread the newspaper first. Paint a background color on the can or mug, if desired. While waiting for the paint to dry, cut out pictures you want to put on the container. In an old, clean margarine tub, mix 1 tablespoon of water with 2 tablespoons of clear gel glue. Brush the back of the picture and the spot where the picture is to be placed on the can. Place the picture where you want it, then carefully brush a layer of glue over the top. Finish putting on all your cool pictures. Welcome to decoupage! Let the pictures dry for a day. Then coat the pencil cup with clear, nontoxic acrylic gloss, according to directions. (You may need an adult's help with this part.) Glue on extras, such as yarn or ribbon, or adorn with paint, rubber stamps, glitter glue, or glitter marker. Let dry for another day.

Make a power-banking variation. Power to the pennies! (Everything counts, you know.) Use an old piggy bank from a garage sale or another unusual container that can be easily opened. Follow the same decoupage directions as above. Make sure to leave an opening for the cash and for necessary withdrawals!

Trip Treasures

◆▷◆▷◆▷◆

Box up all your vacation keepsakes.

If you're planning the adventure of a lifetime, why not put together this special treasure box for the things you collect along the way?

Wrap the lid and bottom of an ordinary shoe box in an extra highway map of the state you're planning to visit. If possible, wrap the lid of the box so your final destination is easy to see (mark it with a bright-colored highlighter). Use a piece of yarn to tie the box securely so you won't lose the special postcards, mementos, and souvenirs of your trip.

What You'll Need
- shoe box
- map of your travel route
- glue
- highlighter
- yarn

Fancy Flowerpot

◀▷◀▷◀▷◀▷

Design your own painted flowerpot to show off a beautiful plant or floral arrangement.

What You'll Need
- clay flowerpot
- dish detergent
- newspaper
- pencil
- acrylic paints and paintbrush

Wash the flowerpot, even if it is new, with dish detergent. Rinse it thoroughly, and place it in the sun to dry. Cover your work surface with newspaper. Sketch a pattern or picture on the flowerpot. You can draw an apple pattern, a picture of your family, or an abstract design. Paint it with acrylic paints.

Let the paint dry. Once the paint is dry, put a plant or a floral arrangement in the flowerpot.

Personalize Your Hats

◆▸◆▸◆▸◆▸

Turn an old baseball cap into a new, stylish hat of your own.
The possibilities are endless.

What You'll Need
- old baseball hat or painter's cap (available at paint supply stores)
- scrap of fabric
- blunt scissors
- craft glue
- fabric paints
- markers
- glitter
- sequins

Cut a circle or square from a scrap of fabric large enough to cover the front emblem of a baseball hat. Glue the fabric over the emblem. Decorate your hat with fabric paints and markers. Make your baseball hat into a fun beach cap. Paint an underwater ocean scene with fish and seaweed. Use the markers to add detail to the picture. Let the paint dry. Glue on glitter and sequins to make the fish sparkle.

Personal Place Mats

◆▸◆▸◆▸◆▸

It doesn't even matter if you get these place mats dirty because they
wipe clean with a damp sponge. Now that's neat.

What You'll Need
- markers
- 12×18-inch piece of poster board
- blunt scissors
- construction paper or old magazines
- craft glue
- grease pencil (optional)

Caution: This project requires adult help.

Use markers to draw a background, such as a beach, on the poster board. Cut out shapes or pictures, such as boats or people, from construction paper or old magazines. Glue the cutouts on the poster board. Have an adult take you to a copy center to have your place mat laminated. Leave a ¼-inch border around the place mat.

Instead of a scene, you could glue on fun things you want to study or draw a maze on your place mat. Once laminated, use a grease pencil to play the game again and again.

Soda Straw Loom Bookmark

◆━◆━◆━◆━◆

Weave this for a special reader in your life.

What You'll Need
- variegated (multicolored) yarn
- blunt scissors
- tape measure
- 6 milkshake straws (the big kind)
- large needle
- masking tape

Cut 6 pieces of yarn. Each piece should be about 5 inches longer than your straws. Use the needle to thread one piece of yarn through each straw. When all the straws have been threaded, tie the tops of all the yarn pieces together. Push the straws up until they touch the knot. Lay the straws on the table, side by side. Put a piece of tape across the tops of the straws, just under the knot, to hold them in place. Turn the straws over; tape the other side in the same place. Cut another piece of yarn about 6 feet long. Tie one end of the yarn onto a straw either on the far left or far right, just below the tape. Weave the yarn over one straw and under the next; when you reach the last straw, go back again. Keep weaving until the whole length of the straws is wrapped in yarn. Tie off the yarn, and trim the end. Take off the masking tape. Slide the straws out of the weaving one by one. Push the weaving up to the knot. Tie an overhand knot in the yarn that was in the straws, just below the weaving.

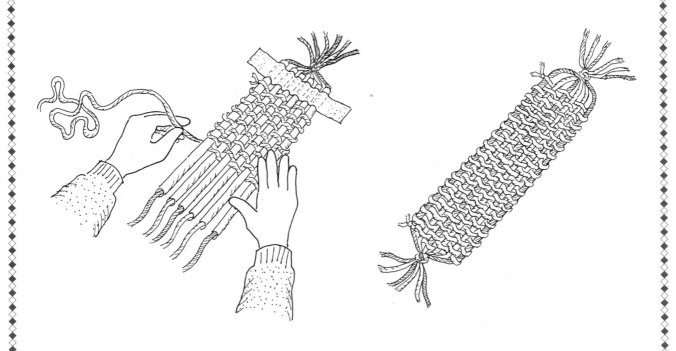

Miniature Garden

◆►◆►◆►◆►

Share a magic miniature garden with a grown-up friend.

What You'll Need
- pieces of sponge, rock, and brick
- water
- old fishbowl or large glass jar
- food coloring
- 4 tablespoons ammonia
- 4 tablespoons liquid bluing
- 4 tablespoons water
- glass jar
- rubber gloves
- salt

Caution: This project requires adult help.

Ask an adult to help you grow this special garden. It will take around 5 to 6 hours. Wet the pieces of sponge, rock, and brick, and arrange them in an old fishbowl or a large glass jar. You might want to stack some of them so that your garden has a variety of heights. Then sprinkle a few drops of food coloring over each piece. Try to use lots of different colors. Ask an adult to help you mix the ammonia, bluing, and water in another glass jar. Carefully pour the mixture over the colored pieces. Do this where there is good ventilation. Whoever is pouring should wear rubber gloves. When the mix has been poured, sprinkle lots of salt over all the pieces. That's all there is to it. Just sit back, relax, and watch your garden bloom!

Bubble Prints

◆►◆►◆►◆►

Usually when you blow bubbles, they pop and disappear. Now you can save your bubbles on a piece of paper.

Mix water, dish soap, and a few drops of food coloring in a plastic cup. Place the plastic cup on the baking sheet. Place the straw in the cup, and blow bubbles through the straw until they spill all over the baking sheet. Remove the cup, and place a piece of paper down over the bubbles. Lift the paper off. The colored bubbles will create a light design on the paper. Let it dry, and then draw in a picture or outline shapes in the design. Use this bubble-printed paper as wrapping paper, book covers, or stationery.

What You'll Need
- ½ cup water
- 1 teaspoon dish soap
- food coloring
- plastic cup
- plastic drinking straw
- baking sheet
- white drawing paper
- markers

T-Shirt Pillows

◆▸◆▸◆▸◆▸

Turn your favorite T-shirt into a huggable pillow. It's so easy,
you'll want to make a set.

What You'll Need
• T-shirt
• needle and thread
• cotton batting

Find a T-shirt with a fun picture on it. Stitch the bottom and the sleeves closed. Stuff your pillow through the neck opening with cotton batting. Then sew the neck closed. Make a set of pillows for your room. If you have a plain T-shirt, make it into a custom pillow with your own design. See the Tie-Dye T-Shirt on page 317.

Letter Writing Kit

◆▸◆▸◆▸◆▸

Combined with the Stationery Set on page 292, this kit makes the perfect gift
for a friend who is moving away.

To make notecards and matching envelopes, see the Stationery Set on page 292. Cut a sheet of construction paper to cover the outside panels and lid of a shoe box. Decorate it to match the notecards and envelopes. Glue the construction paper, with the design facing out, on the shoe box. Cut construction paper slightly larger than the front and back covers of an address book. Decorate them to match the stationery design.

What You'll Need
• notecards and envelopes
• blunt scissors
• construction paper
• shoe box
• markers
• craft glue
• cardboard-covered address book (available at stationery stores)
• pen
• ribbon

Glue the pieces over the address book covers. Fold and trim the edges over the inside of the book. Place all the items and a pen in the box. Wrap ribbon around the box, and tie in a bow.

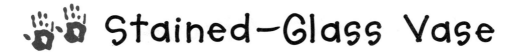

Stained-Glass Vase

◆▸◆▸◆▸◆▸

Make beautiful vases from old glass bottles!

What You'll Need

- glass bottle with a nice shape
- newspaper
- clear gel glue
- water
- tablespoon
- old margarine tub
- mixing spoon
- several light-colored shades of tissue paper
- paintbrush
- clear nontoxic acrylic gloss

Remove all the labels and metal rings from the bottle. Wash and dry it thoroughly. Spread out the newspaper. In the clean margarine tub, mix 2 tablespoons clear gel glue with 1 tablespoon water. Tear off pieces of tissue paper about the size of a quarter. Work with small areas; brush some glue on the bottle in a patch the size of a quarter. Lay a piece of tissue paper on that part of the bottle. Now hold the piece down with your thumb while lightly brushing glue on top of the paper. Carefully add a piece at time, slightly overlapping the edges. You're only going to do 1 layer. Fold some tissue paper over the lip of the bottle all the way around. Finish covering the bottle. Layer pieces under the bottom edge of the bottle, too. Let dry for a day. Coat the bottle with clear acrylic gloss, according to package directions. Let dry.

Clay Pockets

◆▸◆▸◆▸◆▸

Create this special pocket to hide tiny treasures in.

Caution: This project requires adult help.

Roll out a ¼-inch-thick layer of clay on waxed paper. Use a toothpick to make the outline of a 5-inch-diameter circle (the back piece) and a 2½-inch half circle (the pocket) in the clay. Cut both pieces from the clay (have an adult help you with the craft knife). If you want to decorate your clay pocket, press some small items in both clay pieces, or use a toothpick to make tiny impressions, such as baseball stitching.

Place the half-circle pocket piece over the back piece, and pinch the edges together. Then use the straw to punch a hole at the top. Place a piece of crumpled foil into the pocket to hold it open while it dries. With an adult's help, bake clay according to package directions. Once it has cooled, paint with acrylic paints.

What You'll Need

- white polymer clay
- rolling pin
- waxed paper
- ruler
- toothpicks
- craft knife
- keys, coins, or buttons (to make impressions in clay)
- drinking straw
- aluminum foil
- acrylic paints
- paintbrush

Snazzy Scrapbook

Share happy memories with someone, or showcase their awesome vacation souvenirs.

What You'll Need

- 5×7-inch autograph book or journal with unlined pages
- white paper
- pencil
- ruler
- blunt scissors
- ½ yard of fake fur or other novelty fabric
- white glue
- solid-color paper
- fancy scissors that cut in patterns
- different colors of felt
- glitter and regular markers
- glitter glue
- multicolored glue
- ink pad
- ink stamps

Plan a theme for the scrapbook, and choose your supplies accordingly. Open the autograph book or journal, and lay it flat on white paper. Trace around the book (add about ¼ inch to one side—you can trim the fabric later if it is too big), and cut out. Use the white paper as a pattern to cut out the novelty fabric. Stand the book up with its pages open. Coat the front and back covers and spine with white glue. Smear a thin coat of white glue on the backside of the fabric. Line up the corners of one side of the book with the backside of the fabric. Press down with a clean hand inside the book. Close the book, press the fabric around the spine and into the grooves, and then press the second side down. Let dry for a day. Trim fabric if needed.

Meanwhile, using the colored paper, cut out background circles, squares, triangles, etc., for photos or other mementos with the fancy scissors. Decide how you will place them inside the book. Cut out other shapes from felt. Play around with the contents of the book until you're satisfied. Glue everything down with white glue. Decorate the inside and cover of the scrapbook with markers, glitter glue, multicolored glue, and ink stamps.

Personalized Party Plates

❖❖❖❖❖❖

*Make all your party guests feel like guests of honor with
these personalized plates.*

What You'll Need
- paper plates
- markers
- clear plastic wrap
- blunt scissors
- craft glue

Draw a special picture on each paper plate for your guests. If you want to use the plates as place cards, write each guest's name on it. For each plate, cut a circle of clear plastic wrap the same size as the plate. Apply a ring of glue around the rim of 1 plate. Add a dot of glue to the center of the plate. Cover the plate with a circle of plastic wrap to seal your picture. Repeat for the remaining plates. You can use these plates to serve anything that doesn't need to be cut with a knife. Ice cream and cake, cookies, or cheese and crackers all work just fine.

👋 Thank Yous

❖❖❖❖❖❖

*When someone brings you an extra special present, say "thank you"
in an equally special way.*

Make a picture card to thank someone for a birthday or holiday present. Fold a piece of construction paper in half. Write the words *thank you* on the front. Make 1 letter in *thank you* into a picture of the gift you received. If you received a doll, then draw a doll with her arms up for the letter *y*. Write the rest of the letters in colorful

What You'll Need
- construction paper
- markers

markers. You can also make birthday, congratulations, and get-well-soon cards with pictures as the letters. Draw birthday candles to make some letters in *Happy Birthday,* or make the word *soon* into a sickbed for a get-well-soon card.

Button Bonanza

◆▶▶▶▶▶▶

String together colorful buttons to make your own jewelry.
Shorten the necklace if you'd rather make a bracelet.

What You'll Need
- crazy-color buttons with large holes (try a grab bag from the fabric or craft store)
- leather cords or shoelaces
- blunt scissors

Make sure you have enough buttons and cords or shoelaces to make a necklace of the desired length. Tie a knot at the end of the leather cord or shoelace. With the first button face up, thread the cord up through 1 hole and down through the other. Tie a knot after it. Add more buttons in alternating colors and sizes. They can be placed next to each other or spaced apart with knots in between. If your buttons have 4 holes instead of 2, use double laces. At the end of the cord, make a loop large enough to fit over the first button and tie it off. Model your new necklace!

Clothespin Magnets

◆▶▶▶▶▶▶

Design your own clothespin magnet to display your art projects or good grades.

Draw and cut out a ballerina shape on a piece of cardboard or poster board. Decorate the shape. Cut out a piece of tulle or fabric to make a ballerina costume, and glue it on the figure. Add glitter for her crown and toe shoes. Glue the ballerina to a pinch clothespin. Cut a piece of the magnet strip, and glue it to the back of the clothespin. Use your clothespin magnet to hold your artwork on the refrigerator.

What You'll Need
- cardboard or poster board
- markers
- blunt scissors
- tulle netting or fabric scraps
- craft glue
- glitter
- pinch clothespin
- magnet strip

Napkin Rings

◆▷◆▷◆▷◆▷

Coordinate these napkin rings with other table decorations to create a table setting with a theme.

What You'll Need
- construction paper
- blunt scissors
- paper towel tubes
- craft glue
- ruler
- markers

Cut construction paper to fit around a paper towel tube. Glue the paper around the tube. Repeat with other paper towel tubes using different colors of paper. Cut the paper towel tubes into 2-inch rings. Use markers and cutout shapes to decorate each napkin ring. Write each guest's name on a napkin ring to make place cards. Cut out circles or other shapes from construction paper, and glue them to the napkin rings. For birthday parties, make the ring look like a cake. For a picnic, decorate the rings with red and white checkerboards to look like the tablecloth. For an everyday dinner, draw on something that each family member likes to eat.

Paint-a-Gift

◆▷◆▷◆▷◆▷

Grown-ups like presents as much as kids, and they especially like gifts hand-made by you!

Cover your work surface with newspaper. Pin or clip an apron to the cardboard to hold it in place as you paint it. Place some water in a small dish. Paint a design around the edges of the apron with slightly thinned acrylic paints. As you paint, dip the paintbrush in water, then dip the brush in the paint to thin it. Paint cooking utensils for a dad who likes to barbecue or flowers for a mom who likes gardening. If you want, use stencils to make a design. Let the paint dry, then wrap your gift.

What You'll Need
- newspaper
- plain apron
- large piece of cardboard
- straight pins or binder clips
- small dish
- water
- acrylic paints
- paintbrush

Tie-Dye T-Shirt

All eyes will be on you when you wear this cool tie-dyed T-shirt with its bright bursts of color.

What You'll Need
- white T-shirt
- rubber bands
- ruler
- large plastic bag
- rubber gloves
- 1½ cups hot water
- 3 squeeze bottles
- 2 teaspoons red, 1 teaspoon yellow, and 2 teaspoons blue fabric dye
- 6 teaspoons soda ash

Caution: This project requires adult help.

1. To make a bull's-eye design, gather a T-shirt in your hand with the center as one end of the gathered shirt. Tightly wrap a rubber band around the shirt about 2 inches from the center point. Bundle another rubber band about 2 inches down from the first rubber band.

2. Cover your work area with a large plastic bag. Wearing rubber gloves, have an adult help you mix the dye. Pour ½ cup hot water into each squeeze bottle. Add yellow dye to one bottle, red to another bottle, and blue dye to the third bottle. Add 2 teaspoons of soda ash to each bottle. Screw lids onto the bottles. Shake well to mix.

3. Place the rubber-banded T-shirt on your work surface. Squeeze the red dye over the first section, squirting into the folds. Apply the yellow dye to the next section, then squeeze the blue dye about 2 inches beyond the last rubber band. Let the shirt set for about 3 hours.

4. After the shirt has dried, rinse each section until the water runs clear. Remove the rubber bands, and lay the shirt flat to dry.

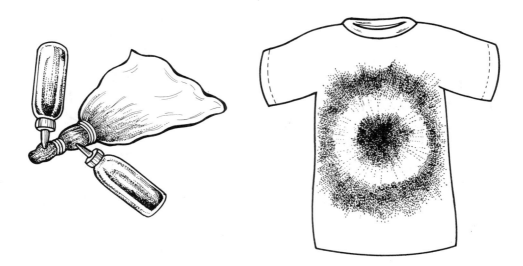

Paper Lanterns

String a series of pretty paper lanterns along an outside porch or window. Watch them sway gently in the wind.

What You'll Need
- 4×6-inch pieces of wrapping or construction paper
- blunt scissors
- clear tape
- string

1. Fold a piece of wrapping or construction paper in half lengthwise. Cut slits along the fold about ½ inch apart.

2. Open the paper, and tape the short edges together with the fold pointing outward.

3. Cut a strip of paper to make a handle. Tape it across the top of the lantern. Now you can hang your lantern with string. Make more lanterns so you can hang a series of them outside or in your room.

1

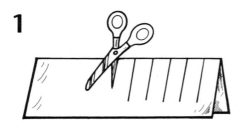

Make cuts in the fold.

3

Tape handle across the top of the lantern.

2

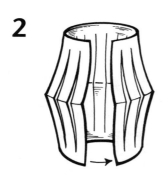

Tape short edges together.

Easy Artist's Easel

◄◆◄◆◄◆►

Make these simple easels to display your artwork—you can create your own art gallery!

What You'll Need
- cardboard box
- tape
- pencil
- yardstick
- heavy-duty scissors or craft knife (adult use only)
- clothespins

Caution: This project requires adult help.

Find a sturdy cardboard box, and tape it shut. On opposite sides, draw a line from the bottom corner to the opposite top corner. Have an adult cut along the diagonals and then across the top and bottom to cut the box in half (see illustration).

Cut 2 small slits at the top of the easel. Attach your artwork by clipping it to the box with the clothespins. You could also use your easel to paint your artwork—just like artists do!

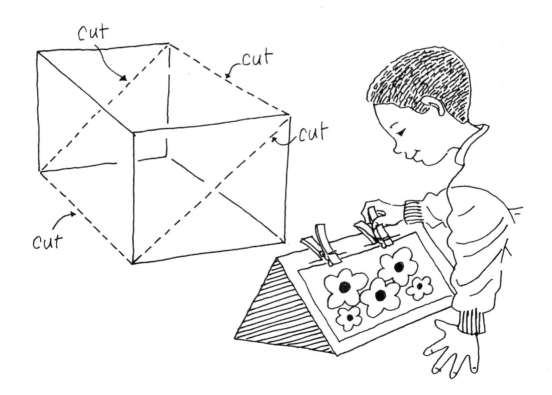

Pop-Up Greeting Card

◆▶◆▶◆▶◆

Give a little extra lift to your message with a special greeting card that springs to life.

What You'll Need
- construction paper
- ruler
- pencil
- blunt scissors
- craft glue
- markers

1. Fold a piece of construction paper in half. Halfway down the fold, make 2 pencil marks about 2 inches apart. At each mark, cut a slit through the fold 1 inch into the paper.

2. Fold the cut flap back and forth several times to crease it well. Bring the flap back to the center. Unfold the page almost completely, and gently push the flap through to the other side. You should have a rectangle that pops out of the paper.

3. Draw a shape or design for your greeting card on another piece of construction paper. Cut it out, and glue it to the front of the pop-out rectangle. Fold another piece of construction paper in half. Trim the pop-up paper so that it is slightly smaller than the second piece of paper. Glue the back of the pop-up paper to the inside of the larger paper. Decorate the front of your greeting card, and write a message inside.

4. If you want to make your pop-up cards into a pop-up gift book, repeat steps 1 and 2 to make several pop-up pages. Then draw and cut out the items for your story from construction paper. Glue those shapes on the pop-out rectangles. Glue the back of 1 page to the front of another. Repeat this until all the pages are glued together. To make a cover, fold another piece of construction paper in half. Glue the first and last pages inside the cover. Decorate the cover of your book.

1   **2**   **3**

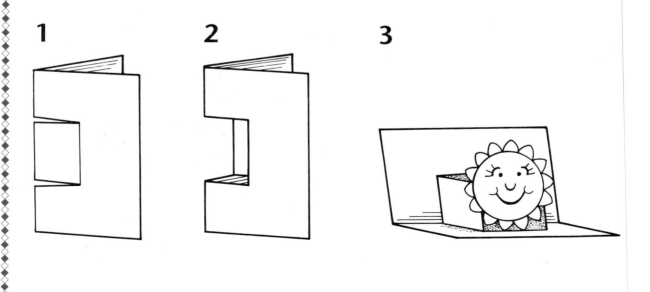

Hair-Clip Holder

Keep your hair—and your room—a little neater with this friendly face.

What You'll Need
- stiff cardboard
- blunt scissors
- markers
- ruler
- yarn
- craft glue

If you're always losing your hair clips and rubber bands, you need someplace to keep them. This fun project is a great idea for organizing your "hair things."

Cut a 4-inch circle from stiff cardboard. This is your hair-clip holder's "face." Draw on eyes, lips, freckles, dimples—anything that makes you smile.

Cut sixteen 20-inch pieces of colored yarn to make your hair-clip holder's "hair." Tie the yarn pieces in the middle with a small piece of matching yarn to form the "part." Glue the part to the top of your cardboard face. You can either braid the dangling strands of yarn hair or leave them loose.

Now you can keep all your hair ties and barrettes safely clipped in your holder's hair until you're ready to use them!

Measure Me Strip

This strip takes only a short time to make, but it gives you years and years of measuring fun.

Draw a scale of inch and foot marks on one side of the pine board. Stand up the board in a corner of your room. Each time you measure yourself, write the date at the measurement mark. Add your baby measurements on the board, too. You can get the measurements from your pediatrician. Have a family member take a picture of you each time you measure yourself. Once the film is developed, cut the picture out and glue the photo to the board next to your measurement mark.

What You'll Need
- 1×4-inch pine board about 6 feet long
- permanent markers
- yardstick
- camera
- color film
- blunt scissors
- craft glue

 Ribbon Basket

Create an all-occasion basket using white ribbons, or select colored ribbons for holiday centerpieces.

What You'll Need

- 8½ yards of 1-inch-wide ribbon
- tape measure
- blunt scissors
- cardboard box (from a small bakery cake)
- aluminum foil
- straight pins
- craft glue
- water
- small dish
- old paintbrush

1. Cut the ribbon into twelve 18-inch strips. Place 6 strips on your work surface side by side, vertically. Take a separate strip, and starting at about 5 inches from one end of the vertical strips, weave it over and under each ribbon horizontally. Repeat with the remaining 5 ribbons. When you are done weaving, the woven part should be centered with the ribbon ends loose.

2. Line a small cardboard box with aluminum foil. Carefully place the ribbon weave in the box. Pin down the bottom to hold it in place. Put the loose ribbon ends up over the sides of the box. Cut three 29-inch pieces of ribbon. Weave 1 piece over and under to form the first row of the sides. Hold in place with pins. Tuck in any excess ribbon. Weave another piece for the next row. Weave the last piece for the third row. Tuck in the ends, and pin in place.

3. Mix equal parts of water and glue in a small dish. Apply a coat of the diluted glue all over the woven ribbons. Once the glue dries, the ribbon should be stiff. Gently peel it from the foil, and admire your basket.

1
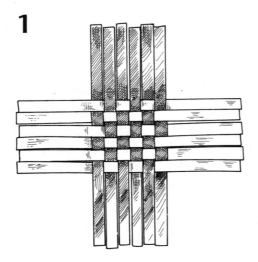

2
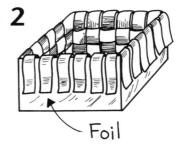
Foil

3

 # Box Cars

◆▶◆▶◆▶◆▶

With a few materials and a little imagination, you can make a race car, a sports car, or even a minivan.

What You'll Need
- old boxes
- blunt scissors
- construction paper
- craft glue
- markers
- plastic milk jug lids or cardboard
- clear plastic cup
- aluminum foil

Save some small boxes from the kitchen or from gifts about the size of a butter box, a cocoa mix box, or a necklace box. Cover the boxes with different colors of construction paper. Decorate the paper-covered boxes with markers. For the wheels, glue on plastic milk jug lids or cut circles from cardboard. Make a windshield from a clear plastic cup cut in half. Glue it to the box. Use aluminum foil to make headlights and bumpers.

 # Recycled Magnets

◆▶◆▶◆▶◆▶

Redecorate old refrigerator magnets to hold up important school papers, special paintings, or party invitations.

Draw musical instruments on a piece of poster board or cardboard. Draw a guitar, a saxophone, or piano keys. Cut out each instrument, and color them in wild colors. If you have flat, rectangular plastic magnets, you can make new "covers" for them. Glue the instruments to the top of the flat plastic magnets. If you have a magnetic strip, cut a small piece and glue (or, if it's adhesive, stick) it to the back of the instrument cutouts. Display your new magnets on the refrigerator.

What You'll Need
- markers
- poster board or cardboard
- blunt scissors
- flat plastic magnets or magnet strips (available at craft stores)
- craft glue

Switch-Plate Covers

◆▷◆▷◆▷◆

Switch on some fun with this stylish room accent!

What You'll Need
- plastic juice or bleach bottle (washed and rinsed well)
- scissors
- screwdriver
- pencil
- craft supplies (sequins, rhinestones, markers, etc.)
- paints
- paintbrushes
- craft glue
- double-sided tape

Caution: This project requires adult help.

Tired of seeing that dull old switch plate every time you flip your lights on and off? Why not make a new design that shines with your own ideas?

Cut a piece of plastic from a clean, washed juice or bleach bottle. Ask an adult to unscrew the faceplate in your room so you can use it as a pattern. Place the faceplate on the plastic, trace around it, and cut out the rectangle. Mark and cut out the center rectangle to make room for the switch. (Have an adult replace the faceplate.)

Decorate the plastic any way that suits your mood. Add sequins or rhinestones if you're in a glamorous mood. Paint tiger stripes if you're feeling wild. Doodle hearts and flowers if you're feeling full of love. Or make it galactic with stars and asteroids if you're an out-of-this-world kid.

When you're done decorating it, attach your new, improved switch plate over the old one (the old faceplate must be in place to keep you safe from electricity) with double-sided tape.

Bolo Tie

◆▷◆▷◆▷◆▶

Both guys and gals can wear this easy Western-style necklace.

What You'll Need
- large Western-style button
- 40-inch-long leather or satin cord or cool shoelace (make sure it's the right thickness for the button)
- metal tips (found in the button department)
- glue (optional)

If your Western-style button has 2 holes, thread both ends of the cord up through 1 hole and down through the other. If the button has 4 holes, thread one end up through 1 hole and down through the other. Then thread the other end of the cord up and down through the hole alongside the first.

Glue the metal tips to the ends of the cords, or just tie a knot at each end. Then take your bolo tie two-stepping!

Pattern Printer

◆▷◆▷◆▷◆▶

Make a potato into a great printing stamp, and turn ordinary paper into decorative gift wrap, book covers, or stationery.

Caution: This project requires adult help.

Cover your work surface with newspaper. Clean a potato, and have an adult help you cut it in half. Draw a shape on the cut surface with a pen. Cut away the edges so that the shape stands out. Place some poster paint on a clean foam food tray. Dip the

potato shape in the paint, and then press it on a piece of paper. Continue stamping the paper until you've created a pattern you like. Let the paint dry.

What You'll Need
- newspaper
- potato
- knife
- ballpoint pen
- poster paints
- foam food tray (from fruits or vegetables only)
- drawing or brown mailing paper

Book Looks

◆▷◆▷◆▷◆▷

Make your history book even more exciting with color!

What You'll Need
- textbooks
- large white paper
- pencil
- ruler
- blunt scissors
- Sunday comics, recycled gift wrap, or your own drawings
- clear adhesive vinyl
- black marker
- clear tape

Lay the open book on the white paper. Trace around the edges of the book with the pencil, allowing for flaps 2 inches deep all the way around the book. Cut out your pattern. Place the pattern on the gift wrap or other decorative paper. Trace around the pattern, and cut out. Peel the backing off a piece of adhesive vinyl that is bigger than the cover. Starting with one end, carefully lay the adhesive vinyl, sticky side down, on the front of the decorative paper. Smooth it out as you go. Cut off the excess adhesive vinyl. Lay the cover face down on the table, and center the book on the cover. Mark, with a black dot, where the corners hit the cover. Cut slits on either side of the spine, and tuck those flaps inside the spine. Line up the corners of the front cover of the book with the dots. Fold in the corners first, then fold in the 2-inch side flaps. Repeat for the back cover. Tape the flaps to each other, not the book.

Clay Accessories

◆▷◆▷◆▷◆▷

It's just like having jewelry for your hair.

Caution: This project requires adult help.

Roll out a thin pancake of blue clay on waxed paper. Ask an adult to cut clay into a rectangular piece slightly larger than the metal barrette. Knead or roll out a small amount of white and yellow clay. Cut tiny stars and a moon from white and yellow clay. Put them on the blue clay piece. Bend the clay to match the curve of the barrette. With an adult's help, bake the clay according to package directions. After the clay piece has cooled, glue it to the back of the barrette.

What You'll Need
- blue, white, and yellow polymer clay
- rolling pin
- waxed paper
- craft knife
- metal barrette
- baking sheet
- craft glue
- toothpicks (for clay buttons)

You can also make your own buttons from clay. After you've rolled out the clay, just cut out small circles for buttons. Use toothpicks to punch 2 holes in the middle of each circle, decorate the buttons with other pieces of clay, and bake. After the clay has cooled, sew the buttons on your favorite shirt. (Once baked, the clay buttons can be machine washed and dried on the gentle cycle.)

Wind Sock

◆◇◆◇◆◇◆

Hang your wind sock on the porch, and watch it dance and swing as it catches the breeze.

What You'll Need

• 26-ounce-size plastic coffee-can lid
• blunt scissors
• ⅔ yard of nylon material
• tape measure
• permanent markers
• needle and thread
• cord

Cut the center out from a plastic coffee-can lid to make a rim. Cut a piece of nylon 15 inches wide on one end, 17 inches wide on the other end, and 12 inches long. Decorate the fabric with permanent markers. Fold the 17-inch wide end over the plastic rim. Sew a stitch around the rim to secure it. Sew the 12-inch long ends together to form a tube.

To add streamers, cut four 1½×24-inch strips of nylon. Sew them to the 15-inch-wide end of the wind sock. To hang the wind sock, cut a 12-inch piece and a 15-inch piece of cord. Carefully cut 2 small holes in the fabric on opposite sides at the 17-inch-wide end. Tie on the cords, then tie the ends together. Hang it from the porch so that it is slightly angled to catch the wind.

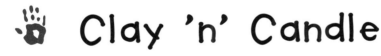

Clay 'n' Candle

◆◇◆◇◆◇◆

A little heart can house the glow.

Form a 3-inch ball of clay into a special shape you like—it could be a circle, a triangle, a heart, or anything else that catches your fancy. Press the base of the candle into the center of the clay shape. Paint the shape if you'd like. Press in glitter and sequins on the surface of the shape, and let the clay dry. Before you know it, you'll have a lovely, handmade candle-holder to brighten up your day (and night). (Remember, never light a candle without adult supervision!)

What You'll Need

• air-drying clay
• ruler
• 6-inch candle
• paint
• paintbrush
• glitter
• sequins

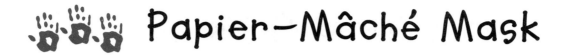

Papier-Mâché Mask

◆▸◆▸◆▸◆

Build an original mask out of newspaper strips, and hang your artwork on the wall.

Caution: This project requires adult help.

1. Cover your work surface with newspaper. Fold several sheets of newspaper into long bands. Using the illustration as a guide, make a mask frame (an oval half) with bands of newspaper stapled together.

2. Mix flour and water together to make a paste. Use 1 cup of flour for each cup of water. Blend until the paste is smooth. Dip a short strip of newspaper in the paste. Rub the strip between your fingers to remove any extra paste. Put the strip over the mask frame, and smooth in place. Repeat until the mask is covered with 4 or 5 layers of strips. To add more dimension to your mask, tape on projections before you add the last layer of newspaper strips. Use rolls or cones for horns, ears, and a nose. Let the mask dry overnight.

3. With an adult's help, cut out the eyes and a mouth. Paint the mask, and let it dry completely. To make your mask shiny, apply a coat of acrylic sealer.

1

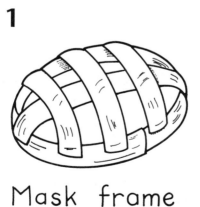

Mask frame

2

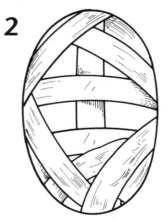

3

Yarn Stationery

Make your letter writing a little more colorful.

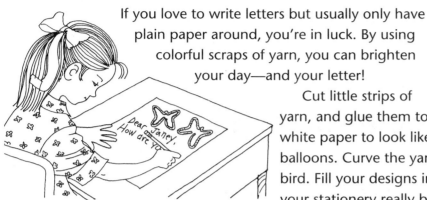

If you love to write letters but usually only have plain paper around, you're in luck. By using colorful scraps of yarn, you can brighten your day—and your letter!

What You'll Need
• yarn scraps
• blunt scissors
• craft glue
• white paper

Cut little strips of yarn, and glue them to white paper to look like pretty flowers or floating balloons. Curve the yarn around to create a cat or a bird. Fill your designs in with more yarn to make your stationery really bright, or create colorful outlines of shapes. The choice is up to you. Let your designs dry for at least 3 days before you write on the paper.

In a Nutshell

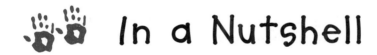

Tiny animal habitats come to life on the half shell.

What You'll Need
• walnut shells (carefully cracked in half and emptied)
• craft glue
• hobby store grass
• tiny plastic animal and nature objects

These tiny animals in nutty habitats are cute and never need to be fed. Cover the inside of half a walnut shell with glue. Sprinkle a thin layer of hobby store grass (it's like green sawdust) inside the nut. Add a tiny paper bush or watering hole, and then glue a small plastic animal in this cozy, fun place. Once the glue is dry, you'll have the world's teeniest pet zone. Take this pocket-size pal everywhere you go, or you can give it as a gift!

MUSIC MANIA

Make some noise! This chapter teaches you how to create great instruments and explore rhythms and sounds. After you've learned how to be melodious, you could stage a performance before an audience of your family and friends. You could even start your own band! And then you'll just have to decide on a catchy name....

 Flowerpot Bells

◄▸◄▸◄▸◄▸

These clay bells ring true, inside or out.

What You'll Need

- newspaper
- small clay flowerpots
- acrylic paint
- paintbrush
- clappers (small, wooden curtain rings; wooden beads; or other solid objects)
- thick string or twine
- coat hanger
- wooden chopstick
- plastic mallet

Whether you ring these inside or hang them outside as chimes, these hand-painted bells will be music to your ears!

Cover your work surface with newspaper. Paint designs on your clay pots with acrylic paints...anything goes. This is your chance to be creative. Once the paint dries, tie 1 or 2 small, wooden curtain rings or beads to a string to make the bell clapper—the object that strikes the inside of the bell to make it ring. Slip the end of the string or twine through the hole in the bottom of the clay pot so the clapper dangles inside the bell. Don't forget to knot the string or twine on the inside of the clay pot to hold the clapper.

Make a few bells, with different clappers, and tie them all to the bottom of a coat hanger so they don't touch. Hang or hold the coat hanger, and play your bells! Experiment with tapping the bells with your fingers, a wooden chopstick, and a plastic mallet to find out what makes the best sound.

Chime away!

Soda Bottle Music

This is so cool your friends will want to try it.

What You'll Need
- newspapers
- 5 or 6 empty glass soda bottles
- water
- dark-colored nail polish
- food coloring
- spoon

Spread out the newspapers. Practice making a tone by blowing into the top of a glass soda bottle. When you have it mastered, fill the bottles with different levels of water. (If you've had some music lessons, you could try tuning the bottles to specific notes.) Arrange the bottles from left to right, low notes to high notes. Practice playing an easy song. Make a water level mark on each bottle with dark-colored nail polish. (Mark the notes, too, if you know them.) Let the polish dry. Using a drop or two of food coloring, put a different color in each bottle. Put your thumb over the end of each bottle, and gently swirl the water to mix the color in. Now you can practice your songs on your soda bottle pipe organ!

When you're out of breath, turn your pipe organ into bells! Take an old metal spoon and tap each bottle. Can you create the same tune with a spoon?

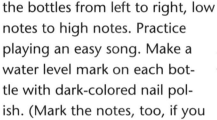

Make It Snappy

Is your favorite song too much fun to keep to yourself? Then get snapping!

Do you find it impossible to sit still when your favorite song comes on the radio? Then go with the flow, and snap your fingers to the beat. Try to pick up the main line of the song and snap with every beat and syllable. Now try it double-time. See if you can cut that rhythm in half. This is a fun exercise in rhythm and a great way to participate in the song!

What You'll Need
- radio or CD player

Air Guitar Plus

◆▶◆▶◆▶◆▶

Playing a rock star has never been easier...or more fun.

What You'll Need
- cardboard appliance box
- pencil
- blunt scissors
- glue
- tempera paints
- paintbrush
- metallic felt-tip marker
- straight pin
- tape measure
- fishing line
- duct tape
- radio

Who hasn't dreamed of being a rock star—a singing sensation dancing across videos and music lovers' hearts. This fun cardboard guitar is like an air guitar—with a little more than air to wrap your fingers around.

Draw a life-size guitar on the long end of an appliance box. You can make an acoustic guitar or an electric guitar shape. Trace around the neck of the guitar on cardboard to make another neck; make this one a bit longer than the original. Cut both pieces out, and glue the second neck to the back of the first neck. This will reinforce your guitar so you can strum wildly! If you've made an acoustic guitar, cut out a hole in the body of the guitar, so it looks like a real guitar.

Paint your guitar however you'd like. You can add your band's name, logo, or whatever you want. Try some swirling designs!

When the paint is dry, draw frets (the lines along the neck of the guitar) with the metallic felt-tip marker.

With a straight pin, make 6 small holes along the top of the neck and 6 holes along the bottom third of the body of the guitar. Measure the length from the top holes to the bottom holes, and add 4 inches. Cut 6 pieces of fishing line that length. Thread a piece of fishing line through the front of a top hole, and tape the line down on the back of the guitar with duct tape; repeat for the bottom hole. Do the same with the other holes and other pieces of line.

Now you're ready to jam—turn on the radio and play along!

 # Can-Can

◆◁◆◁◆◁◆▷

Can you keep the beat? Sure you can-can!

The magic of music is not just in the tune; it's in the rhythm. This coffee can trio of rhythm instruments can help you play along with any of your favorite songs.

Wash and dry the coffee cans. Decorate 3 sheets of paper with colorful drawings of musical notes or fun shapes. You can also use old magazines to cut out pictures of your favorite musical legends or stars, and glue them on the paper (ask for permission first!). Glue your design to the outside of the coffee can, covering the can's brand name and logo.

Now put the uncooked pinto beans in a can, the unpopped popcorn in another, and the uncooked rice in the third. Pop on the plastic lids, and make sure they are securely in place. Tape the lids in place with heavy-duty tape.

Now it's time to shake, shake, shake your way to musical adventure. Notice how different the sounds inside each can are, thanks to the different shapes and densities of the content.

What You'll Need
- 3 small metal coffee cans with plastic lids
- white paper
- color markers
- old magazines
- blunt scissors
- glue
- ½ cup uncooked pinto beans
- ½ cup unpopped popcorn
- ½ cup uncooked rice
- heavy-duty tape

Rubber Band Zither

◆▶◆▶◆▶◆▶

Bet you didn't think you could make music from a box!

Caution: This project requires adult help.

With an adult's help, cut a 4-inch-square hole in the lid of a shoe box. Cut a zigzag edge on each piece of corrugated cardboard, creating "combs." Glue 1 "comb" to one side of the square hole, and glue the other "comb" slightly angled from the square on the other side. Let the glue set overnight. Decorate the box with markers. Stretch rubber bands from the teeth of 1 comb to the teeth of the other comb on the shoe-box lid. Put the lid on the box. Pluck the rubber bands to play your zither.

What You'll Need
- shoe box with lid
- ruler
- scissors
- 2 pieces of corru-gated cardboard, 1×4½ inches each
- craft glue
- markers
- rubber bands

Jingle Bells

◁▶◆▶◆▶◆▶

Turn your body into a musical instrument with jingle bells you can wear as a bracelet.

What You'll Need
- 16 inches of gros-grain ribbon or bias tape
- blunt scissors
- 6 jingle bells
- needle and thread
- 2 sets of snaps

Cut the ribbon or bias tape in half. Sew on 3 jingle bells, evenly spaced apart, on one piece of ribbon or bias tape. Sew a snap on each end. Snap the ends together around your wrist to form a jingle bell bracelet. Use the other piece of ribbon to make a second bracelet. Once you put the bracelets on, shake your arms to make some music. If you want, make jingle bell bracelets for your ankles, too. Listen to them jingle when you march with the band.

Bottle Cap Clinkers

◆▷◆▷◆▷◆▷

Shake some bottle caps for fun and rhythmic beauty.

Caution: This project requires adult help.

Collect dozens of bottle caps from old-fashioned glass soda or beverage bottles. With an adult's help, use the biggest nail to hammer a hole through the center of each cap. Once each cap has a hole, place 4 caps on each 2-inch nail. Make between 4 and 10 nails with caps on them. Hammer the nails halfway into the wood, leaving the bottle caps free to jingle. (If the wood is rough, use the sandpaper to smooth it before hammering nails into it.) Shake the finished rattle for a distinctive sound. Shake, shake, shake it!

What You'll Need
- soda or beverage bottle caps
- hammer
- 1 large nail (larger than a 2-inch nail)
- 2-inch nails with large heads
- long piece of wood
- sandpaper (optional)

Note by Note

◆▷◆▷◆▷◆▷◆▷

Writing a tune is easy if you take it note by note.

What You'll Need
- musical instrument (piano, keyboard, etc.)

Writing tunes might seem like a difficult thing to do, but if you take it 1 note at a time, it can be done. Using a musical instrument with a wide range of notes and tones, pick a number between 1 and 10 and string that many notes together at random, keeping track of the pattern. If you pick 6, use 6 notes in the pattern. Now, using the same notes in a different order, create a new pattern. String the combinations together, and you have a tune of your own composition.

Wood Tap Turn On

◆▷◆▷◆▷◆▷

Tap, tap, tap on wood for a "tone" of fun.

What You'll Need
- 6 to 8 wood pieces
- small hammer
- tape recorder (optional)

Do all wooden doors produce the same knock? Do all blocks of wood sound the same when they are rapped and tapped on? Do they sound identical to the doors? Of course not.

Gather up 6 to 8 wood pieces that are different sizes, shapes, and colors. Tap twice on the first block of wood with your hammer. Listen carefully so you'll remember the tone. Tap on the second. Then the third, and continue until you've tapped on all the blocks. Line up the blocks in musical order (highest-pitched tap to the right, lowest-pitched tap to the left). Now "play" your wooden block instrument for a remarkable sound. For added fun, tape-record your songs!

"Synch" You Very Much

◆▷◆▷◆▷◆▷

For those with a touch of stage fright (that would be most of us!), lip-synching a song is much easier than actually singing it live.

In addition to the pretend singing, dressing up like the band or person that really sings the song is a blast. Not to mention the amusing instrument props you can make. Or the added hamming it up you can do! For a variation, try filming a video of your lip-synch act. You'll have less stage fright and more time to be creative. Act out the story behind the song without pretending to sing it. If your audience roars with applause and laughter, you'll know you have succeeded.

What You'll Need
- tape or CD of a favorite song
- tape or CD player
- instrument props
- creative costumes
- video camera (optional)

Fish Line Music

Make your own instrument that can be strummed!

What You'll Need
- smooth board, 16×6×1 inches
- pencil
- ruler
- hammer
- ten 1-inch nails
- scissors
- nylon fishing line

Caution: This project requires adult help.

Lay a 16×6×1-inch board flat on the table in front of you so that one of the 6-inch sides is nearest you. Draw 5 straight pencil lines down the length of the board about 1 inch apart, beginning 1 inch down from the top and 1 inch in from the left side. Pound a nail about ½ inch deep at the top of each line. (You may need to ask an adult for help with the hammer.)

Cut 5 pieces of nylon fishing line in the following lengths: 14, 12, 10, 8, and 6 inches. Tie a loose slip knot in both ends of each piece of fishing line. Put the slip knot of the 14-inch piece of fishing line over the top left nail on your board, and pull the knot tight. Put the slip knot at the other end of the fishing line over a loose nail, and stretch the line as tightly as you can toward the bottom of the left-most pencil line that you drew. Hammer the nail into the board about ½ inch deep. Nail the other pieces of fishing line onto the board in the same way. Work from left to right on the board, each time using the longest piece of fishing line that you have left.

You now have a musical instrument. Pluck each string with your index finger. Which string has the highest sound? Which has the lowest? Practice with your new instrument, and use it to make music.

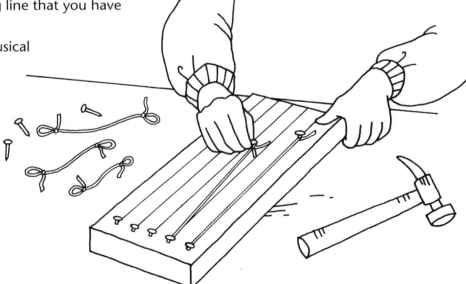

Cue-Card Crazies

Make your audience laugh with this fun-filled performance.

Is it time to put on a class or club program? Or are you and your friends in the mood to entertain your folks? Well, try this fun cue-card performance for a change of pace.

Pick a famous song or poem; "Row, Row, Row Your Boat" is a good example of what would work for this. Have everyone practice singing the song; playing a tape or CD of the song would also work. Illustrate each word or key phrase of the song or poem on large, sturdy pieces of card stock or cardboard.

Pass out the cards, and sing or play the song. Each performer should flip up their word each time the word is sung or said. Practice until everyone gets it right. Now speed up the singing to see if the group can keep up. Before you know it, everyone will be giggling!

Playing with Spoons

Hurray for spoons! What an easy "instrument" to play.

Run a spoon up and down the ridges of a metal can. You'll get a nice sound. Try sliding it across all the textures of a metal kitchen grater. (Be careful not to slide your fingers on the grater!) Think of other kitchen objects that you could use with a spoon to make music. Create your own song using all these instruments, and write your own lyrics. Then perform your musical melody for your family and friends.

Nature's Orchestra

◆▸◆▸◆▸◆▸◆

*You and your friends can strike up the band with these
musical instruments made from natural materials.*

What You'll Need
- nature objects
- cans

With a group of
friends, collect rocks,
gravel, sand, sticks,
shells, and any-
thing else from nature that you can use to
make musical instruments. Use your imagination! (Don't harm live plants or disturb
animals in their habitats during this project.)
Put rocks in cans to shake. Use sticks as
drumsticks. Make a drum from a hollow log
or bark. After everyone has an instrument,
make beautiful music together!

Kool Kazoo

◆▸◆▸◆▸◆▸◆

*You don't need years of practice to make beautiful music. All you need is
this kazoo and a good song to hum.*

Decorate a paper towel tube with markers. You could draw
palm trees or wild stripes and colors. Wrap a piece of
waxed paper over one end of the tube. Secure it
with a rubber band. Carefully cut 2 holes
in the tube.

To play your kazoo, hum your
favorite song into the open end of
the tube. Make more kazoos with tubes that have different
diameters, thicknesses, and lengths to create various
sounds.

What You'll Need
- paper towel tube
- markers
- waxed paper
- rubber band
- blunt scissors

Dandy Drum

◆▸◆▸◆▸◆▸◆

Use your bongo drum to create different sounds with your fingertips or the palm and heel of your hand.

What You'll Need
- oatmeal carton with lid
- construction paper
- blunt scissors
- markers
- craft glue
- ribbon

Cut a piece of construction paper to fit around a clean oatmeal carton. Draw a picture of palm trees on the paper for a Caribbean design. Wrap the paper around the oatmeal carton with the design facing out. Glue it in place. To make a strap, carefully poke a hole in each side of the carton near the top. Remove the lid. Cut a long piece of ribbon. Thread the ends through each hole, and tie a double knot in each end. Put the lid back on the carton. Place the strap over your shoulders, and march around while you beat a rhythm on the lid.

 # Pie Pan Tambourine

◆▸◆▸◆▸◆▸◆

Ring in some fun with this musical craft.

Caution: This project requires adult help.

If keeping time to the music is your favorite pastime, check out this easy-to-make pie pan tambourine.

Punch holes in the edges of an aluminum foil pie pan with a nail. Have an adult help you smooth the sharp edges of the holes with a file or hammer. At each hole, tie a small jingle bell to the pan with yarn or string.

Now jingle those bells to have a rhythmic adventure you won't be able to resist.

What You'll Need
- foil pie pan
- nail
- file or hammer
- jingle bells
- yarn or string

Mix Up Music

If you mix one song with another, can a third song be far behind?

What You'll Need
- radio
- paper
- pencil or pen

If you've ever jumped from radio station to radio station in search of a better tune, you know how much fun this game can be. Turn your radio to the first available familiar tune, and write down the first phrase you hear. Now turn to the next station, and write down the second phrase. Go to the next station, and the next, until you have 6 phrases. When you're done, read the phrases as a new song. Now try to sing it! Did you wind up with a third song that's fun? I'll bet you did!

Plastic Wrap Rap

Music is in the ear of the beholder.

What You'll Need
- plastic wrap from various containers (candy, CDs, toys, etc.)

Have you ever made music with a piece of plastic pressed to your lips? If not, it's about time you did. Take a piece of plastic wrap from a candy box, CD, or shrink-wrapped toy, and hold it tightly between your fingers. Hold the edge of the plastic just below your lips, and blow across it until the plastic whistles. If it doesn't work at first, don't give up. Keep twisting the edge of the plastic toward or away from your lips as you blow until you hear a shrill, almost birdlike squeal. Now try another type of plastic, and keep trying others that are different sizes, thicknesses, and lengths. Do they make the same tones? Gather some friends for a plastic wrap band. It's music of a whole other kind. (Dispose of the plastic wrap when you're done—plastic wrap is a choking hazard!)

Sand Blocks

❖❖❖❖❖❖❖

This one percussion instrument produces two very different sounds—one by tapping the blocks and another by scraping the blocks.

What You'll Need

- 2 wood blocks, each 2 inches thick, 3 inches wide, and 5 inches long
- 2 wood blocks, each 2 inches thick, 2 inches wide, and at least 2 inches long
- saw
- scissors
- sandpaper
- craft glue
- rubber bands

Caution: This project requires adult help.

Ask an adult to help you cut the wood pieces. (If you have an old block set, you can use 2 large and 2 small blocks.) Cut the sandpaper to fit around the bottom and sides of the large block. Wrap the sandpaper around the large block, and glue it in place. Stretch a rubber band around each end to hold the sandpaper in place as the glue dries. To make the handle, glue a small block on top of the large block. Make another sand block with the remaining wood pieces. Let the glue dry overnight.

Hum Along with Me!

❖❖❖❖❖❖❖

This humming instrument is sure to please!

Cut a circle of waxed paper that is 2 inches larger than the top of a foil pie pan. Place the circle on top of the pan, and press the excess paper down over the sides of the pan. Tape the paper onto the pan at 2 opposite points only. To play, place your lips lightly against any edge of this instrument. Hum a tune, and watch the paper vibrate to amplify the sound.

What You'll Need

- waxed paper
- foil pie pan
- blunt scissors
- ruler
- tape

# Instrument Safari

How often do you see signs of music in everyday life?

What You'll Need
- old magazines
- 3-minute timer or egg timer
- blunt scissors
- paper
- glue

Does music influence our everyday lives? Of course it does. But this fun game will help you see just how often it pops up in the magazines you read—and how much you know about it when it does.

You can play this game by yourself or with friends. Get permission to rip apart some old magazines, and set the magazines beside you. Set a timer for 3 minutes—or use an egg timer. See how many signs of music (instruments, notes, song titles, music reviews) you can find, and cut or tear them out. Get 1 point for each sign of music you cut out. For bonus points, name the instruments or sing the songs you've found.

Now for the creative part: Make a collage with all your musical finds to remind you that music is part of your life!

Clap Out a Rhythm

❖▸❖▸❖▸❖

Songs are more than music…clap out a rhythm to find out how.

We all know songs are a series of notes strung together. But have you ever thought about the unusual rhythms of each song? This activity will help you understand them. Pick a simple song, such as "Mary Had a Little Lamb." Now clap out the song as you sing it aloud. Write the words on a piece of paper. Now mark the rhythms, using a straight up-and-down stroke for a short note and a long sideways stroke for a long note. Experiment with other songs; try something more complicated—how about your favorite music star's latest hit. See if you and a friend can guess which song the other is clapping out!

Record the Recorder

❖▸❖▸❖▸❖

Or tape the trumpet! Play and record any instrument or style of music just for the fun of it.

Try an instrument that you're familiar with or experiment with a new one. Anything goes. Try out different styles, such as jazz, blues, rap, pop, rock, or folk. Follow the instructions that came with the instrument, and practice a few times before recording. Put a tape in the recorder, and hit the record button. Play the instrument for as long as you want, turn off the record button, rewind, and push play to listen. Listening to yourself play makes mastering an instrument easier. You could also practice a special song, and then use it as background music for your next musical show! Write your own music or use your favorite song.

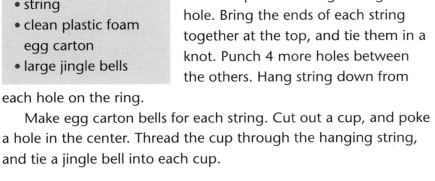

Wind Chimes

◆▶◆▶◆▶◆▶

Hang your wind chime outside and listen to its sounds. It's as if the soft breezes are singing to you.

What You'll Need
• plastic coffee-can lid
• blunt scissors
• ruler
• hole punch
• string
• clean plastic foam egg carton
• large jingle bells

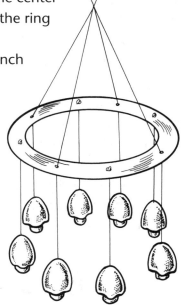

To make the wind chime ring, cut out the center from a plastic coffee-can lid. Make sure the ring is at least ½ inch wide.

To make the wind chime hanger, punch 4 holes evenly spaced around the ring. Thread a piece of string through each hole. Bring the ends of each string together at the top, and tie them in a knot. Punch 4 more holes between the others. Hang string down from each hole on the ring.

Make egg carton bells for each string. Cut out a cup, and poke a hole in the center. Thread the cup through the hanging string, and tie a jingle bell into each cup.

Mood Music Art

Let the music guide your pencil as you create artwork that matches the mood of the music.

Listen to a song on the radio. As you listen to it, draw the way it makes you feel. Use several coloring tools, such as markers, pastel chalks, and colored pencils, to experiment with colors. Think about the colors you would use with fast, slow, or marching music. After you finish that picture, change the station on the radio to find another song with a different tempo. Draw another picture. Keep experimenting with various types of music. Compare the pictures you made for the different kinds of music, such as jazz, country, classical, and rock 'n' roll.

What You'll Need
• radio
• drawing paper
• markers
• pastel chalks
• colored pencils

Animal Sounds

You can create animal sounds just by varying the vibrations on this simple instrument!

Cut the top off of a clean 1-quart milk carton, 4 inches from the bottom. Using scissors, punch a small hole in the center bottom of the carton, and thread the end of the piece of strong string through the hole. On the outside of the carton, tie a knot that will not pull through the hole.

Wet a paper towel, squeezing out the excess water. Hold the milk carton with one hand. With your other hand, put the wet paper towel around the string about 10 inches from the carton. Give the wet towel a quick pull while pressing it with your fingers. It will make a squawking noise that is amplified by the milk carton.

By varying how much string you leave between the wet towel and the carton, you can produce various animal sounds, such as those resembling a rooster's crow and a lion's roar.

What You'll Need
- 1-quart milk carton
- blunt scissors
- ruler
- 24-inch piece strong string
- paper towel
- water

Distinctive Drum

Drum up some distinctive fun.

What You'll Need
- clean, round oatmeal box
- newspaper
- paints
- paintbrush
- construction paper
- blunt scissors
- feathers or charms
- glue
- plastic wrap
- rubber band
- wooden spoons or other kitchen utensils
- rags (optional)

Clean out a small, round oatmeal box. Now you're going to decorate it with things you like or that are important to you. Cover your work surface with newspaper. You could paint your drum or glue construction-paper cutouts, feathers, or charms on it—just express yourself!

Next, wrap the open end of the box with at least 2 layers of clear plastic wrap. Use a very tight rubber band to hold the plastic wrap in place. Wooden spoons or kitchen utensils make great drumsticks to bang out a rhythm—but not TOO hard. You don't want to break the plastic wrap drumhead. If the drum is too loud, you can put a few rags inside to soften the tone.

Dance Party

◆◆◆▶◆◆

Dance to your own drummer, and see if you've got what it takes.

Music video dancers, dancers on Broadway in New York, ballet dancers—dancers of all kinds are incredible athletes. If you don't believe it, try this simple exercise on for size.

Wait for your favorite song to come on the radio. Begin to dance nonstop to the tune's beat. Lift your legs, swing your arms, leap in the air. It doesn't really matter what you do, so long as you keep your body in motion for the whole song. When the song ends, how does your body feel? How fast are you breathing? Is your heart pumping rapidly? Why do you think that's so? Now imagine dancing like that in a 50-minute ballet. You'll have a new respect for the professional dancers you see on TV!

Glass Jar Jingle

◆◆◆▶◆◆

Who knew water could help make music?

Gather together 6 to 8 different-size glass jars with lids. Fill each jar half full of cool water, and tightly close the lids. Use a metal fork to gently strike the jars. Can you hear the music ring? Do all the jars sound the same?

Does the music change when you strike the top, middle, or bottom of the jar? Pour out half the water in each jar, and repeat the experiment. How have the tones changed? Once you're familiar with what note each of your jars will play when softly hit, you can try to play your favorite tunes.

✋ Cheerful Chimes

◇▸◇▸◇▸◇

Nail down some delicate notes.

What You'll Need

- 6-inch block of wood
- sandpaper (optional)
- paint and paint-brush, stickers, or markers (optional)
- cord or yarn
- ruler
- blunt scissors
- different-size nails
- metal dowel

Find a long, flat block of wood that is about 6 inches long. Use sandpaper to smooth the wood if needed.

Paint or decorate the wood with stickers, or draw on it with markers. Cut 8 to 10 pieces of cord or yarn, each about 12 inches long. Tie a piece of cord or yarn every ½ inch along the block of wood. Trim the ends of all the cords so they are even. Tie the different-size nails on the dangling ends of the cord. Cut another length of cord for a hanger, and tie each end to an end of the block of wood.

Hang your chime from a porch or window. Stroke the dangling nails with a metal dowel for a lovely, tinkling sound. And when you're not playing your chimes, the wind will make beautiful music for you!

Triangular Tunes

For a cheerful sound, try playing a triangle. This simple instrument is made of a steel rod in the shape of a triangle open at one of its angles. It is usually hung by a cord and struck with a metal beater. And you thought triangles were just for math class!

Sound that Stretches

Strumming was never so fun!

Caution: This project requires adult help.

Have an adult help you with this project. Decorate either the margarine tub or the metal coffee can with your favorite stickers. Then stretch 5 to 7 rubber bands around the container so that they go over the open end. Practice plucking! Notice how a rubber band makes a high-pitched sound when pulled tightly across the top? It sounds deeper when you loosen it. How does the sound change when you use an empty tissue box instead? Try tuning your "sounds that stretch."

What You'll Need
- large, clean, empty margarine tub or metal coffee can
- stickers
- lots of rubber bands
- empty tissue box

Maraca Music

Keep the beat colorful and lively with these multicolored maracas.

What You'll Need
- small screwdriver
- 2 clear, stiff plastic cups
- colored tape
- pencil
- medium-size colored beads
- ribbon (optional)

Caution: This project requires adult help.

Have an adult help you use the screwdriver to poke a pencil-size hole in the bottom of one of the plastic cups. Wind colored tape around the pencil to make a candy-cane-striped pattern. Slide the pencil into the hole you just made. Wind more colored tape thickly around the pencil to hold it in place. Fill the cup with an assortment of colored beads, and place the other cup rim-to-rim with the first cup to make a closed container. Tape the cups together with colored tape. If you'd like, tie a ribbon around the pencil where it meets the cup's bottom to make pretty streamers. Now you can create a maraca beat that you and your friends can boogie to!

Wacky Washboard

◆▸◆▸◆▸◆▸

Make a cardboard washboard for a musical treat.

What You'll Need
- corrugated card-
  board box
- pencil
- heavy-duty scissors
- paint
- paintbrush
- glue

Caution: This project requires adult help.

The washboard is a scratch-and-thump rhythm instrument that is a special favorite for those who play down-home music. Now you can make a cardboard duplicate.

Using illustration 1 as a guide, draw 2 washboard shapes on the side panel of a large corrugated cardboard box. Make sure you draw and cut out rectangular holes at the top of the instrument. Ask an adult to help you cut out the washboards. Paint one. On the unpainted washboard, peel off the top layer of paper to expose the corrugated ridges. Glue the back of the unpainted washboard (not the corrugated side) to the unpainted side of the other washboard. Let the glue dry completely.

It's time to make music. Rake your fingers across the bumpy surface to create a fun, scratchy sound.

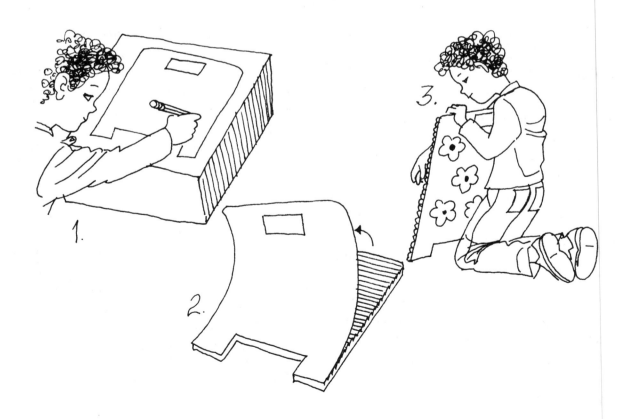

Musical History

▷▶▷▶▷▶

Discover your own musical roots.

In today's hustle and bustle, look-to-the-future world, we often forget to look back. Take time to explore your musical past by following these simple instructions. Ask your parents who your oldest relatives are. Ask if you can visit, write, or e-mail them to ask about the family's musical history. Did grandma play the piano? Did Great-Great-Aunt Minnie buy an organ from a traveling salesman in a covered wagon on the plains? Who were the family singers, and who couldn't carry a tune? If your family emigrated to the United States, do your relatives know or remember songs from the "old country"? If they do, be sure to have your relatives sing them so you can record them!

What You'll Need
• tape recorder
• paper
• pencil or pen

These recordings will be priceless treasures when you're older and have kids of your own to share them with. Be sure to take notes as you talk to these people. Once you start asking questions, you'll probably find out so much more about your family than just its musical history.

Bird Flute

Scientists have discovered the oldest playable musical instrument in the world. It's a flute carved from a bird's wing bone, made more than 9,000 years ago. The flute was discovered with other flutes at an ancient burial site in China.

MONSTROUS MATH

Math is everywhere. That's why it seems so big, so monstrous. But it's definitely not scary. You aren't frightened to buy a toy, are you? Why—it has a price, and that number is math! So get ready to count how many of these math projects you enjoy. You'll be surprised!

Beanbag Bundles

Make your own magic with this bean-bundling fun!

What You'll Need
- resealable plastic sandwich bags
- uncooked beans, peas, or rice
- cardboard boxes or plastic tubs
- colored markers
- paper
- pen or pencil

Fill resealable plastic sandwich bags half-full of uncooked beans (pinto or lima), peas, or rice. Double-bag the bags, and squeeze out excess air, making the bags less likely to spill or break. Decorate cardboard boxes or plastic tubs with brightly colored numbers. The higher the number, the farther away the tub should be from your starting mark. Now toss your beanbags into the tubs, and keep track of how many land in each numbered container. Add the scores for each container, then add the scores for all the containers together. Next, have other players take a turn throwing the beanbags into the containers. The player with the highest score wins. You can compete against your own high score if you're playing alone.

Special Delivery

❖▶❖▶❖▶❖

Yes! It's good news, but can you write it in code so prying eyes won't see the secret before your best friend reads it?

What You'll Need
- paper
- pen or pencil

Afraid that top-secret note you gave your friend in the hallway might fall into enemy hands? Secret codes to the rescue! The simplest way to make up a code is to assign each letter of the alphabet a certain number. For example, look at this code: A=1, B=5, C=9, D=13, E=17, and so on. Do you see how it works? Each letter takes a number that's 4 plus the number of the previous letter. Let your best friend in on your code, and use it to share confidential chat. Codes are also a great way to protect your diary entries from snooping siblings!

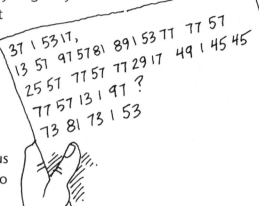

Paper Clip Measurement and Estimation

❖▶❖▶❖▶❖

Estimate and measure common objects with an uncommon measuring tool: a box of paper clips!

What You'll Need
- paper
- pen or pencil
- paper clips

Take a look around your room, and make a list of several objects that are long, short, wide, and narrow. Guess how many paper clips long each object might be. How many paper clips long is a pencil? A shoe? What about your desk? Or your bedroom wall? Write down the name of each object and your estimation. Then measure! You can line paper clips up end to end next to the object to measure it, or you can connect the paper clips to make a measuring chain. Write the number measured next to your estimate. After you have measured all the objects on your list, compare your findings to your estimates. Did you estimate high? Low? Use your discoveries to make new estimates for different objects and test again.

Super-Strong Eggshells

◆▶◆▶◆▶◆

Arches (even ones made of eggshells) are strong because they exert horizontal as well as vertical force to resist the pressure of heavy loads. Don't believe it? Try it for yourself.

What You'll Need
- 4 eggs
- clear tape
- blunt scissors
- telephone books

Carefully break off the small end of the 4 eggs, and pour out the insides (after getting adult permission, of course). Wind a piece of clear tape around the center of each eggshell. Cut through the center of the tape to make 4 dome-shaped shells. Throw away the broken end of each shell. Lay the 4 domes on a table, cut sides down, arranged in the shape of a square. Now it's time to guess how many telephone books you can lay on top of the shells before they break. You'll be surprised!

Weight of Wealth

◆▶◆▶◆▶◆

Show me the money! Then show me how much it weighs!

What You'll Need
- counted coins
- sandwich bags
- grocery store scale
- paper
- pen or pencil

Caution: This project requires adult supervision.

How much does a dollar weigh? Depends on the dollar, of course. Bundle up a dollar's worth of pennies in a sturdy plastic sandwich bag. Do the same for nickels, dimes, and quarters. Make a trip to your local grocery store, and weigh them on the fruit scale (ask permission first!). Jot down the weights in ounces. Now calculate how much $5.00 would weigh. How about $10.00 or $100.00?

Stretch It!

◆◇◆◇◆◇◆

Test a few boundaries with this experiment in fun!

What You'll Need
- samples of flexible materials (cotton, licorice, knit fabrics, elastic, rubber bands)
- yardstick
- paper
- pens or pencils

How far can you stretch a rubber band? How far can you stretch a piece of elastic? How far can you stretch an old T-shirt? Find out with this fun experiment. Measure 5 ordinary items in their "normal" condition. Mark that measurement on paper. Stretch those same items, and record that measurement beside the original. Compare which of the 5 items stretched the most. Graph the results.

Pencil Patterns

◆◇◆◇◆◇◆

Pencil in some fun with the "write" designs.

Using 24 unsharpened pencils, you can experiment with designs and distinctive patterns. How many different arrangements can you make with all the erasers touching? How many unique shapes can you build with only 12 pencils?

What You'll Need
- 24 unsharpened pencils

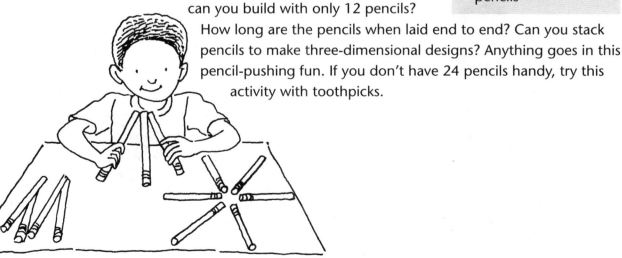

How long are the pencils when laid end to end? Can you stack pencils to make three-dimensional designs? Anything goes in this pencil-pushing fun. If you don't have 24 pencils handy, try this activity with toothpicks.

Mini Miniature Bowling

Practice your math skills by keeping score in this fun game!

What You'll Need

- black crayon
- 10 foam cups
- craft glue
- 2 pieces of cardboard (approximately 10 or more inches square)
- clear tape
- black and red markers
- 4 table tennis balls
- 2 large books
- ruler
- paper
- pen or pencil

Use a black crayon to number the cups from 1 to 10 on the upper inside of each cup. Glue the cups to a piece of cardboard following the illustration below. Allow the glue to dry, then run a strip of tape around all the cups to hold them in place.

Color 2 table tennis balls with a black marker and 2 balls with a red marker. Use a book to prop up your cardboard at a 45-degree angle so the 8 through 10 cups are at floor level and cup number 1 is raised. Make a ramp with the remaining cardboard, book, and tape. Tape one end of the cardboard on the floor, with the book underneath the other end to form a ramp. The angle of this ramp shouldn't be as steep as that of the cups, and the end of the ramp should be 5 to 7 inches away from the cups.

Each player takes a turn rolling the balls up the ramp and into the cups. After rolling 2 balls, a player adds up (the cup numbers are added) and writes down his or her score before the other player bowls. The player with the highest score wins.

Crazy Checkerboard

Make this checkerboard with any two colors you like. Measure two colors of construction paper, and weave them together.

What You'll Need
- 2 pieces of different-colored paper (1 piece, 8×8 inches; 1 piece, 8×10 inches)
- blunt scissors
- ruler
- clear tape
- 8×10-inch cardboard
- craft glue
- cardboard scraps
- markers

Fold the 8×10-inch sheet of paper in half, bringing the 8-inch sides together. Cut 7 slits, 1 inch apart, from the folded edge to within 1 inch of the other edge. Cut out eight strips, 1 inch wide, from the 8×8-inch piece of paper. Unfold the first sheet of paper.

Weave the paper strips through the slits from left to right. Weave over and under the slits. If you started by weaving the first strip over the first slit, weave the second strip under the first slit, the third strip over the first slit, and so on. This will create a checkerboard.

When you have woven all 8 strips through the paper, make the ends of the strips even and straight. Carefully turn the checkerboard over. Place clear tape along the left and right sides of the checkerboard to hold the strips in place. Turn the checkerboard right side up, and glue it to the cardboard.

Cut small circles out of cardboard scraps, stack them 3 or 4 pieces high, and glue them together. Create enough for 2 sets of checkers. Make each set a different color. Now play checkers!

Two by Two

> *It takes two to make a pair and pairs to win this game.*

What You'll Need
- paper
- pens or pencils

Ever notice how many things come in pairs, naturally? Think about it—2 eyes, 2 legs, 2 feet, 2 shoes. The list goes on and on. How far depends on you. Take a walk around your house, your yard, or your neighborhood. How many things can you find that seem to come in pairs? Run out of 2s? Look for natural 4s or dozens or hundreds. Compare your list with a friend's list. This also makes a great party game for teams.

Kite Heights

> *Kite flying soars to new heights when you ask, "How high is high?"*

The next time you fly a kite, take steps to find out just how high it will rise. Before you launch your soaring beauty, mark your string in 10-foot stretches. Measure out 10 feet of string. Color it blue. Measure out the next 10 feet, and color it green. Make the next 10 feet of string red. Keep going with as much of the string as you have the patience to mark. Then launch your kite. Keep track of how many different colors slip through your hands, then multiply that number by 10. (Hint: Make a note on a paper pad of how much string you tied onto your kite so you'll know how high it's gone when it comes to the end of its string.)

What You'll Need
- kite
- string
- yardstick
- colored markers
- paper pad
- pen or pencil

Puzzles for Five Squares

❖❖❖❖❖❖❖

How many shapes can you make with five squares?

What You'll Need
- drawing paper
- ruler
- blunt scissors
- pencil
- construction paper
- tape

To try these puzzles, measure and cut out five 2×2-inch squares out of drawing paper. Arrange the squares into a larger shape so all the squares are touching. The squares must be arranged so that squares with sides touching are lined up corner to corner. There are 12 different ways the 5 squares can be arranged. Find all 12 ways, and record them with pencil and paper by tracing the 12 different shapes onto construction paper. (Trace around the whole shape and also outline each square within the bigger shape.) Next, cut out the 12 different shapes. Eight of the shapes can be folded into boxes that can hold paper clips, buttons, or other small objects! Experiment to figure out which can be turned into boxes. Designate and mark the square that might be the bottom of the box. Then cut along the squares in order to fold and create square boxes. Tape the boxes shut.

Race with Time

◄►◄►◄►◄►

Learn to tell time in no time at all with this fun face-off.

Learning to tell time is easy and fun, thanks to this game. Each player makes their own clock face out of a paper plate, complete with moving minute and hour hands.

Mark the paper plate with the hours, as on a clock. Cut out a big hand and a small hand from colored paper. Attach the hands in the middle of the plate with a paper brad. Now you are ready to play the game! Ask an adult or older friend to shout out times, such as 1:15 or 2:45. The first player to move the hands to show the correct time on his or her clock face wins the round and 5 points. The first person to reach 50 points wins the game. Add more fun to the game: Score extra points for the player who can name an appropriate activity for the time (such as lunch or bedtime) along with marking the time on the clock.

Triangle Treat

◄►◄►◄►◄►

Make a three-sided sensation for mathematical fun.

Triangles are three-sided wonders. Can anyone get enough of them? If you love these geometric gems, why not try this artful game?

Cut colorful card stock into dozens of tiny triangles. Now arrange the triangles into delightful shapes and designs on

the floor, a table, or your desk. Can you make squares from triangles? Patterns? Designs? There's only one way to find out. Get going with a friend for twice the three-sided fun.

Pizza Tic-Tac-Toe

Here's "food" that your parents won't yell at you for playing with!

What You'll Need
- cream-colored felt
- blunt scissors
- ruler
- red felt
- tan felt
- 20 inches brown satin ribbon (⅛ inch wide)
- craft glue

Cut a 5-inch-diameter circle out of the cream-colored felt. This is the crust. For the pepperoni game pieces, cut five 1-inch circles from the red felt. For the mushroom game pieces, cut five 1-inch squares from the tan felt. Trim the tan squares into mushroom shapes.

Cut the ribbon into four 5-inch lengths. Glue the 4 lengths of ribbon to the cream-colored circle to make a tic-tac-toe grid. Trim away any extra ribbon that hangs over the sides of the felt circle.

To play, place the pepperoni and mushroom game pieces within the squares on the grid—just as you would for a regular game of tic-tac-toe.

Now it's time to practice your strategy to achieve victory!

Math War

Make these cards in a flash!

Use a marker to print a number from 1 to 12 on each card (write BIG). You can use the same number more than once. This will make things more fun as you play the game. Decorate the backs of the cards, if you'd like.

What You'll Need
- package of plain index cards (any size, any color)
- colored markers

You'll need at least 2 players for Math War. To play, the dealer gives each player a card until all the cards have been distributed evenly. Each person draws from the top of his pile and lays a card out, face up, on the table. The first person to yell out the correct sum of both numbers on the cards wins that round of play and takes the cards. The game continues until 1 person has all the cards.

Vary the game by changing from addition to subtraction problems, even multiplication!

"Grid" and Bear It

You only need to be able to count to 15 to play this game.

Create your own numbers puzzle. Draw a grid that's 3 squares by 3 squares. Put a number from 1 to 9 in each square. Here's the catch: The numbers in each row have to add up to 15 in every direction—up and down, side to side, and diagonally. Can you find more than one way to make the puzzle work? Play this by yourself, or play it with a friend, competing to see who can be first to create a puzzle that adds up correctly. The answer is on page 364 at the bottom, upside down.

What You'll Need
• paper
• pen or pencil

Artful Numbers

Make a colorful collage of numbers cut out from magazine pictures.

What You'll Need
• old magazines
• blunt scissors
• construction paper
• glue

To start, look through old magazines and cut out bright and colorful numbers you find in pictures and ads (ask for permission first!). Find a variety of numbers in different colors and sizes. Design and arrange the cutout numbers on a piece of construction paper, and glue them in place. One collage can include a random assortment of numbers, or it could have a theme, such as multiples of 4. You can also use the numbers as graphic elements to create figures and objects.

Button, Button

◆▷◆▷◆▷◆▷

Tossing colorful buttons adds up to number-loving fun!

What You'll Need
- paper
- colored markers or crayons
- ruler
- 24 buttons (12 of one color, 12 of another)
- paper
- pen or pencil

Using a blank piece of paper, make a game board with 12 same-size squares. Randomly label each square with the numbers 1 to 12. Once your game board is complete, place it on a table. Place 12 buttons of one color next to the board (don't let them touch), then flick each button with your fingernail onto the board. Add up your score based on where your buttons landed (for example, if all 12 of your buttons landed on the 10 square, give yourself 120 points). Make a note of your score on a piece of paper. Pick up your buttons, and watch your friend flick his or her buttons. You can also play against yourself to better your own score.

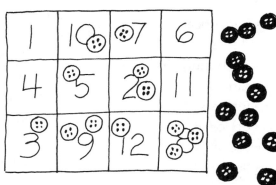

Add a Card

◆▷◆▷◆▷◆▷

Card-carrying math wizards can win this in a flash!

Looking for a new take on adding numbers? It's in the cards! Draw 2 regular playing cards from a standard deck, and deal 2 to your friend. Whoever correctly adds up the combined face value of their cards first wins the round and the point. The player with the most points at the end of the deck wins. Face cards and aces are always worth 10 points. For an added challenge, put a time limit on the simple addition.

What You'll Need
- playing cards
- paper
- pens or pencils

Weigh Cool

Are all things equal when it's time to measure the facts?

What You'll Need
- dowel
- ruler
- knife or scissors
- string
- 2 identical plastic dishes
- measuring cups
- sand
- feathers
- dry cereal
- sugar
- flour
- paper
- pencil

Caution: This project requires adult help.

With a ruler, measure the dowel rod to find the exact middle. Ask an adult to carve a notch in the center of the rod with a knife or scissors. Tie a string around that center notch. Now hang the identical plastic dishes from each side of the dowel with string. Suspend the scale from a safe, still place such as a door frame or a ceiling hook. Now it's time to answer the questions: Are all things equal? Do things that look the same or measure the same actually weigh the same? Measure ¼ cup sand, ¼ cup feathers, ¼ cup dry cereal, ¼ cup sugar, and ¼ cup flour. Examine the things you've measured, and decide if they look like they should weigh the same. Compare the substances using your handmade scale. Make notes about your discovery.

How Do You Measure That?

There are many things that are weighed and measured by scientists today. Some scientists measure the age of coral reefs, some measure the nutrients in cow's manure that will feed crops, and some measure how quickly the universe is expanding. Of course, all these scientists use different tools!

(Answer to "Grid" and Bear It: First row: 3 5 7; second row: 8 1 6; third row: 4 9 2.)

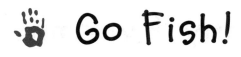 # Go Fish!

◀▶◀▶◀▶◀▶

Fish for higher scores every time you net these colorful swimmers.

What You'll Need
• colored paper
• tape measure
• blunt scissors
• paper clips
• large cardboard box
• magnet
• string
• yardstick or dowel
• colored markers
• paper
• pen or pencil

Cut out 2 dozen 3-inch fish from different colors of paper (the simpler the fish, the easier the fishing). Slip a paper clip on the end of each fish, and toss them into an empty cardboard box. Tie a magnet to an end of a 24-inch string, and dangle it from the end of a yardstick or dowel.

As you cast your line into the box, you'll reel in colorful fish time and time again. Assign each color of fish a point value; for instance, red is 1 point,  blue is 3 points, green is 6 points, etc. Then, as you catch fish, keep adding up your score. For extra fun, decorate the outside of the box with a creative seascape—sunken treasure, flippered flounders, friendly mermaids, and more.

 # Dime a Minute

◀▶◀▶◀▶◀▶

Talk is cheap when your phone calls are local. But try playing this game of "what if."

Everyone's heard the "dime a minute" telephone company ads. How much would your telephone talk cost if local calls were also 10 cents a minute? Keep track of your telephone time for 1 week. Multiply the minutes by 10 cents. If you get paid for jobs around the house, what would you have to do to earn that much money?

What You'll Need
• paper
• pen or pencil

Penny Pyramid

◄►◄►◄►◄►

Stack up your riches in a game that makes cents.

What You'll Need
• several hundred pennies

Set out a square of pennies 10 pennies long and 10 pennies wide. Then make an 8×8-penny square on top of the original square, leaving the outside edge only 1 penny high. Repeat the process with a 6×6-penny square, leaving the outside square 1 penny high, the next square 2 pennies high. Continue until the center 4 pennies are the highest, and then add a triangle of pennies to that layer. Add a single penny in the center to top off the pyramid. Can you figure out how many pennies you used? (Be sure to wash your hands before and after you play.)

Count Me In!

◄►◄►◄►◄►

Go on a numbers hunt, and see how high it takes you.

Here's an activity that will help you see the numbers that are around you all the time. Find something inside or outside the house that you see only 1 of. Now find something you see 2 of. Continue looking for 3 of something, 4 of something, and 5 of something. For example, you may only have 1 kitchen table, but 2 wall clocks, 3 TVs, 4 kitchen chairs, etc. See how high you can count! You might want to challenge a friend to see who can reach the highest number.

Sizing up Body Parts

◆▷◆▷◆▷◆▷

Measure and compare body-part length!

What You'll Need
- yarn
- blunt scissors
- paper
- pen or pencil
- removable tape

Measure and cut yarn pieces that are the same length as your hand, arm, foot, toe, head, and more. With the help of a friend or family member, also cut a strip of yarn that is as long as you are tall. Make a label for each piece of yarn, and tape the body-part label to the piece of yarn. Then tape all the yarn strips on a wall next to one another, and compare the varying lengths of the different parts of your body! For fun, arrange the yarn strips in order, from smallest to tallest.

 # Toothpick Squares

◆▷◆▷◆▷◆▷

Take the toothpick square challenge!

Find the smallest number of toothpicks you can use to make a square. That's easy: 4. But what's the smallest number of toothpicks you can use to make 2 squares with a connecting side? Or 3 squares with connecting sides? What about 4 squares? Take the test! Make a chart with 2 columns. In the first column, list the number of squares you are going to make with toothpicks (with connected sides). In the second column, list the smallest number of toothpicks you can use to make those squares. Now make the toothpick squares, and record your findings on the chart. After constructing several toothpick squares, see if you can find a pattern in the numbers you recorded.

What You'll Need
- toothpicks
- paper
- pen or pencil

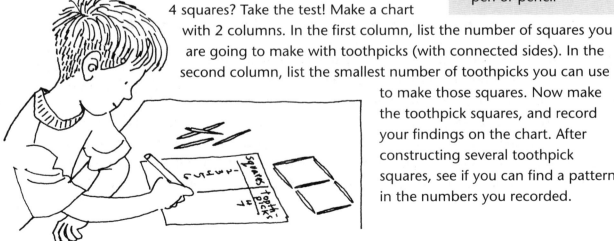

Double Up

Fill 'er up—then fill 'er up again! And again. And again.

What You'll Need
- measuring cups
- bucket
- water
- paper
- pen or pencil

Want an easy way to understand multiplication and division? Double up! Use a measuring cup to fill a bucket with water. Start with ¼ cup. Keep track of how many ¼ cups it takes to fill your bucket to the brim. Write the number down on a piece of paper. Now dump your bucket (in a clean, plugged sink to recycle the water), and fill it up again, this time using a ½-cup measure. How many dips of the cup did it take to fill the bucket this time? Exactly half as many? If not, you spilled. Try it again with a 1-cup measure. You'll have a watery grasp on fractions in no time at all.

How Many Squares?

Figure out how many squares there really are on a checkerboard!

What You'll Need
- checkerboard

This sounds easier than it is! You can easily see all the small squares on a checkerboard, but don't forget about all the other squares that are made by combining the small ones! Don't just count the small squares—count every square! That means each small square counts as 1 square. Each group of 4 squares becomes a bigger square and is counted as 1 square. Each group of 16 squares becomes another square that is counted. Count them all! Try this one day and then on another day—did you come up with the same number of squares each time? Keep trying!

Monumental Number Facts

Collect extremely enormous and staggering number facts.

Set out on a number fact search—write down as many facts as you can that include large numbers. Here are some big-number facts to begin with: People have about 100,000 hairs growing on their heads. There are 525,600 minutes in a year. There are 31,536,000 seconds in a year! One good acre of land can have anywhere from 50,000 to 1,000,000 worms underground. There are more than 800,000 species of insects in the world. There are about 8,000,000 words in the English language. Now, add to the list. How many more big-number facts can you find? Use an encyclopedia, an almanac, online resources, a newspaper, and any other fact finders available! Write down your big-number facts, and keep adding to the collection.

What You'll Need
- paper
- pen or pencil
- reference materials (encyclopedia, newspaper, almanac)

Salad Toss

Toss up a vegetarian treat—lettuce have some fun!

What You'll Need
- colorful card stock or lightweight cardboard
- plastic bowls
- black markers

Make paper salad bits from colorful card stock or lightweight cardboard. Try green paper lettuce leaves, red tomato slices, white onion cubes, and orange carrot chunks. Divide players into 2 teams. Take turns sailing salad bits through the air, trying to land them in the large plastic bowls. The team with the most salad tossed on target wins. For an added challenge, assign each piece of salad a number value. Assign more points for smaller pieces that land in the bowls, fewer points for easier-to-toss lettuce leaves. Tally the totals to determine the winner. You can also play by yourself to keep improving your score!

Cereal Graph

These three-dimensional "graphs" are fun to make, and you can see how easy it is to make a graph with objects as well as numbers.

What You'll Need
- cereal with different colors or shapes
- large sheets of paper
- markers or colored pencils

Be sure to ask for permission before doing this project. Pour out a handful of cereal, and estimate (or guess) which color is the most common (no counting allowed). Arrange the cereal in columns according to color. Place the columns, side by side, onto a

sheet of paper. Now look at the graph to see which color cereal was most common. Was your estimate correct? Will another handful produce the same results? Try the same project a few more times, and write down the results. The same graphing exercise can be done with snack crackers, sorting by shape. For a more challenging option, try a bag of assorted dried beans or a bag of pasta in different shapes or colors.

The Probability of Heads or Tails

Do a probability investigation.

What happens if a coin is flipped 100 times? Which will turn up more: heads or tails? Would the results be different with a different kind of coin? Test the probability of heads and tails turning up with 100 flips! Choose a coin and flip it 100 times, recording the result of each flip. Tally the results. Try the test again with a different kind of coin. Is the result the same or different? To simplify, test a penny, nickel, dime, and quarter, flipping each 20 times and recording the results of each flip. Compare the results. (Be sure to wash your hands before and after play.)

What You'll Need
- coins
- paper
- pen or pencil

Math Potato

◆▶◆▶◆▶◆▶

Play hot potato with numbers, but be careful not to get "burned"!

In the game Hot Potato, players toss a potato or beanbag around in a circle while music is playing. The person who is holding the potato when the music stops is out of the game. Math Potato is a little different. In this game, you toss math problems back and forth as fast as you can. Here's how it works.

The first player starts by calling on another person and then making up a simple math problem, such as 5 + 3. That person must "toss" it to someone else by solving the problem, calling on a new person, and making a new problem out of the solution. For example, Sam says, "Jamie, 5 plus 3 equals _____." Jamie solves the problem by answering "8," then tosses it to Rebecca by saying, "Rebecca, 8 minus 7 equals _____." Rebecca solves the problem, "1," then tosses it back to Sam by saying, "Sam, 1 plus 13 equals _____," and so on. Players who give the wrong answers are out until the next game.

Water Clock Estimation

◆▷◆▷◆▷◆▷

Use water to tell time and also to test your sense of how long things take!

What You'll Need
- paper cup
- straight pin
- cylinder-shaped jar
- digital clock or watch
- water
- permanent marker
- kitchen timer (optional)

Begin by making your time-telling tool, a water clock. To make the clock, carefully pierce a hole in the bottom of the paper cup with a straight pin. Set the cup in the jar so it rests in the rim; the bottom of the cup should not touch the bottom of the jar. With a digital clock or a watch with a second hand nearby, fill the cup with water. Using a permanent marker, record the water level reached at 1-minute intervals on the outside of the jar. Mark off each minute for 15 minutes. Then empty the cup and the jar, and get ready to use the water clock for estimation challenges.

How many minutes does it take you to brush your teeth? How long does it take to make a peanut butter and jelly sandwich? Or to do 25 jumping jacks? Make an estimate, fill the glass with water, do the task, and test out your estimate. You can also make another clock for tracking time for longer periods. Use a larger jar, and this time, mark the water level reached at 15-minute intervals. (You might want to use a kitchen timer to remind you when to record the 15-minute intervals!)

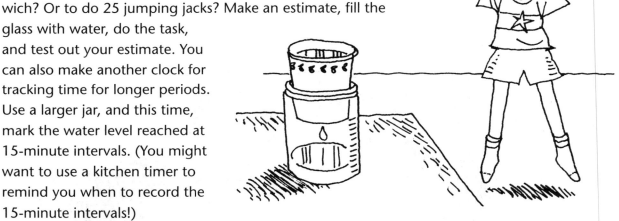

Time to Tell

For more than 22 centuries, human beings have used sundials to tell time. Considering most were made of stone or copper and were large, they wouldn't have made very good wristwatches!

Soda Can Soccer

◄▸►▸►▸►▸►►

Improve your addition skills while kicking.

What You'll Need
- 11 soda cans
- construction paper
- masking tape
- markers
- sand (for weighing down the cans)
- packing tape
- soccer ball
- paper
- pen or pencil

Cover the sides of the cans with construction paper, and write point values on them: mark 1 on a single can, and mark 2 cans with the numbers 2, 3, 5, 7, and 10. Put a little sand in each can to keep it from blowing over. Cover the tops with packing tape.

In a flat, open area, set up the cans along a straight line, putting the lower numbers in the center and the higher numbers toward the ends. Spread the cans out a little. Start from about 10 feet away, on a line with the center can, and call out and point to the cans you are aiming for. Kick the ball toward the cans. You'll only get points for the cans you called and hit. It doesn't count if you call out the 7 and hit the 3, for example.

Rotate with your friends, taking turns catching the ball, resetting the cans, and throwing the ball back for the next shooter. Also, have someone keep score, adding the hits until a player reaches 20 points.

Ups and Downs

◄▸►▸►▸►▸►►

Keep track of temperature changes, just like a real weather forecaster.

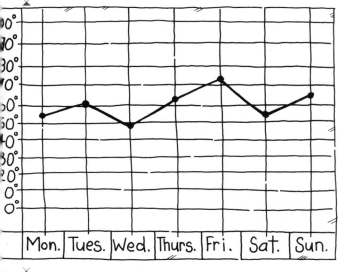

You can watch the news for your weather forecast. But now you can keep track of what the weather has been.

What You'll Need
- outdoor thermometer
- paper
- pen or pencil

Put a thermometer outdoors—out of the sun—and check it at the same time each day. Record the daily temperatures. Make a graph of your temperature readings. Every week, connect the dots on the graph to make a line showing the temperature ups and downs. Which day was the coldest? Which was the warmest? Do you see a trend? Is it getting colder or warmer?

 Multiply the Fun!

◆▷◆▷◆▷◆

It's easy and fun to make these simple math games with file folders and colorful markers. Cover them with clear paper, and they'll stay clean so you can play them over and over again!

What You'll Need
- manila file folders
- colorful markers
- index cards
- clear vinyl adhesive paper
- small toys or coins
- die

For each game you'll need 1 file folder. Open the folder, and draw the game board on the inside, with squares around the outside of the folder. Choose a corner square as the starting point for the game. Label it with an arrow or "START," then number the rest of the squares around the board in order. Label the last square "FINISH."

Fill in most of the squares with different math problems. Figure out the answers to each problem, and put each on a separate index card so players can check their answers as they play. Make the rest of the squares penalty squares. During the game, anyone landing on a penalty square will have to go back a few spaces or start over, for example. (You get to make up the rules!) Decorate the board by drawing colorful pictures or designs with markers, then cover the board with the clear adhesive paper.

Use small toys or coins for game pieces. Once you've developed all the rules and the object of the game (for example, to be the first to get all the way around the board), play the game with a friend by rolling a die to determine how many squares each player will advance. You can create many different board games—1 for addition, 1 for subtraction, 1 for multiplication, etc.

Angular Logic

Capture as many triangles as you can corner!

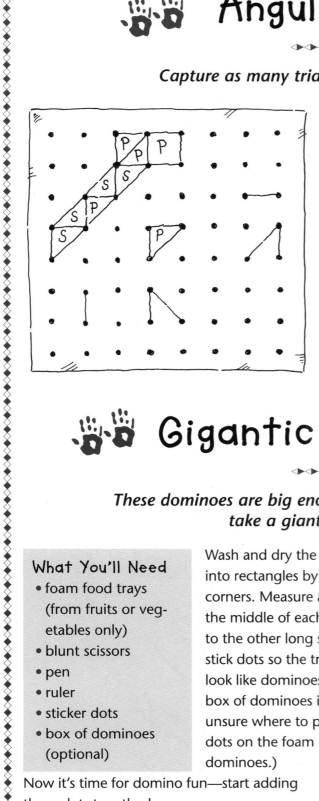

Make a grid of dots (8 across and 8 down makes a good game). Each player takes a turn by drawing 1 line that connects 2 dots (use a ruler, if you want). The object is to make the most triangles.

When you create a triangle, write your first initial in it so you can count each players' triangles later. When you create a triangle, you get to draw another line. Play until there are no more dots to connect. The player with the most triangles wins. (NOTE: Lines cannot cross each other.)

What You'll Need
- paper
- pen or pencil
- ruler (optional)

 # Gigantic Dominoes

These dominoes are big enough for a giant, but it doesn't take a giant to make them!

What You'll Need
- foam food trays (from fruits or vegetables only)
- blunt scissors
- pen
- ruler
- sticker dots
- box of dominoes (optional)

Wash and dry the foam trays. Make the trays into rectangles by cutting off the rounded corners. Measure and draw a line across the middle of each tray, from a long side to the other long side. Add round self-stick dots so the trays look like dominoes. (See a box of dominoes if you're unsure where to place the dots on the foam dominoes.)

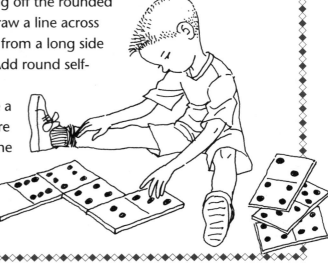

Now it's time for domino fun—start adding those dots together!

Wheel of Time

◆▶◆▶◆▶◆

What time is it in Sydney, Australia, right now? With this activity, you'll be able to tell the time all over the world.

What You'll Need
- large piece of poster board
- blunt scissors
- yardstick
- markers
- thumbtack
- large piece of cardboard

The world is divided into 24 time zones. When it's midnight in one time zone, it can be noon in another time zone—in fact, it can be two different days!

Cut a piece of poster board into a large circle. Draw lines that divide the circle into 24 equal-size wedge-shaped pieces. Write an hour of the day in each time zone. Start with 12 midnite, then 1 A.M., then 2 A.M., and so on. Be sure to continue through the P.M. times also, going in numerical order. Write the hours near the center of the circle. Put a thumbtack in the center of the circle, and attach the circle to a piece of cardboard larger than the circle. On the cardboard, mark sections that correspond to the hours on the poster board. Use the chart below to write in the place names (be sure to write them in the exact order listed). Now you're ready to find out what time it is anywhere in the world.

Check your watch. What time is it where you are? Turn the circle until that time lines up with the name of the city in your time zone. When you line up your time, you can read your time-zone chart to tell you what time it is in London, Paris, Beijing, or Auckland! The world is at your fingertips!

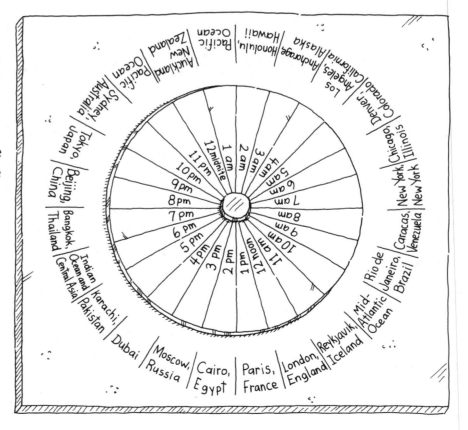

How Tall Is It?

◆▷◆▷◆▷◆▷

How can you measure the height of a tree when it's really tall?
Here's a neat trick to help you do it.

What You'll Need
- yardstick or tape measure
- pencil

You'll need a partner to do this activity. Use a yardstick to measure a straight line 60 feet from the tall tree you want to measure. Then have your partner stand there and hold the yardstick straight up with the bottom touching the ground. (A yardstick will work for trees that are up to about 30 feet tall. For very tall trees, you can do this activity with a metal tape measure instead of a yardstick.)

Walk 6 feet past your partner. (You'll be 66 feet away from the tree.) Lie down with your head at the 66-foot mark. Look up at the tree, and notice where the top of the tree comes to on the yardstick. Have your partner mark that spot. (You'll have to guide your partner to make the mark in the right place by saying, "A little lower...a little higher..." until he or she finds the right place.)

The height of the tree is about 10 times the height marked on the yardstick. For example, if the mark on the yardstick is at 24 inches, the tree is about 240 inches (20 feet) tall. Calculate how tall your tree is by multiplying your yardstick measurement by 10.

 # Geometrical Toothpicks

◆▷◆▷◆▷◆▷

See how many geometric shapes you can build using toothpicks
and modeling clay.

Cover your work surface. Use the modeling clay to attach the ends of the toothpicks together. Can you create a triangle? A square? A rectangle? What about a dodecahedron? Or a geodesic? Try altering the shapes by varying the number of toothpicks that intersect at the clay corners in each shape. More toothpicks intersecting at the clay corners in a shape will create larger and rounder shapes. Try making a shape with 3 toothpicks intersecting at each clay corner, another with 4, and another with 5! Use colored toothpicks to create more decorative geometric sculptures.

What You'll Need
- plastic table covering
- toothpicks
- modeling clay

Round 'n' Round

This miniature Ferris wheel really works! Just carefully count and measure the materials, and be sure to ask an adult for help.

What You'll Need
- cardboard
- pencil
- compass
- scissors
- knitting needle
- 2 wooden or plastic thread spools
- ruler
- glue
- 32 craft sticks
- 8 used wooden matchsticks
- 2 metal coat hangers
- 2×4-inch piece wood cut 16 inches long
- stapler and staples
- 4-inch-long dowel (small enough to fit through hole in spool)
- 8 plastic foam egg carton sections
- strong thread and needle
- markers
- glitter

Caution: This project requires adult help.

Draw two 3-inch circles on the cardboard. Cut out the circles. Using the knitting needle, make a hole large enough for the dowel to fit through the center of each circle. Place a spool over the hole on each circle (make sure the holes in both circles line up), and trace around the spool.

Use a pencil and ruler to measure and divide each circle into 2, then 4, then 8 sections. Glue 8 craft sticks along the lines you have drawn. When these are dry, glue 8 more craft sticks to each circle along the edges between the first 8 sticks you glued on. First glue on 4, leaving every other space unglued. When those are dry, glue on the other 4.

Turn 1 cardboard circle over, and glue the spool over the center hole. Wait for the glue to dry, then glue the second circle to the spool. Make sure the divided sections of each circle line up with the other circle.

Measure the distance between the 2 circles at 1 of the 8 divided sections. Cut 8 wooden matchsticks slightly longer than that length so they will fit tightly. Glue the matchsticks between the 2 craft sticks at each of the 8 sections. This is the wheel.

Bend the tops (hook parts) of 2 coat hangers into circles that are slightly larger than the dowel. Staple a hanger onto each side of the 16-inch-long wooden base (make sure both hangers are the same height).

On cardboard, draw around the second spool 4 times. Cut out the 4 circles. Make a hole with the knitting needle in the center of each circle for the dowel. Push the dowel through a circle, the first hanger, another circle, the wheel's spool, another circle, the second hanger, and the last circle.

Attach each egg carton seat to the matchsticks with a needle and small piece of thread. Make sure the seats clear the base when the wheel turns. Decorate the Ferris wheel with markers, glue, and glitter.

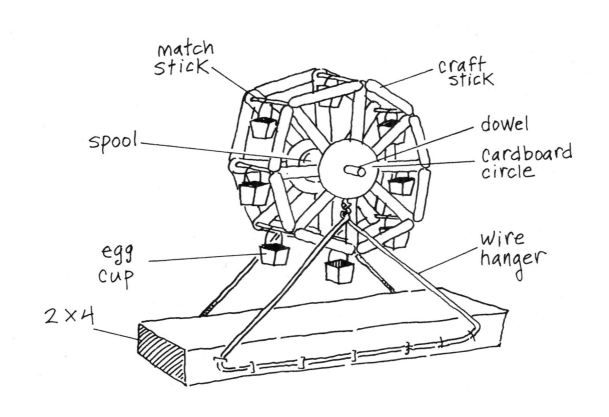

match stick

craft stick

spool

dowel

cardboard circle

egg cup

wire hanger

2×4

That Was No Lightweight Wheel!

Did you know that the first Ferris wheel stood 264 feet high and had 36 cars that carried 60 passengers each—a total of 2,160 riders! This popular ride opened to the public in 1893, weighed 1,200 tons, and was powered by two 1,000 horsepower engines!

String Sensation

Make elegant wall hangings by creating cool geometric shapes out of string.

What You'll Need
- large dinner plate
- paper
- pencil
- blunt scissors
- large board (the size you want your finished artwork)
- colored felt or paper (big enough to cover board)
- craft glue
- 8 glass-head map pins
- string or embroidery floss
- pop-top (from soda can)
- thumbtack

Caution: This project requires adult help.

1. Trace a large dinner plate onto paper to make a circle, then cut out the circle and fold it in half. Fold the circle in half again (into fourths), then again (into eighths). Unfold. Cover a large board by gluing down felt or paper, then place the paper circle in the center of the covered board with 1 fold going straight up and down (imagine folds are numbered 1 through 8, with 1 at the top).

2. Place a pin in the board at the end of every fold, next to the paper circle (the pins should stick up a little). Once all 8 pins are in place, remove the paper circle. Tie one end of the string or floss to pin number 1, and begin winding around the pins in the circle. Go from 1 to 2, 2 to 3, all the way around the circle—making a loop (but not a knot) around each pin. Keep string tight, but don't pull pins loose.

3. After you've looped all the pins in the circle, go around again in this order: 1-3-5-7-1-2-4-6-8-2. Go around the circle a last time, looping pins in this order: 2-5-8-3-6-1-4-7-2. Make a knot when you get back to pin 2, and cut the string.

4. Hang your string art by attaching a pop-top from a soda can (be careful, it might be sharp!) to the back of the board with a thumbtack.

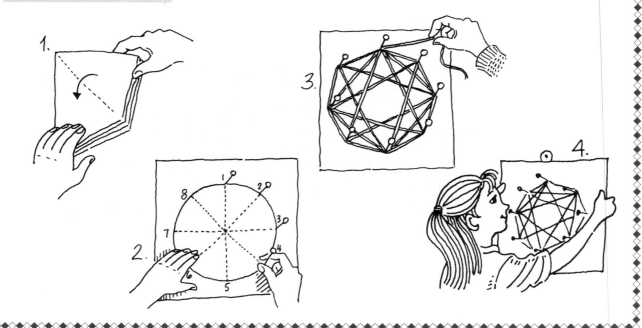

Every Penny Counts!

◆▸◆▸◆▸◆

Find out when most pennies in circulation were minted by taking a sampling and graphing the results.

What You'll Need
- 100 pennies
- poster board
- markers
- ruler
- craft glue (optional)

Sort pennies into piles according to the years they were minted. When you have sorted all your pennies, draw a bar graph on poster board, starting with the first year through the most recent. Then chart how many pennies were minted during each of those years. If you don't want to draw a bar graph, you can glue the pennies directly onto poster board to create a graph. (Just don't forget to remove the pennies from the board and clean them after a few days!)

Remember to wash your hands after counting and sorting all the pennies because coins and bills are very dirty—think of all the hands they've passed through and places they've been!

By the Numbers

◆▸◆▸◆▸◆

Play hopscotch with a 12-way twist.

This version of hopscotch will have you jumping for joy. Make a grid of 12 squares, each 2×2 feet, on a safe sidewalk (be sure to ask for permission first!). Number the squares 1 to 12 (you don't have to number them in any particular order—but be sure numbers aren't more than 1 row away from the previous number). Now hop on 1 foot from square 1 to square 2, square 3, and so on. Each player's turn ends when he or she accidentally steps out of a square or lands out of sequence. No one misses the easy way? Turn up the heat. Make them put their hands behind their backs and repeat the process. Still no flubs? Try jumping to only even-numbered or odd-numbered squares.

What You'll Need
- chalk
- safe sidewalk

AROUND THE WORLD

The world is full of amazing people from many different nations who have many interesting customs. You don't need to be a world traveler to explore those nations and customs—all you need is a curious mind and the fun projects from this chapter. It's time to begin your adventures!

 # Mankala Counting Game

❖ ❖ ❖ ❖ ❖ ❖ ❖

Kids the world over love counting games. This game from Africa is fun for kids of all ages.

What You'll Need
- cardboard egg cartons
- blunt scissors
- tape
- paints
- paintbrush
- 48 small stones

Remove the lid from an egg carton, and tape an extra cup (cut from another carton) to each end. These end cups are used as banks, where players store their winnings. Use the paints and paintbrush to decorate your egg cups if you want, then let the paint dry.

Put 4 stones into each cup, but leave the banks empty. The first player starts the game by taking the stones from any cup. Beginning with the next cup and moving counterclockwise, he drops a stone into each cup. Next, he takes the stones from the cup into which his last stone fell. He continues emptying and depositing stones until his last stone falls into an empty cup. (The first turn is the only time a turn ends this way.)

The second player moves in the same direction, empties the cup of her choice, and redistributes the stones. If her last stone falls into a cup with 3 stones, she wins all the stones in that cup and places them in her bank. But if any stone other than the last one falls into a cup with 3 stones, the first player wins the stones from that cup. Players alternate turns until 4 or fewer stones are left in the carton. The player with the most stones wins.

International Doll Collection

Welcome these tiny children of the world into your home!

What You'll Need

- stiff paper
- small foam balls
- blunt scissors
- glue
- markers
- wiggle eyes
- yarn (optional)
- beads (optional)
- thin wire (optional)
- fabric and felt scraps (optional)
- tiny jewels and sequins (optional)
- cotton balls (optional)

Dress these dolls in traditional costumes to show what children might wear in different parts of the world.

To make the basic doll body, roll a piece of stiff paper into a cone and flatten the top by folding the point inward. For the doll head, trim the base off a foam ball so that it will fit flat on top of the cone. Glue the head on the cone. Draw a face on the head with markers, and glue on wiggle eyes. Decorate your dolls.

For a Native American doll, glue on a braid of black yarn and decorate a strip of paper for a headband. Glue a piece of brown paper with a fringed collar and hem onto the body cone.

Make a necklace out of beads and thin wire to go around the doll's neck.

For a Dutch doll, glue on yellow yarn hair. Draw and cut out the shape of her hat twice, glue the tips together, then glue it on her head. Draw tulips on her dress, and glue a square of fabric on for her apron. You can make tiny earrings from jewels or sequins. Cotton balls can be pulled apart to make fur trim for a Scandinavian doll. Tiny beads can be strung on thin wire to make necklaces for African dolls.

Study pictures of international costumes, and try to copy the fabric patterns on your paper cones. What countries are your dolls from?

Navajo Groaning Stick

◆▶▶▶▶▶

Navajo dancers used these pieces of wood on a whip to make the sound of great winds and distant thunder.

What You'll Need
- lightweight wood (like a shingle or part of a fruit or vegetable crate)
- small saw
- ruler
- drill, or hammer and large nail
- poster paints
- paintbrushes
- 3 feet of heavy twine
- scissors

Caution: This project requires adult help and supervision.

1. Ask an adult to help you cut a 2×6-inch piece of lightweight wood. About 1 inch from a 2-inch side of the piece of wood, have an adult help you drill a hole in the center of the wood or hammer in a large nail (carefully, so the wood doesn't split) to make a hole. If using a nail, remove the nail when the hole is made. Thread one end of heavy twine through the hole. Tie the twine to the wood with several tight knots (ask an adult to make sure the knots are secure). Paint your groaning stick with designs—Navajo symbols such as the thunderbird, lightning, rain, and clouds look nice. Let the paint dry completely.

2. Hold the piece of wood at the point where the twine is attached. Measure the twine from your outstretched arm to your opposite shoulder, and cut the twine that length.

3. To use the stick, wrap some of the twine around your right hand (or your left hand, if you are left-handed). Lift your hand (wrapped in twine) over your head, and swing the groaning stick around. After a few turns it should start to hum and buzz. If not, try adjusting the length of the twine.

Always be careful when you stop spinning the stick. Lower your arm slowly, keeping it outstretched in front of you so it doesn't hit you. Also, always use your groaning stick away from people and other objects!

Faces of the World Necklace

❖❖❖❖❖❖❖

Make these easy homemade beads into an international piece of jewelry.

What You'll Need
- plastic tub
- sand
- white glue
- measuring cups
- mixing spoon
- nail
- waxed paper
- old magazines or catalogs
- blunt scissors
- markers
- colored cord
- tape

Caution: This project requires adult help.

You may want to make several of these cheerful necklaces—once your friends see you wearing one, they will want one of their own!

To make the beads, in the plastic tub mix 1 cup sand with ¼ cup white glue to make the dough. Break off a small piece with your fingers, and roll it into a bead. Make the bead large enough for you to later paste a small picture of a child's face onto the front of it. Carefully (you might need an adult's help) use the nail to poke a hole through the center. If the dough is too mushy, put the bead back and add a little more sand to the mixture. Make as many beads as you wish. Set the beads to dry on waxed paper until they are hard. While the beads dry, cut small pictures of children's faces from old magazines or catalogs (ask for permission first!). Try to choose children from different countries. You can then glue these to the front of the beads. You may want to color the beads with markers, too. Then tape one end of a colored cord that is long enough to go over your head when looped. This will make it easier to string the beads. When you have strung all the beads you want, remove the tape and tie the ends of the cord together. Now wear your new "friends" around the neighborhood, and introduce them to all your best buddies!

Miniature Japanese Sand Garden

◆▷◆▷◆▷◆▷

Create a mini replica of an ancient Zen sand garden. These gardens are used in Japan for quiet meditation, as they were hundreds of years ago.

What You'll Need
- box top
- sand
- rocks or pebbles
- small cardboard rectangles
- blunt scissors

To make your own small garden, fill an empty gift box or shoe box top with clean, damp sand. Place a few rocks or pebbles in the garden, either in small clusters or all alone, to stand for hills and mountains. Then make wavy water ripple lines in the sand with a cardboard comb. To make the combs, cut different-size notches in each of several cardboard pieces. Experiment with each notched cardboard piece, combing through the sand to discover the comb's effects. Pat the sand down after combing to try a new comb or to rearrange your design. Comb a pleasing water design around the mountains, and set the sand garden on a table or desk as a decoration or centerpiece to inspire your own quiet thinking!

 # Turquoise Bracelets

◆▷◆▷◆▷◆▷

Design jewelry that looks like turquoise pieces worn by Native Americans.

Caution: This project requires adult help.

Cut a paper towel tube into 1½-inch-wide bands. Check to see if the tube will slide onto your wrist. If it doesn't, cut the tube so it forms a C. Cover the bracelet with aluminum foil.

Put rubbing alcohol in a small glass bowl. Add a few drops of blue food coloring and 1 drop of green food coloring. Stir the colors to blend them. Color the macaroni shells by placing a few at a time into the glass bowl. Remove the macaroni from the alcohol mixture with a spoon, and place them on a paper towel to dry. Continue until all the macaroni shells are colored. An adult should dispose of the rubbing alcohol when you are done.

When the macaroni shells are dry, glue them to the covered bands to make bracelets. All your friends will want some of your stunning "turquoise and silver" jewelry!

What You'll Need
- paper towel tube
- ruler
- blunt scissors
- aluminum foil
- ½ cup rubbing alcohol
- small glass bowl
- blue and green food coloring
- mixing spoon
- macaroni shells
- paper towels
- craft glue

Chaldean Board Game

◄►◄►◄►◄►

Archaeologists found game boards, which were made more than 4,000 years ago, in the ancient city-state of Ur. Now you can make a game board similar to one the ancient Chaldeans did!

What You'll Need

- 3 boxes (cereal boxes work well, but make sure 1 box is much smaller and the other 2 are the same size)
- glue
- paint
- paintbrush
- marker
- bottle caps

Lay the boxes flat, with the smaller box in the middle connecting the other 2 boxes like a bridge. Glue the boxes together, and paint them however you'd like. When the paint is dry, divide the boxes into squares with a marker or paint (the bridge should be only 1 square wide). Paint designs in the squares if you'd like.

Decorate bottle caps for game pieces. Be sure to make 2 sets of game pieces. Make up rules for your game. For example, see who can hop his or her game pieces to the other end and back again (like checkers). Try to line up your bottle caps to block the bridge so your opponent can't get his bottle caps across.

You're the rule maker—make your game as hard or as easy as you'd like!

Magic Numbers
Math may have been a very popular subject for ancient Chaldeans. That's because they believed that numbers had special powers that could unlock all the secrets of the universe!

Decorative Painted Eggs

◆▶◆▶◆▶◆▶

Paint a portrait, picture, or scene on an egg, and follow in the footsteps of an ancient Chinese tradition.

What You'll Need
- egg
- paper clip
- container
- modeling clay
- watercolors
- paintbrush
- pencil (optional)

Before painting the eggshell, remove the egg inside so your painting can last for a long time. To pierce the shell, unbend a paper clip and wash it. Then, carefully make a small opening in the larger end of the egg by gently piercing the shell. Break the egg yolk inside the egg, and mix the egg so the contents will come out. Pour the egg contents out into a small container, and discard. Gently wash the eggshell. Make a modeling clay collar for the eggshell (see Adorned Eggs on page 486), and set the eggshell, broken side down (and hidden!), in the clay collar. The "egg canvas" is ready for painting. Paint a picture on the blank shell using watercolors, or sketch your drawing on the shell with pencil first and then paint.

Vietnamese Beanbag Toss

◆▶◆▶◆▶◆▶

*Grab a beanbag, and try your talent at **Da-Cau,** a game played by Vietnamese children.*

The object of this game is to balance the game piece on your foot without letting it touch the ground, even when it's tossed! To play, place a beanbag on your foot, kick it up in the air, and then try and

What You'll Need
- beanbag or coin

catch it by getting it to land back on the top of the same foot! If you are playing with a friend, toss the bag back and forth, foot to foot, without letting it land on the ground. To make the game more challenging, play it with a coin instead of a beanbag, just as Vietnamese children do!

Mud Decorating

◄►◄►◄►◄►

Paint with mud like the Korhogo people of the Ivory Coast in Africa.

What You'll Need
- mud or dirt
- plastic spoon
- plastic bowl
- pitcher
- water
- strainer
- paint
- cotton cloth (old sheet, muslin, or handkerchief)
- paintbrush, or leaf or twig
- newspaper or brown grocery bag

To prepare your mud paint, dig up some dirt or mud. Gather together a plastic bowl, pitcher of water, strainer, and plastic spoon. Holding the strainer over the plastic bowl, place a little of the dirt or mud in the strainer, and add some water. Stir the mixture over the plastic bowl, removing pebbles, sticks, leaves, and other pieces that do not fit through the strainer. Continue to add and strain more mud, stopping occasionally to pour off the water that collects at the top of the bowl as mud settles to the bottom. When the mud is fully strained and smooth, add some paint to the mud to create a rich, earthy color. Paint on cotton cloth as the Korhogo do: Place a section of an old sheet or use a piece of muslin or a handkerchief, and paint the material with the mud using a paintbrush or a leaf or a twig. Or, paint on the newspaper or a grocery bag that's been cut open.

Tepee

With your tepee you can sleep outside under the stars and pretend you're a traveler on the Great Plains.

What You'll Need

- 4 wood boards, 1 inch thick, 2 inches wide, and about 4 feet long
- power drill and ⅜-inch drill bit
- 12 inches of cord
- 2⅓ yards of muslin about 44 inches wide
- scissors
- fabric paint
- fabric glue
- needle and strong thread

Caution: This project requires adult help.

1. Have an adult drill a hole 2 inches from the top of each board. Thread the cord through the holes, and tie the boards together to make the tepee frame. Tie the cord in a knot. Spread the boards out to form the frame.

2. Trim one end of the muslin fabric to form a half circle. Cut a U-shape at the center of the straight edge of the muslin. Use fabric paint to decorate the muslin with a Native American design. Let the paint dry. Fold the straight end of the fabric over about 4 inches, and glue a seam to make a pocket. Let the glue set.

3. Slip 2 boards of the tepee frame through the fabric pockets. The tied ends of the boards should poke through the U-shape hole at the top. Sew a piece of thread around the center point of the 2 backboards of the tepee to hold them in place. Stand the frame up, and spread the boards out to form the tepee.

1

Tie boards together to make the tepee frame.

2

Fold the straight end of the fabric over, and glue in place.

3

Slip the boards through the fabric pockets.

Origami Leap Frog

◆►◆►◆►◆►

Origami is the Japanese art of folding paper into objects. Turn a piece of paper into a frog, and race it across the table.

What You'll Need
- one 3×5-inch blank index card
- pencil

1. Follow the illustrations to fold the index card. Fold point A to point D. Unfold and repeat with the other corner, folding point B to point C.

2. Fold the top half of the paper back and then unfold it.

3. Holding the sides at point E and point F, push them in together toward the center of the folds.

4. Press the top half of the paper down, creating a triangle.

5. Fold the point G corner of the triangle up to point I at the top of the triangle, and form a small triangle. Repeat with the other corner of the large triangle at point H.

6. Fold the tiny triangles in half, lengthwise. Then fold each side of the index card in about ¼ inch.

7. Fold the bottom end of the index card up about ¾ inch. Then fold that piece down in half. Turn your frog over, and draw on eyes. Press your finger on the frog's back to make it leap.

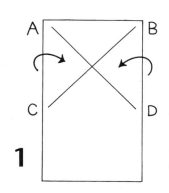

1

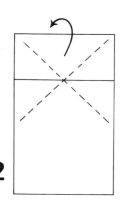

2

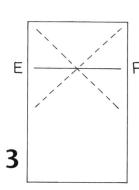

3

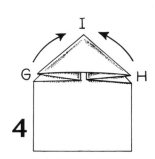

4

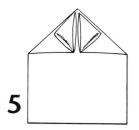

5

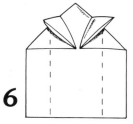

6

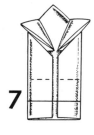

7

Portable Soccer Game

◆▸◆▸◆▸◆▸

Baseball and football aren't the most popular sports in the world—soccer is! Now you can enjoy this game no matter where you live with this portable, tabletop version.

What You'll Need
- berry basket
- blunt scissors
- large rectangular piece of cardboard
- twist ties
- green and white paint (and paintbrush) or markers
- aluminum foil

Cut the berry basket in half; each half will be a goal. Place a berry-basket goal in the middle of the short end of the cardboard. Start on the right side of the berry basket. Poke 2 holes next to each other in the cardboard—one on the inside of the basket, the other on the outside. Repeat for the left side of the basket. Attach the goal to the cardboard by bending a twist tie through each pair of holes in the cardboard and threading the twist tie through the berry basket. Twist the tie ends together underneath the cardboard. Repeat the process for the other short side of the cardboard with the other berry-basket goal.

Paint or use markers to make the cardboard look like a soccer field, using green for grass and white for the boundary lines. Make a ball from foil. Turn your hand into a soccer player—use your pointer and middle fingers as legs to kick the ball.

It's now time to find an opponent and start playing!

Eid ul-Fitr Cards

Eid ul-Fitr is an important Muslim festival, during which people give each other presents and cards. The Muslim religion forbids the drawing of people or animals, so these cards are decorated with beautiful designs made from geometric shapes and patterns.

Caution: This project requires adult help.

Cut a 3-inch square of cardboard with the heavy-duty scissors (you may need adult help with this part). On the cardboard, make a rough pencil sketch of the pattern you want to print. Twist the chenille stems into the shapes that make up your pattern. Brush a thin layer of glue onto your cardboard pattern. While the glue is wet, press the chenille-stem shapes onto the design. Let the glue dry completely.

Use a paintbrush to apply paint to the raised pattern on your cardboard (this is your printing block). Place the printing block on top of a piece of scrap paper, and gently press down on the block. Carefully pull the block away from the paper to see the printed pattern. Practice printing on the scrap paper a few times before printing your designs on folded sheets of construction paper to make cards.

What You'll Need
- cardboard
- heavy-duty scissors
- ruler
- pencil
- chenille stems
- glue brush
- craft glue
- paintbrush
- paints
- scrap paper
- light-colored construction paper

Rakhi (Hindu Plaited Bracelet)

These plaited bracelets are given to family members at Raksha Bandhan, a festival celebrated by most Hindu and Sikh families. You can give your rakhi to a family member or friend, too.

What You'll Need
- strips of fabric, yarn, string, or ribbon
- piece of corkboard or cardboard
- pins
- small circle of cardboard
- aluminum foil
- sequins
- craft glue
- markers
- needle and thread

Use strips of fabric, yarn, string, or ribbon that are more than double the length of the bracelet you want. To make a 3-strand rakhi, knot the ends of 3 pieces together. Pin them to a piece of corkboard or heavy cardboard so they are easier to work with.

Braid the pieces as shown in the diagram below. Continue braiding in this manner until you have braided almost all of the length of ribbon or fabric. To finish the plait, knot the ends together.

Decorate a small circle of cardboard with foil, sequins, and markers. Sew the decorated circle to the middle of the plaited band. To wear the plait as a bracelet, tie it around your wrist.

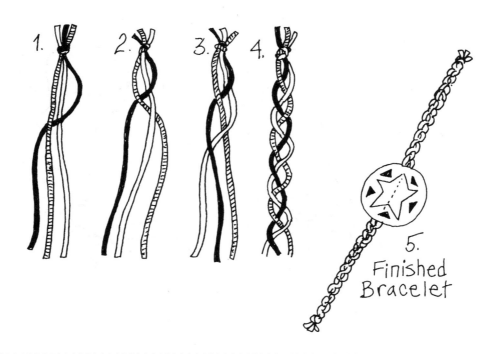

5. Finished Bracelet

Balloon Piñata

*Make a piñata, a Latin American holiday custom, and turn
any occasion into a real party.*

What You'll Need

- newspaper
- water
- flour
- measuring cup
- large bowl
- mixing spoon
- balloon
- paint
- paintbrush
- knife
- hole punch
- yarn
- candy or toys (optional)
- broom handle or bat
- blindfold

Caution: This project requires adult help.

Piñatas were first made by Mexican Indians long before the Spaniards ever explored the Americas. The Spanish explorers helped popularize the piñata after their arrival by bringing the custom back to Spain and Portugal. Today piñatas are widely used in Mexico and in many other parts of the world as part of holiday celebrations. Colorful piñatas are filled with candy or toys and hung as holiday decorations. Later, children play a piñata game. They gather in a circle around the piñata, and players take turns being blindfolded and striking at the piñata with a stick as the other players sing. When the piñata finally breaks, all the players scramble for the goodies!

To make a balloon piñata, tear newspaper into strips. Mix 1 cup of flour for every 1 cup of water together to make a heavy paste. Blow up a balloon, and cover it with strips of newspaper dipped in the flour and water paste (run the strips between your fingers to remove extra paste). Cover the balloon completely. Allow it to dry for a day or 2, turning it occasionally during that time. When the balloon is dry, paint it in bright, decorative colors. Then, with adult help, cut the top off the balloon and punch several holes around the top edge. Thread yarn through the holes, tie them together, and hang up your piñata. Fill the piñata with candy or toys if you want to use it (and break it) for the piñata game!

Sahara Sand Shoes

Make these desert sand shoes like ones the Tuaregs, a wandering desert tribe, make so they can travel on the hot sand and not burn their feet.

What You'll Need
- several large pieces of cardboard (thin and heavy pieces)
- pencil
- scissors
- ruler
- glue
- paint
- paintbrush
- nail
- 2 shoelaces
- four 2-holed buttons (with large holes)

Caution: This project requires adult help.

Trace the shape of your foot onto a piece of heavy cardboard. Draw a paddle shape around the foot pattern—the shape should bulge out at the heel and toes and come in closer at the sides of your foot. Trace your other foot the same way, and make another paddle shape around it.

Have an adult help you cut 4 of these cardboard paddle shapes for each foot. Also cut 4 strips (about 2 inches wide and 4 inches long) from thinner cardboard for shoe straps. Glue 4 paddle shapes together, one on top of the other (using lots of glue), for each shoe. Glue the ends of the 2 cardboard strips (one on each side of the shoe) between the top 2 layers of the paddle shapes. The strips should be angled toward the toes of the shoes. Put something heavy on top of each shoe until the glue dries completely.

Paint designs on the shoes and straps. Place your feet on the shoes. On the top of each sole, make a line between your big toe and second toe. Ask an adult to use a nail to punch 2 holes close together on each line. The holes should go through all the layers of cardboard.

For each shoe and going from the top to the bottom, thread a shoelace through 1 hole, in and out of a button on the bottom, and back through the other hole. Fold the thin cardboard strips inward so they cross over the holes in the sole. Punch 2 holes through the crossed strips. Thread the shoelace through the holes in the strips and through a second button. Try the shoe on. Slide the button down until the shoe fits securely on your foot. Tie the shoelace.

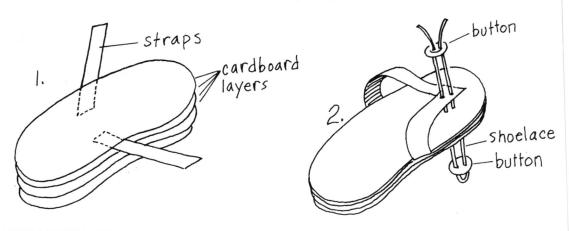

Balloon Fortunes

◆◆◆◆◆◆

People of different cultures have different methods for telling fortunes. The Chinese put paper fortunes in cookies. Create your own fortune-telling method!

What You'll Need
- construction paper
- hole punch
- balloons
- funnel
- paper
- marker or pen
- string
- pins

To make confetti, punch circles out of brightly colored construction paper with a hole punch. Stuff as many as you can into each deflated balloon using a funnel.

Write fortunes on small pieces of paper, and slip them into the balloons. Blow up the balloons (keep your head down while blowing so you don't inhale any confetti), and hang them high but within reach.

During a party or other fun time, hand out pins and let everyone pop a balloon and read their fortune. (Warn people there will be popping balloons before starting this game—some children are afraid of the sound.) And the flying confetti is fun, too!

(Balloons are choking hazards. After popping the balloons, immediately pick up all the balloon pieces to keep them away from young children.)

Ojo de Dios

❖❖❖❖❖❖

***Weave yarn around two sticks or twigs to create
an ancient Mexican "Eye of God."***

What You'll Need
• 2 twigs or craft sticks
• craft glue
• yarn
• blunt scissors

To make your Ojo de Dios, glue 2 craft sticks together to create a cross shape. Or, if you use twigs, cross them and tie them together by winding yarn around the middle diagonally in one direction and then diagonally in the other direction.

After you have formed the cross, tie a strand of yarn to the center and begin to weave it around the arms. Weave the yarn over and around one arm and then over and around the next arm. Continue this around all the arms. Change colors by tying a new piece of yarn to the end of the piece you have been using, and keep winding. Continue until the entire shape is covered, then cut and tuck the end of the yarn into the weaving. Add a dot of glue to hold the end in place.

Hang your Ojo de Dios in your room, or give it as a gift to someone special.

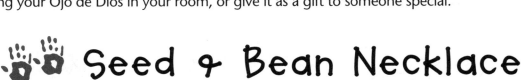

Seed & Bean Necklace

❖❖❖❖❖❖

***String a necklace of beans and seeds, and make nature jewelry as
many people around the world do.***

Caution: This project requires adult help.

Gather together dried beans and seeds from fruits or vegetables (such as melons, squash, or corn). Wash the seeds, and soak the beans and seeds in a bowl of water to soften them; some beans need to soak overnight. Then remove them from the water, and poke a hole in each using the needle and thimble. (Have an adult help you.) Spread the beans and seeds on a paper towel, and let them dry. Thread the needle with thread that is long enough to slip over your head for a necklace. String the seeds and beads in a pattern or design, and then tie the ends of the thread together.

What You'll Need
• dried beans
• seeds from fruits or vegetables
• bowl
• water
• darning needle
• thimble
• paper towels
• buttonhole thread or carpet thread

Little Worry Dolls

◆▸◆▸◆▸◆▸

*Send your worries away by making miniature dolls who will do
all your worrying for you!*

What You'll Need
- aluminum foil
- masking tape
- newspaper
- flour
- water
- large mixing bowl
- measuring cup
- plastic wrap
- gesso (available at an art or craft store)
- paintbrush
- paints

Follow this Central American tradition, and keep a set of worry dolls under your pillow. Each night before going to sleep, whisper a worry to each doll. After your troubles have been told, as the tradition goes, you can forget about them. The dolls will do all the worrying that's needed!

To make the dolls, mold the basic body shape for each doll out of aluminum foil. You can mold the body in 1 piece or create separate body parts and then attach them using masking tape. When the doll's shape is finished, cover the whole surface of the doll with masking tape. Now the dolls are ready for papier-mâché.

Cover your work surface with newspaper. Tear other sheets of newspaper into small, thin strips, and set aside. Make a thick paste out of flour and water in the mixing bowl; mix 1 cup of flour for every cup of water. Dip the newspaper strips into the paste, and run the strips through your fingers to get rid of excess paste. Lay the strips over the dolls. Cover each doll completely by overlapping the newspaper strips. Set the dolls on newspaper, and let them dry for a day. Then cover them with a second coat of newspaper strips, and set them to dry again. (Keep the paste covered with plastic between uses.) When the dolls are fully dry, paint them with gesso. Let them dry again for about 15 minutes. Now paint the dolls in the colors of your choice. Let them dry completely.

Now it's time to tell them all your troubles!

Chocolate Mexicano

▸▸▸▸▸▸

Make delicious Mexican hot chocolate for a breakfast treat.

What You'll Need
- two 3-ounce squares of Mexican chocolate (or 6 ounces of sweet baker's chocolate)
- 6 cups milk
- 1½ teaspoons cinnamon (if using baker's chocolate)
- saucepan
- wooden spoon
- mixing bowl
- eggbeater or electric mixer
- cinnamon sticks for garnish
- cayenne pepper (optional)

Caution: This project requires adult help.

If you can't find Mexican chocolate, you can use sweet baker's chocolate instead. Combine the chocolate, milk, and cinnamon in a saucepan, and cook over low heat. Let an adult in on your secret breakfast treat so they can help you adjust the stove temperature. Stir the mixture constantly so it doesn't burn. When all the chocolate has melted and the mixture is blended, carefully pour the liquid into a large mixing bowl. Using an eggbeater or electric mixer, whip until frothy. (You could also pour the liquid into a blender and whip it that way.) In Mexico, hot chocolate is poured into a large pottery jug and whipped with a wooden beater called a *molinillo* (moh-lee-NEE-yoh). When the hot chocolate is ready, pour it into mugs and garnish with a cinnamon stick. A pinch of cayenne pepper can be added for some real south of the border heat! This recipe serves 4 people.

Buckskin

▸▸▸▸▸▸

Explore the history of Native American symbols by re-creating their beauty on pretend pelts.

Caution: This project requires adult help.

Cut a brown grocery bag in the shape of a pelt. Crumple up the paper until it becomes very soft. Flatten it, then draw a buffalo, sun and moon, or feathers. Color in the picture using pastel chalks. If you want, have an adult spray it with a very light coat of hairspray to set the chalk.

Another idea is to make a ceremonial shield instead of a buckskin. Cut the brown paper bag in a circle instead of a pelt shape. Crumple the paper, then flatten it and draw a Native American design on the paper. Cut out paper strips to create fringe. Glue or tape the paper strips to the paper circle.

What You'll Need
- brown grocery bag
- scissors
- pencil
- pastel chalks
- hairspray (optional)
- craft glue or clear tape

Hawaiian Hula Skirt

You can learn to dance the hula, but it just doesn't look right unless you have a "grass" skirt. Make this simple skirt, and start dancing!

What You'll Need
- rope
- ruler
- scissors
- green raffia

Caution: This project requires adult help.

Measure the rope around your waist, and add a few extra inches. Cut the rope this size. Take a piece of green raffia, and hang it from the rope so the ends are even. Tie a knot to hold the raffia in place. Keep adding and tying pieces of raffia onto the rope until it looks like a grass skirt. When the rope is covered (except for the extra inches), tie it around your waist.

Now it's time for hula dancing! The hula is a dance with hand movements that tell a story. You may not have classes in your area to learn how to dance the hula, but you can make up your own stories. Act them out with your hands, and move your body in a rhythmic pattern.

Teach a few of your friends your new-style hula, and put on a show for the neighborhood or your families!

Dancing with Flowers

Hawaiian hula dancers often wear leis, which are braided or woven necklaces made of natural material such as flowers or shells. That's because the lei is the traditional offering to Laka, goddess of the dance. Leis are also given to people when they visit Hawaii to symbolize friendship.

Japanese Paper Doll

For Hina Matsuri (March 3), make a Japanese paper doll that wears a traditional kimono. In Japan, this day is devoted to dolls.

What You'll Need
- poster board
- ruler
- blunt scissors
- construction paper
- markers or colored pencils
- tape

From poster board, cut out a 7×2-inch rectangle. At the short end of the rectangle, cut out a round head shape. Trim below the head to make sloping shoulders. (This should look like a large, round-headed clothespin.)

For the kimono, cut out a 6-inch square from colored construction paper. For the sash, cut out a 6×⅜-inch rectangle from black paper.

Center the body on top of the kimono. Fold a top corner of the kimono down over the doll's shoulder. Working on the same side of the kimono, fold the paper vertically to cover the doll's body. Use the same method to fold the opposite side of the kimono. Wrap the sash around the doll from front to back, and tape the ends together in the back.

Cut out a wig from the black paper. In the center of the wig, cut a horizontal slit that is wide enough to fit over the doll's head. Fit the wig onto the doll's head. With markers or pencils, draw a face on the doll. Fold down the top ⅜ inch of the kimono to make a collar. Color the collar with a marker or pencil. Lay the kimono flat so the folded collar is face-down.

Make dolls for your friends or to decorate your table for a special March 3 tea party! You don't have to be in Japan to celebrate dolls!

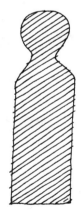
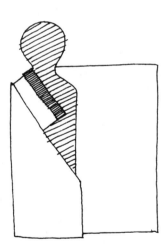

Paper Gondola

▶▶▶▶▶▶

In Venice, Italy, these boats are used just like we use taxis in the United States. Make a miniature gondola, and display it in your room.

What You'll Need
- black construction paper
- blunt scissors
- glue
- gold fadeless or origami paper
- glitter
- ruler
- tape

1. Fold a piece of black construction paper in quarters. With the open fold on the left and the other fold at the bottom, cut out the bow shape (see illustration).

2. Unfold the paper, then glue the ends together to create the bow and stern.

3. To create the beak, fold the gold paper in half, draw a shape similar to the one shown, and cut it out. Glue it to one end of the gondola. Draw a decorative line with glue on the side of the boat, and sprinkle the glue with glitter. To make the gondola stand, fold a 2×8-inch strip of construction paper in half. Cut a notch in the center that is 1 inch wide at the top and 1 inch deep. Tape the ends together, and set your gondola into the notch. *Buon viaggio!*

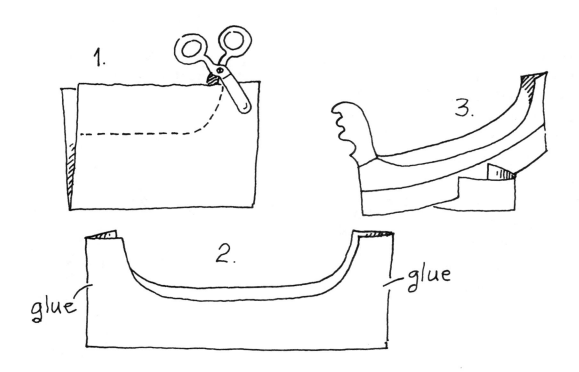

What a Doll

Cornhusk dolls were made by Native Americans in what is now the northeastern United States. Here's how you can make one.

What You'll Need
- cornhusks
- string
- blunt scissors
- markers
- dried flowers (optional)

1. Strip the husks from several ears of corn. Let them dry out for a few days. Make the doll's head by rolling 1 husk into a ball. Put another cornhusk over the rolled-up husk, and use string to tie this piece tightly under the rolled-up husk.

2. Roll a husk lengthwise to make the arms. Tie the roll at each end. Put this roll under the head, and use string to hold the arms in place.

3. Use several husks to make a skirt. Lay these husks in the front and back of the arms, and tie the husks below the arms to hold them in place. Trim the bottom of the skirt with scissors so it is even.

4. To make the blouse, cut a rectangle out of a husk. On a long side of the rectangle, make a cut halfway through to the other side. Put the rectangle behind the doll, with the cut end up. The end of the rectangle that is not cut will be the back of the blouse. Fold the cut end of the rectangle over to the front of the doll. This will be the front of the blouse. Cross the flaps over each other, and use string to tie the blouse in place.

5. Finally, draw a face on your cornhusk doll. You can put dried flowers in its hand or make a bonnet for its head out of cornhusks.

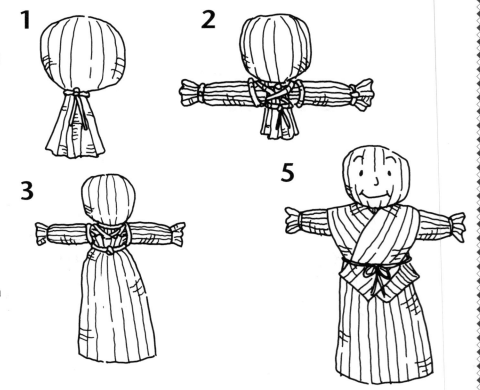

Chili-Pepper Good Luck Charm (Ristra)

◁▷◁▷◁▷▷

Make this colorful Ristra with paper chilies, and hang it in your doorway as a good luck charm and welcome sign.

Cut out about 24 peppers in small (2½ inches long), medium (4¼ inches long), and large (5¼ inches long) shapes from construction paper. Make some peppers yellow, some red, some green, and others orange—be sure you have a good variety of colors and sizes.

Punch a hole in each pepper through the stem. Fold the twine in half, leave a loop at the top, and make a knot. String on the peppers, alternating colors and sizes. Knot the twine after every 2 or 3 peppers. When you're done tying on all the peppers, hang your good luck charm on your bedroom door to welcome your friends.

If you'd like to make more realistic-looking peppers, turn to Silly Sandwiches on page 55. Read the instructions given for stuffing the bread. To "stuff" your peppers, double the number of peppers you cut out, and follow the directions given. After your peppers are stuffed, follow the directions above to string the peppers.

Hot, hot, hot!

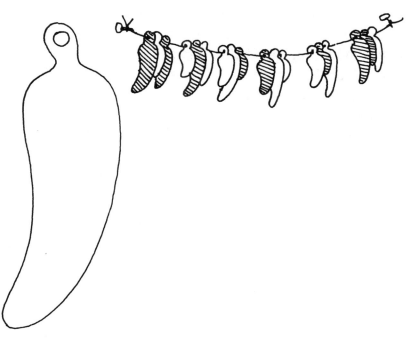

Cultures of the World Book

◆▸◆▸◆▸◆▸

Learn more about people of another culture, and recognize more about yourself at the same time.

What You'll Need

- reference material (encyclopedias, Internet access, personal interviews)
- cereal box
- ruler
- blunt scissors
- 8½×11-inch white paper
- hole punch
- ribbon or string
- construction or contact paper
- glue
- markers

Each page on the right-hand side of this book will contain a picture and some information about people from another culture. Left-hand pages will have a picture and some information about you or someone from your culture. Don't just limit your information to what is different about you and a child from another culture; try to also find things you have in common!

You might want to have a theme for your book, such as food, clothing, or music. (Your teacher might want to have a World's Fair Day and have each student make one of these books. Then the class will have information about many different cultures.) Do your research to decide what you want to put in your book.

To make a book, cut a 9½×6-inch rectangle from the cereal box and place it picture-side up. Fold it in half, matching the 6-inch sides together. Stack 4 sheets of white paper, fold the sheets into quarters, cut along the top, and place the paper inside the folded cardboard. Punch 3 holes along the folded edge, through the paper and cardboard, and thread the ribbon or string through the holes. Tie the ribbon or string to bind the book.

Decorate the outside of the book with markers or cover it with construction or contact paper. Now fill your book with all your information!

✋ Tingmiujang (Eskimo Game)

◆▷◆▷◆▷◆

Use clay to make pieces for this game Eskimo children play to help pass the long, cold winters of the Arctic.

What You'll Need
- air-dry paper clay
- ruler
- large piece vinyl or brown craft paper
- blunt scissors

Use the clay to make 15 birds, about 1 inch long, in the shape of a duck with a simple head and beak, a pointed tail, and a flat bottom (they must have flat bottoms for the game to work). Air-dry the clay overnight or until dry.

For a playing cloth, cut a piece of vinyl or brown craft paper in the shape of an animal pelt. Lay the pelt on the floor, and have your friends sit around it.

Now it's time to play the game! The first player shakes the birds in her or his hands and tosses them up gently and not too high so they fall on the cloth. Some will land upright; others will fall on their sides. Each upright bird is taken by the player its beak points to. The next player shakes and tosses the remaining birds. Again, the upright birds are claimed by the person they face. The game continues until all the birds have been claimed. The player with the most birds wins.

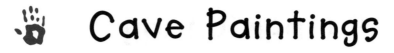# Cave Paintings

◀▶▶▶▶▶

Make a cave painting—it may bring you luck!

What You'll Need
- brown paper grocery bag or brown paper
- pencil
- scratch paper
- wide black marker or charcoal (optional)
- paintbrush
- black and earth-toned tempera paints (red, orange, brown, gold)

Some people who lived in caves painted on the walls of the caves. Most of their pictures were of buffalo, deer, and other wild animals because people thought these drawings would bring them good luck when hunting.

Prepare the surface of the bag or paper so it looks rough and worn: Crinkle the paper, spray it with water in the sink (don't soak it), then let it dry completely. Using a pencil and scratch paper, make a few sample sketches of animals you would like to include in your painting. You don't need to include every detail; make your creatures from simple shapes, such as circles, triangles, and rectangles. Don't worry if your animals don't look exactly like those in photographs; neither do the original cave paintings.

Once you're happy with your sketch, you're ready to draw on the brown paper. After making a rough pencil sketch on the bag, go over the pencil marks with black paint, marker, or charcoal, making sure the lines are thick and strong. Add details, such as eyes, ears, horns, tails, or antlers. When the black lines have dried, paint the figure and background with earth-toned paints.

For more fun, make up a story about your cave painting!

Beaded Beauties

◄◆◄◆◄◆►

Make your own beautiful sand beads to wear, just like the ones worn by African women.

What You'll Need
- sand
- white glue
- mixing spoon
- empty, clean plastic margarine tub
- nail
- foam food tray (from fruits or vegetables only)
- markers, tiny seeds, or glitter
- yarn
- tape

Mix sand and glue in the margarine tub to make sand dough. Make enough dough to roll a number of beads the size you want. With the nail, carefully poke a hole through the center of the bead. If the dough is too soft to make a hole, add more sand until it is stiff enough to make a hole through the bead. Make lots of beads, then let them dry on a foam tray until they are hard.

When the beads have dried, decorate them by coloring them with markers or gluing tiny seeds or bits of glitter to them. To make a necklace, tape one end of a piece of yarn (long enough for a necklace) to the table, and string the beads onto it. Tie the 2 ends of the yarn together when you've strung all your beads.

You've made beautiful beads!

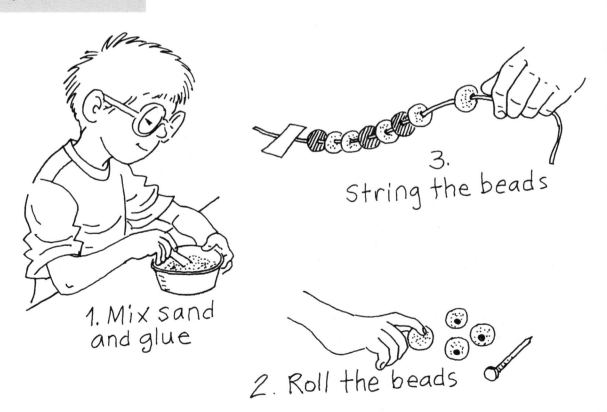

1. Mix sand and glue

2. Roll the beads

3. String the beads

Aloha Hawaiian Lei

Make your own version of the colorful lei Hawaiians give visitors as a way of saying "aloha" or "welcome." Theirs are made of beautiful flowers, but these will last longer.

What You'll Need
- uncooked ziti pasta
- tempera paints
- paintbrush
- waxed paper
- colored crepe paper
- blunt scissors
- 3-foot piece of string
- large sewing needle
- ruler

Color 16 pieces of uncooked ziti using tempera paints. Let them dry on waxed paper. Cut out bunches of flower shapes from colored crepe paper. Loosely tie a knot in one end of a 3-foot piece of string. Thread the other end through the eye of a large sewing needle. Sew through the centers of a dozen or so flowers. String on a piece of painted ziti. Continue sewing on flowers and pasta, stopping 3 inches from the end of the string. Undo the beginning knot, and tie the string ends together with a knot (be sure the lei is long enough to fit over your head). Aloha!

Lei Day

In Hawaii, Don Blanding, a poet and artist, noticed that most leis were being worn by tourists rather than the islanders who made them. So, on May 1, 1928, the first Lei Day was instituted. The following year Lei Day became an official holiday, and every year islanders adorn themselves with leis on that day!

Native American Moccasins

◆▸◆▸◆▸◆▸

In pioneer days, shoes were very expensive and not always easy to obtain. Pioneer families copied the moccasins they saw worn by Native Americans. You can, too!

What You'll Need
- newspaper
- pencil
- ruler
- fabric (such as felt or canvas)
- sewing pins
- scissors
- markers, or embroidery floss and beads
- heavy-duty sewing needle
- strong thread

Caution: This project requires adult help.

1. Stand barefoot on a piece of newspaper, and trace around 1 foot with a pencil. Then, draw a pattern around the traced foot. Find the distance from 1 to 2 and from 3 to 4 by measuring across your instep and dividing that number in half. (Ask an adult if you need help with this calculation.)

2. Pin the pattern on the fabric, trace around it, and cut it out. (If the fabric you are using is very thick, you may need to have an adult cut it for you.) Trace and cut another pattern for your other foot. Decorate the flaps (tops) of the moccasins with markers, embroidered designs, or sewn-on beads.

Fold 1 moccasin in half, with right sides facing in. Use running stitches to sew the front. Gather the stitches a little to fit the shape of your foot. End with several overlapping stitches. Turn the moccasin right side out, and try it on. Use pins to fit the heel seam, then take the moccasin off. Sew the back seam with running stitches to ¾ inch from the bottom. Trim the seam.

3. Cut out a small square from the heel. Flatten the heel, and sew it closed with overcast stitches.

4. For ties, cut 2 strips of fabric, each ½ inch wide and 15 inches long. Then wrap the ties around your ankles just under the top flaps, and tie them in back of the moccasins.

1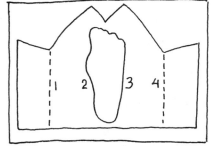

3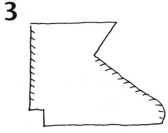

2

4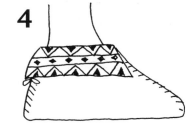

African Tutsi Basket

◆▷◆▷◆▷◆▷

Small baskets like these are made by the Tutsi people of Africa. Now make your own with construction paper!

What You'll Need
- 2 sheets 9×12-inch red construction paper
- ruler
- pencil
- blunt scissors
- 3 sheets 9×12-inch beige construction paper
- craft glue
- 5-inch plate
- clear tape
- 9-inch plate

The Tutsi people of Africa make these baskets by coiling long strands of dried grass around and around, binding them together with thinner strands. The baskets have lids and are used to hold grain. Hold your treasures in your basket!

1. Cut 8 strips of red construction paper, each 12 inches long and ¾ inch wide. With 2 pieces of the beige construction paper, glue the 12-inch-long edges of the pieces together (overlap the edges a little). After the glue has dried, cut 4 strips 16 inches long and ½ inch wide. Then glue 2 red strips together at the middle to form a cross.

2. Do this with all the other red strips until you have 4 red crosses. Place the 4 crosses on top of each other, and fan them out evenly. Glue them in place—they should look like a star.

3. Use the 5-inch plate to draw a circle on the other piece of red construction paper. Cut out the circle, and glue it to the center of the star. This forms the inside bottom of your basket. Fold the rays of the star up at the edge of the circle.

4. Tape a beige strip horizontally across the bottom of 1 ray. Weave the beige strip over and under the rays all the way around. Remove the tape, and glue the ends of the beige strip together. Hold ends together until glue begins to dry. Repeat with remaining beige strips, alternating rays. Push beige strips close together before gluing.

5. After you've finished weaving the beige strips, fold over and glue the red ends to the inside of the basket, forming a rim. Make a pointed lid for the basket by using the 9-inch plate to trace a circle on the last sheet of beige construction paper. Cut out the circle, then cut a pie wedge out of the circle (the bigger the wedge, the taller the lid). Overlap and glue the cut ends together. (Note: If you don't want to use red and beige paper, you can use any 2 colors you would like.)

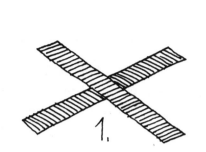

1.

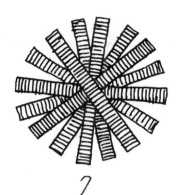

2.

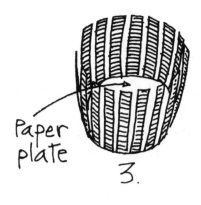

Paper plate

3.

4.

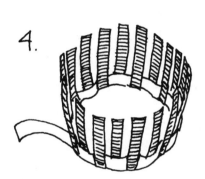

5.

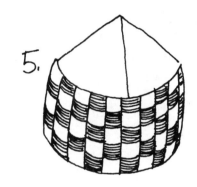

Tall People, Small Baskets

Baskets made by the Tutsi people of central Africa may be small, but the Tutsi people are among the tallest in the world. In fact, the Tutsi are often more than 7 feet in height. The Tutsi live in round grass huts scattered throughout the hilly countryside.

Native American Noisemaker

◆◆◆◆◆◆◆

All children, no matter their nationality or culture, love a good noisemaker!

What You'll Need
- 2-inch coat button with 2 holes
- brown poster paint
- paintbrush
- 2 small pegs or sticks
- 20 inches waxed string or cord

You've probably used noisemakers at parties. But I'll bet you didn't know Native American children used to play with noisemakers that hummed and buzzed—all without electronics! Now you can make one of these fun toys, too.

Paint the large coat button so it looks like clay. Then paint the pegs or sticks. Thread the waxed string or cord through both holes in the button, and tie the ends together. Place the end loops of the cord around the pegs or sticks to make handles. Wind handles in opposite directions until the cord is very twisted. To make the toy hum or buzz, pull the handles apart so the cord untwists. The button will spin, bob up and down, and make a noise!

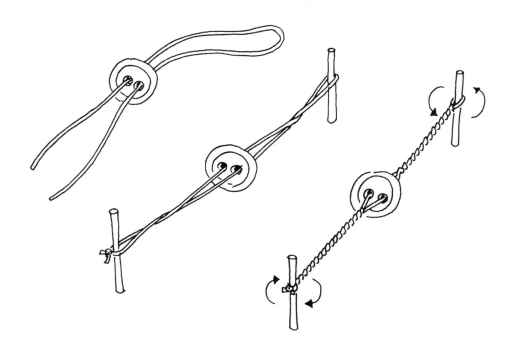

Hindu Rangoli Pattern

◆▶◆▶◆▶◆▶

During the Diwali festival, rangoli patterns, made with colored flour paste, rice, and spices, decorate the entrance to many Hindu homes. You can make a rangoli pattern with glitter.

What You'll Need
- newspaper
- paper
- pencil
- glue
- paintbrush (optional)
- different colors of glitter

Since this project is very messy, first cover your work surface with lots of old newspaper. Draw a fancy design in pencil on a piece of paper. Carefully paint or squeeze a thin line of glue over some parts of the pencil design. Sprinkle 1 color of glitter over the line of glue. To remove excess glitter from the design, carefully tip your glitter design onto another piece of paper and shake off the excess glitter. Make a small paper funnel, and put excess glitter back into the tube. Continue adding several different colors of glitter to your design this way. Let the glued glitter dry completely before you hang your colorful creation.

If you'd like to be more authentic, try using powdered cinnamon, nutmeg, ginger, cloves, uncooked rice, or pasta for your design. (Be sure to ask adult permission before using these supplies!) Apply them to your design on the paper just as you would the glitter.

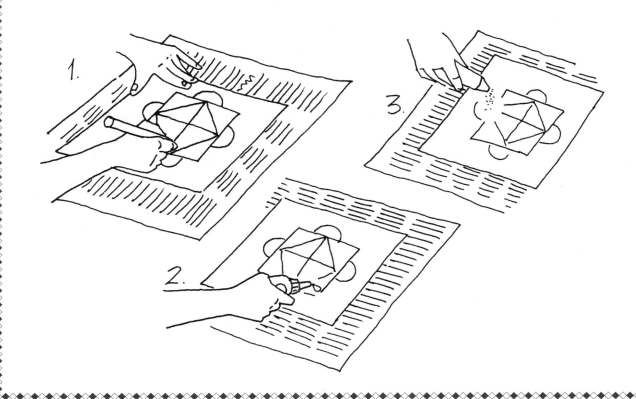

WINTER HOLIDAYS

Winter needn't be boring. Many important religious holidays happen in this season, such as Christmas and Hanukkah, and other important events are remembered at this time also, including the birthday of Martin Luther King, Jr. If you want to make many of your days special this winter season, look to this chapter for celebratory inspiration.

St. Nick Storybook

◄►◄►◄►◄►

Put your friends and family in a story about St. Nick for St. Nicholas Day (December 6).

What You'll Need
- light-colored con-struction paper
- blunt scissors
- pencil
- ruler
- stapler and staples
- thin cardboard
- colored tape
- markers
- glue
- glitter

1. Measure and cut 6 to 10 pieces of light-colored construction paper into 8×6-inch rectangles. Fold the sheets in half. Staple the sheets together in the fold.

2. Cut out 2 pieces of cardboard, 4×3 inches each, for the front and back covers. Use a strip of colored tape for the spine. Place the tape sticky side up, and press the cardboard covers down on it, leaving a gap for the pages of the book. Open the stapled pages flat on top of the covers, and press them onto the tape.

3. Add another thin strip of tape down the center of the pages, and press the tape around to the spine. Draw a decorative line, shape, or outline of St. Nick with glue on the cover, and sprinkle the glue with glitter. As soon as the glue dries, shake the loose glitter onto a sheet of paper. Put the excess glitter back into the bottle to recycle it. Now you are ready to write the story of St. Nick visiting your friends and family!

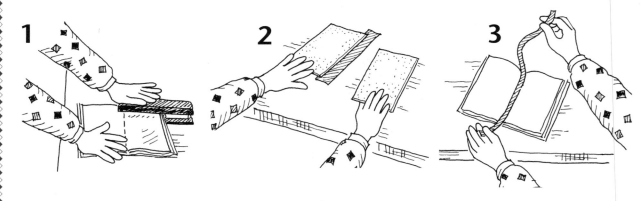

Wire Santa

Twist, wrap, and shape your way into the holiday spirit by creating your very own version of St. Nick.

What You'll Need
- plastic coated wire or green floral wire (both available at craft stores)
- stapler and staples
- cardboard

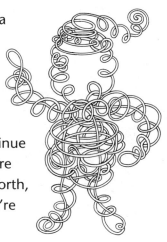

Start by twisting wire to make a face and a beard. Remember: This sculpture is a bit abstract so you don't need to add a lot of detail. Next move down to make the neck, arms, and body. First make the line of the body part, such as the arm, then make loopy twists of wire around it. Continue with the rest of the figure, twisting the wire around to make the legs and boots. Keep looping the wire back and forth, around and around, until the figure has the shape you like. When you're finished, bend the arms and legs to make an interesting position. To display the wire Santa, staple the figure to a piece of cardboard.

St. Nick Charm

Give someone a St. Nick charm on St. Nicholas Day (December 6) for safe travels!

Caution: This project requires adult help.

In Italy sailors put the symbol of St. Nicholas on the prow of their ships for a safe voyage.

What You'll Need
- rolling pin
- drinking glass
- pencil
- cookie sheet
- markers or paints
- thin cord

See the African Gold Weights on page 447 for instructions on how to make clay. Ask an adult to preheat the oven to 300 degrees.

Form a 3-inch ball of the clay mixture, and roll it out with your rolling pin on a floured counter. Press the rim of a drinking glass into the clay to cut out a circular shape. Cut out as many charms as you want. Use a pencil to poke a hole near the top of each circle. Bake the charms on a cookie sheet for 30 minutes. When they cool, use paint or markers to make St. Nick's face. Thread cord through the hole in the charm. Happy trails!

Christmas Card Panorama

Make a festive scene in a box for Christmas Card Day (December 9)!

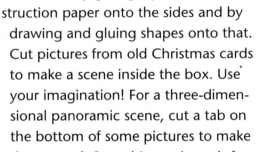

Decorate the box by gluing squares of construction paper onto the sides and by drawing and gluing shapes onto that. Cut pictures from old Christmas cards to make a scene inside the box. Use your imagination! For a three-dimensional panoramic scene, cut a tab on the bottom of some pictures to make them stand. Save this year's cards for a new panorama next year.

What You'll Need
- shoe box
- construction paper
- glue
- crayons
- blunt scissors
- old Christmas cards

Christmas Card Mobile

Display your Christmas cards high above the crowd!

What You'll Need
- 2 wire hangers
- red or green colored tape
- plastic drinking straws
- hole punch
- Christmas cards
- red or green colored string
- artificial mistletoe
- ribbons
- ornaments

Caution: This project requires adult help.

Ask an adult to help you make the base of this mobile. Insert one hanger into the open part of another hanger so that they form a cross shape. Twist the tops together so that they form one hook. Wind colored tape around the base (and the rest of the hangers, if you like). Tape the straws to the base, so they jut out from the base. Cover the straws with the colored tape. These will be the arms of the mobile from which you hang your decorations.

Punch holes at the tops of your Christmas cards. Thread string through the holes, and tie them onto the arms of the mobile. You can also tie on mistletoe, small ornaments, ribbons—use your imagination! Vary the lengths of the string, and alternate cards with other decorations. Ask an adult to help you hang your mobile.

Hanukkah Menorah

◆▶◆▶◆▶

Build a menorah for Hanukkah, the Jewish Festival of Lights.

What You'll Need
- 2 cups flour
- 1 cup salt
- mixing spoon
- mixing bowl
- 1½ cups water
- paint
- paintbrush

Caution: This project requires adult help.

To make your menorah, mix a batch of baker's clay by mixing the flour and salt in the bowl. Add the water, and mix. Form the dough into a ball, and knead it for 5 minutes. Make 9 candle cups by either molding the dough or rolling it out and coiling it around to make a small cup. You will need 8 cups for the 8 nights of Hanukkah and a 9th cup for the special candle that is used to light the other candles. Make a base out of the dough, and attach the candle cups to the base. Place 8 cups in a row and then set the 9th cup higher up and off to the side or in the middle. Let it dry for a few days, or bake at 300 degrees until hard (ask an adult for help). Once it's cool, paint it to express how wonderful you feel about this holiday!

 # Luscious Latkes

◆▶◆▶◆▶

These sweet potato latkes are a twist on traditional Hanukkah pancakes.

What You'll Need
- 4 sweet potatoes
- grater
- 1 onion
- knife
- bowls
- 4 eggs
- eggbeater
- 1 teaspoon cinnamon
- juice of ½ lime
- ½ cup flour
- 1 teaspoon salt
- measuring cups and spoons
- mixing spoon
- ginger (optional)
- butter
- skillet
- oil
- sour cream
- applesauce

Caution: This project requires adult help.

Have an adult help you grate the potatoes and chop the onion. Then beat the eggs. Add the onion, eggs, cinnamon, lime juice, salt, and flour to the potatoes. Mix well. You can add a teaspoon or two of powdered or freshly grated ginger for spice. Have an adult melt several tablespoons of butter in a skillet. Add a little oil to the skillet so the butter doesn't burn. Shape a smooth, flat pancake. Have the adult fry it. It is done when both sides are crispy brown. Serve with sour cream and applesauce!

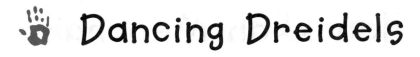

Dancing Dreidels

◆▶◆▶◆▶◆▶

Not all dreidels are made of clay!

What You'll Need
- thin cardboard
- blunt scissors
- ruler
- tape
- paint and paint-brushes
- markers
- pencil
- colored tape
- chocolate Hanukkah gelt

Cut a 12×3-inch rectangle out of thin cardboard. Measure and mark the cardboard at 3, 6, and 9 inches. Fold along those lines to make a box shape. Tape the ends together.

Cut out two 3×3-inch squares of cardboard, and tape them onto the ends of the box. Paint the cardboard in bright colors. When the paint is dry, draw a Hebrew letter on each side (see art below) with a marker. Stick the pencil through the top, down through the bottom of the dreidel. Tape the pencil in place with the colored tape.

To play, everyone puts a chocolate coin (Hanukkah gelt) into the pot. Players then take turns spinning the dreidel. If the dreidel lands with the *nun* facing up, the player gets nothing. If the *gimel* faces up, the player captures the whole pot. If the *hey* faces up, the player takes half the pot. If the *shin* faces up, the player puts a coin into the pot. The letters *nun, gimel, hey,* and *shin* stand for the first letters of the phrase *Nes Gadol Haya Sham,* which means "a great miracle was here."

gimel	shin	nun	hey
ג	שׁ	נ	ה

Star of David Bookmarks

Latkes are not the only use you'll have for potatoes this Hanukkah!

What You'll Need
- firm, raw potatoes
- knife
- paper towels
- marker
- scissors
- ruler
- construction paper
- paints
- paintbrush

Caution: This project requires adult help.

Have an adult help you with the cutting in this project. Choose and wash a firm potato. Cut it in half. Pat the potato dry with a paper towel. Using a marker, draw a Star of David on the white part of the potato half. Carefully cut away the potato around the star outline. When you finish, you will have a raised star.

Cut 12-inch-long rectangles from construction paper to make the bookmarks—cut them a little wider than your potato star shape. Brush a thick, even layer of paint onto the star shape. Carefully press it onto the bookmark where you want a star. Lift the potato straight up—don't wiggle or drag it when you lift it. Print a row of stars along the bookmark. Try painting half the potato shape with one color and the other half a different color!

Shining Tin Menorahs

You can't light this menorah, but its shine will dazzle you!

Double a large piece of foil—the doubled foil should be several inches larger than your piece of cardboard. Cut sheets of newspaper the same size as the cardboard; cut enough newspaper to make a pad (7 to 15 sheets). Put the newspaper pad on the cardboard, and center the foil on top. Fold the excess foil over the edges of the cardboard, and secure them with tape, making sure there are no wrinkles in your foil. Use a knitting needle, spoon handle, or small nail to carefully draw the menorah shape onto the foil. Press firmly but not hard enough to break the foil. Work slowly; once the lines are drawn it isn't easy to erase them. Draw with long, smooth strokes, and don't lift your tool until you have finished a line. When you have finished engraving, glue the back of your menorah onto a slightly larger piece of cardboard to create a frame. Color the cardboard around your engraving with markers. Celebrate a shining silver Hanukkah this year!

What You'll Need
- tinfoil or heavy-duty aluminum foil
- cardboard
- newspaper
- blunt scissors
- tape
- knitting needle, spoon, or small nail
- glue
- markers

Chocolate Hanukkah Balls

◆▶▷▶▷▶▷▶

If you like chocolate and grapes, you'll love these treats!

What You'll Need
- clear glass jar
- blue sand
- white sand
- blue or white ribbon
- seedless grapes
- wooden skewers
- semisweet chocolate chips
- saucepan
- mixing spoon
- saucer of blue and white sprinkles

Caution: This project requires adult help.

These chocolate Hanukkah balls will make a beautiful table decoration, but it won't be long before they turn into dessert!

Prepare the base by washing and drying a large, clear glass jar. Pour alternating layers of blue and white sand into the jar until it is full. Tie a blue or white ribbon around the neck.

Wash and dry a bunch of seedless grapes. Push each grape onto a wooden skewer. Ask an adult to help you melt the chocolate chips in a saucepan over low heat, stirring constantly so the chocolate doesn't burn. When the chocolate is melted, dip each grape into it with a twirling motion so the entire grape is covered with chocolate. Before the chocolate cools, twirl each grape in a saucer of blue and white sprinkles. Poke the ends of the wooden skewers into the jar of sand you prepared earlier. Make a whole bunch and arrange them like flowers. Place the jar on the table for a delicious centerpiece.

Wish Gifts

◆▶▷▶▷▶▷▶

One picture is worth a thousand smiles!

Why not give someone a castle, a giraffe, or a Ferris wheel for Hanukkah? Let someone you love know you're really thinking of them this holiday with this special bag.

Cut out pictures from old magazines or catalogs of presents you'd like to give (be sure to ask for permission first!). Put them on cardboard, trace around the edges of the pictures, and cut out the cardboard shapes. Glue each picture onto its cardboard shape.

All the pictures can then be put into a white paper bag that has been specially decorated for whomever it is for. Write "I Wish I Could Give You . . ." on the outside of the bag. Does your sister want a sports car? Would Dad like a new camera? Even if you're a little short on cash this year, you can give your loved ones just what they really want.

What You'll Need
- old magazines and catalogs
- blunt scissors
- cardboard
- pencil
- glue
- white paper bags
- markers

Hanukkah Candle Cutouts

◆▶▶▶▶▶◀

Make these shimmering candle cutouts to put in your window or doorway—
one for each day of Hanukkah.

What You'll Need
- cardboard
- pencil
- craft knife (adult use only)
- black construction paper
- scissors
- colored cellophane or tissue paper
- tape
- newspaper
- old crayons (yellow, red, orange)
- cheese grater
- waxed paper
- iron and ironing board
- craft glue
- hole punch
- string or yarn

Caution: This project requires adult help.

These are instructions for making 1 candle—but make as many as you'd like to hang. On a rectangle of cardboard, draw candle and flame shapes (see the illustration below). Ask an adult to cut out the shapes using the craft knife; this is your tracing stencil. Make 2 equal-size rectangles from black paper. Use the cardboard to trace the candle and flame shapes onto the black rectangles. Cut out the shapes. Pick a color of cellophane or tissue paper, and cut a rectangle slightly larger than the candle stem. Tape the colored paper to a black rectangle so it covers the cutout stem shape.

Cover your work surface with old newspaper. Carefully grate the crayons to get shavings. Cut two 4-inch squares of waxed paper, and place the shavings on a waxed-paper square. Place the other square on top of the first. Now cover the crayon shavings with more newspaper. Have an adult use an iron (on the dry setting) to press lightly on the newspaper.

When the waxed paper is cool, cut out a piece slightly larger than the candle-flame shape. Tape or glue the waxed paper creation to the black paper so it shines through. To finish, glue the second sheet of black

paper to the back of the first. Punch a hole in the top, thread with string or yarn, and hang.

Easy ID Bracelet

This personalized bracelet is a unique Hanukkah gift for the jewelry lover in the house.

What You'll Need
• paper towel tube
• ruler
• blunt scissors
• paint
• paintbrushes
• markers

Cut 2 inches from a paper towel tube. Cut a slit down one side of the cylinder so that it can be worn on a wrist. Paint the bracelet however you want. When the paint dries, write a friend's or family member's name in large letters on it. You could find out each person's favorite colors and use them. Decorate around the name with tiny polka dots, squiggles, hearts, or any other design. If your friend has a nickname, you can make a nickname ID bracelet!

Edible Menorahs

These menorahs look great and are yummy to eat!

Spread bread with cream cheese or butter, and arrange 8 pretzels on the bread as candles. Poke them through the bread so they stand up. Use the carrot stick as the shammes, the candle that is used to light the other candles. Put the carrot stick behind the other candles. Place raisins as flames at the ends of the carrot and pretzel sticks—you may need to use a dot of cream cheese to make them stay. Use this menorah as a centerpiece for your Hanukkah dinner.

What You'll Need
• bread
• cream cheese or butter
• butter knife
• pretzel sticks
• carrot stick
• raisins

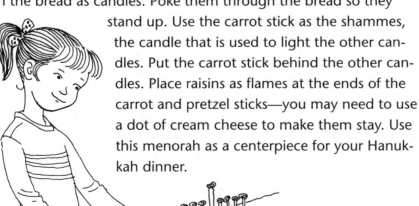

Candy Cane Cookies

◆▶◆▶◆▶◆▶

Make a new kind of candy cane.

What You'll Need

- 4 cups flour
- 2 teaspoons baking powder
- 1 teaspoon salt
- sifter
- mixing bowls
- ¾ cup butter
- 1½ cups sugar
- electric mixer
- 2 eggs
- 2 teaspoons vanilla extract
- 1 teaspoon lemon extract
- red food coloring
- flour (optional)
- cookie sheet

Caution: This project requires adult help.

Have an adult help you with preparation and cooking! Preheat the oven to 375 degrees. Sift together the flour, baking powder, and salt. In another bowl, beat the butter and sugar until the mix is light and fluffy. Beat the eggs into the butter and sugar mixture, then add the vanilla and lemon extracts. Add the flour mixture, in small amounts, to the butter and sugar mixture, until well mixed. Divide the dough in half. Put half in a bowl; add enough red food coloring to make a nice color. Make little balls of red and plain dough. On a clean, floured surface, roll the balls into ropes. Dust your hands with flour if the dough is too sticky. Twist one red rope and one plain rope together, and shape them into a candy cane. Place dough on a cookie sheet; bake for 8 to 10 minutes or until just slightly brown.

Santa's Bag Game

◆▶◆▶◆▶◆

Make up skits about the objects in Santa's bags.

Gather an assortment of small objects, such as toy soldiers, small Christmas ornaments, candy canes, and other tiny toys. Make word cards with Christmas words printed on them. Put the objects and cards in a closed box. Have everyone decorate a white paper bag with crayons. Each person can secretly fill their bag with 3 objects and cards from the box. Close the bags, and put them in a pile. Divide players into small groups. Each group is given a bag that's not their own. Each group shouldn't let the other groups see what's in their bag. Using the objects and cards in the bags, the groups must create a skit. They must refer to their object or word by saying it at least twice during the skit. Audience members then guess which 3 objects and words were in the bag.

What You'll Need
- assorted small objects
- 3×5-inch cards
- pen
- box that closes
- white paper bag
- crayons

"Exploding" Party Favors

◆▶◆▶◆▶◆

Play tug-of-war with these party favors, and watch them explode with candy!

What You'll Need
- gold and silver wrapping paper
- ruler
- blunt scissors
- tape
- small wrapped candies
- colored ribbons

These party favors were popular in France before the mid-1800s! The size of the snapper you want to make will determine how big your paper should be and how much candy you will need. For starters, you might want to use a sheet of wrapping paper that is 6×10 inches. Overlap the paper ½ inch on the long sides to form a tube, and tape the edges together. Put 12 to 15 candies into the middle of the tube. Twist the ends of the paper, about 3 inches from the end. Tie each twist with a piece of ribbon, making a bow with streamers. Open each end of the paper so that it flares outward, and push ends together so the center puffs up. To make your snapper explode candy, hold one end while a friend holds the other. Tug and shake the snapper until the paper breaks.

Straw Star

Weave straws together for a glittering treat.

What You'll Need
- 2 plastic drinking straws
- blunt scissors
- string or yarn
- tape measure
- craft glue
- glitter

Who knew ordinary drinking straws could become glittering holiday stars? It's true—they can be works of art.

Cut the straws in half; be sure the halves are even. Take a long piece of string or yarn in your hand, at least 18 inches long. Criss-cross 4 straw halves so they are in a star pattern, then wrap the string around the middle of the pieces, being careful to keep the string tight in the center. Weave around the straws at the middle, pulling the straws slightly apart as you weave to keep the arms of the star separated. Once you've made the weave secure, knot the string, leaving a little dangling as a hanger. Spread glue on the straw star, and sprinkle it with glitter. Now make enough stars to decorate your house for the holidays!

Wrapping Paper Maker

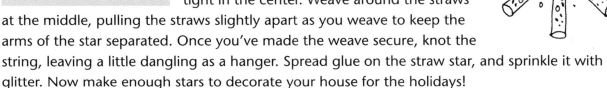

Gifts wrapped in paper you made yourself are extra special.

Cover your work surface. Cut a piece of cardboard so that it is the same length as the rolling pin. Tape one end of the cardboard to the rolling pin, all the way across. Roll the rolling pin so that the cardboard wraps around it, making a tight cardboard cover. When you reach the end of the cardboard, tape it in place. (It may wrap around more than once.) Cut 1-inch Christmas shapes, such as bells, stars, and angels, from the weather stripping. Coat the cardboard rolling pin cover with glue. This is easier if you set each handle on a thick cookbook, so that the rolling pin is hanging between the books. Press the shapes in place, turning the rolling pin as you go, so that your pattern goes all the way around the rolling pin. Let the glue dry. Pour a thin coat of paint on the cookie sheet, roll the Wrapping Paper Maker through it, then roll out a pattern on plain white paper.

What You'll Need
- waterproof table covering
- thin cardboard
- blunt scissors
- rolling pin
- masking tape
- rubber weather stripping (from hardware store)
- pencil
- ruler
- craft glue
- 2 thick cookbooks (optional)
- tempera paints
- cookie sheet
- large pieces of white paper

Secret Santa

◆◆◆◆◆◆

Your old toys could be new treasures for someone special.

Caution: This project requires adult help.

Is your room overflowing with toys and stuffed animals you've out-grown? Why not clean them up and give them to children who are less fortunate? With an adult's help, tape and glue torn game pieces, wash and disinfect soiled action figures, and clean older stuffed ani-mals by putting them inside a pillowcase in a washing machine. Attach a friendly little note with ribbon to each toy, and donate them to your local home-less shelter or YMCA. Also, don't forget well-known drives for new toys, such as Toys for Tots, when it comes time to share your spirit of giving!

What You'll Need
• old toys
• tape
• glue
• cleaning supplies
• ribbon
• construction or notebook paper
• pencil

Wreath of Candy

◆◆◆◆◆◆

Here's a Christmas wreath you'll need to hang out of reach—or else it just might disappear!

What You'll Need
• vinyl-coated wire hanger
• red and green wrapped hard candy
• red and green twist ties
• red and green rib-bon
• scissors

Caution: This project requires adult help.

Traditional wreaths are usually made from pine boughs or pinecones, but this Christmas you might want to try something a little sweeter. Bend the bottom of the hanger into a circle. You might need an adult to help you with this. Attach a twist tie to one end of each candy. Attach the candies to the hanger by twisting the ties onto the hanger. Continue doing this until you have a wreath full of candy. You can also tie ribbon bows onto the wire to make your wreath even prettier.

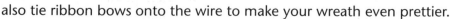

Silver Bell Ornaments

◆▸◆▸◆▸◆

Make your own jingle bells to hang from the Christmas tree.

Caution: This project requires adult help.

These bells may not make music, but they will help make your holidays a singing success!

Cut a single egg carton cup for each bell. String a bead on a string, and secure it with a knot. Ask an adult to help you use a needle to poke the free end of the string through the egg carton cup. Knot the end of the string, making sure the bead swings freely inside the egg cup.

When you have made 3 bells, tie them to a longer string. Paint the bells silver. Tie a ribbon in a bow around the long string.

What You'll Need
- cardboard egg carton
- scissors
- colored string
- pea-size wooden beads
- needle
- silver paint
- paintbrush
- ribbon

Curly Paper Art

◆▸◆▸◆▸◆

You can make just about anything with curly paper, but it looks especially elegant hanging on a Christmas tree.

What You'll Need
- construction paper
- blunt scissors
- clear tape

To make a curly paper ornament, cut 2 long strips and 2 short strips of construction paper. Tape the 2 long and 2 short strips together at the top and bottom. Separate the strips at one end. Cut 2 more short strips. Tape the ends together to form rings. Tape the rings between the long strips. Fanfold some more short strips, and tape them in between. Cut 4 strips and curl them over the edge of a closed pair of scissors. Tape the curly strips to the bottom. Make a loop with a short strip of paper, and tape it to the top of the ornament to hang it.

Christmas Card Puzzles

Make this great puzzle for a little brother, sister, or cousin.

Caution: This project requires adult help.

If your cards are bigger than 6×6 inches, decide which part of the picture you want to be in the puzzle and trim it to a 6-inch square. Lay the blocks together, 3 across and 3 down. Smooth glue across the back of a picture. Make sure it is completely covered. Press it, glue-side down, onto the blocks. Let glue dry for a few minutes. Ask an adult to help you use the craft knife to cut the blocks apart. Trim the paper along the edges of the blocks. Turn up 6 blank sides of the blocks, and repeat with a different card. Repeat with the other cards. When you are finished, each side of the blocks will have a Christmas picture on it, and you will have a 6-picture block puzzle!

What You'll Need
- 6 large, different Christmas cards at least 6×6 inches
- scissors
- ruler
- nine 2×2-inch wooden blocks
- old paintbrush
- glue
- craft knife

Pasta Lace Ornaments

These decorations not only make exquisite Christmas tree ornaments, but they also look pretty hanging in a window.

What You'll Need
- waxed paper
- water
- food coloring
- small bowls
- mixing spoon
- pasta wheels
- elbow macaroni
- craft glue
- ribbon

Cover your work surface with waxed paper. Mix some water and food coloring together in a small bowl. Repeat for other colors. Dip 7 pasta wheels and 6 elbow macaroni pieces in the bowls, alternating colors. Let all pasta pieces dry.

Arrange 6 pasta wheels in a circular pattern with 1 pasta wheel in the center. Apply glue to the sides of the pasta wheels, and glue them together. Glue the 6 elbow macaroni pieces around the circle of pasta wheels. To make the ornament hanger, bring the ends of a small piece of ribbon together to form a loop. Glue the ends to the back of the ornament.

Christmas Seals

Decorate your Christmas cards with homemade Christmas stickers.

What You'll Need
- markers
- white paper
- scissors
- mixing bowl
- 2 tablespoons cold water
- 1 packet plain gelatin
- fork
- 3 tablespoons boiling water
- ½ teaspoon corn syrup
- flavored extract (mint, vanilla, or lemon)
- small paintbrush

Caution: This project requires adult help.

Draw small Christmas pictures, such as Santa, Christmas trees, elves, snow people, candy canes, angels, wrapped presents, and bright stars. Cut out your drawings carefully, getting as close to the edges as you can. When you have finished making your cutouts, pour the cold water into the bowl. Sprinkle the gelatin over it. With adult help, use a fork to mix in the boiling water until the gelatin dissolves. Add the corn syrup and a few drops of extract. With a small brush, paint a thin layer of the gelatin mixture onto the back of each of your cutout drawings. If you have leftover gelatin mixture, place it in a jar in the refrigerator. When you are ready to use it again, place the jar into a bowl of hot water. (Use mixture within two weeks.) Let the stickers dry. When you are ready to use them, lick the back and press onto the surface you are decorating—use them to decorate envelopes, cards, wrapping paper, and presents!

Dancing Sugarplum Fairies

Make your own tiny fairies that dance all by themselves!

Cut out tiny sugarplum fairy shapes from tissue paper—use your imagination about how you think they look! Charge a comb with static electricity by running it through your hair or rubbing it against your clothing for a few minutes.

What You'll Need
- colored tissue paper
- blunt scissors
- comb

Lay the sugarplum fairies on a table. When the comb is held near the fairies, they will wiggle and move around. Do you know the tune to the "Nutcracker Suite"? Hum it for your fairies while they dance!

Keepsake Quilts

You can hang up this sentimental quilt for many Christmases to come.

What You'll Need
- white cardboard
- ruler
- pencil
- blunt scissors
- hole punch
- yarn
- large needle

Caution: This project requires adult help.

You can make a cardboard quilt full of memories by measuring 6×6-inch squares of cardboard and cutting them out. With a hole punch, punch 3 evenly spaced holes on each side inside the borders of each square. Give a square to family and friends. Have them write holiday messages, draw holiday events, or draw portraits of themselves on the squares. Collect the squares. Thread the needle with yarn, and sew the squares together through the holes you punched. You might need an adult to help you get started with the sewing. When the quilt is all sewn, hang it in the family room or on the front door of your house. Bring it out each Christmas, and add more squares for new family memories.

Soft Reindeer Toy

This soft toy makes a cuddly gift for your favorite reindeer lover.

What You'll Need
- heavy, soft brown knee sock
- cotton balls, cotton batting, or foam
- small jingle bells
- rubber band
- pencil
- scraps of brown, black, pink, and white felt
- thin cardboard
- blunt scissors
- glue
- ribbon

Stuff the sock with the cotton or foam and several jingle bells until it is full but loose enough so that the bells have room to move around. Wrap a rubber band tightly around the bottom of the sock to make a neck. Draw and cut out 4 antler shapes from brown felt and 2 antlers from thin cardboard. Glue the felt antlers to either side of the thin cardboard. Glue the antlers to the reindeer's head. Then draw and cut out eyes, a nose, and a mouth from scraps of black, white, and pink felt. Glue them onto the face. Tie a pretty ribbon around the reindeer's neck.

Glitter Ornaments

❖▸❖▸❖▸❖

With a little glue and glitter, you can make a shimmering ornament for each member of your family.

What You'll Need
- waxed paper
- craft glue
- glitter
- thread

Draw an ornament design on a sheet of waxed paper with a thick line of glue. If you can't think of a shape, put a simple picture under the waxed paper and trace it with the glue. Shake glitter over the glue, covering the glue completely. Let it set overnight. The next day, shake off the excess glitter. Peel the waxed paper off, and tie on a piece of thread for the hanger. Make a set of ornaments for your family. Make something that each member of your family uses in his or her hobby such as inline skates or a flower.

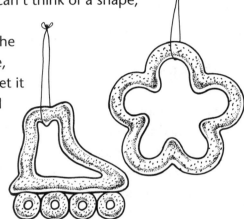

Paper Cutouts #2

❖▸❖▸❖▸❖

Hang these designs on a Christmas tree, in a window, or from a mobile. You can even paste them on a handmade card.

What You'll Need
- drawing paper
- blunt scissors
- ruler

Fold a piece of paper in half. Starting at the fold, cut repeated lines, arches, or L-shapes in the paper as shown. Unfold the paper, and bend every other strip outward. Cut an 8-inch circle from a piece of paper. Fold it in half, and then fold it in half again. Starting at the double-fold, cut curved lines along the curve to ½ inch from the single fold. Open it up, and bend every other strip— one toward you and one away from you on each side. Experiment with other shapes, and use your paper cutouts for ornaments or mobile decorations.

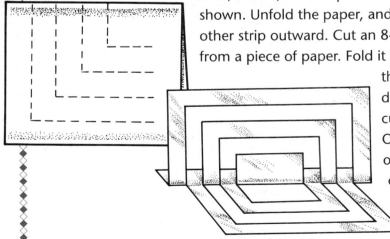

Edible Angels

◄►◄►◄►◄►

These darling angels are almost too sweet to eat.

What You'll Need
• 1 cup peanut butter
• 1 cup honey
• 2½ cups powdered milk
• big bowl
• ruler
• snack chips
• thin licorice string
• raisins or currants
• colored or silver jimmies or cinnamon candies

Wash and dry your hands. To make the clay, put the peanut butter, honey, and powdered milk in a big bowl. Squeeze and knead the ingredients together. If the clay is too sticky, add a little more powdered milk. If it is too dry, add a little more honey or peanut butter. When you have a nice, smooth-feeling clay, shape it into a 3-inch cone to make the angel's body. Add a little ball of clay on top for the angel's head. Carefully press 2 snack chips into the angel's back for wings. Wind a small piece of thin licorice string around the angel's head for a perfect halo. Use raisins or currants to make the face. Colored or silver jimmies or small cinnamon candies can decorate the angel's body. These angels are guaranteed to fly right off the plate and into your mouth!

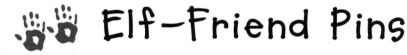

Elf-Friend Pins

►◄►◄►◄►

All of your friends will want an elf-friend when they see these pins!

Offer to crack some walnuts for your mom. Pick out the walnut shells that cracked neatly in half. Dig out the nut meat. Wrap a piece of cotton in a small square of fabric. Gather the edges, and wrap with a rubber band to make a ball. The fabric and cotton ball should just fill the hollow space in the nutshell. Pour a puddle of glue into the nutshell. Set the fabric ball in the glue, rubber band side down. When the glue is dry, stitch the back of a small safety pin to the fabric. You should be able to open and close the pin. Use paint and fine-tipped paintbrushes to paint an elf face on the front of the walnut. Glue on yarn or cotton for hair and beards. Cut out red or green felt elf hats, and glue them on.

What You'll Need
• walnuts
• nutcracker
• scrap fabric
• cotton
• rubber band
• glue
• small safety pin
• needle and thread
• paint and fine-tipped paintbrushes
• yarn
• red or green felt

Clove and Citrus Pomanders

◆▶◆▶◆▶◆

These sweet-smelling, fruity decorations make cheery holiday gifts.

What You'll Need
- oranges or lemons
- thin nail
- cloves
- thin string
- ribbon

Make small holes in the orange skin with the thin nail, covering the entire orange with holes. (If you don't want to cover the whole orange, you can make striped or heart designs on the orange.) Stick a clove in each hole. When you have finished your design, temporarily tie a string around the orange, from the bottom to the top, with a loop at the top for hanging. Hang the pomander in a cool, dry place until the orange begins to shrink a bit. Remove the string when the orange is dry; replace it with a colored ribbon, tied in the same way, with a loop at the top for hanging. For a variation, use a lemon instead of an orange. Make a whole grove of fragrant pomanders for your family and friends!

Pasta Snowflakes

◆▶◆▶◆▶◆

These pasta snowflakes won't melt when you hang them on the tree!

Caution: This project requires adult help.

What You'll Need
- coffee can
- pencil
- paper
- ruler
- waxed paper
- several kinds of dry pasta
- glue
- toothpick
- spray paint
- ribbon or dental floss

Trace around the bottom of a coffee can to make a circle on paper. Use a ruler to make lines across the circle, so that it looks like a pie cut into 8 pieces. This will be your pattern. Put a piece of waxed paper over the pattern, and lay pieces of pasta on top of the waxed paper so that they are all touching. Use the circle and lines you drew to help keep the pattern symmetrical. When you have a design you like, use a toothpick to dab glue between the pasta. After the pasta is glued together, slide the waxed paper to one side and let the glue dry while you make more snowflakes. When the glue is dry, remove the waxed paper, and have an adult help you spray paint the ornaments. Your snowflakes will be fragile, but if they break, you can glue them back together. You can hang your snowflakes with ribbon or dental floss.

Sugarplum Fairy Pillowcases

◄►◄►◄►◄►

These enchanting fairies will bring happy Christmas dreams while everyone sleeps.

What You'll Need

- white pillowcases
- cardboard the size of pillowcase
- pencil
- fabric paints
- paintbrushes

What does a sugarplum fairy look like? Is she wearing a long silver gown? A short blue tunic? Does she have wings or a wand? What color is her hair? Perhaps she is balancing a big sugarplum on the top of her head! However you want her to look, paint her in pretty colors so that any head resting on her will be full of sweet dreams. Wash and dry a spare white pillowcase. Place a piece of cardboard inside so the paint won't bleed through. With a pencil, lightly draw a picture of a sugarplum fairy on the front of the pillowcase. When you finish, color in your outline with fabric paint. After the paint dries, you may want to turn your pillowcase over and paint another sugarplum fairy on the back—for double the dreaming pleasure!

Santa Salad

◄►◄►◄►◄►

This cheery vegetable Santa will brighten up your holiday meal.

Caution: This project requires adult help.

What You'll Need

- tomatoes
- green olives with pimentos
- radishes
- knife
- cottage cheese
- plates

It's easy to put a Santa on every plate at Christmas dinner! Wash all vegetables. Cut tomatoes into ½-inch-thick slices, one for each Santa. Have an adult help you with the sharp knife! Slice a few green olives. Lay 2 tomato slices on a plate, and add the green olives on top of them for Santa's eyes. Cut a radish slice to use for his nose, and cut a radish half moon for his mouth. Carefully spoon cottage cheese on and around the tomato for Santa's hair and beard. If you want, broil the tomato slices in a toaster oven before you begin (ask an adult to help you with this). Hot or cold, these Santas are delicious!

Puzzle Wreath

❖►►►►►►❖

I'll bet you've never seen a wreath like this before!

What You'll Need
- sturdy 9-inch paper plate
- blunt scissors
- hole punch
- yarn
- 1 cup white glue
- large bowl
- green food coloring
- 4 cups old jigsaw puzzle pieces
- mixing spoon
- waxed paper
- small Christmas balls, candy canes, and other Christmas objects

Cut the middle out of the paper plate so that it looks like a wreath. Punch a hole through the top, and tie a loop of yarn through it for a hanger. Put the white glue in a large bowl. Mix in five drops of green food coloring. Pour in the puzzle pieces, and stir until they are completely covered. Lay the plate on some waxed paper. Put spoonfuls of puzzle pieces on the plate. Arrange them so they look nice. Let the wreath dry for several days. When it has dried, glue on small Christmas balls, candy canes, and other Christmas objects!

Frankincense Jars

❖►►►►►►❖

This potpourri jar is pretty enough to give to a king!

Make Christmas stars or other shapes on your jar with glue. Stick rice to the glue. Let glue dry. Measure around the outside of your jar. Cut a piece of aluminum foil long enough to fit around your jar plus an overlap of ½ inch; there should also be a little extra at the top and bottom of the jar. Crush the foil into a ball, then smooth it out again. Using the paintbrush, spread glue evenly on one side of the foil. Carefully place the jar on the edge of the foil. Roll the jar like a rolling pin, so that it wraps itself in foil. Carefully fold the top of the foil into the mouth of the jar, making sure it sticks in place. Fold the bottom of the foil under the jar. Press gently around the jar with your fingers, making sure that the glue sticks everywhere. Tap the foil with the bristles of the fabric brush to bring out the texture of your rice pattern. Fill the jar with sweet potpourri.

What You'll Need
- small jars (baby food jars are fine, but jars of all shapes are good)
- glue
- uncooked rice
- tape measure
- aluminum foil
- blunt scissors
- ruler
- old paintbrush
- fabric brush
- potpourri

Water Glass Carols

◆◀◆◀◆◀◆▶

Serenade your party guests with some tinkly tunes!

Do this inside a large plastic tub in case of breakage. Fill the first glass ⅛ full of water, the second glass ¼ full, the third glass ⅜ full, and so on until the eighth glass is full. (You are adding ⅛ of a cup of water to each glass.) Use a teaspoon to tap on each glass. Add or pour out water to make the musical scale as you sing "do, re, mi, fa, so, la, ti, do." You can add a few drops of food coloring to each glass after your glasses are tuned. Practice tapping out your favorite Christmas songs. Give a holiday concert for family and friends.

What You'll Need
- large plastic tub
- 8 water glasses
- water
- measuring cup
- teaspoons
- food coloring
- simple sheet music

Snowy Christmas Cake House

◆◀◆◀◆◀◆▶

This cake house is as much fun to make as it will be to eat!

What You'll Need
- refrigerated pound cake
- knife
- ruler
- plate
- white frosting
- red and green gumdrops
- small thin squares of chocolate
- toothpicks
- tiny candy canes

Caution: This project requires adult help.

Ask an adult to help you cut four 2-inch squares of pound cake. Using a plate as the base, put the squares together in a box shape to make the 4 walls of the house. Use the frosting as mortar. Cut 2 more squares to use as the sides of the roof, using more frosting as mortar. Cut another square in half, and use each half to carefully close up the front and back of the roof. Frost the house with white frosting so it looks snowy. You can make a chimney of three gumdrops on a toothpick, doors and windows of chocolate squares, and then add snow (frosting) all around the house. Stick candy canes and gumdrops around the house.

Take-One Plate Decoration

This pretty decoration makes a tasty welcome when hung on the front door of your house.

What You'll Need
- 2 aluminum-foil pie plates
- heavy-duty scissors
- colored tape
- glue
- hole punch
- ribbon
- Christmas greenery
- candy canes
- licorice sticks
- pretzel rods
- other candies (optional)
- construction paper
- markers

Caution: This project requires adult help.

Ask an adult to help you cut one pie plate in half. Cover the cut edge with colored tape to make it smooth. Glue it onto the whole pie plate to make a pocket. Punch a hole at the top of the whole plate, and thread it with ribbon to make a hanging loop. Fill the pocket with Christmas greenery, candy canes, licorice sticks, pretzel rods, and any other candies you want. Make a pretty label that says, "Take One." Glue it onto the front of the pocket. Hang the decoration on your front door so that guests will have a welcome treat before they even get inside the house!

Gift-Wrapped Door

Turn your house into a big present!

Measure the height and width of your front door. Double the measurements and add 2 inches so you can wind the ribbon around to the inside of the door. Cut the ribbon that length. Tie the ribbon around the door to look like a gift package, and tape the ends of the ribbon together. Tape one or more large bows onto the ribbon in the center of the door. Add Christmas greenery around the bow(s) with tape. Cut a large gift-tag shape out of cardboard, and a write a holiday message on it. Punch a hole at the top of the gift tag, and attach it to the ribbon with a colorful piece of yarn.

What You'll Need
- tape measure
- wide colored ribbon
- blunt scissors
- tape
- one or several large bows
- Christmas greenery
- cardboard
- marker
- hole punch
- yarn

Christmas Pocket Pixie

◆▸◆▸◆▸◆▸

Who's that peeking out of your pocket?

What You'll Need
- self-hardening clay
- ruler
- large paper clip
- markers

Make a Christmas Pocket Pixie for everyone to wear at your next party. Roll a ½-inch ball of self-hardening clay to make the pixie's head. Press it onto one end of the paper clip. Roll a small cone shape out of clay, and press it on top of the head to make the  pixie's hat. Put a tiny clay ball on top of the cone to make the hat's pom-pom. Color the hat and pom-pom with markers when the clay dries. Draw on a cheerful pixie face. Try to draw a different face on each pixie. Give one pixie big blue eyes, another a long pointy nose, another a missing tooth in his smile. You could write the name of each party guest along the front of each pixie's hat. Invite your guests to clip them onto their pockets or collars.

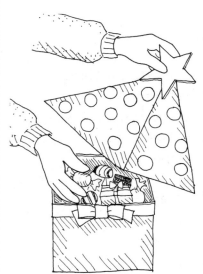# Peek Inside Christmas Tree

◆▸◆▸◆▸◆▸

This Christmas tree has gifts inside instead of under!

Make the base of your tree from the bottom half of a clean milk carton. Glue squares of felt onto it, and trim the edges with ribbons. Cut 4 triangles from thin cardboard that fit over the base. Cover them with green felt. Attach the sides of the triangles, underneath, with masking tape. Fold edges into a Christmas tree shape. This will be the lid for the base. Glue small colored felt circles on the tree to look like Christmas ornaments. Cut a star from cardboard, and cover it with gold foil. Glue the star to the top of your tree. Fill the base with treats or small gifts.

What You'll Need
- half-gallon milk carton
- colored felt
- glue
- ribbons
- thin cardboard
- blunt scissors
- masking tape
- gold foil
- treats or small gifts

Santa Light

Light up the holiday table or a window with this electric Santa.

What You'll Need
- paper bag
- pencil
- blunt scissors
- markers
- cotton balls
- glue
- flashlight
- clay
- saucer
- Santa hat
- tape

Flatten the bag along its creases and turn it so the opening faces you as you draw the face. Draw the outlines of Santa's eyes, nose, and mouth. Cut them out. Use markers to draw on his eyebrows, eyelashes, lips, and cheeks. Glue cotton balls on for hair, mustache, and beard. Stand the flashlight (beam facing up) in clay on a saucer. Put the bag over the flashlight, and add a Santa hat to the bag. When the light is turned on, Santa glows.

Glittering Gift Jewelry

Help someone sparkle this Christmas with beautiful homemade jewelry.

Draw and cut circles, hearts, Christmas trees, and star shapes out of cardboard. Drizzle glue on the shapes, and lay string in tight spirals or circles on the glue. Let the glue dry for several hours. Cover each shape with gold or silver foil, and glue it down in the back. Rub the foil so the string pattern shows through. Glue on gems in attractive designs. If you are making pins, glue a pin backing onto the back of each shape. If you want to make a medallion, tape a loop of thin wire onto the back of the shape; thread gold cord through the loop to make a necklace.

What You'll Need
- corrugated cardboard
- pencil
- blunt scissors
- glue
- string
- gold or silver foil
- flat-backed colored-glass gems
- jewelry pin backings
- tape
- thin wire
- gold cord

Santa Switch Plate

◆▷◆▷◆▷◆▷

Here comes Santa to switch on some fun!

Caution: This project requires adult help.

Draw a jolly Santa on a piece of sturdy cardboard. Make your Santa at least 6 inches tall and about 4 inches wide. Have an adult remove the switch plate. Ask the adult to use it for a guide to mark off the hole for the light switch in the middle of Santa's belly. Have the adult replace the switch plate. Cut out pieces of felt, and glue them onto your drawing. Make sure to leave the hole open for the light switch. Glue on cotton balls for Santa's beard and moustache.

When your Santa is dry, have an adult tape him to your light switch. Every time you give his tummy a tickle, the lights will turn on and off!

What You'll Need
- sturdy cardboard
- ruler
- pencil
- screwdriver
- felt
- blunt scissors
- glue
- cotton balls
- heavy-duty tape

Kwanza Party Favors

◆▷◆▷◆▷◆▷

Make a miniature flag favor for each person you invite to your karamu, or Kwanza celebration feast.

What You'll Need
- white construction paper
- ruler
- blunt scissors
- red, black, and green markers
- craft glue
- toothpicks

Cut small rectangles (about 1½×1 inches) from white paper. Color the top third of each rectangle red, the middle third black, and the bottom third green. Glue each of these flags to a toothpick pole by dabbing glue on the back edge of each square. Then roll the glued edge around a toothpick.

Stick the decorated toothpick in a cupcake or other food to make the flag stand up—and the goodies stand out!

Tie-Dye Party Napkins

◆▸◆▸◆▸◆▸

Make these interesting Kwanza napkins using a traditional African method of fabric dying.

What You'll Need
• wooden clothespin
• white cotton napkins
• string
• vegetable dyes in bowls
• blunt scissors

Wrap the clothespin with a white napkin, and wind string around it. Secure the ends of the string with a knot. Leaving the tip white, dip and dab your napkin in bowls of different-colored dye. You can wait for each color to dry before redipping if you wish or let the colors blend. When the entire napkin is dry, cut away the string and open up the napkin to see the design.

Animal Cracker Magnets

◆▸◆▸◆▸◆▸

Celebrating Kwanza may put you in the mood for an African safari.

Select the animal crackers you want to use. Gently color them with markers in the traditional African colors of red, green, and black. Make sure you don't press too hard while you color, unless you

What You'll Need
• animal crackers
• permanent markers
• clear nail polish
• magnetic strip
• blunt scissors
• glue

want to end up with a headless or tailless beast! Brush a light coat of clear nail polish over the colored crackers. Let dry. Turn crackers over, and coat the back of the beasts with nail polish; let dry. Cut a small piece of magnetic strip for each beast. Attach the magnet to the cracker with glue. Again, be careful when you press on the crackers. Stick your beautiful beasts to the refrigerator!

DEAR KIDS—
I'll BE BACK SOON.
DO YOUR HOMEWORK.
LOVE, MOM

Woven Kwanza Mat

◆◆◆◆◆◆◆

Make a **mkeka,** *one of the seven symbolic items of the African American Kwanza festival.*

What You'll Need
• black, green, and red construction paper
• blunt scissors
• ruler
• tape

The *mkeka* (a woven mat) is the Kwanza symbol of history. To weave a mkeka, cut parallel lines in a piece of black construction paper. Cut the lines starting 1 inch from the bottom edge to 1 inch from the top edge. To make cutting easier, fold the paper in half and cut starting from the middle going toward the edge.

Unfold your black "loom," and cut strips of red and green paper for weaving. Weave the strips of paper in and out of the black loom, alternating red and green strips. After weaving, secure the paper strips in place by taping the back of the mkeka. To make a more decorative mat, you can weave with colored ribbon instead of construction paper.

Sign My Kwanza Tablecloth

◆◆◆◆◆◆◆

Start your own Kwanza tradition with this tablecloth filled with memories and messages.

Decorate the center of your fabric with Kwanza symbols: corn, candles, African animals, silver goblets, the African flag, etc. At the Kwanza party, invite your guests to write their names, the date, and a special Kwanza message. The tablecloth can be brought out, reread, and added to each year.

What You'll Need
• flat twin-size bed sheet or white tablecloth
• fabric markers

Animal Anklet

◆▶▶▶▶▶▶▶

Decorate your ankle with wild beasts!

Roll the clay into grape-size balls. Make giraffes, monkeys, or anything else you want! Use a craft stick to form legs, ears, horns, and trunks. Carefully use small pieces of thin wire to make tails or tusks. Cautiously poke a needle through the back of each animal to make a hole for thread to pass through. Let the animals dry.

Paint the animals. When the paint is dry, brush with a coat of clear varnish or nail polish. Measure a length of wire that will fit comfortably around your ankle. Leave a little extra to make a hook and loop to open and close the anklet. String small beads onto the wire. Thread a needle with colored thread, and make a knot. Thread the needle through a small bead on the anklet and through one of your clay animals. Thread through a few more beads; tie the thread onto the anklet so that the animal hangs down. Repeat this process with the rest of your animals, tying them onto the anklet every inch or so.

What You'll Need
- self-hardening clay
- craft stick
- thin wire
- needle
- paints and paintbrush
- clear varnish or nail polish
- small plastic beads
- blunt scissors
- thread

Kwanza Bag

◆▶▶▶▶▶▶▶

This beautiful bag is a great gift—full or empty!

What You'll Need
- burlap
- blunt scissors
- tape measure
- embroidery thread
- needle
- ribbon or cord
- safety pin
- marker

Cut a 10×14-inch piece of burlap. Along the 14-inch side, fold the burlap down an inch to make a tube. Sew the bottom of this tube closed, leaving the sides open so you can thread a ribbon or cord through it for the bag's drawstring.

Tie the ribbon or cord to a safety pin, and thread it through the tube. Remove the safety pin, and make a knot in both ends of the cord. Use a marker to write the word *Kwanza* on the bag's front. Draw some decorative shapes or lines if you wish. Use embroidery thread to sew along the word *Kwanza* and whatever else you have drawn.

Then fold the bag in half so that the drawstring is at the top and the design is on the inside. Stitch the sides of the bag together, and turn the bag right side out. You can give the empty bag as a gift, or fill it with small toys or Kwanza treats.

Barotse Bowl

Make this traditional craft of the Barotse tribe of Zambia to hold Kwanza treats.

What You'll Need
- newspaper
- ruler
- large bowl
- liquid starch
- round, shallow plastic bowl with lid
- paper towels
- sandpaper
- dark brown paint
- paintbrush
- clear varnish

The Barotse people make beautifully carved wooden bowls to use in the home. To make one for your home, tear newspaper into 1- to 2-inch-wide strips. In a large bowl, soak the strips in liquid starch for 10 minutes. Take the lid off the shallow plastic bowl, and turn the bowl upside down. Paste the strips one by one onto both the bowl's bottom and lid's top until they are entirely covered. Let this layer of newspaper dry. Add three more layers of newspaper strips, letting each layer dry before applying another. Each time you add a layer, change the direction of the strips to make the bowl strong. Use paper towels soaked in starch to form 2 bird shapes. Attach the birds to the top of the lid with more starched paper towels. Let your bowl and lid dry for a couple of days. When ready, lightly sand the edges of the bowl and lid. Paint them dark brown to resemble dark wood. When the paint is dry, paint the bowl and lid with the varnish to seal them. These bowls make lovely gifts.

Kwanza Candle Surprise

◆▶◆▶◆▶

These "pretend" candles in red, green, and black are filled with surprises!
They make perfect party favors for your Kwanza celebration.

What You'll Need
- paper towel tubes
- blunt scissors
- black, red, or green construction paper
- craft glue
- orange or yellow tissue paper
- ruler
- individually wrapped candy
- nuts in the shell
- small prizes
- markers (optional)

Cut each tube in half. Then glue a piece of black, red, or green construction paper around each tube. Cut a 10-inch square of tissue paper, and place candy, nuts, and a small prize in the middle of the square. Gather the tissue paper up around the prize, and push the wrapped candy and prize into the tube so the ends of the tissue stick out like a candle flame. For party favors, make 1 for each person at your table. You could also write each person's name on a candle and use them for name cards for dinner!

 # African Gold Weights

◆▶◆▶◆▶

This ancient form of African money makes a nifty, glittery Kwanza gift!

Caution: This project requires adult help.

To make the clay, mix the salt into the hot water. Ask an adult to help you so you don't burn yourself. When the mixture cools, add 1 cup of flour, and mix until smooth. Add another cup of flour and continue to mix with a spoon. Add the last 1½ to 2 cups flour by kneading the clay with your hands. If the clay is sticky, add more flour. If it is dry, add a little more water, a few drops at a time. Ask an adult to preheat the oven to 300 degrees.

When your clay is ready, roll it flat with a rolling pin on a floured counter. Use a craft stick to draw the outline of each animal; each should be 3 or 4 inches long. For instance, to make a snake, roll a rope and coil it around. Use a spatula to lift the animals off the counter and place them on a cookie sheet. Bake the animals for 30 minutes. When cool, paint the animals gold.

What You'll Need
- 1 cup salt
- 1½ cups hot water
- mixing bowl
- mixing spoon
- 3½ to 4 cups flour
- measuring cup
- rolling pin
- craft stick
- ruler
- spatula
- cookie sheet
- gold paint
- paintbrush

New Year's Garland

Make these lacy garlands out of colored paper, and string them up in your home when it's time to celebrate the New Year.

What You'll Need
- colored construction paper or tissue paper
- blunt scissors
- ruler
- craft glue or glue stick

Cut out twelve 4-inch circles from colored paper. Fold each circle in half, in half again, and finally in half a third time. It should now look like a slice of pie. Cut out a series of small snips from both folded edges. Unfold the snipped circles.

Apply glue along the edge of a circle. (If you are using construction paper, use craft glue; if you are using tissue paper, use a glue stick.) Place a second circle on top of the first so that the edges stick together. Apply glue to the center of the second circle, and place a third circle on top of it. Continue adding the remaining circles, alternately gluing the edges and the centers. When the glue is dry, gently pull the top and bottom circle in opposite directions.

Hang the stretched garland for your New Year's celebration!

Celebrating the New Year

People in the United States celebrate the New Year by throwing confetti into the air. In China, long, lacy garlands decorate the streets for the New Year.

Family Facts

◆▶▶▶▶▶▶

***Who's got the best memory in the family? Test everyone on
Trivia Day (January 4)!***

What You'll Need
- prewritten short descriptions of family experiences and facts on index cards
- white paper
- markers
- timer

Gather up Mom, Dad, and all the kids to play this fun family trivia game. Divide family members into two teams. Each team then writes down 20 short descriptions of experiences or facts related to the family, such as "Ben's high school graduation" or "Nick hates carrots" on index cards. Teams trade their stacks of index cards but can't look at them. Players on each team take turns choosing an index card from their stack and trying to draw it so the rest of the team members can guess what the card says before the timer goes off. Decide as a group how long you want to set the timer for.

Remember, you want to give people enough time to draw and make guesses, but you also want to keep the game exciting!

T-Shirt of Trivia

◆▶▶▶▶▶▶

On Trivia Day, keep them guessing when you wear this puzzling shirt!

What You'll Need
- research books
- white T-shirt
- fabric markers

Trivia Day is a celebration of little-known facts. For every subject in the world, there are tons of trivia! What is your favorite subject? Animal? Music? Sport? Dig up some interesting facts by reading encyclopedias and other informative books

on the topic. Then form questions about the facts you learned. Write the questions on a T-shirt using fabric markers. Write them in interesting patterns on the shirt. Some should be in very tiny letters and others in large letters. For one question, use a combination of words with large letters and words with small letters. Try different types of handwriting. Then challenge your friends to answer the questions on your shirt!

Three Tiny Kings

◆▶◆▶◆▶◆

Make these kings who are no bigger than a thumb for Epiphany!

See if you can find three different nail polish bottles to make your kings. Make sure that they are either empty or that no one will mind if they are turned into little kings! Glue layers of felt onto the body of each bottle to make the kings' robes. Use different colors for each king. Cut and glue ribbons and other trim to the robes to make each one fancy. Paint each bottle top with gold paint. Let paint dry. Pull a thin strip of cotton from a cotton ball, and glue it to the top of the robe to make a fur collar for each king. Cut a small circle of felt to make a face for each king. Draw eyes, nose, mouth, and hair with markers. Glue each face to the bottle, above the fur collar. Try to make each king look wise!

What You'll Need
- 3 empty nail polish bottles with tops
- felt scraps in assorted colors
- glue
- blunt scissors
- ribbons and trim scraps
- gold paint
- paintbrush
- cotton balls
- fine-tipped markers

Star Trivet

◆▶◆▶◆▶◆

Make this beautiful star to protect your table from hot pots.

What You'll Need
- corrugated cardboard
- pencil
- blunt scissors
- glue
- paintbrush
- silver foil
- many metal soda bottle caps
- silver paint

The three Magi were guided by a star. Keep a guiding star in your kitchen all year 'round. Draw and cut a large star from cardboard. Paint the star with a thin layer of glue, and wrap it with foil until it is entirely covered. Glue bottle caps in rows, with the flat side up, to the front of the star. When the glue has dried, paint the bottle caps silver. The star trivet also makes a nice decoration when you are not using it.

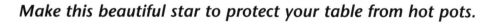

Pop-Me Thank You

◆▶◆▶◆▶◆▶

Burst out with big thanks to someone you love on Thank You Day (January 11).

What You'll Need
- paper
- pen
- fabric ribbon
- balloon
- curling ribbon
- permanent marker

On a small piece of paper, write a thank-you message to the person you want to thank. Roll the paper into a scroll, and tie it with a bit of ribbon. Carefully insert the scroll into the balloon. Blow up the balloon, tie it off, and tie curling ribbon to the end of the balloon. Carefully write "Pop Me" in big letters on the balloon with a marker, deliver the balloon to the person you want to thank, and wait for the bang! (Discard balloon pieces promptly—they are choking hazards for small children.)

Martin's Match Game

◆▶◆▶◆▶◆▶

Use the facts you learn about Dr. King to play a matching game on Dr. Martin Luther King, Jr., Day (on the third Monday in January).

Find out more facts about Dr. King to use in this concentration-type game. Divide 32 index cards into 4 groups. Mark the backs of one group "Open Doors." Mark the backs of the second group "Closed Doors." Mark the backs of the third group with positive situations, including "Peaceful march on Selma." Mark the backs of

What You'll Need
- 32 index cards
- markers
- research books

the fourth group with obstacles, including "Must pay poll tax to vote." Turn all the cards face down and try to match "Open Door" cards with positive situations and "Closed Door" cards with obstacles. If no match is made, the cards are turned face down again. The player with the most matches wins. By the time you are through playing this game, you will be an expert on the extraordinary life of Dr. Martin Luther King, Jr.!

Peace Medals

◄►◄►◄►◄►

Award a medal of peace to a peace-loving friend.

What You'll Need

- 1 cup salt
- 1½ cups hot water
- mixing bowl
- mixing spoon
- 3½ to 4 cups flour
- measuring cup
- rolling pin
- ruler
- drinking glass
- cookie sheet
- gold or silver paint
- paintbrush
- markers
- glue
- glitter
- ribbons
- scissors
- pin backs (optional)

Caution: This project requires adult help.

Honor Dr. King's love of peace by awarding medals to family and friends who have shown great patience or thoughtfulness or who have been helpful in resolving a conflict.

To make the clay: Stir the salt into the hot water. Ask an adult to help with the hot water; be careful that you don't burn yourself. When the mixture cools, add 1 cup flour. Mix until smooth. Add another cup of flour, and continue to mix with a spoon. Add the last 1½ to 2 cups of flour by kneading the clay with your hands. If the clay is sticky, add more flour. If it is dry, add a little more water. Have an adult preheat the oven to 300 degrees.

When your clay is just right for shaping, form a 3-inch ball and roll it out on a floured counter with the rolling pin. Press the rim of a drinking glass onto the flattened clay to cut out a circle. Continue doing this until you have cut out all the medals you want to bake.

Bake the medals on a cookie sheet for 30 minutes. When they cool, paint them gold or silver. When the paint is dry, write messages on them with markers, such as "World Peace." Drizzle glue around the edges, and sprinkle the glue with glitter. Cut two 5-inch pieces of ribbon, and glue them to the back of each medal when they are dry. Glue the pin backs to the medals or a piece of ribbon long enough to fit over your head. Have you done your part for peace? Give yourself a medal!

Peaceful Puppets

❖▶❖▶❖▶

For Dr. Martin Luther King, Jr., Day, why not let these cute puppets bring peace into everyone's hearts?

What You'll Need
- felt
- blunt scissors
- fabric marker
- old colorful socks
- fabric glue
- yarn

It's easy to put on a puppet show about friendship and equality! To make the puppets, cut out 3 circles from felt. Make 2 the same size and 1 slightly smaller. Draw a peace sign on each circle. Glue the larger circles on the toe of a sock to make the eyes and the smaller one below to make the nose of your puppet. Glue on yarn for hair, and cut out a smile from more felt to make the mouth. You can also cut out neckties and buttons or bows from the felt and glue these on, too. Cut 2 small holes on either side of the sock so your fingers can fit through to become the puppet's arms. Then put on a play about peace!

Freedom March Game

❖▶❖▶❖▶

Learn the facts of Dr. King's life while playing a game.

Use research books to learn facts about Dr. King's life. Tape long pieces of poster board together, and draw a winding road of 15 to 20 squares on it. The first square can be marked with the word "Start" and information about Dr. King's birthplace and birth date. The rest of the squares have either "Open Door" or "Closed Door" written in them. The last square is marked "Freedom."

What You'll Need
- research books
- long pieces of poster board
- tape
- markers
- die
- buttons

The Open Doors should also be marked with different successes that Dr. King enjoyed in his fight for freedom, including "Supreme Court declared segregation on buses unconstitutional." The Closed Doors should be marked with setbacks, such as "Dr. King's home bombed." Take turns tossing a die and moving your buttons the number of squares shown on the die. If you land on an "Open Door," you stay there. If you land on a Closed Door, you must go back to Start. The first person to reach "Freedom" wins the game.

Peace Plane

◀◆◀◆◀◆▶

Fly a flock of peaceful doves.

Bring peace into your house and the sky above it with these easy-to-make paper doves. Fold an 8×11-inch piece of white paper in half. Draw the side-view of a dove as shown. Cut off the extra

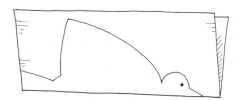

paper around the outline of the dove and its wing. Fold each wing down to make an airplane shape. You can write a peaceful message or quote from Martin Luther King, Jr., such as "I Have a Dream" inside the dove. Let peace fly!

I Have a Dream

◀◆◀◆◀◆▶

Dr. Martin Luther King, Jr., had a dream for his country. What are your dreams for the future?

On January 18, the United States celebrates the vision of Dr. Martin Luther King, Jr. Personalize his message by making your own list of dreams. Use markers or colored pencils to write your dreams on a piece of drawing paper. Some of your dreams may be serious, and some may be silly.

Draw a picture to illustrate each dream you write down. If one of your dreams is for clean air, water, and earth, then draw the world. After you have written down your dreams, display them on a scroll by taping a wood dowel to each edge of the paper.

Lunar New Year Garden

◆◆◆▶▶◀◆◆◆

Plant a narcissus bulb so that it flowers in time for the Chinese Lunar New Year.

What You'll Need
- narcissus bulb
- bowl
- pebbles
- watering can or pitcher
- hyacinth bulb (optional)
- glass (optional)
- paper (optional)
- tape (optional)

The Chinese New Year is celebrated on the first day of the first lunar month (sometime in January or February). The narcissus is a traditional New Year's flower in China; it symbolizes good luck. Start your New Year's garden 4 to 5 weeks before the lunar new year. To "force" the narcissus to bloom early, put pebbles in a shallow bowl. Set the narcissus bulb in the pebbles with the pointy side up. Place the bulb in a sunny window, and make sure the bulb always has water. Flowers will blossom in 4 to 5 weeks. A hyacinth bulb can also be forced to blossom by setting it in a glass of water, with the pointy side up, so that the bottom is sitting in the water. Make a cone-shaped hat to cover the tip. Keep the bulb in a cool place for 8 weeks, making sure it always has enough water. After 8 weeks, move it to a warm spot and watch it bloom.

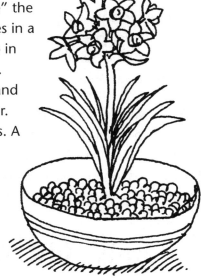

Luck Lantern

◆◆◆▶▶◀◆◆◆

Put this lantern out on the night of the first new moon of the Chinese New Year.

Caution: This project requires adult help.

Good Luck Symbol

Remove the label, and wash and dry the can. Draw the Chinese character for luck on the can with permanent marker, either four times evenly spaced or many times in smaller characters. Leave the lower ¼ of the can blank. Fill the can with water, and freeze. When the water is frozen, take the can from the freezer, and (with adult help) use the hammer and a nail to punch holes to outline the characters. If the ice starts to melt, put the can back in the freezer until it is solid again. When the holes are all punched, let the ice melt. Fill the bottom of the can ¼ full of sand. Put the candle in the sand.

What You'll Need
- empty soup can
- permanent marker
- water
- hammer
- nail
- sand
- small red candle

New Year's Drum

◆▶◆▶◆▶◆

Gong xi fa cai! (It's pronounced Kung hsi fa tsai!) That's how you say "Happy New Year" in the Mandarin Chinese dialect.

What You'll Need
- margarine tub
- craft knife
- large red balloon
- blunt scissors
- large rubber band
- wooden spoons

Caution: This project requires adult help.

Red is considered a very lucky color on the Chinese New Year. Make yourself a red New Year's drum so that you will have it for the Lion Dance or the Dragon Dance!

Have an adult use the craft knife to cut the bottom off the clean margarine tub. Blow up the balloon, then let all the air out of the balloon. Slit the side of the

balloon with scissors, and stretch the rubber over the top of the tub. (Keep balloons away from small children; balloons are choking hazards!) Wrap the rubber band around the rim of the tub to hold the balloon in place. Use wooden spoons to beat the drum.

 # Golden Dragon Puppet

◆▶◆▶◆▶◆

This Golden Dragon has a special trick—make and wear it to find out!

Cut across one of the ties about 15 inches above the point for the dragon's body. Cut the narrow end off both ties 4 inches from the narrow point for the dragon's ears. Use a sponge to press gold fabric paint onto the tie. Let dry. For the dragon's whiskers, glue 2 pieces of red yarn to the point at the wide end of the tie. Cut and glue 2 black felt triangles for the dragon's nose. Cut and glue the dragon's eyes out of white and blue

What You'll Need
- 2 old solid-color neckties
- blunt scissors
- ruler
- gold fabric paint
- sponge
- red yarn
- glue
- felt scraps
- 2 safety pins

felt. Cut and glue the dragon's fangs out of white felt. Make 2 small slits in the tie about 2 inches above the eyes. These slits should be just big enough for the gathered end of the ears to fit in. Pin the ears to the body, hiding the pins in the ear folds.

Frozen Fireworks

The Chinese invented fireworks! Make tissue-paper "fireworks" to celebrate the Chinese New Year.

What You'll Need

- 2 pieces of graph paper
- ruler
- 4 to 6 pieces of colored tissue paper
- glue stick
- poster board
- blunt scissors
- stapler and staples
- paper clip

1. Stack 2 pieces of graph paper. Accordion-fold them along the lines into ¾-inch folds.

2. Unfold and place 4 to 6 pieces of tissue paper between the graph paper; refold to make fold marks in the tissue.

3. Take a piece of folded tissue, and put a line of glue on the inside edge of the first fold. Take the next piece of tissue paper, and place the inside edge of the first fold over the glued edge. Continue in the same way with all the sheets of paper, making one long, continuous pleated sheet.

4. Cut 2 pieces of poster board that are the same length as the tissue sheets but half as wide as the folded edge. Completely cover one side of each poster board with glue. Glue one on top of your stack of tissue and the other on the bottom. At the very top edge, staple the pieces of poster board together (with tissue between). Let the glue dry.

5. Draw fireworks patterns on the edge of the tissue paper. Cut out.

6. Spread fireworks until the poster board sides are back-to-back. Fasten with a paper clip.

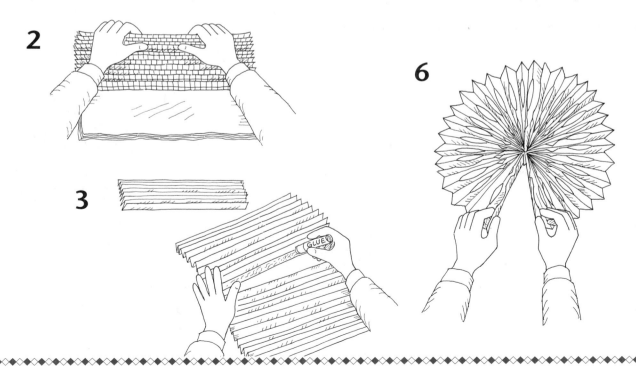

 # Lion Mask

◆▶◆▶◆▶◆▶

*On the third day of the Chinese New Year the Lion Dance begins. Some people
believe putting money in the lion's mouth will bring them luck!*

What You'll Need

- newspaper
- paper plate
- blunt scissors
- stapler and staples
- 2 paper egg-carton
  sections
- tape
- ½ cup white glue
- ½ cup water
- large mixing bowl
- mixing spoon
- tempera paint
- paintbrush
- beads
- sequins
- feathers
- ribbon scraps

1. Cover your work surface. Cut a slit in each side of the paper
plate. Pull the edges of each slit together, and overlap them. Staple
the edges together. This will bend the plate into a face shape.

2. Tape on the egg-carton sections for bulgy eyes. Make a fist-size
ball of newspaper, and tape it in place for the lion's snout. Crumple
up some newspaper, and put it under the mask so it will keep its
form while you work.

3. Tear 7 to 8 newspaper pages into strips. Mix the white glue with
the water in a large mixing bowl. Soak the newspaper strips in the
mixture. When you take the strips out of the mixture, run them
between your fingers to remove the excess liquid. Cover the mask
front with a layer of newspaper strips. Let the mask dry overnight.

4. Add a second layer of strips; smooth the strips over the mask
with your fingers. Let the mask dry overnight.

5. Paint the mask with 2 coats of red tempera paint. Let dry.

6. Paint on the lion's mouth; decorate the mask with beads,
sequins, and feathers. Tape a loop of ribbon to the back of the
mask to hang it on your wall.

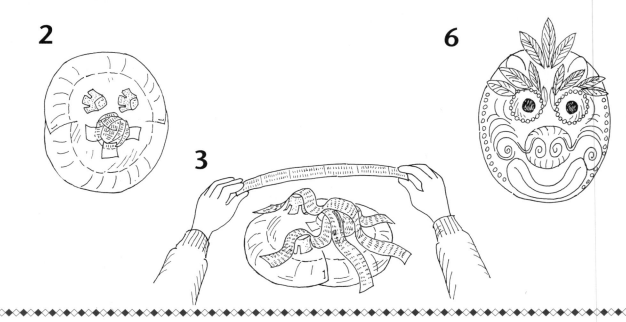

2

3

6

Groundhog Day Shadow Investigation

◆▶◆▶◆▶◆▶

Never celebrated Groundhog Day? Here's a way to make the day special.

What You'll Need
- stiff paper
- ruler
- pencil
- crayons
- blunt scissors
- masking tape
- flashlight

Celebrate Groundhog Day by investigating shadows with a flashlight and a stand-up groundhog drawing. The traditional tale about this day is that the groundhog wakes from his winter hibernation on February 2 (the midpoint of winter) and comes out of his hole. The groundhog is then supposed to take a peek around. If he sees his shadow, it means there will be 6 more weeks of winter cold. If he does not, warm weather is on the way. Though the tale is popular, it is not scientifically accurate! But you can still take advantage of the holiday to learn something about shadow casting.

On a piece of stiff paper, draw a horizontal line about 1½ inches from the bottom for a ground line. Draw a groundhog sitting on the ground line. Color your groundhog, and cut off the excess paper around his outline (but don't cut along the ground line). Fold the bottom of the paper on the ground line so that the bottom becomes a base for a stand-up groundhog. Tape the base to the floor. Darken the room, and shine a flashlight at the groundhog from different angles. Notice what happens to the groundhog's shadow as you change the angle and distance of the light you shine on it.

 # Hidden Shadow Collage Game

◆▶◆▶◆▶◆▶

Race to find the groundhog's shadow for Groundhog Day (February 2) in these tricky collages.

What You'll Need
• old magazines
• blunt scissors
• construction paper
• glue

Have everyone make a board. Cut lots of pictures out of magazines (be sure to ask for permission first!). Glue them onto a piece of construction paper so they completely cover it. Cut out a small groundhog from brown construction paper and another out of black for the shadow. Glue them onto your collage. Now make flaps. To make a flap, cut a small square from a magazine page that will completely cover one of the objects in your collage. Glue down one edge of the flap onto your collage. Continue doing this all over your collage. Let the glue dry. When the flap is lifted, the object is revealed. To play the game, the players exchange boards. When start is called, the players race to find the groundhog and its shadow. If they tear a flap, they lose the game.

 # Four Score Game

◆▶◆▶◆▶◆▶

Even on Abraham Lincoln's birthday (February 12), you don't have to be a president to enjoy this game.

Give each player one sports or stock market page from the newspaper. Set the timer for 5 minutes, and yell "Start." Each player must put a colored dot on every number 4 that they find on their page. Players call out "4 Score" each time they find a 4. The player who has found the most 4s when the timer rings is the winner.

What You'll Need
• sports and/or stock market page of a newspaper for each player
• colored markers
• timer

Lincoln Ring

◆◆◆◆◆◆

Keep President Lincoln at your fingertips all day long.

Cut a thin strip of cardboard long enough to go around your finger; the strip should be a little wider than a penny. Paint the strip with a pretty design. Glue the shiny penny to the front. When the glue is dry, have a friend tape the ring closed on your finger with a small piece of colored tape. Wear the ring on Lincoln's birthday—make sure you do a lot of waving so everyone can enjoy your presidential jewel!

What You'll Need
- thin cardboard
- blunt scissors
- shiny penny
- paint and paintbrush
- glue
- colored tape

Valentine Ideas

◆◆◆◆◆◆

Valentine's Day is a time to say you care about others. Show them how much with these heartfelt ideas.

What You'll Need
- doilies
- blunt scissors
- red and white construction paper
- craft glue
- glitter
- satin ribbon
- craft stick
- plastic sandwich bag (optional)
- Valentine candy (optional)

Doily Cards: Cut heart shapes from doilies, and glue them on red and white construction paper hearts. Use glue to write "Be Mine" on the doily. Cover the glue with glitter. Tie satin ribbon in small bows, and glue them on the doily cards. Once the glue has dried, shake off the excess glitter.

Heart & Arrow Cards: Cut a heart shape from red construction paper. Cut a smaller heart from white construction paper, and glue it on top of the red heart. Make an arrow from a craft stick and construction paper; glue the paper to the craft stick. Glue the arrow to the hearts. Write a valentine message for someone special.

If you want, attach a plastic sandwich bag filled with valentine candy to let your valentine know just how sweet he or she is!

Birch Bark Valentines

❖❖❖❖❖❖

Make special valentines out of natural treasures and your own verse.

What You'll Need

- thin birch bark (use only fallen or loose bark that is peeling off naturally)
- collected natural objects (flowers, rocks, twigs, leaves, etc.)
- pen
- ribbon

Caution: This project requires adult supervision.

With an adult, find a paper birch tree with thin strips of bark that have fallen or are already peeling off. Tear off only what you will use. Be careful not to tear off living bark—you could harm the tree!

Next, take an adult with you on a walk in a park, woodland, or other place where you can find early flowers, feathers, or evergreen twigs. With permission, collect a few natural treasures that you think are pretty. Lay your treasures out at home, and let them inspire a valentine poem. Evergreen twigs may make you think of a friendship that is "ever green." Flowers may stand for a blossoming friendship.

When you have composed your poem, write it on the piece of birch bark. Roll the bark around the feathers, flowers, or whatever objects you have used in your verse. Tie the valentine with a ribbon, and surprise someone on Valentine's Day—or any special day!

Valentine Holder

❖❖❖❖❖❖

Make a valentine holder that looks like a miniature castle.

Cover your work surface with newspaper. Arrange your box or boxes how you would like them to be. Cut the paper towel tubes to different lengths, and arrange them on your boxes. For a castle, use a large tissue box for the main building, then put paper towel rolls on the ends for turrets. When you are happy with the arrangement, it's time to decorate your architecture!

Cut a slit in the top of the main box to place your Valentine's Day cards. Glue construction paper to cover the box(es) and the paper towel tubes. Re-place your box(es) and paper towel tubes, and glue them together. Decorate your building with paint, glitter, stickers, ribbon—whatever you want!

What You'll Need

- newspaper
- tissue box(es)
- paper towel tubes
- blunt scissors
- construction paper
- craft glue
- craft supplies (paint, paintbrush, glitter, stickers, ribbon, etc.)

Valentine's Day Heart Wreath

◆▶◆▶◆▶◆▶

Cover a paper plate with cut-out hearts in various sizes and colors (maybe reds and pinks) for a terrific Valentine's Day decoration!

What You'll Need
- construction paper
- blunt scissors
- ruler
- paper plate
- yarn or ribbon
- craft glue

From the construction paper, cut out hearts in several different sizes (½ inch, 1 inch, 1½ inches, and 2 inches are good sizes). You can choose a color theme (pink and white hearts), or you can make a multi-colored heart wreath. You'll want to cut out a lot of hearts.

Cut the middle out of a paper plate, and throw the middle away. Glue the hearts over the remaining plate to make a valentine wreath. Make small bows with yarn or ribbon, and glue them to the wreath. Make a loop out of yarn or ribbon, and glue it on the back to hang your wreath.

Caramel Nut Sweets

◆▶◆▶◆▶◆▶

Everyone will go nuts for these delicious sweets!

Caution: This project requires adult help.

Ask an adult to preheat the oven to 325 degrees. Grease a cookie sheet, and arrange pecan halves to make the petals of a flower. Put 1 unwrapped caramel candy in the center of each flower. Bake for 5 minutes or until caramels have melted. Grease a metal spatula, and use it to carefully spread the softened caramel over the pecans to coat them. Place the candies on waxed paper. When the candies are cool, wrap them in foil, and give them as Valentine's Day treats.

What You'll Need
- margarine or butter for greasing
- 2 cups pecan halves
- 14-ounce bag of caramels
- cookie sheet
- metal spatula
- waxed paper
- colored foil

Blown-Egg Sachet

◆◆◆◆◆◆

Treat your loved one's nose with this sweetly scented gift on Valentine's Day.

Caution: This project requires adult help.

Ask an adult to help you make the blown egg for your sachet. Stick a hat pin into the top of a raw egg. Carefully dig away tiny pieces of shell to make an opening ⅛ inch wide. Use the pin to stir the egg inside to break the yolk so it can be blown out. Make a tiny hole in the other end of the egg. Blow through the smallest hole so that the egg's insides come out. Make sure you are holding the egg over a bowl while you blow. When the egg is empty, carefully run water through it to clean out the rest of the egg. Let the egg dry. Dip a small piece of cotton in scented oil, and carefully insert the cotton into the egg. Poke more tiny holes in the egg, and insert miniature flowers. Use paint or markers to draw hearts around the flowers. For the base, decorate the egg carton cup red or pink, turn it upside-down, and glue the sachet egg onto it. Happy sniffing!

Valentine's Day Pins

◆▷◆▷◆▷◆

These heart-shaped pins are simple to make. Once you wear one, everyone will want one of their own!

What You'll Need

- dough (1 cup flour, 1 cup warm water, 2 teaspoons cream of tartar, 1 teaspoon oil, ¼ cup salt, food coloring)
- mixing bowl
- mixing spoon
- saucepan
- pot holder
- waxed paper
- heart-shaped cookie cutter
- ¼ cup flour
- cotton swabs (optional)
- pin backs
- craft glue
- paint and paintbrush (optional)
- clear varnish (optional)

Caution: This project requires adult help.

Mix all the dough ingredients, adding the food coloring last. Ask an adult to help you stir this over medium heat on the stove until smooth. Remove the mixture from the pan, and knead it until it is well blended. (Have an adult check to make sure the dough is cool enough to handle!)

To make the valentine pins, use your hands to work the dough on waxed paper until the dough is about ¼ inch thick. Dip the cookie cutter in flour to prevent the dough from sticking, and cut out a heart. If you'd like to personalize the pins, stick the end of a cotton swab in food coloring and write a name on the heart. You can also add other decorations to the pin.

Press the pin back into the heart while the dough is still damp. Allow the pin to dry for a day. (Add a few drops of glue if the pin back isn't stuck well in the dough.) You can paint or apply clear varnish to your heart after it is thoroughly dry.

Queen of Stolen Hearts Game

◆▶◆▶◆▶◆

Be quick and outsmart the Queen—steal her hearts!

What You'll Need
- construction paper
- clear tape
- blunt scissors
- fake jewels
- glitter
- glue
- cardboard tube
- foil
- crepe paper or ribbons
- chair
- tape player, CD player, or radio (optional)

Make a queen's crown out of a band of construction paper that has been taped together at the ends. Cut out and tape triangular shapes around the band to make the crown's points. Glue on fake jewels and glitter. Cover a cardboard tube with foil. Form a ball out of foil, and tape it onto the top of the tube to make the queen's scepter. Tape on crepe paper streamers or ribbons to the other end. Decorate a chair with ribbons and more foil to make a throne. Cut out large hearts from red construction paper.

Now you are ready to play the Stolen Hearts Game. The large hearts are the bases. One person is chosen to be the Queen and sit on the throne. The other players are the Knaves, and they stand on the heart bases. Whoever is left without a heart is the Court Fool. She or he must try to steal a heart whenever the Queen raises her scepter and says "All change hearts." Whoever is left without a heart to stand on must be the new Fool. Players can take turns being the Queen. For variety, the Queen can turn on a tape player, CD player, or the radio when she wants the Knaves to change places; she turns it off when she wants them to grab a heart.

Flowers of Love
The colors of flowers have been used as codes on valentines since they were first sent in the 1400s. Red flowers mean "Our love will last forever." Pink flowers mean "Our love is dying." White flowers mean "Our love is gone."

Chenille Stem Pup

❖▶▶▶▶▶▶▶

This adorable puppy will make your valentine want to bark with delight!

What You'll Need
- red construction paper
- blunt scissors
- ruler
- 3 red chenille stems
- glue
- 2 small wiggle eyes
- marker

Cut a 2×3-inch strip of red construction paper. Hold the 3 chenille stems together so that the ends are even. Roll the paper strip around the middle of the chenille stems. Glue the paper closed. Bend one stem at each end to make the puppy's neck and tail. Curl the tail up so it looks like a little hook. Bend the remaining stems down to make the puppy's feet. Cut a small heart shape out of construction paper to make the puppy's head. Cut out 2 smaller heart shapes to make the puppy's ears; glue them to the larger heart. Glue on the wiggle eyes, and draw a nose and mouth. Glue the head to the puppy's neck. Give your puppy a name, and deliver it to a lucky valentine!

Brokenhearted Puzzle

◀▶▶▶▶▶▶

Tell your valentine to put this broken heart together to get a sweet message.

What You'll Need
- construction paper
- pencil
- blunt scissors
- thin cardboard
- glue
- markers
- envelope

Draw and cut out a large construction-paper heart. Glue it onto a piece of thin cardboard, and cut around the heart when the glue is dry. Write a message in large letters on the heart. Some ideas for messages are: "I Went to Pieces," "Together Forever," or "How Do You Mend a Broken Heart?" You may want to decorate your message and the rest of the heart with pretty designs and colors, maybe with tiny hearts, bluebirds, flowers, and small cupids. When you are finished, cut the heart into several pieces, and put the pieces into a pretty, decorated envelope. Give your broken-heart message puzzle to someone you love for a really special Valentine's Day card.

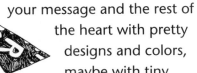

Flying Cupid Mobile

◆◆◆◆◆◆

Flying high over a Valentine's party, or just in your room, watch out for this cupid! He might help someone steal your heart!

What You'll Need
- pencil
- paper
- blunt scissors
- light cardboard
- black fine-tipped marker
- colored markers
- large needle
- clear nylon thread
- dowel

Use cupid's body and wings from this book as a pattern to draw your own. Cut out the paper patterns, and use them to trace the parts onto the cardboard. Mark where the holes for the thread will be with a dot. Cut out the cardboard wings and body. Carefully push the needle through the dots to make holes. Color cupid's body, draw feathers on the wings, and use a black fine-tipped marker to make his eyes and mouth. Sew the wings to the body. Attach a long piece of nylon thread to each of the outside holes on the wings. Tie these threads to the dowel, as shown. Hang up your mobile. Poke cupid's tummy, and watch him fly!

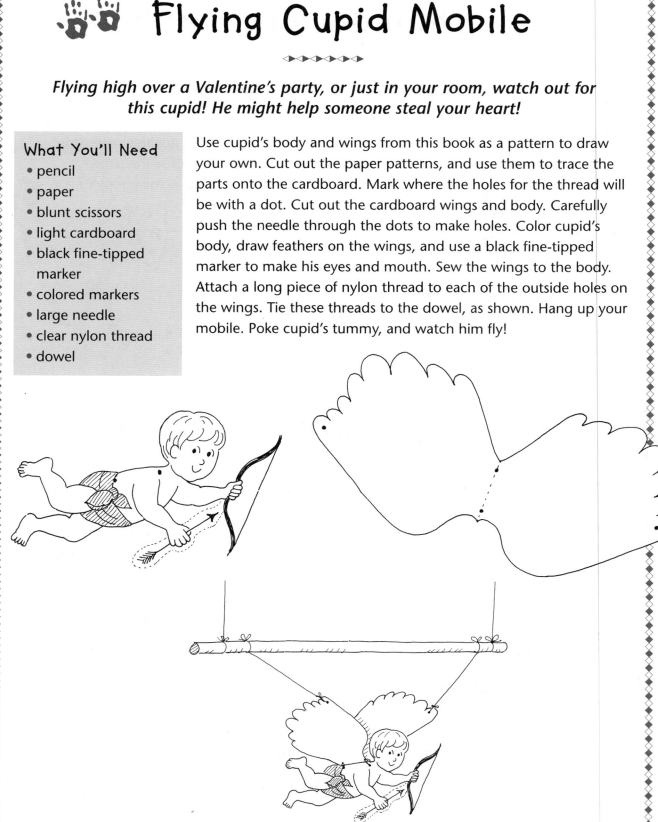

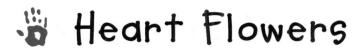

Heart Flowers

♦►♦►♦►♦►►

Give your valentine colorful flowers, even in the middle of winter.

To make the stems of your flowers, twist 2 green chenille stems together. You can make some chenille stems longer by laying them end to end and twisting the ends together. You may want some flowers to be longer than others to give your bouquet more variety.

Cut 2 same-size hearts out of construction paper. You will need 2 hearts for each flower you want to make. Cut each set of hearts different sizes. Staple the hearts front to back around the stem so that the chenille stem is held tightly in place. Then decorate the hearts with markers and by gluing on 1 or 2 tiny candy message hearts. Tie ribbons in bows around the stems, gather the bunch of heart flowers, and wrap them in a tissue-paper cone. Tie the cone with more ribbons to keep the flowers together. Present your heart flowers to your beloved or a special friend!

Rebus Valentine

♦►♦►♦►♦►►

Send your Valentine message in rebus writing, and challenge your friends to figure out the meanings of the picture sentences!

First figure out your Valentine message. Rebus writing uses pictures, objects, or symbols that have names that sound like the words you want to express. To write a rebus message, first write your Valentine greeting on scrap paper. Then figure out pictures and letters you

can use to come up with the sounds for each word. There are many different ways to represent any word. Use your creativity to come up with fun and original pictures for each word of your

message, and then put your friends to the test! For example, "You are the apple of my eye" can be written using a picture of a *ewe* for the word *you,* the letter *R* for the word *are,* a picture of an apple for *apple,* the letter *M* + a picture of an eye for *my,* and a picture of an eye for *eye.* "I like you!" can be written: picture of an eye for *I,* the letter *L* + a picture of a bike – the letter *B* for like, and the letter *U* for *you.* "Be mine!" can be written: picture of a bee for *be,* and the letter *M* + the number *9* – the letter *N* for *mine.*

Swinging Valentine Puppet

◆◇◆◇◆◇◆

This heart-shaped puppet will show you a swinging good time!

What You'll Need

- red construction paper
- blunt scissors
- ruler
- 4 large colored rubber bands
- glue
- stapler and staples
- markers

Cut 2 same-size hearts out of red construction paper. Make sure they are big enough for your hand to fit inside. Cut four 1-inch hearts to use as the puppet's hands and feet. Cut each rubber band to form a long elastic string. Glue the rubber bands to one of the large hearts to make arms and legs (glue 2 at the top sides and 2 at the bottom sides). Staple the 2 large hearts together (with the glued rubber bands on the inside). Remember to leave enough room

for your hand to fit inside. Glue a small heart to each of the loose ends of the rubber bands. Draw a face on your puppet with markers. If you have made several, draw different expressions to make characters for a Valentine's Day play.

Special Valentines

◆◇◆◇◆◇◆

Have you ever sent a secret valentine? It can be even more fun when your secret valentine has a secret meaning!

When paper valentines were first sent in the 1400s, each valentine carried a code. If you sent your sweetheart a valentine with a ribbon on it, that meant "My heart is tied to you." If the valentine had a fan on it, that meant "Open your heart to me." Lace and net are the same word in Latin, so a valentine with a ruffle of lace meant "You have caught my heart in a net." Make your own cards with your own codes. Use colored paper, markers, ribbons, lace, hard candies, and anything else you can think up. Do you think your valentine is sweet? Glue on hard candy as part of your design. You don't have to tell your valentine what your code means!

What You'll Need

- colored paper
- markers
- ribbons
- lace
- hard candies
- glue

"Heart of Gold" Picture Frame

◆▷◆▷◆▷◆▶

Put yourself in someone's heart forever!

Draw and cut out a heart-shaped piece of cardboard to make the frame. You can make your frame big or small, depending on the size of the photo you want to put in it. In the inside of your heart, draw and cut out a smaller heart that is big enough for your photo. Be sure the important part of the photo is visible inside the heart shape. Wind the gold raffia around the frame, going from the outside of the frame in through the middle and then around to the outside again. Cover the frame completely. Secure the ends of raffia on the back of the frame with glue. Place the frame on another piece of cardboard, and trace its outline. Cut the outline out just inside the line to make the back a little smaller than the front. Using the raffia heart as a guide for placement, glue your photo (ask for permission first) to the backing heart. Glue the backing heart to the back of the raffia frame. Using the pattern shown above as a guide, draw and cut out a cardboard stand to fit your frame. Glue it to the back of your frame. It's a golden gift!

What You'll Need
- cardboard
- pencil
- blunt scissors
- gold raffia
- glue
- photo

Love Potion Number Nine

◆▷◆▷◆▷◆▶

Be careful who you get to taste this drink—they may fall in love with you!

What You'll Need
- maraschino cherries
- red food coloring
- ice cube tray
- pink lemonade

Put a maraschino cherry and a drop of red food coloring in each section of an ice cube tray. Fill the tray with water, and freeze. Add one of those ice cubes to a glass of pink lemonade, and serve up some Love Potion Number Nine at a Valentine's party. (Remind everyone to take care not to bite into or swallow the frozen cherries.) Everyone will fall in love with this tasty drink!

Love Knot

◄◆►◄◆►◄◆►

Wearing a love knot on your sleeve means that you have a love that will never end.

What You'll Need
- red felt
- 3×2-inch piece of stiff cardboard
- white glue
- gold braid
- pins
- scissors
- cool-temp glue gun
- pin back

Caution: This project requires adult help.

Glue red felt to the front and back of the cardboard. Glue gold braid to the front of the felt in a sideways figure 8. Hold the braid in place with pins until the glue is dry. Carefully cut around the knot with sharp scissors to make your pin. Have an adult help you to glue the pin back to the back of your love knot with a cool-temp glue gun.

Candy Clips

◄◆►◄◆►◄◆►

These decorative clips tell your valentines exactly how you feel about them.

Paint clips and clothespins red or pink. When the paint dries, glue on tiny felt hearts and candy message hearts. Use the clear nail polish to protect the candy from breaking and to give the Candy Clips a shiny finish. Tie on some thin red, pink, and white curling ribbons. Give these as Valentine's Day presents to friends and family. They make excellent snack bag closers or bookmarks.

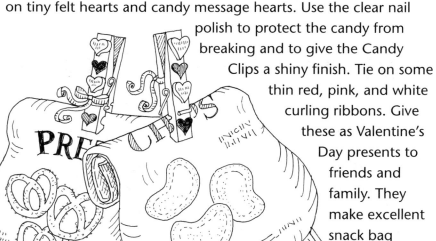

What You'll Need
- metal hair clips or wooden spring clothespins
- paint
- paintbrush
- felt scraps
- candy message hearts
- blunt scissors
- glue
- clear nail polish
- curling ribbons

Secret Heart Valentine

Shhhh! It's a secret, Valentine.

What You'll Need
- colored paper
- ruler
- blunt scissors
- pencil
- glue
- marker

1. Cut 4 paper squares (8×8 inches, 6×6 inches, 4×4 inches, and 1¾×1¾ inches) each in a different color. Cut the smallest square into a heart shape, and set the heart aside. Draw pencil borders from end to end on each side of the 3 larger squares. Make 2-inch borders for the largest square, 1½-inch borders for the middle square, and 1-inch borders for the smallest square. Cut out the corners created on the squares by the intersecting border lines. Cutting out the corners will create a tab on each square side. With scissors, round off the corners of the tabs.

2. Fold the tabs inward along the pencil lines. Using a small drop of glue, paste the smallest square in the middle of the medium square and the medium square in the middle of the largest square. Glue the heart in the middle of the smallest square, and write a tiny message in the heart.

3. Now close the smallest square by tucking each of the 4 semicircular flaps under the other. Close the medium square and then the biggest square in the same way. Your secret hidden heart is ready!

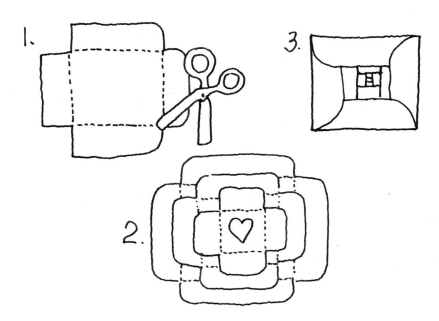

"I Cannot Tell a Lie" Tarts

This dessert will be very popular—and not just with George Washington!

What You'll Need
- 2 chocolate cookies
- 2 clean dishtowels
- rolling pin
- measuring spoons
- muffin cups and pan
- 8 ounces cream cheese
- ⅓ cup sugar
- 1 teaspoon lemon juice
- 1 teaspoon vanilla
- mixing bowl
- electric mixer
- 1 egg
- pot holders
- 20-ounce can cherry pie filling

Caution: This project requires adult help.

Ask an adult to preheat the oven to 375 degrees. To make the cookie crumbs, put plain chocolate cookies between two dishtowels, and crush them with a rolling pin. Place the muffin cups into the muffin pan, and drop 1 tablespoon of cookie crumbs into each. Mix the cream cheese, sugar, lemon juice, and vanilla for 3 minutes with an electric mixer on medium speed. Crack the egg into the mixture, and continue beating for 2 minutes. Put 2 tablespoons of this mixture over the cookie crumbs in each muffin cup. Bake for 15 minutes. Have an adult remove the pan from the oven with pot holders. Let them cool for about 1 hour. Take the muffin cups out of the muffin pan, and put them on a plate. Spoon about 2 tablespoons of cherry pie filling onto each of the muffins. Refrigerate for 2 hours before serving. These tarts are delicious—and that's no lie!

Tricky George

Even George Washington himself couldn't do this trick! Try it on his birthday (February 22).

Tell your friends you'll give them each a dollar if they can pick it up from the floor. But there is a catch; they have to pick it up using your instructions! Have your friends stand with their feet together and heels up against a wall. Put dollar bills on the floor 12 inches in front of their feet. Tell them to pick up the dollars without bending their knees or moving their feet. It is impossible to do! Why? When you are standing against a wall, your center of gravity is over your feet. If you bend forward, you have to move your center of gravity forward in order to keep your balance. Since you can't move your feet during this trick, you're flat out of luck! But that's better than being flat on your face!

What You'll Need
- dollar bills
- ruler
- wall

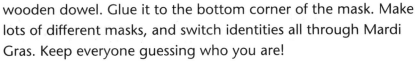

Party Plate Masks

▶▶▶▶▶▶▶

Hide your true identity behind these glittery half-masks for Mardi Gras.

What You'll Need
- paper
- pencil
- shiny or colored plastic-coated paper party plates
- blunt scissors
- glitter glue
- shiny stickers
- hole punch
- curling ribbon
- beads
- paint
- paintbrushes
- elastic string (optional)
- needle (optional)
- wooden dowel (optional)
- glue (optional)

Use our pattern as a starting point for making your own mask. Draw your pattern, and lay it on the paper plate. Trace around the pattern, and cut it out. Carefully cut out the eye holes. Use glitter glue to draw lines around the eye holes. Let the glue dry. Apply shiny stickers to your mask. Punch holes at the bottom corners of your mask, and thread strands of curling ribbon through the holes. String beads on the ends of the ribbons. Decorate your mask with paint. If you want to wear your mask, poke small holes on either side of the mask and thread a loop of elastic string long enough to stretch around your head. If you'd like to hold the mask in front of your face, paint a wooden dowel. Glue it to the bottom corner of the mask. Make lots of different masks, and switch identities all through Mardi Gras. Keep everyone guessing who you are!

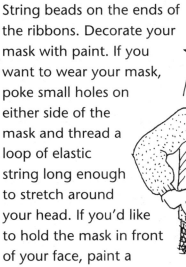

King Cake

❖◀▶◀▶◀▶❖

This delicious Mardi Gras cake has a baked-in surprise!

What You'll Need

- 2 cups flour
- ¼ cup sugar
- 1 package active dry yeast
- measuring cups and spoons
- mixing bowls
- mixing spoon
- ½ cup milk
- saucepan
- ¼ cup butter
- electric mixer
- 3 eggs (at room temperature)
- clean dish towel
- large spoon
- ½ cup each mixed candied fruits and raisins
- 10-inch tube pan
- heat-proof foil-wrapped toy figure
- gold, purple, and green sugar sprinkles

Caution: This project requires adult help.

Mix ¾ cup flour with the sugar and yeast. Pour the milk into a small saucepan, add the butter, and stir over low heat. Slowly add the milk mixture to the flour mixture, and beat until well blended. Add the eggs one by one; beat well after each egg. Add ½ cup flour, and beat until a thick batter is formed. Add the rest of the flour, and beat for 2 minutes. Cover the mixture with a clean dish towel, and set it in a warm place for about 1 hour. Have an adult preheat the oven to 350 degrees. Using a large spoon, fold candied fruits and raisins into the batter. Pour the batter into a greased tube pan, and poke the foil-wrapped toy into the batter. Traditionally, this toy is a baby that represents the Christ child and whoever finds him has good luck for the coming year. Bake the cake for 40 minutes. Let it cool, and cover it with sprinkles.

Clink–Clank Noisemaker

❖◀▶◀▶◀▶❖

Sound off at Mardi Gras with a clink and a clank!

Mark a line across the middle of the top and sides of the tissue box; the line should be across the shorter length of the box. Cut down the line on all 3 sides (don't cut through the bottom). Bend the box so the back sides touch. Glue the jar lids to the outside of each back side. Paint your clink-clank in the Mardi Gras colors of gold, purple, and green. When the paint is dry, draw designs with glue, and sprinkle glitter on top. Shake off the extra glitter, and let the glue dry. Insert your fingers in one half and your thumb in the other half, and make some music!

What You'll Need

- long, empty tissue box
- ruler
- pencil
- blunt scissors
- 2 jar lids
- glue
- paint and paintbrushes
- glitter

Throw–Me Beads

◆▶◆▶◆▶◆

Colorful beads are a tradition at Mardi Gras.

Make a cardboard template of a triangle that has 2 long sides that are 5 inches long and a shorter side that is 1 inch long. Use the template to trace and cut triangles from old magazines or comics (ask for permission first!). Each triangle will be a bead. To make a bead, take a triangle, wrong side up, and roll the wider end around a piece of cord. Work carefully and continue to roll, making sure the bead builds up evenly. Keep rolling the paper tightly until the last 2 inches. Brush the wrong side of the 2 inches with glue, and roll it up. Let the bead dry on the cord. When the glue is dry, give your beads a coat of clear varnish or nail polish to protect them and make them hard. Be sure the beads don't touch each other until they are dry. When dry, thread the beads on embroidery thread to make necklaces, bracelets, and anklets. The traditional Mardi Gras cry is, "Throw me something, Mistuh!" Now you can throw your beads into the air during a parade or party.

What You'll Need
- cardboard
- pencil
- ruler
- old color magazines or comics
- blunt scissors
- stiff cord
- glue
- small paintbrush
- clear varnish or nail polish
- embroidery thread
- large embroidery needle

SPRING INTO SPRING

The flowers are blooming, the birds are chirping, the sun is shining—the signs of spring are everywhere! And there are many wonderful holidays to celebrate at this time of year. So spring into spring!

Japanese Egg Dolls

◆◆◆◆◆◆◆

On March 3 observe Hinamatsuri, a Japanese holiday that celebrates girls, by making your own Hina dolls!

What You'll Need
- 2 raw eggs
- needle
- bowl
- 2 large soda bottle caps
- glue
- colored tissue paper
- black yarn
- paints
- fine paintbrushes

You can make your own Hina dolls to help you celebrate. Use a needle to make a small hole in one end of a raw egg. Stick the needle inside the egg to break the yolk. Make a slightly larger hole in the other end of the egg with the needle. Hold the egg over a bowl, and blow in the small hole until the raw egg comes out the larger hole. You have to blow hard! When the eggshell is empty, gently rinse out the inside and wash the outside. Let it dry completely.

Do the same for the other egg.

Glue the large end of each egg into a soda bottle cap so that it will stand up. Use tissue paper to make kimonos for your dolls. Glue on black yarn for hair. Paint the dolls' faces. If you want, use the raw eggs to bake a cake and have a Hina-matsuri tea party!

Tiny Straw Kite

Paint Hina dolls or peach blossoms on this kite for Hinamatsuri.

Thread 1 long piece of dental floss through 3 straws. Tie the ends of the floss together, which will form the straws into a triangle. Cut 3 pieces of dental floss 2 inches longer than the straws. Thread a piece of floss through each of the last 3 straws, leaving an inch sticking out of each end. Tie together one end of the floss from all 3 straws. You will have a 3-armed star. Tie the floss hanging from the other end of each straw to a corner of the triangle. You will have a 4-sided shape called a tetrahedron. Cover 2 sides of the tetrahedron by gluing tissue paper to the straws. On the triangles with tissue paper, poke small holes in the paper ⅓ of the way from the top of the kite. Thread a piece of floss through each hole, and tie each around the straw. Tie a slightly longer piece of floss around the straw near the bottom ⅓ of the kite. Tie the floss together, then tie a long string to this to fly the kite. Paint a Hina doll or a peach blossom on your kite, and see how high it can fly!

What You'll Need
- dental floss
- 6 straws
- blunt scissors
- ruler
- tissue paper
- glue
- string
- paint
- fine paintbrushes

Purim Movie

Tell the story of Purim with this homemade movie!

What You'll Need
- scrap paper
- pencil
- roll of white butcher paper or shelf paper (or tape paper together to make 60 inches)
- crayons or markers
- two ½-inch dowels, 12 inches long
- tape

Read the story of Queen Esther, Mordecai, and Haman to get ideas for a movie that explains the story of Purim. Make a storyboard before you begin by sketching ideas for each scene in your movie. When you have decided the order of the scenes, draw each picture on a length of butcher paper, starting at one end and continuing until the story is finished. You can write titles, captions, and speech balloons, like a comic strip, too. Leave a few inches of blank paper at either end. Tape each end around a dowel. Then roll the paper onto the dowel that is nearest the end of the story, which will make a scroll. When you are ready to show your movie, hold one end and have a friend hold the other end. Then slowly unroll the paper as you narrate the story that goes with each picture.

Pot o' Gold Game

◆▶▶▶▶▶◀

What brings luck on St. Patrick's Day? The Pot o' Gold Game!

What You'll Need
- yellow, green, and black construction paper
- blunt scissors
- glue
- pennies

This is a game for 2 to 5 people. Use yellow construction paper to make a large circle. Cut 10 quarter-size shamrocks out of green paper. Glue them on the circle in a random pattern. Cut out 10 black banshee spots—these circles should be twice as large as the shamrocks. Glue them on the circle in a random fashion. Stand 5 or 6 feet from the Pot o' Gold. Each player gets to toss a penny a turn. If your penny lands on a lucky shamrock, then you get to keep it. (The penny does not have to be completely on the shamrock; it can be touching the pot. Also, if your penny touches both a shamrock and a banshee spot, it is counted as landing on a banshee spot.) But if it lands on a banshee spot, you have to leave it on the board. (If your penny doesn't land on either a shamrock or banshee spot, you get another chance to throw it. After that, you must leave your penny on the pot.) The next player whose penny lands on a lucky shamrock gets to pick up all the "gold" on the board! The player with the most pennies at the end of the game wins.

Leprechaun's Corsage

◆▶▶▶▶▶◀

You don't have to be Irish to enjoy making and wearing this special green pin!

Thread the needle with a 5-inch length of green yarn. Wrap more yarn around a pencil 30 times. (Not too tight!) Slip the threaded needle under the loops. Pull the pencil out. Tie the ends of the thread around the loops, and pull the knot tight. Cut loops to make a pom-pom. Glue the bottom of the pom-pom into the acorn cap. Glue a safety pin to the back of the acorn cap.

What You'll Need
- thin green yarn
- embroidery needle
- ruler
- blunt scissors
- pencil
- acorn cap
- small safety pin
- glue

Chenille Stem Pals

◆▸◆▸◆▸◆▸

Make some little people even the Irish would love.

What You'll Need
- green chenille stems
- green paper
- blunt scissors
- markers
- cotton balls
- craft glue
- small safety pin (optional)

Bend a green chenille stem in half. Cut a green paper circle, draw a face on it, and add a cottony wisp of a white beard. Cut and glue a hat to the top of his head. Twist a second chenille stem around the body to make wee arms. If you'd like to make a pin out of your friend, glue the back (the side that doesn't open) of a small safety pin to the back of the leprechaun's head.

Limber Liam Leprechaun

◆▸◆▸◆▸◆▸

This little leprechaun might be dancing a jig behind your back— but he'll not so much as hop while you watch him!

What You'll Need
- pink and green crepe paper
- ruler
- blunt scissors
- 5 chenille stems
- cotton ball
- thread
- clear tape
- markers
- green and black felt or cloth scraps
- glue
- spring clothespin

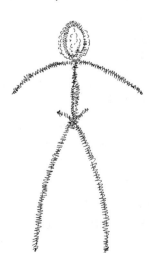

Cut the pink and green crepe paper into 6×1½-inch pieces. Twist the chenille stems together as shown below to make the leprechaun's "bones." Stick a cotton ball on the top of the neck, and wrap it with thread to keep it in place. Wrap the pink crepe paper around the head and the green crepe paper around the figure. Wrap each body part separately so that you can bend the chenille stems at the joints in order to pose your leprechaun. Use more paper on the upper legs or arms to make them thicker; use less on the knees so you can pose them. Secure the ends of crepe paper with clear tape. Use markers to draw a leprechaun face. Make your leprechaun a green suit and black belt out of felt or cloth scraps, and glue them on him. To make him stand up, clip a clothespin to his heel.

Green–Magic Rings

◆▶◆▶◆▶◆▶

You don't have to kiss the Blarney stone to make some magic.

What You'll Need
- plastic screw-on cap
- 3½ inches of narrow elastic
- glue
- clothespins
- 5-inch circle green fabric
- dried rose petals or mint leaves
- jingle bell with small holes
- rubber band

Glue both ends of the elastic inside the cap, on opposite sides. Turn the cap over, and glue the elastic to the outer sides of the cap. Clamp the elastic to the lid with clothespins until the glue is dry. Put rose petals or mint leaves and the jingle bell (the holes in the bell should be small so the dried petals or leaves don't get inside) in the middle of the fabric. Gather the edges, and wrap them with a rubber band to make a ball. Pour glue into the cap. Set the fabric ball in the glue, opening side down. When the glue is dry, slip your finger though the elastic loop under the cap. Shake your ring to make magic.

Leprechaun Bubble Pipe

◁▶◁▶◁▶◁▶

Legend says that fairies catch rides on bubbles made from leprechaun pipes!

Caution: This project requires adult help.

Find a large acorn. With adult help, cut the top off and dig out the meat to make a little bowl. Using the nail, carefully make a hole in the side near the bottom of the bowl, just big enough for the straw to fit through. Put the straw into the hole, and using the cool-temp glue gun (with adult help), fill the area around the straw with glue. Blow gently through the straw to make sure no glue is clogging the hole. Set the bubble pipe aside.

Make some bubble solution by mixing the warm water, green dishwashing liquid, and salt together in a bowl. Stir until the salt dissolves.

Now it's time to give some rides to some fairies! Dip the pipe in the bubble solution, and blow gently.

What You'll Need
- large acorn
- knife
- nail
- straw
- cool-temp glue gun and glue
- 1 cup warm water
- ½ cup green dish-washing liquid
- 1 teaspoon salt
- mixing bowl
- plastic spoon

Mr. and Mrs. Spring

For the Vernal Equinox, make these green pepper people; they're bursting with springtime color!

What You'll Need
- 2 green peppers
- knife
- broccoli
- celery
- peeled potatoes
- green olives
- green food coloring
- small plate
- toothpicks
- bunch of fresh parsley

Caution: This project requires adult help.

Make lunch or dinner full of springtime fun with these green pepper characters sitting on a plate. Wash and dry the green peppers. Have an adult help you with the cutting! Cut off the very top of the peppers, and scoop out the insides. Cut the broccoli, celery, and potatoes into small pieces (keep potatoes in water until ready to cut). Slice the green olives. Color the potatoes by soaking them in a small plate of green food coloring. Stick a triangle-shaped piece of cut and dyed potato on the end of a toothpick and poke it into the pepper body to make a hand and an arm; repeat for other side. Attach pieces of celery to the ends of toothpicks, and stick them into the bottom of the pepper to make feet. Attach other vegetable pieces in this way to make the face: green olive slices for eyes, a broccoli-flower nose, a half-circle of green potato for the mouth, and 2 pieces of potatoes for ears. Fill the peppers with fresh parsley to make hair.

The Great Sphinx
The Great Sphinx, in Egypt, was built so that it directly faces the rising sun on the day of the Vernal Equinox.

Pebble and Sprout Garden

Have springtime right on your table!

What You'll Need
- beet and carrot tops
- knife
- ruler
- pie plate
- pebbles
- water
- small plastic figurines

Caution: This project requires adult help.

Ask an adult to cut the tops from the largest, fattest beets and carrots you can find. The tops should be at least 1 inch long. If there are any greens sprouting from them, cut these off, too. Next, fill a pie plate with pebbles, leaving 1 inch of space at the top. If possible, use all white pebbles or alternate circles of white and dark pebbles for a pretty look. Place the carrot and beet tops on the pebbles with the cut sides down. Add water until it covers the bottom of the vegetables. Stand small plastic figurines in between the pebbles to make a funny springtime scene. Put the arrangement in a place that gets good light but not direct sun. Check the water level each day to make sure the vegetables are always touching the water. In a week, you should see little green sprouts growing from the top of each carrot and beet. You may want to change the water and wash the pebbles after a few weeks. Your arrangement will last a little over a month.

 # Pressed Spring Ornaments

It will be spring forever with these pressed ornaments decorating the house.

What You'll Need
- brown paper
- scissors
- waxed paper
- paper clips
- leaves or flowers
- crayons
- butter knife
- iron and ironing board
- needle and thread

Caution: This project requires adult help.

Cut several shapes, such as a circle, star, leaf, and tulip, out of brown paper. Paper clip 2 pieces of waxed paper onto the shapes, and cut them to match. Put 1 piece aside, and keep one on top of the brown paper. Then arrange a few fresh leaves or flowers on it. With a butter knife, scrape crayon shavings over the leaves and flowers. Make sure you hold the knife facing away from your body. Use different-colored crayons for the shavings. Place the other sheet of waxed paper on top of the crayon shavings. Cover this with another sheet of brown paper. Have an adult help you slide a warm iron over the paper to melt the waxed paper and crayon shavings. Remove the top piece of brown paper. Poke a hole at the top of the waxed paper design with a needle, knot a doubled piece of thread, and pull it through the hole to make a hanging loop. Hang one in each room of the house!

Spring Place Mats

◆▸◆▸◆▸◆▸

These make great gifts, or use them yourself at mealtime.

Caution: This project requires adult help.

For each place mat, measure and cut 2 pieces of clear vinyl adhesive paper into rectangles that are approximately 12×18 inches. Peel the backing off 1 piece of paper, and lay it sticky side up on the table. Place the dried flowers on the sticky side of the paper. Press everything flat with your fingers. Some flowers will work better if you remove the petals and use the petals individually.

Peel the backing off the second piece of adhesive paper. Carefully place it sticky side down over your arrangement. Don't worry about lining up the edges exactly. (TIP: Have an adult help with the adhesive paper. You can each hold 2 corners, and it will be easier to place without causing wrinkles.) Press everything down as flat as possible, and your place mat will look beautiful. Trim the edges with scissors.

Day and Night Flip Stones

◆▸◆▸◆▸◆▸◆

At the time of the Vernal Equinox, the hours of the day equal the hours of the night. Longer days mean it is a great time to go rock hunting!

Find a smooth, round stone. Wash it, and let it dry for several hours. Lay out some old newspapers on your work surface. On one side of the stone, paint a bright-sky-blue background. Make sure you don't get any paint on the other side of the rock. When the blue paint dries, paint a large, smiling sun in the middle of it. When that side dries, paint the other side black. Add a crescent moon when the black background is dry. To protect your painted stones, paint them with clear varnish or nail polish. You might want to do 2 or 3 coats, waiting for each coat to dry before you add another. Now you are ready to play a toss game, much like heads or tails. Take turns calling "day" or "night" and tossing the stone on the grass to see if the side you called lands faceup. Paint other rocks with pretty spring scenes, and give them out as prizes.

Adorned Eggs

Here are two exciting new ways to decorate Easter eggs.

What You'll Need

- 1 tablespoon food coloring
- 1 tablespoon vinegar
- 1 tablespoon cooking oil
- bowls
- mixing spoon
- measuring cups and spoons
- 2 cups water
- hard-boiled eggs
- large spoon
- paper towels
- modeling clay
- rolling pin
- newspaper
- rubber cement

Caution: This project requires adult help.

For marbleized egg decorations, mix the food coloring, vinegar, and cooking oil in a small mixing bowl. Add water, and stir the liquid around quickly until it begins to swirl. Now, using a large spoon, quickly dip a hard-boiled egg into the swirling colored liquid and pull it back out again. Pat the egg dry with a paper towel, and repeat the procedure, this time dipping the egg into a solution of a different color. For a drizzle-decorated egg, combine ½ cup hot water, ½ tablespoon food coloring, and 1 teaspoon vinegar. Let the solution cool.

To make the collar, roll out a snake shape from modeling clay, flatten it, then mold it into a cylinder the egg can sit on. Put the collar on a piece of newspaper. Place the hard-boiled egg on the collar, and drizzle it with rubber cement (have an adult help you, and make sure the room is well ventilated). Let the rubber cement dry. Then, using a spoon, dip the egg into the dye solution. Remove the egg, and pat with a paper towel. Set the egg on the collar. When the dye is dry, rub off the rubber cement.

Carrot Casserole

Make this treat for your favorite Easter bunny!

Caution: This project requires adult help.

Everyone will hop right on over to the table at Easter dinner when they smell this dish! Have an adult preheat the oven to 325 degrees. Wash the carrots. You may need an adult to help cut the carrots into quarter-size rounds. Place the carrots in a baking pan. Sprinkle them with the salt and maple syrup, and dot them with margarine. Cover the pan with foil, and bake for 1 hour and 15 minutes. Before serving, make a circle of fresh parsley to put on top for decoration.

What You'll Need

- 1 pound carrots
- knife
- baking pan
- ½ teaspoon salt
- 2 tablespoons maple syrup
- 2 tablespoons margarine
- aluminum foil
- fresh parsley

Cracked Pictures

▶▶▶▶▶▶

Make beautiful mosaics from Easter eggshells!

What You'll Need
- leftover Easter eggshells
- construction paper
- markers
- craft glue

Wash and dry the shell bits. Collect an assortment of shapes and sizes. A lot of the shells will still have their color, but if you use plain eggshells, color them with markers. Draw the simple outline of an animal, person, or some favorite object on a piece of construction paper. You might want to use a dark piece of paper to contrast with your shells. Glue the shells into the outline. Glue them close together so no paper shows through. When you have filled in the outline completely, let the glue dry. Color in the details with markers.

Mini-Easter Baskets

▶▶▶▶▶▶

These are so simple, you'll want to make plenty to use as table decorations and to give to your friends.

Caution: This project requires adult help.

Separate the individual egg buckets of an egg carton with scissors; an adult may need to help you do this. Use a sharp pencil point to poke a hole on 2 opposite sides of each bucket. Cut a piece of ribbon, and tie each end through a hole to create a handle for the basket. (Instead of ribbon, you could use a chenille stem for the handle; attach each end of the stem to a side of the basket.) Add a bow to the top of the handle. Paint the baskets, if you would like. Fill the basket with plastic Easter grass or shredded green construction paper and Easter goodies.

What You'll Need
- cardboard egg cartons
- scissors
- pencil
- ribbon (or chenille stem)
- paints and paintbrushes (optional)
- plastic Easter grass (or shredded green construction paper)
- Easter goodies

"Bonny" Bonnets

◆▶◆▶◆▶◆▶

When you wear this Easter bonnet, everyone will want one of their own!

What You'll Need

• empty berry basket
• ribbon
• plastic Easter grass
• jelly beans
• silk flowers
• tissue and construc-
  tion paper
• chenille stems
• blunt scissors
• glue
• markers
• pom-poms
• wiggle eyes
• feathers

It wouldn't be Easter without beautiful Easter hats. Make a special hat of your own—it can be silly, pretty, or both. An empty berry basket is the base of the hat. Turn it upside down, and tie ribbons at the bottom of 2 opposite sides. Glue Easter grass all over the basket. Let it dry. To decorate your hat, glue on jelly beans and silk flowers. You can also glue rabbit and egg cutouts to chenille stems and twist them around the basket in various places. The chenille stems will make your cutouts stand up out of the Easter grass. Be creative and make your Easter bonnet full of surprises. Is that a yellow pom-pom chick hiding in the grass?

 # Bunny Hop

◆▶◆▶◆▶◆▶

Egg-ceptional fun for somebunny smart!

Decorate a paper plate with your favorite spring or Easter designs. Put a cardboard box at one end of the room and another box filled with plastic Easter eggs at the other. Keep your feet together to make hopping the only way to go. Fill your paper plate with plastic eggs, and carefully make your way to the box. Deliver your load, then hop back for more. Time yourself to see how quickly you can get the job done. Then try the game again to improve on your personal best. More than 1 person raring to play? Divide into teams for competitive fun.

What You'll Need
• paper plate
• markers
• cardboard boxes
• plastic Easter eggs
• timer

Tissue Paper Pasteup

◆▶◆▶◆▶◆▶

Don't be too careful when you're tearing tissue paper. Your goal is to make soft, fuzzy shapes that blend.

What You'll Need
- colored tissue paper
- drawing paper
- pencil
- craft glue
- water
- small dish
- old paintbrush
- blunt scissors

Tear colored tissue paper into many pieces. Set the torn paper aside. Draw several egg shapes on a piece of drawing paper. Mix equal parts of water and craft glue together in a small dish. Paint the mixture on each shape. Now place torn tissue paper pieces on each shape over the glue. Coat the tissue paper with the diluted glue. Let it dry. The tissue paper creates a bright and fuzzy "paint" for your eggs. Cut the eggs from the paper, and hang them up as Easter decorations.

 # Prickle Chick

◀▶◀▶◀▶◀▶

This little chick is cute on your Easter table, or give it as a fun gift!

Caution: This project requires adult help.

Choose a large pinecone that will stand up by itself. In a well-ventilated room or outside, have an adult help you spray-paint the pinecone yellow. Let the paint dry. Wrap the pinecone in a thin layer of fiberfill. Use a craft stick to poke the fiberfill between the scales of the pinecone. This will give your Prickle Chick a fluffy look. Draw and cut out wings, a beak, 2 feet, and a tail from yellow felt. Glue them in place. Glue a few small feathers on the ends of the wings and tail. Cut 2 circles of white felt for the outer eyes, and glue the wiggle eyes on them. Glue eyes to the chick. Set the Prickle Chick in the center of the table for an Easter decoration!

What You'll Need
- large pinecone
- yellow spray paint
- polyester fiberfill
- craft stick
- pencil
- felt scraps
- pencil
- blunt scissors
- white glue
- feathers (available from a craft store)
- 2 wiggle eyes

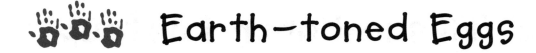

Earth-toned Eggs

The shades made from natural dyes will give your eggs a soft, earthy look.

What You'll Need

- spinach
- broccoli
- blueberries
- coffee
- tea
- cranberries
- beets
- tomatoes
- knife
- enamel pots
- water
- colander
- bowls
- clean cheesecloth or rag
- hard-boiled eggs
- vegetable oil (optional)
- soft cloth (optional)

Caution: This project requires adult help.

Wash and chop up the fruits and vegetables. Have an adult help you with the cutting and with boiling the water. When you have your ingredients ready, put one kind of fruit, vegetable, coffee, or tea in an enamel pot and fill it with water until your ingredient is completely covered. Boil for 10 minutes or longer, depending on how dark you want your color to be. The longer you boil, the darker the color. Just make sure that you don't boil all the water out! Strain the ingredients through a colander into separate bowls lined with cheesecloth or a clean rag. Once your dye has cooled, dip hard-boiled eggs into the liquid for several minutes. Repeat the process with all the ingredients to have cartons of earthy Easter eggs. You can also make your eggs shine by wiping them with a clean, soft cloth that has a few drops of vegetable oil on it.

Alphabet Egg Hunt

Here's an egg hunt with a wordy twist!

Draw lots of eggs on colorful construction paper. You can make them different sizes, anywhere from 2 to 6 inches long. Decorate one side with interesting patterns. Write a letter on the other side. Cut out enough eggs to use all the letters of the alphabet, and then make at least 3 more eggs for each vowel. Make some extra blank eggs. These will be used as "wild" eggs, which means they can be any letter. When you are done creating, hide the eggs inside the house or in the yard. Let the hunt begin! Players try to find as many eggs as they can, but the game isn't over simply by finding the eggs. Everyone has to use their alphabet eggs to make words. The person who can make the most words wins.

What You'll Need

- construction paper
- pencil
- ruler
- blunt scissors
- markers

Jelly Bean Game

Tired of hunting Easter eggs? Bitten the head off each and every chocolate bunny? Then it's time for... the Jelly Bean Game!

What You'll Need
- 3 plastic foam egg cartons
- bottle cap
- blunt scissors
- tape
- red, yellow, and green jelly beans
- 2 plastic spoons

Wash and dry the egg cartons and the bottle cap. Cut the tops and flaps off the egg cartons. Tape the egg cartons together, side by side the long way. When finished, you should have egg cups that are 6 rows across and 6 rows deep. Put a jelly bean in each egg cup—mix the colors randomly. Mark a starting line on the table with tape—about 2 feet away. Holding the bottom of the spoon with your right hand on the table (left, if you are left-handed), put the bottle cap into the bowl of the spoon and press down. Try to flip the bottle cap into an egg cup. If it lands in an egg cup, you get to keep the jelly bean from that cup. Red jelly beans are worth 10 points, yellow jelly beans are worth 5 points, and green jelly beans are worth 1 point. When all the jelly beans have been won, count them up, and see who has the most points. If you eat the jelly beans before the game is over, you lose the points!

Beautiful Bonnet

Make your own Easter bonnet just the color and shape you want.

Pick out some wallpaper or wrapping paper for your bonnet. You will need 2 pieces about the size of half a sheet of newspaper. Spread paste on the back of one piece of wallpaper. Press a piece of newspaper down on it, and smooth it with your hands. Repeat with each piece of newspaper. Paste the final piece of wallpaper down with the print side up. While the paste is still wet, cut a big circle out of the paper. Press the center of the circle over the bowl, and shape it into a hat. Turn the brim up, and brace it while it dries. When your bonnet is dry, decorate it with flowers, buttons, and bows.

What You'll Need
- 2 pieces wallpaper or wrapping paper
- white paste
- 4 sheets of newspaper
- blunt scissors
- a bowl the size of your head
- ribbons
- artificial flowers
- buttons

Twig Easter Basket

This Easter basket is strong enough to hold all the eggs you can find!

What You'll Need
- small green (not dry) branches
- small saw
- tape measure
- twine
- cool-temp glue gun

Caution: This project requires adult help.

Gather some branches that are ¼ to ½ inch thick. Have an adult cut eighteen 9-inch branch pieces and 1 thin, bendable 18-inch piece. Stack your sticks as if you were making a log cabin: Lay 2 branches parallel to each other and then 2 branches across the ends of those. Using a piece of twine for each corner, wrap and tie the sticks at each corner as you go. Make a stack of 3 sticks on each side. Slide the six remaining 9-inch sticks through the lowest space and across to form the bottom of the basket. Tie the sticks in place with twine, then glue them to keep them more firmly in place. Bend the 18-inch branch into a U-shape, and tie it to the basket for a handle. Have an adult use the glue gun to glue the handle in place. Use the basket for an Easter egg hunt, or fill it with flowers and put it on your table for a centerpiece.

Egg Holders

Display your Easter eggs proudly with these animated egg holders. They make a nice surprise for the Easter bunny.

Draw a baby chick with extended strips for "wings" and "feet" on a piece of construction paper. The strips should be at least 7 inches long. Color in the baby chick's features using markers or colored pencils. Cut out the chick shape. If you want, trim the wing strip so the edge is scalloped to make "feathers." Tape the ends of the feet strip together. Stand an Easter egg in the ring. Tape the ends of the wing strip together to "hug" the egg. Make other animal shapes to hold more eggs.

What You'll Need
- construction paper
- markers or colored pencils
- ruler
- blunt scissors
- clear tape

Smart Egg Trick

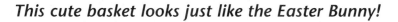

These eggs have a mind of their own!

What You'll Need
- 2 raw eggs
- waterproof markers
- two 8-ounce water glasses
- water
- 4 tablespoons sugar
- spoon
- bowl

You can tell your friends that these eggs have been specially trained by the Easter Bunny to know whether to sink or float in a glass of water. Before performing the trick, decorate 2 raw eggs with waterproof markers. Leave a blank rectangular space on each of your designs so a friend can label the eggs during the trick. Fill the glasses with water to about ¾ inch from the top. Put the sugar in one of the glasses, and mix well. Remember which glass has the sugar in it, but don't tell anyone about this part! When you are ready to perform the trick, tell your friends about your smart eggs. Explain that these eggs can obey written commands. Have a friend use a waterproof marker to label the eggs with the word "sink" on one and the word "float" on the other. After your friend gives you back the eggs, put the "sink" egg in the plain water, and the "float" egg in the sugar water. Watch the eggs obey the commands. If friends wonder how you did it, have them break the eggs into a bowl so they can see that there were no tricks inside the eggs!

Bunny Easter Basket

This cute basket looks just like the Easter Bunny!

What You'll Need
- 1 pint milk carton
- blunt scissors
- white and pink cotton balls
- craft glue
- construction paper
- Easter grass
- Easter goodies

Open the spout of an empty, clean pint milk carton. Lay the carton on a table with the spout side on the table. Cut out the side that is now on the top of the carton. You will have a rectangular hole. Glue white cotton balls all over the remaining milk carton; be sure to cover it completely. The opened spout of the milk carton is the nose of the rabbit. Glue a pink cotton ball on the spout for the nose, and add a pink one in the back for a tail. Cut out 2 paper eyes, and glue them just above the spout. Cut out 2 long ears, and glue them on either side of the carton—your rabbit can be a flop-eared bunny with ears that hang down or the ears can stand up.

Place Easter grass in the hole, and fill the bunny with goodies.

Checkered and Plaid Easter Eggs

◆▶◆▶◆▶◆▶

Have you ever seen a plaid Easter egg? Well, you can make your own plaid or checkered eggs!

What You'll Need
- Easter egg dye
- hard-boiled eggs
- duct tape
- ruler
- blunt scissors

Mix the egg dye according to directions. Dye each egg a solid color. Use the lightest color first. Take the eggs out of the dye bath, and let them dry. Cut ⅛-inch-thick strips of duct tape. Put the tape strips on the colored eggs, running some strips top to bottom and others around the egg. Be sure you leave some eggshell showing. Place the egg into the medium color of dye; let it sit for 20 minutes. Take the egg out, and take off every other strip of tape. Place the egg into the darkest color; let it sit for 20 minutes. Take the egg out. Remove the last strips of tape. Experiment with different patterns.

Mr. Funny Bunny

◆▶◆▶◆▶◆▶

This funny-bunny friend will stand up on your table or on the dresser by your bed.

Fold the middle finger of the glove over the back of the glove. Reach up inside the glove with a safety pin. Push the pin through the fabric from the inside, and pin the finger to the back of the glove. Stuff the rest of the glove with fiberfill all the way to the cuff, so that the fiberfill holds the cuff open. Cut a circle of felt just bigger than the hole in the cuff. Put the sand in the resealable bag, and push it into the glove under the fiberfill. Use the needle and thread to stitch the circle of felt onto the cuff. Pull the thumb and the little finger forward until the tips touch to make the bunny's arms. Pin the bunny's hands together (from behind) with a safety pin. Glue a cotton ball to the tip of the folded-down finger behind the bunny. Glue on yarn whiskers. Use fabric paint to draw the rest of the face.

What You'll Need
- old knit glove
- 2 small safety pins
- polyester fiberfill
- felt
- blunt scissors
- ⅛ cup sand
- resealable plastic bag
- needle
- thread
- cotton ball
- glue
- yarn scraps
- fabric paint
- paintbrush

# Bunny Box

This shadow box has a cotton-ball bunny standing on a hill of jelly eggs.

What You'll Need

- shallow box
- paint
- paintbrush
- plastic Easter grass
- glue
- jelly beans
- cotton balls
- white tissues
- 2 wiggle eyes
- construction paper
- blunt scissors
- jar lid
- self-stick picture hanger

Start with a shallow box such as a handkerchief or tie box, or the lid of a shoe box. Paint the outside of the box a pastel Easter shade. Let the paint dry. Paint the inside a sky-blue color. Glue a layer of plastic grass along the bottom of the box. Glue jelly beans inside the box to make a hill shape. To make your Easter bunny stand on top of the hill, stack two cotton balls, add a tiny puff for the rabbit's cottontail, and glue them down. Twist tissues into 2 floppy ears, and glue them down as well. You can glue on tiny wiggle eyes and construction paper whiskers, nose, and mouth. You might want to give your Easter bunny a big smile or cut its mouth in an O shape, as if it were surprised. Fold construction paper into a basket shape, glue on a strip for a handle, and place it at the bottom of the jelly bean hill, as if it had rolled down. Paint a jar lid to look like a bright, smiling sun, and glue it on. Press a self-stick hanger onto the back of your box, and hang it for all to see.

# Sleeping Chicks

Tuck these sleepy little chicks in their egg cradles.

You can use the plastic egg halves that held your Easter candy for lots of crafts. You can even turn a plastic egg into a tiny cradle! Put a little dab of glue on the bottom of one half of a plastic egg, and set it inside the other half so that one is horizontal and one is vertical. This is your cradle and canopy. Glue 2 wiggle eyes onto a yellow pom. Cut out a tiny orange construction paper beak, and glue this on the pom to make a baby chick. Glue on a little circle of fabric to make a baby cap, and set your little chick in its egg cradle. Use a small square of scrap fabric as a baby blanket.

What You'll Need

- plastic eggs
- glue
- yellow poms
- wiggle eyes
- construction paper
- blunt scissors
- scraps of cloth

One-of-a-Kind Baskets

◆▶▶▶▶▶▶

Make a unique Easter basket for every member of the family.

What You'll Need
- empty oatmeal or milk cartons
- scissors
- paint
- paintbrushes
- glue
- old magazines
- Easter stickers (optional)
- old Easter cards (optional)
- crepe paper (optional)
- colored cord or ribbon
- plastic Easter grass
- treats

Caution: This project requires adult help.

Cut off and throw away the top half of a clean carton. On the bottom half of the carton, poke 2 holes near the top, one on each side, for the handle. (You might need some adult help to do this part.) Paint the carton inside and out. (To paint milk cartons, mix a little white glue into the paint to make the paint adhere better to the waxed surface.) Use a different color for each family member. Look through old magazines to find pictures of things that each family member likes or things that remind you of them. Cut the pictures out (ask for permission first!), and glue them on the basket. Add Easter stickers, pictures from old Easter cards, and thin streamers of crepe paper. When you finish, loop a colored cord or ribbon through the 2 holes

you poked earlier, and tie a bow to make a handle. Fill your baskets with Easter grass and treats.

Spring Bunny

◆▶▶▶▶▶▶

Watch this bunny wiggle, wave, and hop to life.

Cut two 1×8-inch strips of construction paper. Tape one end of each strip together into an L-shape. Fold the bottom strip back over the top strip. Fold the other strip back over the last strip. Continue folding the strips back and forth to make a spring. When you get to the end of the strips, tape the ends together to hold them in place. Make 3 more springs.

Draw a bunny on a piece of construction paper. Glue each spring to the bunny's body for arms and legs. Draw 2 paws and 2 feet on a piece of construction paper, and cut them out. Glue the paws and feet to the spring ends. Glue a cotton ball or pom-pom to the back of the bunny for the tail. Place your spring bunny in an Easter basket, or hang it on the wall.

What You'll Need
- construction paper
- blunt scissors
- ruler
- clear tape
- markers
- craft glue
- cotton ball or white pom-pom

# Eggs Grow on Trees?

This lovely tree is ribboned with egg and flower blossoms.

What You'll Need

- plastic flowerpot
- crepe or tissue paper
- glue
- potting soil
- branch with 5 or 6 shoots
- dried moss
- 4 eggs
- butter knife
- ribbons
- ruler
- scissors
- small fresh flowers
- water
- Easter grass
- miniature chocolate eggs

Caution: This project requires adult help.

Cover a plastic flowerpot with crepe or tissue paper. Glue the paper inside and out, and try to tuck in all the edges so they fit smoothly on the plastic. Fill the pot with soil, and stick a branch with 5 or 6 twiggy shoots into the center. This is the tree. Cover the soil around the tree with moss. Use a butter knife to gently crack the eggs so that you get 2 equal halves. Have an adult help you with this. Carefully wash and dry the shells. Glue an 8-inch piece of ribbon around the bottom and up the sides of each egg half so that enough ribbon is left to tie to a branch in a neat bow. Tie the eggshells to the branches.

Place a small amount of water into some of the eggshells, and place a few small flowers in each. In others, place a bit of Easter grass and a single tiny chocolate egg.

# Doily Baskets

You can use these delicate baskets to hold Easter candy or a special Easter gift.

Fold in the 4 sides of a doily. Stand the sides up, pinching the corners in as you unfold the sides. Hold the pinched corners in place with tape. Cut a strip of construction paper to make a handle for the doily basket. Cut and glue pieces of doily lace to the handle. Tape the ends of the handle to the inside of the basket. Fill your basket with some green plastic grass and holiday goodies. These lacy baskets also make great party favors. Make one for each guest, and fill it with treats.

What You'll Need

- paper doilies
- clear tape
- construction paper
- blunt scissors
- craft glue
- plastic Easter grass
- goodies

Green-Haired Eggheads

◆▷◆▷◆▷◆

Keep the whole family giggling over these funny eggshell people!

What You'll Need
- empty eggshell halves
- waterproof markers
- cotton balls
- sprout seeds
- egg carton

Ask your family to save all their empty eggshell halves for you. Carefully wash and dry the eggshells. Using the markers, draw funny or scary faces on each one. If you wish, write a name on the back of each egghead. Sprinkle a little water on the cotton balls to dampen them. Press cotton balls into each eggshell until the shells are almost full. Poke holes in the cotton, and plant a few sprout seeds in each one. Place your eggshell people in an egg carton, and find a sunny window ledge for them to live on. Make sure the cotton is always damp. In a few days, the seeds will sprout and your eggshell friends will start to grow green hair. When the sprouts have grown a few inches, use them to make green-hair sandwiches for Easter lunch!

Funny Bunny

◆▷◆▷◆▷◆

Turn a baby food jar into a Funny Bunny with this fun craft idea!

Fill a clean baby food jar with cotton balls. Cut out a large heart that is a little taller and wider than the front of the jar. You can draw a face on this heart, if you'd like. Cut out a medium heart that is about 1 inch larger than the base of the jar. Cut out 2 small hearts that are about the size of a penny. Glue the large heart to the front of the jar. The top of the heart should extend beyond the top of the jar and look like ears. Glue the medium heart to the base of the jar so the top of the heart extends beyond the front of the jar. Glue small hearts on the sides of the jar for hands. Glue a cotton ball to the back of the jar for a tail.

What You'll Need
- baby food jar
- cotton balls
- construction paper
- blunt scissors
- markers (optional)
- ruler
- glue

Easter Bunny Races

◆◆◆◆◆◆→

They're off! The bunnies race across the floor... it's the pink bunny... no, it's the blue bunny. It's... it's... lots of fun no matter who wins!

What You'll Need
- 2 pieces of card-board about 12 inches long
- blunt scissors
- markers
- pencil
- two 10-inch pieces of string

Cut 2 Easter bunnies from cardboard, using the illustration as a guide. Color the front and back of the bunnies with markers. With the pencil, carefully punch a hole through the middle of each bunny just below the head—punch from the front to the back so the edges of the hole are smooth. Thread a piece of string through the hole in each rabbit. Tie one end of each string to the leg of a table, just high enough so that the rabbit's legs touch the floor. Back up, taking the rabbits with you, to the end of the string. Stand the rabbits up, making them lean toward the table a little. When you jerk the string, the rabbits will walk toward the table. (Bunnies walk best on smooth floor or low carpet.) The first Easter bunny to reach the table wins!

Egg—streamly Silly Basketball

◆◆◆◆◆◆→

This is a fun game to play with one or more friends on an Easter afternoon.

Tie one end of the rope to the basket's handle. Tie the other end to a tree limb. One player starts the basket swinging. The players then try to toss their plastic eggs into the moving basket while standing on a line 3 to 6 feet away. Who can get the most eggs in? When you have mastered the art of Egg-streamly Silly Basketball, challenge your friends to a game of Egghead. Stand as far or as close as you want. Toss the plastic egg. If you make it in the swinging basket, your friends must make it from the same place you stood. If they miss, they have an E. Keep playing until someone spells "Egghead." For tie-breakers, try special shots, like over the shoulder or between the legs.

What You'll Need
- rope
- large Easter basket
- tree
- 3 plastic Easter eggs for each player

Passover Places

◆▷◆▷◆▷◆▷

Set a special place for each guest at seder.

Everyone will want to keep lifting their plates to look at these beautiful, multicolored place mats. For each place mat, cut a 10×18-inch piece of poster board. You can use colored or plain poster board. Lightly draw your design in pencil on the poster board. You can draw a seder plate, a camel, the map of Israel, or anything else that is meaningful to you about seder. Draw large, simple shapes. Tear colored tissue paper into small pieces to glue inside the outlines of your shapes. Layer the paper to look like a mosaic. The tinier the tissue paper pieces, the more your place mat will have a mosaic look. You can decorate the place mats with markers also, if you wish. When you have finished decorating, cut 2 sheets of adhesive vinyl paper 11×19 inches. Place the poster board onto the sticky side of one sheet, and press the second sheet sticky side down on top. Smooth out any air bubbles, and trim the edges. Cut a scalloped edge for a fancier look. These place mats can be cleaned with a damp sponge and reused.

Making Matzo

◆▷◆▷◆▷◆▷

When the Jews fled slavery in Egypt, they only had time to bake unleavened bread—matzo. Eat this crunchy treat during Passover!

Caution: This project requires adult help.

Ask an adult to preheat the oven to 475 degrees. Mix and knead together the flour and water. When it's smooth and rubbery, roll out the dough on a floured surface. Cut out your dough. Traditional matzo is square, but you can cut your dough in other shapes, such as a camel or a Star of David. Prick designs in the dough with a fork. You can also sprinkle your dough with poppy seeds or sesame seeds for extra flavor. Place the dough on a greased cookie sheet. Bake it for 10 to 15 minutes or until light brown. Let the matzo cool. Serve it with cream cheese, butter, or jam. Regular yeast bread can take hours to make. Now you know how to make something just as tasty—only much faster!

Passover Peek Box

See a miniature scene of the Jews fleeing Egypt in this charming, old-fashioned peek box.

What You'll Need
- thin cardboard
- markers
- ruler
- scissors
- shoe box with lid
- construction paper
- glue
- clear tissue paper or cellophane
- chenille stems
- modeling clay

Caution: This project requires adult supervision.

To re-create the scene in which the Jews fled slavery in Egypt, draw and cut out thin cardboard figures of robed people carrying bags and leading camels. You may want to look at some Bible story illustrations to get ideas. Before you cut out the figures, make sure to add a ½-inch tab at the bottom of each one to glue onto the bottom of the shoe box so your figures will stand. You can also draw and cut out palm trees, a round sun, and several boulders. Before gluing your figures down, line the bottom of the box with sand-colored construction paper. You can line the sides and top of the box with sky-blue construction paper. Then cut a small round hole about 1×1 inch at one end of your box. This is the peek hole. Cut a larger square 3×2 inches at the other end of your box. Glue a square of clear tissue paper or cellophane over this hole on the outside of the box. If you want figures that move in your peek box, cut a slot at the back of the box, and glue a 6- to 8-inch strip of cardboard onto the bottom of the tab on the figure you want to move. Slip the loose end of the cardboard strip through the slot in the peek box, and slide your figure backward and forward. You can make desert birds fly up and down by poking 2 holes ½ inch apart in the lid of your box. Slip a horseshoe-shaped chenille stem into the holes, and glue the free ends onto the back of a bird cutout. Pull the chenille stem up and down to make the bird fly. For variety, add figures made of modeling clay. A peek box is a great way to give a three-dimensional view of a scene. Even something that happened long, long ago can seem real.

Afikomon Hiders

◆►◆►◆►◆►

Hunt for the Afikomon hidden in this decorative slipcover.

The word *afikomon* comes from the Greek word meaning "after-meal" or "dessert." After seder dinner is over, the children try to find the Afikomon, which has been broken in half, wrapped in a napkin, and hidden. Whoever finds it gets a reward, and everyone at the seder tastes a piece of Afikomon for dessert.

To make a pretty slipcover for the Afikomon, use colored embroidery thread to sew the 2 napkins together. Sew 3 edges and leave the 4th open. You can use either an overhand stitch or a running stitch, whichever is easier for you. Turn the slipcover right side out, and slip a piece of cardboard inside before you begin to paint. Draw your design on tracing paper cut to the same size as the slipcover. You can write the word "Afikomon" in large letters to be colored in with a fancy pattern. You might want to draw a large Star of David or a picture of a reward someone might get for finding the Afikomon. Then lay the tracing paper over the slipcover, and trace your design by pressing down hard along the outline with a tracing wheel. Lift off the tracing paper, and use waterproof pens or fabric paint to color your picture. When the Afikomon is found in this beautiful slipcover, the finder will get double the treasure!

A Clean House

Before Passover, many Jews clean their homes of chametz, which is leavening (it makes breads and cakes rise). A complete cleaning of the house is done, sometimes starting weeks before Passover begins. All leavened foods must be taken out of the house, and all crumbs must be cleaned out completely.

 Elijah's Cup

◆▷◆▷◆▷◆▷

The prophet Elijah will visit your house with joy when he can drink from this lovely goblet.

The prophet Elijah is busy at Passover. Think of all the homes he will visit and how many different wine glasses he will sip from! Show him how pleased you are to welcome him into your house with this specially decorated glass.

Wash and dry a drinking glass or wine glass. Trace a circle of felt around the glass, cut it out, and glue it on the bottom

of the glass. Spread old newspaper on your work surface, and paint a design on your glass with acrylic paint. Once the paint is dry, you can write the name "Elijah" in glue as part of your design and sprinkle glitter on it. If you like, glue sequins and fake jewels around the top and bottom of the glass. Make

What You'll Need
• large drinking glass or wine glass (plastic may be used for younger children)
• felt
• markers
• blunt scissors
• glue
• old newspaper
• acrylic paint
• paintbrush
• glitter (optional)
• sequins (optional)
• fake jewels (optional)

Elijah's cup as fancy as you like. These glasses also make nice presents if you are invited to seder at a friend's or relative's home.

Wiggle–Woggle Balloon

◆▷◆▷◆▷◆▷

Invite friends to play a game of catch with this April Fool's balloon!

What You'll Need
• two 10-inch balloons
• water

(Balloons are choking hazards—keep them and any broken pieces away from little children!) To make your tricky balloon, roll one balloon lengthwise and slide it inside the other, leaving only the stem (mouthpiece) sticking out. Place the mouthpiece of the inside balloon over the faucet, and fill the balloon with water until it is about 4 inches across. Tie the stem, and push the balloon the rest of the way inside the outer balloon. Blow up the outer balloon, leaving it a little soft, and tie it. Watch out! This balloon will wiggle-woggle when you toss it. If you start the water balloon rolling around inside before you toss it, the balloon will wiggle-woggle even more! Play wiggle-woggle balloon outside on the grass, away from stickers and thorns.

April Fool's Can

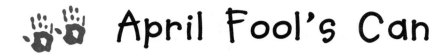

This tricky April Fool's can will amaze your parents and friends.

What You'll Need
- 1-pound coffee can (empty)
- can opener
- 2 plastic coffee-can lids
- hole punch
- large medium-weight rubber band
- blunt scissors
- 2-ounce fishing sinker

Use the can opener to remove both ends of the can. Lay the plastic lids on top of each other. Punch 2 holes about 1 inch apart through both of the lids. Put one lid on the can. Cut the rubber band. Thread the ends through the holes in the lid. Slip the fishing sinker on one of the pieces of rubber band inside the can. Thread the rubber band ends through the holes on the other plastic lid, and tie the ends of the rubber band together. Put the lid on the can. When you push the can, it will roll across the floor— 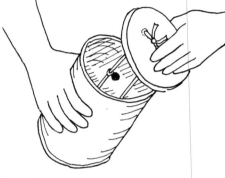 then it will stop and roll back! You may have to experiment with the tension of the rubber band. It should not be so loose that the weight touches the side of the can or so tight that the weight cannot flip around and "wind up" the toy.

Foot Juggling Ball

Use only your feet to play with this April Fool's ball!

(Balloons are choking hazards—keep them and any broken pieces away from little children!) Slide the end of the funnel into the stem (mouthpiece) of the 12-inch balloon. Pour sand into the balloon, tapping with the end of a pencil if the funnel jams, until the balloon is about 4 inches across. Tie the stem. Cut the stems off the 8-inch balloons. One at a time, stretch them over the sand-filled balloon, making sure the hole from the stem is on the opposite side each time. Before you put on the final balloon, use the hole punch to make 4 or 5 holes in it. When you pull it over the ball,

What You'll Need
- funnel
- 12-inch balloon
- sand
- pencil
- three 8-inch balloons
- blunt scissors
- hole punch

the color of the last balloon will show through the holes. See how long you can keep the ball in the air. (Be sure to play outside—your parents might not be happy if the balloon breaks in the house!)

Fairy Castle Book

◆▸◆▸◆▸◆▸

This book is shaped like a fairy castle, complete with a drawbridge and doors that open!

What You'll Need
- construction paper
- paper clips
- pencil
- straight pin
- needle
- colored embroidery thread
- blunt scissors
- glue
- brads (paper fasteners)
- ruler
- tape
- markers

Make this castle-shaped book, and write a fairy tale inside to celebrate the birthday of the famous fairy tale author Hans Christian Andersen on April 2, Children's Book Day. To make a 12-page book, fold 6 sheets of construction paper in half. Make a crease on the center fold, and open the pages. Use paper clips to hold the pages together at the corners. Mark 7 evenly spaced dots along the center fold. Carefully punch holes in the dots with a straight pin. Begin sewing by knotting the thread on the inside of the middle hole. Sew in and out of the holes until you have gone through each hole at least twice. Cut another piece of paper the size of one page, with a border cut at the top to look like a castle. Glue this page onto the front of your book. Draw a smaller castle front, complete with towers and turrets and a large, arch-shaped door on to another page-size paper. Cut the door so it opens in the middle (see illustration). Stick a brad in each door for a door handle.

For the drawbridge, cut out a rectangle that covers the doors for the drawbridge, plus 1 inch longer. Glue the second castle shape on top of the first castle shape. Attach the drawbridge by folding under the extra inch; fit it so the flap folds over the bottom back and so the front of the drawbridge covers the doors. Tape the flap to the back of the cover. Thread a needle with thread, and tie a knot in the end of the thread (do not double thread). Coming from the back of the cover, where the top corner of the drawbridge hits above the door, push thread through the cover and the drawbridge. Pull the drawbridge until it is completely open, and mark the thread. Make a knot at the mark. Repeat for other side of drawbridge. Use different-colored paper for the towers, doors, and drawbridge. Draw on windows, and don't forget to leave room for the title of the story you will write inside.

Cards of Wonder

Send a homemade thank-you card to your favorite author.

Reading about people in other countries can make you feel like you're actually in that place. Make a homemade thank-you card to send to a favorite author of a story set in another place or about people of a nationality different from yours. Fold a piece of construction paper into quarters to make a greeting card shape. With markers, draw characters and scenes from the story on the outside of the card. Inside the card, write down all the things you liked about the story and how glad you are that the author wrote it. You can send your card to the author in care of the company that published the book.

What You'll Need
- construction paper
- markers
- envelope
- postage stamp

Paper Lotus Chain

Celebrate Buddha's birthday on April 8 with this beautiful lotus chain.

What You'll Need
- white paper
- pencil
- blunt scissors
- pink and green tissue paper
- pins
- white glue

Use the patterns below as guides for your own patterns. Make the leaves green and the petals pink. Make stacks of 5 to 10 pieces of tissue paper. You will need 1 green leaf piece for every 2 pink petal pieces. Pin the patterns to the tissue paper, and cut them out. The more pieces you cut, the longer your garland will be. When all of the petals and leaves are cut, lay a green leaf on the table. Put a dot of glue in the middle of the leaf, and press a petal on top of it. Put a dot of glue on each point of the petal, and press another pink petal on top. Put a dot of glue in the middle of the top pink petal, and add a green leaf. Repeat this pattern until you have used all the tissue paper. Remember: Green leaves are glued to petals in the center; petals are glued to petals at the points. Let the glue dry. When you stretch out your creation, you will have a beautiful lotus garland!

Good News Headbands

◆▶◆▶◆▶◆▶

Wear your Earth Day messages around the neighborhood on these recycled headbands.

What You'll Need
- old newspaper
- blunt scissors
- stapler and staples
- crayons
- markers

Cut a strip of old newspaper long enough to wrap around your head with a couple inches left over. When you have the length you want, cut 6 to 8 more strips the same length. Staple them together to make a thick strip. Then staple the ends together to make a headband that fits your head. Think of a good Earth Day message to write in big letters around the band. "Save the Earth!" and "Clean Up Your Earth Today and Every Day!" are some sample messages you might write. Use your imagination to come up with your own slogan. Decorate the headband with drawings of fruits, flowers, birds, fish, animals, trees, and butterflies. As you walk around the neighborhood wearing your Good News Headband, people will surely get the message!

 # Garbage Gobbler

◆▶◆▶◆▶◆▶

Make the planet beautiful and trash-free with this Garbage Gobbler!

Caution: This project requires adult help.

Have an adult help you cut or fold the flaps of a cardboard box so that the top is open. This is the Garbage Gobbler's big, empty belly. Paint the box to look like a fantastic creature. Nobody has ever seen a Garbage Gobbler before, so you can make your creature look however you want. An adult can help you cut a nose, tail, and ears from the extra cardboard. Attach these parts to the Gobbler with glue. When the paint is dry, ask an adult to cut a small hole in the front of the box to attach the rope for the Gobbler's leash. Once you have your Garbage Gobbler ready, walk it around your neighborhood and start filling up its empty belly with trash. Wear work gloves when you pick up trash, and be very careful of broken glass. Also, don't forget to wash your hands after you are done feeding the Garbage Gobbler!

What You'll Need
- large cardboard box
- scissors
- paint
- paintbrushes
- extra cardboard
- glue
- 24 inches of thin rope
- work gloves

Insect Detectives

◆▸◆▸◆▸◆

Do you know all your neighbors? Are you sure?

What You'll Need
- sketch pad
- colored pencils
- magnifying glass

Whether you have a well-kept yard or a forest out back, you can be sure of one thing: There are creepy-crawly creatures living all around you. In fact, unless you live in the arctic, there is a spider not more than 3 feet away from you right now! But don't worry. It's not watching you with its 8 spider eyes. It's looking for insects to eat. Take your sketch pad, pencils, and magnifying glass and go find out who they are! Do you know their names? Each bug you find has an important job to do. It's part of the ecosystem in which they—and you—live. Can you figure out what it eats? What do you think would eat this insect? How do you think this insect is impor- tant to the ecosystem? After drawing them, take your pictures to the library and do a little research for fun!

Animal Alphabet Game

◆▸◆▸◆▸◆

***Earth Day is a day to celebrate all the living things on our planet.
How many kinds of animals can you name?***

This is a game for 2 or more people. It will help you remember different kinds of animals—and maybe help you learn a few more! Count off to decide what order you will play in. Player 1 thinks of an animal, such as elephant. Elephant ends with the letter T, so player 2 must think of an animal that begins with the letter T. Any animal will do, including insects, sea creatures, mammals, reptiles, birds, even dinosaurs and other creatures that once walked the earth. But you can use an animal only once! When the last player thinks of an animal name, the first player must think of an animal that begins with the last letter. If you want to make the game harder, play only sea creatures, land dwellers, or birds.

Animal Tracks

▸▸▸▸▸

For Earth Day, make animal tracks across your letters and notes.

What You'll Need
- paper
- pencil
- block of wood
- double-sided tape
- markers or ink pad
- foam tray (from fruit or vegetables)
- scissors
- paper towels

Caution: This project requires adult help.

Draw some animal tracks—either do some research about your favorite animal or make up your own tracks. Cover a side of the wooden block completely with double-sided tape. You may need to use more than one piece of tape. Don't peel the paper off the front side of the tape yet. Lay a piece of paper over the tracks you have drawn. Trace them with a black marker. This is your pattern. Lay your pattern on top of the clean foam tray. Trace over the tracks with a dull pencil, pressing hard enough to leave marks in the foam. Have an adult help you cut out the tracks with scissors. When all the tracks are cut out, peel the backing off the double-sided tape on the block. Press the tracks onto the tape. Apply color to the stamp with a marker or an ink pad—apply as evenly as possible. Press the stamp firmly onto a piece of paper. Before you use a different color, clean your stamp by pressing it a few times on a damp paper towel, then on a dry paper towel.

Which Day Is It?

There is some dispute about what day is truly Earth Day. John McConnell is the founder of the first Earth Day, which was begun on March 21, 1970. Gaylord Nelson also claims to be the founder of Earth Day; his first Earth Day celebration was April 22, 1970.

May Day Flower Cone

Leave a lovely May Day flower surprise on someone's door as a springtime greeting!

What You'll Need
- decorated paper
- glue
- hole punch
- ribbon
- fresh flowers
- paper towel
- plastic bag

Roll a piece of pretty paper into a cone shape, and glue the edges together to seal it. When the glue has dried, punch 2 holes on opposite sides of the cone. Tie the ends of a piece of ribbon through each of the holes to make a handle. Gather some fresh flowers. Put a wet paper towel around the flower stems, and cover the towel with a plastic bag. Tie ribbon around the plastic bag to seal it, and set the flowers inside the decorative cone. Hang the cone on a family member's bedroom doorknob or on the front door of a neighborhood friend (with a parent's permission).

May Day Garland

Celebrate the blossoming of the spring season with a floral crown!

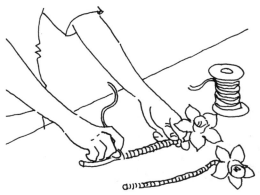

What You'll Need
- fresh flowers
- floral wire

The arrival of spring is celebrated in many European countries on the first day of May. Flower garlands, crowns, and baskets full of flowers are part of many of the celebrations.

To make a flower crown, gather 6 to 10 colorful flowers. Wrap green floral wire around the stem of each flower. Wind the wiry stem of each flower around the stem of the next flower, just beneath the flower. Weave the stem of the last flower around the stem of the first to form a circle. Place the garland on your head to check the fitting before closing the circle. Now don the floral crown, and celebrate spring!

 May Day Baskets

◆▸◆▸◆▸◆▸◆

Make May Day baskets for your neighbors.

What You'll Need
• poster board
• pencil
• ruler
• blunt scissors
• wallpaper with spring pattern
• white paste
• stapler and staples
• fresh flowers

Draw a circle 5 inches across and a strip 10×1 inches on the poster board. Cut them out. Use the poster board circle and strip as patterns. Lay them on the back of the wallpaper. Trace around them. You will need 2 wallpaper circles and 2 wallpaper strips for each basket. Cover one side of your poster board circle with paste, and paste a wallpaper

circle to it with the pretty side up. Cover one side of your poster board strip with paste, and paste a wallpaper strip to it, pretty side up. Turn the strip over, and paste the other wallpaper strip to the other side. Lay your circle on the table wallpaper-side-down. Center the strip, and paste it across the middle of the circle. Paste the last wallpaper circle pretty-side-up on top of the strip. Turn it over. Pull the ends of the strip together to make a handle. (The sides of your basket will curl up.) Staple the handle together at the top. Put fresh flowers in the basket, and give it to your neighbors.

Glorious Garlands

◆▸◆▸◆▸◆▸◆

Guests at May Day festivities were "wreathed": Each wore a crown of green leaves with flowers in their hair. Here's how to make a May Day wreath.

Find a bunch of the same kind of leaves with strong stems. Break off the stems, but hold on to them. Overlap the leaves, and push the broken-off stems through the leaves as if they

What You'll Need
• leaves
• flowers

were pins to hold them together. Make a chain of leaves. When your leaf chain is long enough to fit around your head, fasten the final leaf to the first one. Add flowers by slipping their stems under the stem-pins on the top side of the leaves. (Warning! If you live in an area where poison ivy or poison oak grows, make sure you know what they look like before you go leaf hunting. They could give you a terrible rash!)

Nine Men's Morris

◆◆◆◆◆◆

Nine Men's Morris was one of the most popular May Day games in England.

What You'll Need
- large cardboard square
- marker
- 9 black stones
- 9 white stones
- coin

Copy the Morris board (as seen in the illustration) onto a piece of cardboard. Each player starts with 9 stones of one color. Flip a coin to see who moves first. Take turns putting the stones on the dots on the Morris board one at a time. You can put a stone on any vacant dot. The goal is to make a "mill"—3 of your stones together on any line. Each time you make a mill you get to take one of your opponent's pieces. If your opponent forms a mill, they get to take one of yours. Pieces in a mill are safe— they can't be taken. When all the stones have been placed on the board, the goal is to create new mills by taking turns moving the stones. A stone can be moved one space along any line, but there can't be a stone already sitting on the dot you move to. The game ends when 1 player has just 2 pieces left or when 1 player is unable to move.

May Day Hoops

◆◆◆◆◆◆

Children used to have hoop races on May Day; now you can, too!

Tie as many ribbons as you can to the hoop, all the way around. Make sure the knots are on the inside of the hoop so they won't get in the way when the hoop rolls. Tie a tiny bell to the end of every third or fourth ribbon. Practice rolling your May Day hoop, touching it with the dowel. How fast can you go? Invite your friends to race!

What You'll Need
- plastic hula hoop
- 6-inch ribbons
- small bells
- 12-inch wooden dowel

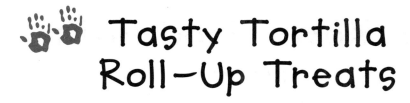

Tasty Tortilla Roll-Up Treats

◆▷◆▷◆▷◆▷

These easy-to-make snacks will help you celebrate the wonderful flavors of Mexico on Cinco de Mayo!

What You'll Need
- flour tortillas
- cream cheese
- table knife
- mild salsa (optional)
- spoon
- tomato
- olives
- lettuce

Caution: This project requires adult help.

Spread a thin layer of cream cheese on a flour tortilla. Spoon a little salsa over the cream cheese (if you don't like spicy foods, you can skip this step). Then put some lettuce, sliced tomatoes (ask an adult to help you slice them), olives, and any other veggies you like on top. Roll the tortilla up, and eat it. Mucho gusto!

Mock Silver Jewelry

◆▷◆▷◆▷◆▷

Dress up for your Cinco de Mayo party with this festive pasta jewelry.

Caution: This project requires adult help.

Use an assortment of pasta. If the pasta you choose doesn't have holes to thread, have an adult make a hole in the pasta with a needle. If you want to make a necklace, cut a length of string and shape it into a loop big enough to fit over your head. Make it a little longer than that so you have enough string to make the knot. Then lay out your pasta shapes along the loop in different

What You'll Need
- dried pasta (tubes, wheels, macaroni, etc.)
- needle
- string
- scissors
- pencil
- turquoise and silver paint
- paintbrushes

arrangements until you get one you like. You might want to write numbers lightly in pencil on the pasta so you know the order in which to string them. Now you can paint the pasta in silver and turquoise. You might paint alternating colors, or paint the whole necklace silver except for the middle 2 pasta pieces. Follow your own design sense! Lay the pasta out to dry in the same arrangement in which you will thread them. When the paint is dry, thread the pasta on the string, and knot the string ends.

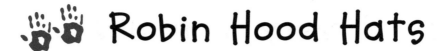

Robin Hood Hats

▶▶▶▶▶▶

Celebrate the coming of spring on May Day just as they did in merry olde England.

What You'll Need
- measuring tape
- paper
- pencil
- green felt
- straight pins
- blunt scissors
- needle and green thread, or stapler and staples
- feather
- small safety pin

Using the measuring tape, measure around your head and add 1 inch. On a piece of paper, draw a line half as long as your measurement. From the middle of your line, measure up 9 inches, and make a dot. Draw a semi-circle (half circle) from the end of the line, through the top dot, to the end of the other side of the line. This half circle is your hat pattern. Stack 2 pieces of green felt, and pin your pattern to them. Cut along the pattern. Stitch or staple ½ inch in from the edge—only along the half circle. Turn up a 1-inch brim. Pin a feather to your hat, and head for Sherwood Forest!

Cinco de Mayo Flowers

▶▶▶▶▶▶

Make a festive floral bouquet to commemorate an important Mexican holiday.

In Spanish, Cinco de Mayo means "the fifth of May." It was on this day in 1862 that a badly outnumbered Mexican army defeated the well-equipped invading French army.

What You'll Need
- different colors of tissue paper
- blunt scissors
- chenille stems
- ribbon or vase

Cut tissue paper circles in a variety of colors in 3 different sizes. For each flower, use 2 small circles, 2 medium circles, and 2 large circles. Place 2 small circles on top of 2 medium circles, and put these on top of the 2 large circles. Make a U with the chenille stem, and push it through all 6 layers so that both ends of the chenille stem go all the way through the pile and stick out behind the large circles. Twist the chenille stem ends together on the bottom of the flower to make it into a stem. Fold up each circle to create a ruffle of petals. (You can make a flower using 1 color, 2 colors, or all different colors!) Make a few flowers, and put them in a vase or tie them together with a ribbon for festive holiday beauty.

Magnets de Mayo

◆▷◆▷◆▷◆▷

These colorful flowers are actually made of corn and beans!

What You'll Need

- assorted dried corn and beans
- green, white, and red paint
- paintbrush
- white, green, or red felt
- blunt scissors
- white glue
- waxed paper
- sticky-backed magnetic strip

Choose an assortment of dried corn and beans to vary the shapes of your flowers. Tiny lentils and corn kernels will make delicate posies, while larger fava beans can become the leaves of a gorgeous bloom. Paint lots of dried beans and corn in the colors of Mexico (green, white, and red), and let them dry. Then arrange 6 to 10 beans and kernels in a flower shape.

Cut a circle of felt a bit larger than your flower. Cover the circle with glue, and arrange your flower on it. Put the felt flower on waxed paper, and cover the flower completely with glue. If some of the glue runs over the edges of your flower, you can break it off when it is dry.

When your flower is dry, peel it off the waxed paper and press a piece of sticky-backed magnetic strip on the back.

Loved One Locket

◆▷◆▷◆▷◆▷

Be close to Mom all year long with this pretty locket.

What You'll Need

- 2 twist-off bottle caps
- colored nail polish
- felt scraps
- blunt scissors
- craft glue
- small photo of your face
- silk cord

Paint both bottle caps inside and out with a light coat of colored nail polish. Paint a side at a time, use even strokes, and let dry for at least 15 minutes before continuing. You may need to add a second coat to cover the bottle cap well.

Cut a small strip of felt in a color that matches the nail polish. Glue an end inside each cap to form a hinge. This will allow the caps to close and form a locket. Cut out and glue another piece of felt inside a cap, and glue a picture of your face, also cut to fit, inside the other cap (ask for permission first!). Cut out a small heart, and glue it inside the first cap.

Make sure the felt hinge is at the top of the locket and your photo is faceup when the cap hangs. You might want to cut out a small felt heart or other decoration to glue to the outside of the locket. When the glue has dried, tie a silk cord around the hinge of the locket. Then tie the ends together to form a loop large enough to fit over an adult head.

Beautiful Baths

Mom will love to relax in a sweet-smelling bath.

Your Mom will thank you again and again for these wonderful homemade bath salts. Put the baking soda in a bowl, and mix in a few drops of flavoring and a few drops of food coloring. Mix them together with a spoon until all the ingredients are well-blended. Choose colors that go well with the flavors, such as green food coloring with mint flavoring and orange food coloring with orange flavoring. Name the different bath salts you create (such as Sweet Vanilla Dream or Minty Refresher), and write the names on the envelopes. Decorate the envelopes with pictures of Mom's favorite things and other pretty pictures. Fill the envelopes with the bath salts.

What You'll Need
- 4 tablespoons baking soda
- bowl
- food flavorings (almond, mint, orange, or vanilla)
- food coloring
- mixing spoon
- envelopes
- markers

Cookie Bouquet

Is your mother one sweet cookie? Then show her!

What You'll Need
- tube of refrigerated cookie dough
- nonstick cooking spray
- cookie sheet
- butter knife
- bamboo skewers
- ruler
- spatula
- florist tape
- ribbons
- florist foam
- artificial leaves

Caution: This project requires adult help.

Pick your mother's favorite kind of cookie dough. Spray the cookie sheet with nonstick spray. Cut the cookie dough into 1-inch-thick slices; you can shape the cookies into flower shapes if you'd like. Push a bamboo skewer point about 1½ inches into the bottom of each cookie. Ask an adult to help you bake the cookies according to directions. Let the cookies cool on the cookie sheet. When cool, use a spatula to lift them off the pan. Wrap the skewers with florist tape, and decorate them with ribbons. Stick the stems into the florist foam. Cover the foam with the leaves.

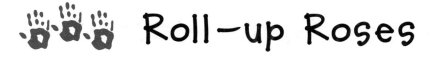

Roll-up Roses

◆▸◆▸◆▸◆▸

Would you like to give your mom a beautiful vase of roses that will never wilt? Spray them with perfume to make them smell sweet!

What You'll Need
- 10×20-inch pieces of crepe or tissue paper
- yardstick
- floral stem wires
- stapler and staples
- florist tape
- vase
- perfume (optional)

1. Lay the yardstick on the long edge of a sheet of crepe or tissue paper. Fold the paper over the yardstick, turning the yardstick as you keep folding. The folds should be a bit loose. Leave 1 inch unwrapped at the bottom (we will call this the fringe).

2. When you are done folding, grab an end of the paper in each hand and push it all to the center of the yardstick. This will give the petals a nice texture. Pull the yardstick out.

3. Make a little loop at the end of a stem wire. Staple the loop onto the folded portion at one end of your paper strip; the fringe of unfolded paper should be just below the staple.

4. Starting with the end where your stem is stapled, roll the paper up. Roll it tightly at first, and then a little more loosely. Gather the fringe and twist it so that it wraps around the stem.

5. Wrap florist tape around the twisted paper fringe and 2 inches down the stem of the rose. Place the rose in a vase, and present to your sweet mom on Mother's Day.

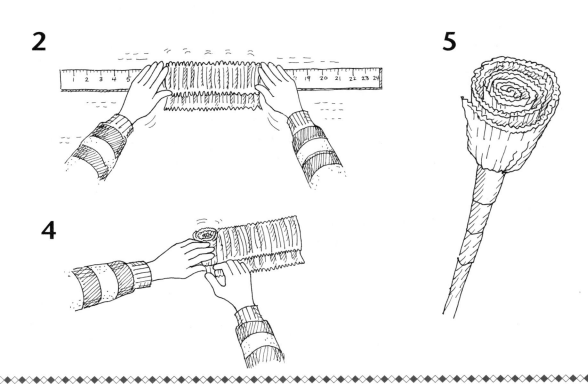

Ribbon Spool Sachet

This present will look pretty and smell great—what more could Mom want?

Take 2 pieces of lovely tissue paper, and spread them out on a flat surface. Place the spool in the center. Sprinkle a good amount of baby powder inside the circular spool.

Draw the tissue paper up around the spool to form a pretty puff. Tie the top of the tissue paper with colorful ribbon. When you give this to Mom, it will remind her that you think no one is quite as sweet as she.

What You'll Need
• tissue paper
• large ribbon spool
• baby powder
• ribbon

Magic Mom Paperweight

Mom will treasure this glittery scene forever!

What You'll Need
• small wide-mouth clear jar with lid
• small china or plastic figure of a woman
• waterproof glue
• other waterproof figures or trinkets
• glycerin or mineral oil
• water
• glitter
• tablespoon
• super glue

Caution: This project requires adult help.

Glue a small figure of a woman onto the inside of your jar. Glue on other tiny, waterproof figures to personalize the scene: How about Mom's favorite cat or dog? Or a small shell or rock from a family vacation? Fake jewels are nice, too. So are miniature plastic trees or flowers that can be found at most hobby or craft shops. Use your imagination to put "Mom" in an interesting and colorful scene. When the glue has dried, fill the jar with mineral oil or glycerin with a small bit of water added. Finish by adding a tablespoon of colored or silver glitter. Screw the top on tightly (have an adult use the super glue to keep the lid on).

Shake up the magic dust—this gift will really show your mother how much you appreciate the magic she makes for you all year long.

Mom and Me Book

This book is sure to bring tears of joy to Mom's eyes!

Caution: This project requires adult help.

Along a seam, cut a side of a brown bag to the bottom. Cut the bottom off the bag. Repeat for all the bags. Unfold the bags. Trim the bags to the size of the cardboard (9-inch squares). Have an adult help you iron the bags with a cool iron to make them lay flat.

Draw a line 1 inch from an edge of each of the cardboard squares. Use the edge of the ruler to bend the cardboard along the line. Bend the cardboard back and forth, until it works like a paper hinge. Put a strip of plastic tape on each side of the cardboard covering the hinge. Glue wrapping paper on the cardboard.

Punch holes in the 1-inch section of the covers; punch a hole 2 inches from the top of the book and another hole 2 inches from the bottom. Punch holes in the paper bag pages to match the cover holes. Stack all the bags between the covers, and clamp them with the clothespins.

Thread the ribbon from the inside to the outside of the cover. Tie the ribbon in a knot, and make a bow. Write a title on the front cover, and decorate it. Fill your book with thoughts and pictures of Mom.

What You'll Need
- 25 small brown paper bags
- scissors
- two 9-inch squares heavy cardboard
- iron and ironing board
- pencil
- metal ruler
- clear plastic tape
- wrapping paper
- craft glue
- hole punch
- 2 clothespins
- ribbon
- markers

Hearts and Flowers Bookmark

◆▶◆▶◆▶◆▶

Give Mom your heart—and the time to enjoy a good book.

What You'll Need
- construction paper
- blunt scissors
- ruler
- clear vinyl adhesive paper
- colorful cord
- paper clip

Cut 3 hearts and 3 flower shapes out of different-colored construction paper. Play with the design of your flowers and hearts. When you are happy with the arrangement, cut two 6-inch squares of the clear adhesive paper. Take the backing off 1 piece, and lay it sticky side up on the table. Carefully arrange the hearts and flowers on the sticky side of the paper. Put a 12-inch piece of colorful satin or metallic cord on the bookmark so there is a small loop above the flowers and some of the cord hangs down from the heart and flower arrangement. Weight the hanging end of the cord with a large paper clip. Take the second sheet of adhesive paper, remove the backing, and cover the other side of your design. Remove the paper clip.

Cut away the excess contact paper, leaving behind your design and the bookmark cord. Your mother will read the love that went into your gift.

Sentimental Journey

◆▶◆▶◆▶◆▶

Tell Mom how much you love her—in an original poem!

Look through family photo albums, or watch videotapes of family celebrations and trips. This is a great way to get inspiration for a Mother's Day poem. Tell her how special an experience was because she was there to share it with you. Ask yourself: What has Mom meant to me? Has she done things for me that no one else has? What do I especially love about her? Think of how happy her smile makes you, how warm and comforting it feels to be hugged by her. Does she help you with your homework? Play games with you? Cook your favorite foods? Your poem does not have to rhyme. A good poem is full of feelings and words that create lively, colorful pictures in the reader's mind. Write your poem on white or colored paper, and draw pictures to go with it.

What You'll Need
- family photo albums or videotapes
- white or colored paper
- markers

Golden Jewelry

These pins take patience to make, but Mom's expression will be worth it!

What You'll Need
- animal crackers
- oval or oblong crackers
- white acrylic spray paint
- small paintbrushes
- sealer
- gold acrylic paint
- glue
- pin backs
- cool-temp glue gun

Caution: This project requires adult help.

Pick an animal cracker and an oval or oblong cracker for the backing. Brush away all loose crumbs and salt from the front and back of the crackers. Have a grown-up spray-paint one side of the crackers white. When dry, have the adult spray-paint the other side. The crackers should be completely white. Paint sealer on the back of the crackers to seal them. Let them dry. Turn them over to seal the top and sides. Let them dry. Paint the animal and the oval cracker with gold acrylic paint. When dry, glue the animal cracker to the middle of the oval cracker. After the glue has dried, add a another coat of gold paint. When the paint is completely dry, seal it by painting it with a thick coat of sealer. When the sealer is dry, have an adult help you glue the pin to the back.

Colored Candleholder

Light up Mom's day with this pretty candleholder.

Wash and dry a small, empty jar. Draw and cut out a small stencil in the shape of a heart or some other pretty design from the cardboard. Make sure your stencil fits on the jar. Tape the stencil down, and use Mom's favorite color of nail polish (with permission!) to paint inside the stencil. Sprinkle salt over the wet polish to make it sparkle when it dries. You may want to paint a design around the whole jar or only on the front and back. Be sure to let each side dry thoroughly before you turn the glass over. When the polish is dry, remove the stencil. Tie a colored ribbon around the neck of the jar, and put a small scented candle inside. Make several candleholders, and put them on the table as a centerpiece to add a fragrant scent to your Mother's Day meal.

What You'll Need
- jar that votive candle will fit in
- cardboard
- pencil
- blunt scissors
- tape
- nail polish
- salt
- ribbon
- scented votive candle

Chocolate Spoons

❖❖❖❖❖❖

Mom will love to stir her coffee with a chocolate spoon.

What You'll Need
- ¼ cup semi-sweet chocolate chips
- microwave-safe cup
- 1½ teaspoons solid shortening
- mixing spoon
- 2 plastic spoons
- drinking glasses
- plastic bags
- ribbon

Caution: This project requires adult help.

Pour the chips into the microwave-safe cup. Add the shortening. Microwave on high for 1 minute. Stir, and continue to microwave for 30 seconds or until the chips are melted. Stir thoroughly. When all the chocolate has melted, use the mixing spoon to coat the chocolate on the front and back of the plastic spoons. Only coat the spoon part, not the handle. Carefully place each plastic spoon on the rim of a drinking glass to dry. It will probably take about 10 minutes for the chocolate to harden. When the spoons are ready, put them in a plastic bag and tie them with a ribbon. These spoons are best when freshly made. Surprise Mom by placing them next to her coffee cup on Mother's Day morning.

Cozy Cases

❖❖❖❖❖❖

Mom will appreciate these soft cases for her glasses and change.

Caution: This project requires adult help.

Find a necktie wide enough to fit a pair of eyeglasses. Cut a 10-inch piece from the widest end (do not include the pointed part at the tie's bottom in your measurement). If there is a tag inside the tie, have an adult carefully cut it out with manicure scissors. Fold the cut edges together, and glue them shut. When dry, fold the tie in half, bringing the end up to just before the tie starts to narrow. Glue the sides together to create an envelope. Use clothespins to hold the sides together until the glue dries. Make a fastener on the open end of the tie by pressing a sticky-backed dot on the inside of the pointed end of the tie, folding it over, and placing another dot on the tie to match up with the first dot. To make the change purse, cut a 5-inch piece of necktie and follow the instructions for the glasses case.

What You'll Need
- old necktie
- blunt scissors
- ruler
- manicure scissors
- blue glue gel
- clothespins
- sticky-backed, hook-and-loop-fabric-fastener dots

Breakfast Bouquet

◆▶◆▶◆▶◆▶

These flowers will last long after Mother's Day is over.

What You'll Need
- blown eggs
- scissors
- paint
- paintbrushes
- construction paper
- glue
- cardboard egg cartons
- pom-poms
- wooden beads
- chenille stems
- florist tape
- crepe paper
- ribbon

Caution: This project requires adult help.

To make the blown eggs for the different flowers, see the instructions for the Blown Egg Sachet on page 464. If you want to make a tulip, using very sharp scissors (you might need an adult's help) carefully cut Vs around the small end of a blown egg. Paint the blown egg light pink with darker pink vertical stripes. For a daisy, glue white paper petals around the base of a yellow egg. Cut a cup out of the egg carton to make the base of a tiger lily. Paint it orange, and glue on orange and brown spotted paper petals. Other flowers can be made by painting egg carton cups in pretty colors and gluing a yellow pom-pom or a wooden bead in the center of each.

Make stems for your flowers using green chenille stems and florist tape. You can also glue on green crepe paper leaves to your stems. Tie your bouquet with a colorful ribbon.

Float a Flower Boat

◆▶◆▶◆▶◆

Decorate a homemade toy boat in honor of soldiers who died at sea.

Draw colorful flowers with waterproof markers on a paper plate. Carefully poke a hole in the center of the plate with a pencil. Poke the open end of a round balloon through the hole. Blow up the balloon (from the back of the plate) until it is full. Knot the balloon. If desired, you can also glue small fresh flowers or wildflowers onto the balloon or plate. Make a few different balloon boats, and send them off to "sea" as a beautiful, flowery thank-you to the men and women who gave their lives to preserve freedom. (Collect the balloons and discard them after you are done; balloons can be harmful to wildlife.)

What You'll Need
- paper plate
- waterproof markers
- pencil
- round balloon
- small fresh flowers or wildflowers (optional)
- glue (optional)

Neighborhood Parade

◆▶◆▶◆▶◆

What would Memorial Day be without a colorful parade?

What You'll Need
- red, white, and blue clothing
- flags or flowers
- empty coffee cans
- wooden spoons
- wagons
- rope
- stuffed animals
- dolls
- red, white, and blue ribbons
- red, white, and blue balloons
- red, white, and blue streamers
- bicycles
- fake flowers
- chenille stems
- paper
- markers

Get the whole neighborhood involved in this festive march around the block. Gather up your pets, too. Tell everyone to wear clothes that are red, white, and blue. You may want to make or carry flags or flowers. Home-made drums can be made by painting empty coffee cans; beat on the lids with a wooden spoon. Tie wagons together with rope, and fill them with stuffed animals and dolls decorated with red, white, and blue ribbons, streamers, and balloons. Weave red, white, and blue streamers into the spokes of your bicycle's wheels. Attach fake flowers to the handlebars with chenille stems. Set a time for your parade to start, and post notices around the neighborhood. When everyone has gathered, pound a beat on one of the drums and lift up those knees in a march.

Traditional Tattoos

❖❖❖❖❖❖❖

On Memorial Day, show your true colors with these patriotic tattoos.

Memorial Day is a day to remember the men and women who died while fighting for our country's freedom. We often place flowers at the graves of soldiers on this day. Make a hand-painted tattoo to show your support for those who died in battle. Some soldiers got tattoos when they were fighting far from home to remind them of their dedication to their country and the people back home who were missed. Maybe you would like to paint on a flower tattoo in memory of a relative who died in battle. Or perhaps you would like to paint a tattoo of the American flag or a bald eagle to show your patriotism. Wear your tattoos to a Memorial Day picnic or parade, and show them off with pride.

What You'll Need
• waterbased face paints
• small paintbrushes

Patriotic Poppies

❖❖❖❖❖❖❖

Memorial Day is also known as Poppy Day.

What You'll Need
• red crepe paper
• ruler
• blunt scissors
• large needle
• green chenille stems

Caution: This project requires adult help.

In the spring, red poppies bloom on European battlefields where thousands of soldiers died in battle. Many veteran's organizations sell poppies to earn money for disabled vets. You can make your own crepe paper poppies.

To make each poppy, cut out three 4-inch circles of red crepe paper. Lay the circles on top of each other, and ask an adult to help you use a needle to make 2 holes next to each other in the center (go through all the circles). Put the end of a chenille stem through one hole, bend the chenille stem, and bring the end down through the other hole. Twist the end around the long part of the chenille stem to secure it. Pull the crepe paper petals slightly away from each other to form the poppy.

SUMMER SHINES

Summer is a blast—all that sunshine, all those outdoor games, all the picnic fun! This chapter gives you even more exciting projects to do and make for all those fun-in-the-sun summer holidays.

Progressive Mining Flag Game

◆▸◆▸◆▸◆

Play a unique version of this popular Victorian game on Flag Day (June 1).

What You'll Need
- small containers
- sand
- ruler
- paper
- blunt scissors
- markers
- wooden skewers
- glue
- plastic straws
- empty cups or bowls

This game requires a steady hand while playing. To make the game, fill small containers with sand. These are known as "mines." For every 2 players there must be 1 mine. Cut a 4×3-inch square of paper for each of the mines. On each square, draw one of the different stages of the American flag, beginning with the original design up to our present-day flag. Glue the end of each paper flag to a wooden skewer, and when the glue dries, stick a flag into each of the mines. Cut a little off the end of each straw (1 for each player) to make a shovel shape. Players then take turns using the plastic straws to remove a bit of sand and placing it in an empty cup or bowl. Whichever team makes the flag fall while removing sand loses the game.

Magnet Movie Theater

Invite your friends to a movie—right inside your house!

What You'll Need
- shoe box
- construction paper
- old magazines or catalogs, or paper
- markers
- blunt scissors
- glue
- paper clips
- magnets
- fabric
- flashlight

Do you like movies? Have you ever thought of making your own? To celebrate Children's Day (on the second Sunday in June), why not make up a science fiction or fantasy movie, such as *The Hundred-Foot Child Who Saved the World.* To make your movie theater, cover a shoe box inside and out with colorful construction paper. You may want to write the name of your movie theater on the sides of the box. Cut out pictures you want for the background of your movie. Does your movie take place in a city? Cut out or draw buildings, and glue them to the inside of the box. If you want something to move—people, animals, clouds, or vehicles—glue a paper clip to the back

of the object. Then, when you tell the story of your movie, put your cutout against the background and press a magnet against the back of the shoe box behind the paper clip. When you let go of the cutout, the magnet will hold it up. Slide 2 magnets around the back of the shoe box to make 2 characters move. You can also cut out fabric curtains and glue the top edge to the top of the box. Turn out the lights before your movie starts, and have a friend shine a flashlight onto the "screen" just as you flip the curtains up. (Our illustration shows the top cut off the box to better show the inside scene.)

 # Carp Kite

◄►◄►◄►◄►

Celebrate Children's Day—Japanese style!

What You'll Need
- wire coat hanger
- tissue paper
- tape
- construction paper
- blunt scissors
- markers
- ruler
- spool of string

Caution: This project requires adult help.

In Japan on Children's Day, carp kites are flown. The carp is the symbol of strength, courage, and determination because of the way it leaps upstream. These are qualities parents wish for their children. You can draw a carp on a kite to fly on Children's Day.

To make the kite, ask an adult to help you bend a coat hanger into a diamond shape. Have them bend the hook part so it won't poke anyone. Then cover the wire by wrapping it with a layer of tissue paper. Tape the ends of the tissue paper to secure it. Cut a diamond shape out of construction paper that is a little larger than the coat-hanger diamond. Draw the carp with the markers. Tape the paper to the coat hanger so that the diamond-shaped opening is covered. Ask an adult to help you poke a hole at each of the corners of the diamond. Cut three 20-inch lengths of string. Tie one each to the top and side holes. Tie one end of a spool of string to the bottom hole to make the flying string. Then tie the free ends of the top and side strings to the flying string near where it meets the kite. This will help your kite fly. Take your carp out and run!

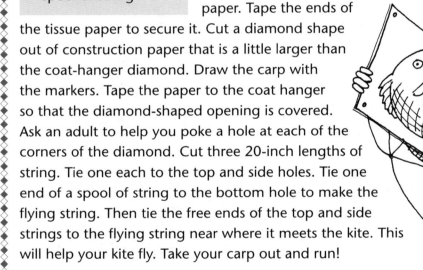

New Child Welcome Tray

New parents will really appreciate this gift.

What You'll Need
- 4 or 5 small jars of different sizes (one with a shaker top for powder)
- stickers or decals
- paints
- paintbrushes
- cotton balls
- pins
- baby oil
- baby powder
- round or rectangular aluminum foil cake pan
- ribbon
- glue

Collect some small empty jars of different sizes. You can use jars that once held peanut butter, spices, baby food, mustard, relish, or pickles. Just make sure that they are washed and dried well to get rid of any smell. Decorate the clean jars with stickers or decals, or paint on flowers or other cheery designs. Then label each lid (Cotton Balls, Baby Lotion, Baby Oil, Diaper Pins, etc.) with the new baby supplies. Put those supplies in each jar. Put baby powder in a spice jar with a shaker top. Next, glue a ribbon around the edge of a foil cake pan. Arrange the jars in the pan and take them over to the new baby's house to welcome her or him into the world.

 # Kid Talk

Put on a special talk show—by kids, for kids, and about kids!

Think about the kinds of problems and challenges that children face and what you can do to make life better for children. Write down your ideas, and then act out a TV talk show to discuss them. One person can be the host, and everyone else can be guests or members of the studio audience. One person can videotape, if you have a video camera. Think of a name for your show. You may want to play music while someone announces the beginning of the show. The host can sit at a table with her or his guests. The studio audience can sit in rows of chairs facing the host and guests. The guests can play experts, such as teachers or politicians, or they can play parents and children. Members of the studio audience can ask questions when the host calls on them. Practice your TV show, and then invite a real audience to watch it!

What You'll Need
- paper
- pen or pencil
- chairs
- desk or table
- video camera or audio cassette player (optional)

Famous Children Game

❖❖❖❖❖❖❖

Do you know the names of famous children? Play this game and find out!

This game will give you and your friends a real mental workout. One player is "It" and must think of a famous child. The famous child could be a movie star, a sports figure, a character in a book or play, or someone that is currently in the news. The famous child must be familiar to everyone playing the game. "It" then says "I'm thinking of a famous child whose name starts with *W*" (or whatever letter). The other players take turns asking questions about the famous child that can be answered either yes or no. They may ask a total of 20 questions. Whoever guesses correctly gets to be "It" in the next round of the game. Who was the famous child? Tiny Tim in *A Christmas Carol?* Little Red Riding Hood?

Slamming Caps Game

❖❖❖❖❖❖❖

Play this popular, old-fashioned game of Milk Caps, or POGs, with your friends.

What You'll Need
- corrugated card-board
- small jar tops
- pencil
- blunt scissors
- copies of school pictures, or magazine or catalog pictures of children's faces
- paints (optional)
- paintbrush (optional)

Back in the 1930s, when milk was delivered in bottles, children collected the milk bottle caps and played a game with them. You can make your own Milk Caps, or POGs, to use in a special Children's Day game.

To make POGs, trace around a small jar top placed on corrugated cardboard. Cut them out. Glue on either pictures of school friends or children's faces cut from an old magazine or catalog (ask for permission first!). Leave the other sides of the POGs blank or paint them a solid color. To play the game, stack 10 or more POGs in a column. Toss a small jar top, or slammer, at the column. If a POG lands with the child's face up, the person who tossed the slammer gets 1 point. If the POG lands with the blank side up, the player gets 0 points. You can also play for POGs instead of points. Most of the fun of this game is collecting and trading the POGs. See if you can get an entire set of POGs with the faces of your classmates!

Special Seed Bracelets

◄►◄►◄►◄►

Let the world see your friendship when you and a friend wear these matching bracelets on Friendship Day (June 15).

What You'll Need
- watermelon seeds
- cookie sheet
- large needle
- paints
- paintbrushes
- elastic thread
- blunt scissors

Caution: This project requires adult help.

Wash lots of watermelon seeds. Use the dark brown seeds; the white ones may not be firm enough. Spread the seeds out on a cookie sheet, and let them dry overnight. When they are dry, have an adult help you carefully poke a hole through the top of each seed with a large needle. To make matching bracelets, decide with your friend what colors you should paint the seeds. You might want to use both of your favorite colors, alternating them when you thread them on the elastic to show how you and your friend always take turns. When you paint the seeds, paint one side of the seeds, and let the paint dry. Then turn the seeds over, and paint the other side. You can paint each side of your seeds a different color, and you can draw dots or tiny hearts on your seeds. Use your imagination! Thread the seeds onto enough elastic to make a bracelet. Knot the elastic. You and your friend can then slip your bracelets onto your wrists and declare your friendship to be forever.

Live Longer
According to researchers, people who have life-long, meaningful friendships live longer and healthier than those without life-long friends.

Best Friend's House Game

Race to your friend's house—without using your feet!

What You'll Need
- 2 oatmeal carton lids
- blunt scissors
- 2 shoe-box lids
- glue
- construction paper
- ruler
- markers
- clear tape
- 6 marbles

You and your friend should carefully cut the oatmeal lids on one side to make an opening for the marbles to pass through. After the lid is cut, it should look like a big letter C. Glue this C near one end of the inside of your shoe-box lids. If you want, you can first line your lids with colored construction paper. Cut out a 12×5-inch rectangle of construction paper, and fold it into a square shape to make the walls of a house. Before taping it together, draw on windows and doors, and each of you should write your name and address on your house. Cut out the door so that it will fit over the cutout in the oatmeal lid. Fold another rectangle over the square to make a roof, and tape the roof and the base of the house together. Glue the house over the oatmeal lid, with the door lining up with the opening of the C. Decorate the path to your house with markers. Draw driveways, trees, sidewalks, and people. To play the game, place 3 marbles in each shoe-box lid. To start, both of you say "Come on over to my house!" Each person races to get all their marbles into the house by moving their lid.

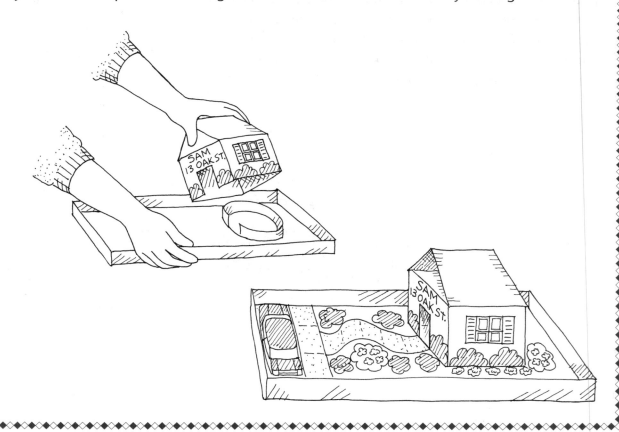

Logs for Lincoln Cake

❯❯❯❯❯❯❯

You don't have to be a president to enjoy this cake!

What You'll Need
- metal coffee can
- chocolate cake mix
- butter knife
- chocolate frosting
- chocolate sprinkles
- toasted coconut
- construction paper
- blunt scissors
- marker
- toothpicks
- tape

Caution: This project requires adult help.

Juneteenth (June 19) celebrates the day east Texas enforced President Lincoln's Emancipation Proclamation that abolished slavery. Share a log-shaped cake with friends to remember this smart and caring president.

Have an adult smooth the edges of the coffee can so you won't cut yourself. Wash and dry the empty can. Grease the inside of the can; the can will be used as a pan to make the cake into a log shape. Follow the directions on the cake mix. Pour the batter into the coffee can. Bake according to the directions on the box, but ask an adult to insert a knife into the center of the cake from time to time to check doneness. If the knife comes out clean, the cake is done. Let cool for 10 minutes, then run a knife around the edges and remove the cake.

When the cake has cooled, frost it with chocolate frosting and add chocolate sprinkles and toasted coconut to make the cake look like bark. Cut squares of construction paper, and write on messages such as "Happy Freedom Day!" or "Thanks, President Lincoln!" Tape the signs to toothpicks. Stick the signs in the top of the cake.

Race to Freedom Game

❯❯❯❯❯❯❯

Play this fast-paced game at your Juneteenth picnic.

Make a big sign from poster board, and write the word *Freedom* on it. Place it 50 to 100 yards away from the start of the race. Divide players into 2 teams. Players from both teams wait at 10- to 20-yard intervals on the course between the starting line and *Freedom*. (This is best played on grass or soft carpeting.) The first player skates on 2 paper plates while balancing a corncob on a spoon. When this player reaches the next player, he or she hands the

What You'll Need
- poster board
- markers
- corncobs
- spoons
- paper plates

skates, corncob, and spoon to the next player on the course, and so on until the final player makes it to *Freedom*. If the corncob falls off the spoon at any time, that player must return to the beginning, and his or her team starts again. Whichever team reaches *Freedom* first wins!

Pack of Log Sandwiches

◆▷◆▷◆▷◆▷

Make and fill your own picnic basket.

What You'll Need
- 2 cereal boxes
- blunt scissors
- tape
- wrapping paper
- construction paper
- glue
- yarn
- stapler and staples
- whole wheat bread (pre-sliced)
- rolling pin
- peanut butter
- butter knife
- plastic wrap
- napkins

To make the picnic basket, take out the inner bags of the cereal boxes, and cut a side panel from each box. Cut off the top flaps from both boxes. Slide one box halfway inside the other. Tape the boxes together where they meet. Cover the boxes with wrapping paper. Glue on cutout designs such as stars, the word *Juneteenth*, and the number 19 from construction paper. Staple a length of yarn across the top of the basket to make a handle. To make a log sandwich, flatten a slice of whole wheat bread with a rolling pin. Spread the slice with peanut butter, and roll it up into a cylinder shape. Wrap your "logs" in plastic wrap, and stack them and napkins inside your picnic basket.

 # Freedom Flag

◆▷◆▷◆▷◆▷

Wave the flag of freedom high!

To make it, staple the short edge of the fabric to a wooden dowel. Leave 2 inches of dowel showing at the top, and tie on yarn or ribbon streamers to the top. The rest of the dowel will be your flag's handle. Decorate your flag by cutting the word *Freedom* out of felt or fabric scraps and gluing them onto the canvas. Paint designs around the word with fabric paint. You might want to draw President Lincoln or the state of Texas on your flag. Think of what Juneteenth means to you and what pictures you can draw to show your feelings. Then wave your flag with pride as you march down the street.

What You'll Need
- 24×18-inch piece of heavy cotton or canvas
- stapler and staples
- 36-inch length of ½-inch dowel
- yarn or ribbons
- felt or fabric scraps
- blunt scissors
- fabric paint
- paintbrushes

Free-Form Freedom Rap

Write a rap song to celebrate freedom.

What You'll Need
• paper
• pencil
• wooden blocks

Freedom is something to sing about! Write a rhyming poem, and make up your own freedom rap song. Brainstorm a list of words and ideas that remind you of freedom and the holiday of June-teenth. Then think of words that rhyme with this list. For example, June and moon, free and honeybee, nineteen and keen. Write rhyming sentences that use these words, such as: "One fine June, I saw a beautiful moon. The date was June nineteen, and it sure was keen. Because now I am free, just like the honeybee!" When you finish your rhyme, clap out a rhythm with wooden blocks, and say it like a rap. Teach it to a friend, and make up a dance to go with it!

Lincoln's Cabin

Re-create Lincoln's log cabin for a centerpiece at your Juneteenth party.

Wash and dry the milk carton; cut off the top half. Glue brown construction paper to cover it inside and out. Cut out windows and doors or draw them on with a marker. Then cut and fold a piece of cardboard in half to form the roof. Attach it to the base of the cabin with tape or glue. Now you are ready to add the logs. You can glue on small straight twigs, or you can make logs by rolling a piece of brown paper around a pencil, taping the paper, and then sliding the pencil out. Glue logs in rows on all the sides of the house, leaving spaces for the windows and doors. Set the cabin on a plate, and surround it with leaves.

What You'll Need
• empty milk carton
• blunt scissors
• brown construction paper
• glue
• markers
• cardboard
• tape
• small straight twigs (optional)
• pencil
• plate
• leaves

Goddess of Liberty Crown

◄▷◄▷◄▷►

Be the Goddess of Liberty at the Juneteenth parade!

Cut out a 10-inch-high piece of construction paper that will be long enough to fit around your head plus a few inches to staple it closed. Cut long, pointed triangle shapes in the long end of the paper to make a crown shape. Cut 2 different-colored pieces of construction paper the same length and with the same pointed triangle shapes at the top. One piece should be 8 inches high, and the other should be 6 inches high. Glue each piece onto the next largest piece, and staple all the ends together. Now you have a beautiful layered crown. Use markers to write Goddess of Liberty on your crown. Decorate it with pretty designs. Put it on your head, and march proudly in the next Juneteenth parade!

What You'll Need
- construction paper
- blunt scissors
- ruler
- glue
- stapler and staples
- markers

Number 19 Mobile

◄▷◄▷◄▷◄▷►

The number 19 is a very lucky number for millions of people!

What You'll Need
- thin cardboard
- pencil
- blunt scissors
- paints
- paintbrushes
- old magazines
- small decorative objects
- glue
- large needle
- string
- hanger
- markers

Draw and cut out a very large number 1 and a number 9 from thin cardboard. Paint one side of both, let them dry, then paint the other side. While you are waiting for the paint to dry, look through old magazines and find pictures that remind you of freedom, which could include happy faces, birds flying, and people dancing. Gather other decorative objects, such as shells, ribbon, feathers, tiny flags, and other small items. Arrange your pictures and objects in a pleasing design on top of the number 19, and glue them down. Poke a small hole in the tops of the 1 and 9, and tie them to a hanger with string. Draw other figures and objects that remind you of free- dom on more cardboard, and cut them out. Poke holes in the tops of these, and tie them onto the hanger with string to make a mobile with number 19 as the middle. How about drawing President Lincoln!

Flame-Jumping Contest

▶▶▶▶▶

Play this old-fashioned game on the summer solstice,
and try not to get "burned"!

Draw and cut out a cardboard flame 15 inches high by 10 inches wide. Decorate the flame with markers. Cut out and decorate another piece of cardboard that is 20 inches square. Fold this piece in half to make a stand 10 inches high. To play the game, fasten the cardboard flame with clothespins to the cardboard stand. Start by pinning the flame so that its bottom is level with the bottom of the stand. Each player must then jump over it without knocking it over or touching it and getting "burned." Each time all the players have successfully leapt over the flame, the flame is repinned an inch higher. How high can you jump? If this flame game is too easy for you, make a taller flame!

What You'll Need
- corrugated cardboard
- blunt scissors
- ruler
- pencil
- markers
- clothespins

Just Dewy, Dear

In Lithuania, the summer solstice celebration is called Rasa, which means dew. In the region of Svencionis, young women would get up early and wash with the dew on the grass. They would then go back to sleep to dream of their future mate!

Clowny Cones

These cool, sweet clowns bring the circus right to your summer solstice party.

What You'll Need
- paper doily
- paper plate
- ice cream
- ice cream scooper
- gumdrops
- chocolate chips
- round hard candies
- sugar ice cream cone

For each clown, put a paper doily on a small paper plate. Place a scoop of ice cream on top of the doily. Use gumdrops or chocolate chips for the clown's eyes and nose. Carefully break a round hard candy in half for a smiling mouth. You can also use the whole candy if you want your clown to look surprised. You can use 2 more round candy halves for eyebrows. Give your clown a sugar cone hat with a gumdrop stuck on the tip. Keep your clowns in the freezer until you are ready to serve them. Your party guests will be laughing all the way to the table!

Sun Bread

Celebrate the sun with a sunny treat!

Caution: This project requires adult help.

To make this delicious bread, ask an adult to preheat the oven to 325 degrees. Beat the margarine, maple syrup, and egg for 1 minute at medium speed. Mix the other ingredients together in a separate bowl. Add the two mixtures together, and mix with a spoon until smooth. Pour the batter into a greased loaf pan, and bake for 1 hour. Let the bread cool for about 15 minutes, then remove it from the pan to finish cooling. Gently press more sunflower seeds onto the top of your bread to make a sunflower design. Serve with peanut butter or jam, and wear your sunglasses while you eat!

What You'll Need
- 2 tablespoons margarine
- 1 cup maple syrup
- 1 egg
- electric mixer
- 2 mixing bowls
- ¾ cup orange juice
- 2 tablespoons grated orange rind
- 1 tablespoon baking powder
- ½ teaspoon salt
- 2 cups whole wheat flour
- 1 cup sunflower seeds
- mixing spoon
- loaf pan

Fuzzy Flowers

These flowers don't ever need watering—and they'll remind you of summer long after the solstice has passed!

What You'll Need
- heavy worsted yarn in different colors
- blunt scissors
- ruler
- dowel or rolling pin at least 2 inches in diameter
- chenille stems
- ribbon or vase

These pinwheel-shaped flowers are nice and soft. To make one, lay a piece of yarn (about 4 inches long) straight along the length of the dowel or rolling pin. Next, wind another piece of yarn around the dowel and the first piece of yarn about 30 times. Tie the ends of the 4-inch piece of yarn together—which will hold the wound yarn together. Slide the yarn off the dowel. Now you have a round yarn flower! To make a stem for your flower, bend the end of a chenille stem, hook it into the flower, and twist the end. Make a bunch of these fuzzy flowers, and tie them together with a ribbon or put them in a vase to make a fantastic, fuzzy bouquet!

Sculptures of Ice

Here's a fun way to make your own sculpture and cool off at the same time!

Add a few drops of food coloring to water that you have put into empty plastic containers or milk cartons. Freeze overnight. The next day, spread large garbage bags on a picnic table (in the shade!), and put a frozen container on each. Peel off or have an adult cut away the containers. Now you are ready to sculpt. Use your hands and your mouth to make wild and crazy shapes. Even the family dog might enjoy cooling off while licking one of these ice sculptures!

What You'll Need
- empty plastic containers or milk cartons
- water
- food coloring
- garbage bags

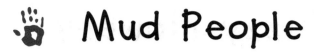

Mud People

◄▸◄▸◄▸◄▸

Have some earthy summer fun!

What You'll Need
- old clothes
- pail of water
- small spade
- dirt
- leaves
- twigs
- flower tops
- grass
- pebbles
- wildflowers

For the summer solstice or on a sunny day, put on some old clothes that you are allowed to get dirty. Grab a pail of water and a spade, and head for a place where it is okay to dig. A great way to celebrate the longest day of summer is to make some friends to join in the fun. Your new friends will be made of mud, but that won't be a problem—until it rains! Dig up a nice pile of earth, and add enough water to make clay. Roll balls to make heads, and roll out longer shapes to make bodies. Give your mud people arms and legs made of stiff leaf stems or tiny twigs. You can add flower tops for hair, and stick on bits of leaves and grass for clothes. Find tiny pebbles to use for eyes and noses. Line up your mud people in a circle, and pick a bunch of wildflowers to put in the center. Before heading back to the house, make sure you clean up so all that nice summer mud stays outside where it belongs!

If It Rains Game

◄▸◄▸◄▸◄▸

Whatever the weather, you'll be ready to play!

Don't worry if the sun is hiding on summer solstice—you can still invite your friends over for a great time. If it rains, that just means there will be lots of umbrellas around to play this fun game. All you need

What You'll Need
- rubber-tipped child's umbrella
- table tennis balls

is an open umbrella, set upside down on a bare floor. A carpeted area will not work for this game. Each player is given a table tennis ball and must stand 5 feet from the umbrella. One at a time, players try to bounce their ball once before it lands in the umbrella. A player scores 1 point for each ball that stays without bouncing out again. Be sure to use an umbrella with rubber-tipped spines so no one gets poked!

 # Dandy Desk Organizer

❖◆❖◆❖◆❖

Dad will love this dandy desk organizer for Father's Day!

What You'll Need
- cereal box
- construction paper
- clear and colored tape or glue
- assorted cardboard food containers (orange juice cans, small cereal boxes, etc.)
- blunt scissors
- stickers
- markers or crayons

Use tape or glue to cover a large cereal box with construction paper. Arrange the assorted clean food containers on the cereal box, and carefully trace the outlines. Cut out each shape so the containers will fit into the cereal box.

Cover the containers with construction paper, insert them in the cereal box, and glue or tape them in place. Now decorate everything; you can use stickers, markers, crayons, construction paper cutouts—anything you think Dad would like!

 # "A Hug for You" Card

❖◆❖◆❖◆❖

Give your dad a double hug—one for real and one he can carry around with him all day.

To make the card, cut out a large plate-sized head shape and draw on hair and a face so that it looks like you. Cut out an 18×4-inch rectangle. This will be the arms. Glue the head to the arms.

Trace around your hands on a separate sheet of paper, and cut out the hand shapes. Glue a hand to the end of each arm. Fold the arms in so that the hands overlap. Inside the arms write a message for Dad, such as "Here is a big loving hug for you on Father's Day!"

What You'll Need
- construction paper
- blunt scissors
- markers
- ruler
- craft glue

HERE IS A BIG LOVING HUG FOR YOU ON FATHER'S DAY

Mini Golf

If your dad is a golfer, he'll love having his own golf course!

The only limit to the challenge of this golf course is your imagination. You can make the course inside or outside your house. Generally, there are either 9 or 18 holes in a course, but make yours as large as you have space for. To make a golf club, attach a new sponge to the end of a long stick with colored tape. To make the course, you will want to set up obstacles before each of the holes. To make a hole, lay a small empty juice can on its side. Paint the can, and write the number of the hole on it.

You can make the obstacles in lots of different ways. For example, a tunnel can be made by cutting the bottoms from lidless oatmeal containers and taping them together. Turn a shoe box upside down, and cut an arch on either side of it big enough for the golf ball to pass through. If you are outdoors, you can pour sand inside a hula hoop to make a sand trap. Make tents of corrugated cardboard, and build towers from blocks. Set up foil pie plates in a daisy pattern with just enough room for a golf ball to pass through the petals. Use small rocks to hold things down if you are outdoors and it is a windy day.

Keep score to see how many strokes it takes to get your golf ball in each of the holes. Remember: The winner will be the person with the lowest score. Challenge Dad to get a birdie—or a hole in one!

 I Love Dad Game

◆▶◆▶◆▶◆▶

Watch Dad's smile grow bigger and bigger as this game goes on and on.

Here's a game that's also like a show—just for Dad. Gather your family members together. Dad will be the audience. The first player says, "I love Dad with an *A* because he is so Athletic" (or whatever nice thing you want to say about Dad that starts with *A*). The next player repeats what the first player says and then says, "I love Dad with a *B* because he is so Brave" (or another word that starts with a *B*). Players keep repeating what has already been said and adding to it until they have gone all the way to *Z*. (When you get to the letter *X*, you can cheat a little and say something like "because he is so X-tra great"). You might want to have a dictionary handy, just in case. This will surely be one of the best shows Dad has ever seen!

Best Dad Badge

◆▶◆▶◆▶◆▶

Everyone will know how much you love Dad when he wears this Best Dad Badge.

Alphabet macaroni are fun to eat, and they are also great three-dimensional letters to write things with. You can use them to write "Best Dad" or other messages on these easy-to-make Father's Day badges. Cut a 4×1-inch rectangle out of cardboard. Paint one side, let it dry, then paint the other side, and let it dry. Glue the alphabet macaroni to one side of the cardboard to spell out your message. You can use markers to color the noodles. When the glue dries, turn the cardboard over, and tape a large safety pin to the back (be sure the pin can be opened before

What You'll Need
• dried alphabet macaroni
• ruler
• cardboard
• blunt scissors
• paints
• paintbrushes
• glue
• markers
• large safety pin
• tape

you tape it down). Pin the badge to a dad-sized T-shirt, and place it somewhere Dad will find it. Bet he gives you a big Best Dad smile!

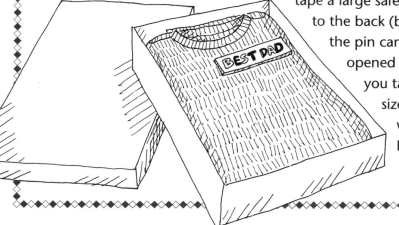

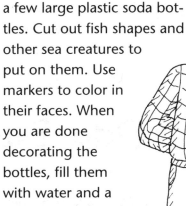

Bottle Fishing Game

Even if you live in the middle of the desert, you can still go fishing!

What You'll Need

- long wooden stick or branch
- paint
- paintbrush
- string
- blunt scissors
- ruler
- small plastic lid
- colored tape
- clear plastic soda bottle
- markers
- water
- blue food coloring

To make a fishing rod, paint a long, thin wooden stick or branch, and tie a 24-inch piece of string to one end. Cut out the middle of a small plastic lid (a pint-size yogurt container works great) until just the outer ring is left. Cover the ring with colored tape, and tie it onto the free end of your string. (You could make 2 rods—one for you and one for your dad!) Use more colored tape to decorate a few large plastic soda bottles. Cut out fish shapes and other sea creatures to put on them. Use markers to color in their faces. When you are done decorating the bottles, fill them with water and a few drops of blue food coloring. When you are ready to go fishing with Dad, tell him to keep one hand behind his back while he tries to fit the plastic ring over a bottle's neck. You and Dad might also want to each put one hand on the fishing rod to see how many fish the 2 of you can catch together!

All About Dad Poster

◆▶◆▶◆▶

Dad will be so surprised to find out how much you know about him.

What You'll Need
- construction paper
- blunt scissors
- markers
- cardboard
- gold or silver foil
- ribbon
- glue
- snapshots
- old magazines and catalogs
- poster board

Think of all the things you love about your dad, and write them down on pieces of colored construction paper cut into different shapes. Make medals by covering cardboard circles with foil and gluing ribbon to the back. Cut out a smaller circle of paper to glue on the foil, and write what the medal is for, such as "Best Hugger" or "Best Gardener." Gather up extra snapshots of Dad (ask for permission first!), or ask an adult to make photocopies of them. Cut out pictures of Dad's favorite things from old magazines or catalogs (ask for permission first!). Draw pictures of the 2 of you together, having a good time. Lay everything out in different arrangements on your poster board. After you find a pattern you like, glue the pieces down and write "ALL ABOUT DAD" at the top. Add the date and your own message to Dad in one of the bottom corners, such as "Happy Father's Day!"

Dad's Bookmark

◆▶◆▶◆▶

For Father's Day, make Dad his own special bookmark. He'll love it!

Using the self-hardening clay, make the object that you want to be on top of the bookmark—maybe a bowling ball, a fish, a golf ball, or anything you think Dad would like! Push the nonclipping end of the paper clip into the back of the clay object. Let the clay dry.

Once the clay is dry, add some craft glue where the clay meets the paper clip to hold the clay in place. When the glue is dry, paint the clay any way you'd like. Is Dad's favorite color red? Paint a red fish—remember, you can use your imagination to create this bookmark!

What You'll Need
- self-hardening clay
- large paper clip
- craft glue
- paint
- paintbrush

Greatest Dad Statue

Dad will get a big kick out of seeing a statue of himself right in your own yard!

What You'll Need
- full-length photo of Dad
- blunt scissors
- thin cardboard
- pencil
- glue
- thin wooden skewer
- tape
- plaster of paris
- water
- plastic bowl
- empty plastic or card-board container 6 to 8 inches high
- paints
- paintbrushes
- small towel

Find a full-length photograph of your dad (ask for permission first!), and cut it out. Lay it on thin cardboard. Trace around the figure, cut out the shape, and glue the photo and cardboard together. Tape the figure to a wooden skewer. Mix 2 parts plaster of paris to 1 part water in a plastic bowl. Pour the mixture into an empty plastic or cardboard container. When the mixture reaches the top of the container, smooth it flat with a piece of cardboard. Poke the wooden skewer into the center of the plaster of paris mixture. In about an hour, the plaster should be dry. Then remove the container. Paint the base of the statue, and write "Greatest Dad" on it. Erect your statue in the backyard, cover it with a small towel, and invite Dad out to the big unveiling! (Throw unused plaster of paris into the trash. Never pour it down a drain—it will clog it!) If it rains, don't forget to bring your statue inside!

Giant Dad Cookies

◆◆◆◆◆◆

Make Dad's day a little sweeter with these cookies painted with love.

What You'll Need
- 4 cups flour
- 2 teaspoons baking powder
- 1 teaspoon salt
- 2 mixing bowls
- measuring cups and spoons
- electric beater
- ¾ cup butter
- 1½ cups sugar
- rolling pin
- empty coffee can with top and bottom cut out
- 2 eggs
- 2 teaspoons vanilla extract
- 1 teaspoon lemon extract
- 4 egg yolks
- small bowls
- food coloring
- spoons
- paintbrushes
- spatula
- cookie sheet

Caution: This project requires adult help.

Preheat the oven to 375 degrees. Mix together the flour, baking powder, and salt. In another bowl, cream the butter and sugar together with an electric beater until it is fluffy. Mix in the 2 eggs and the extracts. Add the flour mixture a little at a time, and stir until well blended. Roll out the dough. Use a coffee can to cut out circles—have an adult smooth down the can's edges first. To make each color of the cookie paint, mix an egg yolk in a small bowl with a few drops of food coloring. Write sweet messages such as "I Love My Dad," and paint pictures on your giant cookies. Carefully lift the cookies with a spatula, and bake them on a cookie sheet for about 10 minutes or until they are slightly brown.

 # Gingerbread Freshener

◆◆◆◆◆◆

Dad's car will smell great with this hanging from the rearview mirror.

What You'll Need
- sandpaper
- gingerbread man cookie cutter
- pencil
- blunt scissors
- cinnamon sticks
- cheese grater
- clear glue (optional)
- twine or ribbon

On the smooth side of a piece of sandpaper, place a gingerbread man cookie cutter. Trace the shape with a pencil, and cut it out.

Over the rough side of the sandpaper, grate a cinnamon stick with a cheese grater. (Don't scrape your knuckles on the grater!) The cinnamon should stick in the crevices of the sandpaper, but you can also spread a little clear glue on the sandpaper before you grate the cinnamon.

Use the scissors to punch a small hole in the top of the gingerbread man's head. Put a piece of twine or ribbon through the hole so you can hang Dad's new air freshener.

Happy Family Dolls

These dolls always land on their feet!

What You'll Need
- small rubber ball
- craft knife
- plaster of paris
- disposable container
- construction paper
- markers
- scissors
- tape
- glue

Caution: This project requires adult help.

Ask an adult to cut the ball in half to form 2 bowl shapes. Prepare the plaster of paris in the disposable container according to the package instructions. Pour plaster into each ball half, and let it harden. (Dispose of unused plaster of paris in the trash!) While you are waiting, draw and cut out 2 faces from construction paper. Make 1 face to look like your

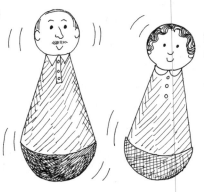

Dad and 1 face to look like you. Make 2 paper cones (choose colors that will contrast with the faces) to fit on top of the rubber balls—they will look like upside-down ice cream cones. Close the cones with tape, and glue them onto each half of the rubber balls. Glue a face onto each tip of the cones. These happy dolls are made like a Japanese folk toy called the *daruma*. "Wishing" darumas are made without eyes. If you want, don't draw eyes on your Dad's doll right away. Have your Dad make a wish, and then draw one eye. When his wish comes true, he can draw on the other eye. In the meantime, just have fun playing with your happy dolls.

Mouse Mitt

Protect Dad's mouse from dust—and cats!

Ask your Mom for permission to make a cover for Dad's computer mouse. To make your Mouse Mitt, place the computer mouse on a piece of felt that is Dad's favorite color. Draw a large computer mouse shape around it. Make your shape about twice the size of the real computer mouse. Cut out the shape, and then cut another one from a second piece of felt that is Dad's other favorite color.

What You'll Need
- felt
- blunt scissors
- stapler and staples
- glue

Put the computer mouse between the 2 pieces, and staple all the sides together except for the one with the mouse's "tail" (computer cord) poking out. Now cut out shapes from felt to glue onto your Mouse Mitt. You can cut out the word *Dad* or make the face of an animal. Now Dad's mouse won't get dirty (or run away) while it's waiting for him to use it!

Dad Snack

◆▶◆▶◆▶◆▶

Even dads like a snack now and then!

What You'll Need

- unsweetened dry cereal
- pretzel sticks
- mixed nuts
- small rice crackers
- bowl
- spoon
- seasoning salt
- garlic salt
- Worcestershire sauce
- measuring cup and spoon
- margarine
- oil
- saucepan
- baking sheet
- jar
- stickers
- ribbon

Caution: This project requires adult help.

Make Dad a jar of delicious Dad Snack. It's easy and guaranteed to be a tasty hit. Just mix 1 box of cereal with handfuls of pretzel sticks, nuts, and small crackers. How much you use depends on how large your jar is. Add 1 tablespoon each of seasoning salt, garlic salt, and Worcestershire sauce. Add the seasonings a little at a time, tasting to make sure the mix is not too salty. Remember, you can always add more seasoning later. Have an adult help you with the stove. Melt ½ cup margarine with ½ cup oil in a saucepan over low heat. When the margarine melts, pour it over the cereal mixture. Then spread the mix on a baking sheet, and put it in the oven for 1½ hours at 250 degrees. Stir the mixture every 15 minutes or so. When the mix has cooled, fill a clean jar with it. Decorate the jar with stickers. Tie a ribbon around the jar's neck, and leave it beside Dad's favorite chair.

 # Dad's Shadow Picture

◆▶◆▶◆▶◆▶

Have Dad sit for this special silhouette portrait.

Tell Dad you are going to give him his shadow for a Father's Day present. He won't believe it, but you can assure him that what you say is true. Attach a large piece of white paper to a wall. Place a chair several feet away from it. Invite Dad to sit in the chair so that you have a side view of his face. Turn off the lights in the room, and shine the clip light on Dad so that the shadow of his profile falls onto the white paper. Now trace around the shadow. When you finish, cut out the outline of Dad's shadow and lay it on a piece of black paper. Then cut out the shape from the black paper to give Dad his shadow!

What You'll Need

- large white paper
- tape
- clip light
- pencil
- blunt scissors
- large black paper

Paper Cup Race

◆▶◆▶◆▶◆

Make this homemade game, and play it with Dad on his day.

What You'll Need
- large cardboard box
- blunt scissors
- paints
- paintbrushes
- paper cups
- table
- tape
- string

This game will get you breathing hard! Remove the top of a large cardboard box. Paint the box lots of bright colors, and write the words "Happy Father's Day" on the bottom of the inside. Let the paint dry. Poke a hole in the bottom of 2 paper cups. Paint the cups or use some that have colorful designs already on them. Set the box on its side on a table. Make sure that the open end is several inches away from the edge of the table. Tape a length of string to the top of the left side of the box. The string should be long enough so that it reaches the table edge. Thread a paper cup onto the string, with the open part facing you. Tape the other end of the string to the table edge. Repeat with another string and paper cup on the top of the right side of the box. Now you are ready to race with Dad! The paper cups should be resting on the table edge with the openings facing you. At the count of 3, blow into the cups and see who can make their cup reach the top of the box first. Is Dad winning? Well, that's what Father's Day is all about!

Maple Leaf Toss

Here's a great way to use all those unmatched socks and celebrate Canada Day (July 1)!

What You'll Need
- large cardboard box
- red and white paint
- paintbrush
- red and white socks
- sand
- red fabric paint
- measuring tape

To make the game, first decorate a big cardboard box to look like the Canadian flag. Gather up all the unmatched red and white socks that you can find, and fill them with sand. Tie the end of each sock securely. If you only have white socks, you can paint a red maple leaf on some. To start the game, players stand 5 feet away from the box and toss the socks in. Players score 1 point for each white sock

and 2 points for each red (or maple leaf) sock that they get into the box without tipping it over. After each turn, players move back 1 foot. Keep playing until someone reaches 50 points. This is an outdoor game—Mom and Dad won't appreciate sand in the house!

# Red and White Game

This is a good memory game—once you play, you'll always remember the colors of Canada!

You can play this game with a big group or just 2 people. Hang up a big red and white Canadian flag to get everyone in the mood. Then have all the players make a list of all the red or white things they can think of in 5 minutes. It can be anything as long as it is mostly red or white or both. Each player reads her or his list aloud and crosses off items that everyone else has listed (everyone has to cross them off, too). One point is gained for things that another player has listed (as long as it's not on everyone's list). Two points are gained for things no one else has listed. The player with the most points wins the game.

What You'll Need
- Canadian flag (optional)
- paper
- pencils or pens
- timer

 Canada Day Flag

◄►◄►◄►◄►

On July 1 (Canada Day), wave a Canadian flag you created using construction paper and paint.

What You'll Need
- red paint
- paint tray or pie tin
- large maple leaf
- white construction paper
- paintbrush
- 12-inch stick
- tape

Pour some red paint into a tray or pie tin, and dip the leaf into the paint to coat 1 side of it thoroughly. Press the leaf in the center of the white paper, and carefully lift the leaf up. Paint the outside ends of the paper to make the Canadian flag (see illustration). When the paint is dry, tape your flag to the stick. Proudly wave the Canadian flag to celebrate Canada Day on July 1!

Patriotic Collage

◄►◄►◄►◄►

What does Independence Day mean to you? Gather up symbolic objects and create your own patriotic collage.

Look through old magazines for pictures of patriotic symbols, such as the American flag, stars, bells, eagles, and historical monuments. You can also look for pictures of people saluting, soldiers marching, or lawmakers speaking. Cut out the pictures (ask for permission first!). Cut scraps of red, white, and blue fabric into stars and stripes. Glue the pictures and the fabric to a piece of construction paper in a random arrangement. Cover the sheet of paper with the pictures and fabric pieces overlapping. Let the glue dry.

What You'll Need
- old magazines
- blunt scissors
- red, white, and blue fabric scraps
- construction paper
- craft glue

United States Celery

❖❖❖❖❖❖

Can a vegetable be patriotic? Do this experiment and find out!

What You'll Need
- celery stalks with white part attached
- knife
- 3 glasses
- water
- red and blue food coloring

Caution: This project requires adult help.

Tell your friends that you know a vegetable that can celebrate Independence Day by turning the colors of the American flag. Ask an adult to help you make several slits in the lower part of 3 celery stalks (choose celery stalks that are not much taller than the glasses you are going to use). Fill 3 glasses with water. Put a few drops of red food coloring in the first glass, a few drops of blue in the second, and leave the third glass clear. Place a stalk of celery into each of the glasses. One celery stalk will turn red, 1 will turn blue, and 1 will remain white (choose one of the center, light-colored stalks to put in this glass). When you're done with the experiment, you can have an all-American snack!

Patriotic Wiggle Stars

❖❖❖❖❖❖

These gelatin stars make a shimmering red, white, and blue holiday dessert.

Caution: This project requires adult help.

These colorful stars are almost too pretty to eat. Mix up separate batches of red and blue gelatin, and pour them into shallow baking pans. (Have an adult help you with the hot water.) Set the pans in the refrigerator for several hours until the gelatin is firm. Use a star-shaped cookie cutter to make stars, and gently lift the stars out of the pans with a spatula. Arrange the stars in alternating rows of red and blue stars on a large serving platter. Squirt a button of whipped cream in the center of each star. People say that the stars and stripes will last forever, but once everyone sees these stars, forever will be just a spoon away!

What You'll Need
- packages of raspberry and blueberry gelatin
- water
- spoon
- 2 mixing bowls
- 2 glass baking pans
- star-shaped cookie cutter
- spatula
- large serving platter
- whipped cream

Stars and Stripes Forever

Create a red, white, and blue magnet that looks like a miniature U.S. flag. Then compare it to the real stars and stripes!

What You'll Need
- toothpicks
- red marker
- plastic lid
- craft glue
- scrap of blue construction paper
- ruler
- blunt scissors
- tiny gold stars or glitter
- strip of sticky-backed magnet

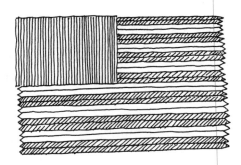

Use the red marker to color 14 toothpicks. Arrange the toothpicks on the plastic lid, starting with 2 red toothpicks across the top, then 2 natural-colored toothpicks. Alternate 2 toothpicks of each color to create the stripes of the U.S. flag. Use glue to hold the toothpicks together. Don't add too much glue or the red color on the toothpicks will bleed.

Glue a 1-inch square of blue paper to the upper left corner of your flag. Cover the blue paper with a thin layer of glue, then sprinkle it with tiny stars or glitter. (Or, if you want, break more toothpicks in half, and glue them vertically to the original toothpicks.) You probably won't fit 50 stars on this small flag, so just add as many as you can.

When your flag has dried completely, peel it from the lid. Trim any excess glue with scissors. Then stick a piece of sticky-backed magnet on the back of the flag. Hang your flag on the refrigerator for everyone to see!

After you've made the U.S. flag, which represents our country, create a flag that represents YOU. Use any colored markers you like, as well as different colored pieces of construction paper, glitter, stars, or other tiny decorations.

Long May She Wave

Here's a riddle to stump your friends: What is the one place where the American flag flies 24 hours a day, is never raised or lowered, and is never saluted? Answer: The Moon!

Fight for Independence Game

◆▶◆▶◆▶◆▶

Even bad weather can't spoil the fun of this game.

Here's a great 2-person game for a rainy day. To make the game board, cut a piece of thick cardboard into a 20×20-inch square. Mark off 25 squares, 5 across and 5 down, so that the board looks like a checkerboard. Paint the squares different colors. Then draw and cut 20 thin cardboard circles a little smaller than the size of a square. Paint 10 circles blue with a white star, and paint 10 circles white with a red cross. The blue circles (markers) will represent the United States (1 player), and the red will represent Great Britain (the other player). Players line up their markers in 2 rows closest to them. Each player takes a turn moving 1 marker at a time. Markers can move forward, backward, and diagonally, but only to an empty square. If a player's marker is fenced in so it cannot move, the other player gets 5 points. The first player to get all their markers into the other player's 2 rows wins 10 points. Play until someone gets 50 points.

What You'll Need
- thick cardboard
- ruler
- blunt scissors
- pencil
- paint
- paintbrushes
- thin cardboard

Patriotic Eyeglasses

You'll have perfect red-and-blue vision when you wear these fancy eyeglasses.

What You'll Need
- ruler
- thin white cardboard
- pencil
- blunt scissors
- red and blue cellophane
- glue
- white chenille stems
- red and blue markers
- glitter glue

Cut a cardboard rectangle a little longer than the width of your face. Your rectangle should be at least 2 inches deep. Your glasses can be any shape you want: circles, squares, triangles, or big Independence Day stars. Draw and cut out 2 eye holes on the glasses. Cut out a piece of red and a piece of blue cellophane a little larger than each eye hole. Glue a piece of cellophane over the inside of each eye hole to make the colored lenses. Next, carefully poke a small hole at either end of the eyeglasses, and fasten a chenille stem in each. Hook the free ends of the stems over your ears. Use red and blue markers to decorate your eyeglass frames. Use glitter glue for sparkly fireworks.

Yankee Doodle Bell Game

◆▷◆▷◆▷◆▷

Dress up as a Yankee Doodle Dandy, and try your skill at ringing the liberty bell!

What You'll Need
- paper bag
- old newspapers
- paints
- paintbrushes
- yarn
- glue
- old broomstick
- tape
- construction paper
- blunt scissors
- bell with string attached
- beanbag

Make Yankee Doodle's hobby horse by stuffing a paper bag with newspaper and painting on a face. Glue on yarn for the horse's mane, then tape the end of the bag around the broomstick. Fold a piece of construction paper into a tricornered cap, and draw and cut out a feather to stick in it. Then take turns being Yankee Doodle Dandy by wearing the hat while you ride the hobby horse. Tie the bell to the limb of a tree. As Yankee Doodle Dandy rides by, she or he must try to ring the bell by tossing a beanbag at it without stopping. Each Yankee Doodle Dandy gets 3 tries. You get 2 points each time you ring the bell. Whoever gets 10 points first wins the game.

High-Flying Rocket

Launch a patriotic rocket in your own backyard!

What You'll Need

- plastic drinking straws
- blunt scissors
- long red, white, and blue balloons
- rubber bands
- paper
- ruler
- markers
- pencil

This balloon rocket will fly high in the air, just like fireworks.

To make a rocket, cut a straw in half. Fold the tip of 1 straw in half, and insert it into the end of the other straw half until it is all the way inside. Slide the neck of a balloon over one end of your double straw, and secure it with a rubber band.

Cut a 3-inch square piece of paper, and fold it in half. This will be your rocket's fin, which you can decorate with patriotic designs. Use a pencil to poke a hole through the middle of the fin, and slide it over the double straw.

To make your rocket fly, hold the rubber band around the balloon's neck and blow through the straw. When the balloon is full of air, let your rocket go! Make sure that no one is in the way before you let go. Your rocket should fly high. Experiment with different shapes and sizes of rocket fins. The fin controls the rocket's path.

Get your friends together for some high-flying fun! (Balloons are choking hazards—be sure to keep them away from small children! Discard all broken balloons immediately.)

Watermelon Slush

This cool and refreshing drink is as fun to make as it is to drink!

Caution: This project requires adult help.

What You'll Need

- 8 ice cubes
- blender
- mixing spoon
- 2 cups seedless watermelon
- 1 teaspoon honey
- glasses
- marshmallows
- blueberries
- toothpicks

The sun is hot, and everyone is extra thirsty. A nice juicy slice of watermelon would taste great, but why not take that watermelon and try something new? Put the ice cubes in a blender, and turn it on high. Have an adult help you get the ice thoroughly crushed by turning the blender off and mixing the ice with a spoon before turning it on again. Add chunks of watermelon. Make sure you have taken out all the seeds. Add the honey, and blend well. Pour into tall glasses that you have chilled in the freezer. Garnish each drink with a marshmallow sandwiched between 2 blueberries on a toothpick. Lay the toothpick across the rim.

Independent Noses

◆▸◆▸◆▸◆▸

Be as nosey as you like when you play this game!

Caution: This project requires adult help.

This is a fun game for a big group. You can play it outside or inside. Hang an old white bed sheet to make a curtain. Cut (be sure Mom or Dad has given an OK for this!) a small hole into it about nose high. Have an adult help with the cutting. Divide the group into 2 teams. One team will paint their noses red and the other will paint theirs blue. Wait until everyone's noses are dry before starting the game.

What You'll Need
• old white bed sheet
• blunt scissors
• red and blue non-toxic face paints

Have 1 team go behind the sheet, and the players take turns putting their noses into the hole. The other team tries to guess whose nose it is. Score 3 points for each correct guess. After the game is over you will really know your noses!

Glitterworks

◆▸◆▸◆▸◆▸

Capture the feel of the rocket's red glare without ever lighting a match.

What You'll Need
• newspaper
• black construction paper
• pencil
• glue
• glitter

Many people love fireworks. They are part of what makes July 4 so exciting. So why not express your love of those explosive sky lights with glitter?

Cover your work surface with newspaper. Be creative—try to draw your favorite fireworks display using black construction paper and a pencil. The pencil marks will show a little—as shiny imprints. Trace your explosion with a thin line of glue. Sprinkle glitter on the glue. Let the glue dry for 5 minutes, then carefully shake the excess glitter off the page and into the glitter container to recycle it.

Flag Windsock

◆◆◆▶▶▶

You'll feel free as the breeze when you catch the wind in this decorative windsock.

What You'll Need
- tissue paper
- blunt scissors
- glue stick
- large plastic dry-cleaner's bag
- plastic-coated hangers or thick wire
- tape
- pole
- ribbons (optional)

Cut out a large square of blue tissue paper. Draw and cut out white tissue-paper stars, and glue them to the blue background. Glue this onto a plastic dry-cleaner's bag. Cut out red and white tissue paper stripes, and glue these to the bag to make the American flag. Make a large hoop from a plastic-coated hanger or thick wire. Have an adult help you with this. Fold about 2 inches of the bag over the loop, and tape it. Attach the windsock to a pole with loose wire loops so your windsock can change direction in the wind. Tie long red, white, and blue ribbons to the top of the pole to make streamers if you'd like. (Keep plastic bags away from small children—plastic is a choking hazard!)

Lady Liberty Costume

◆◆◆▶▶▶

Won't everyone be surprised when they see the Statue of Liberty?

Caution: This project requires adult help.

Make a long green wig from yarn held in place by a green headband. Make a crown (the base should be long enough to go around your head) out of green poster board, staple the ends, and tuck the base of the crown into the headband to hold it more tightly in place. Roll brown construction paper into a cone, and tape it in place for a torch. Have an adult help you spray-paint the batting orange, and glue it to the top of the torch. Paint your face and arms with nontoxic green face paint. Wrap a green bedsheet around you like a sari or a toga, pull on a pair of sandals, grab a green notebook to use as a stone tablet (the original tablet is inscribed with the Declaration of Independence), and march down the street holding your torch high!

What You'll Need
- green yarn
- green headband
- green poster board
- stapler and staples
- brown construction paper
- tape
- cotton batting
- orange spray paint
- glue
- nontoxic green face paint
- green bedsheet
- sandals
- green notebook

❦ Red, White, and Blue Bugs

◆▸◆▸◆▸◆▸◆

You won't mind having these cute bugs at your Independence Day picnic.

What You'll Need
- peanuts in the shell
- red, white, and blue paint
- paintbrushes
- wiggle eyes
- dried maple seeds (or brown construction paper and blunt scissors)
- glue
- hairpins
- wire cutters
- hat pins

Caution: This project requires adult help.

These patriotic bugs can sit at your Independence Day picnic table without bugging anyone. To make the body, paint a whole peanut shell red, white, and blue. Glue on 2 wiggle eyes and 2 dried maple seeds for the wings. (If you don't have maple seeds, cut wings from construction paper.) Ask an adult to cut hairpins in half to make 6 legs. Bend the ends of the hairpins to make feet. Then poke the legs into the sides of the peanut body. Carefully poke 2 hat pins into the bug's head for its antennae. Make a whole line of bugs leading up to a big cake centerpiece!

❦ Special Tablecloths

◆▸◆▸◆▸◆▸◆

Add some color to the dinner table with special tablecloths you make yourself.

Make a special tablecloth for your dinner table. Color a paper tablecloth with markers. Decorate it with your favorite foods, such as pizza, ice cream cones, or fried chicken. For a Fourth of July picnic, find out what's on the menu. Draw a border of corn-on-the-cob, hamburgers and hot dogs, or watermelon slices. You can even cut a special design in the edges with scissors. If you want, place your tablecloth over a brightly colored tablecloth to show off the decorative edge.

What You'll Need
- paper tablecloth
- markers
- blunt scissors (optional)

Fireworks Picture

After you experience the spectacular display of the Fourth of July fireworks, re-create the colorful bursts and blasts in a picture.

What You'll Need
- construction paper
- blunt scissors
- craft glue
- hole punch
- aluminum foil

Cut building shapes from assorted colors of construction paper. Cut out skyscrapers, small buildings, or houses to match your town. To make your town's skyline, glue the building shapes along the bottom of the black construction paper sheet. Use a hole punch to make confetti dots from aluminum foil and assorted colors of construction paper. Glue the colored dots over the night-time skyline to re-create a magnificent fireworks display.

Crêpes Bastille

Oo la la! What a delicious treat for Bastille Day (July 14)!

Caution: This project requires adult help.

Before the French Revolution, the colors of the French flag were white and blue. After the revolution, the flag's colors were changed to red, blue, and white. Make these crêpes to show France's colors after the revolution.

Mix the flour, sugar, and salt. Add the milk, water, eggs, and butter. Mix with an electric beater until smooth. Heat a heavy nonstick skillet until it is very hot. Pour in a few tablespoons of the batter, then quickly tilt the pan so that the batter is evenly spread. Cook about 30 seconds until the crêpe is light brown, then flip and cook another 20 seconds. Fill each crêpe with raspberry and blueberry preserves, then roll them up. Sprinkle with powdered sugar, and enjoy!

What You'll Need
- 1 cup flour
- 1 tablespoon sugar
- ¼ teaspoon salt
- mixing spoon and bowl
- 1 cup milk
- ⅓ cup water
- 3 eggs
- 3 tablespoons melted butter
- electric beater
- nonstick skillet
- spatula
- raspberry and blueberry preserves
- powdered sugar

Steal the Bastille Game

Have great fun playing a game while collecting money for children in need!

What You'll Need
- large heavy drawing paper
- markers
- large outdoor play area
- red and blue bandannas (enough for each player to wear 1)
- 2 rubber bands
- stone (optional)
- pennies

The Bastille was a French prison that was dismantled in the first serious act of the French Revolution. To play a game of Steal the Bastille on Bastille Day (July 14), have 2 teams each draw a large picture of the Bastille. A great place to play the game would be a large backyard or field with lots of trees and bushes to hide behind. Before beginning play, the players on 1 team tie red bandannas around their heads. The other team's players tie blue bandannas around their heads. Each team stakes out a prison and a safe territory, which should be marked and shown to both teams. Clearly mark a dividing line between the 2 territories. Clearly mark outer boundaries, too. Outer boundaries are lines that cannot be crossed. Now each team should hide their Bastille picture somewhere on their territory by rolling it up and putting a rubber band around it. The picture may need to be weighted down with stones if it is a windy day. Once the game begins, players must try to find and steal each other's Bastille. If a player is tagged in the other team's territory, he or she is captured and must stay in prison until another of his team members finds and tags him. Once the Bastille picture is found, it must be torn up by the team that finds it and resold to the team it was stolen from for a penny a piece. (When the original Bastille was dismantled, the pieces were sold as souvenirs.) You can donate the pennies to UNICEF for children in need!

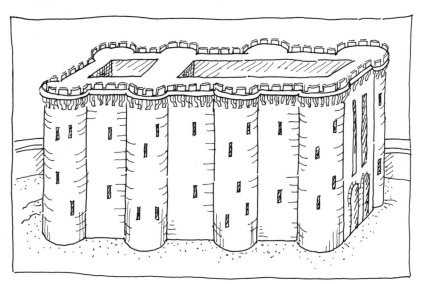

Family Paper Dolls

◆◆◆◆◆◆◆

Make everyone in your family into a doll!

What You'll Need
- construction paper
- pencil
- blunt scissors
- family photographs
- glue
- markers
- old wrapping paper

For Family Day (on the second Sunday in August), draw the head and body shape of each member of your family on construction paper that matches their skin tone. The dolls will probably be different sizes, just like the members of your family. Cut out the dolls. Find photographs of family members' heads that will be the right size for the cutout bodies (make sure it is all right to cut these photos). Carefully cut out the heads, and glue them onto the dolls. Use markers to draw under-

clothes on the dolls. Trace around each doll on wrapping paper to make clothing and shoes. Before you cut out the clothes and shoes, add small tabs that can be folded over the doll's body to attach them. You can make lots of different outfits for your family. Does each family member have a favorite outfit? Draw and color it on white construction paper. Then dress up your doll family, and invite your real family to meet themselves!

Family Shoes Game

◆◆◆◆◆◆◆

The family can get to know one another better with this thoughtful game.

The day before Family Day, decorate a large cardboard box by painting it in bright colors. Each family member might want to contribute to part of the design. Let the box dry overnight. On Family Day, have each member put one of their shoes into the box. Use a scarf to blindfold family members one at a time, and have them reach into the box and pick out a shoe. If they pick their own shoe, they should put it back and try again. When everyone has picked someone else's shoe, they have to think of 3 nice surprises they can do for the shoe's owner on Family Day.

What You'll Need
- cardboard box large enough for 1 shoe of each family member
- paints
- paintbrushes
- family members' shoes
- scarf

Tree of Hands

This special family tree will win a place in everyone's heart—hands down!

What You'll Need
- large poster board
- paints
- paintbrushes
- construction paper
- pencil
- blunt scissors
- glue
- marker

Family trees are a great way to remember the names and birthdays of everyone in the family. It will be neat to see all the different hand sizes of family members in this unique family tree.

Paint a large brown tree trunk on a poster board. Add branches on both sides, enough for every member of the family to have their own branch. You can add more at the bottom for later generations. Trace each family member's hand on different-colored construction paper, and cut out. When the paint on the poster board has dried, glue the construction-paper hands onto the branches, starting with the oldest members of the family at the top branches and working your way down. Have each family member sign their name, and write their birth date on their paper hand. When everyone is finished, you may want to decorate the background around the tree. Hang your family tree in the family room, and add more names as more people are born into the family.

Star-Fall Sleepover

Before movie stars or TV stars, there were other stars—heroes, monsters, and animals—who marched across the night sky.

Invite your friends for a special camp out on the Night of the Falling Stars (August 11)—and plan to stay up very late. Before the day of your camp out arrives, read about the origin of constellation names—you can tell the exciting stories to your friends while you wait for falling stars! If you can, spend the night at least 20 miles from the nearest large city. You will be able to see the stars more clearly. Before dark, put red cellophane over your flashlights. This will help your eyes stay adjusted to the dark so you can see the stars better. The biggest, best, and brightest falling stars will probably be seen between midnight and 2:00 A.M. No bright lights or campfires allowed!

What You'll Need
- mythology book
- sleeping bags
- pillows
- flashlights
- red cellophane
- rubber bands

Falling Stars

For ages untold, humans have looked up at the summer night sky in amazement as the stars themselves seemed to fall from the sky!

What You'll Need
- waxed paper
- white glue in bottle with a pointed top
- glitter
- string

Ancient people didn't know what we do now—that once a year the earth's orbit passes though a giant field of space rocks called the Perseids (rocks left in the wake of a passing comet). They are called the Perseids because they seem to come from the constellation Perseus. The rocks burn up as they smash into our atmosphere—and we call them falling stars.

Draw 5-pointed star outlines, including 3 lines for a "tail," on waxed paper with glue. Make the glue lines wide and thick. Sprinkle the glue with glitter until the lines are completely covered. Let your stars dry for 2 days. When completely dry, peel the stars off the waxed paper and hang up your falling stars with string.

FALL HOLIDAYS

Crisp leaves crunching underfoot, buying new clothes for school, going apple picking, deciding on the best Halloween costume ever—this season is full of fun and excitement. Look to this chapter in order to fall for fall holidays.

 Butter Churn

Work your muscles the old-fashioned way by making your own butter on Labor Day.

What You'll Need
- whipping cream
- jar with tight-fitting lid
- bread or crackers
- butter knife

Not too long ago, people in this country couldn't just drive to the store to buy a pound of butter. They had to make the butter themselves! Here's your chance to experience some good old-fashioned labor and make yourself some delicious, creamy butter. It's easy, but hard work, so have lots of friends around to help.

To start, let a pint of whipping cream sit at room temperature for about an hour. Cold whipping cream cannot be used for this recipe. When the cream is ready, pour it into a jar with a very tight-fitting lid. Have an adult help you close the jar if you aren't sure it is tight enough. Taking turns with your friends, shake the jar as hard as you can. After a little while, the butterfat in the cream will start to clump together and form a lump. There may be a little watery liquid left over. This is known as the buttermilk. When a large lump has formed, put the jar in the refrigerator until the butter is firm. You can drain off the buttermilk into a glass and drink it. Then set the butter on the table and serve it with some fresh bread or crackers. See? All that hard work was worth it!

Field Holler

◄▷◄▷◄▷◄▷

You'll be surprised how fast your chores get done once you start singing while you work.

Lots of people sing or whistle while they work to make the time go faster. Workers in the fields used to set up a steady rhythm and sing about the jobs they were doing. You can set up your own chant or "field holler" to sing while you work by first deciding on a beat. You might want to use a One, Two, One-Two-Three rhythm or maybe use a simple sing-song One-and-Two-and-Three-and-Four. If you are cleaning a room with a friend, sing about the tasks that you both are doing, such as: "You are dusting and I will sweep, getting rid of dirt we sure won't keep! I will wash the windows today, and you will throw all the trash away!" You can make up three or four different verses and repeat them over and over, changing the melody or volume every couple of verses. Try whispering the lyrics or harmonizing. Before you know it, your chores will be over—but you'll still be singing!

"Good Work" Sign

◄▷◄▷◄▷◄▷

Remind your favorite worker of the good work they've done.

What You'll Need
- embroidery canvas
- pencil
- different-colored raffia
- wool needle
- thin cardboard
- blunt scissors
- glue

Write the words *Good Work* on a piece of embroidery canvas. You can add other simple line drawings if you wish, such as stars, to show that a job has been done well. Then sew the words and pictures with different-colored strands of raffia. Use long stitches for straight lines and small stitches for going around curves, such as for letters in the word *Good.* Cut a piece of thin cardboard into a frame shape, and glue it over your canvas so it frames your artwork. Glue another piece of cardboard to the back. When it is dry, give the sign to your favorite worker to hang in his or her workplace.

When I Was Young Book

◆▷◆▷◆▷◆▷◆

***Show your grandparents how much you care on Grandparent's Day
(on the first Sunday after Labor Day), with this book.***

What You'll Need
- paper and pen, or tape recorder
- construction paper
- stapler and staples
- markers
- old magazines (optional)
- blunt scissors (optional)
- glue (optional)

Your grandparents have led a long and full life. They probably have had experiences that seem unbelievable to you. What did your grandparents do for fun when they were your age? What sorts of clothes did they wear? What did they dream they would be when they grew up? Get to know your grandparents. Ask them to tell you stories about their lives when they were your age, and take notes or tape-record the conversation. Then staple folded sheets of construction paper together to make a book. Write a story inside about some of the things your grandparents told you. Draw or cut out pictures from old magazines (ask for permission first!), and glue them to the construction paper to illustrate their story. Write a title on the cover of your book, such as "When I Was Young" or "The Story of Grandpa and Grandma." This is one book that the whole family will cherish forever!

Cup of Love

◆▷◆▷◆▷◆▷◆

***You'll make the nicest "drink" any grandparent could have
on Grandparent's Day!***

Paint the cup or mug with the words and phrases that tell your grandparents how you feel about them. You can write surprise messages of love on the inside of the cup and underneath it. Write short things, such as "I Love You" or "You're Nice." Paint pretty designs on the cup, or glue on conversation hearts, jewels, decals, ribbons, and glitter. When the paint and glue dry, fill the cup with a froth of pink tissue paper and more conversation hearts to make the cup look as though it is overflowing with love.

What You'll Need
- plain white mug or tea cup and saucer
- acrylic paint
- paintbrush
- conversation hearts
- fake jewels
- decals
- ribbons
- glitter
- glue
- pink tissue paper

Your Biggest Fan

◆▶◆▶◆▶◆▶

Help Grandma beat the heat with this pretty, lacy fan on Grandparent's Day.

What You'll Need

- 10-inch length of 1-inch-wide edging lace (3 yard package of lace seam binding)
- liquid starch
- 2 pieces of shiny 4×10-inch wrapping paper
- small paintbrush
- glue
- water
- bowl
- ruler
- pencil
- paper clip
- 14-inch length of ¼-inch-wide velvet or satin ribbon

1. To make the fan, first dip the lace in liquid starch, smooth it out, and hang it to dry.

2. When the lace is dry, brush on a ¼-inch-wide line of glue along one 10-inch edge of paper on the blank side. Lay the bottom, straight edge of lace along the glued edge, and press it flat.

3. When the glue is dry, brush slightly thinned glue (add a little water to the glue to thin it) over the blank sides of both pieces of paper. Press them together, smoothing the paper carefully. You might want to put a book on top until the glue is dry.

4. When dry, measure and draw very light pencil lines on the paper to make ½-inch-wide sections. Fold along the pencil lines to make accordion pleats.

5. Then brush a ½-inch line of glue along the edge opposite the lace. Press the pleats together at this point, and fold the bottom up against the rest of the fan to make a little handle.

6. Glue the folded part to the fan, and clamp with a paper clip until the glue dries. Tie a bow with the ribbon, and glue it to the bottom of the fan. Won't Grandma feel cool now?

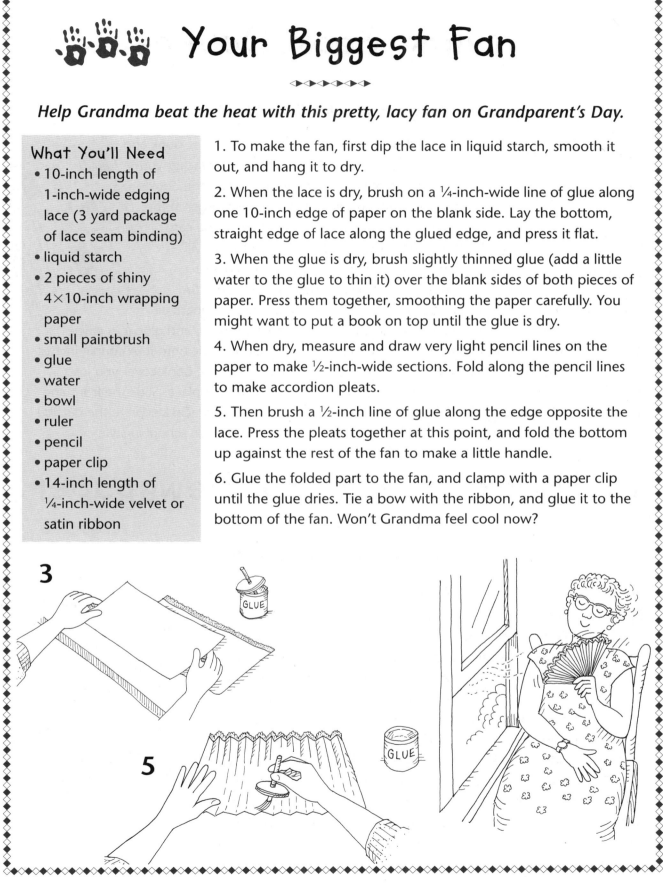

Styling Book Covers

These covers make schoolbooks look great.

What You'll Need
- thin cardboard
- blunt scissors
- ruler
- felt or fabric
- glue
- elastic strips

For each book you want to cover, open the book and lay it flat with the back and front covers facing you. Cut a piece of thin cardboard to fit over the book's surface. Cut your piece about ½ inch larger at the sides. Make 2 creases in the middle of the cardboard (the width of the spine) so that it will bend easily when the book is opened and closed. Glue a piece of felt or fabric onto the cardboard. Make sure the cloth is at least 1 inch larger than the cardboard all around. Fold the extra felt or fabric on the other side of the cardboard, and glue it in place. Cover the remaining cardboard by gluing another piece of felt or fabric onto it. A couple inches from either end, sew an elastic strip top to bottom on the inside of the book cover you just made—be sure the elastic is stretched a bit so the book cover stays in place. Slide the front and back covers of your schoolbook into these strips to hold the book in place. Decorate the outside of your new book cover with felt or fabric cutouts. This year, go back to school in style!

Back-to-School Newspaper

Find out all the school news that's fit to print!

Caution: This project requires adult help.

What You'll Need
- paper
- pen, typewriter, or computer
- markers, old magazines (and blunt scissors and glue), or camera with film
- copy machine
- stapler and staples

To get your stories, interview classmates and teachers to find out what they did over the summer and what they hope to accomplish this year at school. Remember that a good newspaper story always answers the questions: who, what, when, where, why (and sometimes how). You can write your stories by hand or use a typewriter or computer. Illustrate your stories with funny cartoons that you draw or that you cut out from old magazines. If you have a camera, you could also take pictures of the people who are in the stories. Think of a name for your newspaper, and write it across the top of the first page in big, bold letters. Give all your stories headlines. Ask an adult to copy your newspaper so you have one for everyone in your class. Staple the pages together, and hand them out.

Apple of Hope

Make a giant papier mâché apple, and fill it with messages telling of your hopes for the New Year.

What You'll Need

- balloon
- rubber band
- newspaper
- ruler
- liquid starch
- bowl
- paper towels
- stiff cardboard
- pen or pencil
- blunt scissors
- paints
- paintbrushes
- glue
- green construction paper
- paper

To make the apple, blow up a large, round balloon. Fasten the end with a rubber band. Tear newspaper into strips that are 1 to 2 inches wide. Soak the strips in liquid starch for 10 minutes. Then paste the strips onto the balloon until the whole balloon is covered. Let the paper dry. Add 3 more layers of newspaper strips, letting each layer dry before adding the next. Each time you add a layer, change the direction of the strips to make your apple strong. Soak 1- to 2-inch strips of paper towels in the liquid starch, and add 2 layers of these strips to form more of an apple shape. Cut a 1×4-inch piece of stiff cardboard for the stem. Wrap starched newspaper strips around it. Let your apple and stem dry for a few days. Remove the rubber band, and the balloon inside will lose its air. Then draw a line all around the top third of the apple. Cut along this line. Cut a hole in the top half that is a little smaller than the stem you made. Wedge the stem in the hole so that it forms a tight seal and can be used as a handle. Paint the stem brown and the apple a rosy red color. You could even glue on some green construction paper leaves. Paint the inside of your apple white. Have family and friends write messages telling their hopes for the New Year, and put them inside the apple. Take turns reading the messages aloud at the Rosh Hashanah seder.

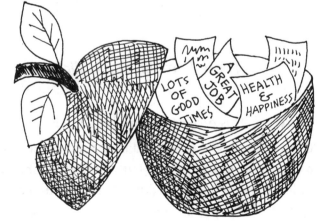

Honey Cards

◆▶◆▶◆▶◆▶

Send out lots of these honey-sweet New Year's cards.

What You'll Need
- heavy paper
- pencil
- blunt scissors
- felt
- glue
- permanent markers

It's traditional to send out New Year's cards at Rosh Hashanah wishing your friends and family a sweet year. To make a honey of a card, draw a large honey jar along the edge of a folded piece of heavy paper. Cut out the honey jar shape on all the edges except the folded one. Trace the jar shape on a piece of felt, and cut out 2 felt jar shapes that you can glue onto the front and back of your card. Glue them on. Cut and glue an oval shape out of felt to use as the honey jar's label. Write *HONEY* on it with a marker. Inside the card, draw pictures and write the message, "May your New Year be as sweet as honey!" Everyone will agree that this is one sweet card!

Dried Apples

◆▶◆▶◆▶◆▶

These leftover apple slices are dried and enjoyed for weeks into the Rosh Hashanah.

Caution: This project requires adult help.

Long ago, people preserved their food without refrigerators. Here's a great way to use up any leftover Rosh Hashanah apples that didn't get eaten. Ask an adult to help you peel, core, and slice the apples. Then loop pieces of string through the circular apple slices. Tape or tie the other ends of the string to a coat hanger, and hang the slices in a warm, dry place. In 2 weeks, the apples will have dried out and will be a sweet and chewy treat!

What You'll Need
- apples
- knife
- string
- coat hangers
- tape (optional)

Blow Your Own Shofar

Ring in Rosh Hashanah with this colorful shofar!

What You'll Need
- plastic funnel
- colored tape
- 30-inch length of rubber hose
- scissors

Caution: This project requires adult help.

You need a lot of practice to be able to blow a shofar. Here's an easy way you can make those holiday sounds with a shofar of your own. Decorate the funnel with colored tape. You might want to wind strips around the funnel to cover it entirely, or you could use little cutout shapes. Push the funnel into one end of the hose, and tape it in place. Then make a large loop in the hose, and tape it in place—be sure you have a few straight inches left over for the part where you hold the horn and blow. Wind strips of colored tape around the hose to decorate it. Wind a couple inches of colored tape at the mouthpiece at the straight end of the hose opposite the funnel. Now you are ready to blow! Just hold the horn, and blow into the mouthpiece end, making your lips vibrate against it. Blow hard or softly to make different tones. Make your lips tighter, and see what sort of a shofar sound comes out now!

Chai Charm

For Yom Kippur, give three cheers for life!

In ancient times, many Jewish people cut stones to make seals for traders, farmers, and merchants. They also cut stones to make charms to wear around the neck or wrist. You can practice an ancient tradition and make a Chai charm. Chai is the symbol for life and is a traditional New Year's symbol.

What You'll Need
- self-hardening clay
- pencil
- craft stick
- gold or silver paint
- paintbrush
- clear varnish or nail polish
- thin leather cord

To make your charm, roll a piece of self-hardening clay into a ball and flatten it to the size of a half dollar. Poke a hole at the top for the cord. Lightly trace the Chai symbol (see our illustration) onto one side of the clay. With a craft stick, carefully shape the clay around this symbol so that the Chai is slightly raised up from the rest of the clay. Let the clay dry. Paint the Chai with gold or silver paint. When dry, coat the charm with clear varnish or nail polish. Thread a thin leather cord through the hole, and wear your charm for a lucky life.

Truth or Lies Game

Challenge your friends to find out the truth about their country.

How much do you and your friends know about the United States? Play this game to find out. The leader of the game must write a list of facts about America. (For example: There are 50 states in America. Native Americans were the first people to live in this country. The first president of the United States was George Washington.) The leader should also write a list of lies about America. (For example: France is the name of an American state. Each president has 2 vice presidents.) When the leader has a list of around 20 facts and lies, the game is ready to begin. The leader quickly calls out facts and lies from the lists. It is good if the leader can call out the facts and lies in a kind of rhythm, like a rap. Players respond by clapping in rhythm 3 times if the statement is true, and not at all if the statement is false. Keep the pace lively. Anyone who claps at the wrong time is out, and the last one left is the leader next time around.

What You'll Need
- prewritten true and false facts about America

American Medals

On Citizenship Day (September 17), present your favorite American with a patriotic medal.

What You'll Need
- plaster of paris
- water
- empty plastic tub
- spoon
- disposable plastic cups
- pencil
- markers or paints (and paintbrush)
- clear nail polish
- cord

Citizenship Day is a time to celebrate new citizens of the United States. It is also a day to remind us of the rights and privileges that have been guaranteed by the U.S. Constitution. You can present a new citizen with one of these homemade medals or simply wear the medal yourself and celebrate your pride in being an American.

Mix plaster of paris and water in an empty plastic tub until it is thick and smooth. Pour ½ inch of the mix into a small plastic cup. Quickly poke a pencil at one edge to make a hole to thread the necklace cord through. When the plaster has dried, peel away the plastic cup. Paint your medal on both sides, and let it dry. You can now draw or paint patriotic messages such as "I Am an American," "U.S.A. All the Way!," or "Life, Liberty, and Happiness." Protect your medal with a coat of clear nail polish after the paint has dried.

Thread enough cord through the hole to make a loop large enough for your head to pass through. You are now ready to wear or give away your medal with pride.

World on a Pencil

On World Gratitude Day (September 21), keep the whole world in mind as you write.

These special pencils will remind you what a fantastic planet you live on. To make one, copy the outline of the continents onto the foam ball. Use a globe to help you get the shapes right. When you finish, outline the continents with a black, fine-tipped marker. Color them with different-colored markers. Color the space around them blue to make seas and oceans. Poke the end of a pencil into the bottom of your model world, and add a little glue to keep the world on. Now you have a nifty way to write pen pals all around the world.

What You'll Need
- foam craft ball
- pencil
- globe
- permanent markers
- glue

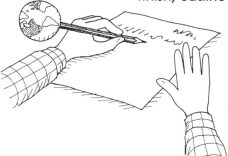

"Leave" a Treat

Bring a little autumn beauty to someone who needs it.

What You'll Need
- colorful autumn leaves
- crayons with paper peeled off
- blank white paper
- clear adhesive vinyl (optional)

Busy grown-ups sometimes forget to stop and watch the leaves change color when autumn rolls around. You can remind your favorite adult how beautiful the seasons can be. Gather flat, flexible autumn leaves that have just fallen from their branches. Select colors of crayons similar to the colors of the leaves. One by one, slip the leaves under a blank piece of paper, and gently rub the side of a crayon back and forth across the surface of the paper over the leaf. An image of the leaf will appear. Repeat the process with other leaves of various shapes and colors until your page is a colorful fall collage. Share it with a busy friend. If you'd like, cover your collage with clear adhesive vinyl for a place mat or more permanent art.

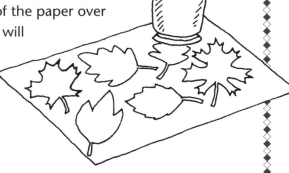

Autumn Jewel Bracelets

◆◀◆◀◆◀◆▶

You can make this bracelet only during the autumn season.

What You'll Need
- roll of wide masking tape
- nature

Take a walk, and make a bracelet at the same time! Pick a nice, sunny day for your walk. Ask a grown-up friend to walk with you out in the woods or in a field where there are lots of little natural "gems" (such as baby pinecones, leaves, little pebbles, seed pods, and moss) to collect for your bracelet. Before leaving on your walk, have your friend attach a loop of wide masking tape, sticky side out, around your wrist. Then, as you walk, pick up pretty bits of nature and stick them onto the tape. Make a bracelet of tiny wild flowers and acorn tops or small feathers and fuzzy grass!

Apple Bread

◆◀◆◀◆◀◆▶

The tastes of fall harvest are mixed together in this yummy bread.

Caution: This project requires adult help.

Have an adult preheat the oven to 350 degrees. Mix the flour, cornmeal, salt, and baking soda together in a bowl. Add the water and the maple syrup, and mix everything until it is smooth. Fold in the applesauce, raisins, and walnuts. Pour the batter into a greased loaf pan, and bake for about 35 minutes. Have an adult stick a butter knife in the center of the bread to tell if it is done. If the knife comes out clean, take the pan out of the oven. If not, let the bread cook a few minutes longer. This bread is nice when served with baked beans and a big green salad. Or, have it with a little cinnamon butter for dessert!

What You'll Need
- 2 cups whole wheat flour
- 1 cup cornmeal
- ½ teaspoon salt
- 1 teaspoon baking soda
- mixing bowl
- mixing spoon
- 1 cup water
- 1 cup maple syrup
- ¾ cup unsweetened applesauce
- ¾ cup raisins
- ½ cup chopped walnuts
- loaf pan
- butter knife

Harvest Place Mats

◆▶◆▶◆▶

Create decorative place mats that symbolize harvest time.

What You'll Need

- onion, apple, mushroom, garlic clove, brussels sprout, cabbage wedge, or other fruits and vegetables
- knife
- table covering
- foam food trays (from fruits or vegetables only)
- paint
- construction paper
- clear adhesive vinyl
- scissors

Caution: This project requires adult help.

These festive mealtime decorations can be used to celebrate any of the many international harvest festivals. Make the harvest place mats by printing with fruits and vegetables. Choose several fruits or vegetables, and cut each in half. (Have an adult help you with the cutting.) Cover the table. Pour several colors of paint into clean foam food trays. Choose fall colors or create your own personal color scheme. Dip the cut side of the fruit or vegetable into the paint, and make a print on a sheet of construction paper. Make several prints on the paper. You can cover each sheet of paper with a combination of fruit and vegetable prints or a single fruit printed with different colors. Let the paint dry, and then seal the place mats in clear adhesive vinyl. To seal, cut 2 pieces of clear adhesive vinyl slightly larger than the construction paper place mat. Peel the white paper off a sheet, and place the adhesive vinyl on a table, sticky side up. Carefully lay the place mat on top of the adhesive vinyl, and gently rub it so it sticks. Then peel the white paper off the second sheet of adhesive vinyl, and carefully place it, sticky side down, on top of the unsealed side of the place mat. Gently rub to seal, and trim the edges if necessary. Now the easy-to-clean place mats are ready for a holiday meal!

Sweet Squash Soup

This sweet and creamy soup is great on a cool autumn day.

What You'll Need
- 1 butternut and 1 acorn squash
- vegetable peeler
- knife
- saucepan
- water
- 1 chopped onion
- 1 tablespoon oil
- frying pan
- 1 vegetable bouillon cube
- blender
- ½ teaspoon basil
- ¼ teaspoon cinnamon
- ¼ teaspoon nutmeg
- lowfat milk

Caution: This project requires adult help.

Have an adult help you peel the squash, remove the seeds, and cut it into chunks. When that is done, place the squash chunks in a large saucepan, cover them with water, and cook them over a medium flame for about 20 minutes or until mushy. Do not drain the liquid out of the pot. While the squash is cooking, have an adult help you brown the onion in the oil in a frying pan. Then put the squash, bouillon cube, and some of the cooked liquid into a blender. Blend it until smooth, and pour it back into the saucepan. Mix in the onions and the seasonings and enough lowfat milk to make the soup as thick or thin as you like. Stir and heat—then it's time to eat!

Autumn Treasure Box

Display nature's treasures!

With different colors, lightly paint the squares of each compartment of a plastic utility box and set aside. While you are waiting for the paint to dry, go on a nature walk and collect small treasures to put in each compartment. Look for unusual pebbles, seeds, and dried berries or leaves. Try to get an assortment of shapes and colors. Then arrange your treasures in the painted box in a pleasant display. Set the box on a windowsill so light can shine through. The paint will make the box look like stained glass.

What You'll Need
- clear plastic utility box with separate compartments and clear lid
- acrylic paint
- paintbrush
- pebbles
- dried seed husks
- dried berries or leaves
- other found nature treasures

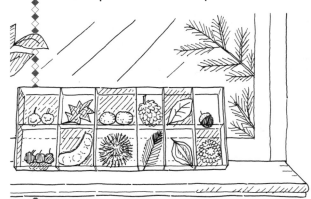

Terrific Totems

Make your own totem pole on Native American Day.

What You'll Need

- shoe boxes, oatmeal containers, cardboard tubes, corks, spools, and egg cartons
- glue
- stones
- paints
- paintbrushes
- construction paper
- blunt scissors
- rocks, craft feathers, leaves, and shells

Stack empty shoe boxes, oatmeal containers, cardboard tubes, corks, spools, and egg cartons, and glue them together. If your pole is a little tippy, weight the bottom container with a few stones. Paint your pole in bright colors. You can paint on different Native American designs or glue on construction paper cutouts. Glue on small rocks, feathers, leaves, and shells. Here are some ideas to choose from and what they symbolize to Native Americans: beaver = water, canoe paddle = transportation, deer = food and clothing, fiery flames = campfire, handshake = friendship, thunderbird = tribal crest. What things in nature do you especially love? Make up your own ideas for what these things symbolize, and add them to your totem pole.

 # Native American Wall Hanging

This wall hanging is easy to make, and it looks so authentic!

Run glue along the top border of a cloth napkin, and fold the edge over a knitting needle. You can use clothespins to hold the napkin while the glue dries. Cut different geometric shapes from colored tape. Use triangles, squares, rectangles, and hexagons, and form symmetrical patterns with them on the napkin. Lots of traditional Native American designs have one pattern that repeats over and over in a pleasing way. Look through books to find patterns that you want to copy, or make up one of your own. Tie fishing line to either end of the knitting needle to make a hanging loop. Hang your design to brighten your home!

What You'll Need

- old cloth napkin (plain or solid-colored)
- plastic knitting needle
- glue
- clothespins
- colored cloth tape
- blunt scissors
- fishing line

# Little Canoe

This canoe will make you dream of deep rivers and wide lakes!

What You'll Need
- 8×12-inch piece of heavy paper
- pencil
- blunt scissors
- needle and embroidery thread
- markers
- toothpicks
- ruler
- thin cardboard

Fold a piece of heavy paper in half lengthwise. Draw a canoe shape on it, and cut the extra paper away. Don't cut the fold, however. Sew each pair of ends of the canoe together with an overhand stitch. Draw Native American designs on the sides of the canoe. You might draw the sun, the moon, a bow and arrow, or a deer. After decorating the canoe, insert 2 or 3 toothpicks horizontally inside the canoe at 2- or 3-inch intervals to hold the sides

apart. Draw and cut out paddles from thin cardboard. You can also draw and cut out a couple of traditional Native American people to ride in the canoe.

Kick Stick Game

You'll need fast feet to play this Zuni Indian game.

This is a great outdoor game. If you are camping, you may want to use real branches instead of dowels, just as the Zunis did. The 2 branches must be straight, about 12 inches long and 1 inch thick. Peel off some of the bark from one of the branches so that it looks different. If you are using dowels, paint one red and one green. To make the Kick Stick playing field, have a group of your friends stand in a large circle or make a circle of white cornmeal on a large area of pavement or dirt. Both players then stand back to back at a point on the circle. When someone else shouts "Go!," the 2 players must kick their sticks around the circle in opposite directions until they return to the starting point. If a player kicks her or his stick out of the circle, or if the stick touches the other player's stick or another person, they must start again. When the game is over, the players shake hands.

What You'll Need
- 12-inch wooden dowels or branches
- ruler
- paint
- paintbrush
- white cornmeal (optional)

Owner Sticks

◆▶◆▶◆▶◆▶

The Crow Indians used sticks like these to identify their belongings.

To make your Owner Stick, draw symbols that best show what you are like, such as a lion if you feel you are a brave person or a flower if you think you are sweet. Draw lots of different symbols on 1 stick. You can also tape on craft feathers and strings of beads. Wind soft pieces of leather or suede around your sticks. Make a cross by taping 2 sticks together with colored tape. Decorate your owner stick however you like, but make sure that it really shows how unique you are. You may want to make up an Indian name, such as Little Running Deer, and sign it on your stick. If you go camping, drive your Owner Stick into the ground next to your tent to let everyone know you're there!

What You'll Need
- craft sticks
- markers
- colored tape
- craft feathers
- colored string
- beads
- scrap pieces of soft leather or suede

Native Necklace

◆▶◆▶◆▶◆▶

Make traditional jewelry for boys and girls.

What You'll Need
- ravel-free burlap scraps
- blunt scissors
- embroidery thread and needle
- thin wire
- ribbon
- beads

Cut 4 different geometric shapes out of burlap. Sew around the edges so they don't unravel. Embroider the shapes with cross-stitches in geometric patterns. Use a different bright-colored thread for each pattern. Attach the burlap shapes with wire so that they hang down in a long line. Cut a piece of wide ribbon into fringe, and sew on the bottom of the last shape. Sew a thin ribbon to each side of the top shape and tie in a knot; make sure the loop is long enough to pass over your head. Add more beads to hang down from the shapes with short pieces of wire if you like. Experiment with different shapes, and make necklaces for all your friends to wear for this special day.

Ring Toss Toy

◆▷◆▷◆▷◆▷

This was a favorite toy among the Sioux and Cheyenne Indians.

What You'll Need
- cardboard
- pencil
- blunt scissors
- 1-inch wooden dowel
- crayons or markers
- colored tape
- paint (optional)
- 12-inch piece of colored string
- small plastic ring
- needle

You can carry this game with you and play it just about anywhere. Using cardboard, draw and cut out a round head with horns and a neck. Make sure the neck is as wide as the wooden dowel you want to use, but narrower than the head. Decorate the head to look like a fierce bull. Tape the neck to the top of the wooden dowel (you can paint the dowel first or you can leave it plain). Tie a small plastic ring to one end of a string. Poke a small hole in the top of the bull's head, and thread the other end of the string through the hole and knot it. Now try to flick the ring so that it lands on one of the horns. Keep score by yourself or with a friend by counting the number of flicks it takes to ring the horn. This time, the lowest score wins!

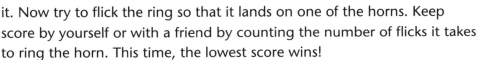

Native American Leaf Mosaics

◆▷◆▷◆▷◆▷

Use nature to "paint" a scene.

Put leaves in heavy books, and leave them alone for a week or two until they are dry. While you are waiting, you can draw different Native American scenes, such as a tepee on a river bank with a canoe parked out front. Draw only the outlines of your scene, because you are going to "color" them in and add details by using bits and pieces of dried leaves. When the leaves are dry, tear them into small pieces. Glue the bits inside the lines to fill in the shapes. It's okay if the colors don't match the things that you have drawn.

What You'll Need
- leaves of different colors
- heavy books
- pencil
- white construction paper
- glue

Corn and Bean Fry Cakes

Make a delicious meal from two traditional Native American foods.

What You'll Need

- 2 cups cornmeal
- ½ teaspoon salt
- large frying pan
- wooden spoon
- 2 cups boiling water
- waxed paper
- 1 cup cooked pinto beans
- 1 tablespoon miso
- bowl
- masher or fork
- ¼ cup oil
- spatula
- plate
- paper towels
- sour cream or plain yogurt
- chopped scallions

Caution: This project requires adult help.

Ask an adult to help you fry up these delicious little cakes for lunch or dinner. Mix the cornmeal and salt in a pan. Have the adult slowly stir in the boiling water. It is important to stir slowly so the batter doesn't get lumpy. Cook the mixture over low heat for about 5 to 10 minutes, until it is thick. Drop 8 equal-size portions of the cornmeal mix onto a piece of waxed paper. Let them sit until they are cool enough to touch. Divide each portion in half, and with your hands, make a little round cake out of each half. Put the beans and the miso in a bowl, and mash them together until you have a fairly smooth paste. It's okay if there are a few lumps in this. Place 2 tablespoons of the bean mixture on 8 of the cornmeal cakes. Put the other 8 cakes on top to make little bean sandwiches. Press around the edges with a fork to seal so that the bean mix is hidden inside the cornmeal cakes. Pour the oil in the frying pan, and have the adult heat the oil on medium-high heat until the oil is sizzling. Have an adult fry the cornmeal cakes until golden brown. Flip them over, and brown the other side. Add more oil if you need to. Let the cakes drain on a plate covered with paper towels. Top each with a dab of sour cream or plain yogurt and a sprinkle of chopped scallions.

Chief Plenty Coups

Plenty Coups, or "Bull Who Goes into the Wind," had a dream when he was a child about the destruction of the Crow way of life and the buffalo herds his people needed for survival. He grew up to become the leader of the Crow Nation, and he led his people through the hard times that he had seen in his dream.

Snakey Stick Game

◆◇◆◇◆◇◆

Toss the sticks, and try your luck!

What You'll Need
- 3 ice cream sticks or craft sticks
- red and blue markers

Here's a traditional Native American game that the whole family will enjoy. Draw a red snake pattern on one side of two of the ice cream or craft sticks. These are the snake sticks. Draw a blue dot pattern on one side of the other stick. This stick is the man stick. Now you are ready to play. Hold the sticks in one hand, and toss them up into the air. If all the patterned sides land face up, score 4 points. If all the plain sides land face up, score 4 points. If you get 2 snakes and 1 plain facing up, score 6 points. If you get 2 plain and 1 snake facing up, score 6 points. If you get a man and 2 plains, score 3 points. If you get a plain, a snake, and a man face up, score 0 points.

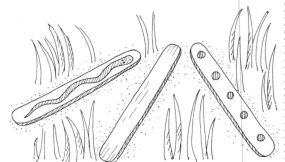

Comanche Dart Game

◆◇◆◇◆◇◆

Make your own darts, and hit the moving target—if you can!

This dart game was especially popular with Comanche children. You can make your own darts by sticking a toothpick in a cork and painting it in a bright color. Draw and cut out a construction paper feather, and tape it onto the toothpick. Make lots of darts! To play the game, one person rolls a ball down a hill while the other players try to hit the ball with their darts. Each time someone hits the ball, they score 10 points. Play until someone reaches 100 points, then play again. Hold a Comanche dart tournament!

What You'll Need
- toothpicks
- corks
- paints and paintbrush
- pencil
- construction paper
- blunt scissors
- tape
- outdoor hill
- rubber ball

Hot Candy Apples

◆◇◆◇◆◇◆

These apples make a fiery fall treat—especially great for Oktoberfest!

What You'll Need

- 1½ cups sugar
- ½ cup corn syrup
- ½ cup hot cinnamon candies
- ¾ cup water
- ¼ teaspoon salt
- saucepan
- mixing spoon
- water
- bowl
- baking pan
- 1 teaspoon red food coloring
- 1 teaspoon cinnamon
- 1 teaspoon ginger
- 6 wooden skewers
- 6 tart apples
- waxed paper

Caution: This project requires adult help.

Mix the sugar, syrup, cinnamon candies, water, and salt in a saucepan. Stir over medium heat until it comes to a boil. You must stir the mixture constantly so it does not burn. After the mix boils, stop stirring and wait until the syrup forms a solid ball when a bit is dropped into cold water. Remove the saucepan from the stove, and carefully place the saucepan in a pan of very hot water. Add the food coloring and dry spices, and stir. Carefully stick a skewer into the bottom of each apple. Swirl the apple into the syrup until it is entirely covered. Let the apples harden on waxed paper. Serve these at an Oktoberfest gathering with plenty of ice-cold apple cider.

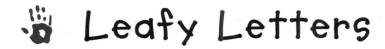

Leafy Letters

◆◇◆◇◆◇◆

Use the beautiful autumn leaves to make your own stationery.

What You'll Need

- food coloring
- small paper plates
- leaves
- paper

Leaves, leaves, leaves! They're everywhere and in every color. Celebrate the glory of autumn by gathering lots of different-shaped leaves to make leafy prints. This stationery is so easy and lovely you'll want to write lots of letters this fall. Pour a little food coloring onto a paper plate. Dip one leaf at a time into the coloring, and gently press it onto the paper wherever you want a leaf print. Carefully lift the leaf off the paper so the print is sharp and clear. Allow the stationery to dry thoroughly, then write notes and poems about the beauty of autumn. Send them to everyone you care about.

Apple Girl

◆▸◆▸◆▸◆

Not only does she have apple cheeks, her whole head's an apple!

Caution: This project requires adult help.

To make this doll, peel a medium-size apple (you may need adult help for this). Use your fingers to press in eyes, a nose, and a mouth. Let the apple dry in a cool, dry place for about 2 weeks until it is brown and small. When it is ready, poke a skewer into the bottom of the apple. To make the doll's dress, fold 3 pieces of tissue paper in half and make a little hole in the middle. Slide the tissues onto the stick. To make the doll's arms, roll up 2 or 3 pieces of tissue paper and tie the ends with embroidery thread. Slip the arms up horizontally underneath the dress, then tie the dress at the waist with thread so the arms stay in place. You can glue on yarn hair and make a hat from a tiny sock with a pom glued to the top. Name your doll, and introduce her to your friends. Can they guess what her head is made of?

What You'll Need
- apple
- knife
- craft stick or wooden skewer
- tissue paper
- embroidery thread
- glue
- yarn
- child's sock
- colored pom

Silly Applesauce Faces

◆▸◆▸◆▸◆

These silly faces are quite yummy.

What You'll Need
- 1 cup applesauce
- 1 cup plain yogurt
- bowls
- mixing spoon
- nuts
- raisins
- cinnamon
- toasted coconut
- cinnamon candies

October is the best apple season! It's a great time for picking apples, jumping into leaves, and working up a big appetite. When you and your friends are really hungry, invite them in for a silly snack.

Put the applesauce into a bowl, and add the yogurt. Stir the mixture until it is smooth. Then divide it evenly into 3 bowls. Gently add raisins and nuts to make a silly face. Use a spoon to sprinkle cinnamon freckles. Toasted coconut makes great moustaches, beards, eyebrows, and hair. Add a cluster of cinnamon candies on each cheek to give your silly face a rosy autumn glow!

Pumpkin-Head Twirlers

This pumpkin-head person never tires of going round and round.

This is an amusing and acrobatic toy. To make it, draw a little person about 4 inches tall on a piece of thin cardboard. Instead of the usual head, draw a pumpkin with a face on it. Give it a funny hat if you want. Use the markers to decorate it. Cut out the pumpkin-head person, and tape chenille stems to its back to form arms and legs. Use 1 horseshoe-shaped piece for both arms and another horseshoe-shaped piece for both legs. Wrap the ends of the arms around a drinking straw so your pumpkin-head person is holding on like a trapeze artist. When you twirl the ends of the straw, watch the tricks begin! Make another pumpkin-head person, and wrap the ends of its legs around the straw. Make a whole circus of pumpkin-head performers!

What You'll Need
- thin cardboard
- pencil
- ruler
- markers
- blunt scissors
- chenille stems
- tape
- plastic drinking straws

That's One Big Party!
Munich has the largest Oktoberfest celebration in the world. The first Oktoberfest in Munich was held in 1810. Today, Oktoberfest in Munich has over 7 million visitors during the 16-day celebration!

Discover It Game

◆▷◆▷◆▷◆▶

This is an exciting race against time!

What You'll Need
- thin cardboard
- black and colored felt
- ruler
- blunt scissors
- glue
- fine-tipped marker
- timer

Glue a square of black felt onto a 20×20-inch piece of cardboard. Use a fine-tipped marker to draw simple shapes, such as Spain, North America, Columbus's ships, Columbus, spice bottles, the sun, and ocean waves on the colored felt. Cut out each shape, and then cut each shape again into 2 or 3 pieces. To play the game, one player makes a simple scene by putting the shapes on the black felt board (they will stick). The other player studies the scene for a few minutes. The first player then takes the scene away and scrambles the pieces. Set the timer for 5 minutes. The other player must put the felt pieces back together to make the scene before the timer runs out. Make 2 games, and race each other to see who can discover faster.

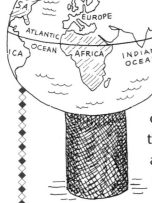

Big, Round World Box

◆▷◆▷◆▷◆▶

This box is a great gift for your favorite explorer.

Caution: This project requires adult help.

Blow up a balloon, and fasten the end with a rubber band. Tear newspaper into strips that are 1 to 2 inches wide. Soak the strips in liquid starch for 10 minutes. Paste the strips onto all of the balloon. Dry between layers. Add 3 more layers, each time changing the direction of the strips. Let dry for a couple of days. Remove the rubber band, and the balloon will deflate. Copy the shapes of countries from a map or another globe onto your globe. Paint each a different color, and label it. Label the oceans, too. (Try not to have any lettering near the center of the globe because you are going to make a cut there.) When dry, draw a light chalk line all around the middle. Cut along this line. Paint the inside of your box one color. Glue or tape construction paper around a can to make a stand.

What You'll Need
- large, round balloon
- rubber band
- newspapers
- ruler
- liquid starch
- large bowl
- map or globe
- paints
- paintbrush
- markers
- chalk
- craft knife
- small metal can
- construction paper
- glue or tape

Race to the New World

On Columbus Day, play this game to find out which boat will win the race: the Nina, the Pinta, or the Santa Maria.

What You'll Need
- adhesive vinyl paper in various colors
- waterproof markers
- large plastic tub
- blunt scissors
- water
- foam blocks
- toothpicks

Here's a fun game to play outside in nice weather. To make the game, draw the scenes of Columbus's journey from the Old World to the New World on adhesive paper. You may first want to stick a strip of blue adhesive paper around the top 4 to 5 inches of a deep plastic tub to look like the sky. Then you can draw things like islands with palm trees, clouds, birds, fish jumping into the air, sailboats, and pirate ships on more adhesive paper. Do some research to find out what else Columbus might have seen on his journey. Cut out the figures you drew, and stick them onto the blue paper. Label one side "Old World" and the opposite side "New World" with waterproof markers. When you have finished creating your scene, cover the whole thing with clear adhesive paper. Then fill the tub with water to just a little below the bottom edge of the adhesive paper.

Make Columbus's boats next: the Nina, the Pinta, and the Santa Maria. Make each boat by poking a toothpick into a small foam block. You can use more adhesive paper to cut a sail for each boat. Label each boat with its name. If you like, decorate the boats with waterproof markers or more adhesive paper. Now you are ready to race. Line up the boats in the Old World, and blow them over to the New. Which boat will get there first?

Tiny Secret Box

These miniature scenes will touch someone's heart.

What You'll Need

- empty sliding matchbox
- construction paper or fabric scraps
- blunt scissors
- old magazines
- markers
- glue

There is something irresistible about a miniature scene hidden away in a tiny box. It's almost as though you are telling someone a lovely little secret. Maybe you know someone who has been sick in bed or a senior citizen who lives alone. These boxes would be a sweet way to help them celebrate this Sweetest Day.

Slide the top off an empty matchbox. Line the box with pretty paper or a square of soft fabric. Cut out or draw tiny pictures to make a little scene to glue inside the box. Does the person you are giving this gift to love the ocean? Make a cheery beach scene inside your box. Finish your box by gluing construction paper to the outside of the matchbox and writing a little message to your friend, such as "You're Sweet" or "I'll Never Forget You."

You're Sweet Tarts

Bake someone nice a delicious goody for Sweetest Day.

Caution: This project requires adult help.

Spread some scrumptious cheer to people who have been kind to you lately. Ask an adult to preheat the oven to 350 degrees. Cream the flour and butter together. Add the water and salt, and blend well. Roll the dough into small balls, and press each one into a muffin tin cup with your clean fingers. Bake about 10 minutes or until the tart crust is a light, golden brown. When the crust has

What You'll Need

- 1 cup flour
- ⅓ cup butter
- mixing bowl
- mixing spoon
- 2 tablespoons water
- ¼ teaspoon salt
- small muffin tin
- fruit preserves
- nuts
- powdered sugar
- construction paper
- scissors
- markers
- tape
- toothpicks

cooled, spoon fruit preserves into each until the tarts are full. Sprinkle nuts and powdered sugar on top. Draw and cut out heart shapes, and tape them onto toothpicks. Write messages for the people you give the tarts to, such as "Thanks for being so nice." They'll be glad they were!

Sugar Cube Sculptures

Sugar is sweet—but it can also be art!

What You'll Need
- cardboard
- blunt scissors
- markers
- old newspapers
- sugar cubes
- thick poster paints
- paintbrushes
- glue

Sweetest Day started as a way to remember the orphans and shut-ins who felt forgotten or neglected. One small kind act or gift can mean so much to a person who needs attention—a homemade gift is always especially appreciated. These sugar cube sculptures will make a unique present for someone you want to remember.

Cut a square or circle of cardboard to make the base for your sculpture. If you want, write a message to the person you are giving the sculpture to on this base. Cover your work area with old newspapers. Paint sugar cubes in a variety of colors; let them dry. When they are ready, glue the cubes together to make interesting shapes on top of the base. You might want to build a little sugar cube house or castle or stack the sugar cubes in a pattern of repeating colors. Think about whom you are giving your sculpture to, and let thoughts of them guide your imagination to create a truly original work of art. (Don't eat the sugar cubes. They are for your art project, not for eating!)

Flower of Candy

◆▷◆▷◆▷◆▷

The center of this big paper flower is made of sweet, colorful candy.

What You'll Need
- crepe paper
- ruler
- blunt scissors
- small bowl
- wrapped candies

Whoever receives this colorful flower will not soon forget it—or you! To make a big flower of candy, fold a 6-inch-wide strip of crepe paper in half lengthwise. Cut petal shapes all along the edge that is not folded. Arrange the petals in a small bowl. Fill the center of the flower with pretty candies. Give this sweet flower to someone sweet. Delicious!

World Coloring Book

◆▷◆▷◆▷◆▷

For United Nations Day (October 24), add color to all the places in the world that you would like to visit!

This coloring book will not be the only one in the world—but it will be all about the world! Use encyclopedias to research facts about different countries that you would like to visit. Staple together 10 or 12 sheets of white paper to make a book. For each page, write a short caption that includes a fact you have learned during your research. Then draw a simple outline of something that relates to the caption. Give your book as a present to a friend so they can color in your outlines. If you researched France, you can draw the Eiffel Tower. Underneath it you can write, "The Eiffel Tower was built for the Paris International Exhibition and was designed by Alexandre Gustave Eiffel."

What You'll Need
- encyclopedias and other research books
- white paper
- stapler and staples
- black marker

United Buttons

Make your own international fashion statement.

Caution: This project requires adult help.

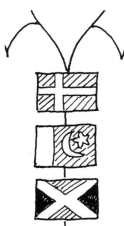

Add miniature flags to your favorite button-down shirt. Look in reference books to find pictures of flags from different countries. Trace and cut out 2×1-inch rectangles from strong craft foam. Make a rectangle for each button you want to cover. Use permanent markers to color each button cover like a different flag. Then take a pencil and mark the width of the button holes from your shirt in the middle of each button cover (on the unpainted side). Have an adult cut slits for the buttons on the lines you just drew. Put on your shirt, and button it. Slip the button covers over the buttons, and unite all the nations!

What You'll Need
- reference books
- strong craft foam squares
- ruler
- pencil
- scissors
- permanent markers
- craft knife

Terrific Trading Cards

Make your own trading cards to trade with your friends.

What You'll Need
- thin cardboard
- playing card
- pencil
- blunt scissors
- tracing paper
- map
- pen
- markers or colored pencils
- research books

The United Nations is the peacekeeper for the world. Trading is one way in which people cooperate.

Lay a playing card on cardboard, trace around it, and cut it out. Repeat this for as many cards as you want to make. Then trace the outline of a country or a state by placing tracing paper over a map. Transfer the outline by placing the tracing paper on the cardboard and pressing down hard with a pen. Remove the tracing paper, and go over the indentations you made with the pen on the cardboard. Write the name of the country or state inside the outline. Color the card with markers or colored pencils.

On the back of the card, draw pictures that show something found in that country or state, such as official trees, birds, or special foods that are prepared there. Write interesting facts about this place under your pictures. Trade these cards with your friends, and collect the world!

Colorful Collection Box

❖❖❖❖❖❖

This collection box is so pretty everyone will want to put something in it on UNICEF Day (October 31).

Do you know what UNICEF (United Nations Children's Fund) does? They collect money to give to needy children all over the world. Many people help UNICEF by doing some of the money collecting for the organization. It's easy to make your own collection box. Just use a shoe box or other small box, and cut a small slot in the lid. Paint the box a pretty color inside and out. When the paint is dry, decorate your box by cutting out pictures of children from magazines and catalogs (ask for permission first!). Glue the pictures all over the box. Cut out large letters that spell the word *UNICEF,* and glue these to the top of the box. Put the box on your dining-room table. Whenever you find a coin, you can put it in the box. Whenever you or your family members feel grateful for all you have, you can put in money to send to UNICEF.

What You'll Need
- shoe box or other small box with lid
- blunt scissors
- paints
- paintbrushes
- old magazines and catalogs
- glue

Paperweight Faces

❖❖❖❖❖❖

These smiling children's faces hold down everyone's papers.

What You'll Need
- smooth, flat stones
- paints
- paintbrushes
- marker
- clear varnish
- shoe box

Everyone needs a paperweight—especially one as charming as these smiling children paperweights! Gather some smooth, flat stones. Try to find ones that are round or oval-shaped. Paint each one of your stones a different skin tone. There are so many different colors of skin to choose from! Give each face different-colored eyes and all kinds of hairstyles, colors, and textures. The variety is endless! When the fronts of your stones have a smiling child's face on them, let them dry. Then paint the back a pretty color, let it dry, and use a marker to write "I Gave to UNICEF!" on it. Let the stones dry, and then paint one or more coats of clear varnish on it to protect the paint. Carefully arrange the paperweights in a shoe box. Now you are ready to sell your paperweights to friends and family. Donate your profits to UNICEF!

I Gave to UNICEF!

Really Haunted House

Create a house of horrors, and give your friends a silly scare!

Lead your blindfolded friends one by one through this scary room. To make a first-class scary haunted house, cover folding chairs and tables or boxes with a big, open sheet to make a long tunnel. Tape rubber spiders and bats to the inside for your friends to feel while a scary tape plays. Outside the tunnel, place bowls of clammy substances to dip your guests' hands into. Give those substances scary names: intestines (cold, cooked noodles), eyeballs (peeled grapes), witch hair (an old mop head), brains (greased broccoli), monster hands (rubber gloves filled with wet sand), and hearts (chopped gelatin). Flick a flashlight on and off, and play scary cassettes or CDs of cackles and screeches that you have prerecorded. Tickle your friends' arms with a feather, and tell them that it is a vampire bat. Have them walk through a curtain of hanging strings—tell them that it is a spider web. When you finish, take off the blindfold and let them see just how scary the haunted house really is. You'll all have a good, long cackle.

What You'll Need
- blindfold
- small tables, chairs, or boxes
- large sheet
- rubber creatures
- tape
- bowls
- cold, cooked noodles
- peeled grapes
- old mop head
- chilled, greased broccoli
- rubber gloves filled with wet sand
- chopped gelatin
- flashlight
- sound-effects cassettes or CDs
- feather
- string

Pipe Cleaner Ears

These ears are great for Halloween costumes.

What You'll Need
- 6 or 7 pipe cleaners
- blunt scissors
- construction paper
- markers
- craft glue
- yarn (optional)

Twist the ends of 2 or 3 pipe cleaners together in a band. Make sure the band fits around your head. Trim off any excess. Take 4 pipe cleaners, and attach them to the band. Twist them together at the top to make a "hat."

Cut and color 2 rabbit ears in a fold-over pattern from a piece of construction paper. Fold them over the top pipe cleaners, and glue the sides together. To create more, make other animal ears or antennae that stick up or hang from the band, or tie yarn to the pipe cleaners to make a wig.

Halloween Hello

◆▷◆▷◆▷◆

Cheerful holiday greetings can make all seasons bright.

What You'll Need
- tiny pumpkins
- permanent markers
- ribbon

Buy tiny pumpkins from your local grocery store or produce stand. Decorate them with cheerful, smiling faces and curls of brightly colored ribbon on the stems. Pass them out to less-fortunate families and senior citizens in your

neighborhood. Your local police department or YMCA can help distribute them, making sure they land in households that really need some holiday cheer. For holiday cheer throughout the year, make decorated evergreen branches, colored eggs, paper shamrocks, and other seasonal symbols.

Dried Apple Creatures

◆▷◆▷◆▷◆▷◆

Dried apple people make great puppet heads and fun sculptures. At Halloween, hang them from the ceiling as shrunken heads.

Caution: This project requires adult help.

Ask an adult to help you peel and core an apple. Cut a face in the apple. Set in 2 cloves for the eyes. Mix together 1 part lemon juice, 1 part warm water, and 1 to 2 teaspoons of salt in a small bowl. Dip the whole apple in the mixture to help preserve it. Let it dry in a warm, dry place for a few days. Notice that once it is dry, the apple shrinks and wrinkles, making its face look different from the one you originally cut. Glue on yarn hair and a cardboard hat to decorate your apple creature. If you want, add chenille stems to make glasses or antennas or use fabric scraps for clothes.

What You'll Need
- apples
- knife
- cloves
- lemon juice
- water
- salt
- measuring spoon
- small bowl
- mixing spoon
- yarn
- cardboard
- craft glue
- chenille stems or fabric scraps (optional)

Halloween Hood

◆▶◆▶◆▶

This Halloween hood is a parent pleaser that's also fun to wear!

What You'll Need

- 12×18-inch piece of gray felt
- black marker
- ruler
- blunt scissors
- fabric glue
- pink felt
- 2 buttons
- needle
- gray thread
- 6 chenille stems

1. Make a mouse costume with this hood. Fold the gray felt in half horizontally. Refer to the illustration to draw the hood, tie strings, and ear patterns on the felt. Follow the dimensions shown. Cut out all the pieces.

2. To make the hood, bring side A and side B of the hood piece together and glue them at the seam. Let the glue set. Cut a hole in each front corner of the hood. Thread the tie strings through the holes, and tie the ends in a knot.

3. Glue the gray felt ears on the hood. Cut 2 inner ear pieces from pink felt, and glue the pieces to the gray ears. Sew 2 buttons on the hood at the front rim for the eyes. Glue 3 chenille stems on each side for whiskers.

1

← 5" →

6"

6"

9"

8"

← 3" →

Cut out the felt pieces.

2

A   B

Bring side A and side B together.

3

Decorate the hood with felt ears, button eyes, and whiskers.

Woven Pumpkin

◀▶◀▶◀▶◀▶

Make something different for Halloween this year. Weave a three-dimensional pumpkin from construction paper.

What You'll Need
- 4 strips of orange construction paper, 1×24 inches each
- clear tape
- green construction paper
- pencil
- blunt scissors

1. Arrange orange construction paper strips as shown, overlapping them in the center. Secure the strips with tape.

2. To make a pumpkin sphere, start with the bottom strip and bring the ends together to form a circle. Hold the ends in place with tape. Repeat with the remaining strips. Work from the bottom strip up, and attach the ends together at the top of the sphere.

3. Draw a pumpkin stem shape on a piece of green construction paper. Cut out the stem, and tape it to the top of the pumpkin.

1

Arrange strips, overlapping the centers.

2

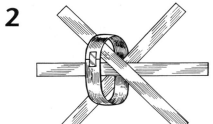

Tape ends of bottom strip together to form a circle.

3

Add a green paper stem to top of pumpkin sphere.

Hats: Wild & Styled

Old birthday or holiday wrapping paper makes great dress-up hats for Halloween or just for fun.

What You'll Need
- wrapping paper
- blunt scissors
- craft glue
- water
- small dish
- old paintbrush
- balloon or large ball
- feathers, ribbons, glitter, or rhinestones

Make a serious hat for parties, a silly hat just for laughs, or a theme hat for a Halloween costume. Cut out 2 big, identical circles of wrapping paper. Mix equal parts of water and glue together in a small dish. Coat the blank side of 1 piece of wrapping paper with glue. Place the other piece, blank side down, over the glue. Place it on your head, and form it into a hat shape while the glue is still wet. Once you've shaped the hat, place it over a blown-up balloon or a ball. Let it set overnight. When it's dry, decorate it with feathers, ribbons, glitter, or rhinestones.

Marvelous Monster

Beware! There are monsters everywhere!

Caution: This project requires adult help.

Ask an adult to cut a 2½-inch slit in the middle of the tennis ball. Cut 2 triangle-shaped mouth pieces from felt; the base of the triangles should be 2½ inches wide. Put glue on the top and bottom edges of the ball's slit. Glue the edges of the triangles into the slit to form a beak. Slide a pencil into the slit to keep it open while the glue dries. Cut eyes from felt, and glue them in place. Use felt or yarn tentacles to decorate your monster. When the glue is dry, squeeze the monster's sides to make it open its mouth. Fill it up with small candies or toys!

What You'll Need
- tennis ball
- craft knife
- ruler
- black, green, and orange felt
- scissors
- white glue
- pencil
- yarn
- small candies or toys

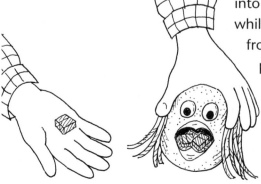

Baked Witch's Fingers

These witchy fingers magically point out how hungry you are!

What You'll Need
- 2 cookie sheets
- 1½ cups warm water
- 1 package dry yeast
- mixing bowl
- mixing spoon
- 1 teaspoon salt
- 1 tablespoon sugar
- 5 cups white flour
- 1 egg
- 1 tablespoon water
- small jar
- pastry brush
- coarse salt
- metal spatula
- red jam
- paintbrush

Caution: This project requires adult help.

Make long and crooked witchy fingers, and serve them at your next Halloween party. Have an adult preheat the oven to 350 degrees. Grease 2 cookie sheets. Mix together the warm water and the yeast. Stir in the salt, sugar, and flour to make dough. On a floured surface, pull off pieces of the dough and roll them between your palms to make ropes. Shape each rope into the long, crooked finger of a witch. Make the tip of the finger as pointy as you can. Lay the fingers on the cookie sheets so that they don't touch each other. Put the egg and 1 tablespoon of water into a tightly closed jar, and shake it up very hard. Use a pastry brush to brush this egg glaze onto each finger. Sprinkle the glaze with coarse salt, and bake for 25 minutes. Loosen the fingers with a metal spatula. When the witch's fingers have cooled, paint red jam fingernails on their pointy tips!

Blood-Red Eyeballs

It's your party—you can scream if you want to!

Caution: This project requires adult help.

With an adult's help, heat the white chocolate until it is melted. Hold a maraschino cherry by the stem, and dip it ⅔ of the way into the chocolate. Dip it several times, so that the chocolate coating is nice and thick and the red of the cherry doesn't show through. Set it on the waxed paper while the chocolate cools. When the white chocolate is cool, melt the dark chocolate. Pull the stems from the cherries, and using a spoon, fill the hole with an "iris" of dark chocolate. Arrange all the eyes on the plate. Just try not to think about all those eyeballs following your every move!

What You'll Need
- white chocolate
- maraschino cherries
- dark chocolate
- waxed paper
- spoon
- plate

Floating Ghosts Game

Watch out for low-flying ghosts when you play this game.

What You'll Need
- black construction paper
- tape
- white balloons
- black permanent marker

Caution: This project requires adult help.

Your party guests can each make their own ghost to use in this fun game. Give each player a piece of black construction paper, and have them tape it to make a tube. Have everyone blow up a white balloon. (Younger children may need an adult to help them do this.) Each player draws a silly or scary ghost face on their balloon with a black marker. To play the game, players lie on their backs with their ghost balloon on top of their black tube. When someone says "Go," players have to blow through their tubes. Whoever keeps their ghost up in the air (it can't touch the tube) for the longest time is the winner. (Balloons are choking hazards for small children—be sure they are supervised when playing with balloons!)

Spider Ball

On Halloween when werewolves howl and crazed creatures crawl, ghosties and ghoulies play spider ball! Play it by yourself, or with a fiend . . . er, friend.

To make a spider's web paddle, cut the center out of the plastic lid, leaving a 1-inch rim all the way around. Tie black yarn to the ring, leaving a 2-inch tail. Wrap the ring with yarn until it is completely covered. Be sure the tail is not covered! Tie the yarn, and trim the end. Tie the white yarn to the 2-inch tail. Stretch the yarn across the ring to the other side, and pull it fairly tight. Wrap it around and tie a knot, then stretch it across in a different direction and repeat to form a web. Repeat until you have a nice tight web. Now, using the markers, draw a big, black spider (with red eyes) on the table tennis ball. Her long, black legs should wrap around the "egg-sack" ball. Bounce the spider ball on the web. How many times can you bounce it in a row?

What You'll Need
- large plastic coffee-can lid (or any large plastic lid)
- blunt scissors
- ruler
- black and white yarn
- table tennis ball
- black and red markers

Ogre Costume

Even your best friend won't recognize you in this scary getup!

What You'll Need
- ratty jeans
- mismatched shoes and socks
- newspaper
- small towel
- string
- sweater
- old oversized T-shirt
- blunt scissors
- fabric markers
- rope
- cold cream
- cotton balls
- sweet corn syrup
- liquid foundation
- eye pencil
- face paint
- burlap bag
- reflective tape
- old woolen ski cap
- twigs and leaves

Every Halloween party should have at least one ogre around to liven things up. You will need to wear old, mismatched clothes and shoes. If your father has a pair of old shoes, wear those and stuff them with newspapers so that your feet don't slip out. Ogres are some of the world's worst dressers! You might even want to wear the shoes on the wrong feet because ogres are not too smart, either. For the ogre's hump, fold a small towel in quarters and tie it up. Put the towel on your shoulder, and tie more string around it and your shoulders to hold it in place. Put on a tight sweater to keep your hump really secure. To make the ogre's tunic, cut the sleeves off an old T-shirt that is too big for you (remember to ask first!). The dirtier and more full of holes, the better! You can also paint blood or snakes on it with fabric markers. Use a rope to belt it around your waist. To make a lumpy ogre face, apply a thin layer of cold cream. Then glue thin wisps of cotton to your face with sweet corn syrup. Put the lumps on your nose and cheeks. Carefully dab liquid foundation on the cotton and then over the rest of your face. When the makeup dries, use an eye pencil to draw a scary third eye in the middle of your forehead. Smudge green face paint around your real eyes. You can also draw thin red lines above and below all 3 eyes for a really sickly ogre look. Draw black scar lines with dots on either side of the lines to look like stitch marks. Color your lips gray. Use a burlap bag for your trick-or-treat bag. Put reflective tape on the front and back of your costume for safety if you are going to be walking around in the dark. Finish off your costume by tucking all your hair up in an old woolen ski cap. Have some twigs and leaves sticking out so it looks like you've been doing scary ogre things in the deep, dark woods!

Trick-or-Treat Jug

◆◆◆◆◆◆◆

Design a rainproof candy jug to match your costume. Not only will it carry all your goodies, but you can also give your friends a fright!

What You'll Need
- plastic milk jug
- scissors
- permanent markers
- black felt
- craft glue
- 2 screws
- ruler
- brass paper fasteners

Caution: This project requires adult help.

With an adult's help, cut off the top half of a plastic milk jug. Set it aside. Decorate the bottom half of the milk jug to make a trick-or-treat basket. Use markers to draw on a Frankenstein face. Cut a strip of black felt for his hair. Glue it to the basket. Have an adult poke 2 holes near the bottom of the basket. Insert a screw in each hole for Frankenstein's bolts. Cut 2 small pieces of felt. Glue them over the ends of the screws on the inside of the basket. Cut a 1-inch-wide strip from the top half of the jug. Punch holes in the handle ends and the sides of the basket. Use brass paper fasteners to attach the handle to the basket.

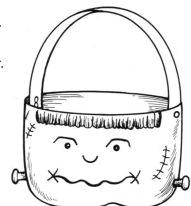

Halloween Mural

◆◆◆◆◆◆◆

This mural is a fun way to tell picture stories. Ask friends to help out— there's space for everyone!

A mural is a large wall painting that tells a story or creates a scene. To make your holiday mural, tape a long piece of paper on the wall. Spread newspaper out along the floor. Starting at one end of the paper, paint a Halloween scene. Make a picket fence with jack-o'-lanterns, black cats, goblins, and a harvest moon. Add more items to "tell" a spooky or fun Halloween story. Follow your ideas right across the mural. Let the paint dry. This is a great project for a Halloween party. Have your friends each paint an area of the mural.

What You'll Need
- butcher paper or heavy wrapping paper
- masking tape
- newspaper
- poster paints and paintbrushes

Dancing Jack-O'-Lantern

Put on a Halloween show for the trick-or-treaters with this dancing pumpkin pal!

To make a dancing jack-o'-lantern, cut out a round pumpkin shape for the body and a smaller pumpkin shape for the head. Cut out rectangles for the arms and legs. Cut out small pumpkin shapes for

the hands and feet. Paint all of the shapes with glow-in-the-dark paint, adding jack-o'-lantern faces on the head and hands. Using the paper fasteners, attach the hands to the arms and the legs to the feet. Then attach arms and legs to the body. Charge up the glow paint by shining a light on it. Turn off all the lights, and stand in front of the window with the curtains drawn behind you. Wear black or dark clothes, gloves, and a hat so you are almost invisible. Move the jack-o'-lantern's head, arms, and legs to make him dance. Anyone who looks in the window will see something very spooky!

What You'll Need
- poster board
- blunt scissors
- glow-in-the-dark paints
- paintbrush
- paper fasteners
- dark clothes

Scary Bug Game

All the bug lovers in the house will have fun playing this scary game of chance.

What You'll Need
- die
- paper
- blunt scissors
- markers
- tape

This game will be fun during a Halloween party. Cut small squares of paper to cover a die. Mark each square with one of these letters: *B, H, L, E, A, T.* These letters stand for the body, head, legs, eyes, antennae, and tail of the Scary Bug. Tape each square onto one side of the die. Then give each player a piece of drawing paper. Have a lot of colored markers for them to choose from. To play the game, a player rolls the die. That player draws the body part starting with whichever letter is face up. The next player rolls the die and draws whatever body part that starts with the letter rolled. Play continues until someone draws the entire Scary Bug to win the game. At the end of the game, everyone can color their bug drawings and hang them up as Halloween decorations.

Candy Skeleton

◆◆◆◆◆◆

This minty ghoul will be a favorite...until you gobble him up.

Bend a chenille stem in half. Cut a skull out of white paper, and use a black marker to give it facial features. Slip 3 candies down the chenille stem to the center of the skeleton's body for his ribs. Below the candies, pull the legs out so the candies stay on the body.

Wrap a second chenille stem just above the candies to form bony arms. Put a white gumdrop on the end of each leg for feet. Glue the paper skull to the top of the chenille stem (where it is bent in half), and the magic is complete.

What You'll Need
• white chenille stems
• white paper
• blunt scissors
• black marker
• wintergreen or peppermint candy with holes in the middle
• white gumdrops
• craft glue

Butterfly Mask

◆◆◆◆◆◆

People will be wondering who's behind this mask long after you have flown away.

What You'll Need
• cardboard egg carton
• blunt scissors
• poster board
• paints
• paintbrushes
• markers
• glue
• sequins
• glitter
• feathers
• needle
• elastic string

Caution: This project requires adult help.

Not all Halloween costumes are scary—some are actually quite beautiful. To transform yourself into a beautiful butterfly, cut out a 2-cup section from an egg carton for the eye mask. Make holes in the bottoms of the cups so you can see through them. Cut out 2 butterfly wings (add tabs to the inside of the wings to attach them to the mask) from poster board. Paint or color the wings and the eye mask in pretty colors, and glue on sequins, glitter (on the wings only), and feathers in an attractive design. To attach the wings to the eye mask, carefully cut a small slit on the top of each egg cup just large enough for you to snugly fit the tabs of the butterfly wings into. Glue the tabs in place. Ask an adult to poke a tiny hole on the side of each egg cup with the needle. Thread the elastic string through the holes. Knot the ends of the string in the holes. You don't need a lot of elastic because it will stretch—experiment with different lengths to see what fits your head. Put on your mask, and flap your wings!

Zombie Costume

On Halloween night, dress up like one of the walking dead!

What You'll Need
- old, torn-up shirt
- fabric paint
- old, dark pants that can get smeared with dirt
- dirt
- old, beat-up shoes and socks
- cold cream
- gray eye shadow
- black eye crayon
- white eye crayon
- blue and red makeup sticks
- cold spaghetti
- lightweight chains
- burlap sack
- silver reflective tape

Turn into a scary zombie for Halloween. Start with an old, torn-up shirt, and draw a jagged, "bloody" slit over the chest. Dribble more red paint down from the slit so it looks like dried blood. If anyone asks how you were killed, tell them in a scary voice that someone stabbed you! Put on old, dark pants, and smear them with dirt. Dirty up some old shoes and socks, and put those on, too. Remember, zombies have to climb through 6 feet of earth to get out of a grave! For the zombie face, cover your face with a thin layer of cold cream; then smooth on gray eye shadow. Color your nostrils and lips black, and smudge more black all around your eyes. You can add white circles around your eyes, too. To make a scar, draw a crooked smudge of blue and dark red. Draw a thin black line through it and tiny black dots on either side to look like the holes left by stitches. You can also paint your hands gray. Make it look like you have maggots crawling all over you by putting short pieces of cold, cooked spaghetti in your hair and on your costume. Drape some lightweight chains around you, and rattle them as you walk. Your trick or treat bag can be a burlap sack. Have someone put some reflective tape on the front and back of your costume so you can have a safe as well as a scary Halloween.

Spiderweb Pictures

◆▶◆▶◆▶◆▶

Spiders can be scary, but don't be afraid of these creepy friends.
Wherever you put them, that's where they'll stay.

What You'll Need
- construction paper
- markers or colored pencils
- black pom-pom
- craft glue
- 2 sequins

Draw a small circle in the middle of a sheet of construction paper. Draw another circle around it. Keep adding bigger circles until you have drawn 4 or 5 circles total. Draw lines from the center circle to the edges of the paper. Draw some lines from the center circle to the edges of the other inner circles. To make the spider, glue a black pom-pom to the web. Glue 2 sequins to the pom-pom for eyes. Draw in the spider's 8 long legs. If you want, color in all the spaces in the web with bright colors to make it look like a stained-glass web.

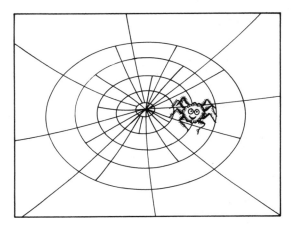

 Halloween Ornaments

◆▶◆▶◆▶◆▶

Scare up a few of these recycled ornaments and start a new family tradition—
Halloween trees!

Here are some ideas for rainproof ornaments made with recyclables. To make a ghost, cut a 10- to 12-inch circle from a white plastic bag. Poke a tiny hole in the center. Crumple up a piece of newspaper into a tight ball. Tie black yarn around the ball. Pull the yarn through the hole on the plastic circle for the ornament hanger. Tie another piece of yarn around the plastic under the newspaper ball. Draw a ghost's face on the bag. To make a pumpkin, cut a circle from orange fabric. Wrap it around an old tennis ball. Tie it closed with yarn. Draw a face on the fabric. Hang your ornaments on a Halloween tree.

What You'll Need
- white plastic bags
- blunt scissors
- ruler
- newspaper
- black yarn
- black permanent marker
- orange fabric
- old tennis ball

Pitch the Pumpkin Game

If you've ever wanted to catch the Halloween spirit, here's your chance.

What You'll Need
- 2 bleach bottles
- heavy-duty scissors
- permanent markers
- resealable sandwich bags
- 1 cup dry beans
- fabric
- rubber band

Caution: This project requires adult help.

Wash the bleach bottles well, and dry them. Have an adult help you cut the bottoms from the bottles to form catcher's scoops. Decorate the handles with permanent markers.

Fill a sandwich bag with the dry beans, and seal the bag. Using scraps of Halloween fabric, wrap the bag in the fabric and use a rubber band to hold the fabric in place. (If you don't have Halloween fabric, use markers to decorate plain white fabric in a fun Halloween style.)

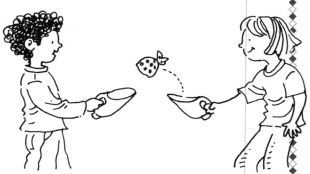

You're ready to start your game. Toss and catch the beanbag with your scoops. Whoever drops the beanbag first loses a piece of Halloween candy.

Box Costume

Turn an oversize box into a great Halloween costume. Make animals, cars, buildings, or even furniture!

What You'll Need
- large cardboard box
- scissors
- markers
- newspaper
- poster paints and paintbrush
- masking tape
- wide cloth ribbon
- stapler and staples

Caution: This project requires adult help.

With an adult's help, cut the bottom and top off of a cardboard box. Use the top and bottom pieces to make a horse's head and tail for a carousel horse costume. Draw the shape of a horse's head and tail on the cardboard pieces. Decorate the shapes with markers, and cut them out. Cover your work surface with newspaper. Paint the horse body with poster paints. After the paint has dried, tape the head and tail to the box body.

Make suspenders to hold the horse costume around your body. With an adult's help, staple a long piece of wide ribbon to an inside corner of the box. Staple the other end of the ribbon to the opposite inside corner. Staple a second piece of ribbon to the inside of the remaining corners so the ribbon suspenders cross over one another.

Spooky Spider

◆▸◆▸◆▸◆▸

Hang a few of these spiders around the house to spook up your Halloween!

What You'll Need

- plastic foam egg carton cup
- scissors
- black permanent marker
- chenille stems
- needle
- black thread

Caution: This project requires adult help.

Spiders look scary, but most are great to have around because they eat pesky bugs. You can make your spider look scary, friendly, silly, or even sad!

Cut out an egg cup from a plastic foam egg carton. Draw the spider's face on one of the sides. Then poke 4 black chenille stems through one side and out the other. Bend them so that your spider can stand up. Have an adult help you sew a thread up through the inside of the spider's head. Leave the free end of the thread long enough to hang your spider. Your spider may even fool a few bugs!

Mummy Pin

◆▸◆▸◆▸◆▸

Wear this silly, scary pin when you go trick or treating.

You can make this pin almost as quickly as you can say the word *Mummy*.

Wind white embroidery floss around a craft stick over and over. The more floss you wind on, the fatter your mummy will be! Make sure you wrap more floss around the middle. When you are finished winding, use glue to fasten the floss end to the back of the mummy. Glue 2 wiggle eyes to the front of the mummy, and glue a jewelry pin on the back.

What You'll Need

- wooden craft stick
- white embroidery floss
- craft glue
- 2 wiggle eyes
- jewelry pin

Make a whole group of mummy pins, and pin them in a big M shape on the back of your Halloween costume. *M* is for Mummy!

Scary Sounds

Disguise your voice and fool the witch in this scary party game.

What You'll Need
- blindfold
- witch hat
- 4 or more players

See how good you are at making monster sounds when you try to fool the witch. The game begins with one person wearing a witch hat and a blindfold. This person is the "witch" and must be seated facing away from the rest of the players. The rest of the players are the "monsters." Each monster takes a turn creeping up to the witch and disguising their voice to make scary monster sounds. They can also say scary monster sayings such as "I'm coming to get you!" The witch must try to guess who each monster is. If the monster gets caught, he or she must take the witch's place.

Alien Eggs

One look at these eggs and you will know they could never have been laid by an earthly creature!

Push 3 to 4 large wrapped candies and a medium-size toy inside a deflated balloon. (Important: Don't use small candies or toys! Make sure that the candies and toys are too big to fit back through the nozzle of the balloon—so you have no danger of inhaling the objects. You should have to stretch the nozzle to get them inside.) Blow up the balloon until it is about 6 inches across. Tie the balloon. Mix the white glue and water. Put the string in the glue/water mixture. Pull the string between your fingers to squeeze out some of the glue; wrap the balloon in a spider's web of string. Allow to dry in a warm place for at least a day. When the glue is thoroughly dry, pop the balloon. Carefully take out the broken balloon pieces. (Balloons are choking hazards—keep them away from small children!)

What You'll Need
- wrapped candies
- Halloween toys (creepy bugs and monsters)
- 12-inch balloons
- ½ cup white glue
- ¼ cup water
- string

Ghostly Fingers Punch

A ghostly hand floats in a punch bowl!

What You'll Need
- disposable gloves
- yellow food coloring
- lemonade
- orange juice
- carbonated water
- punch bowl
- blunt scissors

Serve this punch at your next Halloween party, and watch the surprise on your friends' faces. Wash a pair of disposable gloves inside and out. Fill them with water, add a few drops of yellow food coloring to the water, and knot the opening closed. Freeze your gloves for several hours or overnight. Just before the party, pour enough lemonade, orange juice,

and carbonated water to fill a large punch bowl. Then take your frozen gloves from the freezer and cut away the gloves. Place the frozen hands into the punch, and let the party begin.

Scary Bone Hunt

Hunt for bones, and make them into scary glowing "bone" people.

Invite your friends to a scary bone hunt this Halloween. First draw and cut out lots of different-size bones from cardboard. Hide them around the Halloween party room. Be creative with your hiding places—bones can be tucked inside books, under rugs and chair cushions, even slipped inside a bushy plant. If you are having your bone hunt outdoors, you might want to weight the bones down with small pebbles so they don't blow away. When all of the bones have been found, lay out newspapers and paint the bones with glow-in-the-dark paint. When the paint is dry, use glow-in-the-dark paints and markers to make faces on the bones. These scary bone people are great party favors for your guests to take home.

What You'll Need
- white cardboard
- pencil
- blunt scissors
- glow-in-the-dark paint and markers
- paintbrushes
- newspapers

Visible/Invisible Game

You won't believe your eyes in this secret game of camouflage!

What You'll Need
- 12 small objects (piece of embroidery thread, nail, marble, button, piece of ribbon, thimble, postage stamp, pencil, etc.)
- list of objects and pencil for each player
- timer

To set up the game, all the players except one must leave the room. That one player then places a dozen small objects in plain sight near other objects that can camouflage them. For example, she or he might put a piece of thread on a curtain that is the same color or place a pencil along the bottom edge of a cabinet. When all the objects are hidden, the player who hid them gives each of the other players a list of what they must find. The players race to find the objects but when they spy one, they don't tell anyone. They write down on their list where they saw it hidden. After 5 minutes, all the players stop looking. Whoever found the most objects is the winner. (Hint: Whoever is hiding the objects should keep a list for her or himself to remember where the objects are hidden!)

Wriggling Snake

This snake isn't dangerous—until it gets out of your pocket!

Here's a great Halloween "trick" to perform when earning "treats." Tell your audience that you have a live snake in your pocket. Some-

What You'll Need
- 5-inch piece of stretchy plastic wrap
- large paper clip

time before the trick, hold one end of a piece of plastic wrap and twist the other end into a rope shape. Make sure when you are twisting the wrap that you wind it very tight. Roll the twisted wrap up so it forms a round, flat coil. For the snake's head, make a small knot in the free end of the coil. Hold the coil together with a large paper clip. When you are about to let your snake out of your pocket, reach your hand in and remove the paper clip, but hold the coil so it doesn't unwind. Once the snake is in your hand without the paper clip, it will wriggle and writhe as it unwinds. Getting the clip off in secret will take a little practice. This trick looks very good with colored plastic wrap!

Paper Plate Monster

◆▶◆▶◆▶◆▶

Keep this big-mouthed monster away from all your Halloween treats, or else!

What You'll Need
- white paper plate
- poster board
- blunt scissors
- glue
- chenille stems
- crayons or markers
- ribbon

To make this scary decoration, fold a dinner-size paper plate in half for the giant mouth. Cut out a few 3-inch-long, arch-shaped eyes out of the poster board—remember: Monsters can have more than 2 eyes! Carefully cut slits in the top half of the mouth, and stick the eyes into the slits. Fold the bottom edge of the slit, and glue it to the inside of the mouth to hold the eyes in place. Make antennae or horns out of the chenille stems, and attach them to  the mouth in the same way as you did the eyes. Cut out arms, legs, or tentacles. Glue them to the underside of the mouth so that they stick out. Color your monster with wild colors. You might want to glue a long ribbon inside the mouth for the monster's tongue. Put your monster on the kitchen table, and tell everyone to watch their treats!

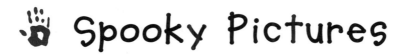 Spooky Pictures

◆▶◆▶◆▶◆▶

These are the scariest pictures you'll ever make by blowing through a straw!

These spooky pictures can be a little messy to make, so cover your table with newspaper before you begin. For each picture, pour a teaspoon of tempera paint onto a piece of paper. Gently blow at the paint through a drinking straw to make weird, scary shapes. If you want, you can add teaspoons of different colors of paint on top of the first color. These pictures will always be a big surprise. Is that a spider? Is that a witch riding a broom? Take turns with your friends describing the things you see in each picture.

What You'll Need
- newspaper
- drawing paper
- teaspoon
- thinned tempera paint
- drinking straw

Magic Glove

To your audience, this is no ordinary glove. Only you know the real truth.

What You'll Need
- long shiny glove
- playing cards
- table
- ring
- toothpick

Before doing this trick, tell your audience that the glove on your hand has magic Halloween powers. Lay your gloved hand on a table, and push a card under it. Keep pushing cards under it until there are 10 cards. Say "Abracadabra," and slowly lift your hand. All the cards will raise up with your hand! How did you do it? Everyone will want to know. Your secret is this: The ring you are wearing on the middle finger of your glove has a toothpick stuck in it along the underside of your hand. The toothpick holds the first card, and the rest of the cards hold the others as you push them in one by one. Now that's magic!

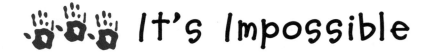

It's Impossible

Practice makes perfect before you perform this tricky trick.

You may want to wear the Magician Costume (on the next page) you made for this trick. Before you perform the trick, however, you will need to practice. To set up the trick, place a strip of paper on top of a closed ketchup bottle so that one end of the paper hangs over longer than the other side. Stack checkers or poker chips on top of the paper. The higher the stack, the more impressed your audience will be. Start practicing with just a few checkers or chips though, and work your way up. To remove the strip without knock-

What You'll Need
- ketchup bottle with cap
- 1½×3-inch strip of paper
- checkers or poker chips

ing the checkers or chips off the bottle, lick your index finger so that it will stick to the paper. Grasp the longer end of the paper between your index finger and your thumb. Quickly bring your hand down toward the table. You must remove the paper as quickly as possible. If you hesitate, the stack will fall! When you are ready to perform your trick, tell your audience that you have special powers on Halloween. Show them how you set up the trick and how easy it is to knock the stack over. Challenge a member of the audience to perform the trick. The stack will crash. Then you, the powerful Halloween magician, will show them your magic!

# Magician Costume

◆◆◆◆◆◆◆

Wear this costume while you perform some Halloween magic.

What You'll Need

- two 15×4-inch strips of shiny material
- 2 fake jeweled pins
- black crepe paper
- bath towel
- blunt scissors
- needle and thread
- black ribbon

If you want to put on a magic show this Halloween, you'll need to be dressed in the right costume. To make a magician's turban, drape a strip of the shiny material over your head so that the middle of the fabric is in the middle of your head and the ends hang down on either side of your body. Bring the ends up over the top of your head, and cross them in front to make a big X. Tuck the ends into the back of the fabric where it meets your head. If you have a big, jeweled pin, attach it to the middle of your turban. To make a sash, tie another strip of fabric around your waist and let the ends hang off to one side. Make a cape from crepe paper; use a bath towel for a pattern by laying it on the crepe paper and cutting around it. Fasten the cape around your neck with another large, jeweled pin, or sew a black ribbon to each of the top corners of the cape, and tie them in a bow around your neck. Now you're ready to do some hocus pocus!

What's in a Name?

Perhaps one of the most famous early magicians was escape artist Harry Houdini. His actual name was Ehrich Weiss, but he changed it after reading an autobiography by the French magician Jean Robert-Houdin. He wanted to be just like Robert-Houdin, so he added the letter i, which means "like," to his name; so he became Houdini.

 Ghostly Gobble Game

❖▸❖▸❖▸❖▸

This is a tasty way to turn yourself into a ghost!

What You'll Need
- strings
- coat hangers
- powdered donuts

This game is a silly way to serve dessert after a Halloween dinner. Attach strings to coat hangers that are hung in your Halloween party room. Tie a powdered donut to the end of each string. (You may want to cover the floor with an old shower curtain or newspapers, or do this game outside—it can get a little messy). Invite your guests to eat the donuts while keeping their hands behind their backs. The powdered sugar will get all over everyone's faces and turn them into ghostly gobblers!

Colored Face Powder

❖▸❖▸❖▸❖▸

Mix up a batch of makeup for your favorite ghoul.

Here's how you can mix up your own Halloween makeup. To make face powder, wrap a piece of colored chalk in a plastic bag. Pound it with a rolling pin. Be careful that you do not break the plastic bag. When you have broken the chalk into small pieces, pour it into the larger of two nesting metal bowls. Put the smaller bowl inside the larger one and move it around in circles to grind the chalk into a fine powder. (You will need to press fairly hard to do this.) After the chalk is ground into an even powder, mix in the cornstarch. You can experiment with different amounts of chalk and cornstarch to see which feels best on your skin. You can make another kind of powder by putting the talcum powder into a cup and mixing in 5 or 6 drops of food coloring. Mix the food coloring well, so that it is spread evenly in the powder. Use the cotton balls to apply your ghoulish powders—look great from head to toe in your Halloween costume!

What You'll Need
- colored nontoxic chalk
- plastic bags
- rolling pin
- 2 nesting metal bowls
- ½ cup cornstarch
- 1 tablespoon talcum powder
- cup
- food coloring
- mixing spoon
- cotton balls

Dracula Costume

◆▶◆▶◆▶◆▶

Your neighbors will scream when the famous Count Dracula shows up at their house!

What You'll Need
- white dress shirt
- dark pants, shoes, socks, and bow tie
- 2 yards black material
- blunt scissors
- sewing supplies
- black ribbon
- 2 large rubber bands
- reflective tape
- hair gel
- nontoxic face paints
- fangs
- fake blood
- black bag

Count Dracula may be a monster, but he is also a snazzy dresser. Put on a white dress shirt, and dark pants, shoes, socks, and a bow tie. Cut out a cape; make the bottom of the cape scalloped, just like bat wings. Sew black ribbons at the top corners to tie the cape around your neck. Sew a rubber band on each side where the cape hits your wrist so the fabric will swirl nicely when you move your arms. Put a V for vampire, or write "The Count" on the back of your cape with reflective tape. Slick back your hair with hair gel, and paint your face with white face paint. Smudge dark circles under your eyes—Count Dracula is always up all night! Slip some plastic fangs in your mouth, and drip a little fake blood down your chin or the corners of your lips to show everyone just what the Count has been drinking. Color your lips black and then add a coat of red. Don't forget your trick or treat bag—black, of course!

Souling

On All Souls' Day (a day when lost souls wander the earth) people used to go Souling, a game that was half trick-or-treat and half truth-or-dare.

What You'll Need
- cookies or candies
- napkins
- straws
- 2 masks
- 2 sheets

Invite your friends over for a party. Put a treat on a napkin by their plate. Warn them not to eat it! When the meal is done, draw straws to see who will be the wandering souls. The 2 guests who draw the short straws must put on masks and wrap up in a sheet. As they walk around the table, the soulers chant: "A soul cake, a soul cake, please, give us a soul cake, one for Peter, two for Paul, three for Him who made us all. If you haven't got a soul cake, a half-penny will do, if you haven't got a half-penny, then God bless you!" When they say "you!" they tap someone on the shoulder. That person can either give them the treat on the napkin or keep it for themselves. If they keep it, however, the wandering souls can command them to do something funny or tell a secret.

Day of the Dead Cookies

On the Day of the Dead (November 2), Mexicans honor the dead with a celebration of life.

Caution: This project requires adult help.

To make your own skull-shaped cookies, start by measuring and mixing together the margarine, butter, sugar, egg, and vanilla. When thoroughly blended, add the flour, baking powder, and salt. Chill the dough in the refrigerator for an hour. After the dough is chilled, roll it out to approximately ⅛ inch thickness. Cut skull shapes out of the dough with a dull knife. Place cookies on an ungreased cookie sheet. Have an

What You'll Need
- ¼ cup margarine
- ¼ cup butter
- ⅓ cup sugar
- 1 egg
- ½ teaspoon vanilla
- mixing bowl
- mixing spoon
- 1 cup flour
- ½ teaspoon baking powder
- ½ teaspoon salt
- rolling pin
- dull knife
- spatula
- cookie sheet
- canned icing

adult help you bake the cookies at 400 degrees for 6 to 8 minutes. When cookies are cool, decorate them using the icing. (Makes approximately 2 dozen cookies.)

Wooden Spoon Soldiers

◆◆◆◆◆◆

This army will be sure to protect all the ice cream at your Veteran's Day party!

What You'll Need
- wooden ice cream spoons
- markers
- construction paper
- blunt scissors
- glue
- aluminum foil
- ribbon

Bring this army to your Veteran's Day picnic to protect the food and decorate the table. Before you make your army, decide what colors the uniforms will be. It will look more realistic if you have all your soldiers wearing the same outfit. Color a hat and face on the top part of each spoon. Cut out hats from construction paper, and glue them on. Color the uniforms onto each spoon handle. Don't forget to color the backs of your spoons, too. Make tiny badges of honor from foil and bits of ribbon, and glue them onto your bravest soldiers. When the glue dries—1, 2, 3, march!

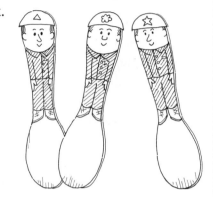

Victorious Veteran Pins

◆◆◆◆◆◆

Award these colorful pins to the brave veterans at the parade on Veteran's Day (November 11)!

It is traditional to honor brave soldiers with medals, pins, and ribbons. Long after the war, you can show veterans that you have not forgotten their courageous acts. Make these victory pins, and give them to your local veteran's association to distribute.

What You'll Need
- large safety pins
- colored beads to fit on pins
- white glue
- waxed paper
- ribbon
- blunt scissors

To make one, thread colored beads onto the pin side of a large safety pin. You could use only red, white, and blue beads for a patriotic flair! Or you can use purple for a Purple Heart pin or white for peace. Glue the beads onto the pin. Let them dry on waxed paper. Tie a little ribbon onto the other arm of each pin. Don't forget to make a pin for your shirt, too!

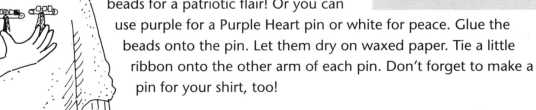

Patriotic Raindrops

❖❖❖❖❖

Here's some raindrops you'll want to let right in the house!

What You'll Need
- ½ cup white grape juice
- saucepan
- 1 package unflavored gelatin
- mixing spoon
- 2 bowls
- red and blue food coloring
- mini marshmallows
- cookie sheet
- waxed paper

Caution: This project requires adult help.

If the parade's rained out, you can still be patriotic. Make a batch of red and blue raindrops, and serve them up with white marshmallows. Put the grape juice in a small saucepan, and have an adult cook it on medium heat until it boils. Sprinkle the gelatin on the fruit juice, and mix it until the gelatin dissolves. Be careful; this mixture is hot. Have an adult pour the mixture into 2 bowls. Put a few drops of red food coloring in one bowl and a few drops of blue in the other. Spoon 1-inch raindrop shapes onto the waxed paper. Let them cool for about 20 minutes, then peel them off the paper. Put them on a plate with some mini marshmallows for a victorious Veteran's Day dessert!

Marching Songs

❖❖❖❖❖❖

Get everybody marching to your tune!

Everyone loves marching songs. If you have ever marched to "Yankee Doodle Dandy" or "When the Saints Go Marching In" you know how much fun these songs add to a parade. You can make up your own Veteran's Day marching songs. Think of themes that go with the holiday, and make up titles such as "Peace Forever" or "War No More." Then write the lyrics to your song. These songs

What You'll Need
- drum
- tambourine
- other percussion instruments

work well if the phrases rhyme. When you sing the marching songs, call out the lyrics in a loud, clear voice. Use a drum, tambourine, or other percussion instrument to keep the beat while you sing. To get yourself started, sing these lyrics while you pound your drum: "Today's the day when we all say: No more war! War go away! All our soldiers are home to stay!"

"Thankful" Message Box

◆◇◆◇◆◇◆

Help the family get into the Thanksgiving spirit with this message box.

What You'll Need
- shoe box
- tissue box
- paints
- paintbrush
- assorted decorative art supplies
- pencil
- string
- tape
- small slips of notepaper

The week before Thanksgiving, paint and decorate an empty shoe box and tissue box. Tie one end of a string around a pencil, and tape the other end to the tissue box. Set a stack of notepaper next to the pencil. Invite family and friends to write down what they are thankful for, and put the slips inside the tissue box. On Thanksgiving Day, take turns reading the slips aloud. The shoe box can be used to store the slips, adding a new bunch of "thankful messages" each year. You may want to paint traditional Thanksgiving symbols on your boxes; you could draw turkeys, pilgrims, Native Americans, and harvest foods, such as corn, pumpkin, squash, and apples. You can print the words "Give Thanks" around the opening of the tissue box and the words "Our Thanks" on top.

 # Harvest Candleholders

◆◇◆◇◆◇◆

Can a fruit be a candleholder? You bet!

Caution: This project requires adult help.

Choose the right fruit for these candleholders by making sure the fruit can sit securely on a plate. Use an apple, orange, or grapefruit. Have an adult help you make a hole in your fruit that is large enough for a taper candle to fit snugly inside. The hole should go almost to the bottom of the fruit. Have the adult light the candle and drip some warm wax into the hole.

What You'll Need
- apple, orange, or grapefruit
- apple corer or knife
- candles
- raisins and toothpicks or cloves

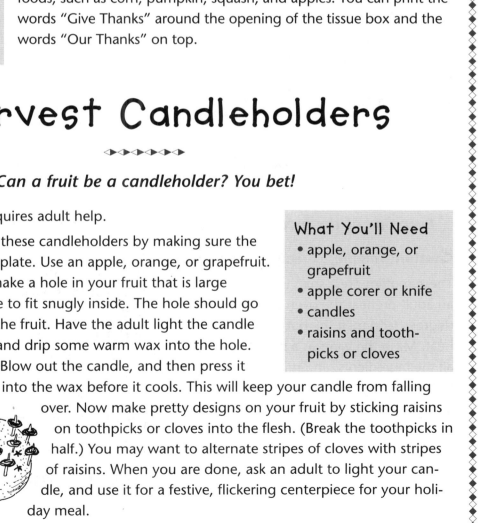

Blow out the candle, and then press it into the wax before it cools. This will keep your candle from falling over. Now make pretty designs on your fruit by sticking raisins on toothpicks or cloves into the flesh. (Break the toothpicks in half.) You may want to alternate stripes of cloves with stripes of raisins. When you are done, ask an adult to light your candle, and use it for a festive, flickering centerpiece for your holiday meal.

Pilgrim Seed Pictures

It will take patient hands to make this 3-D picture.

What You'll Need
- poster board
- markers
- glue
- sunflower and pumpkin seeds
- lentils
- uncooked spaghetti

From tiny seeds grow mighty trees—and mighty pilgrims, too! Draw a large outline of a pilgrim on a piece of poster board. Give him a hat, knee breeches, a shirt with a collar or a short jacket, a belt, long stockings, and shoes. Glue the seeds one at a time to fill in the outline. Overlap the seeds to fill in all the gaps. Use sunflower seeds for the black hat, shoes, and belt. You can color pumpkin seeds with markers to fill in other areas. Lentils can be used for the eyes, nose, and mouth. Break pieces of uncooked spaghetti to glue on for the hair. You will have to work carefully to make this picture, but you'll have the patience of a pilgrim when you are through!

Yummy Yammy Muffins

Everyone at the breakfast table will be thanking you for these yummy treats!

Caution: This project requires adult help.

These muffins are a snap to make. Have an adult preheat the oven to 350 degrees, and melt the butter over low heat. Mash the yams in a bowl. Combine all the ingredients, and mix well. Pour the batter into muffin cups in a muffin tin. Bake for about 20 minutes. Let cool a little before serving with honey or jam. Breakfast has never been so yummy, or so yammy!

What You'll Need
- 4 tablespoons sweet butter
- saucepan
- 1 cup canned yams
- fork
- mixing bowl
- 1¾ cups whole wheat flour
- ½ teaspoon salt
- ½ cup brown sugar
- 2 teaspoons baking powder
- 2 eggs
- 4 tablespoons sweet butter
- ¾ cup milk
- 1 teaspoon cinnamon
- 1 teaspoon nutmeg
- muffin tin and cups
- honey or jam

Stand-up Pilgrims

Put these pilgrims all around the house in surprising places.

What You'll Need
- stiff cardboard
- pencil
- ruler
- markers
- felt
- glue
- blunt scissors

For each pilgrim, draw a 6- to 8-inch-high person. At the bottom of each figure, draw a rectangular base a little wider than the person's body. Draw on hats, breeches, buckled shoes, and long dresses such as the pilgrims wore. You could also cut out the pilgrims' clothes from felt and glue them onto your figure. Then cut out your pilgrim with its rectangular base attached. Cut a vertical slit in the bottom center of the rectangular base. Then cut out another same-size rectangle from cardboard, make a vertical slit in the middle of the top, and insert it into the other slit to make a cross-shaped base. Now, who's that standing around? Why, it's Miles Standish!

Mosaic Planters

The fall harvest can decorate your spring planters!

What You'll Need
- paper
- crayons
- assortment of dried beans
- empty can
- sandpaper
- white glue
- small paintbrush
- shellac or clear nail polish
- dried flowers

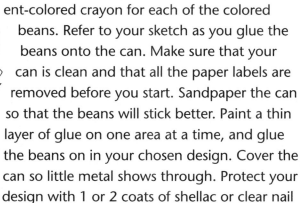

Before you begin to make these planters, sketch out pattern ideas on paper first. Look at your beans and arrange them on a table, then copy the design you like on paper, using a different-colored crayon for each of the colored beans. Refer to your sketch as you glue the beans onto the can. Make sure that your can is clean and that all the paper labels are removed before you start. Sandpaper the can so that the beans will stick better. Paint a thin layer of glue on one area at a time, and glue the beans on in your chosen design. Cover the can so little metal shows through. Protect your design with 1 or 2 coats of shellac or clear nail polish. Fill the can with dried flowers for a harvest theme decoration. Or use the can in a few months when you start your spring seedlings.

Tiny Turkey Pillows

Place these tiny pillows on the couch or an easy chair for a soft, turkey touch.

What You'll Need
- old knit glove
- cotton balls or batting
- glue
- clothespins
- craft feathers
- yellow and red felt
- blunt scissors
- 2 wiggle eyes
- fabric paint

To make your turkey pillow, stuff an old knit glove with cotton balls or batting until it is full. Glue the bottom edges together. Hold the edges shut with clothespins until the glue dries.

Glue colorful craft feathers between and around the fingers of the glove. Cut a beak from yellow felt and a wattle (the turkey's red throat) from red felt. Glue them on the side of the thumb. Decorate your bird by gluing on wiggle eyes. You can also paint details on the turkey's body with fabric paint.

You might want to paint a name on your turkey. How about Tillie? Terwilliger? Thomasina?

Orangey Popcorn Balls

This snack is a pretty Thanksgiving centerpiece when piled into a pyramid.

Caution: This project requires adult help.

Have an adult help you pop the popcorn. After the corn is popped, mix the gelatin, sugar, corn syrup, and a few drops of food coloring together in a saucepan. Have the adult heat and stir until the mix reaches a full boil. The adult should pour the syrup over the popcorn. Stir it well to thoroughly coat all the kernels. Let the popcorn cool a few minutes. Now for the really fun part! Butter your hands (be sure the popcorn is cool enough for you to handle because the butter will draw out its heat), and shape the popcorn into orange-size balls. Arrange the balls in a stacked pyramid shape on a serving platter or in a large bowl. If you have trouble balancing the popcorn balls, use a little dab of honey as "glue." Dot your pyramid with fresh cranberries to add even more Thanksgiving color. Don't forget to eat this centerpiece for dessert!

What You'll Need
- 1½ cups popcorn kernels
- cooking oil
- 1 package orange gelatin
- 1 cup sugar
- 1 cup corn syrup
- orange food coloring
- mixing spoon
- saucepan
- butter
- serving platter or large bowl
- honey
- cranberries

Turkey Costume

Entertain the Thanksgiving crowd at your house by turning into a giant turkey!

What You'll Need
- cardboard box
- paint
- paintbrushes
- blunt scissors
- glue
- tissue paper
- cardboard
- craft feathers
- T-shirt
- tights

Make a turkey head by painting a cardboard box (large enough to fit your head inside) red. Cut out holes for the eyes. Tear off yellow, orange, and red tissue paper feathers, and glue them on the box, leaving the eye holes free. Cut a triangle-shaped beak from cardboard, paint it yellow, and glue it underneath the eyes on the front of the box. You can also cut the turkey wattle from cardboard, paint it red, and attach it to the bottom front of the box. Glue craft feathers onto an old red T-shirt, and put on some red tights to complete the costume. Now, practice your gobble and start talking turkey!

Thanksgiving Napkin Rings

These napkin rings are a perfect addition to the Thanksgiving table.

Measure and cut the tubes so each ring measures 2 inches in length. (Make enough so everyone coming to dinner has a napkin ring.) Cut the same number of 2-inch-wide colored paper strips. Glue the paper strips to the tubes.

Now decide how you want to decorate your napkin rings. You could make each different, or you could make them all the same. Draw a turkey, autumn leaves, pumpkins, or something else you're thankful for on construction paper, and cut it out. Glue it to the ring. Use markers, paint, ribbon, beads, and feathers to decorate the rings. Here is your chance to be really creative and fanciful.

What You'll Need
- paper towel tubes
- ruler
- blunt scissors
- construction paper
- craft glue
- craft supplies (markers, paint, paintbrush, ribbon, beads, feathers, etc.)

Tabletop Gobbler

Make an edible centerpiece for your Thanksgiving table!

What You'll Need
- apple
- orange slices, raisins, cranberries, carrots, celery, and other fruit you'd like to use
- knife
- toothpicks

Caution: This project requires adult help.

Place the apple on a table with the stem on the table. This is the body of the turkey. Have an adult help you cut up the fruit and vegetables you have chosen. Then start working on your turkey. Use the toothpicks to stick the pieces onto the turkey.

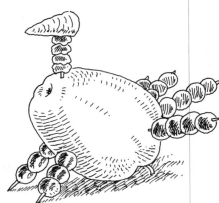

He needs a tail, a head, a wattle (the red thing that hangs down his neck), a beak, eyes, feet, and anything else you can think of. Use your imagination, and don't worry if your turkey doesn't look like the real thing. It will be a wonderful decoration for your table! And you can eat your turkey for a healthy snack. (Note: Don't eat the cranberries; they are very tart.)

Indian Corn Painting

Indian corn makes great fall decorations, but did you know that it makes a great painting tool, too?

Caution: This project requires adult help.

Make a fall painting with Indian corn as your paintbrush. Cover your work surface with newspaper. Pour poster paint on paper plates. Have an adult use a knife to cut the corn into 3-inch sections. Dip the cut end of 1 corncob in poster paint. Stamp it on a piece of drawing paper to create a flowerlike pattern. Roll a 3-inch corncob in some poster paint. Then roll it on the paper for a unique dotted design. Use this technique to fill in a picture or to create patterned paper.

What You'll Need
- newspaper
- poster paints
- paper plates
- 1 or 2 ears of Indian corn
- knife
- drawing paper

Cornucopia Copies

◁▷◁▷◁▷

A cornucopia is a horn of plenty. Make yours overflow with fruit and flowers plus plenty of color and texture.

What You'll Need
- corrugated cardboard
- pencil
- blunt scissors
- poster board
- craft glue
- newspaper
- poster paints
- palette or paint tray
- brayer
- drawing paper

Draw a horn shape on a piece of corrugated cardboard. Draw fruit shapes, such as a pear, a banana, grapes, and apples on cardboard. Carefully peel a layer of paper off the side of the cardboard you have not drawn on to expose the inside ridges. Cut out the shapes. Glue the horn on a piece of poster board. Glue the fruit shapes on the poster board in front of the horn. Let the glue set.

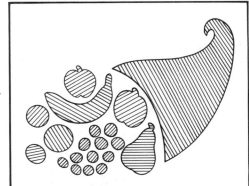

Cover your work surface with newspaper. Place poster paint on a palette or paint tray. Roll the brayer in the paint, then roll it over the cardboard shapes. Place a piece of paper over the painted surface. Gently rub the paper with your hands. Remove the paper, and let the paint dry.

Balloon Parade

◁▷◁▷◁▷

Hold your own Thanksgiving Day Parade!

Caution: This project requires adult help.

Blow up lots of different-size, colored, and shaped balloons. You may need an adult to help you do this. Carefully glue several balloons together to make animals and your favorite cartoon characters. Draw on faces and clothes. Tie a long string to each animal or character, and march your balloony creations outside in a neighborhood Thanksgiving Day Parade. Make a big turkey and a pilgrim. Make your family dog. Is that Superwoman flying so high in the sky?! (Caution: Balloons are choking hazards. Keep them away from small children and pick up all broken pieces immediately!)

What You'll Need
- balloons in assorted sizes, shapes, and colors
- glue
- permanent markers
- string

Pin the Tail on the Turkey

◆▷◆▷◆▷◆▶

Help the Thanksgiving turkey get a tail!

What You'll Need
- large poster board
- crayons
- construction paper
- blunt scissors
- double-sided tape
- bandanna

Draw a large, silly-looking turkey without any tail feathers on a piece of poster board. Hang it on the back of a door or on a wall. Draw lots of turkey tail feathers on construction paper, and cut them out. Put a small piece of double-sided tape on the end of each feather. To play pin the tail on the turkey, use a bandanna to blindfold players one at a time. Twirl them around 3 times, and point them in the direction of the turkey. Who can pin the tail on the turkey?

Turkey Blow-Ups

◆▷◆▷◆▷◆▶

These turkeys are full of hot air!

These turkeys come in all the colors of the rainbow. Blow up lots of different-colored round or oval balloons. Then cut strips of poster board to make stands for the balloons to rest on. Cut some strips 3 inches wide and 6 inches long. Cut other strips 1½ inches wide and 10 inches long. This will give the height and look of your turkeys more variety. Glue the ends of each strip together. Draw a line of glue around the top edge of each stand, and gently press a balloon onto it. Draw turkey heads and tails, and cut them out of the poster board. Add a little extra flap at the bottom of the neck and the base of the tail. These flaps can be bent and glued onto each end of the balloon to form the turkey. Make a whole flock of these terrific party decorations! (Balloons are choking hazards—keep them away from small children!)

What You'll Need
- round or oval balloons
- poster board
- blunt scissors
- ruler
- glue
- markers

Harvest Corn Doll

◆━◆━◆━◆━◆━▶

Cornhusk dolls have been traditional autumn ornaments in England for hundreds of years. Introduce the tradition to your family!

What You'll Need
- cornhusks
- bowl of water
- yarn
- blunt scissors
- permanent marker
- glue
- fabric scraps (optional)

Carefully peel the husks off 2 ears of corn. Place the husks in a bowl of water, and soak them until they soften. Remove them from the water, but allow them to remain damp. Start to make your doll by rolling a cornhusk into a ball for the doll's head. Layer 4 more cornhusks, and fold them over the head. Tie a piece of yarn under the head. Layer 2 more cornhusks, and roll them together lengthwise. Slip these under the head to create arms. Tie yarn at each end to make hands. Tie another piece of yarn under the arms to secure them in place and to make the doll's waist. Cut the ends of the husks hanging below the doll's waist to make legs. Tie yarn near the bottom of each leg to make feet. When the husks are dry, draw a face on the doll using a permanent marker. (Be sure the husks are dry—otherwise the markers might bleed.) Make hair for your doll with yarn, and glue it on. Keep the doll natural in his or her cornhusk clothing, or create a more decorative outfit by cutting out scraps of fabric and gluing them on the doll.

Salt and Pepper Pilgrims

◆━◆━◆━◆━◆━▶

Now you'll always have pilgrims at your holiday table!

At the very first Thanksgiving there were no salt and pepper shakers. But there were pilgrims! Now you can have pilgrims at your Thanksgiving with these nifty shakers that you make from spice jars. Make sure that each jar is washed and dried well. Paint a male pilgrim on one and a female pilgrim on the other. Label one jar "Salt" and one jar "Pepper." Now fill them up to decorate your Thanksgiving table!

What You'll Need
- 2 clean, empty spice jars with shaker tops
- paints
- paintbrushes
- salt
- pepper

Turkey Day Decoration

Turn a ball of clay and a handful of cotton swabs into a fat turkey with a tailful of feathers.

What You'll Need
- modeling clay
- stiff paper
- blunt scissors
- crayons or markers
- newspaper
- paper cups
- paint
- cotton swabs

This clay turkey can be used as a colorful Thanksgiving decoration on a holiday dinner table, in a window, or even peeking out of a bookshelf. To make the turkey, roll some modeling clay into a ball for the turkey's body. Cut a turkey head and neck shape from a piece of stiff paper. Draw the turkey's eyes, and color the head, beak, wattle, and neck. Insert the stiff paper head and neck piece into the clay body. Now you're ready for the tail! Lay newspaper on your work surface. Pour a small amount of several different colors of paint into different cups. Place the turkey and paint cups on the newspaper. Dip 1 side of the cotton swab in a paint cup, then insert the other end into the turkey's rump. Keep dipping and inserting until the turkey's tail is colorful and full.

Turkey Feathers Game

Know your feathered friends—or lose the game!

Gather together 5 or more players for this fast-paced game. One person is the leader, who will say "Turkey Feathers, Turkey Feathers" while flapping his or her arms. Other players should flap their arms, too. The leader keeps calling out "Turkey Feathers" again and again, sometimes naming other creatures—some that have feathers and some that do not. For example, the leader may say, "Chicken Feathers, Pig Feathers, Dog Feathers, Turkey Feathers, Turkey Feathers, Mouse Feathers, Robin Feathers" while flapping and flapping his or her arms. Any other player who flaps her or his arms when a nonfeathered creature, such as pig or dog or mouse, is called is out. The last person still playing when everyone else is out gets to be the leader for the next round.

Yam Vines

◆▶◆▶◆▶◆▶

Save the tops from your Thanksgiving yams, and watch them grow!

Caution: This project requires adult help.

The top of a long, skinny yam will work best for this. Cut off the bottom third of the yam (have an adult help you). Scrub the top well with warm water and a brush. Then stick 4 toothpicks into the center of the yam top so that it will sit in a jar full of water with half of it poking out the top. The cut part should be fully in the water. Place the jar in bright light, but not direct sunlight. Check your yam every day to make sure that the water always covers the cut part. Turn your yam so that all sides get even light. After about a week, you will see stringy white roots growing out of the cut part. Soon, purplish leaves will sprout from the top. If your water gets cloudy, pour it out and refill the jar. The yam vine will grow fast, and soon the leaves will be bright green. Transfer the plant to larger and larger jars as the vine grows and grows and grows.

What You'll Need
- yam (or sweet potato)
- knife
- vegetable brush
- toothpicks
- jar
- water

Fruity Turkeys

◆▶◆▶◆▶◆▶

These gobblers will be gobbled up in a hurry!

What You'll Need
- oranges
- knife
- spoon
- 1 cup fresh or frozen cranberries
- ¼ cup honey
- blender
- small carrot sticks
- cherry tomatoes or radishes
- toothpicks
- raisins or currants
- small plate
- leafy lettuce

Caution: This project requires adult help.

Is there a vegetarian in your family? A vegetarian is someone who doesn't eat meat. Even a vegetarian will enjoy this special turkey! Cut an orange in half, and scoop out the insides. You might need an adult to help you do this. Put the pulp, cranberries, and honey into the blender. Mix well. Spoon the mixture into the orange halves. Use small carrot sticks to form the turkey's tail feathers. Stick a cherry tomato or a radish on a toothpick for the turkey's head. Raisins or currants stuck on bits of broken toothpick can be poked into the tomato or radish for the turkey's eyes. Two bits of broken toothpick can be used for the turkey's beak. Set your turkey on a plate, and surround it with lots of leafy lettuce. Everyone will agree that this turkey is gobble-gobblin' good!

Index

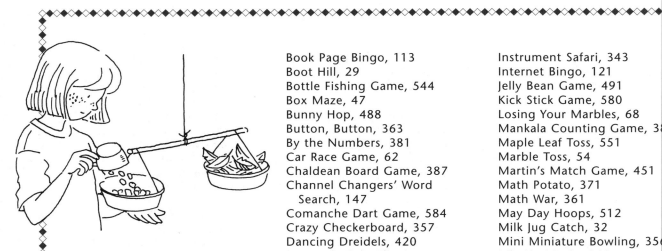

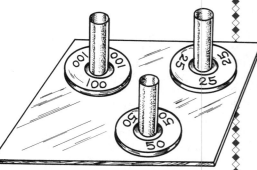

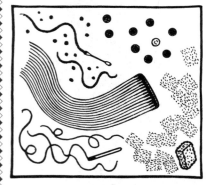